Guy de Maupassant was a master of brevity. Born in 1850, he turned everyday moments into unforgettable stories. Whether delving into romance, greed, or human folly, Maupassant had a gift for bringing characters to life with a few well-chosen words. His works remain timeless snapshots of human nature, perfect for when you need a little wisdom or a lot of heart.

Maupassant Complete Short Stories II

Guy de Maupassant

Om Books International

This edition first published in 2025 by

Om Books International

Corporate & Editorial Office
A-12, Sector 64, Noida 201 301
Uttar Pradesh, India
Phone: +91 120 477 4100
Email: editorial@ombooks.com
Website: www.ombooksinternational.com

Sales Office
107, Ansari Road, Darya Ganj,
New Delhi 110 002, India
Phone: +91 11 4000 9000
Fax: +91 11 2327 8091
Email: sales@ombooks.com
Website: www.ombooks.com

ISBN: 978-93-6395-551-6

Printed in India

10 9 8 7 6 5 4 3 2 1

Table of Contents

VOLUME VII

THE FALSE GEMS

Monsieur Lantin had met the young girl at a reception at the house of the second head of his department, and had fallen head over heels in love with her.

She was the daughter of a provincial tax collector, who had been dead several years. She and her mother came to live in Paris, where the latter, who made the acquaintance of some of the families in her neighborhood, hoped to find a husband for her daughter.

They had very moderate means, and were honorable, gentle, and quiet.

The young girl was a perfect type of the virtuous woman in whose hands every sensible young man dreams of one day intrusting his happiness. Her simple beauty had the charm of angelic modesty, and the imperceptible smile which constantly hovered about the lips seemed to be the reflection of a pure and lovely soul. Her praises resounded on every side. People never tired of repeating: "Happy the man who wins her love! He could not find a better wife."

Monsieur Lantin, then chief clerk in the Department of the Interior, enjoyed a snug little salary of three thousand five hundred francs, and he proposed to this model young girl, and was accepted.

He was unspeakably happy with her. She governed his household with such clever economy that they seemed to live in luxury. She lavished the most delicate attentions on her husband, coaxed and fondled him; and so great was her charm that six years after their marriage, Monsieur Lantin discovered that he loved his wife even more than during the first days of their honeymoon.

He found fault with only two of her tastes: Her love for the theatre, and her taste for imitation jewelry. Her friends (the wives of some petty officials) frequently procured for her a box at the theatre, often for the first representations of the new plays; and her husband was obliged to accompany her, whether he wished it or not, to these entertainments which bored him excessively after his day's work at the office.

After a time, Monsieur Lantin begged his wife to request some lady of her acquaintance to accompany her, and to bring her home after the theatre. She opposed this arrangement, at first; but, after much persuasion, finally consented, to the infinite delight of her husband.

Now, with her love for the theatre, came also the desire for ornaments. Her costumes remained as before, simple, in good taste, and always modest; but she soon began to adorn her ears with huge rhinestones, which glittered and sparkled like real diamonds. Around her neck she wore strings of false pearls, on her arms bracelets of imitation gold, and combs set with glass jewels.

Her husband frequently remonstrated with her, saying:

"My dear, as you cannot afford to buy real jewelry, you ought to appear adorned with your beauty and modesty alone, which are the rarest ornaments of your sex."

But she would smile sweetly, and say:

"What can I do? I am so fond of jewelry. It is my only weakness. We cannot change our nature."

Then she would wind the pearl necklace round her fingers, make the facets of the crystal gems sparkle, and say:

"Look! are they not lovely? One would swear they were real."

Monsieur Lantin would then answer, smilingly:

"You have bohemian tastes, my dear."

Sometimes, of an evening, when they were enjoying a tete-a-tete by the fireside, she would place on the tea table the morocco leather box containing the "trash," as Monsieur Lantin called it. She would examine the false gems with a passionate attention, as though they imparted some deep and secret joy; and she often persisted in passing a necklace around her husband's neck, and, laughing heartily, would exclaim: "How droll you look!" Then she would throw herself into his arms, and kiss him affectionately.

One evening, in winter, she had been to the opera, and returned home chilled through and through. The next morning she coughed, and eight days later she died of inflammation of the lungs.

Monsieur Lantin's despair was so great that his hair became white in one month. He wept unceasingly; his heart was broken as he remembered her smile, her voice, every charm of his dead wife.

Time did not assuage his grief. Often, during office hours, while his colleagues were discussing the topics of the day, his eyes would suddenly fill with tears, and he would give vent to his grief in heartrending sobs. Everything in his wife's room remained as it was during her lifetime; all her furniture, even her clothing, being left as it was on the day of her death. Here he was wont to seclude himself daily and think of her who had been his treasure-the joy of his existence.

But life soon became a struggle. His income, which, in the hands of his wife, covered all household expenses, was now no longer sufficient for his own immediate wants; and he wondered how she could have managed to buy such excellent wine and the rare delicacies which he could no longer procure with his modest resources.

He incurred some debts, and was soon reduced to absolute poverty. One morning, finding himself without a cent in his pocket, he resolved to sell something, and immediately the thought occurred to him of disposing of his wife's paste jewels, for he cherished in his heart a sort of rancor against these "deceptions," which had always irritated him in the past. The very sight of them spoiled, somewhat, the memory of his lost darling.

To the last days of her life she had continued to make purchases, bringing home new gems almost every evening, and he turned them over some time before finally deciding to sell the heavy necklace, which she seemed to prefer, and which, he thought, ought to be worth about six or seven francs; for it was of very fine workmanship, though only imitation.

He put it in his pocket, and started out in search of what seemed a reliable jeweler's shop. At length he found one, and went in, feeling a little ashamed to expose his misery, and also to offer such a worthless article for sale.

"Sir," said he to the merchant, "I would like to know what this is worth."

The man took the necklace, examined it, called his clerk, and made some remarks in an undertone; he then put the ornament back on the counter, and looked at it from a distance to judge of the effect.

Monsieur Lantin, annoyed at all these ceremonies, was on the point of saying: "Oh! I know well enough it is not worth anything," when the jeweler said: "Sir, that necklace is worth from twelve to fifteen thousand francs; but I could not buy it, unless you can tell me exactly where it came from."

The widower opened his eyes wide and remained gaping, not comprehending the merchant's meaning. Finally he stammered: "You say—are you sure?" The other replied, drily: "You can try elsewhere and see if any one will offer you more. I consider it worth fifteen thousand at the most. Come back; here, if you cannot do better."

Monsieur Lantin, beside himself with astonishment, took up the necklace and left the store. He wished time for reflection.

Once outside, he felt inclined to laugh, and said to himself: "The fool! Oh, the fool! Had I only taken him at his word! That jeweler cannot distinguish real diamonds from the imitation article."

A few minutes after, he entered another store, in the Rue de la Paix. As soon as the proprietor glanced at the necklace, he cried out:

"Ah, parbleu! I know it well; it was bought here."

Monsieur Lantin, greatly disturbed, asked:

"How much is it worth?"

"Well, I sold it for twenty thousand francs. I am willing to take it back for eighteen thousand, when you inform me, according to our legal formality, how it came to be in your possession."

This time, Monsieur Lantin was dumfounded. He replied:

"But—but—examine it well. Until this moment I was under the impression that it was imitation."

The jeweler asked:

"What is your name, sir?"

"Lantin—I am in the employ of the Minister of the Interior. I live at number sixteen Rue des Martyrs."

The merchant looked through his books, found the entry, and said: "That necklace was sent to Madame Lantin's address, sixteen Rue des Martyrs, July 20, 1876."

The two men looked into each other's eyes—the widower speechless with astonishment; the jeweler scenting a thief. The latter broke the silence.

"Will you leave this necklace here for twenty-four hours?" said he; "I will give you a receipt."

Monsieur Lantin answered hastily: "Yes, certainly." Then, putting the ticket in his pocket, he left the store.

He wandered aimlessly through the streets, his mind in a state of dreadful confusion. He tried to reason, to understand. His wife could not afford to purchase such a costly ornament. Certainly not.

But, then, it must have been a present!—a present!—a present, from whom? Why was it given her?

He stopped, and remained standing in the middle of the street. A horrible doubt entered his mind—She? Then, all the other jewels must have been presents, too! The earth seemed to tremble beneath him—the tree before him to be falling; he threw up his arms, and fell to the ground, unconscious. He recovered his senses in a pharmacy, into which the passers-by had borne him. He asked to be taken home, and, when he reached the house, he shut himself up in his room, and wept until nightfall. Finally, overcome with fatigue, he went to bed and fell into a heavy sleep.

The sun awoke him next morning, and he began to dress slowly to go to the office. It was hard to work after such shocks. He sent a letter to his employer, requesting to be excused. Then he remembered that he had to return to the jeweler's. He did not like the idea; but he could not leave the necklace with that man. He dressed and went out.

It was a lovely day; a clear, blue sky smiled on the busy city below. Men of leisure were strolling about with their hands in their pockets.

Monsieur Lantin, observing them, said to himself: "The rich, indeed, are happy. With money it is possible to forget even the deepest sorrow. One can go where one pleases, and in travel find that distraction which is the surest cure for grief. Oh if I were only rich!"

He perceived that he was hungry, but his pocket was empty. He again remembered the necklace. Eighteen thousand francs! Eighteen thousand francs! What a sum!

He soon arrived in the Rue de la Paix, opposite the jeweler's. Eighteen thousand francs! Twenty times he resolved to go in, but shame kept him back. He was hungry, however—very hungry—and not a cent in his pocket. He decided quickly, ran across the street, in order not to have time for reflection, and rushed into the store.

The proprietor immediately came forward, and politely offered him a chair; the clerks glanced at him knowingly.

"I have made inquiries, Monsieur Lantin," said the jeweler, "and if you are still resolved to dispose of the gems, I am ready to pay you the price I offered."

"Certainly, sir," stammered Monsieur Lantin.

Whereupon the proprietor took from a drawer eighteen large bills, counted, and handed them to Monsieur Lantin, who signed a receipt; and, with trembling hand, put the money into his pocket.

As he was about to leave the store, he turned toward the merchant, who still wore the same knowing smile, and lowering his eyes, said:

"I have—I have other gems, which came from the same source. Will you buy them, also?"

The merchant bowed: "Certainly, sir."

Monsieur Lantin said gravely: "I will bring them to you." An hour later, he returned with the gems.

The large diamond earrings were worth twenty thousand francs; the bracelets, thirty-five thousand; the rings, sixteen thousand; a set of emeralds and sapphires, fourteen thousand; a gold chain with solitaire pendant, forty thousand—making the sum of one hundred and forty-three thousand francs.

The jeweler remarked, jokingly:

"There was a person who invested all her savings in precious stones."

Monsieur Lantin replied, seriously:

"It is only another way of investing one's money."

That day he lunched at Voisin's, and drank wine worth twenty francs a bottle. Then he hired a carriage and made a tour of the

Bois. He gazed at the various turnouts with a kind of disdain, and could hardly refrain from crying out to the occupants:

"I, too, am rich!—I am worth two hundred thousand francs."

Suddenly he thought of his employer. He drove up to the bureau, and entered gaily, saying:

"Sir, I have come to resign my position. I have just inherited three hundred thousand francs."

He shook hands with his former colleagues, and confided to them some of his projects for the future; he then went off to dine at the Cafe Anglais.

He seated himself beside a gentleman of aristocratic bearing; and, during the meal, informed the latter confidentially that he had just inherited a fortune of four hundred thousand francs.

For the first time in his life, he was not bored at the theatre, and spent the remainder of the night in a gay frolic.

Six months afterward, he married again. His second wife was a very virtuous woman; but had a violent temper. She caused him much sorrow.

FASCINATION

I can tell you neither the name of the country, nor the name of the man. It was a long, long way from here on a fertile and burning shore. We had been walking since the morning along the coast, with the blue sea bathed in sunlight on one side of us, and the shore covered with crops on the other. Flowers were growing quite close to the waves, those light, gentle, lulling waves. It was very warm, a soft warmth permeated with the odor of the rich, damp, fertile soil. One fancied one was inhaling germs.

I had been told, that evening, that I should meet with hospitality at the house of a Frenchman who lived in an orange grove at the end of a promontory. Who was he? I did not know. He had come there one morning ten years before, and had bought land which he planted with vines and sowed with grain. He had worked, this man, with passionate energy, with fury. Then as he went on from month to month, year to year, enlarging his boundaries, cultivating incessantly the strong virgin soil, he accumulated a fortune by his indefatigable labor.

But he kept on working, they said. Rising at daybreak, he would remain in the fields till evening, superintending everything without ceasing, tormented by one fixed idea, the insatiable desire for money, which nothing can quiet, nothing satisfy. He now appeared to be very rich. The sun was setting as I reached his house. It was situated as described, at the end of a promontory in the midst of a grove of orange trees. It was a large square house, quite plain, and overlooked the sea. As I approached, a man wearing a long beard appeared in the doorway. Having greeted him, I asked if he would give me shelter for the night. He held out his hand and said, smiling:

"Come in, monsieur, consider yourself at home."

He led me into a room, and put a man servant at my disposal with the perfect ease and familiar graciousness of a man-of-the-world. Then he left me saying:

"We will dine as soon as you are ready to come downstairs."

We took dinner, sitting opposite each other, on a terrace facing the sea. I began to talk about this rich, distant, unknown land. He smiled, as he replied carelessly:

"Yes, this country is beautiful. But no country satisfies one when they are far from the one they love."

"You regret France?"

"I regret Paris."

"Why do you not go back?"

"Oh, I will return there."

And gradually we began to talk of French society, of the boulevards, and things Parisian. He asked me questions that showed he knew all about these things, mentioned names, all the familiar names in vaudeville known on the sidewalks.

"Whom does one see at Tortoni's now?

"Always the same crowd, except those who died." I looked at him attentively, haunted by a vague recollection. I certainly had seen that head somewhere. But where? And when? He seemed tired, although he was vigorous; and sad, although he was determined. His long, fair beard fell on his chest. He was somewhat bald and had heavy eyebrows and a thick mustache.

The sun was sinking into the sea, turning the vapor from the earth into a fiery mist. The orange blossoms exhaled their powerful, delicious fragrance. He seemed to see nothing besides me, and gazing steadfastly he appeared to discover in the depths of my mind the far-away, beloved and well-known image of the wide, shady pavement leading from the Madeleine to the Rue Drouot.

"Do you know Boutrelle?"

"Yes, indeed."

"Has he changed much?"

"Yes, his hair is quite white."

"And La Ridamie?"

"The same as ever."

"And the women? Tell me about the women. Let's see. Do you know Suzanne Verner?"

"Yes, very much. But that is over."

"Ah! And Sophie Astier?"

"Dead."

"Poor girl. Did you—did you know—"

But he ceased abruptly: And then, in a changed voice, his face suddenly turning pale, he continued:

"No, it is best that I should not speak of that any more, it breaks my heart."

Then, as if to change the current of his thoughts he rose.

"Would you like to go in?" he said.

"Yes, I think so."

And he preceded me into the house. The downstairs rooms were enormous, bare and mournful, and had a deserted look. Plates and glasses were scattered on the tables, left there by the dark-skinned servants who wandered incessantly about this spacious dwelling.

Two rifles were banging from two nails, on the wall; and in the corners of the rooms were spades, fishing poles, dried palm leaves, every imaginable thing set down at random when people came home in the evening and ready to hand when they went out at any time, or went to work.

My host smiled as he said:

"This is the dwelling, or rather the kennel, of an exile, but my own room is cleaner. Let us go there."

As I entered I thought I was in a second-hand store, it was so full of things of all descriptions, strange things of various kinds that one felt must be souvenirs. On the walls were two pretty paintings by well-known artists, draperies, weapons, swords and pistols, and exactly in the middle, on the principal panel, a square of white satin in a gold frame.

Somewhat surprised, I approached to look at it, and perceived a hairpin fastened in the centre of the glossy satin. My host placed his hand on my shoulder.

"That," said he, "is the only thing that I look at here, and the only thing that I have seen for ten years. M. Prudhomme said: 'This sword is the most memorable day of my life.' I can say: 'This hairpin is all my life.'"

I sought for some commonplace remark, and ended by saying: "You have suffered on account of some woman?"

He replied abruptly:

"Say, rather, that I am suffering like a wretch."

"But come out on my balcony. A name rose to my lips just now which I dared not utter; for if you had said 'Dead' as you did of Sophie Astier, I should have fired a bullet into my brain, this very day."

We had gone out on the wide balcony from whence we could see two gulfs, one to the right and the other to the left, enclosed by high gray mountains. It was just twilight and the reflection of the sunset still lingered in the sky.

He continued:

"Is Jeanne de Limours still alive?"

His eyes were fastened on mine and were full of a trembling anxiety. I smiled.

"Parbleu—she is prettier than ever."

"Do you know her?"

"Yes."

He hesitated and then said:

"Very well?"

"No."

He took my hand.

"Tell me about her," he said.

"Why, I have nothing to tell. She is one of the most charming women, or, rather, girls, and the most admired in Paris. She leads a delightful existence and lives like a princess, that is all."

"I love her," he murmured in a tone in which he might have said "I am going to die." Then suddenly he continued:

"Ah! For three years we lived in a state of terror and delight. I almost killed her five or six times. She tried to pierce my eyes with that hairpin that you saw just now. Look, do you see that little white spot beneath my left eye? We loved each other. How can I explain that infatuation? You would not understand it."

"There must be a simple form of love, the result of the mutual impulse of two hearts and two souls. But there is also assuredly an atrocious form, that tortures one cruelly, the result of the occult blending of two unlike personalities who detest each other at the same time that they adore one another."

"In three years this woman had ruined me. I had four million francs which she squandered in her calm manner, quietly, eat them up with a gentle smile that seemed to fall from her eyes on to her lips."

"You know her? There is something irresistible about her. What is it? I do not know. Is it those gray eyes whose glance penetrates you like a gimlet and remains there like the point of an arrow? It is more likely the gentle, indifferent and fascinating smile that she wears like a mask. Her slow grace pervades you little by little; exhales from her like a perfume, from her slim figure that scarcely sways as she passes you, for she seems to glide rather than walk; from her pretty voice with its slight drawl that would seem to be the music of her smile; from her gestures, also, which are never exaggerated, but always appropriate, and intoxicate your vision with their harmony. For three years she was the only being that existed for me on the earth! How I suffered; for she deceived me as she deceived everyone! Why? For no reason; just for the pleasure of deceiving. And when I found it out, when I treated her as a common girl and a beggar, she said quietly: 'Are we married?'

"Since I have been here I have thought so much about her that at last I understand her. She is Manon Lescaut come back to life. It is Marion, who could not love without deceiving; Marion for whom love, amusement, money, are all one."

He was silent. After a few minutes he resumed:

"When I had spent my last sou on her she said simply:

"'You understand, my dear boy, that I cannot live on air and weather. I love you very much, better than anyone, but I must live. Poverty and I could not keep house together."

"And if I should tell you what a horrible life I led with her! When I looked at her I would just as soon have killed her as kissed her. When I looked at her … I felt a furious desire to open my arms to embrace and strangle her. She had, back of her eyes, something false and intangible that made me execrate her; and that was, perhaps, the reason I loved her so well. The eternal feminine, the odious and seductive feminine, was stronger in her than in any other woman. She was full of it, overcharged, as with a venomous and intoxicating fluid. She was a woman to a greater extent than any one has ever been."

"And when I went out with her she would look at all men in such a manner that she seemed to offer herself to each in a single glance. This exasperated me, and still it attached me to her all the more. This creature in just walking along the street belonged to everyone, in spite of me, in spite of herself, by the very fact of her nature, although she had a modest, gentle carriage. Do you understand?

"And what torture! At the theatre, at the restaurant she seemed to belong to others under my very eyes. And as soon as I left her she did belong to others.

"It is now ten years since I saw her and I love her better than ever."

Night spread over the earth. A strong perfume of orange blossoms pervaded the air. I said:

"Will you see her again?"

"Parbleu! I now have here, in land and money, seven to eight thousand francs. When I reach a million I shall sell out and go away. I shall have enough to live on with her for a year—one whole year. And then, good-bye, my life will be finished."

"But after that?" I asked.

"After that, I do not know. That will be all, I may possibly ask her to take me as a valet de chambre."

YVETTE SAMORIS

"The Comtesse Samoris."

"That lady in black over there?"

"The very one. She's wearing mourning for her daughter, whom she killed."

"You don't mean that seriously? How did she die?"

"Oh! it is a very simple story, without any crime in it, any violence."

"Then what really happened?"

"Almost nothing. Many courtesans are born to be virtuous women, they say; and many women called virtuous are born to be courtesans—is that not so? Now, Madame Samoris, who was born a courtesan, had a daughter born a virtuous woman, that's all."

"I don't quite understand you."

"I'll—explain what I mean. The comtesse is nothing but a common, ordinary parvenue originating no one knows where. A Hungarian or Wallachian countess or I know not what. She appeared one winter in apartments she had taken in the Champs Elysees, that quarter for adventurers and adventuresses, and opened her drawing-room to the first comer or to any one that turned up.

"I went there. Why? you will say. I really can't tell you. I went there, as every one goes to such places because the women are facile and the men are dishonest. You know that set composed of filibusters with varied decorations, all noble, all titled, all unknown at the embassies, with the exception of those who are spies. All talk of their honor without the slightest occasion for doing so, boast of their ancestors, tell you about their lives, braggarts, liars, sharpers, as dangerous as the false cards they have up their sleeves, as delusive as their names—in short, the aristocracy of the bagnio.

"I adore these people. They are interesting to study, interesting to know, amusing to understand, often clever, never commonplace like public functionaries. Their wives are always pretty, with a slight flavor of foreign roguery, with the mystery of their existence, half of it perhaps spent in a house of correction. They have, as a rule, magnificent eyes and incredible hair. I adore them also.

"Madame Samoris is the type of these adventuresses, elegant, mature and still beautiful. Charming feline creatures, you feel that they are vicious to the marrow of their bones. You find them very amusing when you visit them; they give card parties; they have dances and suppers; in short, they offer you all the pleasures of social life.

"And she had a daughter—a tall, fine-looking girl, always ready for amusement, always full of laughter and reckless gaiety—a true adventuress' daughter—but, at the same time, an innocent, unsophisticated, artless girl, who saw nothing, knew nothing, understood nothing of all the things that happened in her father's house.

"The girl was simply a puzzle to me. She was a mystery. She lived amid those infamous surroundings with a quiet, tranquil ease that was either terribly criminal or else the result of innocence. She sprang from the filth of that class like a beautiful flower fed on corruption."

"How do you know about them?"

"How do I know? That's the funniest part of the business! One morning there was a ring at my door, and my valet came up to tell me that M. Joseph Bonenthal wanted to speak to me. I said directly:

"'And who is this gentleman?' My valet replied: 'I don't know, monsieur; perhaps 'tis some one that wants employment.' And so it was. The man wanted me to take him as a servant. I asked him where he had been last. He answered: 'With the Comtesse Samoris.' 'Ah!' said I, 'but my house is not a bit like hers.' 'I know that well, monsieur,' he said, 'and that's the very reason I want to take service with monsieur. I've had enough of these people: a man may stay a little while with them, but he won't remain long with them.' I required an additional man servant at the time and so I took him.

"A month later Mademoiselle Yvette Samoris died mysteriously, and here are all the details of her death I could gather from Joseph, who got them from his sweetheart, the comtesse's chambermaid.

"It was a ball night, and two newly arrived guests were chatting behind a door. Mademoiselle Yvette, who had just been dancing, leaned against this door to get a little air.

"They did not see her approaching, but she heard what they were saying. And this was what they said:

"'But who is the father of the girl?'

"'A Russian, it appears; Count Rouvaloff. He never comes near the mother now.'

"'And who is the reigning prince to-day?'

"'That English prince standing near the window; Madame Samoris adores him. But her adoration of any one never lasts longer than a month or six weeks. Nevertheless, as you see, she has a large circle of admirers. All are called—and nearly all are chosen. That kind of thing costs a good deal, but—hang it, what can you expect?'

"'And where did she get this name of Samoris?'

"'From the only man perhaps that she ever loved—a Jewish banker from Berlin who goes by the name of Samuel Morris.'

"'Good. Thanks. Now that I know what kind of woman she is and have seen her, I'm off!'

"What a shock this was to the mind of a young girl endowed with all the instincts of a virtuous woman! What despair overwhelmed that simple soul! What mental tortures quenched her unbounded gaiety, her delightful laughter, her exultant satisfaction with life! What a conflict took place in that youthful heart up to the moment when the last guest had left! Those were things that Joseph could not tell me. But, the same night, Yvette abruptly entered her mother's room just as the comtesse was getting into bed, sent out the lady's maid, who was close to the door, and, standing erect and pale and with great staring eyes, she said:

"'Mamma, listen to what I heard a little while ago during the ball.'

"And she repeated word for word the conversation just as I told it to you.

"The comtesse was so stunned that she did not know what to say in reply at first. When she recovered her self-possession she denied everything and called God to witness that there was no truth in the story.

"The young girl went away, distracted but not convinced. And she began to watch her mother.

"I remember distinctly the strange alteration that then took place in her. She became grave and melancholy. She would fix on us her great earnest eyes as if she wanted to read what was at the bottom of our hearts. We did not know what to think of her and used to imagine that she was looking out for a husband.

"One evening she overheard her mother talking to her admirer and later saw them together, and her doubts were confirmed. She was heartbroken, and after telling her mother what she had seen, she said coldly, like a man of business laying down the terms of an agreement:

"'Here is what I have determined to do, mamma: We will both go away to some little town, or rather into the country. We will live there quietly as well as we can. Your jewelry alone may be called a fortune. If you wish to marry some honest man, so much the better; still better will it be if I can find one. If you don't consent to do this, I will kill myself.'

"This time the comtesse ordered her daughter to go to bed and never to speak again in this manner, so unbecoming in the mouth of a child toward her mother.

"Yvette's answer to this was: 'I give you a month to reflect. If, at the end of that month, we have not changed our way of living, I will kill myself, since there is no other honorable issue left to my life.'

"And she left the room.

"At the end of a month the Comtesse Samoris had resumed her usual entertainments, as though nothing had occurred. One day, under the pretext that she had a bad toothache, Yvette purchased a few drops of chloroform from a neighboring chemist. The next day she purchased more, and every time she went out she managed to procure small doses of the narcotic. She filled a bottle with it.

"One morning she was found in bed, lifeless and already quite cold, with a cotton mask soaked in chloroform over her face.

"Her coffin was covered with flowers, the church was hung in white. There was a large crowd at the funeral ceremony.

"Ah! well, if I had known—but you never can know—I would have married that girl, for she was infernally pretty."

"And what became of the mother?"

"Oh! she shed a lot of tears over it. She has only begun to receive visits again for the past week."

"And what explanation is given of the girl's death?"

"Oh! they pretended that it was an accident caused by a new stove, the mechanism of which got out of order. As a good many such accidents have occurred, the thing seemed probable enough."

A VENDETTA

The widow of Paolo Saverini lived alone with her son in a poor little house on the outskirts of Bonifacio. The town, built on an outjutting part of the mountain, in places even overhanging the sea, looks across the straits, full of sandbanks, towards the southernmost coast of Sardinia. Beneath it, on the other side and almost surrounding it, is a cleft in the cliff like an immense corridor which serves as a harbor, and along it the little Italian and Sardinian fishing boats come by a circuitous route between precipitous cliffs as far as the first houses, and every two weeks the old, wheezy steamer which makes the trip to Ajaccio.

On the white mountain the houses, massed together, makes an even whiter spot. They look like the nests of wild birds, clinging to this peak, overlooking this terrible passage, where vessels rarely venture. The wind, which blows uninterruptedly, has swept bare the forbidding coast; it drives through the narrow straits and lays waste both sides. The pale streaks of foam, clinging to the black rocks, whose countless peaks rise up out of the water, look like bits of rag floating and drifting on the surface of the sea.

The house of widow Saverini, clinging to the very edge of the precipice, looks out, through its three windows, over this wild and desolate picture.

She lived there alone, with her son Antonia and their dog "Semillante," a big, thin beast, with a long rough coat, of the sheep-dog breed. The young man took her with him when out hunting.

One night, after some kind of a quarrel, Antoine Saverini was treacherously stabbed by Nicolas Ravolati, who escaped the same evening to Sardinia.

When the old mother received the body of her child, which the neighbors had brought back to her, she did not cry, but she stayed there for a long time motionless, watching him. Then, stretching her wrinkled hand over the body, she promised him a vendetta. She did not wish anybody near her, and she shut herself up beside the body with the dog, which howled continuously, standing at the foot of the bed, her head stretched towards her master and her tail between her legs. She did not move any more than did the mother, who, now leaning over the body with a blank stare, was weeping silently and watching it.

The young man, lying on his back, dressed in his jacket of coarse cloth, torn at the chest, seemed to be asleep. But he had blood all over him; on his shirt, which had been torn off in order to administer the first aid; on his vest, on his trousers, on his face, on his hands. Clots of blood had hardened in his beard and in his hair.

His old mother began to talk to him. At the sound of this voice the dog quieted down.

"Never fear, my boy, my little baby, you shall be avenged. Sleep, sleep; you shall be avenged. Do you hear? It's your mother's promise! And she always keeps her word, your mother does, you know she does."

Slowly she leaned over him, pressing her cold lips to his dead ones.

Then Semillante began to howl again with a long, monotonous, penetrating, horrible howl.

The two of them, the woman and the dog, remained there until morning.

Antoine Saverini was buried the next day and soon his name ceased to be mentioned in Bonifacio.

He had neither brothers nor cousins. No man was there to carry on the vendetta. His mother, the old woman, alone pondered over it.

On the other side of the straits she saw, from morning until night, a little white speck on the coast. It was the little Sardinian village Longosardo, where Corsican criminals take refuge when they are too closely pursued. They compose almost the entire population of this hamlet, opposite their native island, awaiting the time to return, to go back to the "maquis." She knew that Nicolas Ravolati had sought refuge in this village.

All alone, all day long, seated at her window, she was looking over there and thinking of revenge. How could she do anything without help—she, an invalid and so near death? But she had promised, she had sworn on the body. She could not forget, she could not wait. What could she do? She no longer slept at night; she had neither rest nor peace of mind; she thought persistently. The dog, dozing at her feet, would sometimes lift her head and howl. Since her master's death she often howled thus, as though she were calling him, as though her beast's soul, inconsolable too, had also retained a recollection that nothing could wipe out.

One night, as Semillante began to howl, the mother suddenly got hold of an idea, a savage, vindictive, fierce idea. She thought it over until morning. Then, having arisen at daybreak she went to church. She prayed, prostrate on the floor, begging the Lord to help her, to support her, to give to her poor, broken-down body the strength which she needed in order to avenge her son.

She returned home. In her yard she had an old barrel, which acted as a cistern. She turned it over, emptied it, made it fast to the ground with sticks and stones. Then she chained Semillante to this improvised kennel and went into the house.

She walked ceaselessly now, her eyes always fixed on the distant coast of Sardinia. He was over there, the murderer.

All day and all night the dog howled. In the morning the old woman brought her some water in a bowl, but nothing more; no soup, no bread.

Another day went by. Semillante, exhausted, was sleeping. The following day her eyes were shining, her hair on end and she was pulling wildly at her chain.

All this day the old woman gave her nothing to eat. The beast, furious, was barking hoarsely. Another night went by.

Then, at daybreak, Mother Saverini asked a neighbor for some straw. She took the old rags which had formerly been worn by her husband and stuffed them so as to make them look like a human body.

Having planted a stick in the ground, in front of Semillante's kennel, she tied to it this dummy, which seemed to be standing up. Then she made a head out of some old rags.

The dog, surprised, was watching this straw man, and was quiet, although famished. Then the old woman went to the store and bought a piece of black sausage. When she got home she started a fire in the yard, near the kennel, and cooked the sausage. Semillante, frantic, was jumping about, frothing at the mouth, her eyes fixed on the food, the odor of which went right to her stomach.

Then the mother made of the smoking sausage a necktie for the dummy. She tied it very tight around the neck with string, and when she had finished she untied the dog.

With one leap the beast jumped at the dummy's throat, and with her paws on its shoulders she began to tear at it. She would fall back with a piece of food in her mouth, then would jump again, sinking her fangs into the string, and snatching few pieces of meat she would fall back again and once more spring forward. She was tearing up the face with her teeth and the whole neck was in tatters.

The old woman, motionless and silent, was watching eagerly. Then she chained the beast up again, made her fast for two more days and began this strange performance again.

For three months she accustomed her to this battle, to this meal conquered by a fight. She no longer chained her up, but just pointed to the dummy.

She had taught her to tear him up and to devour him without even leaving any traces in her throat.

Then, as a reward, she would give her a piece of sausage.

As soon as she saw the man, Semillante would begin to tremble. Then she would look up to her mistress, who, lifting her finger, would cry, "Go!" in a shrill tone.

When she thought that the proper time had come, the widow went to confession and, one Sunday morning she partook of communion with an ecstatic fervor. Then, putting on men's clothes and looking like an old tramp, she struck a bargain with a Sardinian fisherman who carried her and her dog to the other side of the straits.

In a bag she had a large piece of sausage. Semillante had had nothing to eat for two days. The old woman kept letting her smell the food and whetting her appetite.

They got to Longosardo. The Corsican woman walked with a limp. She went to a baker's shop and asked for Nicolas Ravolati. He had taken up his old trade, that of carpenter. He was working alone at the back of his store.

The old woman opened the door and called:

"Hallo, Nicolas!"

He turned around. Then releasing her dog, she cried:

"Go, go! Eat him up! eat him up!"

The maddened animal sprang for his throat. The man stretched out his arms, clasped the dog and rolled to the ground. For a few seconds he squirmed, beating the ground with his feet. Then he stopped moving, while Semillante dug her fangs into his throat and tore it to ribbons. Two neighbors, seated before their door, remembered perfectly having seen an old beggar come out with a thin, black dog which was eating something that its master was giving him.

At nightfall the old woman was at home again. She slept well that night.

MY TWENTY-FIVE DAYS

I had just taken possession of my room in the hotel, a narrow den between two papered partitions, through which I could hear every sound made by my neighbors; and I was beginning to arrange my clothes and linen in the wardrobe with a long mirror, when I opened the drawer which is in this piece of furniture. I immediately noticed a roll of paper. Having opened it, I spread it out before me, and read this title:

My Twenty-five Days.

It was the diary of a guest at the watering place, of the last occupant of my room, and had been forgotten at the moment of departure.

These notes may be of some interest to sensible and healthy persons who never leave their own homes. It is for their benefit that I transcribe them without altering a letter.

"CHATEL-GUYON, July 15th.

"At the first glance it is not lively, this country. However, I am going to spend twenty-five days here, to have my liver and stomach treated, and to get thin. The twenty-five days of any one taking the baths are very like the twenty-eight days of the reserves; they are all devoted to fatigue duty, severe fatigue duty. To-day I have done nothing as yet; I have been getting settled. I have made the acquaintance of the locality and of the doctor. Chatel-Guyon consists of a stream in which flows yellow water, in the midst of several hillocks on which are a casino, some houses, and some stone crosses. On the bank of the stream, at the end of the valley, may be seen a square building surrounded by a little garden; this is the bathing establishment. Sad people wander around this building—the invalids. A great silence reigns in the walks shaded by trees, for this is not a pleasure resort, but a true health resort; one takes care of one's health as a business, and one gets well, so it seems.

"Those who know affirm, even, that the mineral springs perform true miracles here. However, no votive offering is hung around the cashier's office.

"From time to time a gentleman or a lady comes over to a kiosk with a slate roof, which shelters a woman of smiling and gentle aspect, and a spring boiling in a basin of cement: Not a word is exchanged between the invalid and the female custodian of the healing water. She hands the newcomer a little glass in which air bubbles sparkle in the transparent liquid. The guest drinks and goes off with a grave step to resume his interrupted walk beneath the trees.

"No noise in the little park, no breath of air in the leaves; no voice passes through this silence. One ought to write at the entrance to this district: 'No one laughs here; they take care of their health.'

"The people who chat resemble mutes who merely open their mouths to simulate sounds, so afraid are they that their voices might escape.

"In the hotel, the same silence. It is a big hotel, where you dine solemnly with people of good position, who have nothing to say to each other. Their manners bespeak good breeding, and their faces reflect the conviction of a superiority of which it might be difficult for some to give actual proofs.

"At two o'clock I made my way up to the Casino, a little wooden hut perched on a hillock, which one reaches by a goat path. But the view from that height is admirable. Chatel-Guyon is situated in a very narrow valley, exactly between the plain and the mountain. I perceive, at the left, the first great billows of the mountains of Auvergne, covered with woods, and here and there big gray patches, hard masses of lava, for we are at the foot of the extinct volcanoes. At the right, through the narrow cut of the valley, I discover a plain, infinite as the sea, steeped in a bluish fog which lets one only dimly discern the villages, the towns, the yellow fields of ripe grain, and the green squares of meadowland shaded with apple trees. It is the Limagne, an immense level, always enveloped in a light veil of vapor.

"The night has come. And now, after having dined alone, I write these lines beside my open window. I hear, over there, in front of me, the little orchestra of the Casino, which plays airs just as a foolish bird might sing all alone in the desert.

"A dog barks at intervals. This great calm does one good. Goodnight.

"July 16th.—Nothing new. I have taken a bath and then a shower bath. I have swallowed three glasses of water, and I have walked along the paths in the park, a quarter of an hour between each glass, then half an hour after the last. I have begun my twenty-five days.

"July 17th.—Remarked two mysterious, pretty women who are taking their baths and their meals after every one else has finished.

"July 18th.—Nothing new.

"July 19th.—Saw the two pretty women again. They have style and a little indescribable air which I like very much.

"July 20th.—Long walk in a charming wooded valley, as far as the Hermitage of Sans-Souci. This country is delightful, although sad; but so calm; so sweet, so green. One meets along the mountain roads long wagons loaded with hay, drawn by two cows at a slow pace or held back by them in going down the slopes with a great effort of their heads, which are yoked together. A man with a big black hat on his head is driving them with a slender stick, tipping them on the side or on the forehead; and often with a simple gesture, an energetic and serious gesture, he suddenly halts them when the excessive load precipitates their journey down the too rugged descents.

"The air is good to inhale in these valleys. And, if it is very warm, the dust bears with it a light odor of vanilla and of the stable, for so many cows pass over these routes that they leave reminders everywhere. And this odor is a perfume, when it would be a stench if it came from other animals.

"July 21st.—Excursion to the valley of the Enval. It is a narrow gorge inclosed by superb rocks at the very foot of the mountain. A stream flows amid the heaped-up boulders.

"As I reached the bottom of this ravine I heard women's voices, and I soon perceived the two mysterious ladies of my hotel, who were chatting, seated on a stone.

"The occasion appeared to me a good one, and I introduced myself without hesitation. My overtures were received without embarrassment. We walked back together to the hotel. And we talked about Paris. They knew, it seemed, many people whom I knew, too. Who can they be?

"I shall see them to-morrow. There is nothing more amusing than such meetings as this.

"July 22d.—Day passed almost entirely with the two unknown ladies. They are very pretty, by Jove!—one a brunette and the other a blonde. They say they are widows. H'm?

"I offered to accompany them to Royat tomorrow, and they accepted my offer.

"Chatel-Guyon is less sad than I thought on my arrival.

"July 23d.—Day spent at Royat. Royat is a little patch of hotels at the bottom of a valley, at the gate of Clermont-Ferrand. A great many people there. A large park full of life. Superb view of the Puyde-Dome, seen at the end of a perspective of valleys.

"My fair companions are very popular, which is flattering to me. The man who escorts a pretty woman always believes himself crowned with an aureole; with much more reason, the man who is accompanied by one on each side of him. Nothing is so pleasant as to dine in a fashionable restaurant with a female companion at whom everybody stares, and there is nothing better calculated to exalt a man in the estimation of his neighbors.

"To go to the Bois, in a trap drawn by a sorry nag, or to go out into the boulevard escorted by a plain woman, are the two most humiliating things that could happen to a sensitive heart that values the opinion of others. Of all luxuries, woman is the rarest and the most distinguished; she is the one that costs most and which we desire most; she is, therefore the one that we should seek by preference to exhibit to the jealous eyes of the world.

"To exhibit to the world a pretty woman leaning on your arm is to excite, all at once, every kind of jealousy. It is as much as to say: 'Look here! I am rich, since I possess this rare and costly object; I have taste, since I have known how to discover this pearl; perhaps, even, I am loved by her, unless I am deceived by her, which would still prove that others also consider her charming.

"But, what a disgrace it is to walk about town with an ugly woman!

"And how many humiliating things this gives people to understand!

"In the first place, they assume she must be your wife, for how could it be supposed that you would have an unattractive sweetheart? A true woman may be ungraceful; but then, her ugliness implies a thousand disagreeable things for you. One supposes you must be a notary or a magistrate, as these two professions have a monopoly of grotesque and well-dowered spouses. Now, is this not distressing to a man? And then, it seems to proclaim to the public that you have the odious courage, and are even under a legal obligation, to caress that ridiculous face and that ill-shaped body, and that you will, without doubt, be shameless enough to make a mother of this by no means desirable being—which is the very height of the ridiculous.

"July 24th.—I never leave the side of the two unknown widows, whom I am beginning to know quite well. This country is delightful and our hotel is excellent. Good season. The treatment is doing me an immense amount of good.

"July 25th.—Drive in a landau to the lake of Tazenat. An exquisite and unexpected jaunt decided on at luncheon. We started immediately on rising from table. After a long journey through the mountains we suddenly perceived an admirable little lake, quite round, very blue, clear as glass, and situated at the bottom of an extinct crater. One side of this immense basin is barren, the other is wooded. In the midst of the trees is a small house where sleeps a good-natured, intellectual man, a sage who passes his days in this Virgilian region. He opens his dwelling for us. An idea comes into my head. I exclaim:

"'Supposing we bathe?'

"'Yes,' they said, 'but costumes.'

"'Bah! we are in the wilderness.'

"And we did bathe!

"If I were a poet, how I would describe this unforgettable vision of those lissome young forms in the transparency of the water! The high, sloping sides shut in the lake, motionless, gleaming and round, as a silver coin; the sun pours into it a flood of warm light; and along the rocks the fair forms move in the almost invisible water in which the swimmers seemed suspended. On the sand at the bottom of the lake one could see their shadows as they moved along.

"July 26th.—Some persons seem to look with shocked and disapproving eyes at my rapid intimacy with the two fair widows. There are some people, then, who imagine that life consists in being bored. Everything that appears to be amusing becomes immediately a breach of good breeding or morality. For them duty has inflexible and mortally tedious rules.

"I would draw their attention, with all respect, to the fact that duty is not the same for Mormons, Arabs Zulus, Turks, Englishmen, and Frenchmen, and that there are very virtuous people among all these nations.

"I will cite a single example. As regards women, duty begins in England at nine years of age; in France at fifteen. As for me, I take a little of each people's notion of duty, and of the whole I make a result comparable to the morality of good King Solomon.

"July 27th.—Good news. I have lost 620 grams in weight. Excellent, this water of Chatel-Guyon! I am taking the widows to dine at Riom. A sad town whose anagram constitutes it an objectionable neighbor to healing springs: Riom, Mori.

"July 28th.—Hello, how's this! My two widows have been visited by two gentlemen who came to look for them. Two widowers, without doubt. They are leaving this evening. They have written to me on fancy notepaper.

"July 29th.—Alone! Long excursion on foot to the extinct crater of Nachere. Splendid view.

"July 30th.—Nothing. I am taking the treatment.

"July 31st.—Ditto. Ditto. This pretty country is full of polluted streams. I am drawing the notice of the municipality to the abominable sewer which poisons the road in front of the hotel. All the kitchen refuse of the establishment is thrown into it. This is a good way to breed cholera.

"August 1st.—Nothing. The treatment.

"August 2d.—Admirable walk to Chateauneuf, a place of sojourn for rheumatic patients, where everybody is lame. Nothing can be queerer than this population of cripples!

"August 3d.—Nothing. The treatment.

"August 4th.—Ditto. Ditto.

"August 5th.—Ditto. Ditto.

"August 6th.—Despair! I have just weighed myself. I have gained 310 grams. But then?

"August 7th.—Drove sixty-six kilometres in a carriage on the mountain. I will not mention the name of the country through respect for its women.

"This excursion had been pointed out to me as a beautiful one, and one that was rarely made. After four hours on the road, I arrived at a rather pretty village on the banks of a river in the midst of an admirable wood of walnut trees. I had not yet seen a forest of walnut trees of such dimensions in Auvergne. It constitutes, moreover, all the wealth of the district, for it is planted on the village common. This common was formerly only a hillside covered with brushwood. The authorities had tried in vain to get it cultivated. There was scarcely enough pasture on it to feed a few sheep.

"To-day it is a superb wood, thanks to the women, and it has a curious name: it is called the Sins of the Cure.

"Now I must say that the women of the mountain districts have the reputation of being light, lighter than in the plain. A bachelor who meets them owes them at least a kiss; and if he does not take more he is only a blockhead. If we consider this fairly, this way of looking at the matter is the only one that is logical and reasonable. As woman, whether she be of the town or the country, has her natural mission to please man, man should always show her that she pleases him. If he abstains from every sort of demonstration, this means that he considers her ugly; it is almost an insult to her. If I were a woman, I would not receive, a second time, a man who failed to show me respect at our first meeting, for I would consider that he had failed in appreciation of my beauty, my charm, and my feminine qualities.

"So the bachelors of the village X often proved to the women of the district that they found them to their taste, and, as the cure was unable to prevent these demonstrations, as gallant as they were natural, he resolved to utilize them for the benefit of the general prosperity. So he imposed as a penance on every woman who had gone wrong that she should plant a walnut tree on the common. And every night lanterns were seen moving about like will-o'-the-wisps on the hillock, for the erring ones scarcely like to perform their penance in broad daylight.

"In two years there was no longer any room on the lands belonging to the village, and to-day they calculate that there are more than three thousand trees around the belfry which rings out the services amid their foliage. These are the Sins of the Cure.

"Since we have been seeking for so many ways of rewooding France, the Administration of Forests might surely enter into some arrangement with the clergy to employ a method so simple as that employed by this humble cure.

"August 7th.—Treatment.

"August 8th.—I am packing up my trunks and saying good-by to the charming little district so calm and silent, to the green mountain, to the quiet valleys, to the deserted Casino, from which you can see, almost veiled by its light, bluish mist, the immense plain of the Limagne.

"I shall leave to-morrow."

Here the manuscript stopped. I will add nothing to it, my impressions of the country not having been exactly the same as those of my predecessor. For I did not find the two widows!

"THE TERROR"

You say you cannot possibly understand it, and I believe you. You think I am losing my mind? Perhaps I am, but for other reasons than those you imagine, my dear friend.

Yes, I am going to be married, and will tell you what has led me to take that step.

I may add that I know very little of the girl who is going to become my wife to-morrow; I have only seen her four or five times. I know that there is nothing unpleasing about her, and that is enough for my purpose. She is small, fair, and stout; so, of course, the day after to-morrow I shall ardently wish for a tall, dark, thin woman.

She is not rich, and belongs to the middle classes. She is a girl such as you may find by the gross, well adapted for matrimony, without any apparent faults, and with no particularly striking qualities. People say of her:

"Mlle. Lajolle is a very nice girl," and tomorrow they will say: "What a very nice woman Madame Raymon is." She belongs, in a word, to that immense number of girls whom one is glad to have for one's wife, till the moment comes when one discovers that one happens to prefer all other women to that particular woman whom one has married.

"Well," you will say to me, "what on earth did you get married for?"

I hardly like to tell you the strange and seemingly improbable reason that urged me on to this senseless act; the fact, however, is that I am afraid of being alone.

I don't know how to tell you or to make you understand me, but my state of mind is so wretched that you will pity me and despise me.

I do not want to be alone any longer at night. I want to feel that there is some one close to me, touching me, a being who can speak and say something, no matter what it be.

I wish to be able to awaken somebody by my side, so that I may be able to ask some sudden question, a stupid question even, if I feel inclined, so that I may hear a human voice, and feel that there is some waking soul close to me, some one whose reason is at work; so that when I hastily light the candle I may see some human face by my side—because—because —I am ashamed to confess it—because I am afraid of being alone.

Oh, you don't understand me yet.

I am not afraid of any danger; if a man were to come into the room, I should kill him without trembling. I am not afraid of ghosts, nor do I believe in the supernatural. I am not afraid of dead people, for I believe in the total annihilation of every being that disappears from the face of this earth.

Well—yes, well, it must be told: I am afraid of myself, afraid of that horrible sensation of incomprehensible fear.

You may laugh, if you like. It is terrible, and I cannot get over it. I am afraid of the walls, of the furniture, of the familiar objects; which are animated, as far as I am concerned, by a kind of animal life. Above all, I am afraid of my own dreadful thoughts, of my reason, which seems as if it were about to leave me, driven away by a mysterious and invisible agony.

At first I feel a vague uneasiness in my mind, which causes a cold shiver to run all over me. I look round, and of course nothing is to be seen, and I wish that there were something there, no matter what, as long as it were something tangible. I am frightened merely because I cannot understand my own terror.

If I speak, I am afraid of my own voice. If I walk, I am afraid of I know not what, behind the door, behind the curtains, in the cupboard, or under my bed, and yet all the time I know there is nothing anywhere, and I turn round suddenly because I am afraid of what is behind me, although there is nothing there, and I know it.

I become agitated. I feel that my fear increases, and so I shut myself up in my own room, get into bed, and hide under the clothes;

and there, cowering down, rolled into a ball, I close my eyes in despair, and remain thus for an indefinite time, remembering that my candle is alight on the table by my bedside, and that I ought to put it out, and yet—I dare not do it.

It is very terrible, is it not, to be like that?

Formerly I felt nothing of all that. I came home quite calm, and went up and down my apartment without anything disturbing my peace of mind. Had any one told me that I should be attacked by a malady—for I can call it nothing else—of most improbable fear, such a stupid and terrible malady as it is, I should have laughed outright. I was certainly never afraid of opening the door in the dark. I went to bed slowly, without locking it, and never got up in the middle of the night to make sure that everything was firmly closed.

It began last year in a very strange manner on a damp autumn evening. When my servant had left the room, after I had dined, I asked myself what I was going to do. I walked up and down my room for some time, feeling tired without any reason for it, unable to work, and even without energy to read. A fine rain was falling, and I felt unhappy, a prey to one of those fits of despondency, without any apparent cause, which make us feel inclined to cry, or to talk, no matter to whom, so as to shake off our depressing thoughts.

I felt that I was alone, and my rooms seemed to me to be more empty than they had ever been before. I was in the midst of infinite and overwhelming solitude. What was I to do? I sat down, but a kind of nervous impatience seemed to affect my legs, so I got up and began to walk about again. I was, perhaps, rather feverish, for my hands, which I had clasped behind me, as one often does when walking slowly, almost seemed to burn one another. Then suddenly a cold shiver ran down my back, and I thought the damp air might have penetrated into my rooms, so I lit the fire for the first time that year, and sat down again and looked at the flames. But soon I felt that I could not possibly remain quiet, and so I got up again and determined to go out, to pull myself together, and to find a friend to bear me company.

I could not find anyone, so I walked to the boulevard to try and meet some acquaintance or other there.

It was wretched everywhere, and the wet pavement glistened in the gaslight, while the oppressive warmth of the almost impalpable rain lay heavily over the streets and seemed to obscure the light of the lamps.

I went on slowly, saying to myself: "I shall not find a soul to talk to."

I glanced into several cafes, from the Madeleine as far as the Faubourg Poissoniere, and saw many unhappy-looking individuals sitting at the tables who did not seem even to have enough energy left to finish the refreshments they had ordered.

For a long time I wandered aimlessly up and down, and about midnight I started for home. I was very calm and very tired. My janitor opened the door at once, which was quite unusual for him, and I thought that another lodger had probably just come in.

When I go out I always double-lock the door of my room, and I found it merely closed, which surprised me; but I supposed that some letters had been brought up for me in the course of the evening.

I went in, and found my fire still burning so that it lighted up the room a little, and, while in the act of taking up a candle, I noticed somebody sitting in my armchair by the fire, warming his feet, with his back toward me.

I was not in the slightest degree frightened. I thought, very naturally, that some friend or other had come to see me. No doubt the porter, to whom I had said I was going out, had lent him his own key. In a moment I remembered all the circumstances of my return, how the street door had been opened immediately, and that my own door was only latched and not locked.

I could see nothing of my friend but his head, and he had evidently gone to sleep while waiting for me, so I went up to him to rouse him. I saw him quite distinctly; his right arm was hanging down and his legs were crossed; the position of his head, which was somewhat inclined to the left of the armchair, seemed to indicate that he was asleep. "Who can it be?" I asked myself. I could not see clearly, as the room was rather dark, so I put out my hand to touch him on the shoulder, and it came in contact with the back of the chair. There was nobody there; the seat was empty.

I fairly jumped with fright. For a moment I drew back as if confronted by some terrible danger; then I turned round again, impelled by an imperious standing upright, panting with fear, so upset that I could not collect my thoughts, and ready to faint.

But I am a cool man, and soon recovered myself. I thought: "It is a mere hallucination, that is all," and I immediately began to reflect on this phenomenon. Thoughts fly quickly at such moments.

I had been suffering from an hallucination, that was an incontestable fact. My mind had been perfectly lucid and had acted regularly and logically, so there was nothing the matter with the brain. It was only my eyes that had been deceived; they had had a vision, one of those visions which lead simple folk to believe in miracles. It was a nervous seizure of the optical apparatus, nothing more; the eyes were rather congested, perhaps.

I lit my candle, and when I stooped down to the fire in doing so I noticed that I was trembling, and I raised myself up with a jump, as if somebody had touched me from behind.

I was certainly not by any means calm.

I walked up and down a little, and hummed a tune or two. Then I double-locked the door and felt rather reassured; now, at any rate, nobody could come in.

I sat down again and thought over my adventure for a long time; then I went to bed and blew out my light.

For some minutes all went well; I lay quietly on my back, but presently an irresistible desire seized me to look round the room, and I turned over on my side.

My fire was nearly out, and the few glowing embers threw a faint light on the floor by the chair, where I fancied I saw the man sitting again.

I quickly struck a match, but I had been mistaken; there was nothing there. I got up, however, and hid the chair behind my bed, and tried to get to sleep, as the room was now dark; but I had not forgotten myself for more than five minutes, when in my dream I saw all the scene which I had previously witnessed as clearly as if it were reality. I woke up with a start, and having lit the candle, sat up in bed, without venturing even to try to go to sleep again.

Twice, however, sleep overcame me for a few moments in spite of myself, and twice I saw the same thing again, till I fancied I was going mad. When day broke, however, I thought that I was cured, and slept peacefully till noon.

It was all past and over. I had been feverish, had had the nightmare. I know not what. I had been ill, in fact, but yet thought I was a great fool.

I enjoyed myself thoroughly that evening. I dined at a restaurant and afterward went to the theatre, and then started for home. But as I got near the house I was once more seized by a strange feeling of uneasiness. I was afraid of seeing him again. I was not afraid of him, not afraid of his presence, in which I did not believe; but I was afraid of being deceived again. I was afraid of some fresh hallucination, afraid lest fear should take possession of me.

For more than an hour I wandered up and down the pavement; then, feeling that I was really too foolish, I returned home. I breathed so hard that I could hardly get upstairs, and remained standing outside my door for more than ten minutes; then suddenly I had a courageous impulse and my will asserted itself. I inserted my key into the lock, and went into the apartment with a candle in my hand. I kicked open my bedroom door, which was partly open, and cast a frightened glance toward the fireplace. There was nothing there. A-h! What a relief and what a delight! What a deliverance! I walked up and down briskly and boldly, but I was not altogether reassured, and kept turning round with a jump; the very shadows in the corners disquieted me.

I slept badly, and was constantly disturbed by imaginary noises, but did not see him; no, that was all over.

Since that time I have been afraid of being alone at night. I feel that the spectre is there, close to me, around me; but it has not appeared to me again.

And supposing it did, what would it matter, since I do not believe in it, and know that it is nothing?

However, it still worries me, because I am constantly thinking of it. His right arm hanging down and his head inclined to the left like a man who was asleep—I don't want to think about it!

Why, however, am I so persistently possessed with this idea? His feet were close to the fire!

He haunts me; it is very stupid, but who and what is he? I know that he does not exist except in my cowardly imagination, in my fears, and in my agony. There—enough of that!

Yes, it is all very well for me to reason with myself, to stiffen my backbone, so to say; but I cannot remain at home because I know he is there. I know I shall not see him again; he will not show himself again; that is all over. But he is there, all the same, in my thoughts. He remains invisible, but that does not prevent his being there. He is behind the doors, in the closed cupboard, in the wardrobe, under the bed, in every dark corner. If I open the door or the cupboard, if I take the candle to look under the bed and throw a light on the dark places he is there no longer, but I feel that he is behind me. I turn round, certain that I shall not see him, that I shall never see him again; but for all that, he is behind me.

It is very stupid, it is dreadful; but what am I to do? I cannot help it.

But if there were two of us in the place I feel certain that he would not be there any longer, for he is there just because I am alone, simply and solely because I am alone!

LEGEND OF MONT ST. MICHEL

I had first seen it from Cancale, this fairy castle in the sea. I got an indistinct impression of it as of a gray shadow outlined against the misty sky. I saw it again from Avranches at sunset. The immense stretch of sand was red, the horizon was red, the whole boundless bay was red. The rocky castle rising out there in the distance like a weird, seignorial residence, like a dream palace, strange and beautiful-this alone remained black in the crimson light of the dying day.

The following morning at dawn I went toward it across the sands, my eyes fastened on this, gigantic jewel, as big as a mountain, cut like a cameo, and as dainty as lace. The nearer I approached the greater my admiration grew, for nothing in the world could be more wonderful or more perfect.

As surprised as if I had discovered the habitation of a god, I wandered through those halls supported by frail or massive columns, raising my eyes in wonder to those spires which looked like rockets starting for the sky, and to that marvellous assemblage of towers, of gargoyles, of slender and charming ornaments, a regular fireworks of stone, granite lace, a masterpiece of colossal and delicate architecture.

As I was looking up in ecstasy a Lower Normandy peasant came up to me and told me the story of the great quarrel between Saint Michael and the devil.

A sceptical genius has said: "God made man in his image and man has returned the compliment."

This saying is an eternal truth, and it would be very curious to write the history of the local divinity of every continent as well as the history of the patron saints in each one of our provinces. The negro has his ferocious man-eating idols; the polygamous Mahometan fills his paradise with women; the Greeks, like a practical people, deified all the passions.

Every village in France is under the influence of some protecting saint, modelled according to the characteristics of the inhabitants.

Saint Michael watches over Lower Normandy, Saint Michael, the radiant and victorious angel, the sword-carrier, the hero of Heaven, the victorious, the conqueror of Satan.

But this is how the Lower Normandy peasant, cunning, deceitful and tricky, understands and tells of the struggle between the great saint and the devil.

To escape from the malice of his neighbor, the devil, Saint Michael built himself, in the open ocean, this habitation worthy of an archangel; and only such a saint could build a residence of such magnificence.

But as he still feared the approaches of the wicked one, he surrounded his domains by quicksands, more treacherous even than the sea.

The devil lived in a humble cottage on the hill, but he owned all the salt marshes, the rich lands where grow the finest crops, the wooded valleys and all the fertile hills of the country, while the saint ruled only over the sands. Therefore Satan was rich, whereas Saint Michael was as poor as a church mouse.

After a few years of fasting the saint grew tired of this state of affairs and began to think of some compromise with the devil, but the matter was by no means easy, as Satan kept a good hold on his crops.

He thought the thing over for about six months; then one morning he walked across to the shore. The demon was eating his soup in front of his door when he saw the saint. He immediately rushed toward him, kissed the hem of his sleeve, invited him in and offered him refreshments.

Saint Michael drank a bowl of milk and then began: "I have come here to propose to you a good bargain."

The devil, candid and trustful, answered: "That will suit me."

"Here it is. Give me all your lands."

Satan, growing alarmed, wished to speak "But—"

The saint continued: "Listen first. Give me all your lands. I will take care of all the work, the ploughing, the sowing, the fertilizing, everything, and we will share the crops equally. How does that suit you?"

The devil, who was naturally lazy, accepted. He only demanded in addition a few of those delicious gray mullet which are caught around the solitary mount. Saint Michael promised the fish.

They grasped hands and spat on the ground to show that it was a bargain, and the saint continued: "See here, so that you will have nothing to complain of, choose that part of the crops which you prefer: the part that grows above ground or the part that stays in the ground." Satan cried out: "I will take all that will be above ground."

"It's a bargain!" said the saint. And he went away.

Six months later, all over the immense domain of the devil, one could see nothing but carrots, turnips, onions, salsify, all the plants whose juicy roots are good and savory and whose useless leaves are good for nothing but for feeding animals.

Satan wished to break the contract, calling Saint Michael a swindler.

But the saint, who had developed quite a taste for agriculture, went back to see the devil and said:

"Really, I hadn't thought of that at all; it was just an accident, no fault of mine. And to make things fair with you, this year I'll let you take everything that is under the ground."

"Very well," answered Satan.

The following spring all the evil spirit's lands were covered with golden wheat, oats as big as beans, flax, magnificent colza, red clover, peas, cabbage, artichokes, everything that develops into grains or fruit in the sunlight.

Once more Satan received nothing, and this time he completely lost his temper. He took back his fields and remained deaf to all the fresh propositions of his neighbor.

A whole year rolled by. From the top of his lonely manor Saint Michael looked at the distant and fertile lands and watched the devil direct the work, take in his crops and thresh the wheat. And he grew angry, exasperated at his powerlessness.

As he was no longer able to deceive Satan, he decided to wreak vengeance on him, and he went out to invite him to dinner for the following Monday.

"You have been very unfortunate in your dealings with me," he said; "I know it, but I don't want any ill feeling between us, and I expect you to dine with me. I'll give you some good things to eat."

Satan, who was as greedy as he was lazy, accepted eagerly. On the day appointed he donned his finest clothes and set out for the castle.

Saint Michael sat him down to a magnificent meal. First there was a 'vol-au-vent', full of cocks' crests and kidneys, with meat-balls, then two big gray mullet with cream sauce, a turkey stuffed with chestnuts soaked in wine, some salt-marsh lamb as tender as cake, vegetables which melted in the mouth and nice hot pancake which was brought on smoking and spreading a delicious odor of butter.

They drank new, sweet, sparkling cider and heady red wine, and after each course they whetted their appetites with some old apple brandy.

The devil drank and ate to his heart's content; in fact he took so much that he was very uncomfortable, and began to retch.

Then Saint Michael arose in anger and cried in a voice like thunder: "What! before me, rascal! You dare—before me—"

Satan, terrified, ran away, and the saint, seizing a stick, pursued him. They ran through the halls, turning round the pillars, running up the staircases, galloping along the cornices, jumping from gargoyle to gargoyle. The poor devil, who was woefully ill, was running about madly and trying hard to escape. At last he found himself at the top of the last terrace, right at the top, from which could be seen the immense bay, with its distant towns, sands and pastures. He could no longer escape, and the saint came up behind him and gave him a furious kick, which shot him through space like a cannonball.

He shot through the air like a javelin and fell heavily before the town of Mortain. His horns and claws stuck deep into the rock, which keeps through eternity the traces of this fall of Satan.

He stood up again, limping, crippled until the end of time, and as he looked at this fatal castle in the distance, standing out against the setting sun, he understood well that he would always be vanquished in this unequal struggle, and he went away limping, heading for distant countries, leaving to his enemy his fields, his hills, his valleys and his marshes.

And this is how Saint Michael, the patron saint of Normandy, vanquished the devil.

Another people would have dreamed of this battle in an entirely different manner.

A NEW YEAR'S GIFT

Jacques de Randal, having dined at home alone, told his valet he might go out, and he sat down at his table to write some letters.

He ended every year in this manner, writing and dreaming. He reviewed the events of his life since last New Year's Day, things that were now all over and dead; and, in proportion as the faces of his friends rose up before his eyes, he wrote them a few lines, a cordial New Year's greeting on the first of January.

So he sat down, opened a drawer, took out of it a woman's photograph, gazed at it a few moments, and kissed it. Then, having laid it beside a sheet of notepaper, he began:

"MY DEAR IRENE: You must by this time have received the little souvenir I sent you addressed to the maid. I have shut myself up this evening in order to tell you——"

The pen here ceased to move. Jacques rose up and began walking up and down the room.

For the last ten months he had had a sweetheart, not like the others, a woman with whom one engages in a passing intrigue, of the theatrical world or the demi-monde, but a woman whom he loved and won. He was no longer a young man, although he was still comparatively young for a man, and he looked on life seriously in a positive and practical spirit.

Accordingly, he drew up the balance sheet of his passion, as he drew up every year the balance sheet of friendships that were ended or freshly contracted, of circumstances and persons that had entered into his life.

His first ardor of love having grown calmer, he asked himself with the precision of a merchant making a calculation what was the state of his heart with regard to her, and he tried to form an idea of what it would be in the future.

He found there a great and deep affection; made up of tenderness, gratitude and the thousand subtleties which give birth to long and powerful attachments.

A ring at the bell made him start. He hesitated. Should he open the door? But he said to himself that one must always open the door on New Year's night, to admit the unknown who is passing by and knocks, no matter who it may be.

So he took a wax candle, passed through the antechamber, drew back the bolts, turned the key, pulled the door back, and saw his sweetheart standing pale as a corpse, leaning against the wall.

He stammered:

"What is the matter with you?"

She replied:

"Are you alone?"

"Yes."

"Without servants?"

"Yes."

"You are not going out?"

"No."

She entered with the air of a woman who knew the house. As soon as she was in the drawing-room, she sank down on the sofa, and, covering her face with her hands, began to weep bitterly.

He knelt down at her feet, and tried to remove her hands from her eyes, so that he might look at them, and exclaimed:

"Irene, Irene, what is the matter with you? I implore you to tell me what is the matter with you?"

Then, amid her sobs, she murmured:

"I can no longer live like this."

"Live like this? What do you mean?"

"Yes. I can no longer live like this. I have endured so much. He struck me this afternoon."

"Who? Your husband?"

"Yes, my husband."

"Ah!"

He was astonished, having never suspected that her husband could be brutal. He was a man of the world, of the better class, a clubman, a lover of horses, a theatergoer and an expert swordsman; he was known, talked about, appreciated everywhere, having very courteous manners, a very mediocre intellect, an absence of education and of the real culture needed in order to think like all well-bred people, and finally a respect for conventionalities.

He appeared to devote himself to his wife, as a man ought to do in the case of wealthy and well-bred people. He displayed enough of anxiety about her wishes, her health, her dresses, and, beyond that, left her perfectly free.

Randal, having become Irene's friend, had a right to the affectionate hand-clasp which every husband endowed with good manners owes to his wife's intimate acquaintance. Then, when Jacques, after having been for some time the friend, became the lover, his relations with the husband were more cordial, as is fitting.

Jacques had never dreamed that there were storms in this household, and he was bewildered at this unexpected revelation.

He asked:

"How did it happen? Tell me."

Thereupon she related a long story, the entire history of her life since the day of her marriage, the first disagreement arising out of a mere nothing, then becoming accentuated at every new difference of opinion between two dissimilar dispositions.

Then came quarrels, a complete separation, not apparent, but real; next, her husband showed himself aggressive, suspicious, violent. Now, he was jealous, jealous of Jacques, and that very day, after a scene, he had struck her.

She added with decision: "I will not go back to him. Do with me what you like."

Jacques sat down opposite to her, their knees touching. He took her hands:

"My dear love, you are going to commit a gross, an irreparable folly. If you want to leave your husband, put him in the wrong, so that your position as a woman of the world may be saved."

She asked, as she looked at him uneasily:

"Then, what do you advise me?"

"To go back home and to put up with your life there till the day when you can obtain either a separation or a divorce, with the honors of war."

"Is not this thing which you advise me to do a little cowardly?"

"No; it is wise and sensible. You have a high position, a reputation to protect, friends to preserve and relations to deal with. You must not lose all these through a mere caprice."

She rose up, and said with violence:

"Well, no! I cannot stand it any longer! It is at an end! it is at an end!"

Then, placing her two hands on her lover's shoulders, and looking him straight in the face, she asked:

"Do you love me?"

"Yes."

"Really and truly?"

"Yes."

"Then take care of me."

He exclaimed:

"Take care of you? In my own house? Here? Why, you are mad. It would mean losing you forever; losing you beyond hope of recall! You are mad!"

She replied, slowly and seriously, like a woman who feels the weight of her words:

"Listen, Jacques. He has forbidden me to see you again, and I will not play this comedy of coming secretly to your house. You must either lose me or take me."

"My dear Irene, in that case, obtain your divorce, and I will marry you."

"Yes, you will marry me in—two years at the soonest. Yours is a patient love."

"Look here! Reflect! If you remain here he'll come to-morrow to take you away, seeing that he is your husband, seeing that he has right and law on his side."

"I did not ask you to keep me in your own house, Jacques, but to take me anywhere you like. I thought you loved me enough to do that. I have made a mistake. Good-by!"

She turned round and went toward the door so quickly that he was only able to catch hold of her when she was outside the room:

"Listen, Irene."

She struggled, and would not listen to him. Her eyes were full of tears, and she stammered:

"Let me alone! let me alone! let me alone!"

He made her sit down by force, and once more falling on his knees at her feet, he now brought forward a number of arguments and counsels to make her understand the folly and terrible risk of her project. He omitted nothing which he deemed necessary to convince her, finding even in his very affection for her incentives to persuasion.

As she remained silent and cold as ice, he begged of her, implored of her to listen to him, to trust him, to follow his advice.

When he had finished speaking, she only replied:

"Are you disposed to let me go away now? Take away your hands, so that I may rise to my feet."

"Look here, Irene."

"Will you let me go?"

"Irene—is your resolution irrevocable?"

"Will you let me go."

"Tell me only whether this resolution, this mad resolution of yours, which you will bitterly regret, is irrevocable?"

"Yes—let me go!"

"Then stay. You know well that you are at home here. We shall go away to-morrow morning."

She rose to her feet in spite of him, and said in a hard tone:

"No. It is too late. I do not want sacrifice; I do not want devotion."

"Stay! I have done what I ought to do; I have said what I ought to say. I have no further responsibility on your behalf. My conscience is at peace. Tell me what you want me to do, and I will obey."'

She resumed her seat, looked at him for a long time, and then asked, in a very calm voice:

"Well, then, explain."

"Explain what? What do you wish me to explain?"

"Everything—everything that you thought about before changing your mind. Then I will see what I ought to do."

"But I thought about nothing at all. I had to warn you that you were going to commit an act of folly. You persist; then I ask to share in this act of folly, and I even insist on it."

"It is not natural to change one's mind so quickly."

"Listen, my dear love. It is not a question here of sacrifice or devotion. On the day when I realized that I loved you, I said to myself what every lover ought to say to himself in the same case: 'The man who loves a woman, who makes an effort to win her, who gets her, and who takes her, enters into a sacred contract with himself and with her. That is, of course, in dealing with a woman like you, not a woman with a fickle heart and easily impressed.'

"Marriage which has a great social value, a great legal value, possesses in my eyes only a very slight moral value, taking into account the conditions under which it generally takes place.

"Therefore, when a woman, united by this lawful bond, but having no attachment to her husband, whom she cannot love, a woman whose heart is free, meets a man whom she cares for, and gives herself to him, when a man who has no other tie, takes a woman in this way, I say that they pledge themselves toward each other by this mutual and free agreement much more than by the 'Yes' uttered in the presence of the mayor.

"I say that, if they are both honorable persons, their union must be more intimate, more real, more wholesome, than if all the sacraments had consecrated it.

"This woman risks everything. And it is exactly because she knows it, because she gives everything, her heart, her body, her soul, her honor, her life, because she has foreseen all miseries, all dangers all catastrophes, because she dares to do a bold act, an intrepid act, because she is prepared, determined to brave everything—her husband, who might kill her, and society, which may cast her out. This is why she is worthy of respect in the midst of her conjugal infidelity; this is why her lover, in taking her, should also foresee everything, and prefer her to every one else whatever may happen. I have nothing more to say. I spoke in the beginning like a sensible man whose duty it was to warn you; and now I am only a man—a man who loves you—Command, and I obey."

Radiant, she closed his mouth with a kiss, and said in a low tone:

"It is not true, darling! There is nothing the matter! My husband does not suspect anything. But I wanted to see, I wanted to know, what you would do. I wished for a New Year's gift—the gift of your heart—another gift besides the necklace you sent me. You have given it to me. Thanks! thanks! God be thanked for the happiness you have given me!"

FRIEND PATIENCE

What became of Leremy?"

"He is captain in the Sixth Dragoons."

"And Pinson?"

"He's a subprefect."

"And Racollet?"

"Dead."

We were searching for other names which would remind us of the youthful faces of our younger days. Once in a while we had met some of these old comrades, bearded, bald, married, fathers of several children, and the realization of these changes had given us an unpleasant shudder, reminding us how short life is, how everything passes away, how everything changes. My friend asked me:

"And Patience, fat Patience?"

I almost, howled:

"Oh! as for him, just listen to this. Four or five years ago I was in Limoges, on a tour of inspection, and I was waiting for dinner time. I was seated before the big cafe in the Place du Theatre, just bored to death. The tradespeople were coming by twos, threes or fours, to take their absinthe or vermouth, talking all the time of their own or other people's business, laughing loudly, or lowering their voices in order to impart some important or delicate piece of news.

"I was saying to myself: 'What shall I do after dinner?' And I thought of the long evening in this provincial town, of the slow, dreary walk through unknown streets, of the impression of deadly gloom which these provincial people produce on the lonely traveller, and of the whole oppressive atmosphere of the place.

"I was thinking of all these things as I watched the little jets of gas flare up, feeling my loneliness increase with the falling shadows.

"A big, fat man sat down at the next table and called in a stentorian voice:

"'Waiter, my bitters!'

"The 'my' came out like the report of a cannon. I immediately understood that everything was his in life, and not another's; that he had his nature, by Jove, his appetite, his trousers, his everything, his, more absolutely and more completely than anyone else's. Then he looked round him with a satisfied air. His bitters were brought, and he ordered:

"'My newspaper!'

"I wondered: 'Which newspaper can his be?' The title would certainly reveal to me his opinions, his theories, his principles, his hobbies, his weaknesses.

"The waiter brought the Temps. I was surprised. Why the Temps, a serious, sombre, doctrinaire, impartial sheet? I thought:

"'He must be a serious man with settled and regular habits; in short, a good bourgeois.'

"He put on his gold-rimmed spectacles, leaned back before beginning to read, and once more glanced about him. He noticed me, and immediately began to stare at me in an annoying manner. I was even going to ask the reason for this attention, when he exclaimed from his seat:

"'Well, by all that's holy, if this isn't Gontran Lardois.'

"I answered:

"'Yes, monsieur, you are not mistaken.'

"Then he quickly rose and came toward me with hands outstretched:

"'Well, old man, how are you?'

"As I did not recognize him at all I was greatly embarrassed. I stammered:

"'Why-very well-and-you?'

"He began to laugh "'I bet you don't recognize me.'

"'No, not exactly. It seems—however—'

"He slapped me on the back:

"'Come on, no joking! I am Patience, Robert Patience, your friend, your chum.'

"I recognized him. Yes, Robert Patience, my old college chum. It was he. I took his outstretched hand:

"'And how are you?'

"'Fine!'

"His smile was like a paean of victory.

"He asked:

"'What are you doing here?'

"I explained that I was government inspector of taxes.

"He continued, pointing to my red ribbon:

"'Then you have-been a success?'

"I answered:

"'Fairly so. And you?'

"'I am doing well!'

"'What are you doing?'

"'I'm in business.'

"'Making money?'

"'Heaps. I'm very rich. But come around to lunch, to-morrow noon, 17 Rue du Coq-qui-Chante; you will see my place.'

"He seemed to hesitate a second, then continued:

"'Are you still the good sport that you used to be?'

"'I—I hope so.'

"'Not married?'

"'No.'

"'Good. And do you still love a good time and potatoes?'

"I was beginning to find him hopelessly vulgar. Nevertheless, I answered "'Yes.'

"'And pretty girls?'

"'Most assuredly.'

"He began to laugh good-humoredly.

"'Good, good! Do you remember our first escapade, in Bordeaux, after that dinner at Routie's? What a spree!'

"I did, indeed, remember that spree; and the recollection of it cheered me up. This called to mind other pranks. He would say:

"'Say, do you remember the time when we locked the proctor up in old man Latoque's cellar?'

"And he laughed and banged the table with his fist, and then he continued:

"'Yes-yes-yes-and do you remember the face of the geography teacher, M. Marin, the day we set off a firecracker in the globe, just as he was haranguing about the principal volcanoes of the earth?'

"Then suddenly I asked him:

"'And you, are you married?'

"He exclaimed:

"'Ten years, my boy, and I have four children, remarkable youngsters; but you'll see them and their mother.'

"We were talking rather loud; the people around us looked at us in surprise.

"Suddenly my friend looked at his watch, a chronometer the size of a pumpkin, and he cried:

"'Thunder! I'm sorry, but I'll have to leave you; I am never free at night.'

"He rose, took both my hands, shook them as though he were trying to wrench my arms from their sockets, and exclaimed:

"'So long, then; till to-morrow noon!'

"'So long!'

"I spent the morning working in the office of the collector-general of the Department. The chief wished me to stay to luncheon, but I told him that I had an engagement with a friend. As he had to go out, he accompanied me.

"I asked him:

"'Can you tell me how I can find the Rue du Coq-qui-Chante?'

"He answered:

"'Yes, it's only five minutes' walk from here. As I have nothing special to do, I will take you there.'

"We started out and soon found ourselves there. It was a wide, fine-looking street, on the outskirts of the town. I looked at the houses and I noticed No. 17. It was a large house with a garden behind it. The facade, decorated with frescoes, in the Italian style, appeared to me as being in bad taste. There were goddesses holding vases, others swathed in clouds. Two stone cupids supported the number of the house.

"I said to the treasurer:

"'Here is where I am going.'

"I held my hand out to him. He made a quick, strange gesture, said nothing and shook my hand.

"I rang. A maid appeared. I asked:

"'Monsieur Patience, if you please?'

"She answered:

"'Right here, sir. Is it to monsieur that you wish to speak?'

"'Yes.'

"The hall was decorated with paintings from the brush of some local artist. Pauls and Virginias were kissing each other under palm trees bathed in a pink light. A hideous Oriental lantern was ranging from the ceiling. Several doors were concealed by bright hangings.

"But what struck me especially was the odor. It was a sickening and perfumed odor, reminding one of rice powder and the mouldy smell of a cellar. An indefinable odor in a heavy atmosphere as oppressive as that of public baths. I followed the maid up a marble stairway, covered with a green, Oriental carpet, and was ushered into a sumptubus parlor.

"Left alone, I looked about me.

"The room was richly furnished, but in the pretentious taste of a parvenu. Rather fine engravings of the last century represented women with powdered hair dressed high surprised by gentlemen in interesting positions. Another lady, lying in a large bed, was teasing with her foot a little dog, lost in the sheets. One drawing showed four feet, bodies concealed behind a curtain. The large room, surrounded by soft couches, was entirely impregnated with that enervating and insipid odor which I had already noticed. There seemed to be something suspicious about the walls, the hangings, the exaggerated luxury, everything.

"I approached the window to look into the garden. It was very big, shady, beautiful. A wide path wound round a grass plot in the midst of which was a fountain, entered a shrubbery and came out farther away. And, suddenly, yonder, in the distance, between two clumps of bushes, three women appeared. They were walking slowly, arm in arm, clad in long, white tea-gowns covered with lace. Two were blondes and the other was dark-haired. Almost immediately they disappeared again behind the trees. I stood there entranced, delighted with this short and charming apparition, which brought to my mind a whole world of poetry. They had scarcely allowed themselves to be seen, in just the proper light, in that frame of foliage, in the midst of that mysterious, delightful park. It seemed to me that I had suddenly seen before me the great ladies of the last century, who were depicted in the engravings on the wall. And I began to think of the happy, joyous, witty and amorous times when manners were so graceful and lips so approachable.

"A deep voice made me jump. Patience had come in, beaming, and held out his hands to me.

"He looked into my eyes with the sly look which one takes when divulging secrets of love, and, with a Napoleonic gesture, he showed me his sumptuous parlor, his park, the three women, who had reappeared in the back of it, then, in a triumphant voice, where the note of pride was prominent, he said:

"'And to think that I began with nothing—my wife and my sister-in-law!'"

ABANDONED

"I really think you must be mad, my dear, to go for a country walk in such weather as this. You have had some very strange notions for the last two months. You drag me to the seaside in spite of myself, when you have never once had such a whim during all the forty-four years that we have been married. You chose Fecamp, which is a very dull town, without consulting me in the matter, and now you are seized with such a rage for walking, you who hardly ever stir out on foot, that you want to take a country walk on the hottest day of the year. Ask d'Apreval to go with you, as he is ready to gratify all your whims. As for me, I am going back to have a nap."

Madame de Cadour turned to her old friend and said:

"Will you come with me, Monsieur d'Apreval?"

He bowed with a smile, and with all the gallantry of former years:

"I will go wherever you go," he replied.

"Very well, then, go and get a sunstroke," Monsieur de Cadour said; and he went back to the Hotel des Bains to lie down for an hour or two.

As soon as they were alone, the old lady and her old companion set off, and she said to him in a low voice, squeezing his hand:

"At last! at last!"

"You are mad," he said in a whisper. "I assure you that you are mad. Think of the risk you are running. If that man—"

She started.

"Oh! Henri, do not say that man, when you are speaking of him."

"Very well," he said abruptly, "if our son guesses anything, if he has any suspicions, he will have you, he will have us both in his power. You have got on without seeing him for the last forty years. What is the matter with you to-day?"

They had been going up the long street that leads from the sea to the town, and now they turned to the right, to go to Etretat. The white road stretched in front of him, then under a blaze of brilliant sunshine, so they went on slowly in the burning heat. She had taken her old friend's arm, and was looking straight in front of her, with a fixed and haunted gaze, and at last she said:

"And so you have not seen him again, either?"

"No, never."

"Is it possible?"

"My dear friend, do not let us begin that discussion again. I have a wife and children and you have a husband, so we both of us have much to fear from other people's opinion."

She did not reply; she was thinking of her long past youth and of many sad things that had occurred. How well she recalled all the details of their early friendship, his smiles, the way he used to linger, in order to watch her until she was indoors. What happy days they were, the only really delicious days she had ever enjoyed, and how quickly they were over!

And then—her discovery—of the penalty she paid! What anguish!

Of that journey to the South, that long journey, her sufferings, her constant terror, that secluded life in the small, solitary house on the shores of the Mediterranean, at the bottom of a garden, which she did not venture to leave. How well she remembered those long days which she spent lying under an orange tree, looking up at the round, red fruit, amid the green leaves. How she used to long to go out, as far as the sea, whose fresh breezes came to her over the wall, and whose small waves she could hear lapping on the beach. She dreamed of its immense blue expanse sparkling under the sun, with the white sails of the small vessels, and a mountain on the horizon. But she did not dare to go outside the gate. Suppose anybody had recognized her!

And those days of waiting, those last days of misery and expectation! The impending suffering, and then that terrible night! What misery she had endured, and what a night it was! How she had groaned and screamed! She could still see the pale face of her lover, who kissed her hand every moment, and the clean-shaven face of the doctor and the nurse's white cap.

And what she felt when she heard the child's feeble cries, that wail, that first effort of a human's voice!

And the next day! the next day! the only day of her life on which she had seen and kissed her son; for, from that time, she had never even caught a glimpse of him.

And what a long, void existence hers had been since then, with the thought of that child always, always floating before her. She had never seen her son, that little creature that had been part of herself, even once since then; they had taken him from her, carried him away, and had hidden him. All she knew was that he had been brought up by some peasants in Normandy, that he had become a peasant himself, had married well, and that his father, whose name he did not know, had settled a handsome sum of money on him.

How often during the last forty years had she wished to go and see him and to embrace him! She could not imagine to herself that he had grown! She always thought of that small human atom which she had held in her arms and pressed to her bosom for a day.

How often she had said to M. d'Apreval: "I cannot bear it any longer; I must go and see him."

But he had always stopped her and kept her from going. She would be unable to restrain and to master herself; their son would guess it and take advantage of her, blackmail her; she would be lost.

"What is he like?" she said.

"I do not know. I have not seen him again, either."

"Is it possible? To have a son and not to know him; to be afraid of him and to reject him as if he were a disgrace! It is horrible."

They went along the dusty road, overcome by the scorching sun, and continually ascending that interminable hill.

"One might take it for a punishment," she continued; "I have never had another child, and I could no longer resist the longing to see him, which has possessed me for forty years. You men cannot understand that. You must remember that I shall not live much longer, and suppose I should never see him, never have seen him! ... Is it possible? How could I wait so long? I have thought about him every day since, and what a terrible existence mine has been! I have never awakened, never, do you understand, without my first thoughts being of him, of my child. How is he? Oh, how guilty I feel toward him! Ought one to fear what the world may say in a case like this? I ought to have left everything to go after him, to bring him up and to show my love for him. I should certainly have been much happier, but I did not dare, I was a coward. How I have suffered! Oh, how those poor, abandoned children must hate their mothers!"

She stopped suddenly, for she was choked by her sobs. The whole valley was deserted and silent in the dazzling light and the overwhelming heat, and only the grasshoppers uttered their shrill, continuous chirp among the sparse yellow grass on both sides of the road.

"Sit down a little," he said.

She allowed herself to be led to the side of the ditch and sank down with her face in her hands. Her white hair, which hung in curls on both sides of her face, had become tangled. She wept, overcome by profound grief, while he stood facing her, uneasy and not knowing what to say, and he merely murmured: "Come, take courage."

She got up.

"I will," she said, and wiping her eyes, she began to walk again with the uncertain step of an elderly woman.

A little farther on the road passed beneath a clump of trees, which hid a few houses, and they could distinguish the vibrating and regular blows of a blacksmith's hammer on the anvil; and presently they saw a wagon standing on the right side of the road in front of a low cottage, and two men shoeing a horse under a shed.

Monsieur d'Apreval went up to them.

"Where is Pierre Benedict's farm?" he asked.

"Take the road to the left, close to the inn, and then go straight on; it is the third house past Poret's. There is a small spruce fir close to the gate; you cannot make a mistake."

They turned to the left. She was walking very slowly now, her legs threatened to give way, and her heart was beating so violently that she felt as if she should suffocate, while at every step she murmured, as if in prayer:

"Oh! Heaven! Heaven!"

Monsieur d'Apreval, who was also nervous and rather pale, said to her somewhat gruffly:

"If you cannot manage to control your feelings, you will betray yourself at once. Do try and restrain yourself."

"How can I?" she replied. "My child! When I think that I am going to see my child."

They were going along one of those narrow country lanes between farmyards, that are concealed beneath a double row of beech trees at either side of the ditches, and suddenly they found themselves in front of a gate, beside which there was a young spruce fir.

"This is it," he said.

She stopped suddenly and looked about her. The courtyard, which was planted with apple trees, was large and extended as far as the small thatched dwelling house. On the opposite side were the stable, the barn, the cow house and the poultry house, while the gig, the wagon and the manure cart were under a slated outhouse. Four calves were grazing under the shade of the trees and black hens were wandering all about the enclosure.

All was perfectly still; the house door was open, but nobody was to be seen, and so they went in, when immediately a large black dog came out of a barrel that was standing under a pear tree, and began to bark furiously.

There were four bee-hives on boards against the wall of the house.

Monsieur d'Apreval stood outside and called out:

"Is anybody at home?"

Then a child appeared, a little girl of about ten, dressed in a chemise and a linen, petticoat, with dirty, bare legs and a timid and cunning look. She remained standing in the doorway, as if to prevent any one going in.

"What do you want?" she asked.

"Is your father in?"

"No."

"Where is he?"

"I don't know."

"And your mother?"

"Gone after the cows."

"Will she be back soon?"

"I don't know."

Then suddenly the lady, as if she feared that her companion might force her to return, said quickly:

"I shall not go without having seen him."

"We will wait for him, my dear friend."

As they turned away, they saw a peasant woman coming toward the house, carrying two tin pails, which appeared to be heavy and which glistened brightly in the sunlight.

She limped with her right leg, and in her brown knitted jacket, that was faded by the sun and washed out by the rain, she looked like a poor, wretched, dirty servant.

"Here is mamma," the child said.

When she got close to the house, she looked at the strangers angrily and suspiciously, and then she went in, as if she had not seen them. She looked old and had a hard, yellow, wrinkled face, one of those wooden faces that country people so often have.

Monsieur d'Apreval called her back.

"I beg your pardon, madame, but we came in to know whether you could sell us two glasses of milk."

She was grumbling when she reappeared in the door, after putting down her pails.

"I don't sell milk," she replied.

"We are very thirsty," he said, "and madame is very tired. Can we not get something to drink?"

The peasant woman gave them an uneasy and cunning glance and then she made up her mind.

"As you are here, I will give you some," she said, going into the house, and almost immediately the child came out and brought two chairs, which she placed under an apple tree, and then the mother, in turn, brought out two bowls of foaming milk, which she gave to the visitors. She did not return to the house, however, but remained standing near them, as if to watch them and to find out for what purpose they had come there.

"You have come from Fecamp?" she said.

"Yes," Monsieur d'Apreval replied, "we are staying at Fecamp for the summer."

And then, after a short silence, he continued:

"Have you any fowls you could sell us every week?"

The woman hesitated for a moment and then replied:

"Yes, I think I have. I suppose you want young ones?"

"Yes, of course."

"'What do you pay for them in the market?"

D'Apreval, who had not the least idea, turned to his companion:

"What are you paying for poultry in Fecamp, my dear lady?"

"Four francs and four francs fifty centimes," she said, her eyes full of tears, while the farmer's wife, who was looking at her askance, asked in much surprise:

"Is the lady ill, as she is crying?"

He did not know what to say, and replied with some hesitation:

"No—no—but she lost her watch as we came along, a very handsome watch, and that troubles her. If anybody should find it, please let us know."

Mother Benedict did not reply, as she thought it a very equivocal sort of answer, but suddenly she exclaimed:

"Oh, here is my husband!"

She was the only one who had seen him, as she was facing the gate. D'Apreval started and Madame de Cadour nearly fell as she turned round suddenly on her chair.

A man bent nearly double, and out of breath, stood there, ten-yards from them, dragging a cow at the end of a rope. Without taking any notice of the visitors, he said:

"Confound it! What a brute!"

And he went past them and disappeared in the cow house.

Her tears had dried quickly as she sat there startled, without a word and with the one thought in her mind, that this was her son, and D'Apreval, whom the same thought had struck very unpleasantly, said in an agitated voice:

"Is this Monsieur Benedict?"

"Who told you his name?" the wife asked, still rather suspiciously.

"The blacksmith at the corner of the highroad," he replied, and then they were all silent, with their eyes fixed on the door of the cow house, which formed a sort of black hole in the wall of the building. Nothing could be seen inside, but they heard a vague noise, movements and footsteps and the sound of hoofs, which were deadened by the straw on the floor, and soon the man reappeared in the door, wiping his forehead, and came toward the house with long, slow strides. He passed the strangers without seeming to notice them and said to his wife:

"Go and draw me a jug of cider; I am very thirsty."

Then he went back into the house, while his wife went into the cellar and left the two Parisians alone.

"Let us go, let us go, Henri," Madame de Cadour said, nearly distracted with grief, and so d'Apreval took her by the arm, helped her to rise, and sustaining her with all his strength, for he felt that she was nearly fainting, he led her out, after throwing five francs on one of the chairs.

As soon as they were outside the gate, she began to sob and said, shaking with grief:

"Oh! oh! is that what you have made of him?"

He was very pale and replied coldly:

"I did what I could. His farm is worth eighty thousand francs, and that is more than most of the sons of the middle classes have."

They returned slowly, without speaking a word. She was still crying; the tears ran down her cheeks continually for a time, but by degrees they stopped, and they went back to Fecamp, where they found Monsieur de Cadour waiting dinner for them. As soon as he saw them, he began to laugh and exclaimed:

"So my wife has had a sunstroke, and I am very glad of it. I really think she has lost her head for some time past!"

Neither of them replied, and when the husband asked them, rubbing his hands:

"Well, I hope that, at least, you have had a pleasant walk?"

Monsieur d'Apreval replied:

"A delightful walk, I assure you; perfectly delightful."

THE MAISON TELLIER

They went there every evening about eleven o'clock, just as they would go to the club. Six or eight of them; always the same set, not fast men, but respectable tradesmen, and young men in government or some other employ, and they would drink their Chartreuse, and laugh with the girls, or else talk seriously with Madame Tellier, whom everybody respected, and then they would go home at twelve o'clock! The younger men would sometimes stay later.

It was a small, comfortable house painted yellow, at the corner of a street behind Saint Etienne's Church, and from the windows one could see the docks full of ships being unloaded, the big salt marsh, and, rising beyond it, the Virgin's Hill with its old gray chapel.

Madame Tellier, who came of a respectable family of peasant proprietors in the Department of the Eure, had taken up her profession, just as she would have become a milliner or dressmaker. The prejudice which is so violent and deeply rooted in large towns, does not exist in the country places in Normandy. The peasant says:

"It is a paying-business," and he sends his daughter to keep an establishment of this character just as he would send her to keep a girls' school.

She had inherited the house from an old uncle, to whom it had belonged. Monsieur and Madame Tellier, who had formerly been innkeepers near Yvetot, had immediately sold their house, as they thought that the business at Fecamp was more profitable, and they arrived one fine morning to assume the direction of the enterprise, which was declining on account of the absence of the proprietors. They were good people enough in their way, and soon made themselves liked by their staff and their neighbors.

Monsieur died of apoplexy two years later, for as the new place kept him in idleness and without any exercise, he had grown excessively stout, and his health had suffered. Since she had been a widow, all the frequenters of the establishment made much of her; but people said that, personally, she was quite virtuous, and even the girls in the house could not discover anything against her. She was tall, stout and affable, and her complexion, which had become pale in the dimness of her house, the shutters of which were scarcely ever opened, shone as if it had been varnished. She had a fringe of curly false hair, which gave her a juvenile look, that contrasted strongly with the ripeness of her figure. She was always smiling and cheerful, and was fond of a joke, but there was a shade of reserve about her, which her occupation had not quite made her lose. Coarse words always shocked her, and when any young fellow who had been badly brought up called her establishment a hard name, she was angry and disgusted.

In a word, she had a refined mind, and although she treated her women as friends, yet she very frequently used to say that "she and they were not made of the same stuff."

Sometimes during the week she would hire a carriage and take some of her girls into the country, where they used to enjoy themselves on the grass by the side of the little river. They were like a lot of girls let out from school, and would run races and play childish games. They had a cold dinner on the grass, and drank cider, and went home at night with a delicious feeling of fatigue, and in the carriage they kissed Madame' Tellier as their kind mother, who was full of goodness and complaisance.

The house had two entrances. At the corner there was a sort of tap-room, which sailors and the lower orders frequented at night, and she had two girls whose special duty it was to wait on them with the assistance of Frederic, a short, light-haired, beardless fellow, as strong as a horse. They set the half bottles of wine and the jugs of beer on the shaky marble tables before the customers, and then urged the men to drink.

The three other girls—there were only five of them—formed a kind of aristocracy, and they remained with the company on the first floor, unless they were wanted downstairs and there was nobody on the first floor. The salon de Jupiter, where the tradesmen used to meet, was papered in blue, and embellished with a large drawing representing Leda and the swan. The room was reached by a winding staircase, through a narrow door opening on the street, and above this door a lantern inclosed in wire, such as one still sees in some towns, at the foot of the shrine of some saint, burned all night long.

The house, which was old and damp, smelled slightly of mildew. At times there was an odor of eau de Cologne in the passages, or sometimes from a half-open door downstairs the noisy mirth of the common men sitting and drinking rose to the first floor, much to the disgust of the gentlemen who were there. Madame Tellier, who was on friendly terms with her customers, did not leave the room, and took much interest in what was going on in the town, and they regularly told her all the news. Her serious conversation was a change from the ceaseless chatter of the three women; it was a rest from the obscene jokes of those stout individuals who every evening indulged in the commonplace debauchery of drinking a glass of liqueur in company with common women.

The names of the girls on the first floor were Fernande, Raphaele, and Rosa, the Jade. As the staff was limited, madame had endeavored that each member of it should be a pattern, an epitome of the feminine type, so that every customer might find as nearly as possible the realization of his ideal. Fernande represented the handsome blonde; she was very tall, rather fat, and lazy; a country girl, who could not get rid of her freckles, and whose short, light, almost colorless, tow-like hair, like combed-out hemp, barely covered her head.

Raphaele, who came from Marseilles, played the indispensable part of the handsome Jewess, and was thin, with high cheekbones, which were covered with rouge, and black hair covered with pomatum, which curled on her forehead. Her eyes would have been handsome, if the right one had not had a speck in it. Her Roman nose came down over a square jaw, where two false upper teeth contrasted strangely with the bad color of the rest.

Rosa was a little roll of fat, nearly all body, with very short legs, and from morning till night she sang songs, which were alternately risque or sentimental, in a harsh voice; told silly, interminable tales, and only stopped talking in order to eat, and left off eating in order to talk; she was never still, and was active as a squirrel, in spite of her embonpoint and her short legs; her laugh, which was a torrent of shrill cries, resounded here and there, ceaselessly, in a bedroom, in the loft, in the cafe, everywhere, and all about nothing.

The two women on the ground floor, Lodise, who was nicknamed La Cocotte, and Flora, whom they called Balancoise, because she limped a little, the former always dressed as the Goddess of Liberty, with a tri-colored sash, and the other as a Spanish woman, with a string of copper coins in her carroty hair, which jingled at every uneven step, looked like cooks dressed up for the carnival. They were like all other women of the lower orders, neither uglier nor better looking than they usually are.

They looked just like servants at an inn, and were generally called "the two pumps."

A jealous peace, which was, however, very rarely disturbed, reigned among these five women, thanks to Madame Tellier's conciliatory wisdom, and to her constant good humor, and the establishment, which was the only one of the kind in the little town, was very much frequented. Madame Tellier had succeeded in giving it such a respectable appearance, she was so amiable and obliging to everybody, her good heart was so well known, that she was treated with a certain amount of consideration. The regular customers spent money on her, and were delighted when she was especially friendly toward them, and when they met during the day, they would say: "Until this evening, you know where," just as men say: "At the club, after dinner." In a word, Madame Tellier's house was somewhere to go to, and they very rarely missed their daily meetings there.

One evening toward the end of May, the first arrival, Monsieur Poulin, who was a timber merchant, and had been mayor, found the door shut. The lantern behind the grating was not alight; there was not a sound in the house; everything seemed dead. He knocked, gently at first, but then more loudly, but nobody answered the door. Then he went slowly up the street, and when he got to the market place he met Monsieur Duvert, the gunmaker, who was going to the same place, so they went back together, but did not meet with any better success. But suddenly they heard a loud noise, close to them, and on going round the house, they saw a number of English and French sailors, who were hammering at the closed shutters of the taproom with their fists.

The two tradesmen immediately made their escape, but a low "Pst!" stopped them; it was Monsieur Tournevau, the fish curer, who had recognized them, and was trying to attract their attention. They told him what had happened, and he was all the more annoyed, as he was a married man and father of a family, and only went on Saturdays. That was his regular evening, and now he should be deprived of this dissipation for the whole week.

The three men went as far as the quay together, and on the way they met young Monsieur Philippe, the banker's son, who frequented the place regularly, and Monsieur Pinipesse, the collector, and they all returned to the Rue aux Juifs together, to make a last attempt. But the exasperated sailors were besieging the house, throwing stones at the shutters, and shouting, and the five first-floor customers went away as quickly as possible, and walked aimlessly about the streets.

Presently they met Monsieur Dupuis, the insurance agent, and then Monsieur Vasse, the Judge of the Tribunal of Commerce, and they took a long walk, going to the pier first of all, where they sat down in a row on the granite parapet and watched the rising tide, and when the promenaders had sat there for some time, Monsieur Tournevau said:

"This is not very amusing!"

"Decidedly not," Monsieur Pinipesse replied, and they started off to walk again.

After going through the street alongside the hill, they returned over the wooden bridge which crosses the Retenue, passed close to the railway, and came out again on the market place, when, suddenly, a quarrel arose between Monsieur Pinipesse, the collector, and Monsieur Tournevau about an edible mushroom which one of them declared he had found in the neighborhood.

As they were out of temper already from having nothing to do, they would very probably have come to blows, if the others had not interfered. Monsieur Pinipesse went off furious, and soon another altercation arose between the ex-mayor, Monsieur

Poulin, and Monsieur Dupuis, the insurance agent, on the subject of the tax collector's salary and the profits which he might make. Insulting remarks were freely passing between them, when a torrent of formidable cries was heard, and the body of sailors, who were tired of waiting so long outside a closed house, came into the square. They were walking arm in arm, two and two, and formed a long procession, and were shouting furiously. The townsmen hid themselves in a doorway, and the yelling crew disappeared in the direction of the abbey. For a long time they still heard the noise, which diminished like a storm in the distance, and then silence was restored. Monsieur Poulin and Monsieur Dupuis, who were angry with each other, went in different directions, without wishing each other good-by.

The other four set off again, and instinctively went in the direction of Madame Tellier's establishment, which was still closed, silent, impenetrable. A quiet, but obstinate drunken man was knocking at the door of the lower room, antd then stopped and called Frederic, in a low voice, but finding that he got no answer, he sat down on the doorstep, and waited the course of events.

The others were just going to retire, when the noisy band of sailors reappeared at the end of the street. The French sailors were shouting the "Marseillaise," and the Englishmen "Rule Britannia." There was a general lurching against the wall, and then the drunken fellows went on their way toward the quay, where a fight broke out between the two nations, in the course of which an Englishman had his arm broken and a Frenchman his nose split.

The drunken man who had waited outside the door, was crying by that time, as drunken men and children cry when they are vexed, and the others went away. By degrees, calm was restored in the noisy town; here and there, at moments, the distant sound of voices could be heard, and then died away in the distance.

One man only was still wandering about, Monsieur Tournevau, the fish curer, who was annoyed at having to wait until the following Saturday, and he hoped something would turn up, he did not know what; but he was exasperated at the police for thus allowing an establishment of such public utility, which they had under their control, to be closed.

He went back to it and examined the walls, trying to find out some reason, and on the shutter he saw a notice stuck up. He struck a wax match and read the following, in a large, uneven hand: "Closed on account of the Confirmation."

Then he went away, as he saw it was useless to remain, and left the drunken man lying on the pavement fast asleep, outside that inhospitable door.

The next day, all the regular customers, one after the other, found some reason for going through the street, with a bundle of papers under their arm to keep them in countenance, and with a furtive glance they all read that mysterious notice:

"Closed on account of the Confirmation."

PART II

Madame Tellier had a brother, who was a carpenter in their native place, Virville, in the Department of Eure. When she still kept the inn at Yvetot, she had stood godmother to that brother's daughter, who had received the name of Constance—Constance Rivet; she herself being a Rivet on her father's side. The carpenter, who knew that his sister was in a good position, did not lose sight of her, although they did not meet often, for they were both kept at home by their occupations, and lived a long way from each other. But as the girl was twelve years old, and going to be confirmed, he seized that opportunity to write to his sister, asking her to come and be present at the ceremony. Their old parents were dead, and as she could not well refuse her goddaughter, she accepted the invitation. Her brother, whose name was Joseph, hoped that by dint of showing his sister attention, she might be induced to make her will in the girl's favor, as she had no children of her own.

His sister's occupation did not trouble his scruples in the least, and, besides, nobody knew anything about it at Virville. When they spoke of her, they only said: "Madame Tellier is living at Fecamp," which might mean that she was living on her own private income. It was quite twenty leagues from Fecamp to Virville, and for a peasant, twenty leagues on land is as long a journey as crossing the ocean would be to city people. The people at Virville had never been further than Rouen, and nothing attracted the people from Fecamp to a village of five hundred houses in the middle of a plain, and situated in another department; at any rate, nothing was known about her business.

But the Confirmation was coming on, and Madame Tellier was in great embarrassment. She had no substitute, and did not at all care to leave her house, even for a day; for all the rivalries between the girls upstairs and those downstairs would infallibly break out. No doubt Frederic would get drunk, and when he was in that state, he would knock anybody down for a mere word. At last, however, she made up her mind to take them all with her, with the exception of the man, to whom she gave a holiday until the next day but one.

When she asked her brother, he made no objection, but undertook to put them all up for a night, and so on Saturday morning the eight-o'clock express carried off Madame Tellier and her companions in a second-class carriage. As far as Beuzeville they were alone, and chattered like magpies, but at that station a couple got in. The man, an old peasant, dressed in a blue blouse with a turned-down collar, wide sleeves tight at the wrist, ornamented with white embroidery, wearing an old high hat with long nap, held an enormous green umbrella in one hand, and a large basket in the other, from which the heads of three frightened ducks protruded. The woman, who sat up stiffly in her rustic finery, had a face like a fowl, with a nose that was as pointed as a bill. She sat down opposite her husband and did not stir, as she was startled at finding herself in such smart company.

There was certainly an array of striking colors in the carriage. Madame Tellier was dressed in blue silk from head to foot, and had on a dazzling red imitation French cashmere shawl. Fernande was puffing in a Scotch plaid dress, of which her companions had laced the bodice as tight as they could, forcing up her full bust, that was continually heaving up and down. Raphaele, with a bonnet covered with feathers, so that it looked like a bird's nest, had on a lilac dress with gold spots on it, and there was something Oriental about it that suited her Jewish face. Rosa had on a pink skirt with largo flounces, and looked like a very fat child, an obese dwarf; while the two Pumps looked as if they had cut their dresses out of old flowered curtains dating from the Restoration.

As soon as they were no longer alone in the compartment, the ladies put on staid looks, and began to talk of subjects which might give others a high opinion of them. But at Bolbeck a gentleman with light whiskers, a gold chain, and wearing two or three rings, got in, and put several parcels wrapped in oilcloth on the rack over his head. He looked inclined for a joke, and seemed a good-hearted fellow.

"Are you ladies changing your quarters?" he said, and that question embarrassed them all considerably. Madame Tellier, however, quickly regained her composure, and said sharply, to avenge the honor of her corps:

"I think you might try and be polite!"

He excused himself, and said: "I beg your pardon, I ought to have said your nunnery."

She could not think of a retort, so, perhaps thinking she had said enough, madame gave him a dignified bow and compressed her lips.

Then the gentleman, who was sitting between Rosa and the old peasant, began to wink knowingly at the ducks whose heads were sticking out of the basket, and when he felt that he had fixed the attention of his public, he began to tickle them under the bills and spoke funnily to them to make the company smile.

"We have left our little pond, quack! quack! to make the acquaintance of the little spit, qu-ack! qu-ack!"

The unfortunate creatures turned their necks away, to avoid his caresses, and made desperate efforts to get out of their wicker prison, and then, suddenly, all at once, uttered the most lamentable quacks of distress. The women exploded with laughter. They leaned forward and pushed each other, so as to see better; they were very much interested in the ducks, and the gentleman redoubled his airs, his wit and his teasing.

Rosa joined in, and leaning over her neighbor's legs, she kissed the three animals on the head, and immediately all the girls wanted to kiss them, in turn, and as they did so the gentleman took them on his knee, jumped them up and down and pinched their arms. The two peasants, who were even in greater consternation than their poultry, rolled their eyes as if they were possessed, without venturing to move, and their old wrinkled faces had not a smile, not a twitch.

Then the gentleman, who was a commercial traveller, offered the ladies suspenders by way of a joke, and taking up one of his packages, he opened it. It was a joke, for the parcel contained garters. There were blue silk, pink silk, red silk, violet silk, mauve silk garters, and the buckles were made of two gilt metal cupids embracing each other. The girls uttered exclamations of delight and looked at them with that gravity natural to all women when they are considering an article of dress. They consulted one another by their looks or in a whisper, and replied in the same manner, and Madame Tellier was longingly handling a pair of orange garters that were broader and more imposing looking than the rest; really fit for the mistress of such an establishment.

The gentleman waited, for he had an idea.

"Come, my kittens," he said, "you must try them on."

There was a torrent of exclamations, and they squeezed their petticoats between their legs, but he quietly waited his time and said: "Well, if you will not try them on I shall pack them up again."

And he added cunningly: "I offer any pair they like to those who will try them on."

But they would not, and sat up very straight and looked dignified.

But the two Pumps looked so distressed that he renewed his offer to them, and Flora, especially, visibly hesitated, and he insisted: "Come, my dear, a little courage! Just look at that lilac pair; it will suit your dress admirably."

That decided her, and pulling up her dress she showed a thick leg fit for a milkmaid, in a badly fitting, coarse stocking. The commercial traveller stooped down and fastened the garter. When he had done this, he gave her the lilac pair and asked: "Who next?"

"I! I!" they all shouted at once, and he began on Rosa, who uncovered a shapeless, round thing without any ankle, a regular "sausage of a leg," as Raphaele used to say.

Lastly, Madame Tellier herself put out her leg, a handsome, muscular Norman leg, and in his surprise and pleasure, the commercial traveller gallantly took off his hat to salute that master calf, like a true French cavalier.

The two peasants, who were speechless from surprise, glanced sideways out of the corner of one eye, and they looked so exactly like fowls that the man with the light whiskers, when he sat up, said: "Co—co—ri—co" under their very noses, and that gave rise to another storm of amusement.

The old people got out at Motteville with their basket, their ducks and their umbrella, and they heard the woman say to her husband as they went away:

"They are no good and are off to that cursed place, Paris."

The funny commercial traveller himself got out at Rouen, after behaving so coarsely that Madame Tellier was obliged sharply to put him in his right place, and she added, as a moral: "This will teach us not to talk to the first comer."

At Oissel they changed trains, and at a little station further on Monsieur Joseph Rivet was waiting for them with a large cart with a number of chairs in it, drawn by a white horse.

The carpenter politely kissed all the ladies and then helped them into his conveyance.

Three of them sat on three chairs at the back, Raphaele, Madame Tellier and her brother on the three chairs in front, while Rosa, who had no seat, settled herself as comfortably as she could on tall Fernande's knees, and then they set off.

But the horse's jerky trot shook the cart so terribly that the chairs began to dance and threw the travellers about, to the right and to the left, as if they were dancing puppets, which made them scream and make horrible grimaces.

They clung on to the sides of the vehicle, their bonnets fell on their backs, over their faces and on their shoulders, and the white horse went on stretching out his head and holding out his little hairless tail like a rat's, with which he whisked his buttocks from time to time.

Joseph Rivet, with one leg on the shafts and the other doubled under him, held the reins with his elbows very high, and kept uttering a kind of clucking sound, which made the horse prick up its ears and go faster.

The green country extended on either side of the road, and here and there the colza in flower presented a waving expanse of yellow, from which arose a strong, wholesome, sweet and penetrating odor, which the wind carried to some distance.

The cornflowers showed their little blue heads amid the rye, and the women wanted to pick them, but Monsieur Rivet refused to stop.

Then, sometimes, a whole field appeared to be covered with blood, so thick were the poppies, and the cart, which looked as if it were filled with flowers of more brilliant hue, jogged on through fields bright with wild flowers, and disappeared behind the trees of a farm, only to reappear and to go on again through the yellow or green standing crops, which were studded with red or blue.

One o'clock struck as they drove up to the carpenter's door. They were tired out and pale with hunger, as they had eaten nothing since they left home. Madame Rivet ran out and made them alight, one after another, and kissed them as soon as they were on the ground, and she seemed as if she would never tire of kissing her sister-in-law, whom she apparently wanted to monopolize. They had lunch in the workshop, which had been cleared out for the next day's dinner.

The capital omelet, followed by boiled chitterlings and washed down with good hard cider, made them all feel comfortable.

Rivet had taken a glass so that he might drink with them, and his wife cooked, waited on them, brought in the dishes, took them out and asked each of them in a whisper whether they had everything they wanted. A number of boards standing against the walls and heaps of shavings that had been swept into the corners gave out a smell of planed wood, a smell of a carpenter's shop, that resinous odor which penetrates to the lungs.

They wanted to see the little girl, but she had gone to church and would not be back again until evening, so they all went out for a stroll in the country.

It was a small village, through which the highroad passed. Ten or a dozen houses on either side of the single street were inhabited by the butcher, the grocer, the carpenter, the innkeeper, the shoemaker and the baker.

The church was at the end of the street and was surrounded by a small churchyard, and four immense lime-trees, which stood just outside the porch, shaded it completely. It was built of flint, in no particular style, and had a slate-roofed steeple. When you got past it, you were again in the open country, which was varied here and there by clumps of trees which hid the homesteads.

Rivet had given his arm to his sister, out of politeness, although he was in his working clothes, and was walking with her in a dignified manner. His wife, who was overwhelmed by Raphaele's gold-striped dress, walked between her and Fernande, and roly-poly Rosa was trotting behind with Louise and Flora, the Seesaw, who was limping along, quite tired out.

The inhabitants came to their doors, the children left off playing, and a window curtain would be raised, so as to show a muslin cap, while an old woman with a crutch, who was almost blind, crossed herself as if it were a religious procession, and they all gazed for a long time at those handsome ladies from town, who had come so far to be present at the confirmation of Joseph Rivet's little girl, and the carpenter rose very much in the public estimation.

As they passed the church they heard some children singing. Little shrill voices were singing a hymn, but Madame Tellier would not let them go in, for fear of disturbing the little cherubs.

After the walk, during which Joseph Rivet enumerated the principal landed proprietors, spoke about the yield of the land and the productiveness of the cows and sheep, he took his tribe of women home and installed them in his house, and as it was very small, they had to put them into the rooms, two and two.

Just for once Rivet would sleep in the workshop on the shavings; his wife was to share her bed with her sister-in-law, and Fernande and Raphaele were to sleep together in the next room. Louise and Flora were put into the kitchen, where they had a mattress on the floor, and Rosa had a little dark cupboard to herself at the top of the stairs, close to the loft, where the candidate for confirmation was to sleep.

When the little girl came in she was overwhelmed with kisses; all the women wished to caress her with that need of tender expansion, that habit of professional affection which had made them kiss the ducks in the railway carriage.

They each of them took her on their knees, stroked her soft, light hair and pressed her in their arms with vehement and spontaneous outbursts of affection, and the child, who was very good and religious, bore it all patiently.

As the day had been a fatiguing one for everybody, they all went to bed soon after dinner. The whole village was wrapped in that perfect stillness of the country, which is almost like a religious silence, and the girls, who were accustomed to the noisy evenings of their establishment, felt rather impressed by the perfect repose of the sleeping village, and they shivered, not with cold, but with those little shivers of loneliness which come over uneasy and troubled hearts.

As soon as they were in bed, two and two together, they clasped each other in their arms, as if to protect themselves against this feeling of the calm and profound slumber of the earth. But Rosa, who was alone in her little dark cupboard, felt a vague and painful emotion come over her.

She was tossing about in bed, unable to get to sleep, when she heard the faint sobs of a crying child close to her head, through the partition. She was frightened, and called out, and was answered by a weak voice, broken by sobs. It was the little girl, who was always used to sleeping in her mother's room, and who was afraid in her small attic.

Rosa was delighted, got up softly so as not to awaken any one, and went and fetched the child. She took her into her warm bed, kissed her and pressed her to her bosom, lavished exaggerated manifestations of tenderness on her, and at last grew calmer herself and went to sleep. And till morning the candidate for confirmation slept with her head on Rosa's bosom.

At five o'clock the little church bell, ringing the Angelus, woke the women, who usually slept the whole morning long.

The villagers were up already, and the women went busily from house to house, carefully bringing short, starched muslin dresses or very long wax tapers tied in the middle with a bow of silk fringed with gold, and with dents in the wax for the fingers.

The sun was already high in the blue sky, which still had a rosy tint toward the horizon, like a faint remaining trace of dawn. Families of fowls were walking about outside the houses, and here and there a black cock, with a glistening breast, raised his head, which was crowned by his red comb, flapped his wings and uttered his shrill crow, which the other cocks repeated.

Vehicles of all sorts came from neighboring parishes, stopping at the different houses, and tall Norman women dismounted, wearing dark dresses, with kerchiefs crossed over the bosom, fastened with silver brooches a hundred years old.

The men had put on their blue smocks over their new frock-coats or over their old dress-coats of green-cloth, the two tails of which hung down below their blouses. When the horses were in the stable there was a double line of rustic conveyances along the road: carts, cabriolets, tilburies, wagonettes, traps of every shape and age, tipping forward on their shafts or else tipping backward with the shafts up in the air.

The carpenter's house was as busy as a bee-hive. The women, in dressing-jackets and petticoats, with their thin, short hair, which looked faded and worn, hanging down their backs, were busy dressing the child, who was standing quietly on a table, while Madame Tellier was directing the movements of her battalion. They washed her, did her hair, dressed her, and with the help of a number of pins, they arranged the folds of her dress and took in the waist, which was too large.

Then, when she was ready, she was told to sit down and not to move, and the women hurried off to get ready themselves.

The church bell began to ring again, and its tinkle was lost in the air, like a feeble voice which is soon drowned in space. The candidates came out of the houses and went toward the parochial building, which contained the two schools and the mansion house, and which stood quite at one end of the village, while the church was situated at the other.

The parents, in their very best clothes, followed their children, with embarrassed looks, and those clumsy movements of a body bent by toil.

The little girls disappeared in a cloud of muslin, which looked like whipped cream, while the lads, who looked like embryo waiters in a cafe and whose heads shone with pomatum, walked with their legs apart, so as not to get any dust or dirt on their black trousers.

It was something for a family, to be proud of, when a large number of relatives, who had come from a distance, surrounded the child, and the carpenter's triumph was complete.

Madame Tellier's regiment, with its leader at its head, followed Constance; her father gave his arm to his sister, her mother walked by the side of Raphaele, Fernande with Rosa and Louise and Flora together, and thus they proceeded majestically through the village, like a general's staff in full uniform, while the effect on the village was startling.

At the school the girls ranged themselves under the Sister of Mercy and the boys under the schoolmaster, and they started off, singing a hymn as they went. The boys led the way, in two files, between the two rows of vehicles, from which the horses had been taken out, and the girls followed in the same order; and as all the people in the village had given the town ladies the precedence out of politeness, they came immediately behind the girls, and lengthened the double line of the procession still more, three on the right and three on the left, while their dresses were as striking as a display of fireworks.

When they went into the church the congregation grew quite excited. They pressed against each other, turned round and jostled one another in order to see, and some of the devout ones spoke almost aloud, for they were so astonished at the sight of those ladies whose dresses were more elaborate than the priest's vestments.

The mayor offered them his pew, the first one on the right, close to the choir, and Madame Tellier sat there with her sister-in-law, Fernande and Raphaele. Rosa, Louise and Flora occupied the second seat, in company with the carpenter.

The choir was full of kneeling children, the girls on one side and the boys on the other, and the long wax tapers which they held looked like lances pointing in all directions, and three men were standing in front of the lectern, singing as loud as they could.

They prolonged the syllables of the sonorous Latin indefinitely, holding on to "Amens" with interminable "a-a's," which the reed stop of the organ sustained in a monotonous, long-drawn-out tone.

A child's shrill voice took up the reply, and from time to time a priest sitting in a stall and wearing a biretta got up, muttered something and sat down again, while the three singers continued, their eyes fixed on the big book of plain chant lying open before them on the outstretched wings of a wooden eagle.

Then silence ensued and the service went on. Toward the close Rosa, with her head in both hands, suddenly thought of her mother, her village church and her first communion. She almost fancied that that day had returned, when she was so small and was almost hidden in her white dress, and she began to cry.

First of all she wept silently, and the tears dropped slowly from her eyes, but her emotion in creased with her recollections, and she began to sob. She took out her pocket handkerchief, wiped her eyes and held it to her mouth, so as not to scream, but it was in vain. A sort of rattle escaped her throat, and she was answered by two other profound, heartbreaking sobs, for her two neighbors, Louise and Flora, who were kneeling near her, overcome by similar recollections, were sobbing by her side, amid a flood of tears; and as tears are contagious, Madame Tellier soon in turn found that her eyes were wet, and on turning to her sister-in-law, she saw that all the occupants of her seat were also crying.

Soon, throughout the church, here and there, a wife, a mother, a sister, seized by the strange sympathy of poignant emotion, and affected at the sight of those handsome ladies on their knees, shaken with sobs was moistening her cambric pocket handkerchief and pressing her beating heart with her left hand.

Just as the sparks from an engine will set fire to dry grass, so the tears of Rosa and of her companions infected the whole congregation in a moment. Men, women, old men and lads in new smocks were soon all sobbing, and something superhuman seemed to be hovering over their heads—a spirit, the powerful breath of an invisible and all powerful Being.

Suddenly a species of madness seemed to pervade the church, the noise of a crowd in a state of frenzy, a tempest of sobs and stifled cries. It came like gusts of wind which blow the trees in a forest, and the priest, paralyzed by emotion, stammered out incoherent prayers, without finding words, ardent prayers of the soul soaring to heaven.

The people behind him gradually grew calmer. The cantors, in all the dignity of their white surplices, went on in somewhat uncertain voices, and the reed stop itself seemed hoarse, as if the instrument had been weeping; the priest, however, raised his hand to command silence and went and stood on the chancel steps, when everybody was silent at once.

After a few remarks on what had just taken place, and which he attributed to a miracle, he continued, turning to the seats where the carpenter's guests were sitting; "I especially thank you, my dear sisters, who have come from such a distance, and whose presence among us, whose evident faith and ardent piety have set such a salutary example to all. You have edified my parish; your emotion has warmed all hearts; without you, this great day would not, perhaps, have had this really divine character. It is sufficient, at times, that there should be one chosen lamb, for the Lord to descend on His flock."

His voice failed him again, from emotion, and he said no more, but concluded the service.

They now left the church as quickly as possible; the children themselves were restless and tired with such a prolonged tension of the mind. The parents left the church by degrees to see about dinner.

There was a crowd outside, a noisy crowd, a babel of loud voices, where the shrill Norman accent was discernible. The villagers formed two ranks, and when the children appeared, each family took possession of their own.

The whole houseful of women caught hold of Constance, surrounded her and kissed her, and Rosa was especially demonstrative. At last she took hold of one hand, while Madame Tellier took the other, and Raphaele and Fernande held up her long muslin skirt, so that it might not drag in the dust; Louise and Flora brought up the rear with Madame Rivet; and the child, who was very silent and thoughtful, set off for home in the midst of this guard of honor.

Dinner was served in the workshop on long boards supported by trestles, and through the open door they could see all the enjoyment that was going on in the village. Everywhere they were feasting, and through every window were to be seen tables surrounded by people in their Sunday best, and a cheerful noise was heard in every house, while the men sat in their shirt-sleeves, drinking glass after glass of cider.

In the carpenter's house the gaiety maintained somewhat of an air of reserve, the consequence of the emotion of the girls in the morning, and Rivet was the only one who was in a jolly mood, and he was drinking to excess. Madame Tellier looked at the clock every moment, for, in order not to lose two days running, they must take the 3:55 train, which would bring them to Fecamp by dark.

The carpenter tried very hard to distract her attention, so as to keep his guests until the next day, but he did not succeed, for she never joked when there was business on hand, and as soon as they had had their coffee she ordered her girls to make haste and get ready, and then, turning to her brother, she said:

"You must put in the horse immediately," and she herself went to finish her last preparations.

When she came down again, her sister-in-law was waiting to speak to her about the child, and a long conversation took place, in which, however, nothing was settled. The carpenter's wife was artful and pretended to be very much affected, and Madame Tellier, who was holding the girl on her knee, would not pledge herself to anything definite, but merely gave vague promises—she would not forget her, there was plenty of time, and besides, they would meet again.

But the conveyance did not come to the door and the women did not come downstairs. Upstairs they even heard loud laughter, romping, little screams, and much clapping of hands, and so, while the carpenter's wife went to the stable to see whether the cart was ready, madame went upstairs.

Rivet, who was very drunk, was plaguing Rosa, who was half choking with laughter. Louise and Flora were holding him by the arms and trying to calm him, as they were shocked at his levity after that morning's ceremony; but Raphaele and Fernande were urging him on, writhing and holding their sides with laughter, and they uttered shrill cries at every rebuff the drunken fellow received.

The man was furious, his face was red, and he was trying to shake off the two women who were clinging to him, while he was pulling Rosa's skirt with all his might and stammering incoherently.

But Madame Tellier, who was very indignant, went up to her brother, seized him by the shoulders, and threw him out of the room with such violence that he fell against the wall in the passage, and a minute afterward they heard him pumping water on his head in the yard, and when he reappeared with the cart he was quite calm.

They started off in the same way as they had come the day before, and the little white horse started off with his quick, dancing trot. Under the hot sun, their fun, which had been checked during dinner, broke out again. The girls now were amused at the jolting of the cart, pushed their neighbors' chairs, and burst out laughing every moment.

There was a glare of light over the country, which dazzled their eyes, and the wheels raised two trails of dust along the highroad. Presently, Fernande, who was fond of music, asked Rosa to sing something, and she boldly struck up the "Gros Cure de Meudon," but Madame Tellier made her stop immediately, as she thought it a very unsuitable song for such a day, and she added:

"Sing us something of Beranger's." And so, after a moment's hesitation, Rosa began Beranger's song "The Grandmother" in her worn-out voice, and all the girls, and even Madame Tellier herself, joined in the chorus:

"How I regret
My dimpled arms,
My nimble legs,
And vanished charms."

"That is first rate," Rivet declared, carried away by the rhythm, and they shouted the refrain to every verse, while Rivet beat time on the shaft with his foot, and with the reins on the back of the horse, who, as if he himself were carried away by the rhythm, broke into a wild gallop, and threw all the women in a heap, one on top of the other, on the bottom of the conveyance.

They got up, laughing as if they were mad, and the Gong went on, shouted at the top of their voices, beneath the burning sky, among the ripening grain, to the rapid gallop of the little horse, who set off every time the refrain was sung, and galloped a hundred yards, to their great delight, while occasionally a stone-breaker by the roadside sat up and looked at the load of shouting females through his wire spectacles.

When they got out at the station, the carpenter said:

"I am sorry you are going; we might have had some good times together." But Madame Tellier replied very sensibly: "Everything has its right time, and we cannot always be enjoying ourselves." And then he had a sudden inspiration:

"Look here, I will come and see you at Fecamp next month." And he gave Rosa a roguish and knowing look.

"Come," his sister replied, "you must be sensible; you may come if you like, but you are not to be up to any of your tricks."

He did not reply, and as they heard the whistle of the train, he immediately began to kiss them all. When it came to Rosa's turn, he tried to get to her mouth, which she, however, smiling with her lips closed, turned away from him each time by a rapid movement of her head to one side. He held her in his arms, but he could not attain his object, as his large whip, which he was holding in his hand and waving behind the girl's back in desperation, interfered with his movements.

"Passengers for Rouen, take your seats!" a guard cried, and they got in. There was a slight whistle, followed by a loud whistle from the engine, which noisily puffed out its first jet of steam, while the wheels began to turn a little with a visible effort, and Rivet left the station and ran along by the track to get another look at Rosa, and as the carriage passed him, he began to crack his whip and to jump, while he sang at the top of his voice:

"How I regret
My dimpled arms,
My nimble legs,
And vanished charms."

And then he watched a white pocket-handkerchief, which somebody was waving, as it disappeared in the distance.

PART III

They slept the peaceful sleep of a quiet conscience, until they got to Rouen, and when they returned to the house, refreshed and rested, Madame Tellier could not help saying:

"It was all very well, but I was longing to get home."

They hurried over their supper, and then, when they had put on their usual evening costume, waited for their regular customers, and the little colored lamp outside the door told the passers-by that Madame Tellier had returned, and in a moment the news spread, nobody knew how or through whom.

Monsieur Philippe, the banker's son, even carried his friendliness so far as to send a special messenger to Monsieur Tournevau, who was in the bosom of his family.

The fish curer had several cousins to dinner every Sunday, and they were having coffee, when a man came in with a letter in his hand. Monsieur Tournevau was much excited; he opened the envelope and grew pale; it contained only these words in pencil:

"The cargo of cod has been found; the ship has come into port; good business for you. Come immediately."

He felt in his pockets, gave the messenger two sons, and suddenly blushing to his ears, he said: "I must go out." He handed his wife the laconic and mysterious note, rang the bell, and when the servant came in, he asked her to bring him has hat and overcoat immediately. As soon as he was in the street, he began to hurry, and the way seemed to him to be twice as long as usual, in consequence of his impatience.

Madame Tellier's establishment had put on quite a holiday look. On the ground floor, a number of sailors were making a deafening noise, and Louise and Flora drank with one and the other, and were being called for in every direction at once.

The upstairs room was full by nine o'clock. Monsieur Vasse, the Judge of the Tribunal of Commerce, Madame Tellier's regular but Platonic wooer, was talking to her in a corner in a low voice, and they were both smiling, as if they were about to come to an understanding.

Monsieur Poulin, the ex-mayor, was talking to Rosa, and she was running her hands through the old gentleman's white whiskers.

Tall Fernande was on the sofa, her feet on the coat of Monsieur Pinipesse, the tax collector, and leaning back against young Monsieur Philippe, her right arm around his neck, while she held a cigarette in her left hand.

Raphaele appeared to be talking seriously with Monsieur Dupuis, the insurance agent, and she finished by saying: "Yes, I will, yes."

Just then, the door opened suddenly, and Monsieur Tournevau came in, and was greeted with enthusiastic cries of "Long live Tournevau!" And Raphaele, who was dancing alone up and down the room, went and threw herself into his arms. He seized her in a vigorous embrace and, without saying a word, lifted her up as if she had been a feather.

Rosa was chatting to the ex-mayor, kissing him and puffing; both his whiskers at the same time, in order to keep his head straight.

Fernanad and Madame Tellier remained with the four men, and Monsieur Philippe exclaimed: "I will pay for some champagne; get three bottles, Madame Tellier." And Fernande gave him a hug, and whispered to him: "Play us a waltz, will you?" So he rose and sat down at the old piano in the corner, and managed to get a hoarse waltz out of the depths of the instrument.

The tall girl put her arms round the tax collector, Madame Tellier let Monsieur Vasse take her round the waist, and the two couples turned round, kissing as they danced. Monsieur Vasse, who had formerly danced in good society, waltzed with such elegance that Madame Tellier was quite captivated.

Frederic brought the champagne; the first cork popped, and Monsieur Philippe played the introduction to a quadrille, through which the four dancers walked in society fashion, decorously, with propriety, deportment, bows and curtsies, and then they began to drink.

Monsieur Philippe next struck up a lively polka, and Monsieur Tournevau started off with the handsome Jewess, whom he held without letting her feet touch the ground. Monsieur Pinipesse and Monsieur Vasse had started off with renewed vigor, and from time to time one or other couple would stop to toss off a long draught of sparkling wine, and that dance was threatening to become never-ending, when Rosa opened the door.

"I want to dance," she exclaimed. And she caught hold of Monsieur Dupuis, who was sitting idle on the couch, and the dance began again.

But the bottles were empty. "I will pay for one," Monsieur Tournevau said. "So will I," Monsieur Vasse declared. "And. I will do the same," Monsieur Dupuis remarked.

They all began to clap their hands, and it soon became a regular ball, and from time to time Louise and Flora ran upstairs quickly and had a few turns, while their customers downstairs grew impatient, and then they returned regretfully to the tap-room. At midnight they were still dancing.

Madame Tellier let them amuse themselves while she had long private talks in corners with Monsieur Vasse, as if to settle the last details of something that had already been settled.

At last, at one o'clock, the two married men, Monsieur Tournevau and Monsieur Pinipesse, declared that they were going home, and wanted to pay. Nothing was charged for except the champagne, and that cost only six francs a bottle, instead of ten, which was the usual price, and when they expressed their surprise at such generosity, Madame Tellier, who was beaming, said to them:

"We don't have a holiday every day."

DENIS

To Leon Chapron.

Marambot opened the letter which his servant Denis gave him and smiled.

For twenty years Denis has been a servant in this house. He was a short, stout, jovial man, who was known throughout the countryside as a model servant. He asked:

"Is monsieur pleased? Has monsieur received good news?"

M. Marambot was not rich. He was an old village druggist, a bachelor, who lived on an income acquired with difficulty by selling drugs to the farmers. He answered:

"Yes, my boy. Old man Malois is afraid of the law-suit with which I am threatening him. I shall get my money to-morrow. Five thousand francs are not liable to harm the account of an old bachelor."

M. Marambot rubbed his hands with satisfaction. He was a man of quiet temperament, more sad than gay, incapable of any prolonged effort, careless in business.

He could undoubtedly have amassed a greater income had he taken advantage of the deaths of colleagues established in more important centers, by taking their places and carrying on their business. But the trouble of moving and the thought of all the preparations had always stopped him. After thinking the matter over for a few days, he would be satisfied to say:

"Bah! I'll wait until the next time. I'll not lose anything by the delay. I may even find something better."

Denis, on the contrary, was always urging his master to new enterprises. Of an energetic temperament, he would continually repeat:

"Oh! If I had only had the capital to start out with, I could have made a fortune! One thousand francs would do me."

M. Marambot would smile without answering and would go out in his little garden, where, his hands behind his back, he would walk about dreaming.

All day long, Denis sang the joyful refrains of the folk-songs of the district. He even showed an unusual activity, for he cleaned all the windows of the house, energetically rubbing the glass, and singing at the top of his voice.

M. Marambot, surprised at his zeal, said to him several times, smiling:

"My boy, if you work like that there will be nothing left for you to do to-morrow."

The following day, at about nine o'clock in the morning, the postman gave Denis four letters for his master, one of them very heavy. M. Marambot immediately shut himself up in his room until late in the afternoon. He then handed his servant four letters for the mail. One of them was addressed to M. Malois; it was undoubtedly a receipt for the money.

Denis asked his master no questions; he appeared to be as sad and gloomy that day as he had seemed joyful the day before.

Night came. M. Marambot went to bed as usual and slept.

He was awakened by a strange noise. He sat up in his bed and listened. Suddenly the door opened, and Denis appeared, holding in one hand a candle and in the other a carving knife, his eyes staring, his face contracted as though moved by some deep emotion; he was as pale as a ghost.

M. Marambot, astonished, thought that he was sleep-walking, and he was going to get out of bed and assist him when the servant blew out the light and rushed for the bed. His master stretched out his hands to receive the shock which knocked him over on his back; he was trying to seize the hands of his servant, whom he now thought to be crazy, in order to avoid the blows which the latter was aiming at him.

He was struck by the knife; once in the shoulder, once in the forehead and the third time in the chest. He fought wildly, waving his arms around in the darkness, kicking and crying:

"Denis! Denis! Are you mad? Listen, Denis!"

But the latter, gasping for breath, kept up his furious attack always striking, always repulsed, sometimes with a kick, sometimes with a punch, and rushing forward again furiously.

M. Marambot was wounded twice more, once in the leg and once in the stomach. But, suddenly, a thought flashed across his mind, and he began to shriek:

"Stop, stop, Denis, I have not yet received my money!"

The man immediately ceased, and his master could hear his labored breathing in the darkness.

M. Marambot then went on:

"I have received nothing. M. Malois takes back what he said, the law-suit will take place; that is why you carried the letters to the mail. Just read those on my desk."

With a final effort, he reached for his matches and lit the candle.

He was covered with blood. His sheets, his curtains, and even the walls, were spattered with red. Denis, standing in the middle of the room, was also bloody from head to foot.

When he saw the blood, M. Marambot thought himself dead, and fell unconscious.

At break of day he revived. It was some time, however, before he regained his senses, and was able to understand or remember. But, suddenly, the memory of the attack and of his wounds returned to him, and he was filled with such terror that he closed his eyes in order not to see anything. After a few minutes he grew calmer and began to think. He had not died immediately, therefore he might still recover. He felt weak, very weak; but he had no real pain, although he noticed an uncomfortable smarting sensation in several parts of his body. He also felt icy cold, and all wet, and as though wrapped up in bandages. He thought that this dampness came from the blood which he had lost; and he shivered at the dreadful thought of this red liquid which had come from his veins and covered his bed. The idea of seeing this terrible spectacle again so upset him that he kept his eyes closed with all his strength, as though they might open in spite of himself.

What had become of Denis? He had probably escaped.

But what could he, Marambot, do now? Get up? Call for help? But if he should make the slightest motions, his wounds would undoubtedly open up again and he would die from loss of blood.

Suddenly he heard the door of his room open. His heart almost stopped. It was certainly Denis who was coming to finish him up. He held his breath in order to make the murderer think that he had been successful.

He felt his sheet being lifted up, and then someone feeling his stomach. A sharp pain near his hip made him start. He was being very gently washed with cold water. Therefore, someone must have discovered the misdeed and he was being cared for. A wild joy seized him; but prudently, he did not wish to show that he was conscious. He opened one eye, just one, with the greatest precaution.

He recognized Denis standing beside him, Denis himself! Mercy! He hastily closed his eye again.

Denis! What could he be doing? What did he want? What awful scheme could he now be carrying out?

What was he doing? Well, he was washing him in order to hide the traces of his crime! And he would now bury him in the garden, under ten feet of earth, so that no one could discover him! Or perhaps under the wine cellar! And M. Marambot began to tremble like a leaf. He kept saying to himself: "I am lost, lost!" He closed his eyes so as not to see the knife as it descended for the final stroke. It did not come. Denis was now lifting him up and bandaging him. Then he began carefully to dress the wound on his leg, as his master had taught him to do.

There was no longer any doubt. His servant, after wishing to kill him, was trying to save him.

Then M. Marambot, in a dying voice, gave him the practical piece of advice:

"Wash the wounds in a dilute solution of carbolic acid!"

Denis answered:

"This is what I am doing, monsieur."

M. Marambot opened both his eyes. There was no sign of blood either on the bed, on the walls, or on the murderer. The wounded man was stretched out on clean white sheets.

The two men looked at each other.

Finally M. Marambot said calmly:

"You have been guilty of a great crime."

Denis answered:

"I am trying to make up for it, monsieur. If you will not tell on me, I will serve you as faithfully as in the past."

This was no time to anger his servant. M. Marambot murmured as he closed his eyes:

"I swear not to tell on you."

Denis saved his master. He spent days and nights without sleep, never leaving the sick room, preparing drugs, broths, potions, feeling his pulse, anxiously counting the beats, attending him with the skill of a trained nurse and the devotion of a son.

He continually asked:

"Well, monsieur, how do you feel?"

M. Marambot would answer in a weak voice:

"A little better, my boy, thank you."

And when the sick man would wake up at night, he would often see his servant seated in an armchair, weeping silently.

Never had the old druggist been so cared for, so fondled, so spoiled. At first he had said to himself:

"As soon as I am well I shall get rid of this rascal."

He was now convalescing, and from day to day he would put off dismissing his murderer. He thought that no one would ever show him such care and attention, for he held this man through fear; and he warned him that he had left a document with a lawyer denouncing him to the law if any new accident should occur.

This precaution seemed to guarantee him against any future attack; and he then asked himself if it would not be wiser to keep this man near him, in order to watch him closely.

Just as formerly, when he would hesitate about taking some larger place of business, he could not make up his mind to any decision.

"There is always time," he would say to himself.

Denis continued to show himself an admirable servant. M. Marambot was well. He kept him.

One morning, just as he was finishing breakfast, he suddenly heard a great noise in the kitchen. He hastened in there. Denis was struggling with two gendarmes. An officer was taking notes on his pad.

As soon as he saw his master, the servant began to sob, exclaiming:

"You told on me, monsieur, that's not right, after what you had promised me. You have broken your word of honor, Monsieur Marambot; that is not right, that's not right!"

M. Marambot, bewildered and distressed at being suspected, lifted his hand:

"I swear to you before the Lord, my boy that I did not tell on you. I haven't the slightest idea how the police could have found out about your attack on me."

The officer started:

"You say that he attacked you, M. Marambot?"

The bewildered druggist answered:

"Yes—but I did not tell on him—I haven't said a word—I swear it—he has served me excellently from that time on—"

The officer pronounced severely:

"I will take down your testimony. The law will take notice of this new action, of which it was ignorant, Monsieur Marambot. I was commissioned to arrest your servant for the theft of two ducks surreptitiously taken by him from M. Duhamel of which act there are witnesses. I shall make a note of your information."

Then, turning toward his men, he ordered:

"Come on, bring him along!"

The two gendarmes dragged Denis out.

The lawyer used a plea of insanity, contrasting the two misdeeds in order to strengthen his argument. He had clearly proved that the theft of the two ducks came from the same mental condition as the eight knife-wounds in the body of Maramlot. He had cunningly analyzed all the phases of this transitory condition of mental aberration, which could, doubtless, be cured by a few months' treatment in a reputable sanatorium. He had spoken in enthusiastic terms of the continued devotion of this faithful servant, of the care with which he had surrounded his master, wounded by him in a moment of alienation.

Touched by this memory, M. Marambot felt the tears rising to his eyes.

The lawyer noticed it, opened his arms with a broad gesture, spreading out the long black sleeves of his robe like the wings of a bat, and exclaimed:

"Look, look, gentleman of the jury, look at those tears. What more can I say for my client? What speech, what argument, what reasoning would be worth these tears of his master? They, speak louder than I do, louder than the law; they cry: 'Mercy, for the poor wandering mind of a while ago! They implore, they pardon, they bless!"

He was silent and sat down.

Then the judge, turning to Marambot, whose testimony had been excellent for his servant, asked him:

"But, monsieur, even admitting that you consider this man insane, that does not explain why you should have kept him. He was none the less dangerous."

Marambot, wiping his eyes, answered:

"Well, your honor, what can you expect? Nowadays it's so hard to find good servants—I could never have found a better one."

Denis was acquitted and put in a sanatorium at his master's expense.

MY WIFE

It had been a stag dinner. These men still came together once in a while without their wives as they had done when they were bachelors. They would eat for a long time, drink for a long time; they would talk of everything, stir up those old and joyful memories which bring a smile to the lip and a tremor to the heart. One of them was saying: "Georges, do you remember our excursion to Saint-Germain with those two little girls from Montmartre?"

"I should say I do!"

And a little detail here or there would be remembered, and all these things brought joy to the hearts.

The conversation turned on marriage, and each one said with a sincere air: "Oh, if it were to do over again!" Georges Duportin added: "It's strange how easily one falls into it. You have fully decided never to marry; and then, in the springtime, you go to the country; the weather is warm; the summer is beautiful; the fields are full of flowers; you meet a young girl at some friend's house—crash! all is over. You return married!"

Pierre Letoile exclaimed: "Correct! that is exactly my case, only there were some peculiar incidents—"

His friend interrupted him: "As for you, you have no cause to complain. You have the most charming wife in the world, pretty, amiable, perfect! You are undoubtedly the happiest one of us all."

The other one continued: "It's not my fault."

"How so?"

"It is true that I have a perfect wife, but I certainly married her much against my will."

"Nonsense!"

"Yes—this is the adventure. I was thirty-five, and I had no more idea of marrying than I had of hanging myself. Young girls seemed to me to be inane, and I loved pleasure.

"During the month of May I was invited to the wedding of my cousin, Simon d'Erabel, in Normandy. It was a regular Normandy wedding. We sat down at the table at five o'clock in the evening and at eleven o'clock we were still eating. I had been paired off, for the occasion, with a Mademoiselle Dumoulin, daughter of a retired colonel, a young, blond, soldierly person, well formed, frank and talkative. She took complete possession of me for the whole day, dragged me into the park, made me dance willy-nilly, bored me to death. I said to myself: 'That's all very well for to-day, but tomorrow I'll get out. That's all there is to it!'

"Toward eleven o'clock at night the women retired to their rooms; the men stayed, smoking while they drank or drinking while they smoked, whichever you will.

"Through the open window we could see the country folks dancing. Farmers and peasant girls were jumping about in a circle yelling at the top of their lungs a dance air which was feebly accompanied by two violins and a clarinet. The wild song of the peasants often completely drowned the sound of the instruments, and the weak music, interrupted by the unrestrained voices, seemed to come to us in little fragments of scattered notes. Two enormous casks, surrounded by flaming torches, contained drinks for the crowd. Two men were kept busy rinsing the glasses or bowls in a bucket and immediately holding them under the spigots, from which flowed the red stream of wine or the golden stream of pure cider; and the parched dancers, the old ones quietly, the girls panting, came up, stretched out their arms and grasped some receptacle, threw back their heads and poured down their throats the drink which they preferred. On a table were bread, butter, cheese and sausages. Each one would step up from time to time and swallow a mouthful, and under the starlit sky this healthy and violent exercise was a pleasing sight, and made one also feel like drinking from these enormous casks and eating the crisp bread and butter with a raw onion.

"A mad desire seized me to take part in this merrymaking, and I left my companions. I must admit that I was probably a little tipsy, but I was soon entirely so.

"I grabbed the hand of a big, panting peasant woman and I jumped her about until I was out of breath.

"Then I drank some wine and reached for another girl. In order to refresh myself afterward, I swallowed a bowlful of cider, and I began to bounce around as if possessed.

"I was very light on my feet. The boys, delighted, were watching me and trying to imitate me; the girls all wished to dance with me, and jumped about heavily with the grace of cows.

"After each dance I drank a glass of wine or a glass of cider, and toward two o'clock in the morning I was so drunk that I could hardly stand up.

"I realized my condition and tried to reach my room. Everybody was asleep and the house was silent and dark.

"I had no matches and everybody was in bed. As soon as I reached the vestibule I began to, feel dizzy. I had a lot of trouble to find the banister. At last, by accident, my hand came in contact with it, and I sat down on the first step of the stairs in order to try to gather my scattered wits.

"My room was on the second floor; it was the third door to the left. Fortunately I had not forgotten that. Armed with this knowledge, I arose, not without difficulty, and I began to ascend, step by step. In my hands I firmly gripped the iron railing in order not to fall, and took great pains to make no noise.

"Only three or four times did my foot miss the steps, and I went down on my knees; but thanks to the energy of my arms and the strength of my will, I avoided falling completely.

"At last I reached the second floor and I set out in my journey along the hall, feeling my way by the walls. I felt one door; I counted: 'One'; but a sudden dizziness made me lose my hold on the wall, make a strange turn and fall up against the other wall. I wished to turn in a straight line: The crossing was long and full of hardships. At last I reached the shore, and, prudently, I began to travel along again until I met another door. In order to be sure to make no mistake, I again counted out loud: 'Two.' I started out on my walk again. At last I found the third door. I said: 'Three, that's my room,' and I turned the knob. The door opened. Notwithstanding my befuddled state, I thought: 'Since the door opens, this must be home.' After softly closing the door, I stepped out in the darkness. I bumped against something soft: my easy-chair. I immediately stretched myself out on it.

"In my condition it would not have been wise to look for my bureau, my candles, my matches. It would have taken me at least two hours. It would probably have taken me that long also to undress; and even then I might not have succeeded. I gave it up.

"I only took my shoes off; I unbuttoned my waistcoat, which was choking me, I loosened my trousers and went to sleep.

"This undoubtedly lasted for a long time. I was suddenly awakened by a deep voice which was saying: 'What, you lazy girl, still in bed? It's ten o'clock!'

"A woman's voice answered: 'Already! I was so tired yesterday.'

"In bewilderment I wondered what this dialogue meant. Where was I? What had I done? My mind was wandering, still surrounded by a heavy fog. The first voice continued: 'I'm going to raise your curtains.'

"I heard steps approaching me. Completely at a loss what to do, I sat up. Then a hand was placed on my head. I started. The voice asked: 'Who is there?' I took good care not to answer. A furious grasp seized me. I in turn seized him, and a terrific struggle ensued. We were rolling around, knocking over the furniture and crashing against the walls. A woman's voice was shrieking: 'Help! help!'

"Servants, neighbors, frightened women crowded around us. The blinds were open and the shades drawn. I was struggling with Colonel Dumoulin.

"I had slept beside his daughter's bed!

"When we were separated, I escaped to my room, dumbfounded. I locked myself in and sat down with my feet on a chair, for my shoes had been left in the young girl's room.

"I heard a great noise through the whole house, doors being opened and closed, whisperings and rapid steps.

"After half an hour some one knocked on my door. I cried: 'Who is there?' It was my uncle, the bridegroom's father. I opened the door:

"He was pale and furious, and he treated me harshly: 'You have behaved like a scoundrel in my house, do you hear?' Then he added more gently 'But, you young fool, why the devil did you let yourself get caught at ten o'clock in the morning? You go to sleep like a log in that room, instead of leaving immediately—immediately after.'

"I exclaimed: 'But, uncle, I assure you that nothing occurred. I was drunk and got into the wrong room.'

"He shrugged his shoulders! 'Don't talk nonsense.' I raised my hand, exclaiming: 'I swear to you on my honor.' My uncle continued: 'Yes, that's all right. It's your duty to say that.'

"I in turn grew angry and told him the whole unfortunate occurrence. He looked at me with a bewildered expression, not knowing what to believe. Then he went out to confer with the colonel.

"I heard that a kind of jury of the mothers had been formed, to which were submitted the different phases of the situation.

"He came back an hour later, sat down with the dignity of a judge and began: 'No matter what may be the situation, I can see only one way out of it for you; it is to marry Mademoiselle Dumoulin.'

"I bounded out of the chair, crying: 'Never! never!'

"Gravely he asked: 'Well, what do you expect to do?'

"I answered simply: 'Why—leave as soon as my shoes are returned to me.'

"My uncle continued: 'Please do not jest. The colonel has decided to blow your brains out as soon as he sees you. And you may be sure that he does not threaten idly. I spoke of a duel and he answered: "No, I tell you that I will blow his brains out."'

"'Let us now examine the question from another point of view. Either you have misbehaved yourself—and then so much the worse for you, my boy; one should not go near a young girl—or else, being drunk, as you say, you made a mistake in the room. In this case, it's even worse for you. You shouldn't get yourself into such foolish situations. Whatever you may say, the poor girl's reputation is lost, for a drunkard's excuses are never believed. The only real victim in the matter is the girl. Think it over.'

"He went away, while I cried after him: 'Say what you will, I'll not marry her!'

"I stayed alone for another hour. Then my aunt came. She was crying. She used every argument. No one believed my story. They could not imagine that this young girl could have forgotten to lock her door in a house full of company. The colonel had struck her. She had been crying the whole morning. It was a terrible and unforgettable scandal. And my good aunt added: 'Ask for her hand, anyhow. We may, perhaps, find some way out of it when we are drawing up the papers.'

"This prospect relieved me. And I agreed to write my proposal. An hour later I left for Paris. The following day I was informed that I had been accepted.

"Then, in three weeks, before I had been able to find any excuse, the banns were published, the announcement sent out, the contract signed, and one Monday morning I found myself in a church, beside a weeping young girl, after telling the magistrate that I consented to take her as my companion—for better, for worse.

"I had not seen her since my adventure, and I glanced at her out of the corner of my eye with a certain malevolent surprise. However, she was not ugly—far from it. I said to myself: 'There is some one who won't laugh every day.'

"She did not look at me once until, the evening, and she did not say a single word.

"Toward the middle of the night I entered the bridal chamber with the full intention of letting her know my resolutions, for I was now master. I found her sitting in an armchair, fully dressed, pale and with red eyes. As soon as I entered she rose and came slowly toward me saying: 'Monsieur, I am ready to do whatever you may command. I will kill myself if you so desire'

"The colonel's daughter was as pretty as she could be in this heroic role. I kissed her; it was my privilege.

"I soon saw that I had not got a bad bargain. I have now been married five years. I do not regret it in the least."

Pierre Letoile was silent. His companions were laughing. One of them said: "Marriage is indeed a lottery; you must never choose your numbers. The haphazard ones are the best."

Another added by way of conclusion: "Yes, but do not forget that the god of drunkards chose for Pierre."

THE UNKNOWN

We were speaking of adventures, and each one of us was relating his story of delightful experiences, surprising meetings, on the train, in a hotel, at the seashore. According to Roger des Annettes, the seashore was particularly favorable to the little blind god.

Gontran, who was keeping mum, was asked what he thought of it.

"I guess Paris is about the best place for that," he said. "Woman is like a precious trinket, we appreciate her all the more when we meet her in the most unexpected places; but the rarest ones are only to be found in Paris."

He was silent for a moment, and then continued:

"By Jove, it's great! Walk along the streets on some spring morning. The little women, daintily tripping along, seem to blossom out like flowers. What a delightful, charming sight! The dainty perfume of violet is everywhere. The city is gay, and everybody notices the women. By Jove, how tempting they are in their light, thin dresses, which occasionally give one a glimpse of the delicate pink flesh beneath!

"One saunters along, head up, mind alert, and eyes open. I tell you it's great! You see her in the distance, while still a block away; you already know that she is going to please you at closer quarters. You can recognize her by the flower on her hat, the toss of her head, or her gait. She approaches, and you say to yourself: 'Look out, here she is!' You come closer to her and you devour her with your eyes.

"Is it a young girl running errands for some store, a young woman returning from church, or hastening to see her lover? What do you care? Her well-rounded bosom shows through the thin waist. Oh, if you could only take her in your arms and fondle and kiss her! Her glance may be timid or bold, her hair light or dark. What difference does it make? She brushes against you, and a cold shiver runs down your spine. Ah, how you wish for her all day! How many of these dear creatures have I met this way, and how wildly in love I would have been had I known them more intimately.

"Have you ever noticed that the ones we would love the most distractedly are those whom we never meet to know? Curious, isn't it? From time to time we barely catch a glimpse of some woman, the mere sight of whom thrills our senses. But it goes no further. When I think of all the adorable creatures that I have elbowed in the streets of Paris, I fairly rave. Who are they! Where are they? Where can I find them again? There is a proverb which says that happiness often passes our way; I am sure that I have often passed alongside the one who could have caught me like a linnet in the snare of her fresh beauty."

Roger des Annettes had listened smilingly. He answered: "I know that as well as you do. This is what happened to me. About five years ago, for the first time I met, on the Pont de la Concorde, a young woman who made a wonderful impression on me. She was dark, rather stout, with glossy hair, and eyebrows which nearly met above two dark eyes. On her lip was a scarcely perceptible down, which made one dream-dream as one dreams of beloved woods, on seeing a bunch of wild violets. She had a small waist and a well-developed bust, which seemed to present a challenge, offer a temptation. Her eyes were like two black spots on white enamel. Her glance was strange, vacant, unthinking, and yet wonderfully beautiful.

"I imagined that she might be a Jewess. I followed her, and then turned round to look at her, as did many others. She walked with a swinging gait that was not graceful, but somehow attracted one. At the Place de la Concorde she took a carriage, and I stood there like a fool, moved by the strongest desire that had ever assailed me.

"For about three weeks I thought only of her; and then her memory passed out of my mind.

"Six months later I descried her in the Rue de la Paix again. On seeing her I felt the same shock that one experiences on seeing a once dearly loved woman. I stopped that I might better observe her. When she passed close enough to touch me I felt as though I were standing before a red hot furnace. Then, when she had passed by, I noticed a delicious sensation, as of a cooling breeze blowing over my face. I did not follow her. I was afraid of doing something foolish. I was afraid of myself.

"She haunted all my dreams.

"It was a year before I saw her again. But just as the sun was going down on one beautiful evening in May I recognized her walking along the Avenue des Champs-Elysees. The Arc de Triomphe stood out in bold relief against the fiery glow of the sky. A golden haze filled the air; it was one of those delightful spring evenings which are the glory of Paris.

"I followed her, tormented by a desire to address her, to kneel before her, to pour forth the emotion which was choking me. Twice I passed by her only to fall back, and each time as I passed by I felt this sensation, as of scorching heat, which I had noticed in the Rue de la Paix.

"She glanced at me, and then I saw her enter a house on the Rue de Presbourg. I waited for her two hours and she did not come out. Then I decided to question the janitor. He seemed not to understand me. 'She must be visiting some one,' he said.

"The next time I was eight months without seeing her. But one freezing morning in January, I was walking along the Boulevard Malesherbes at a dog trot, so as to keep warm, when at the corner I bumped into a woman and knocked a small package out of her hand. I tried to apologize. It was she!

"At first I stood stock still from the shock; then having returned to her the package which she had dropped, I said abruptly:

"'I am both grieved and delighted, madame, to have jostled you. For more than two years I have known you, admired you, and had the most ardent wish to be presented to you; nevertheless I have been unable to find out who you are, or where you live. Please excuse these foolish words. Attribute them to a passionate desire to be numbered among your acquaintances. Such sentiments can surely offend you in no way! You do not know me. My name is Baron Roger des Annettes. Make inquiries about me, and you will find that I am a gentleman. Now, if you refuse my request, you will throw me into abject misery. Please be good to me and tell me how I can see you.'

"She looked at me with her strange vacant stare, and answered smilingly:

"'Give me your address. I will come and see you.'

"I was so dumfounded that I must have shown my surprise. But I quickly gathered my wits together and gave her a visiting card, which she slipped into her pocket with a quick, deft movement.

"Becoming bolder, I stammered:

"'When shall I see you again?'

"She hesitated, as though mentally running over her list of engagements, and then murmured:

"'Will Sunday morning suit you?'

"'I should say it would!'

"She went on, after having stared at me, judged, weighed and analyzed me with this heavy and vacant gaze which seemed to leave a quieting and deadening impression on the person towards whom it was directed.

"Until Sunday my mind was occupied day and night trying to guess who she might be and planning my course of conduct towards her. I finally decided to buy her a jewel, a beautiful little jewel, which I placed in its box on the mantelpiece, and left it there awaiting her arrival.

"I spent a restless night waiting for her.

"At ten o'clock she came, calm and quiet, and with her hand outstretched, as though she had known me for years. Drawing up a chair, I took her hat and coat and furs, and laid them aside. And then, timidly, I took her hand in mine; after that all went on without a hitch.

"Ah, my friends! what a bliss it is, to stand at a discreet distance and watch the hidden pink and blue ribbons, partly concealed, to observe the hazy lines of the beloved one's form, as they become visible through the last of the filmy garments! What a delight it is to watch the ostrich-like modesty of those who are in reality none too modest. And what is so pretty as their motions!

"Her back was turned towards me, and suddenly, my eyes were irresistibly drawn to a large black spot right between her shoulders. What could it be? Were my eyes deceiving me? But no, there it was, staring me in the face! Then my mind reverted to the faint down on her lip, the heavy eyebrows almost meeting over her coal-black eyes, her glossy black hair—I should have been prepared for some surprise.

"Nevertheless I was dumfounded, and my mind was haunted by dim visions of strange adventures. I seemed to see before me one of the evil genii of the Thousand and One Nights, one of these dangerous and crafty creatures whose mission it is to drag men down to unknown depths. I thought of Solomon, who made the Queen of Sheba walk on a mirror that he might be sure that her feet were not cloven.

"And when the time came for me to sing of love to her, my voice forsook me. At first she showed surprise, which soon turned to anger; and she said, quickly putting on her wraps:

"'It was hardly worth while for me to go out of my way to come here.'

"I wanted her to accept the ring which I had bought for her, but she replied haughtily: 'For whom do you take me, sir?' I blushed to the roots of my hair. She left without saying another word.

"There is my whole adventure. But the worst part of it is that I am now madly in love with her. I can't see a woman without thinking of her. All the others disgust me, unless they remind me of her. I cannot kiss a woman without seeing her face before me, and without suffering the torture of unsatisfied desire. She is always with me, always there, dressed or nude, my true love. She is there, beside the other one, visible but intangible. I am almost willing to believe that she was bewitched, and carried a talisman between her shoulders.

"Who is she? I don't know yet. I have met her once or twice since. I bowed, but she pretended not to recognize me. Who is she? An Oriental? Yes, doubtless an oriental Jewess! I believe that she must be a Jewess! But why? Why? I don't know!"

THE APPARITION

The subject of sequestration of the person came up in speaking of a recent lawsuit, and each of us had a story to tell—a true story, he said. We had been spending the evening together at an old family mansion in the Rue de Grenelle, just a party of intimate friends. The old Marquis de la Tour-Samuel, who was eighty-two, rose, and, leaning his elbow on the mantelpiece, said in his somewhat shaky voice:

"I also know of something strange, so strange that it has haunted me all my life. It is now fifty-six years since the incident occurred, and yet not a month passes that I do not see it again in a dream, so great is the impression of fear it has left on my mind. For ten minutes I experienced such horrible fright that ever since then a sort of constant terror has remained with me. Sudden noises startle me violently, and objects imperfectly distinguished at night inspire me with a mad desire to flee from them. In short, I am afraid of the dark!

"But I would not have acknowledged that before I reached my present age. Now I can say anything. I have never receded before real danger, ladies. It is, therefore, permissible, at eighty-two years of age, not to be brave in presence of imaginary danger.

"That affair so completely upset me, caused me such deep and mysterious and terrible distress, that I never spoke of it to any one. I will now tell it to you exactly as it happened, without any attempt at explanation.

"In July, 1827, I was stationed at Rouen. One day as I was walking along the quay I met a man whom I thought I recognized without being able to recall exactly who he was. Instinctively I made a movement to stop. The stranger perceived it and at once extended his hand.

"He was a friend to whom I had been deeply attached as a youth. For five years I had not seen him; he seemed to have aged half a century. His hair was quite white and he walked bent over as though completely exhausted. He apparently understood my surprise, and he told me of the misfortune which had shattered his life.

"Having fallen madly in love with a young girl, he had married her, but after a year of more than earthly happiness she died suddenly of an affection of the heart. He left his country home on the very day of her burial and came to his town house in Rouen, where he lived, alone and unhappy, so sad and wretched that he thought constantly of suicide.

"'Since I have found you again in this manner,' he said, 'I will ask you to render me an important service. It is to go and get me out of the desk in my bedroom—our bedroom—some papers of which I have urgent need. I cannot send a servant or a business clerk, as discretion and absolute silence are necessary. As for myself, nothing on earth would induce me to reenter that house. I will give you the key of the room, which I myself locked on leaving, and the key of my desk, also a few words for my gardener, telling him to open the chateau for you. But come and breakfast with me tomorrow and we will arrange all that.'

"I promised to do him the slight favor he asked. It was, for that matter, only a ride which I could make in an hour on horseback, his property being but a few miles distant from Rouen.

"At ten o'clock the following day I breakfasted, tete-a-tete, with my friend, but he scarcely spoke.

"He begged me to pardon him; the thought of the visit I was about to make to that room, the scene of his dead happiness, overcame him, he said. He, indeed, seemed singularly agitated and preoccupied, as though undergoing some mysterious mental struggle.

"At length he explained to me exactly what I had to do. It was very simple. I must take two packages of letters and a roll of papers from the first right-hand drawer of the desk, of which I had the key. He added:

"'I need not beg you to refrain from glancing at them.'

"I was wounded at that remark and told him so somewhat sharply. He stammered:

"'Forgive me, I suffer so,' and tears came to his eyes.

"At about one o'clock I took leave of him to accomplish my mission.

"'The weather was glorious, and I trotted across the fields, listening to the song of the larks and the rhythmical clang of my sword against my boot. Then I entered the forest and walked my horse. Branches of trees caressed my face as I passed, and now and then I caught a leaf with my teeth and chewed it, from sheer gladness of heart at being alive and vigorous on such a radiant day.

"As I approached the chateau I took from my pocket the letter I had for the gardener, and was astonished at finding it sealed. I was so irritated that I was about to turn back without having fulfilled my promise, but reflected that I should thereby display undue susceptibility. My friend in his troubled condition might easily have fastened the envelope without noticing that he did so.

"The manor looked as if it had been abandoned for twenty years. The open gate was falling from its hinges, the walks were overgrown with grass and the flower beds were no longer distinguishable.

"The noise I made by kicking at a shutter brought out an old man from a side door. He seemed stunned with astonishment at seeing me. On receiving my letter, he read it, reread it, turned it over and over, looked me up and down, put the paper in his pocket and finally said:

"'Well, what is it you wish?'

"I replied shortly:

"'You ought to know, since you have just read your master's orders. I wish to enter the chateau.'

"He seemed overcome.

"'Then you are going in—into her room?'

"I began to lose patience.

"'Damn it! Are you presuming to question me?'

"He stammered in confusion:

"'No—sir—but—but it has not been opened since—since the-death. If you will be kind enough to wait five minutes I will go and—and see if—'

"I interrupted him angrily:

"'See here, what do you mean by your tricks?

"'You know very well you cannot enter the room, since here is the key!'

"He no longer objected.

"'Then, sir, I will show you the way.'

"'Show me the staircase and leave me. I'll find my way without you.'

"'But—sir—indeed—'

"This time I lost patience, and pushing him aside, went into the house.

"I first went through the kitchen, then two rooms occupied by this man and his wife. I then crossed a large hall, mounted a staircase and recognized the door described by my friend.

"I easily opened it, and entered the apartment. It was so dark that at first I could distinguish nothing. I stopped short, disagreeably affected by that disagreeable, musty odor of closed, unoccupied rooms. As my eyes slowly became accustomed to the darkness I saw plainly enough a large and disordered bedroom, the bed without sheets but still retaining its mattresses and pillows, on one of which was a deep impression, as though an elbow or a head had recently rested there.

"The chairs all seemed out of place. I noticed that a door, doubtless that of a closet, had remained half open.

"I first went to the window, which I opened to let in the light, but the fastenings of the shutters had grown so rusty that I could not move them. I even tried to break them with my sword, but without success. As I was growing irritated over my useless efforts and could now see fairly well in the semi-darkness, I gave up the hope of getting more light, and went over to the writing desk.

"I seated myself in an armchair and, letting down the lid of the desk, I opened the drawer designated. It was full to the top. I needed but three packages, which I knew how to recognize, and began searching for them.

"I was straining my eyes in the effort to read the superscriptions when I seemed to hear, or, rather, feel, something rustle back of me. I paid no attention, believing that a draught from the window was moving some drapery. But in a minute or so another movement, almost imperceptible, sent a strangely disagreeable little shiver over my skin. It was so stupid to be affected, even slightly, that self-respect prevented my turning around. I had just found the second package I needed and was about to lay my hand on the third when a long and painful sigh, uttered just at my shoulder, made me bound like a madman from my seat and land several feet off. As I jumped I had turned round my hand on the hilt of my sword, and, truly, if I had not felt it at my side I should have taken to my heels like a coward.

"A tall woman dressed in white, stood gazing at me from the back of the chair where I had been sitting an instant before.

"Such a shudder ran through all my limbs that I nearly fell backward. No one who has not experienced it can understand that frightful, unreasoning terror! The mind becomes vague, the heart ceases to beat, the entire body grows as limp as a sponge.

"I do not believe in ghosts, nevertheless I collapsed from a hideous dread of the dead, and I suffered, oh! I suffered in a few moments more than in all the rest of my life from the irresistible terror of the supernatural. If she had not spoken I should have died perhaps. But she spoke, she spoke in a sweet, sad voice that set my nerves vibrating. I dare not say that I became master of myself and recovered my reason. No! I was terrified and scarcely knew what I was doing. But a certain innate pride, a remnant of soldierly instinct, made me, almost in spite of myself, maintain a bold front. She said:

"'Oh, sir, you can render me a great service.'

"I wanted to reply, but it was impossible for me to pronounce a word. Only a vague sound came from my throat. She continued:

"'Will you? You can save me, cure me. I suffer frightfully. I suffer, oh! how I suffer!' and she slowly seated herself in my armchair, still looking at me.

"'Will you?' she said.

"I nodded in assent, my voice still being paralyzed.

"Then she held out to me a tortoise-shell comb and murmured:

"'Comb my hair, oh! comb my hair; that will cure me; it must be combed. Look at my head—how I suffer; and my hair pulls so!'

"Her hair, unbound, very long and very black, it seemed to me, hung over the back of the armchair and touched the floor.

"Why did I promise? Why did I take that comb with a shudder, and why did I hold in my hands her long black hair that gave my skin a frightful cold sensation, as though I were handling snakes? I cannot tell.

"That sensation has remained in my fingers, and I still tremble in recalling it.

"I combed her hair. I handled, I know not how, those icy locks. I twisted, knotted, and unknotted, and braided them. She sighed, bowed her head, seemed happy. Suddenly she said, 'Thank you!' snatched the comb from my hands and fled by the door that I had noticed ajar.

"Left alone, I experienced for several seconds the horrible agitation of one who awakens from a nightmare. At length I regained my senses. I ran to the window and with a mighty effort burst open the shutters, letting a flood of light into the room. Immediately I sprang to the door by which that being had departed. I found it closed and immovable!

"Then the mad desire to flee overcame me like a panic the panic which soldiers know in battle. I seized the three packets of letters on the open desk, ran from the room, dashed down the stairs four steps at a time, found myself outside, I know not how, and, perceiving my horse a few steps off, leaped into the saddle and galloped away.

"I stopped only when I reached Rouen and alighted at my lodgings. Throwing the reins to my orderly, I fled to my room and shut myself in to reflect. For an hour I anxiously asked myself if I were not the victim of a hallucination. Undoubtedly I had had one of those incomprehensible nervous attacks those exaltations of mind that give rise to visions and are the stronghold of the supernatural. And I was about to believe I had seen a vision, had a hallucination, when, as I approached the window, my eyes fell, by chance, upon my breast. My military cape was covered with long black hairs! One by one, with trembling fingers, I plucked them off and threw them away.

"I then called my orderly. I was too disturbed, too upset to go and see my friend that day, and I also wished to reflect more fully upon what I ought to tell him. I sent him his letters, for which he gave the soldier a receipt. He asked after me most particularly, and, on being told I was ill—had had a sunstroke—appeared exceedingly anxious. Next morning I went to him, determined to tell him the truth. He had gone out the evening before and had not yet returned. I called again during the day; my friend was still absent. After waiting a week longer without news of him, I notified the authorities and a judicial search was instituted. Not the slightest trace of his whereabouts or manner of disappearance was discovered.

"A minute inspection of the abandoned chateau revealed nothing of a suspicious character. There was no indication that a woman had been concealed there.

"After fruitless researches all further efforts were abandoned, and for fifty-six years I have heard nothing; I know no more than before."

VOLUME VIII

CLOCHETTE

How strange those old recollections are which haunt us, without our being able to get rid of them.

This one is so very old that I cannot understand how it has clung so vividly and tenaciously to my memory. Since then I have seen so many sinister things, which were either affecting or terrible, that I am astonished at not being able to pass a single day without the face of Mother Bellflower recurring to my mind's eye, just as I knew her formerly, now so long ago, when I was ten or twelve years old.

She was an old seamstress who came to my parents' house once a week, every Thursday, to mend the linen. My parents lived in one of those country houses called chateaux, which are merely old houses with gable roofs, to which are attached three or four farms lying around them.

The village, a large village, almost a market town, was a few hundred yards away, closely circling the church, a red brick church, black with age.

Well, every Thursday Mother Clochette came between half-past six and seven in the morning, and went immediately into the linen-room and began to work. She was a tall, thin, bearded or rather hairy woman, for she had a beard all over her face, a surprising, an unexpected beard, growing in improbable tufts, in curly bunches which looked as if they had been sown by a madman over that great face of a gendarme in petticoats. She had them on her nose, under her nose, round her nose, on her chin, on her cheeks; and her eyebrows, which were extraordinarily thick and long, and quite gray, bushy and bristling, looked exactly like a pair of mustaches stuck on there by mistake.

She limped, not as lame people generally do, but like a ship at anchor. When she planted her great, bony, swerving body on her sound leg, she seemed to be preparing to mount some enormous wave, and then suddenly she dipped as if to disappear in an abyss, and buried herself in the ground. Her walk reminded one of a storm, as she swayed about, and her head, which was always covered with an enormous white cap, whose ribbons fluttered down her back, seemed to traverse the horizon from north to south and from south to north, at each step.

I adored Mother Clochette. As soon as I was up I went into the linen-room where I found her installed at work, with a foot-warmer under her feet. As soon as I arrived, she made me take the foot-warmer and sit upon it, so that I might not catch cold in that large, chilly room under the roof.

"That draws the blood from your throat," she said to me.

She told me stories, whilst mending the linen with her long crooked nimble fingers; her eyes behind her magnifying spectacles, for age had impaired her sight, appeared enormous to me, strangely profound, double.

She had, as far as I can remember the things which she told me and by which my childish heart was moved, the large heart of a poor woman. She told me what had happened in the village, how a cow had escaped from the cow-house and had been found the next morning in front of Prosper Malet's windmill, looking at the sails turning, or about a hen's egg which had been found in the church belfry without any one being able to understand what creature had been there to lay it, or the story of Jean-Jean Pila's dog, who had been ten leagues to bring back his master's breeches which a tramp had stolen whilst they were hanging up to dry out of doors, after he had been in the rain. She told me these simple adventures in such a manner, that in my mind they assumed the proportions of never-to-be-forgotten dramas, of grand and mysterious poems; and the ingenious stories invented by the poets which my mother told me in the evening, had none of the flavor, none of the breadth or vigor of the peasant woman's narratives.

Well, one Tuesday, when I had spent all the morning in listening to Mother Clochette, I wanted to go upstairs to her again during the day after picking hazelnuts with the manservant in the wood behind the farm. I remember it all as clearly as what happened only yesterday.

On opening the door of the linen-room, I saw the old seamstress lying on the ground by the side of her chair, with her face to the ground and her arms stretched out, but still holding her needle in one hand and one of my shirts in the other. One of her legs in a blue stocking, the longer one, no doubt, was extended under her chair, and her spectacles glistened against the wall, as they had rolled away from her.

I ran away uttering shrill cries. They all came running, and in a few minutes I was told that Mother Clochette was dead.

I cannot describe the profound, poignant, terrible emotion which stirred my childish heart. I went slowly down into the drawing-room and hid myself in a dark corner, in the depths of an immense old armchair, where I knelt down and wept. I remained there a long time, no doubt, for night came on. Suddenly somebody came in with a lamp, without seeing me, however, and I heard my father and mother talking with the medical man, whose voice I recognized.

He had been sent for immediately, and he was explaining the causes of the accident, of which I understood nothing, however. Then he sat down and had a glass of liqueur and a biscuit.

He went on talking, and what he then said will remain engraved on my mind until I die! I think that I can give the exact words which he used.

"Ah!" said he, "the poor woman! She broke her leg the day of my arrival here, and I had not even had time to wash my hands after getting off the diligence before I was sent for in all haste, for it was a bad case, very bad.

"She was seventeen, and a pretty girl, very pretty! Would any one believe it? I have never told her story before, and nobody except myself and one other person who is no longer living in this part of the country ever knew it. Now that she is dead, I may be less discreet.

"Just then a young assistant-teacher came to live in the village; he was a handsome, well-made fellow, and looked like a non-commissioned officer. All the girls ran after him, but he paid no attention to them, partly because he was very much afraid of his superior, the schoolmaster, old Grabu, who occasionally got out of bed the wrong foot first.

"Old Grabu already employed pretty Hortense who has just died here, and who was afterwards nicknamed Clochette. The assistant master singled out the pretty young girl, who was, no doubt, flattered at being chosen by this impregnable conqueror; at any rate, she fell in love with him, and he succeeded in persuading her to give him a first meeting in the hay-loft behind the school, at night, after she had done her day's sewing.

"She pretended to go home, but instead of going downstairs when she left the Grabus' she went upstairs and hid among the hay, to wait for her lover. He soon joined her, and was beginning to say pretty things to her, when the door of the hay-loft opened and the schoolmaster appeared, and asked: 'What are you doing up there, Sigisbert?' Feeling sure that he would be caught, the young schoolmaster lost his presence of mind and replied stupidly: 'I came up here to rest a little amongst the bundles of hay, Monsieur Grabu.'

"The loft was very large and absolutely dark, and Sigisbert pushed the frightened girl to the further end and said: 'Go over there and hide yourself. I shall lose my position, so get away and hide yourself.'

"When the schoolmaster heard the whispering, he continued: 'Why, you are not by yourself?' 'Yes, I am, Monsieur Grabu!' 'But you are not, for you are talking.' 'I swear I am, Monsieur Grabu.' 'I will soon find out,' the old man replied, and double locking the door, he went down to get a light.

"Then the young man, who was a coward such as one frequently meets, lost his head, and becoming furious all of a sudden, he repeated: 'Hide yourself, so that he may not find you. You will keep me from making a living for the rest of my life; you will ruin my whole career. Do hide yourself!' They could hear the key turning in the lock again, and Hortense ran to the window which looked out on the street, opened it quickly, and then said in a low and determined voice: 'You will come and pick me up when he is gone,' and she jumped out.

"Old Grabu found nobody, and went down again in great surprise, and a quarter of an hour later, Monsieur Sigisbert came to me and related his adventure. The girl had remained at the foot of the wall unable to get up, as she had fallen from the second story, and I went with him to fetch her. It was raining in torrents, and I brought the unfortunate girl home with me, for the right leg was broken in three places, and the bones had come trough the flesh. She did not complain, and merely said, with admirable resignation: 'I am punished, well punished!'

"I sent for assistance and for the work-girl's relatives and told them a, made-up story of a runaway carriage which had knocked her down and lamed her outside my door. They believed me, and the gendarmes for a whole month tried in vain to find the author of this accident.

"That is all! And I say that this woman was a heroine and belonged to the race of those who accomplish the grandest deeds of history.

"That was her only love affair, and she died a virgin. She was a martyr, a noble soul, a sublimely devoted woman! And if I did not absolutely admire her, I should not have told you this story, which I would never tell any one during her life; you understand why."

The doctor ceased. Mamma cried and papa said some words which I did not catch; then they left the room and I remained on my knees in the armchair and sobbed, whilst I heard a strange noise of heavy footsteps and something knocking against the side of the staircase.

They were carrying away Clochette's body.

THE KISS

My Little Darling: So you are crying from morning until night and from night until morning, because your husband leaves you; you do not know what to do and so you ask your old aunt for advice; you must consider her quite an expert. I don't know as much as you think I do, and yet I am not entirely ignorant of the art of loving, or, rather, of making one's self loved, in which you are a little lacking. I can admit that at my age.

You say that you are all attention, love, kisses and caresses for him. Perhaps that is the very trouble; I think you kiss him too much.

My dear, we have in our hands the most terrible power in the world: LOVE.

Man is gifted with physical strength, and he exercises force. Woman is gifted with charm, and she rules with caresses. It is our weapon, formidable and invincible, but we should know how to use it.

Know well that we are the mistresses of the world! To tell the history of Love from the beginning of the world would be to tell the history of man himself: Everything springs from it, the arts, great events, customs, wars, the overthrow of empires.

In the Bible you find Delila, Judith; in fables we find Omphale, Helen; in history the Sabines, Cleopatra and many others.

Therefore we reign supreme, all-powerful. But, like kings, we must make use of delicate diplomacy.

Love, my dear, is made up of imperceptible sensations. We know that it is as strong as death, but also as frail as glass. The slightest shock breaks it, and our power crumbles, and we are never able to raise it again.

We have the power of making ourselves adored, but we lack one tiny thing, the understanding of the various kinds of caresses. In embraces we lose the sentiment of delicacy, while the man over whom we rule remains master of himself, capable of judging the foolishness of certain words. Take care, my dear; that is the defect in our armor. It is our Achilles' heel.

Do you know whence comes our real power? From the kiss, the kiss alone! When we know how to hold out and give up our lips we can become queens.

The kiss is only a preface, however, but a charming preface. More charming than the realization itself. A preface which can always be read over again, whereas one cannot always read over the book.

Yes, the meeting of lips is the most perfect, the most divine sensation given to human beings, the supreme limit of happiness: It is in the kiss alone that one sometimes seems to feel this union of souls after which we strive, the intermingling of hearts, as it were.

Do you remember the verses of Sully-Prudhomme:

Caresses are nothing but anxious bliss,
Vain attempts of love to unite souls through a kiss.

One caress alone gives this deep sensation of two beings welded into one—it is the kiss. No violent delirium of complete possession is worth this trembling approach of the lips, this first moist and fresh contact, and then the long, lingering, motionless rapture.

Therefore, my dear, the kiss is our strongest weapon, but we must take care not to dull it. Do not forget that its value is only relative, purely conventional. It continually changes according to circumstances, the state of expectancy and the ecstasy of the mind. I will call attention to one example.

Another poet, Francois Coppee, has written a line which we all remember, a line which we find delightful, which moves our very hearts.

After describing the expectancy of a lover, waiting in a room one winter's evening, his anxiety, his nervous impatience, the terrible fear of not seeing her, he describes the arrival of the beloved woman, who at last enters hurriedly, out of breath, bringing with her part of the winter breeze, and he exclaims:

Oh! the taste of the kisses first snatched through the veil.

Is that not a line of exquisite sentiment, a delicate and charming observation, a perfect truth? All those who have hastened to a clandestine meeting, whom passion has thrown into the arms of a man, well do they know these first delicious kisses through the veil; and they tremble at the memory of them. And yet their sole charm lies in the circumstances, from being late, from the anxious expectancy, but from the purely—or, rather, impurely, if you prefer—sensual point of view, they are detestable.

Think! Outside it is cold. The young woman has walked quickly; the veil is moist from her cold breath. Little drops of water shine in the lace. The lover seizes her and presses his burning lips to her liquid breath. The moist veil, which discolors and carries the dreadful odor of chemical dye, penetrates into the young man's mouth, moistens his mustache. He does not taste the lips of his beloved, he tastes the dye of this lace moistened with cold breath. And yet, like the poet, we would all exclaim:

Oh! the taste of the kisses first snatched through the veil.

Therefore, the value of this caress being entirely a matter of convention, we must be careful not to abuse it.

Well, my dear, I have several times noticed that you are very clumsy. However, you were not alone in that fault; the majority of women lose their authority by abusing the kiss with untimely kisses. When they feel that their husband or their lover is a little tired, at those times when the heart as well as the body needs rest, instead of understanding what is going on within him, they persist in giving inopportune caresses, tire him by the obstinacy of begging lips and give caresses lavished with neither rhyme nor reason.

Trust in the advice of my experience. First, never kiss your husband in public, in the train, at the restaurant. It is bad taste; do not give in to your desires. He would feel ridiculous and would never forgive you.

Beware of useless kisses lavished in intimacy. I am sure that you abuse them. For instance, I remember one day that you did something quite shocking. Probably you do not remember it.

All three of us were together in the drawing-room, and, as you did not stand on ceremony before me, your husband was holding you on his knees and kissing you at great length on the neck, the lips and throat. Suddenly you exclaimed: "Oh! the fire!" You had been paying no attention to it, and it was almost out. A few lingering embers were glowing on the hearth. Then he rose, ran to the woodbox, from which he dragged two enormous logs with great difficulty, when you came to him with begging lips, murmuring:

"Kiss me!" He turned his head with difficulty and tried to hold up the logs at the same time. Then you gently and slowly placed your mouth on that of the poor fellow, who remained with his neck out of joint, his sides twisted, his arms almost dropping off, trembling with fatigue and tired from his desperate effort. And you kept drawing out this torturing kiss, without seeing or understanding. Then when you freed him, you began to grumble: "How badly you kiss!" No wonder!

Oh, take care of that! We all have this foolish habit, this unconscious need of choosing the most inconvenient moments. When he is carrying a glass of water, when he is putting on his shoes, when he is tying his scarf—in short, when he finds himself in any uncomfortable position —then is the time which we choose for a caress which makes him stop for a whole minute in the middle of a gesture with the sole desire of getting rid of us!

Do not think that this criticism is insignificant. Love, my dear, is a delicate thing. The least little thing offends it; know that everything depends on the tact of our caresses. An ill-placed kiss may do any amount of harm.

Try following my advice.

Your old aunt,

COLLETTE.

This story appeared in the Gaulois in November, 1882, under the pseudonym of "Maufrigneuse."

THE LEGION OF HONOR

HOW HE GOT THE LEGION OF HONOR

From the time some people begin to talk they seem to have an overmastering desire or vocation.

Ever since he was a child, M. Caillard had only had one idea in his head —to wear the ribbon of an order. When he was still quite a small boy he used to wear a zinc cross of the Legion of Honor pinned on his tunic, just as other children wear a soldier's cap, and he took his mother's hand in the street with a proud air, sticking out his little chest with its red ribbon and metal star so that it might show to advantage.

His studies were not a success, and he failed in his examination for Bachelor of Arts; so, not knowing what to do, he married a pretty girl, as he had plenty of money of his own.

They lived in Paris, as many rich middle-class people do, mixing with their own particular set, and proud of knowing a deputy, who might perhaps be a minister some day, and counting two heads of departments among their friends.

But M. Caillard could not get rid of his one absorbing idea, and he felt constantly unhappy because he had not the right to wear a little bit of colored ribbon in his buttonhole.

When he met any men who were decorated on the boulevards, he looked at them askance, with intense jealousy. Sometimes, when he had nothing to do in the afternoon, he would count them, and say to himself: "Just let me see how many I shall meet between the Madeleine and the Rue Drouot."

Then he would walk slowly, looking at every coat with a practiced eye for the little bit of red ribbon, and when he had got to the end of his walk he always repeated the numbers aloud.

"Eight officers and seventeen knights. As many as that! It is stupid to sow the cross broadcast in that fashion. I wonder how many I shall meet going back?"

And he returned slowly, unhappy when the crowd of passers-by interfered with his vision.

He knew the places where most were to be found. They swarmed in the Palais Royal. Fewer were seen in the Avenue de l'Opera than in the Rue de la Paix, while the right side of the boulevard was more frequented by them than the left.

They also seemed to prefer certain cafes and theatres. Whenever he saw a group of white-haired old gentlemen standing together in the middle of the pavement, interfering with the traffic, he used to say to himself:

"They are officers of the Legion of Honor," and he felt inclined to take off his hat to them.

He had often remarked that the officers had a different bearing to the mere knights. They carried their head differently, and one felt that they enjoyed a higher official consideration and a more widely extended importance.

Sometimes, however, the worthy man would be seized with a furious hatred for every one who was decorated; he felt like a Socialist toward them.

Then, when he got home, excited at meeting so many crosses—just as a poor, hungry wretch might be on passing some dainty provision shop—he used to ask in a loud voice:

"When shall we get rid of this wretched government?"

And his wife would be surprised, and ask:

"What is the matter with you to-day?"

"I am indignant," he replied, "at the injustice I see going on around us. Oh, the Communards were certainly right!"

After dinner he would go out again and look at the shops where the decorations were sold, and he examined all the emblems of various shapes and colors. He would have liked to possess them all, and to have walked gravely at the head of a procession, with his crush hat under his arm and his breast covered with decorations, radiant as a star, amid a buzz of admiring whispers and a hum of respect.

But, alas! he had no right to wear any decoration whatever.

He used to say to himself: "It is really too difficult for any man to obtain the Legion of Honor unless he is some public functionary. Suppose I try to be appointed an officer of the Academy!"

But he did not know how to set about it, and spoke on the subject to his wife, who was stupefied.

"Officer of the Academy! What have you done to deserve it?"

He got angry. "I know what I am talking about. I only want to know how to set about it. You are quite stupid at times."

She smiled. "You are quite right. I don't understand anything about it."

An idea struck him: "Suppose you were to speak to M. Rosselin, the deputy; he might be able to advise me. You understand I cannot broach the subject to him directly. It is rather difficult and delicate, but coming from you it might seem quite natural."

Mme. Caillard did what he asked her, and M. Rosselin promised to speak to the minister about it; and then Caillard began to worry him, till the deputy told him he must make a formal application and put forward his claims.

"What were his charms?" he said. "He was not even a Bachelor of Arts." However, he set to work and produced a pamphlet, with the title, "The People's Right to Instruction," but he could not finish it for want of ideas.

He sought for easier subjects, and began several in succession. The first was, "The Instruction of Children by Means of the Eye." He wanted gratuitous theatres to be established in every poor quarter of Paris for little children. Their parents were to take them there when they were quite young, and, by means of a magic lantern, all the notions of human knowledge were to be imparted to them. There were to be regular courses. The sight would educate the mind, while the pictures would remain impressed on the brain, and thus science would, so to say, be made visible. What could be more simple than to teach universal history, natural history, geography, botany, zoology, anatomy, etc., etc., in this manner?

He had his ideas printed in pamphlets, and sent a copy to each deputy, ten to each minister, fifty to the President of the Republic, ten to each Parisian, and five to each provincial newspaper.

Then he wrote on "Street Lending-Libraries." His idea was to have little pushcarts full of books drawn about the streets. Everyone would have a right to ten volumes a month in his home on payment of one sou.

"The people," M. Caillard said, "will only disturb itself for the sake of its pleasures, and since it will not go to instruction, instruction must come to it," etc., etc.

His essays attracted no attention, but he sent in his application, and he got the usual formal official reply. He thought himself sure of success, but nothing came of it.

Then he made up his mind to apply personally. He begged for an interview with the Minister of Public Instruction, and he was received by a young subordinate, who was very grave and important, and kept touching the knobs of electric bells to summon ushers, and footmen, and officials inferior to himself. He declared to M. Caillard that his matter was going on quite favorably, and advised him to continue his remarkable labors, and M. Caillard set at it again.

M. Rosselin, the deputy, seemed now to take a great interest in his success, and gave him a lot of excellent, practical advice. He, himself, was decorated, although nobody knew exactly what he had done to deserve such a distinction.

He told Caillard what new studies he ought to undertake; he introduced him to learned societies which took up particularly obscure points of science, in the hope of gaining credit and honors thereby; and he even took him under his wing at the ministry.

One day, when he came to lunch with his friend—for several months past he had constantly taken his meals there—he said to him in a whisper as he shook hands: "I have just obtained a great favor for you. The Committee of Historical Works is going to intrust you with a commission. There are some researches to be made in various libraries in France."

Caillard was so delighted that he could scarcely eat or drink, and a week later he set out. He went from town to town, studying catalogues, rummaging in lofts full of dusty volumes, and was hated by all the librarians.

One day, happening to be at Rouen, he thought he should like to go and visit his wife, whom he had not seen for more than a week, so he took the nine o'clock train, which would land him at home by twelve at night.

He had his latchkey, so he went in without making any noise, delighted at the idea of the surprise he was going to give her. She had locked herself in. How tiresome! However, he cried out through the door:

"Jeanne, it is I!"

She must have been very frightened, for he heard her jump out of her bed and speak to herself, as if she were in a dream. Then she went to her dressing room, opened and closed the door, and went quickly up and down her room barefoot two or three times, shaking the furniture till the vases and glasses sounded. Then at last she asked:

"Is it you, Alexander?"

"Yes, yes," he replied; "make haste and open the door."

As soon as she had done so, she threw herself into his arms, exclaiming:

"Oh, what a fright! What a surprise! What a pleasure!"

He began to undress himself methodically, as he did everything, and took from a chair his overcoat, which he was in the habit of hanging up in the hall. But suddenly he remained motionless, struck dumb with astonishment—there was a red ribbon in the buttonhole:

"Why," he stammered, "this—this—this overcoat has got the ribbon in it!"

In a second, his wife threw herself on him, and, taking it from his hands, she said:

"No! you have made a mistake—give it to me."

But he still held it by one of the sleeves, without letting it go, repeating in a half-dazed manner:

"Oh! Why? Just explain—Whose overcoat is it? It is not mine, as it has the Legion of Honor on it."

She tried to take it from him, terrified and hardly able to say:

"Listen—listen! Give it to me! I must not tell you! It is a secret. Listen to me!"

But he grew angry and turned pale.

"I want to know how this overcoat comes to be here? It does not belong to me."

Then she almost screamed at him:

"Yes, it does; listen! Swear to me—well—you are decorated!"

She did not intend to joke at his expense.

He was so overcome that he let the overcoat fall and dropped into an armchair.

"I am—you say I am—decorated?"

"Yes, but it is a secret, a great secret."

She had put the glorious garment into a cupboard, and came to her husband pale and trembling.

"Yes," she continued, "it is a new overcoat that I have had made for you. But I swore that I would not tell you anything about it, as it will not be officially announced for a month or six weeks, and you were not to have known till your return from your business journey. M. Rosselin managed it for you."

"Rosselin!" he contrived to utter in his joy. "He has obtained the decoration for me? He—Oh!"

And he was obliged to drink a glass of water.

A little piece of white paper fell to the floor out of the pocket of the overcoat. Caillard picked it up; it was a visiting card, and he read out:

"Rosselin-Deputy."

"You see how it is," said his wife.

He almost cried with joy, and, a week later, it was announced in the Journal Officiel that M. Caillard had been awarded the Legion of Honor on account of his exceptional services.

THE TEST

The Bondels were a happy family, and although they frequently quarrelled about trifles, they soon became friends again.

Bondel was a merchant who had retired from active business after saving enough to allow him to live quietly; he had rented a little house at Saint-Germain and lived there with his wife. He was a quiet man with very decided opinions; he had a certain degree of education and read serious newspapers; nevertheless, he appreciated the gaulois wit. Endowed with a logical mind, and that practical common sense which is the master quality of the industrial French bourgeois, he thought little, but clearly, and reached a decision only after careful consideration of the matter in hand. He was of medium size, with a distinguished look, and was beginning to turn gray.

His wife, who was full of serious qualities, had also several faults. She had a quick temper and a frankness that bordered upon violence. She bore a grudge a long time. She had once been pretty, but had now become too stout and too red; but in her neighborhood at Saint-Germain she still passed for a very beautiful woman, who exemplified health and an uncertain temper.

Their dissensions almost always began at breakfast, over some trivial matter, and they often continued all day and even until the following day. Their simple, common, limited life imparted seriousness to the most unimportant matters, and every topic of conversation became a subject of dispute. This had not been so in the days when business occupied their minds, drew their hearts together, and gave them common interests and occupation.

But at Saint-Germain they saw fewer people. It had been necessary to make new acquaintances, to create for themselves a new world among strangers, a new existence devoid of occupations. Then the monotony of loneliness had soured each of them a little; and the quiet happiness which they had hoped and waited for with the coming of riches did not appear.

One June morning, just as they were sitting down to breakfast, Bondel asked:

"Do you know the people who live in the little red cottage at the end of the Rue du Berceau?"

Madame Bondel was out of sorts. She answered:

"Yes and no; I am acquainted with them, but I do not care to know them."

"Why not? They seem to be very nice."

"Because—"

"This morning I met the husband on the terrace and we took a little walk together."

Seeing that there was danger in the air, Bendel added: "It was he who spoke to me first."

His wife looked at him in a displeased manner. She continued: "You would have done just as well to avoid him."

"Why?"

"Because there are rumors about them."

"What kind?"

"Oh! rumors such as one often hears!"

M. Bondel was, unfortunately, a little hasty. He exclaimed:

"My dear, you know that I abhor gossip. As for those people, I find them very pleasant."

She asked testily: "The wife also?"

"Why, yes; although I have barely seen her."

The discussion gradually grew more heated, always on the same subject for lack of others. Madame Bondel obstinately refused to say what she had heard about these neighbors, allowing things to be understood without saying exactly what they were. Bendel would shrug his shoulders, grin, and exasperate his wife. She finally cried out: "Well! that gentleman is deceived by his wife, there!"

The husband answered quietly: "I can't see how that affects the honor of a man."

She seemed dumfounded: "What! you don't see?—you don't see?—well, that's too much! You don't see!—why, it's a public scandal! he is disgraced!"

He answered: "Ah! by no means! Should a man be considered disgraced because he is deceived, because he is betrayed, robbed? No, indeed! I'll grant you that that may be the case for the wife, but as for him—"

She became furious, exclaiming: "For him as well as for her. They are both in disgrace; it's a public shame."

Bondel, very calm, asked: "First of all, is it true? Who can assert such a thing as long as no one has been caught in the act?"

Madame Bondel was growing uneasy; she snapped: "What? Who can assert it? Why, everybody! everybody! it's as clear as the nose on your face. Everybody knows it and is talking about it. There is not the slightest doubt."

He was grinning: "For a long time people thought that the sun revolved around the earth. This man loves his wife and speaks of her tenderly and reverently. This whole business is nothing but lies!"

Stamping her foot, she stammered: "Do you think that that fool, that idiot, knows anything about it?"

Bondel did not grow angry; he was reasoning clearly: "Excuse me. This gentleman is no fool. He seemed to me, on the contrary, to be very intelligent and shrewd; and you can't make me believe that a man with brains doesn't notice such a thing in his own house, when the neighbors, who are not there, are ignorant of no detail of this liaison—for I'll warrant that they know everything."

Madame Bondel had a fit of angry mirth, which irritated her husband's nerves. She laughed: "Ha! ha! ha! they're all the same! There's not a man alive who could discover a thing like that unless his nose was stuck into it!"

The discussion was wandering to other topics now. She was exclaiming over the blindness of deceived husbands, a thing which he doubted and which she affirmed with such airs of personal contempt that he finally grew angry. Then the discussion became an angry quarrel, where she took the side of the women and he defended the men. He had the conceit to declare: "Well, I swear that if I had ever been deceived, I should have noticed it, and immediately, too. And I should have taken away your desire for such things in such a manner that it would have taken more than one doctor to set you on foot again!"

Boiling with anger, she cried out to him: "You! you! why, you're as big a fool as the others, do you hear!"

He still maintained: "I can swear to you that I am not!"

She laughed so impertinently that he felt his heart beat and a chill run down his back. For the third time he said:

"I should have seen it!"

She rose, still laughing in the same manner. She slammed the door and left the room, saying: "Well! if that isn't too much!"

Bondel remained alone, ill at ease. That insolent, provoking laugh had touched him to the quick. He went outside, walked, dreamed. The realization of the loneliness of his new life made him sad and morbid. The neighbor, whom he had met that morning, came to him with outstretched hands. They continued their walk together. After touching on various subjects they came to talk of their wives. Both seemed to have something to confide, something inexpressible, vague, about these beings associated with their lives; their wives. The neighbor was saying:

"Really, at times, one might think that they bear some particular ill-will toward their husband, just because he is a husband. I love my wife—I love her very much; I appreciate and respect her; well! there are times when she seems to have more confidence and faith in our friends than in me."

Bondel immediately thought: "There is no doubt; my wife was right!"

When he left this man he began to think things over again. He felt in his soul a strange confusion of contradictory ideas, a sort of interior burning; that mocking, impertinent laugh kept ringing in his ears and seemed to say: "Why; you are just the same as the others, you fool!" That was indeed bravado, one of those pieces of impudence of which a woman makes use when she dares everything, risks everything, to wound and humiliate the man who has aroused her ire. This poor man must also be one of those deceived husbands, like so many others. He had said sadly: "There are times when she seems to have more confidence and faith in our friends than in me." That is how a husband formulated his observations on the particular attentions of his wife for another man. That was all. He had seen nothing more. He was like the rest—all the rest!

And how strangely Bondel's own wife had laughed as she said: "You, too —you, too." How wild and imprudent these creatures are who can arouse such suspicions in the heart for the sole purpose of revenge!

He ran over their whole life since their marriage, reviewed his mental list of their acquaintances, to see whether she had ever appeared to show more confidence in any one else than in himself. He never had suspected any one, he was so calm, so sure of her, so confident.

But, now he thought of it, she had had a friend, an intimate friend, who for almost a year had dined with them three times a week. Tancret, good old Tancret, whom he, Bendel, loved as a brother and whom he continued to see on the sly, since his wife, he did not know why, had grown angry at the charming fellow.

He stopped to think, looking over the past with anxious eyes. Then he grew angry at himself for harboring this shameful insinuation of the defiant, jealous, bad ego which lives in all of us. He blamed and accused himself when he remembered the visits and the demeanor of this friend whom his wife had dismissed for no apparent reason. But, suddenly, other memories returned to him, similar ruptures due to the vindictive character of Madame Bondel, who never pardoned a slight. Then he laughed frankly at himself for the doubts which he had nursed; and he remembered the angry looks of his wife as he would tell her, when he returned at night: "I saw good old Tancret, and he wished to be remembered to you," and he reassured himself.

She would invariably answer: "When you see that gentleman you can tell him that I can very well dispense with his remembrances." With what an irritated, angry look she would say these words! How well one could feel that she did not and would not forgive—and he had suspected her even for a second? Such foolishness!

But why did she grow so angry? She never had given the exact reason for this quarrel. She still bore him that grudge! Was it?—But no—no—and Bondel declared that he was lowering himself by even thinking of such things.

Yes, he was undoubtedly lowering himself, but he could not help thinking of it, and he asked himself with terror if this thought which had entered into his mind had not come to stop, if he did not carry in his heart the seed of fearful torment. He knew himself; he was a man to think over his doubts, as formerly he would ruminate over his commercial operations, for days and nights, endlessly weighing the pros and the cons.

He was already becoming excited; he was walking fast and losing his calmness. A thought cannot be downed. It is intangible, cannot be caught, cannot be killed.

Suddenly a plan occurred to him; it was bold, so bold that at first he doubted whether he would carry it out.

Each time that he met Tancret, his friend would ask for news of Madame Bondel, and Bondel would answer: "She is still a little angry." Nothing more. Good Lord! What a fool he had been! Perhaps!

Well, he would take the train to Paris, go to Tancret, and bring him back with him that very evening, assuring him that his wife's mysterious anger had disappeared. But how would Madame Bondel act? What a scene there would be! What anger! what scandal! What of it?—that would be revenge! When she should come face to face with him, unexpectedly, he certainly ought to be able to read the truth in their expressions.

He immediately went to the station, bought his ticket, got into the car, and as soon as he felt him self being carried away by the train, he felt a fear, a kind of dizziness, at what he was going to do. In order not to weaken, back down, and return alone, he tried not to think of the matter any longer, to bring his mind to bear on other affairs, to do what he had decided to do with a blind resolution; and he began to hum tunes from operettas and music halls until he reached Paris.

As soon as he found himself walking along the streets that led to Tancret's, he felt like stopping, He paused in front of several shops, noticed the prices of certain objects, was interested in new things, felt like taking a glass of beer, which was not his usual custom; and as he approached his friend's dwelling he ardently hoped not meet him. But Tancret was at home, alone, reading. He jumped up in surprise, crying: "Ah! Bondel! what luck!"

Bondel, embarrassed, answered: "Yes, my dear fellow, I happened to be in Paris, and I thought I'd drop in and shake hands with you."

"That's very nice, very nice! The more so that for some time you have not favored me with your presence very often."

"Well, you see—even against one's will, one is often influenced by surrounding conditions, and as my wife seemed to bear you some ill-will"

"Jove! 'seemed'—she did better than that, since she showed me the door."

"What was the reason? I never heard it."

"Oh! nothing at all—a bit of foolishness—a discussion in which we did not both agree."

"But what was the subject of this discussion?"

"A lady of my acquaintance, whom you may perhaps know by name, Madame Boutin."

"Ah! really. Well, I think that my wife has forgotten her grudge, for this very morning she spoke to me of you in very pleasant terms."

Tancret started and seemed so dumfounded that for a few minutes he could find nothing to say. Then he asked: "She spoke of me—in pleasant terms?"

"Yes."

"You are sure?"

"Of course I am. I am not dreaming."

"And then?"

"And then—as I was coming to Paris I thought that I would please you by coming to tell you the good news."

"Why, yes—why, yes—"

Bondel appeared to hesitate; then, after a short pause, he added: "I even had an idea."

"What is it?"

"To take you back home with me to dinner."

Tancret, who was naturally prudent, seemed a little worried by this proposition, and he asked: "Oh! really—is it possible? Are we not exposing ourselves to—to—a scene?"

"No, no, indeed!"

"Because, you know, Madame Bendel bears malice for a long time."

"Yes, but I can assure you that she no longer bears you any ill—will. I am even convinced that it will be a great pleasure for her to see you thus, unexpectedly."

"Really?"

"Yes, really!"

"Well, then! let us go along. I am delighted. You see, this misunderstanding was very unpleasant for me."

They set out together toward the Saint-Lazare station, arm in arm. They made the trip in silence. Both seemed absorbed in deep meditation. Seated in the car, one opposite the other, they looked at each other without speaking, each observing that the other was pale.

Then they left the train and once more linked arms as if to unite against some common danger. After a walk of a few minutes they stopped, a little out of breath, before Bondel's house. Bondel ushered his friend into the parlor, called the servant, and asked: "Is madame at home?"

"Yes, monsieur."

"Please ask her to come down at once."

They dropped into two armchairs and waited. Both were filled with the same longing to escape before the appearance of the much-feared person.

A well-known, heavy tread could be heard descending the stairs. A hand moved the knob, and both men watched the brass handle turn. Then the door opened wide, and Madame Bondel stopped and looked to see who was there before she entered. She looked, blushed, trembled, retreated a step, then stood motionless, her cheeks aflame and her hands resting against the sides of the door frame.

Tancret, as pale as if about to faint, had arisen, letting fall his hat, which rolled along the floor. He stammered out: "Mon Dieu—madame—it is I—I thought—I ventured—I was so sorry—"

As she did not answer, he continued: "Will you forgive me?"

Then, quickly, carried away by some impulse, she walked toward him with her hands outstretched; and when he had taken, pressed, and held these two hands, she said, in a trembling, weak little voice, which was new to her husband:

"Ah! my dear friend—how happy I am!"

And Bondel, who was watching them, felt an icy chill run over him, as if he had been dipped in a cold bath.

FOUND ON A DROWNED MAN

Madame, you ask me whether I am laughing at you? You cannot believe that a man has never been in love. Well, then, no, no, I have never loved, never!

Why is this? I really cannot tell. I have never experienced that intoxication of the heart which we call love! Never have I lived in that dream, in that exaltation, in that state of madness into which the image of a woman casts us. I have never been pursued, haunted, roused to fever heat, lifted up to Paradise by the thought of meeting, or by the possession of, a being who had suddenly become for me more desirable than any good fortune, more beautiful than any other creature, of more consequence than the whole world! I have never wept, I have never suffered on account of any of you. I have not passed my nights sleepless, while thinking of her. I have no experience of waking thoughts bright with thought and memories of her. I have never known the wild rapture of hope before her arrival, or the divine sadness of regret when she went from me, leaving behind her a delicate odor of violet powder.

I have never been in love.

I have also often asked myself why this is. And truly I can scarcely tell. Nevertheless I have found some reasons for it; but they are of a metaphysical character, and perhaps you will not be able to appreciate them.

I suppose I am too critical of women to submit to their fascination. I ask you to forgive me for this remark. I will explain what I mean. In every creature there is a moral being and a physical being. In order to love, it would be necessary for me to find a harmony between these two beings which I have never found. One always predominates; sometimes the moral, sometimes the physical.

The intellect which we have a right to require in a woman, in order to love her, is not the same as the virile intellect. It is more, and it is less. A woman must be frank, delicate, sensitive, refined, impressionable. She has no need of either power or initiative in thought, but she must have kindness, elegance, tenderness, coquetry and that faculty of assimilation which, in a little while, raises her to an equality with him who shares her life. Her greatest quality must be tact, that subtle sense which is to the mind what touch is to the body. It reveals to her a thousand little things, contours, angles and forms on the plane of the intellectual.

Very frequently pretty women have not intellect to correspond with their personal charms. Now, the slightest lack of harmony strikes me and pains me at the first glance. In friendship this is not of importance. Friendship is a compact in which one fairly shares defects and merits. We may judge of friends, whether man or woman, giving them credit for what is good, and overlooking what is bad in them, appreciating them at their just value, while giving ourselves up to an intimate, intense and charming sympathy.

In order to love, one must be blind, surrender one's self absolutely, see nothing, question nothing, understand nothing. One must adore the weakness as well as the beauty of the beloved object, renounce all judgment, all reflection, all perspicacity.

I am incapable of such blindness and rebel at unreasoning subjugation. This is not all. I have such a high and subtle idea of harmony that nothing can ever fulfill my ideal. But you will call me a madman. Listen to me. A woman, in my opinion, may have an exquisite soul and charming body without that body and that soul being in perfect harmony with one another. I mean that persons who have noses made in a certain shape should not be expected to think in a certain fashion. The fat have no right to make use of the same words and phrases as the thin. You, who have blue eyes, madame, cannot look at life and judge of things and events as if you had black eyes. The shade of your eyes should correspond, by a sort of fatality, with the shade of your thought. In perceiving these things, I have the scent of a bloodhound. Laugh if you like, but it is so.

And yet, once I imagined that I was in love for an hour, for a day. I had foolishly yielded to the influence of surrounding circumstances. I allowed myself to be beguiled by a mirage of Dawn. Would you like me to tell you this short story?

I met, one evening, a pretty, enthusiastic little woman who took a poetic fancy to spend a night with me in a boat on a river. I would have preferred a room and a bed; however, I consented to the river and the boat.

It was in the month of June. My fair companion chose a moonlight night in order the better to stimulate her imagination.

We had dined at a riverside inn and set out in the boat about ten o'clock. I thought it a rather foolish kind of adventure, but as my companion pleased me I did not worry about it. I sat down on the seat facing her; I seized the oars, and off we starred.

I could not deny that the scene was picturesque. We glided past a wooded isle full of nightingales, and the current carried us rapidly over the river covered with silvery ripples. The tree toads uttered their shrill, monotonous cry; the frogs croaked in the grass by the river's bank, and the lapping of the water as it flowed on made around us a kind of confused murmur almost imperceptible, disquieting, and gave us a vague sensation of mysterious fear.

The sweet charm of warm nights and of streams glittering in the moonlight penetrated us. It was delightful to be alive and to float along thus, and to dream and to feel at one's side a sympathetic and beautiful young woman.

I was somewhat affected, somewhat agitated, somewhat intoxicated by the pale brightness of the night and the consciousness of my proximity to a lovely woman.

"Come and sit beside me," she said.

I obeyed.

She went on:

"Recite some poetry for me."

This appeared to be rather too much. I declined; she persisted. She certainly wanted to play the game, to have a whole orchestra of sentiment, from the moon to the rhymes of poets. In the end I had to yield, and, as if in mockery, I repeated to her a charming little poem by Louis Bouilhet, of which the following are the last verses:

"I hate the poet who with tearful eye
Murmurs some name while gazing tow'rds a star,
Who sees no magic in the earth or sky,
Unless Lizette or Ninon be not far.

"The bard who in all Nature nothing sees
Divine, unless a petticoat he ties
Amorously to the branches of the trees
Or nightcap to the grass, is scarcely wise.

"He has not heard the Eternal's thunder tone,
The voice of Nature in her various moods,
Who cannot tread the dim ravines alone,
And of no woman dream mid whispering woods."

I expected some reproaches. Nothing of the sort. She murmured:

"How true it is!"

I was astonished. Had she understood?

Our boat had gradually approached the bank and become entangled in the branches of a willow which impeded its progress. I placed my arm round my companion's waist, and very gently approached my lips towards her neck. But she repulsed me with an abrupt, angry movement.

"Have done, pray! How rude you are!"

I tried to draw her toward me. She resisted, caught hold of the tree, and was near flinging us both into the water. I deemed it prudent to cease my importunities.

She said:

"I would rather capsize you. I feel so happy. I want to dream. This is so delightful." Then, in a slightly malicious tone, she added:

"Have you already forgotten the verses you repeated to me just now?"

She was right. I became silent.

She went on:

"Come, now!"

And I plied the oars once more.

I began to think the night long and my position ridiculous.

My companion said to me:

"Will you make me a promise?"

"Yes. What is it?"

"To remain quiet, well-behaved and discreet, if I permit you—"

"What? Say what you mean!"

"Here is what I mean: I want to lie down on my back at the bottom of the boat with you by my side. But I forbid you to touch me, to embrace me —in short—to caress me."

I promised. She said warningly:

"If you move, 'I'll capsize the boat."

And then we lay down side by side, our eyes turned toward the sky, while the boat glided slowly through the water. We were rocked by its gentle motion. The slight sounds of the night came to us more distinctly in the bottom of the boat, sometimes causing us to start. And I felt springing up within me a strange, poignant emotion, an infinite tenderness, something like an irresistible impulse to open my arms in order to embrace, to open my heart in order to love, to give myself, to give my thoughts, my body, my life, my entire being to some one.

My companion murmured, like one in a dream:

"Where are we; Where are we going? It seems to me that I am leaving the earth. How sweet it is! Ah, if you loved me—a little!!!"

My heart began to throb. I had no answer to give. It seemed to me that I loved her. I had no longer any violent desire. I felt happy there by her side, and that was enough for me.

And thus we remained for a long, long time without stirring. We had clasped each other's hands; some delightful force rendered us motionless, an unknown force stronger than ourselves, an alliance, chaste, intimate, absolute, of our beings lying there side by side, belonging to each other without contact. What was this? How do I know? Love, perhaps?

Little by little the dawn appeared. It was three o'clock in the morning. Slowly a great brightness spread over the sky. The boat knocked up against something. I rose up. We had come close to a tiny islet.

But I remained enchanted, in an ecstasy. Before us stretched the firmament, red, pink, violet, spotted with fiery clouds resembling golden vapor. The river was glowing with purple and three houses on one side of it seemed to be burning.

I bent toward my companion. I was going to say, "Oh! look!" But I held my tongue, quite dazed, and I could no longer see anything except her. She, too, was rosy, with rosy flesh tints with a deeper tinge that was partly a reflection of the hue of the sky. Her tresses were rosy; her eyes were rosy; her teeth were rosy; her dress, her laces, her smile, all were rosy. And in truth I believed, so overpowering was the illusion, that the dawn was there in the flesh before me.

She rose softly to her feet, holding out her lips to me; and I moved toward her, trembling, delirious feeling indeed that I was going to kiss Heaven, to kiss happiness, to kiss a dream that had become a woman, to kiss the ideal which had descended into human flesh.

She said to me: "You have a caterpillar in your hair." And, suddenly, I felt as sad as if I had lost all hope in life.

That is all, madame. It is puerile, silly, stupid. But I am sure that since that day it would be impossible for me to love. And yet—who can tell?

[The young man upon whom this letter was found was yesterday taken out of the Seine between Bougival and Marly. An obliging bargeman, who had searched the pockets in order to ascertain the name of the deceased, brought this paper to the author.]

THE ORPHAN

Mademoiselle Source had adopted this boy under very sad circumstances. She was at the time thirty-six years old. Being disfigured through having as a child slipped off her nurse's lap into the fireplace and burned her face shockingly, she had determined not to marry, for she did not want any man to marry her for her money.

A neighbor of hers, left a widow just before her child was born, died in giving birth, without leaving a sou. Mademoiselle Source took the new-born child, put him out to nurse, reared him, sent him to a boarding-school, then brought him home in his fourteenth year, in order to have in her empty house somebody who would love her, who would look after her, and make her old age pleasant.

She had a little country place four leagues from Rennes, and she now dispensed with a servant; her expenses having increased to more than double since this orphan's arrival, her income of three thousand francs was no longer sufficient to support three persons.

She attended to the housekeeping and cooking herself, and sent out the boy on errands, letting him also occupy himself in cultivating the garden. He was gentle, timid, silent, and affectionate. And she experienced a deep happiness, a fresh happiness when he kissed her without surprise or horror at her disfigurement. He called her "Aunt," and treated her as a mother.

In the evening they both sat down at the fireside, and she made nice little dainties for him. She heated some wine and toasted a slice of bread, and it made a charming little meal before going to bed. She often took him on her knees and covered him with kisses, murmuring tender words in his ear. She called him: "My little flower, my cherub, my adored angel, my divine jewel." He softly accepted her caresses, hiding his head on the old maid's shoulder. Although he was now nearly fifteen, he had remained small and weak, and had a rather sickly appearance.

Sometimes Mademoiselle Source took him to the city, to see two married female relatives of hers, distant cousins, who were living in the suburbs, and who were the only members of her family in existence. The two women had always found fault with her, for having adopted this boy, on account of the inheritance; but for all that, they gave her a cordial welcome, having still hopes of getting a share for themselves, a third, no doubt, if what she possessed were only equally divided.

She was happy, very happy, always occupied with her adopted child. She bought books for him to improve his mind, and he became passionately fond of reading.

He no longer climbed on her knee to pet her as he had formerly done; but, instead, would go and sit down in his little chair in the chimney-corner and open a volume. The lamp placed at the edge of the Tittle table above his head shone on his curly hair, and on a portion of his forehead; he did not move, he did not raise his eyes or make any gesture. He read on, interested, entirely absorbed in the story he was reading.

Seated opposite to him, she would gaze at him earnestly, astonished at his studiousness, often on the point of bursting into tears.

She said to him occasionally: "You will fatigue yourself, my treasure!" hoping that he would raise his head, and come across to embrace her; but he did not even answer her; he had not heard or understood what she was saying; he paid no attention to anything save what he read in those pages.

For two years he devoured an incalculable number of volumes. His character changed.

After this, he asked Mademoiselle Source several times for money, which she gave him. As he always wanted more, she ended by refusing, for she was both methodical and decided, and knew how to act rationally when it was necessary to do so. By dint of entreaties he obtained a large sum from her one night; but when he begged her for more a few days later, she showed herself inflexible, and did not give way to him further, in fact.

He appeared to be satisfied with her decision.

He again became quiet, as he had formerly been, remaining seated for entire hours, without moving, plunged in deep reverie. He now did not even talk to Madame Source, merely answering her remarks with short, formal words. Nevertheless, he was agreeable and attentive in his manner toward her; but he never embraced her now.

She had by this time grown slightly afraid of him when they sat facing one another at night on opposite sides of the fireplace. She wanted to wake him up, to make him say something, no matter what, that would break this dreadful silence, which was like the darkness of a wood. But he did not appear to listen to her, and she shuddered with the terror of a poor feeble woman when she had spoken to him five or six times successively without being able to get a word out of him.

What was the matter with him? What was going on in that closed-up head? When she had remained thus two or three hours opposite him, she felt as if she were going insane, and longed to rush away and to escape into the open country in order to avoid that mute, eternal companionship and also some vague danger, which she could not define, but of which she had a presentiment.

She frequently wept when she was alone. What was the matter with him? When she expressed a wish, he unmurmuringly carried it into execution. When she wanted anything brought from the city, he immediately went there to procure it. She had no complaint to make of him; no, indeed! And yet—

Another year flitted by, and it seemed to her that a fresh change had taken place in the mind of the young man. She perceived it; she felt it; she divined it. How? No matter! She was sure she was not mistaken; but she could not have explained in what manner the unknown thoughts of this strange youth had changed.

It seemed to her that, until now, he had been like a person in a hesitating frame of mind, who had suddenly arrived at a determination. This idea came to her one evening as she met his glance, a fixed, singular glance which she had not seen in his face before.

Then he commenced to watch her incessantly, and she wished she could hide herself in order to avoid that cold eye riveted on her.

He kept staring at her, evening after evening, for hours together, only averting his eyes when she said, utterly unnerved:

"Do not look at me like that, my child!"

Then he would lower his head.

But the moment her back was turned she once more felt that his eyes were upon her. Wherever she went, he pursued her with his persistent gaze.

Sometimes, when she was walking in her little garden, she suddenly noticed him hidden behind a bush, as if he were lying in wait for her; and, again, when she sat in front of the house mending stockings while he was digging some vegetable bed, he kept continually watching her in a surreptitious manner, as he worked.

It was in vain that she asked him:

"What's the matter with you, my boy? For the last three years, you have become very different. I don't recognize you. Do tell me what ails you, and what you are thinking of."

He invariably replied, in a quiet, weary tone:

"Why, nothing ails me, aunt!"

And when she persisted:

"Ah! my child, answer me, answer me when I speak to you. If you knew what grief you caused me, you would always answer, and you would not look at me that way. Have you any trouble? Tell me! I'll comfort you!"

He went away, with a tired air, murmuring:

"But there is nothing the matter with me, I assure you."

He had not grown much, having always a childish look, although his features were those of a man. They were, however, hard and badly cut. He seemed incomplete, abortive, only half finished, and disquieting as a mystery. He was a self-contained, unapproachable being, in whom there seemed always to be some active, dangerous mental labor going on. Mademoiselle Source was quite conscious of all this, and she could not sleep at night, so great was her anxiety. Frightful terrors, dreadful nightmares assailed her. She shut herself up in her own room, and barricaded the door, tortured by fear.

What was she afraid of? She could not tell.

She feared everything, the night, the walls, the shadows thrown by the moon on the white curtains of the windows, and, above all, she feared him.

Why?

What had she to fear? Did she know what it was?

She could live this way no longer! She felt certain that a misfortune threatened her, a frightful misfortune.

She set forth secretly one morning, and went into the city to see her relatives. She told them about the matter in a gasping voice. The two women thought she was going mad and tried to reassure her.

She said:

"If you knew the way he looks at me from morning till night. He never takes his eyes off me! At times, I feel a longing to cry for help, to call in the neighbors, so much am I afraid. But what could I say to them? He does nothing but look at me."

The two female cousins asked:

"Is he ever brutal to you? Does he give you sharp answers?"

She replied:

"No, never; he does everything I wish; he works hard: he is steady; but I am so frightened that I care nothing for that. He is planning something, I am certain of that—quite certain. I don't care to remain all alone like that with him in the country."

The relatives, astonished at her words, declared that people would be amazed, would not understand; and they advised her to keep silent about her fears and her plans, without, however, dissuading her from coming to reside in the city, hoping in that way that the entire inheritance would eventually fall into their hands.

They even promised to assist her in selling her house, and in finding another, near them.

Mademoiselle Source returned home. But her mind was so much upset that she trembled at the slightest noise, and her hands shook whenever any trifling disturbance agitated her.

Twice she went again to consult her relatives, quite determined now not to remain any longer in this way in her lonely dwelling. At last, she found a little cottage in the suburbs, which suited her, and she privately bought it.

The signature of the contract took place on a Tuesday morning, and Mademoiselle Source devoted the rest of the day to the preparations for her change of residence.

At eight o'clock in the evening she got into the diligence which passed within a few hundred yards of her house, and she told the conductor to put her down in the place where she usually alighted. The man called out to her as he whipped his horses:

"Good evening, Mademoiselle Source—good night!"

She replied as she walked on:

"Good evening, Pere Joseph." Next morning, at half-past seven, the postman who conveyed letters to the village noticed at the cross-road, not far from the high road, a large splash of blood not yet dry. He said to himself: "Hallo! some boozer must have had a nose bleed."

But he perceived ten paces farther on a pocket handkerchief also stained with blood. He picked it up. The linen was fine, and the postman, in alarm, made his way over to the ditch, where he fancied he saw a strange object.

Mademoiselle Source was lying at the bottom on the grass, her throat cut with a knife.

An hour later, the gendarmes, the examining magistrate, and other authorities made an inquiry as to the cause of death.

The two female relatives, called as witnesses, told all about the old maid's fears and her last plans.

The orphan was arrested. After the death of the woman who had adopted him, he wept from morning till night, plunged, at least to all appearance, in the most violent grief.

He proved that he had spent the evening up to eleven o'clock in a cafe. Ten persons had seen him, having remained there till his departure.

The driver of the diligence stated that he had set down the murdered woman on the road between half-past nine and ten o'clock.

The accused was acquitted. A will, drawn up a long time before, which had been left in the hands of a notary in Rennes, made him sole heir. So he inherited everything.

For a long time, the people of the country boycotted him, as they still suspected him. His house, that of the dead woman, was looked upon as accursed. People avoided him in the street.

But he showed himself so good-natured, so open, so familiar, that gradually these horrible doubts were forgotten. He was generous, obliging, ready to talk to the humblest about anything, as long as they cared to talk to him.

The notary, Maitre Rameau, was one of the first to take his part, attracted by his smiling loquacity. He said at a dinner, at the tax collector's house:

"A man who speaks with such facility and who is always in good humor could not have such a crime on his conscience."

Touched by his argument, the others who were present reflected, and they recalled to mind the long conversations with this man who would almost compel them to stop at the road corners to listen to his ideas, who insisted on their going into his house when they were passing by his garden, who could crack a joke better than the lieutenant of the gendarmes himself, and who possessed such contagious gaiety that, in spite of the repugnance with which he inspired them, they could not keep from always laughing in his company.

All doors were opened to him after a time.

He is to-day the mayor of his township.

THE BEGGAR

He had seen better days, despite his present misery and infirmities.

At the age of fifteen both his legs had been crushed by a carriage on the Varville highway. From that time forth he begged, dragging himself along the roads and through the farmyards, supported by crutches which forced his shoulders up to his ears. His head looked as if it were squeezed in between two mountains.

A foundling, picked up out of a ditch by the priest of Les Billettes on the eve of All Saints' Day and baptized, for that reason, Nicholas Toussaint, reared by charity, utterly without education, crippled in consequence of having drunk several glasses of brandy given him by the baker (such a funny story!) and a vagabond all his life afterward—the only thing he knew how to do was to hold out his hand for alms.

At one time the Baroness d'Avary allowed him to sleep in a kind of recess spread with straw, close to the poultry yard in the farm adjoining the chateau, and if he was in great need he was sure of getting a glass of cider and a crust of bread in the kitchen. Moreover, the old lady often threw him a few pennies from her window. But she was dead now.

In the villages people gave him scarcely anything—he was too well known. Everybody had grown tired of seeing him, day after day for forty years, dragging his deformed and tattered person from door to door on his wooden crutches. But he could not make up his mind to go elsewhere, because he knew no place on earth but this particular corner of the country, these three or four villages where he had spent the whole of his miserable existence. He had limited his begging operations and would not for worlds have passed his accustomed bounds.

He did not even know whether the world extended for any distance beyond the trees which had always bounded his vision. He did not ask himself the question. And when the peasants, tired of constantly meeting him in their fields or along their lanes, exclaimed: "Why don't you go to other villages instead of always limping about here?" he did not answer, but slunk away, possessed with a vague dread of the unknown—the dread of a poor wretch who fears confusedly a thousand things—new faces, taunts, insults, the suspicious glances of people who do not know him and the policemen walking in couples on the roads. These last he always instinctively avoided, taking refuge in the bushes or behind heaps of stones when he saw them coming.

When he perceived them in the distance, 'With uniforms gleaming in the sun, he was suddenly possessed with unwonted agility—the agility of a wild animal seeking its lair. He threw aside his crutches, fell to the ground like a limp rag, made himself as small as possible and crouched like a hare under cover, his tattered vestments blending in hue with the earth on which he cowered.

He had never had any trouble with the police, but the instinct to avoid them was in his blood. He seemed to have inherited it from the parents he had never known.

He had no refuge, no roof for his head, no shelter of any kind. In summer he slept out of doors and in winter he showed remarkable skill in slipping unperceived into barns and stables. He always decamped before his presence could be discovered. He knew all the holes through which one could creep into farm buildings, and the handling of his crutches having made his arms surprisingly muscular he often hauled himself up through sheer strength of wrist into hay-lofts, where he sometimes remained for four or five days at a time, provided he had collected a sufficient store of food beforehand.

He lived like the beasts of the field. He was in the midst of men, yet knew no one, loved no one, exciting in the breasts of the peasants only a sort of careless contempt and smoldering hostility.

They nicknamed him "Bell," because he hung between his two crutches like a church bell between its supports.

For two days he had eaten nothing. No one gave him anything now. Every one's patience was exhausted. Women shouted to him from their doorsteps when they saw him coming:

"Be off with you, you good-for-nothing vagabond! Why, I gave you a piece of bread only three days ago!"

And he turned on his crutches to the next house, where he was received in the same fashion.

The women declared to one another as they stood at their doors:

"We can't feed that lazy brute all the year round!"

And yet the "lazy brute" needed food every day.

He had exhausted Saint-Hilaire, Varville and Les Billettes without getting a single copper or so much as a dry crust. His only hope was in Tournolles, but to reach this place he would have to walk five miles along the highroad, and he felt so weary that he could hardly drag himself another yard. His stomach and his pocket were equally empty, but he started on his way.

It was December and a cold wind blew over the fields and whistled through the bare branches of the trees; the clouds careered madly across the black, threatening sky. The cripple dragged himself slowly along, raising one crutch after the other with a painful effort, propping himself on the one distorted leg which remained to him.

Now and then he sat down beside a ditch for a few moments' rest. Hunger was gnawing his vitals, and in his confused, slow-working mind he had only one idea-to eat-but how this was to be accomplished he did not know. For three hours he continued his painful journey. Then at last the sight of the trees of the village inspired him with new energy.

The first peasant he met, and of whom he asked alms, replied:

"So it's you again, is it, you old scamp? Shall I never be rid of you?"

And "Bell" went on his way. At every door he got nothing but hard words. He made the round of the whole village, but received not a halfpenny for his pains.

Then he visited the neighboring farms, toiling through the muddy land, so exhausted that he could hardly raise his crutches from the ground. He met with the same reception everywhere.

It was one of those cold, bleak days, when the heart is frozen and the temper irritable, and hands do not open either to give money or food.

When he had visited all the houses he knew, "Bell" sank down in the corner of a ditch running across Chiquet's farmyard. Letting his crutches slip to the ground, he remained motionless, tortured by hunger, but hardly intelligent enough to realize to the full his unutterable misery.

He awaited he knew not what, possessed with that vague hope which persists in the human heart in spite of everything. He awaited in the corner of the farmyard in the biting December wind, some mysterious aid from Heaven or from men, without the least idea whence it was to arrive. A number of black hens ran hither and thither, seeking their food in the earth which supports all living things. Ever now and then they snapped up in their beaks a grain of corn or a tiny insect; then they continued their slow, sure search for nutriment.

"Bell" watched them at first without thinking of anything. Then a thought occurred rather to his stomach than to his mind—the thought that one of those fowls would be good to eat if it were cooked over a fire of dead wood.

He did not reflect that he was going to commit a theft. He took up a stone which lay within reach, and, being of skillful aim, killed at the first shot the fowl nearest to him. The bird fell on its side, flapping its wings. The others fled wildly hither and thither, and "Bell," picking up his crutches, limped across to where his victim lay.

Just as he reached the little black body with its crimsoned head he received a violent blow in his back which made him let go his hold of his crutches and sent him flying ten paces distant. And Farmer Chiquet, beside himself with rage, cuffed and kicked the marauder with all the fury of a plundered peasant as "Bell" lay defenceless before him.

The farm hands came up also and joined their master in cuffing the lame beggar. Then when they were tired of beating him they carried him off and shut him up in the woodshed, while they went to fetch the police.

"Bell," half dead, bleeding and perishing with hunger, lay on the floor. Evening came—then night—then dawn. And still he had not eaten.

About midday the police arrived. They opened the door of the woodshed with the utmost precaution, fearing resistance on the beggar's part, for Farmer Chiquet asserted that he had been attacked by him and had had great, difficulty in defending himself.

The sergeant cried:

"Come, get up!"

But "Bell" could not move. He did his best to raise himself on his crutches, but without success. The police, thinking his weakness feigned, pulled him up by main force and set him between the crutches.

Fear seized him—his native fear of a uniform, the fear of the game in presence of the sportsman, the fear of a mouse for a cat-and by the exercise of almost superhuman effort he succeeded in remaining upright.

"Forward!" said the sergeant. He walked. All the inmates of the farm watched his departure. The women shook their fists at him the men scoffed at and insulted him. He was taken at last! Good riddance! He went off between his two guards. He mustered sufficient energy—the energy of despair—to drag himself along until the evening, too dazed to know what was happening to him, too frightened to understand.

People whom he met on the road stopped to watch him go by and peasants muttered:

"It's some thief or other."

Toward evening he reached the country town. He had never been so far before. He did not realize in the least what he was there for or what was to become of him. All the terrible and unexpected events of the last two days, all these unfamiliar faces and houses struck dismay into his heart.

He said not a word, having nothing to say because he understood nothing. Besides, he had spoken to no one for so many years past that he had almost lost the use of his tongue, and his thoughts were too indeterminate to be put into words.

He was shut up in the town jail. It did not occur to the police that he might need food, and he was left alone until the following day. But when in the early morning they came to examine him he was found dead on the floor. Such an astonishing thing!

THE RABBIT

Old Lecacheur appeared at the door of his house between five and a quarter past five in the morning, his usual hour, to watch his men going to work.

He was only half awake, his face was red, and with his right eye open and the left nearly closed, he was buttoning his braces over his fat stomach with some difficulty, at the same time looking into every corner of the farmyard with a searching glance. The sun darted its oblique rays through the beech trees by the side of the ditch and athwart the apple trees outside, and was making the cocks crow on the dunghill, and the pigeons coo on the roof. The smell of the cow stable came through the open door, and blended in the fresh morning air with the pungent odor of the stable, where the horses were neighing, with their heads turned toward the light.

As soon as his trousers were properly fastened, Lecacheur came out, and went, first of all, toward the hen house to count the morning's eggs, for he had been afraid of thefts for some time; but the servant girl ran up to him with lifted arms and cried:

"Master! master! they have stolen a rabbit during the night."

"A rabbit?"

"Yes, master, the big gray rabbit, from the hutch on the left"; whereupon the farmer completely opened his left eye, and said, simply:

"I must see about that."

And off he went to inspect it. The hutch had been broken open and the rabbit was gone. Then he became thoughtful, closed his right eye again, and scratched his nose, and after a little consideration, he said to the frightened girl, who was standing stupidly before her master:

"Go and fetch the gendarmes; say I expect them as soon as possible."

Lecacheur was mayor of the village, Pavigny-le-Gras, and ruled it like a master, on account of his money and position, and as soon as the servant had disappeared in the direction of the village, which was only about five hundred yards off, he went into the house to have his morning coffee and to discuss the matter with his wife, whom he found on her knees in front of the fire, trying to make it burn quickly, and as soon as he got to the door, he said:

"Somebody has stolen the gray rabbit."

She turned round so suddenly that she found herself sitting on the floor, and looking at her husband with distressed eyes, she said:

"What is it, Cacheux? Somebody has stolen a rabbit?"

"The big gray one."

She sighed.

"What a shame! Who can have done it?"

She was a little, thin, active, neat woman, who knew all about farming. Lecacheur had his own ideas about the matter.

"It must be that fellow, Polyte."

His wife got up suddenly and said in a furious voice:

"He did it! he did it! You need not look for any one else. He did it! You have said it, Cacheux!"

All her peasant's fury, all her avarice, all her rage of a saving woman against the man of whom she had always been suspicious, and against the girl whom she had always suspected, showed themselves in the contraction of her mouth, and the wrinkles in the cheeks and forehead of her thin, exasperated face.

"And what have you done?" she asked.

"I have sent for the gendarmes."

This Polyte was a laborer, who had been employed on the farm for a few days, and who had been dismissed by Lecacheur for an insolent answer. He was an old soldier, and was supposed to have retained his habits of marauding and debauchery from his campaigns in Africa. He did anything for a livelihood, but whether he were a mason, a navvy, a reaper, whether he broke stones or lopped trees, he was always lazy, and so he remained nowhere for long, and had, at times, to change his neighborhood to obtain work.

From the first day that he came to the farm, Lecacheur's wife had detested him, and now she was sure that he had committed the theft.

In about half an hour the two gendarmes arrived. Brigadier Senateur was very tall and thin, and Gendarme Lenient short and fat. Lecacheur made them sit down, and told them the affair, and then they went and saw the scene of the theft, in order to verify the fact that the hutch had been broken open, and to collect all the proofs they could. When they got back to the kitchen, the mistress brought in some wine, filled their glasses, and asked with a distrustful look:

"Shall you catch him?"

The brigadier, who had his sword between his legs, appeared thoughtful. Certainly, he was sure of taking him, if he was pointed out to him, but if not, he could not answer for being able to discover him, himself, and after reflecting for a long time, he put this simple question:

"Do you know the thief?"

And Lecacheur replied, with a look of Normandy slyness in his eyes:

"As for knowing him, I do not, as I did not see him commit the theft. If I had seen him, I should have made him eat it raw, skin and flesh, without a drop of cider to wash it down. But as for saying who it is, I cannot, although I believe it is that good-for-nothing Polyte."

Then he related at length his troubles with Polyte, his leaving his service, his bad reputation, things which had been told him, accumulating insignificant and minute proofs, and then, the brigadier, who had been listening very attentively while he emptied his glass and filled it again with an indifferent air, turned to his gendarme and said:

"We must go and look in the cottage of Severin's wife." At which the gendarme smiled and nodded three times.

Then Madame Lecacheur came to them, and very quietly, with all a peasant's cunning, questioned the brigadier in her turn. That shepherd Severin, a simpleton, a sort of brute who had been brought up and had grown up among his bleating flocks, and who knew scarcely anything besides them in the world, had nevertheless preserved the peasant's instinct for saving, at the bottom of his heart. For years and years he must have hidden in hollow trees and crevices in the rocks all that he earned, either as a shepherd or by curing animals' sprains—for the bonesetter's secret had been handed down to him by the old shepherd whose place he took-by touch or word, and one day he bought a small property, consisting of a cottage and a field, for three thousand francs.

A few months later it became known that he was going to marry a servant, notorious for her bad morals, the innkeeper's servant. The young fellows said that the girl, knowing that he was pretty well off, had been to his cottage every night, and had taken him, captured him, led him on to matrimony, little by little night by night.

And then, having been to the mayor's office and to church, she now lived in the house which her man had bought, while he continued to tend his flocks, day and night, on the plains.

And the brigadier added:

"Polyte has been sleeping there for three weeks, for the thief has no place of his own to go to!"

The gendarme made a little joke:

"He takes the shepherd's blankets."

Madame Lecacheur, who was seized by a fresh access of rage, of rage increased by a married woman's anger against debauchery, exclaimed:

"It is she, I am sure. Go there. Ah, the blackguard thieves!"

But the brigadier was quite unmoved.

"One minute," he said. "Let us wait until twelve o'clock, as he goes and dines there every day. I shall catch them with it under their noses."

The gendarme smiled, pleased at his chief's idea, and Lecacheur also smiled now, for the affair of the shepherd struck him as very funny; deceived husbands are always a joke.

Twelve o'clock had just struck when the brigadier, followed by his man, knocked gently three times at the door of a little lonely house, situated at the corner of a wood, five hundred yards from the village.

They had been standing close against the wall, so as not to be seen from within, and they waited. As nobody answered, the brigadier knocked again in a minute or two. It was so quiet that the house seemed uninhabited; but Lenient, the gendarme, who had very quick ears, said that he heard somebody moving about inside, and then Senateur got angry. He would not allow any one to resist the authority of the law for a moment, and, knocking at the door with the hilt of his sword, he cried out:

"Open the door, in the name of the law."

As this order had no effect, he roared out:

"If you do not obey, I shall smash the lock. I am the brigadier of the gendarmerie, by G—! Here, Lenient."

He had not finished speaking when the door opened and Senateur saw before him a fat girl, with a very red, blowzy face, with drooping breasts, a big stomach and broad hips, a sort of animal, the wife of the shepherd Severin, and he went into the cottage.

"I have come to pay you a visit, as I want to make a little search," he said, and he looked about him. On the table there was a plate, a jug of cider and a glass half full, which proved that a meal was in progress. Two knives were lying side by side, and the shrewd gendarme winked at his superior officer.

"It smells good," the latter said.

"One might swear that it was stewed rabbit," Lenient added, much amused.

"Will you have a glass of brandy?" the peasant woman asked.

"No, thank you; I only want the skin of the rabbit that you are eating."

She pretended not to understand, but she was trembling.

"What rabbit?"

The brigadier had taken a seat, and was calmly wiping his forehead.

"Come, come, you are not going to try and make us believe that you live on couch grass. What were you eating there all by yourself for your dinner?"

"I? Nothing whatever, I swear to you. A mite of butter on my bread."

"You are a novice, my good woman. A mite of butter on your bread. You are mistaken; you ought to have said: a mite of butter on the rabbit. By G—, your butter smells good! It is special butter, extra good butter, butter fit for a wedding; certainly, not household butter!"

The gendarme was shaking with laughter, and repeated:

"Not household butter certainly."

As Brigadier Senateur was a joker, all the gendarmes had grown facetious, and the officer continued:

"Where is your butter?"

"My butter?"

"Yes, your butter."

"In the jar."

"Then where is the butter jar?"

"Here it is."

She brought out an old cup, at the bottom of which there was a layer of rancid salt butter, and the brigadier smelled of it, and said, with a shake of his head:

"It is not the same. I want the butter that smells of the rabbit. Come, Lenient, open your eyes; look under the sideboard, my good fellow, and I will look under the bed."

Having shut the door, he went up to the bed and tried to move it; but it was fixed to the wall, and had not been moved for more than half a century, apparently. Then the brigadier stooped, and made his uniform crack. A button had flown off.

"Lenient," he said.

"Yes, brigadier?"

"Come here, my lad, and look under the bed; I am too tall. I will look after the sideboard."

He got up and waited while his man executed his orders.

Lenient, who was short and stout, took off his kepi, laid himself on his stomach, and, putting his face on the floor, looked at the black cavity under the bed, and then, suddenly, he exclaimed:

"All right, here we are!"

"What have you got? The rabbit?"

"No, the thief."

"The thief! Pull him out, pull him out!"

The gendarme had put his arms under the bed and laid hold of something, and he was pulling with all his might, and at last a foot, shod in a thick boot, appeared, which he was holding in his right hand. The brigadier took it, crying:

"Pull! Pull!"

And Lenient, who was on his knees by that time, was pulling at the other leg. But it was a hard job, for the prisoner kicked out hard, and arched up his back under the bed.

"Courage! courage! pull! pull!" Senateur cried, and they pulled him with all their strength, so that the wooden slat gave way, and he came out as far as his head; but at last they got that out also, and they saw the terrified and furious face of Polyte, whose arms remained stretched out under the bed.

"Pull away!" the brigadier kept on exclaiming. Then they heard a strange noise, and as the arms followed the shoulders, and the hands the arms, they saw in the hands the handle of a saucepan, and at the end of the handle the saucepan itself, which contained stewed rabbit.

"Good Lord! good Lord!" the brigadier shouted in his delight, while Lenient took charge of the man; the rabbit's skin, an overwhelming proof, was discovered under the mattress, and then the gendarmes returned in triumph to the village with their prisoner and their booty.

A week later, as the affair had made much stir, Lecacheur, on going into the mairie to consult the schoolmaster, was told that the shepherd Severin had been waiting for him for more than an hour, and he found him sitting on a chair in a corner, with his stick between his legs. When he saw the mayor, he got up, took off his cap, and said:

"Good-morning, Maitre Cacheux"; and then he remained standing, timid and embarrassed.

"What do you want?" the former said.

"This is it, monsieur. Is it true that somebody stole one of your rabbits last week?"

"Yes, it is quite true, Severin."

"Who stole the rabbit?"

"Polyte Ancas, the laborer."

"Right! right! And is it also true that it was found under my bed?"

"What do you mean, the rabbit?"

"The rabbit and then Polyte."

"Yes, my poor Severin, quite true, but who told you?"

"Pretty well everybody. I understand! And I suppose you know all about marriages, as you marry people?"

"What about marriage?"

"With regard to one's rights."

"What rights?"

"The husband's rights and then the wife's rights."

"Of course I do."

"Oh! Then just tell me, M'sieu Cacheux, has my wife the right to go to bed with Polyte?"

"What, to go to bed with Polyte?"

"Yes, has she any right before the law, and, seeing that she is my wife, to go to bed with Polyte?"

"Why, of course not, of course not."

"If I catch him there again, shall I have the right to thrash him and her also?"

"Why—why—why, yes."

"Very well, then; I will tell you why I want to know. One night last week, as I had my suspicions, I came in suddenly, and they were not behaving properly. I chucked Polyte out, to go and sleep somewhere else; but that was all, as I did not know what my rights were. This time I did not see them; I only heard of it from others. That is over, and we will not say any more about it; but if I catch them again—by G—, if I catch them again, I will make them lose all taste for such nonsense, Maitre Cacheux, as sure as my name is Severin."

HIS AVENGER

When M. Antoine Leuillet married the widow, Madame Mathilde Souris, he had already been in love with her for ten years.

M. Souris has been his friend, his old college chum. Leuillet was very much attached to him, but thought he was somewhat of a simpleton. He would often remark: "That poor Souris who will never set the world on fire."

When Souris married Miss Mathilde Duval, Leuillet was astonished and somewhat annoyed, as he was slightly devoted to her, himself. She was the daughter of a neighbor, a former proprietor of a draper's establishment who had retired with quite a small fortune. She married Souris for his money.

Then Leuillet thought he would start a flirtation with his friend's wife. He was a good-looking man, intelligent and also rich. He thought it would be all plain sailing, but he was mistaken. Then he really began to admire her with an admiration that his friendship for the husband obliged him to keep within the bounds of discretion, making him timid and embarrassed. Madame Souris believing that his presumptions had received a wholesome check now treated him as a good friend. This went on for nine years.

One morning a messenger brought Leuillet a distracted note from the poor woman. Souris had just died suddenly from the rupture of an aneurism. He was dreadfully shocked, for they were just the same age. But almost immediately a feeling of profound joy, of intense relief, of emancipation filled his being. Madame Souris was free.

He managed, however, to assume the sad, sympathetic expression that was appropriate, waited the required time, observed all social appearances. At the end of fifteen months he married the widow.

This was considered to be a very natural, and even a generous action. It was the act of a good friend of an upright man.

He was happy at last, perfectly happy.

They lived in the most cordial intimacy, having understood and appreciated each other from the first. They had no secrets from one another and even confided to each other their most secret thoughts. Leuillet loved his wife now with a quiet and trustful affection; he loved her as a tender, devoted companion who is an equal and a confidante. But there lingered in his mind a strange and inexplicable bitterness towards the defunct Souris, who had first been the husband of this woman, who had had the flower of her youth and of her soul, and had even robbed her of some of her poetry. The memory of the dead husband marred the happiness of the living husband, and this posthumous jealousy tormented his heart by day and by night.

The consequence was he talked incessantly of Souris, asked about a thousand personal and secret minutia, wanted to know all about his habits and his person. And he sneered at him even in his grave, recalling with self-satisfaction his whims, ridiculing his absurdities, dwelling on his faults.

He would call to his wife all over the house:

"Hallo, Mathilde!"

"Here I am, dear."

"Come here a moment."

She would come, always smiling, knowing well that he would say something about Souris and ready to flatter her new husband's inoffensive mania.

"Tell me, do you remember one day how Souris insisted on explaining to me that little men always commanded more affection than big men?"

And he made some remarks that were disparaging to the deceased, who was a small man, and decidedly flattering to himself, Leuillet, who was a tall man.

Mme. Leuillet allowed him to think he was right, quite right, and she laughed heartily, gently ridiculing her former husband for the sake of pleasing the present one, who always ended by saying:

"All the same, what a ninny that Souris was!"

They were happy, quite happy, and Leuillet never ceased to show his devotion to his wife.

One night, however, as they lay awake, Leuillet said as he kissed his wife:

"See here, dearie."

"Well?"

"Was Souris—I don't exactly know how to say it—was Souris very loving?"

She gave him a kiss for reply and murmured "Not as loving as you are, mon chat."

He was flattered in his self-love and continued:

"He must have been—a ninny—was he not?"

She did not reply. She only smiled slyly and hid her face in her husband's neck.

"He must have been a ninny and not—not—not smart?"

She shook her head slightly to imply, "No—not at all smart."

He continued:

"He must have been an awful nuisance, eh?"

This time she was frank and replied:

"Oh yes!"

He kissed her again for this avowal and said:

"What a brute he was! You were not happy with him?"

"No," she replied. "It was not always pleasant."

Leuillet was delighted, forming in his mind a comparison, much in his own favor, between his wife's former and present position. He was silent for a time, and then with a burst of laughter he asked:

"Tell me?"

"What?"

"Will you be frank, very frank with me?"

"Why yes, my dear."

"Well then, tell me truly did you never feel tempted to—to—to deceive that imbecile Souris?"

Mme. Leuillet said: "Oh!" pretending to be shocked and hid her face again on her husband's shoulder. But he saw that she was laughing.

"Come now, own up," he persisted. "He looked like a ninny, that creature! It would be funny, so funny! Good old Souris! Come, come, dearie, you do not mind telling me, me, of all people."

He insisted on the "me" thinking that if she had wished to deceive Souris she would have chosen him, and he was trembling in anticipation of her avowal, sure that if she had not been a virtuous woman she would have encouraged his own attentions.

But she did not answer, laughing still, as at the recollection of something exceedingly comical.

Leuillet, in his turn began to laugh, thinking he might have been the lucky man, and he muttered amid his mirth: "That poor Souris, that poor Souris, oh, yes, he looked like a fool!"

Mme. Leuillet was almost in spasms of laughter.

"Come, confess, be frank. You know I will not mind."

Then she stammered out, almost choking with laughter: "Yes, yes."

"Yes, what?" insisted her husband. "Come, tell all."

She was quieter now and putting her mouth to her husband's ear, she whispered: "Yes, I did deceive him."

He felt a chill run down his back and to his very bones, and he stammered out, dumfounded: "You—you—deceived him—criminally?"

She still thought he was amused and replied: "Yes—yes, absolutely."

He was obliged to sit up to recover his breath, he was so shocked and upset at what he had heard.

She had become serious, understanding too late what she had done.

"With whom?" said Leuillet at length.

She was silent seeking some excuse.

"A young man," she replied at length.

He turned suddenly toward her and said drily:

"I did not suppose it was the cook. I want to know what young man, do you hear?"

She did not answer.

He snatched the covers from her face, repeating:

"I want to know what young man, do you hear?"

Then she said sorrowfully: "I was only in fun." But he was trembling with rage. "What? How? You were only in fun? You were making fun of me, then? But I am not satisfied, do you hear? I want the name of the young man!"

She did not reply, but lay there motionless.

He took her by the arm and squeezed it, saying: "Do you understand me, finally? I wish you to reply when I speak to you."

"I think you are going crazy," she said nervously, "let me alone!"

He was wild with rage, not knowing what to say, exasperated, and he shook her with all his might, repeating:

"Do you hear me, do you hear me?"

She made an abrupt effort to disengage herself and the tips of her fingers touched her husband's nose. He was furious, thinking she had tried to hit him, and he sprang upon her holding her down; and boxing her ears with all his might, he cried: "Take that, and that, there, there, wretch!"

When he was out of breath and exhausted, he rose and went toward the dressing table to prepare a glass of eau sucree with orange flower, for he felt as if he should faint.

She was weeping in bed, sobbing bitterly, for she felt as if her happiness was over, through her own fault.

Then, amidst her tears, she stammered out:

"Listen, Antoine, come here, I told you a lie, you will understand, listen."

And prepared to defend herself now, armed with excuses and artifice, she raised her disheveled head with its nightcap all awry.

Turning toward her, he approached, ashamed of having struck her, but feeling in the bottom of his heart as a husband, a relentless hatred toward this woman who had deceived the former husband, Souris.

MY UNCLE JULES

A white-haired old man begged us for alms. My companion, Joseph Davranche, gave him five francs. Noticing my surprised look, he said:

"That poor unfortunate reminds me of a story which I shall tell you, the memory of which continually pursues me. Here it is:

"My family, which came originally from Havre, was not rich. We just managed to make both ends meet. My father worked hard, came home late from the office, and earned very little. I had two sisters.

"My mother suffered a good deal from our reduced circumstances, and she often had harsh words for her husband, veiled and sly reproaches. The poor man then made a gesture which used to distress me. He would pass his open hand over his forehead, as if to wipe away perspiration which did not exist, and he would answer nothing. I felt his helpless suffering. We economized on everything, and never would accept an invitation to dinner, so as not to have to return the courtesy. All our provisions were bought at bargain sales. My sisters made their own gowns, and long discussions would arise on the price of a piece of braid worth fifteen centimes a yard. Our meals usually consisted of soup and beef, prepared with every kind of sauce.

"They say it is wholesome and nourishing, but I should have preferred a change.

"I used to go through terrible scenes on account of lost buttons and torn trousers.

"Every Sunday, dressed in our best, we would take our walk along the breakwater. My father, in a frock coat, high hat and kid gloves, would offer his arm to my mother, decked out and beribboned like a ship on a holiday. My sisters, who were always ready first, would await the signal for leaving; but at the last minute some one always found a spot on my father's frock coat, and it had to be wiped away quickly with a rag moistened with benzine.

"My father, in his shirt sleeves, his silk hat on his head, would await the completion of the operation, while my mother, putting on her spectacles, and taking off her gloves in order not to spoil them, would make haste.

"Then we set out ceremoniously. My sisters marched on ahead, arm in arm. They were of marriageable age and had to be displayed. I walked on the left of my mother and my father on her right. I remember the pompous air of my poor parents in these Sunday walks, their stern expression, their stiff walk. They moved slowly, with a serious expression, their bodies straight, their legs stiff, as if something of extreme importance depended upon their appearance.

"Every Sunday, when the big steamers were returning from unknown and distant countries, my father would invariably utter the same words:

"'What a surprise it would be if Jules were on that one! Eh?'

"My Uncle Jules, my father's brother, was the only hope of the family, after being its only fear. I had heard about him since childhood, and it seemed to me that I should recognize him immediately, knowing as much about him as I did. I knew every detail of his life up to the day of his departure for America, although this period of his life was spoken of only in hushed tones.

"It seems that he had led a bad life, that is to say, he had squandered a little money, which action, in a poor family, is one of the greatest crimes. With rich people a man who amuses himself only sows his wild oats. He is what is generally called a sport. But among needy families a boy who forces his parents to break into the capital becomes a good-for-nothing, a rascal, a scamp. And this distinction is just, although the action be the same, for consequences alone determine the seriousness of the act.

"Well, Uncle Jules had visibly diminished the inheritance on which my father had counted, after he had swallowed his own to the last penny. Then, according to the custom of the times, he had been shipped off to America on a freighter going from Havre to New York.

"Once there, my uncle began to sell something or other, and he soon wrote that he was making a little money and that he soon hoped to be able to indemnify my father for the harm he had done him. This letter caused a profound emotion in the family. Jules, who up to that time had not been worth his salt, suddenly became a good man, a kind-hearted fellow, true and honest like all the Davranches.

"One of the captains told us that he had rented a large shop and was doing an important business.

"Two years later a second letter came, saying: 'My dear Philippe, I am writing to tell you not to worry about my health, which is excellent. Business is good. I leave to-morrow for a long trip to South America. I may be away for several years without sending you any news. If I shouldn't write, don't worry. When my fortune is made I shall return to Havre. I hope that it will not be too long and that we shall all live happily together . . . .'

"This letter became the gospel of the family. It was read on the slightest provocation, and it was shown to everybody.

"For ten years nothing was heard from Uncle Jules; but as time went on my father's hope grew, and my mother, also, often said:

"'When that good Jules is here, our position will be different. There is one who knew how to get along!'

"And every Sunday, while watching the big steamers approaching from the horizon, pouring out a stream of smoke, my father would repeat his eternal question:

"'What a surprise it would be if Jules were on that one! Eh?'

"We almost expected to see him waving his handkerchief and crying:

"'Hey! Philippe!'

"Thousands of schemes had been planned on the strength of this expected return; we were even to buy a little house with my uncle's money—a little place in the country near Ingouville. In fact, I wouldn't swear that my father had not already begun negotiations.

"The elder of my sisters was then twenty-eight, the other twenty-six. They were not yet married, and that was a great grief to every one.

"At last a suitor presented himself for the younger one. He was a clerk, not rich, but honorable. I have always been morally certain that Uncle Jules' letter, which was shown him one evening, had swept away the young man's hesitation and definitely decided him.

"He was accepted eagerly, and it was decided that after the wedding the whole family should take a trip to Jersey.

"Jersey is the ideal trip for poor people. It is not far; one crosses a strip of sea in a steamer and lands on foreign soil, as this little island belongs to England. Thus, a Frenchman, with a two hours' sail, can observe a neighboring people at home and study their customs.

"This trip to Jersey completely absorbed our ideas, was our sole anticipation, the constant thought of our minds.

"At last we left. I see it as plainly as if it had happened yesterday. The boat was getting up steam against the quay at Granville; my father, bewildered, was superintending the loading of our three pieces of baggage; my mother, nervous, had taken the arm of my unmarried sister, who seemed lost since the departure of the other one, like the last chicken of a brood; behind us came the bride and groom, who always stayed behind, a thing that often made me turn round.

"The whistle sounded. We got on board, and the vessel, leaving the breakwater, forged ahead through a sea as flat as a marble table. We watched the coast disappear in the distance, happy and proud, like all who do not travel much.

"My father was swelling out his chest in the breeze, beneath his frock coat, which had that morning been very carefully cleaned; and he spread around him that odor of benzine which always made me recognize Sunday. Suddenly he noticed two elegantly dressed ladies to whom two gentlemen were offering oysters. An old, ragged sailor was opening them with his knife and passing them to the gentlemen, who would then offer them to the ladies. They ate them in a dainty manner, holding the shell on a fine handkerchief and advancing their mouths a little in order not to spot their dresses. Then they would drink the liquid with a rapid little motion and throw the shell overboard.

"My father was probably pleased with this delicate manner of eating oysters on a moving ship. He considered it good form, refined, and, going up to my mother and sisters, he asked:

"'Would you like me to offer you some oysters?'

"My mother hesitated on account of the expense, but my two sisters immediately accepted. My mother said in a provoked manner:

"'I am afraid that they will hurt my stomach. Offer the children some, but not too much, it would make them sick.' Then, turning toward me, she added:

"'As for Joseph, he doesn't need any. Boys shouldn't be spoiled.'

"However, I remained beside my mother, finding this discrimination unjust. I watched my father as he pompously conducted my two sisters and his son-in-law toward the ragged old sailor.

"The two ladies had just left, and my father showed my sisters how to eat them without spilling the liquor. He even tried to give them an example, and seized an oyster. He attempted to imitate the ladies, and immediately spilled all the liquid over his coat. I heard my mother mutter:

"'He would do far better to keep quiet.'

"But, suddenly, my father appeared to be worried; he retreated a few steps, stared at his family gathered around the old shell opener, and quickly came toward us. He seemed very pale, with a peculiar look. In a low voice he said to my mother:

"'It's extraordinary how that man opening the oysters looks like Jules.'

"Astonished, my mother asked:

"'What Jules?'

"My father continued:

"'Why, my brother. If I did not know that he was well off in America, I should think it was he.'

"Bewildered, my mother stammered:

"'You are crazy! As long as you know that it is not he, why do you say such foolish things?'

"But my father insisted:

"'Go on over and see, Clarisse! I would rather have you see with your own eyes.'

"She arose and walked to her daughters. I, too, was watching the man. He was old, dirty, wrinkled, and did not lift his eyes from his work.

"My mother returned. I noticed that she was trembling. She exclaimed quickly:

"'I believe that it is he. Why don't you ask the captain? But be very careful that we don't have this rogue on our hands again!'

"My father walked away, but I followed him. I felt strangely moved.

"The captain, a tall, thin man, with blond whiskers, was walking along the bridge with an important air as if he were commanding the Indian mail steamer.

"My father addressed him ceremoniously, and questioned him about his profession, adding many compliments:

"'What might be the importance of Jersey? What did it produce? What was the population? The customs? The nature of the soil?' etc., etc.

"'You have there an old shell opener who seems quite interesting. Do you know anything about him?'

"The captain, whom this conversation began to weary, answered dryly:

"'He is some old French tramp whom I found last year in America, and I brought him back. It seems that he has some relatives in Havre, but that he doesn't wish to return to them because he owes them money. His name is Jules—Jules Darmanche or Darvanche or something like that. It seems that he was once rich over there, but you can see what's left of him now.'

"My father turned ashy pale and muttered, his throat contracted, his eyes haggard.

"'Ah! ah! very well, very well. I'm not in the least surprised. Thank you very much, captain.'

"He went away, and the astonished sailor watched him disappear. He returned to my mother so upset that she said to him:

"'Sit down; some one will notice that something is the matter.'

"He sank down on a bench and stammered:

"'It's he! It's he!'

"Then he asked:

"'What are we going to do?'

"She answered quickly:

"'We must get the children out of the way. Since Joseph knows everything, he can go and get them. We must take good care that our son-in-law doesn't find out.'

"My father seemed absolutely bewildered. He murmured:

"'What a catastrophe!'

"Suddenly growing furious, my mother exclaimed:

"'I always thought that that thief never would do anything, and that he would drop down on us again! As if one could expect anything from a Davranche!'

"My father passed his hand over his forehead, as he always did when his wife reproached him. She added:

"'Give Joseph some money so that he can pay for the oysters. All that it needed to cap the climax would be to be recognized by that beggar. That would be very pleasant! Let's get down to the other end of the boat, and take care that that man doesn't come near us!'

"They gave me five francs and walked away.

"Astonished, my sisters were awaiting their father. I said that mamma had felt a sudden attack of sea-sickness, and I asked the shell opener:

"'How much do we owe you, monsieur?'

"I felt like laughing: he was my uncle! He answered:

"'Two francs fifty.'

"I held out my five francs and he returned the change. I looked at his hand; it was a poor, wrinkled, sailor's hand, and I looked at his face, an unhappy old face. I said to myself:

"'That is my uncle, the brother of my father, my uncle!'

"I gave him a ten-cent tip. He thanked me:

"'God bless you, my young sir!'

"He spoke like a poor man receiving alms. I couldn't help thinking that he must have begged over there! My sisters looked at me, surprised at my generosity. When I returned the two francs to my father, my mother asked me in surprise:

"'Was there three francs' worth? That is impossible.'

"I answered in a firm voice

"'I gave ten cents as a tip.'

"My mother started, and, staring at me, she exclaimed:

"'You must be crazy! Give ten cents to that man, to that vagabond—'

"She stopped at a look from my father, who was pointing at his son-in-law. Then everybody was silent.

"Before us, on the distant horizon, a purple shadow seemed to rise out of the sea. It was Jersey.

"As we approached the breakwater a violent desire seized me once more to see my Uncle Jules, to be near him, to say to him something consoling, something tender. But as no one was eating any more oysters, he had disappeared, having probably gone below to the dirty hold which was the home of the poor wretch."

THE MODEL

Curving like a crescent moon, the little town of Etretat, with its white cliffs, its white, shingly beach and its blue sea, lay in the sunlight at high noon one July day. At either extremity of this crescent its two "gates," the smaller to the right, the larger one at the left, stretched forth—one a dwarf and the other a colossal limb—into the water, and the bell tower, almost as tall as the cliff, wide below, narrowing at the top, raised its pointed summit to the sky.

On the sands beside the water a crowd was seated watching the bathers. On the terrace of, the Casino another crowd, seated or walking, displayed beneath the brilliant sky a perfect flower patch of bright costumes, with red and blue parasols embroidered with large flowers in silk.

On the walk at the end of the terrace, other persons, the restful, quiet ones, were walking slowly, far from the dressy throng.

A young man, well known and celebrated as a painter, Jean Sumner, was walking with a dejected air beside a wheeled chair in which sat a young woman, his wife. A manservant was gently pushing the chair, and the crippled woman was gazing sadly at the brightness of the sky, the gladness of the day, and the happiness of others.

They did not speak. They did not look at each other.

"Let us stop a while," said the young woman.

They stopped, and the painter sat down on a camp stool that the servant handed him.

Those who were passing behind the silent and motionless couple looked at them compassionately. A whole legend of devotion was attached to them. He had married her in spite of her infirmity, touched by her affection for him, it was said.

Not far from there, two young men were chatting, seated on a bench and looking out into the horizon.

"No, it is not true; I tell you that I am well acquainted with Jean Sumner."

"But then, why did he marry her? For she was a cripple when she married, was she not?"

"Just so. He married her—he married her—just as every one marries, parbleu! because he was an idiot!"

"But why?"

"But why—but why, my friend? There is no why. People do stupid things just because they do stupid things. And, besides, you know very well that painters make a specialty of foolish marriages. They almost always marry models, former sweethearts, in fact, women of doubtful reputation, frequently. Why do they do this? Who can say? One would suppose that constant association with the general run of models would disgust them forever with that class of women. Not at all. After having posed them they marry them. Read that little book, so true, so cruel and so beautiful, by Alphonse Daudet: 'Artists' Wives.'

"In the case of the couple you see over there the accident occurred in a special and terrible manner. The little woman played a frightful comedy, or, rather, tragedy. She risked all to win all. Was she sincere? Did she love Jean? Shall we ever know? Who is able to determine precisely how much is put on and how much is real in the actions of a woman? They are always sincere in an eternal mobility of impressions. They are furious, criminal, devoted, admirable and base in obedience to intangible emotions. They tell lies incessantly without intention, without knowing or understanding why, and in spite of it all are absolutely frank in their feelings and sentiments, which they display by violent, unexpected, incomprehensible, foolish resolutions which overthrow our arguments, our customary poise and all our selfish plans. The unforeseenness and suddenness of their determinations will always render them undecipherable enigmas as far as we are concerned. We continually ask ourselves:

"'Are they sincere? Are they pretending?'

"But, my friend, they are sincere and insincere at one and the same time, because it is their nature to be extremists in both and to be neither one nor the other.

"See the methods that even the best of them employ to get what they desire. They are complex and simple, these methods. So complex that we can never guess at them beforehand, and so simple that after having been victimized we cannot help being astonished and exclaiming: 'What! Did she make a fool of me so easily as that?'

"And they always succeed, old man, especially when it is a question of getting married.

"But this is Sumner's story:

"The little woman was a model, of course. She posed for him. She was pretty, very stylish-looking, and had a divine figure, it seems. He fancied that he loved her with his whole soul. That is another strange thing. As soon as one likes a woman one sincerely believes that they could not get along without her for the rest of their life. One knows that one has felt the same way before and that disgust invariably succeeded gratification; that in order to pass one's existence side by side with another there must be not a brutal, physical passion which soon dies out, but a sympathy of soul, temperament and temper. One should know how to determine in the enchantment to which one is subjected whether it proceeds from the physical, from a certain sensuous intoxication, or from a deep spiritual charm.

"Well, he believed himself in love; he made her no end of promises of fidelity, and was devoted to her.

"She was really attractive, gifted with that fashionable flippancy that little Parisians so readily affect. She chattered, babbled, made foolish remarks that sounded witty from the manner in which they were uttered. She used graceful gesture's which were calculated to attract a painter's eye. When she raised her arms, when she bent over, when she got into a carriage, when she held out her hand to you, her gestures were perfect and appropriate.

"For three months Jean never noticed that, in reality, she was like all other models.

"He rented a little house for her for the summer at Andresy.

"I was there one evening when for the first time doubts came into my friend's mind.

"As it was a beautiful evening we thought we would take a stroll along the bank of the river. The moon poured a flood of light on the trembling water, scattering yellow gleams along its ripples in the currents and all along the course of the wide, slow river.

"We strolled along the bank, a little enthused by that vague exaltation that these dreamy evenings produce in us. We would have liked to undertake some wonderful task, to love some unknown, deliciously poetic being. We felt ourselves vibrating with raptures, longings, strange aspirations. And we were silent, our beings pervaded by the serene and living coolness of the beautiful night, the coolness of the moonlight, which seemed to penetrate one's body, permeate it, soothe one's spirit, fill it with fragrance and steep it in happiness.

"Suddenly Josephine (that is her name) uttered an exclamation:

"'Oh, did you see the big fish that jumped, over there?'

"He replied without looking, without thinking:

"'Yes, dear.'

"She was angry.

"'No, you did not see it, for your back was turned.'

"He smiled.

"'Yes, that's true. It is so delightful that I am not thinking of anything.'

"She was silent, but at the end of a minute she felt as if she must say something and asked:

"'Are you going to Paris to-morrow?'

"'I do not know,' he replied.

"She was annoyed again.

"'Do you think it is very amusing to walk along without speaking? People talk when they are not stupid.'

"He did not reply. Then, feeling with her woman's instinct that she was going to make him angry, she began to sing a popular air that had harassed our ears and our minds for two years:

"'Je regardais en fair.'

"He murmured:

"'Please keep quiet.'

"She replied angrily:

"'Why do you wish me to keep quiet?'

"'You spoil the landscape for us!' he said.

"Then followed a scene, a hateful, idiotic scene, with unexpected reproaches, unsuitable recriminations, then tears. Nothing was left unsaid. They went back to the house. He had allowed her to talk without replying, enervated by the beauty of the scene and dumfounded by this storm of abuse.

"Three months later he strove wildly to free himself from those invincible and invisible bonds with which such a friendship chains our lives. She kept him under her influence, tyrannizing over him, making his life a burden to him. They quarreled continually, vituperating and finally fighting each other.

"He wanted to break with her at any cost. He sold all his canvases, borrowed money from his friends, realizing twenty thousand francs (he was not well known then), and left them for her one morning with a note of farewell.

"He came and took refuge with me.

"About three o'clock that afternoon there was a ring at the bell. I went to the door. A woman sprang toward me, pushed me aside, came in and went into my atelier. It was she!

"He had risen when he saw her coming.

"She threw the envelope containing the banknotes at his feet with a truly noble gesture and said in a quick tone:

"'There's your money. I don't want it!'

"She was very pale, trembling and ready undoubtedly to commit any folly. As for him, I saw him grow pale also, pale with rage and exasperation, ready also perhaps to commit any violence.

"He asked:

"'What do you want?'

"She replied:

"'I do not choose to be treated like a common woman. You implored me to accept you. I asked you for nothing. Keep me with you!'

"He stamped his foot.

"'No, that's a little too much! If you think you are going—'

"I had seized his arm.

"'Keep still, Jean... Let me settle it.'

"I went toward her and quietly, little by little, I began to reason with her, exhausting all the arguments that are used under similar circumstances. She listened to me, motionless, with a fixed gaze, obstinate and silent.

"Finally, not knowing what more to say, and seeing that there would be a scene, I thought of a last resort and said:

"'He loves you still, my dear, but his family want him to marry some one, and you understand—'

"She gave a start and exclaimed:

"'Ah! Ah! Now I understand:

"And turning toward him, she said:

"'You are—you are going to get married?'

"He replied decidedly" 'Yes.'

"She took a step forward.

"'If you marry, I will kill myself! Do you hear?'

"He shrugged his shoulders and replied:

"'Well, then kill yourself!'

"She stammered out, almost choking with her violent emotion:

"'What do you say? What do you say? What do you say? Say it again!'

"He repeated:

"'Well, then kill yourself if you like!'

"With her face almost livid, she replied:

"'Do not dare me! I will throw myself from the window!'

"He began to laugh, walked toward the window, opened it, and bowing with the gesture of one who desires to let some one else precede him, he said:

"'This is the way. After you!'

"She looked at him for a second with terrible, wild, staring eyes. Then, taking a run as if she were going to jump a hedge in the country, she rushed past me and past him, jumped over the sill and disappeared.

"I shall never forget the impression made on me by that open window after I had seen that body pass through it to fall to the ground. It appeared to me in a second to be as large as the heavens and as hollow as space. And I drew back instinctively, not daring to look at it, as though I feared I might fall out myself.

"Jean, dumfounded, stood motionless.

"They brought the poor girl in with both legs broken. She will never walk again.

"Jean, wild with remorse and also possibly touched with gratitude, made up his mind to marry her.

"There you have it, old man."

It was growing dusk. The young woman felt chilly and wanted to go home, and the servant wheeled the invalid chair in the direction of the village. The painter walked beside his wife, neither of them having exchanged a word for an hour.

This story appeared in Le Gaulois, December 17, 1883.

A VAGABOND

He was a journeyman carpenter, a good workman and a steady fellow, twenty-seven years old, but, although the eldest son, Jacques Randel had been forced to live on his family for two months, owing to the general lack of work. He had walked about seeking work for over a month and had left his native town, Ville-Avary, in La Manche, because he could find nothing to do and would no longer deprive his family of the bread they needed themselves, when he was the strongest of them all. His two sisters earned but little as charwomen. He went and inquired at the town hall, and the mayor's secretary told him that he would find work at the Labor Agency, and so he started, well provided with papers and certificates, and carrying another pair of shoes, a pair of trousers and a shirt in a blue handkerchief at the end of his stick.

And he had walked almost without stopping, day and night, along interminable roads, in sun and rain, without ever reaching that mysterious country where workmen find work. At first he had the fixed idea that he must only work as a carpenter, but at every carpenter's shop where he applied he was told that they had just dismissed men on account of work being so slack, and, finding himself at the end of his resources, he made up his mind to undertake any job that he might come across on the road. And so by turns he was a navvy, stableman, stonecutter; he split wood, lopped the branches of trees, dug wells, mixed mortar, tied up fagots, tended goats on a mountain, and all for a few pence, for he only obtained two or three days' work occasionally by offering himself at a shamefully low price, in order to tempt the avarice of employers and peasants.

And now for a week he had found nothing, and had no money left, and nothing to eat but a piece of bread, thanks to the charity of some women from whom he had begged at house doors on the road. It was getting dark, and Jacques Randel, jaded, his legs failing him, his stomach empty, and with despair in his heart, was walking barefoot on the grass by the side of the road, for he was taking care of his last pair of shoes, as the other pair had already ceased to exist for a long time. It was a Saturday, toward the end of autumn. The heavy gray clouds were being driven rapidly through the sky by the gusts of wind which whistled among the trees, and one felt that it would rain soon. The country was deserted at that hour on the eve of Sunday. Here and there in the fields there rose up stacks of wheat straw, like huge yellow mushrooms, and the fields looked bare, as they had already been sown for the next year.

Randel was hungry, with the hunger of some wild animal, such a hunger as drives wolves to attack men. Worn out and weakened with fatigue, he took longer strides, so as not to take so many steps, and with heavy head, the blood throbbing in his temples, with red eyes and dry mouth, he grasped his stick tightly in his hand, with a longing to strike the first passer by who might be going home to supper.

He looked at the sides of the road, imagining he saw potatoes dug up and lying on the ground before his eyes; if he had found any he would have gathered some dead wood, made a fire in the ditch and have had a capital supper off the warm, round vegetables with which he would first of all have warmed his cold hands. But it was too late in the year, and he would have to gnaw a raw beetroot which he might pick up in a field as he had done the day before.

For the last two days he had talked to himself as he quickened his steps under the influence of his thoughts. He had never thought much hitherto, as he had given all his mind, all his simple faculties to his mechanical work. But now fatigue and this desperate search for work which he could not get, refusals and rebuffs, nights spent in the open air lying on the grass, long fasting, the contempt which he knew people with a settled abode felt for a vagabond, and that question which he was continually asked, "Why do you not remain at home?" distress at not being able to use his strong arms which he felt so full of vigor, the recollection of the relations he had left at home and who also had not a penny, filled him by degrees with rage, which had been accumulating every day, every hour, every minute, and which now escaped his lips in spite of himself in short, growling sentences.

As he stumbled over the stones which tripped his bare feet, he grumbled: "How wretched! how miserable! A set of hogs—to let a man die of hunger—a carpenter—a set of hogs—not two sous—not two sous—and now it is raining—a set of hogs!"

He was indignant at the injustice of fate, and cast the blame on men, on all men, because nature, that great, blind mother, is unjust, cruel and perfidious, and he repeated through his clenched teeth:

"A set of hogs" as he looked at the thin gray smoke which rose from the roofs, for it was the dinner hour. And, without considering that there is another injustice which is human, and which is called robbery and violence, he felt inclined to go into one of those houses to murder the inhabitants and to sit down to table in their stead.

He said to himself: "I have no right to live now, as they are letting me die of hunger, and yet I only ask for work—a set of hogs!" And the pain in his limbs, the gnawing in his heart rose to his head like terrible intoxication, and gave rise to this simple thought in his brain: "I have the right to live because I breathe and because the air is the common property of everybody. So nobody has the right to leave me without bread!"

A fine, thick, icy cold rain was coming down, and he stopped and murmured: "Oh, misery! Another month of walking before I get home." He was indeed returning home then, for he saw that he should more easily find work in his native town, where he was known—and he did not mind what he did—than on the highroads, where everybody suspected him. As the carpentering business was not prosperous, he would turn day laborer, be a mason's hodman, a ditcher, break stones on the road. If he only earned a franc a day, that would at any rate buy him something to eat.

He tied the remains of his last pocket handkerchief round his neck to prevent the cold rain from running down his back and chest, but he soon found that it was penetrating the thin material of which his clothes were made, and he glanced about him with the agonized look of a man who does not know where to hide his body and to rest his head, and has no place of shelter in the whole world.

Night came on and wrapped the country in obscurity, and in the distance, in a meadow, he saw a dark spot on the grass; it was a cow, and so he got over the ditch by the roadside and went up to her without exactly knowing what he was doing. When he got close to her she raised her great head to him, and he thought: "If I only had a jug I could get a little milk." He looked at the cow and the cow looked at him and then, suddenly giving her a kick in the side, he said: "Get up!"

The animal got up slowly, letting her heavy udders bang down. Then the man lay down on his back between the animal's legs and drank for a long time, squeezing her warm, swollen teats, which tasted of the cowstall, with both hands, and he drank as long as she gave any milk. But the icy rain began to fall more heavily, and he saw no place of shelter on the whole of that bare plain. He was cold, and he looked at a light which was shining among the trees in the window of a house.

The cow had lain down again heavily, and he sat down by her side and stroked her head, grateful for the nourishment she had given him. The animal's strong, thick breath, which came out of her nostrils like two jets of steam in the evening air, blew on the workman's face, and he said: "You are not cold inside there!" He put his hands on her chest and under her stomach to find some warmth there, and then the idea struck him that he might pass the night beside that large, warm animal. So he found a comfortable place and laid his head on her side, and then, as he was worn out with fatigue, fell asleep immediately.

He woke up, however, several times, with his back or his stomach half frozen, according as he put one or the other against the animal's flank. Then he turned over to warm and dry that part of his body which had remained exposed to the night air, and soon went soundly to sleep again. The crowing of a cock woke him; the day was breaking, it was no longer raining, and the sky was bright. The cow was resting with her muzzle on the ground, and he stooped down, resting on his hands, to kiss those wide, moist nostrils, and said: "Good-by, my beauty, until next time. You are a nice animal. Good-by." Then he put on his shoes and went off, and for two hours walked straight before him, always following the same road, and then he felt so tired that he sat down on the grass. It was broad daylight by that time, and the church bells were ringing; men in blue blouses, women in white caps, some on foot, some in carts, began to pass along the road, going to the neighboring villages to spend Sunday with friends or relations.

A stout peasant came in sight, driving before him a score of frightened, bleating sheep, with the help of an active dog. Randel got up, and raising his cap, said: "You do not happen to have any work for a man who is dying of hunger?" But the other, giving an angry look at the vagabond, replied: "I have no work for fellows whom I meet on the road."

And the carpenter went back and sat down by the side of the ditch again. He waited there for a long time, watching the country people pass and looking for a kind, compassionate face before he renewed his request, and finally selected a man in an overcoat, whose stomach was adorned with a gold chain. "I have been looking for work," he said, "for the last two months and cannot find any, and I have not a sou in my pocket." But the would-be gentleman replied: "You should have read the notice which is stuck up at the entrance to the village: 'Begging is prohibited within the boundaries of this parish.' Let me tell you that I am the mayor, and if you do not get out of here pretty quickly I shall have you arrested."

Randel, who was getting angry, replied: "Have me arrested if you like; I should prefer it, for, at any rate, I should not die of hunger." And he went back and sat down by the side of his ditch again, and in about a quarter of an hour two gendarmes appeared on the road. They were walking slowly side by side, glittering in the sun with their shining hats, their yellow accoutrements and their metal buttons, as if to frighten evildoers, and to put them to flight at a distance. He knew that they were coming after him, but he did not move, for he was seized with a sudden desire to defy them, to be arrested by them, and to have his revenge later.

They came on without appearing to have seen him, walking heavily, with military step, and balancing themselves as if they were doing the goose step; and then, suddenly, as they passed him, appearing to have noticed him, they stopped and looked at him angrily and threateningly, and the brigadier came up to him and asked: "What are you doing here?" "I am resting," the man replied calmly. "Where do you come from?" "If I had to tell you all the places I have been to it would take me more than an hour." "Where are you going to?" "To Ville-Avary." "Where is that?" "In La Manche." "Is that where you belong?" "It is." "Why did you leave it?" "To look for work."

The brigadier turned to his gendarme and said in the angry voice of a man who is exasperated at last by an oft-repeated trick: "They all say that, these scamps. I know all about it." And then he continued: "Have you any papers?" "Yes, I have some." "Give them to me."

Randel took his papers out of his pocket, his certificates, those poor, worn-out, dirty papers which were falling to pieces, and gave them to the soldier, who spelled them through, hemming and hawing, and then, having seen that they were all in order, he gave them back to Randel with the dissatisfied look of a man whom some one cleverer than himself has tricked.

After a few moments' further reflection, he asked him: "Have you any money on you?" "No." "None whatever?" "None." "Not even a sou?" "Not even a son!" "How do you live then?" "On what people give me." "Then you beg?" And Randel answered resolutely: "Yes, when I can."

Then the gendarme said: "I have caught you on the highroad in the act of vagabondage and begging, without any resources or trade, and so I command you to come with me." The carpenter got up and said: "Wherever you please." And, placing himself between the two soldiers, even before he had received the order to do so, he added: "Well, lock me up; that will at any rate put a roof over my head when it rains."

And they set off toward the village, the red tiles of which could be seen through the leafless trees, a quarter of a league off. Service was about to begin when they went through the village. The square was full of people, who immediately formed two lines to see the criminal pass. He was being followed by a crowd of excited children. Male and female peasants looked at the prisoner between the two gendarmes, with hatred in their eyes and a longing to throw stones at him, to tear his skin with their nails, to trample him under their feet. They asked each other whether he had committed murder or robbery. The butcher, who was an ex-'spahi', declared that he was a deserter. The tobacconist thought that he recognized him as the man who had that very morning passed a bad half-franc piece off on him, and the ironmonger declared that he was the murderer of Widow Malet, whom the police had been looking for for six months.

In the municipal court, into which his custodians took him, Randel saw the mayor again, sitting on the magisterial bench, with the schoolmaster by his side. "Aha! aha!" the magistrate exclaimed, "so here you are again, my fine fellow. I told you I should have you locked up. Well, brigadier, what is he charged with?"

"He is a vagabond without house or home, Monsieur le Maire, without any resources or money, so he says, who was arrested in the act of begging, but he is provided with good testimonials, and his papers are all in order."

"Show me his papers," the mayor said. He took them, read them, reread, returned them and then said: "Search him." So they searched him, but found nothing, and the mayor seemed perplexed, and asked the workman:

"What were you doing on the road this morning?" "I was looking for work." "Work? On the highroad?" "How do you expect me to find any if I hide in the woods?"

They looked at each other with the hatred of two wild beasts which belong to different hostile species, and the magistrate continued: "I am going to have you set at liberty, but do not be brought up before me again." To which the carpenter replied: "I would rather you locked me up; I have had enough running about the country." But the magistrate replied severely: "be silent." And then he said to the two gendarmes: "You will conduct this man two hundred yards from the village and let him continue his journey."

"At any rate, give me something to eat," the workman said, but the other grew indignant: "Have we nothing to do but to feed you? Ah! ah! ah! that is rather too much!" But Randel went on firmly: "If you let me nearly die of hunger again, you will force me to commit a crime, and then, so much the worse for you other fat fellows."

The mayor had risen and he repeated: "Take him away immediately or I shall end by getting angry."

The two gendarmes thereupon seized the carpenter by the arms and dragged him out. He allowed them to do it without resistance, passed through the village again and found himself on the highroad once more; and when the men had accompanied him two hundred yards beyond the village, the brigadier said: "Now off with you and do not let me catch you about here again, for if I do, you will know it."

Randel went off without replying or knowing where he was going. He walked on for a quarter of an hour or twenty minutes, so stupefied that he no longer thought of anything. But suddenly, as he was passing a small house, where the window was half open, the smell of the soup and boiled meat stopped him suddenly, and hunger, fierce, devouring, maddening hunger, seized him and almost drove him against the walls of the house like a wild beast.

He said aloud in a grumbling voice: "In Heaven's name! they must give me some this time!" And he began to knock at the door vigorously with his stick, and as no one came he knocked louder and called out: "Hey! hey! you people in there, open the door!" And then, as nothing stirred, he went up to the window and pushed it wider open with his hand, and the close warm air of the kitchen, full of the smell of hot soup, meat and cabbage, escaped into the cold outer air, and with a bound the carpenter was in the house. Two places were set at the table, and no doubt the proprietors of the house, on going to church, had left their dinner on the fire, their nice Sunday boiled beef and vegetable soup, while there was a loaf of new bread on the chimney-piece, between two bottles which seemed full.

Randel seized the bread first of all and broke it with as much violence as if he were strangling a man, and then he began to eat voraciously, swallowing great mouthfuls quickly. But almost immediately the smell of the meat attracted him to the fireplace, and, having taken off the lid of the saucepan, he plunged a fork into it and brought out a large piece of beef tied with a string. Then he took more cabbage, carrots and onions until his plate was full, and, having put it on the table, he sat down before it, cut the meat into four pieces, and dined as if he had been at home. When he had eaten nearly all the meat, besides a quantity of vegetables, he felt thirsty and took one of the bottles off the mantelpiece.

Scarcely had he poured the liquor into his glass when he saw it was brandy. So much the better; it was warming and would instill some fire into his veins, and that would be all right, after being so cold; and he drank some. He certainly enjoyed it, for he had grown unaccustomed to it, and he poured himself out another glassful, which he drank at two gulps. And then almost immediately he felt quite merry and light-hearted from the effects of the alcohol, just as if some great happiness filled his heart.

He continued to eat, but more slowly, and dipping his bread into the soup. His skin had become burning, and especially his forehead, where the veins were throbbing. But suddenly the church bells began to ring. Mass was over, and instinct rather than fear, the instinct of prudence, which guides all beings and makes them clear-sighted in danger, made the carpenter get up. He put the remains of the loaf into one pocket and the brandy bottle into the other, and he furtively went to the window and looked out into the road. It was still deserted, so he jumped out and set off walking again, but instead of following the highroad he ran across the fields toward a wood he saw a little way off.

He felt alert, strong, light-hearted, glad of what he had done, and so nimble that he sprang over the enclosure of the fields at a single bound, and as soon as he was under the trees he took the bottle out of his pocket again and began to drink once more, swallowing it down as he walked, and then his ideas began to get confused, his eyes grew dim, and his legs as elastic as springs, and he started singing the old popular song:

"Oh! what joy, what joy it is,
To pick the sweet, wild strawberries."

He was now walking on thick, damp, cool moss, and that soft carpet under his feet made him feel absurdly inclined to turn head over heels as he used to do when a child, so he took a run, turned a somersault, got up and began over again. And between each time he began to sing again:

"Oh! what joy, what joy it is,
To pick the sweet, wild strawberries."

Suddenly he found himself above a deep road, and in the road he saw a tall girl, a servant, who was returning to the village with two pails of milk. He watched, stooping down, and with his eyes as bright as those of a dog who scents a quail, but she saw him raised her head and said: "Was that you singing like that?" He did not reply, however, but jumped down into the road, although it was a fall of at least six feet and when she saw him suddenly standing in front of her, she exclaimed: "Oh! dear, how you frightened me!"

But he did not hear her, for he was drunk, he was mad, excited by another requirement which was more imperative than hunger, more feverish than alcohol; by the irresistible fury of the man who has been deprived of everything for two months, and who is drunk; who is young, ardent and inflamed by all the appetites which nature has implanted in the vigorous flesh of men.

The girl started back from him, frightened at his face, his eyes, his half-open mouth, his outstretched hands, but he seized her by the shoulders, and without a word, threw her down in the road.

She let her two pails fall, and they rolled over noisily, and all the milk was spilt, and then she screamed lustily, but it was of no avail in that lonely spot.

When she got up the thought of her overturned pails suddenly filled her with fury, and, taking off one of her wooden sabots, she threw it at the man to break his head if he did not pay her for her milk.

But he, mistaking the reason of this sudden violent attack, somewhat sobered, and frightened at what he had done, ran off as fast as he could, while she threw stones at him, some of which hit him in the back.

He ran for a long time, very long, until he felt more tired than he had ever been before. His legs were so weak that they could scarcely carry him; all his ideas were confused, he lost recollection of everything and could no longer think about anything, and so he sat down at the foot of a tree, and in five minutes was fast asleep. He was soon awakened, however, by a rough shake, and, on opening his eyes, he saw two cocked hats of shiny leather bending over him, and the two gendarmes of the morning, who were holding him and binding his arms.

"I knew I should catch you again," said the brigadier jeeringly. But Randel got up without replying. The two men shook him, quite ready to ill treat him if he made a movement, for he was their prey now. He had become a jailbird, caught by those hunters of criminals who would not let him go again.

"Now, start!" the brigadier said, and they set off. It was late afternoon, and the autumn twilight was setting in over the land, and in half an hour they reached the village, where every door was open, for the people had heard what had happened. Peasants and peasant women and girls, excited with anger, as if every man had been robbed and every woman attacked, wished to see the wretch brought back, so that they might overwhelm him with abuse. They hooted him from the first house in the village until they reached the Hotel de Ville, where the mayor was waiting for him to be himself avenged on this vagabond, and as soon as he saw him approaching he cried:

"Ah! my fine fellow! here we are!" And he rubbed his hands, more pleased than he usually was, and continued: "I said so. I said so, the moment I saw him in the road."

And then with increased satisfaction:

"Oh, you blackguard! Oh, you dirty blackguard! You will get your twenty years, my fine fellow!"

THE FISHING HOLE

"Cuts and wounds which caused death." Such was the charge upon which Leopold Renard, upholsterer, was summoned before the Court of Assizes.

Round him were the principal witnesses, Madame Flameche, widow of the victim, and Louis Ladureau, cabinetmaker, and Jean Durdent, plumber.

Near the criminal was his wife, dressed in black, an ugly little woman, who looked like a monkey dressed as a lady.

This is how Renard (Leopold) recounted the drama.

"Good heavens, it is a misfortune of which I was the prime victim all the time, and with which my will has nothing to do. The facts are their own commentary, Monsieur le President. I am an honest man, a hard-working man, an upholsterer, living in the same street for the last sixteen years, known, liked, respected and esteemed by all, as my neighbors can testify, even the porter's wife, who is not amiable every day. I am fond of work, I am fond of saving, I like honest men and respectable amusements. That is what has ruined me, so much the worse for me; but as my will had nothing to do with it, I continue to respect myself.

"Every Sunday for the last five years my wife and I have spent the day at Passy. We get fresh air, and, besides, we are fond of fishing. Oh! we are as fond of it as we are of little onions. Melie inspired me with that enthusiasm, the jade, and she is more enthusiastic than I am, the scold, seeing that all the mischief in this business is her fault, as you will see immediately.

"I am strong and mild tempered, without a pennyworth of malice in me. But she! oh! la! la! she looks like nothing; she is short and thin. Very well, she does more mischief than a weasel. I do not deny that she has some good qualities; she has some, and very important ones for a man in business. But her character! Just ask about it in the neighborhood, and even the porter's wife, who has just sent me about my business—she will tell you something about it.

"Every day she used to find fault with my mild temper: 'I would not put up with this! I would not put up with that.' If I had listened to her, Monsieur le President, I should have had at least three hand-to-hand fights a month … ."

Madame Renard interrupted him: "And for good reasons, too; they laugh best who laugh last."

He turned toward her frankly: "Well, I can't blame you, since you were not the cause of it."

Then, facing the President again, he said:

"I will continue. We used to go to Passy every Saturday evening, so as to begin fishing at daybreak the next morning. It is a habit which has become second nature with us, as the saying is. Three years ago this summer I discovered a place, oh! such a spot. Oh, dear, dear! In the shade, eight feet of water at least and perhaps ten, a hole with cavities under the bank, a regular nest for fish and a paradise for the fisherman. I might look upon that fishing hole as my property, Monsieur le President, as I was its Christopher Columbus. Everybody in the neighborhood knew it, without making any opposition. They would say: 'That is Renard's place'; and nobody would have gone there, not even Monsieur Plumeau, who is well known, be it said without any offense, for poaching on other people's preserves.

"Well, I returned to this place of which I felt certain, just as if I had owned it. I had scarcely got there on Saturday, when I got into Delila, with my wife. Delila is my Norwegian boat, which I had built by Fournaire, and which is light and safe. Well, as I said, we got into the boat and we were going to set bait, and for setting bait there is none to be compared with me, and they all know it. You want to know with what I bait? I cannot answer that question; it has nothing to do with the accident. I cannot answer; that is my secret. There are more than three hundred people who have asked me; I have been offered glasses of brandy and liqueur, fried fish, matelotes, to make me tell. But just go and try whether the chub will come. Ah! they have tempted my stomach to get at my secret, my recipe. Only my wife knows, and she will not tell it any more than I will. Is not that so, Melie?"

The president of the court interrupted him.

"Just get to the facts as soon as you can," and the accused continued: "I am getting to them, I am getting to them. Well, on Saturday, July 8, we left by the twenty-five past five train and before dinner we went to set bait as usual. The weather promised to keep fine and I said to Melie: 'All right for tomorrow.' And she replied: 'If looks like it,' We never talk more than that together.

"And then we returned to dinner. I was happy and thirsty, and that was the cause of everything. I said to Melie: 'Look here, Melie, it is fine weather, suppose I drink a bottle of 'Casque a meche'.' That is a weak white wine which we have christened so, because if you drink too much of it it prevents you from sleeping and takes the place of a nightcap. Do you understand me?

"She replied: 'You can do as you please, but you will be ill again and will not be able to get up tomorrow.' That was true, sensible and prudent, clear-sighted, I must confess. Nevertheless I could not resist, and I drank my bottle. It all came from that.

"Well, I could not sleep. By Jove! it kept me awake till two o'clock in the morning, and then I went to sleep so soundly that I should not have heard the angel sounding his trump at the last judgment.

"In short, my wife woke me at six o'clock and I jumped out of bed, hastily put on my trousers and jersey, washed my face and jumped on board Delila. But it was too late, for when I arrived at my hole it was already occupied! Such a thing had never happened to me in three years, and it made me feel as if I were being robbed under my own eyes. I said to myself: 'Confound it all! confound it!' And then my wife began to nag at me. 'Eh! what about your 'Casque a meche'? Get along, you drunkard! Are you satisfied, you great fool?' I could say nothing, because it was all true, but I landed all the same near the spot and tried to profit by what was left. Perhaps after all the fellow might catch nothing and go away.

"He was a little thin man in white linen coat and waistcoat and a large straw hat, and his wife, a fat woman, doing embroidery, sat behind him.

"When she saw us take up our position close to them she murmured: 'Are there no other places on the river?' My wife, who was furious, replied: 'People who have any manners make inquiries about the habits of the neighborhood before occupying reserved spots.'

"As I did not want a fuss, I said to her: 'Hold your tongue, Melie. Let them alone, let them alone; we shall see.'

"Well, we fastened Delila under the willows and had landed and were fishing side by side, Melie and I, close to the two others. But here, monsieur, I must enter into details.

"We had only been there about five minutes when our neighbor's line began to jerk twice, thrice; and then he pulled out a chub as thick as my thigh; rather less, perhaps, but nearly as big! My heart beat, the perspiration stood on my forehead and Melie said to me: 'Well, you sot, did you see that?'

"Just then Monsieur Bru, the grocer of Poissy, who is fond of gudgeon fishing, passed in a boat and called out to me: 'So somebody has taken your usual place, Monsieur Renard?' And I replied: 'Yes, Monsieur Bru, there are some people in this world who do not know the rules of common politeness.'

"The little man in linen pretended not to hear, nor his fat lump of a wife, either."

Here the president interrupted him a second time: "Take care, you are insulting the widow, Madame Flameche, who is present."

Renard made his excuses: "I beg your pardon, I beg your pardon; my anger carried me away. Well, not a quarter of an hour had passed when the little man caught another chub, and another almost immediately, and another five minutes later.

"Tears were in my eyes, and I knew that Madame Renard was boiling with rage, for she kept on nagging at me: 'Oh, how horrid! Don't you see that he is robbing you of your fish? Do you think that you will catch anything? Not even a frog, nothing whatever. Why, my hands are tingling, just to think of it.'

"But I said to myself: 'Let us wait until twelve o'clock. Then this poacher will go to lunch and I shall get my place again. As for me, Monsieur le President, I lunch on that spot every Sunday.

We bring our provisions in Delila. But there! At noon the wretch produced a chicken in a newspaper, and while he was eating, he actually caught another chub!

"Melie and I had a morsel also, just a bite, a mere nothing, for our heart was not in it.

"Then I took up my newspaper to aid my digestion. Every Sunday I read the Gil Blas in the shade by the side of the water. It is Columbine's day, you know; Columbine, who writes the articles in the Gil Blas. I generally put Madame Renard into a rage by pretending to know this Columbine. It is not true, for I do not know her and have never seen her, but that does not matter. She writes very well, and then she says things that are pretty plain for a woman. She suits me and there are not many of her sort.

"Well, I began to tease my wife, but she got angry immediately, and very angry, so I held my tongue. At that moment our two witnesses who are present here, Monsieur Ladureau and Monsieur Durdent, appeared on the other side of the river. We knew each other by sight. The little man began to fish again and he caught so many that I trembled with vexation and his wife said: 'It is an uncommonly good spot, and we will come here always, Desire.' As for me, a cold shiver ran down my back, and Madame Renard kept repeating: 'You are not a man; you have the blood of a chicken in your veins'; and suddenly I said to her: 'Look here, I would rather go away or I shall be doing something foolish.'

"And she whispered to me, as if she had put a red-hot iron under my nose: 'You are not a man. Now you are going to run away and surrender your place! Go, then, Bazaine!'

"I felt hurt, but yet I did not move, while the other fellow pulled out a bream: Oh, I never saw such a large one before, never! And then my wife began to talk aloud, as if she were thinking, and you can see her tricks. She said: 'That is what one might call stolen fish, seeing that we set the bait ourselves. At any rate, they ought to give us back the money we have spent on bait.'

"Then the fat woman in the cotton dress said in her turn: 'Do you mean to call us thieves, madame?' Explanations followed and compliments began to fly. Oh, Lord! those creatures know some good ones. They shouted so loud that our two witnesses, who were on the other bank, began to call out by way of a joke: 'Less noise over there; you will interfere with your husbands' fishing.'

"The fact is that neither the little man nor I moved any more than if we had been two tree stumps. We remained there, with our eyes fixed on the water, as if we had heard nothing; but, by Jove! we heard all the same. 'You are a thief! You are nothing better than a tramp! You are a regular jade!' and so on and so on. A sailor could not have said more.

"Suddenly I heard a noise behind me and turned round. It was the other one, the fat woman, who had attacked my wife with her parasol. Whack, whack! Melie got two of them. But she was furious, and she hits hard when she is in a rage. She caught the fat woman by the hair and then thump! thump! slaps in the face rained down like ripe plums. I should have let them fight it out: women together, men together. It does not do to mix the blows. But the little man in the linen jacket jumped up like a devil and was going to rush at my wife. Ah! no, no, not that, my friend! I caught the gentleman with the end of my fist, and crash! crash! One on the nose, the other in the stomach. He threw up his arms and legs and fell on his back into the river, just into the hole.

"I should have fished him out most certainly, Monsieur le President, if I had had time. But, to make matters worse, the fat woman had the upper hand and was pounding Melie for all she was worth. I know I ought not to have interfered while the man was in the water, but I never thought that he would drown and said to myself: 'Bah, it will cool him.'

"I therefore ran up to the women to separate them and all I received was scratches and bites. Good Lord, what creatures! Well, it took me five minutes, and perhaps ten, to separate those two viragos. When I turned round there was nothing to be seen.

"The water was as smooth as a lake and the others yonder kept shouting: 'Fish him out! fish him out!' It was all very well to say that, but I cannot swim and still less dive.

"At last the man from the dam came and two gentlemen with boathooks, but over a quarter of an hour had passed. He was found at the bottom of the hole, in eight feet of water, as I have said. There he was, the poor little man, in his linen suit! Those are the facts such as I have sworn to. I am innocent, on my honor."

The witnesses having given testimony to the same effect, the accused was acquitted.

THE SPASM

The hotel guests slowly entered the dining-room and took their places. The waiters did not hurry themselves, in order to give the late comers a chance and thus avoid the trouble of bringing in the dishes a second time. The old bathers, the habitues, whose season was almost over, glanced, gazed toward the door whenever it opened, to see what new faces might appear.

This is the principal distraction of watering places. People look forward to the dinner hour in order to inspect each day's new arrivals, to find out who they are, what they do, and what they think. We always have a vague desire to meet pleasant people, to make agreeable acquaintances, perhaps to meet with a love adventure. In this life of elbowings, unknown strangers assume an extreme importance. Curiosity is aroused, sympathy is ready to exhibit itself, and sociability is the order of the day.

We cherish antipathies for a week and friendships for a month; we see people with different eyes, when we view them through the medium of acquaintanceship at watering places. We discover in men suddenly, after an hour's chat, in the evening after dinner, under the trees in the park where the healing spring bubbles up, a high intelligence and astonishing merits, and a month afterward we have completely forgotten these new friends, who were so fascinating when we first met them.

Permanent and serious ties are also formed here sooner than anywhere else. People see each other every day; they become acquainted very quickly, and their affection is tinged with the sweetness and unrestraint of long-standing intimacies. We cherish in after years the dear and tender memories of those first hours of friendship, the memory of those first conversations in which a soul was unveiled, of those first glances which interrogate and respond to questions and secret thoughts which the mouth has not as yet uttered, the memory of that first cordial confidence, the memory of that delightful sensation of opening our hearts to those who seem to open theirs to us in return.

And the melancholy of watering places, the monotony of days that are all alike, proves hourly an incentive to this heart expansion.

Well, this evening, as on every other evening, we awaited the appearance of strange faces.

Only two appeared, but they were very remarkable, a man and a woman —father and daughter. They immediately reminded me of some of Edgar Poe's characters; and yet there was about them a charm, the charm associated with misfortune. I looked upon them as the victims of fate. The man was very tall and thin, rather stooped, with perfectly white hair, too white for his comparatively youthful physiognomy; and there was in his bearing and in his person that austerity peculiar to Protestants. The daughter, who was probably twenty-four or twenty-five, was small in stature, and was also very thin, very pale, and she had the air of one who was worn out with utter lassitude. We meet people like this from time to time, who seem too weak for the tasks and the needs of daily life, too weak to move about, to walk, to do all that we do every day. She was rather pretty; with a transparent, spiritual beauty. And she ate with extreme slowness, as if she were almost incapable of moving her arms.

It must have been she, assuredly, who had come to take the waters.

They sat facing me, on the opposite side of the table; and I at once noticed that the father had a very singular, nervous twitching.

Every time he wanted to reach an object, his hand described a sort of zigzag before it succeeded in reaching what it was in search of, and after a little while this movement annoyed me so that I turned aside my head in order not to see it.

I noticed, too, that the young girl, during meals, wore a glove on her left hand.

After dinner I went for a stroll in the park of the bathing establishment. This led toward the little Auvergnese station of Chatel-Guyon, hidden in a gorge at the foot of the high mountain, from which flowed so many boiling springs, arising from the deep bed of extinct volcanoes. Over yonder, above our heads, the domes of extinct craters lifted their ragged peaks above the rest in the long mountain chain. For Chatel-Guyon is situated at the entrance to the land of mountain domes.

Beyond it stretches out the region of peaks, and, farther on again the region of precipitous summits.

The "Puy de Dome" is the highest of the domes, the Peak of Sancy is the loftiest of the peaks, and Cantal is the most precipitous of these mountain heights.

It was a very warm evening, and I was walking up and down a shady path, listening to the opening, strains of the Casino band, which was playing on an elevation overlooking the park.

And I saw the father and the daughter advancing slowly in my direction. I bowed as one bows to one's hotel companions at a watering place; and the man, coming to a sudden halt, said to me:

"Could you not, monsieur, tell us of a nice walk to take, short, pretty, and not steep; and pardon my troubling you?"

I offered to show them the way toward the valley through which the little river flowed, a deep valley forming a gorge between two tall, craggy, wooded slopes.

They gladly accepted my offer.

And we talked, naturally, about the virtue of the waters.

"Oh," he said, "my daughter has a strange malady, the seat of which is unknown. She suffers from incomprehensible nervous attacks. At one time the doctors think she has an attack of heart disease, at another time they imagine it is some affection of the liver, and at another they declare it to be a disease of the spine. To-day this protean malady, that assumes a thousand forms and a thousand modes of attack, is attributed to the stomach, which is the great caldron and regulator of the body. This is why we have come here. For my part, I am rather inclined to think it is the nerves. In any case it is very sad."

Immediately the remembrance of the violent spasmodic movement of his hand came back to my mind, and I asked him:

"But is this not the result of heredity? Are not your own nerves somewhat affected?"

He replied calmly:

"Mine? Oh, no-my nerves have always been very steady."

Then, suddenly, after a pause, he went on:

"Ah! You were alluding to the jerking movement of my hand every time I try to reach for anything? This arises from a terrible experience which I had. Just imagine, this daughter of mine was actually buried alive!"

I could only utter, "Ah!" so great were my astonishment and emotion.

He continued:

"Here is the story. It is simple. Juliette had been subject for some time to serious attacks of the heart. We believed that she had disease of that organ, and were prepared for the worst.

"One day she was carried into the house cold, lifeless, dead. She had fallen down unconscious in the garden. The doctor certified that life was extinct. I watched by her side for a day and two nights. I laid her with my own hands in the coffin, which I accompanied to the cemetery, where she was deposited in the family vault. It is situated in the very heart of Lorraine.

"I wished to have her interred with her jewels, bracelets, necklaces, rings, all presents which she had received from me, and wearing her first ball dress.

"You may easily imagine my state of mind when I re-entered our home. She was the only one I had, for my wife had been dead for many years. I found my way to my own apartment in a half-distracted condition, utterly exhausted, and sank into my easy-chair, without the capacity to think or the strength to move. I was nothing better now than a suffering, vibrating machine, a human being who had, as it were, been flayed alive; my soul was like an open wound.

"My old valet, Prosper, who had assisted me in placing Juliette in her coffin, and aided me in preparing her for her last sleep, entered the room noiselessly, and asked:

"'Does monsieur want anything?'

"I merely shook my head in reply.

"'Monsieur is wrong,' he urged. 'He will injure his health. Would monsieur like me to put him to bed?'

"I answered: 'No, let me alone!'

"And he left the room.

"I know not how many hours slipped away. Oh, what a night, what a night! It was cold. My fire had died out in the huge grate; and the wind, the winter wind, an icy wind, a winter hurricane, blew with a regular, sinister noise against the windows.

"How many hours slipped away? There I was without sleeping, powerless, crushed, my eyes wide open, my legs stretched out, my body limp, inanimate, and my mind torpid with despair. Suddenly the great doorbell, the great bell of the vestibule, rang out.

"I started so that my chair cracked under me. The solemn, ponderous sound vibrated through the empty country house as through a vault. I turned round to see what the hour was by the clock. It was just two in the morning. Who could be coming at such an hour?

"And, abruptly, the bell again rang twice. The servants, without doubt, were afraid to get up. I took a wax candle and descended the stairs. I was on the point of asking: 'Who is there?'

"Then I felt ashamed of my weakness, and I slowly drew back the heavy bolts. My heart was throbbing wildly. I was frightened. I opened the door brusquely, and in the darkness I distinguished a white figure, standing erect, something that resembled an apparition.

"I recoiled petrified with horror, faltering:

"'Who-who-who are you?'

"A voice replied:

"'It is I, father.'

"It was my daughter.

"I really thought I must be mad, and I retreated backward before this advancing spectre. I kept moving away, making a sign with my hand,' as if to drive the phantom away, that gesture which you have noticed—that gesture which has remained with me ever since.

"'Do not be afraid, papa,' said the apparition. 'I was not dead. Somebody tried to steal my rings and cut one of my fingers; the blood began to flow, and that restored me to life.'

"And, in fact, I could see that her hand was covered with blood.

"I fell on my knees, choking with sobs and with a rattling in my throat.

"Then, when I had somewhat collected my thoughts, though I was still so bewildered that I scarcely realized the awesome happiness that had befallen me, I made her go up to my room and sit dawn in my easy-chair; then I rang excitedly for Prosper to get him to rekindle the fire and to bring some wine, and to summon assistance.

"The man entered, stared at my daughter, opened his mouth with a gasp of alarm and stupefaction, and then fell back dead.

"It was he who had opened the vault, who had mutilated and then abandoned my daughter; for he could not efface the traces of the theft. He had not even taken the trouble to put back the coffin into its place, feeling sure, besides, that he would not be suspected by me, as I trusted him absolutely.

"You see, monsieur, that we are very unfortunate people."

He was silent.

The night had fallen, casting its shadows over the desolate, mournful vale, and a sort of mysterious fear possessed me at finding myself by the side of those strange beings, of this young girl who had come back from the tomb, and this father with his uncanny spasm.

I found it impossible to make any comment on this dreadful story. I only murmured:

"What a horrible thing!"

Then, after a minute's silence, I added:

"Let us go indoors. I think it is growing cool."

And we made our way back to the hotel.

IN THE WOOD

As the mayor was about to sit down to breakfast, word was brought to him that the rural policeman, with two prisoners, was awaiting him at the Hotel de Ville. He went there at once and found old Hochedur standing guard before a middle-class couple whom he was regarding with a severe expression on his face.

The man, a fat old fellow with a red nose and white hair, seemed utterly dejected; while the woman, a little roundabout individual with shining cheeks, looked at the official who had arrested them, with defiant eyes.

"What is it? What is it, Hochedur?"

The rural policeman made his deposition: He had gone out that morning at his usual time, in order to patrol his beat from the forest of Champioux as far as the boundaries of Argenteuil. He had not noticed anything unusual in the country except that it was a fine day, and that the wheat was doing well, when the son of old Bredel, who was going over his vines, called out to him: "Here, Daddy Hochedur, go and have a look at the outskirts of the wood. In the first thicket you will find a pair of pigeons who must be a hundred and thirty years old between them!"

He went in the direction indicated, entered the thicket, and there he heard words which made him suspect a flagrant breach of morality. Advancing, therefore, on his hands and knees as if to surprise a poacher, he had arrested the couple whom he found there.

The mayor looked at the culprits in astonishment, for the man was certainly sixty, and the woman fifty-five at least, and he began to question them, beginning with the man, who replied in such a weak voice that he could scarcely be heard.

"What is your name?"

"Nicholas Beaurain."

"Your occupation?"

"Haberdasher, in the Rue des Martyrs, in Paris."

"What were you doing in the wood?"

The haberdasher remained silent, with his eyes on his fat paunch, and his hands hanging at his sides, and the mayor continued:

"Do you deny what the officer of the municipal authorities states?"

"No, monsieur."

"So you confess it?"

"Yes, monsieur."

"What have you to say in your defence?"

"Nothing, monsieur."

"Where did you meet the partner in your misdemeanor?"

"She is my wife, monsieur."

"Your wife?"

"Yes, monsieur."

"Then—then—you do not live together-in Paris?"

"I beg your pardon, monsieur, but we are living together!"

"But in that case—you must be mad, altogether mad, my dear sir, to get caught playing lovers in the country at ten o'clock in the morning."

The haberdasher seemed ready to cry with shame, and he muttered: "It was she who enticed me! I told her it was very stupid, but when a woman once gets a thing into her head—you know—you cannot get it out."

The mayor, who liked a joke, smiled and replied: "In your case, the contrary ought to have happened. You would not be here, if she had had the idea only in her head."

Then Monsieur Beauain was seized with rage and turning to his wife, he said: "Do you see to what you have brought us with your poetry? And now we shall have to go before the courts at our age, for a breach of morals! And we shall have to shut up the shop, sell our good will, and go to some other neighborhood! That's what it has come to."

Madame Beaurain got up, and without looking at her husband, she explained herself without embarrassment, without useless modesty, and almost without hesitation.

"Of course, monsieur, I know that we have made ourselves ridiculous. Will you allow me to plead my cause like an advocate, or rather like a poor woman? And I hope that you will be kind enough to send us home, and to spare us the disgrace of a prosecution.

"Years ago, when I was young, I made Monsieur Beaurain's acquaintance one Sunday in this neighborhood. He was employed in a draper's shop, and I was a saleswoman in a ready-made clothing establishment. I remember it as if it were yesterday. I used to come and spend Sundays here occasionally with a friend of mine, Rose Leveque, with whom I lived in the Rue Pigalle, and Rose had a sweetheart, while I had none. He used to bring us here, and one Saturday he told me laughing that he should bring a friend with him the next day. I quite understood what he meant, but I replied that it would be no good; for I was virtuous, monsieur.

"The next day we met Monsieur Beaurain at the railway station, and in those days he was good-looking, but I had made up my mind not to encourage him, and I did not Well, we arrived at Bezons. It was a lovely day, the sort of day that touches your heart. When it is fine even now, just as it used to be formerly, I grow quite foolish, and when I am in the country I utterly lose my head. The green grass, the swallows flying so swiftly, the smell of the grass, the scarlet poppies, the daisies, all that makes me crazy. It is like champagne when one is not accustomed to it!

"Well, it was lovely weather, warm and bright, and it seemed to penetrate your body through your eyes when you looked and through your mouth when you breathed. Rose and Simon hugged and kissed each other every minute, and that gave me a queer feeling! Monsieur Beaurain and I walked behind them, without speaking much, for when people do not know each other, they do not find anything to talk about. He looked timid, and I liked to see his embarrassment. At last we got to the little wood; it was as cool as in a bath there, and we four sat down. Rose and her lover teased me because I looked rather stern, but you will understand that I could not be otherwise. And then they began to kiss and hug again, without putting any more restraint upon themselves than if we had not been there; and then they whispered together, and got up and went off among the trees, without saying a word. You may fancy what I looked like, alone with this young fellow whom I saw for the first time. I felt so confused at seeing them go that it gave me courage, and I began to talk. I asked him what his business was, and he said he was a linen draper's assistant, as I told you just now. We talked for a few minutes, and that made him bold, and he wanted to take liberties with me, but I told him sharply to keep his place. Is not that true, Monsieur Beaurain?"

Monsieur Beaurain, who was looking at his feet in confusion, did not reply, and she continued: "Then he saw that I was virtuous, and he began to make love to me nicely, like an honorable man, and from that time he came every Sunday, for he was very much in love with me. I was very fond of him also, very fond of him! He was a good-looking fellow, formerly, and in short he married me the next September, and we started in business in the Rue des Martyrs.

"It was a hard struggle for some years, monsieur. Business did not prosper, and we could not afford many country excursions, and, besides, we had got out of the way of them. One has other things in one's head, and thinks more of the cash box than of pretty speeches, when one is in business. We were growing old by degrees without perceiving it, like quiet people who do not think much about love. One does not regret anything as long as one does not notice what one has lost.

"And then, monsieur, business became better, and we were tranquil as to the future! Then, you see, I do not exactly know what went on in my mind, no, I really do not know, but I began to dream like a little boarding-school girl. The sight of the little carts full of flowers which are drawn about the streets made me cry; the smell of violets sought me out in my easy-chair, behind my cash box, and made my heart beat! Then I would get up and go out on the doorstep to look at the blue sky between the roofs. When one looks up at the sky from the street, it looks like a river which is descending on Paris, winding as it flows, and the swallows pass to and fro in it like fish. These ideas are very stupid at my age! But how can one help it, monsieur, when one has worked all one's life? A moment comes in which one perceives that one could have done something else, and that one regrets, oh! yes, one feels intense regret! Just think, for twenty years I might have gone and had kisses in the woods, like other women. I used to think how delightful it would be to lie under the trees and be in love with some one! And I thought of it every day and every night! I dreamed of the moonlight on the water, until I felt inclined to drown myself.

"I did not venture to speak to Monsieur Beaurain about this at first. I knew that he would make fun of me, and send me back to sell my needles and cotton! And then, to speak the truth, Monsieur Beaurain never said much to me, but when I looked in the glass, I also understood quite well that I no longer appealed to any one!

"Well, I made up my mind, and I proposed to him an excursion into the country, to the place where we had first become acquainted. He agreed without mistrusting anything, and we arrived here this morning, about nine o'clock.

"I felt quite young again when I got among the wheat, for a woman's heart never grows old! And really, I no longer saw my husband as he is at present, but just as he was formerly! That I will swear to you, monsieur. As true as I am standing here I was crazy. I began to kiss him, and he was more surprised than if I had tried to murder him. He kept saying to me: 'Why, you must be mad! You are mad this morning! What is the matter with you?' I did not listen to him, I only listened to my own heart, and I made him come into the wood with me. That is all. I have spoken the truth, Monsieur le Maire, the whole truth."

The mayor was a sensible man. He rose from his chair, smiled, and said: "Go in peace, madame, and when you again visit our forests, be more discreet."

MARTINE

It came to him one Sunday after mass. He was walking home from church along the by-road that led to his house when he saw ahead of him Martine, who was also going home.

Her father walked beside his daughter with the important gait of a rich farmer. Discarding the smock, he wore a short coat of gray cloth and on his head a round-topped hat with wide brim.

She, laced up in a corset which she wore only once a week, walked along erect, with her squeezed-in waist, her broad shoulders and prominent hips, swinging herself a little. She wore a hat trimmed with flowers, made by a milliner at Yvetot, and displayed the back of her full, round, supple neck, reddened by the sun and air, on which fluttered little stray locks of hair.

Benoist saw only her back; but he knew well the face he loved, without, however, having ever noticed it more closely than he did now.

Suddenly he said: "Nom d'un nom, she is a fine girl, all the same, that Martine." He watched her as she walked, admiring her hastily, feeling a desire taking possession of him. He did not long to see her face again, no. He kept gazing at her figure, repeating to himself: "Nom d'un nom, she is a fine girl."

Martine turned to the right to enter "La Martiniere," the farm of her father, Jean Martin, and she cast a glance behind her as she turned round. She saw Benoist, who looked to her very comical. She called out: "Good-morning, Benoist." He replied: "Good-morning, Martine; good-morning, mait Martin," and went on his way.

When he reached home the soup was on the table. He sat down opposite his mother beside the farm hand and the hired man, while the maid servant went to draw some cider.

He ate a few spoonfuls, then pushed away his plate. His mother said:

"Don't you feel well?"

"No. I feel as if I had some pap in my stomach and that takes away my appetite."

He watched the others eating, as he cut himself a piece of bread from time to time and carried it lazily to his mouth, masticating it slowly. He thought of Martine. "She is a fine girl, all the same." And to think that he had not noticed it before, and that it came to him, just like that, all at once, and with such force that he could not eat.

He did not touch the stew. His mother said:

"Come, Benoist, try and eat a little; it is loin of mutton, it will do you good. When one has no appetite, they should force themselves to eat."

He swallowed a few morsels, then, pushing away his plate, said:

"No. I can't go that, positively."

When they rose from table he walked round the farm, telling the farm hand he might go home and that he would drive up the animals as he passed by them.

The country was deserted, as it was the day of rest. Here and there in a field of clover cows were moving along heavily, with full bellies, chewing their cud under a blazing sun. Unharnessed plows were standing at the end of a furrow; and the upturned earth ready for the seed showed broad brown patches of stubble of wheat and oats that had lately been harvested.

A rather dry autumn wind blew across the plain, promising a cool evening after the sun had set. Benoist sat down on a ditch, placed his hat on his knees as if he needed to cool off his head, and said aloud in the stillness of the country: "If you want a fine girl, she is a fine girl."

He thought of it again at night, in his bed, and in the morning when he awoke.

He was not sad, he was not discontented, he could not have told what ailed him. It was something that had hold of him, something fastened in his mind, an idea that would not leave him and that produced a sort of tickling sensation in his heart.

Sometimes a big fly is shut up in a room. You hear it flying about, buzzing, and the noise haunts you, irritates you. Suddenly it stops; you forget it; but all at once it begins again, obliging you to look up. You cannot catch it, nor drive it away, nor kill it, nor make it keep still. As soon as it settles for a second, it starts off buzzing again.

The recollection of Martine disturbed Benoist's mind like an imprisoned fly.

Then he longed to see her again and walked past the Martiniere several times. He saw her, at last, hanging out some clothes on a line stretched between two apple trees.

It was a warm day. She had on only a short skirt and her chemise, showing the curves of her figure as she hung up the towels. He remained there, concealed by the hedge, for more than an hour, even after she had left. He returned home more obsessed with her image than ever.

For a month his mind was full of her, he trembled when her name was mentioned in his presence. He could not eat, he had night sweats that kept him from sleeping.

On Sunday, at mass, he never took his eyes off her. She noticed it and smiled at him, flattered at his appreciation.

One evening, he suddenly met her in the road. She stopped short when she saw him coming. Then he walked right up to her, choking with fear and emotion, but determined to speak to her. He began falteringly:

"See here, Martine, this cannot go on like this any longer."

She replied as if she wanted to tease him:

"What cannot go on any longer, Benoist?"

"My thinking of you as many hours as there are in the day," he answered.

She put her hands on her hips.

"I do not oblige you to do so."

"Yes, it is you," he stammered; "I cannot sleep, nor rest, nor eat, nor anything."

"What do you need to cure you of all that?" she asked.

He stood there in dismay, his arms swinging, his eyes staring, his mouth agape.

She hit him a punch in the stomach and ran off.

From that day they met each other along the roadside, in byroads or else at twilight on the edge of a field, when he was going home with his horses and she was driving her cows home to the stable.

He felt himself carried, cast toward her by a strong impulse of his heart and body. He would have liked to squeeze her, strangle her, eat her, make her part of himself. And he trembled with impotence, impatience, rage, to think she did not belong to him entirely, as if they were one being.

People gossiped about it in the countryside. They said they were engaged. He had, besides, asked her if she would be his wife, and she had answered "Yes."

They, were waiting for an opportunity to talk to their parents about it.

But, all at once, she stopped coming to meet him at the usual hour. He did not even see her as he wandered round the farm. He could only catch a glimpse of her at mass on Sunday. And one Sunday, after the sermon, the priest actually published the banns of marriage between Victoire-Adelaide Martin and Josephin-Isidore Vallin.

Benoist felt a sensation in his hands as if the blood had been drained off. He had a buzzing in the ears; and could hear nothing; and presently he perceived that his tears were falling on his prayer book.

For a month he stayed in his room. Then he went back to his work.

But he was not cured, and it was always in his mind. He avoided the roads that led past her home, so that he might not even see the trees in the yard, and this obliged him to make a great circuit morning and evening.

She was now married to Vallin, the richest farmer in the district. Benoist and he did not speak now, though they had been comrades from childhood.

One evening, as Benoist was passing the town hall, he heard that she was enceinte. Instead of experiencing a feeling of sorrow, he experienced, on the contrary, a feeling of relief. It was over, now, all over. They were more separated by that than by her marriage. He really preferred that it should be so.

Months passed, and more months. He caught sight of her, occasionally, going to the village with a heavier step than usual. She blushed as she saw him, lowered her head and quickened her pace. And he turned out of his way so as not to pass her and meet her glance.

He dreaded the thought that he might one morning meet her face to face, and be obliged to speak to her. What could he say to her now, after all he had said formerly, when he held her hands as he kissed her hair beside her cheeks? He often thought of those meetings along the roadside. She had acted horridly after all her promises.

By degrees his grief diminished, leaving only sadness behind. And one day he took the old road that led past the farm where she now lived. He looked at the roof from a distance. It was there, in there, that she lived with another! The apple trees were in bloom, the cocks crowed on the dung hill. The whole dwelling seemed empty, the farm hands had gone to the fields to their spring toil. He stopped near the gate and looked into the yard. The dog was asleep outside his kennel, three calves were walking slowly, one behind the other, towards the pond. A big turkey was strutting before the door, parading before the turkey hens like a singer at the opera.

Benoist leaned against the gate post and was suddenly seized with a desire to weep. But suddenly, he heard a cry, a loud cry for help coming from the house. He was struck with dismay, his hands grasping the wooden bars of the gate, and listened attentively. Another cry, a prolonged, heartrending cry, reached his ears, his soul, his flesh. It was she who was crying like that! He darted inside, crossed the grass patch, pushed open the door, and saw her lying on the floor, her body drawn up, her face livid, her eyes haggard, in the throes of childbirth.

He stood there, trembling and paler than she was, and stammered:

"Here I am, here I am, Martine!"

She replied in gasps:

"Oh, do not leave me, do not leave me, Benoist!"

He looked at her, not knowing what to say, what to do. She began to cry out again:

"Oh, oh, it is killing me. Oh, Benoist!"

She writhed frightfully.

Benoist was suddenly seized with a frantic longing to help her, to quiet her, to remove her pain. He leaned over, lifted her up and laid her on her bed; and while she kept on moaning he began to take off her clothes, her jacket, her skirt and her petticoat. She bit her fists to keep from crying out. Then he did as he was accustomed to doing for cows, ewes, and mares: he assisted in delivering her and found in his hands a large infant who was moaning.

He wiped it off and wrapped it up in a towel that was drying in front of the fire, and laid it on a bundle of clothes ready for ironing that was on the table. Then he went back to the mother.

He took her up and placed her on the floor again, then he changed the bedclothes and put her back into bed. She faltered:

"Thank you, Benoist, you have a noble heart." And then she wept a little as if she felt regretful.

He did not love her any longer, not the least bit. It was all over. Why? How? He could not have said. What had happened had cured him better than ten years of absence.

She asked, exhausted and trembling:

"What is it?"

He replied calmly:

"It is a very fine girl."

Then they were silent again. At the end of a few moments, the mother, in a weak voice, said:

"Show her to me, Benoist."

He took up the little one and was showing it to her as if he were holding the consecrated wafer, when the door opened, and Isidore Vallin appeared.

He did not understand at first, then all at once he guessed.

Benoist, in consternation, stammered out:

"I was passing, I was just passing by when I heard her crying out, and I came—there is your child, Vallin!"

Then the husband, his eyes full of tears, stepped forward, took the little mite of humanity that he held out to him, kissed it, unable to speak from emotion for a few seconds; then placing the child on the bed, he held out both hands to Benoist, saying:

"Your hand upon it, Benoist. From now on we understand each other. If you are willing, we will be a pair of friends, a pair of friends!" And Benoist replied: "Indeed I will, certainly, indeed I will."

ALL OVER

Compte de Lormerin had just finished dressing. He cast a parting glance at the large mirror which occupied an entire panel in his dressing-room and smiled.

He was really a fine-looking man still, although quite gray. Tall, slight, elegant, with no sign of a paunch, with a small mustache of doubtful shade, which might be called fair, he had a walk, a nobility, a "chic," in short, that indescribable something which establishes a greater difference between two men than would millions of money. He murmured:

"Lormerin is still alive!"

And he went into the drawing-room where his correspondence awaited him.

On his table, where everything had its place, the work table of the gentleman who never works, there were a dozen letters lying beside three newspapers of different opinions. With a single touch he spread out all these letters, like a gambler giving the choice of a card; and he scanned the handwriting, a thing he did each morning before opening the envelopes.

It was for him a moment of delightful expectancy, of inquiry and vague anxiety. What did these sealed mysterious letters bring him? What did they contain of pleasure, of happiness, or of grief? He surveyed them with a rapid sweep of the eye, recognizing the writing, selecting them, making two or three lots, according to what he expected from them. Here, friends; there, persons to whom he was indifferent; further on, strangers. The last kind always gave him a little uneasiness. What did they want from him? What hand had traced those curious characters full of thoughts, promises, or threats?

This day one letter in particular caught his eye. It was simple, nevertheless, without seeming to reveal anything; but he looked at it uneasily, with a sort of chill at his heart. He thought: "From whom can it be? I certainly know this writing, and yet I can't identify it."

He raised it to a level with his face, holding it delicately between two fingers, striving to read through the envelope, without making up his mind to open it.

Then he smelled it, and snatched up from the table a little magnifying glass which he used in studying all the niceties of handwriting. He suddenly felt unnerved. "Whom is it from? This hand is familiar to me, very familiar. I must have often read its tracings, yes, very often. But this must have been a long, long time ago. Whom the deuce can it be from? Pooh! it's only somebody asking for money."

And he tore open the letter. Then he read:

MY DEAR FRIEND:

You have, without doubt, forgotten me, for it is now twenty-five years since we saw each other. I was young; I am old.

When I bade you farewell, I left Paris in order to follow into the provinces my husband, my old husband, whom you used to call "my hospital." Do you remember him? He died five years ago, and now I am returning to Paris to get my daughter married, for I have a daughter, a beautiful girl of eighteen, whom you have never seen.

I informed you of her birth, but you certainly did not pay much attention to so trifling an event.

You are still the handsome Lormerin; so I have been told. Well, if you still recollect little Lise, whom you used to call Lison, come and dine with her this evening, with the elderly Baronne de Vance your ever faithful friend, who, with some emotion, although happy, reaches out to you a devoted hand, which you must clasp, but no longer kiss, my poor Jaquelet.

LISE DE VANCE.

Lormerin's heart began to throb. He remained sunk in his armchair with the letter on his knees, staring straight before him, overcome by a poignant emotion that made the tears mount up to his eyes!

If he had ever loved a woman in his life it was this one, little Lise, Lise de Vance, whom he called "Ashflower," on account of the strange color of her hair and the pale gray of her eyes. Oh! what a dainty, pretty, charming creature she was, this frail baronne, the wife of that gouty, pimply baron, who had abruptly carried her off to the provinces, shut her up, kept her in seclusion through jealousy, jealousy of the handsome Lormerin.

Yes, he had loved her, and he believed that he too, had been truly loved. She familiarly gave him, the name of Jaquelet, and would pronounce that word in a delicious fashion.

A thousand forgotten memories came back to him, far, off and sweet and melancholy now. One evening she had called on him on her way home from a ball, and they went for a stroll in the Bois de Boulogne, she in evening dress, he in his dressing-jacket. It was springtime; the weather was beautiful. The fragrance from her bodice embalmed the warm air-the odor of her bodice, and perhaps, too, the fragrance of her skin. What a divine night! When they reached the lake, as the moon's rays fell across the branches into the water, she began to weep. A little surprised, he asked her why.

"I don't know. The moon and the water have affected me. Every time I see poetic things I have a tightening at the heart, and I have to cry."

He smiled, affected himself, considering her feminine emotion charming—the unaffected emotion of a poor little woman, whom every sensation overwhelms. And he embraced her passionately, stammering:

"My little Lise, you are exquisite."

What a charming love affair, short-lived and dainty, it had been and over all too quickly, cut short in the midst of its ardor by this old brute of a baron, who had carried off his wife, and never let any one see her afterward.

Lormerin had forgotten, in fact, at the end of two or three months. One woman drives out another so quickly in Paris, when one is a bachelor! No matter; he had kept a little altar for her in his heart, for he had loved her alone! He assured himself now that this was so.

He rose, and said aloud: "Certainly, I will go and dine with her this evening!"

And instinctively he turned toward the mirror to inspect himself from head to foot. He reflected: "She must look very old, older than I look." And he felt gratified at the thought of showing himself to her still handsome, still fresh, of astonishing her, perhaps of filling her with emotion, and making her regret those bygone days so far, far distant!

He turned his attention to the other letters. They were of no importance.

The whole day he kept thinking of this ghost of other days. What was she like now? How strange it was to meet in this way after twenty-five years! But would he recognize her?

He made his toilet with feminine coquetry, put on a white waistcoat, which suited him better with the coat than a black one, sent for the hairdresser to give him a finishing touch with the curling iron, for he had preserved his hair, and started very early in order to show his eagerness to see her.

The first thing he saw on entering a pretty drawing-room newly furnished was his own portrait, an old faded photograph, dating from the days when he was a beau, hanging on the wall in an antique silk frame.

He sat down and waited. A door opened behind him. He rose up abruptly, and, turning round, beheld an old woman with white hair who extended both hands toward him.

He seized them, kissed them one after the other several times; then, lifting up his head, he gazed at the woman he had loved.

Yes, it was an old lady, an old lady whom he did not recognize, and who, while she smiled, seemed ready to weep.

He could not abstain from murmuring:

"Is it you, Lise?"

She replied:

"Yes, it is I; it is I, indeed. You would not have known me, would you? I have had so much sorrow—so much sorrow. Sorrow has consumed my life. Look at me now—or, rather, don't look at me! But how handsome you have kept—and young! If I had by chance met you in the street I would have exclaimed: 'Jaquelet!'. Now, sit down and let us, first of all, have a chat. And then I will call my daughter, my grown-up daughter. You'll see how she resembles me—or, rather, how I resembled her—no, it is not quite that; she is just like the 'me' of former days—you shall see! But I wanted to be alone with you first. I feared that there would be some emotion on my side, at the first moment. Now it is all over; it is past. Pray be seated, my friend."

He sat down beside her, holding her hand; but he did not know what to say; he did not know this woman—it seemed to him that he had never seen her before. Why had he come to this house? What could he talk about? Of the long ago? What was there in common between him and her? He could no longer recall anything in presence of this grandmotherly face. He could no longer recall all the nice, tender things, so sweet, so bitter, that had come to his mind that morning when he thought of the other, of little Lise, of the dainty Ashflower. What, then, had become of her, the former one, the one he had loved? That woman of far-off dreams, the blonde with gray eyes, the young girl who used to call him "Jaquelet" so prettily?

They remained side by side, motionless, both constrained, troubled, profoundly ill at ease.

As they talked only commonplaces, awkwardly and spasmodically and slowly, she rose and pressed the button of the bell.

"I am going to call Renee," she said.

There was a tap at the door, then the rustle of a dress; then a young voice exclaimed:

"Here I am, mamma!"

Lormerin remained bewildered as at the sight of an apparition. He stammered:

"Good-day, mademoiselle"

Then, turning toward the mother:

"Oh! it is you!"

In fact, it was she, she whom he had known in bygone days, the Lise who had vanished and come back! In her he found the woman he had won twenty-five years before. This one was even younger, fresher, more childlike.

He felt a wild desire to open his arms, to clasp her to his heart again, murmuring in her ear:

"Good-morning, Lison!"

A man-servant announced:

"Dinner is ready, madame."

And they proceeded toward the dining-room.

What passed at this dinner? What did they say to him, and what could he say in reply? He found himself plunged in one of those strange dreams which border on insanity. He gazed at the two women with a fixed idea in his mind, a morbid, self-contradictory idea:

"Which is the real one?"

The mother smiled again repeating over and over:

"Do you remember?" And it was in the bright eyes of the young girl that he found again his memories of the past. Twenty times he opened his mouth to say to her: "Do you remember, Lison?" forgetting this white-haired lady who was looking at him tenderly.

And yet, there were moments when, he no longer felt sure, when he lost his head. He could see that the woman of to-day was not exactly the woman of long ago. The other one, the former one, had in her voice, in her glances, in her entire being, something which he did not find again. And he made prodigious efforts of mind to recall his lady love, to seize again what had escaped from her, what this resuscitated one did not possess.

The baronne said:

"You have lost your old vivacity, my poor friend."

He murmured:

"There are many other things that I have lost!"

But in his heart, touched with emotion, he felt his old love springing to life once more, like an awakened wild beast ready to bite him.

The young girl went on chattering, and every now and then some familiar intonation, some expression of her mother's, a certain style of speaking and thinking, that resemblance of mind and manner which people acquire by living together, shook Lormerin from head to foot. All these things penetrated him, making the reopened wound of his passion bleed anew.

He got away early, and took a turn along the boulevard. But the image of this young girl pursued him, haunted him, quickened his heart, inflamed his blood. Apart from the two women, he now saw only one, a young one, the old one come back out of the past, and he loved her as he had loved her in bygone years. He loved her with greater ardor, after an interval of twenty-five years.

He went home to reflect on this strange and terrible thing, and to think what he should do.

But, as he was passing, with a wax candle in his hand, before the glass, the large glass in which he had contemplated himself and admired himself before he started, he saw reflected there an elderly, gray-haired man; and suddenly he recollected what he had been in olden days, in the days of little Lise. He saw himself charming and handsome, as he had been when he was loved! Then, drawing the light nearer, he looked at himself more closely, as one inspects a strange thing with a magnifying glass, tracing the wrinkles, discovering those frightful ravages, which he had not perceived till now.

And he sat down, crushed at the sight of himself, at the sight of his lamentable image, murmuring:

"All over, Lormerin!"

THE PARROT

I

Everybody in Fecamp knew Mother Patin's story. She had certainly been unfortunate with her husband, for in his lifetime he used to beat her, just as wheat is threshed in the barn.

He was master of a fishing bark and had married her, formerly, because she was pretty, although poor.

Patin was a good sailor, but brutal. He used to frequent Father Auban's inn, where he would usually drink four or five glasses of brandy, on lucky days eight or ten glasses and even more, according to his mood. The brandy was served to the customers by Father Auban's daughter, a pleasing brunette, who attracted people to the house only by her pretty face, for nothing had ever been gossiped about her.

Patin, when he entered the inn, would be satisfied to look at her and to compliment her politely and respectfully. After he had had his first glass of brandy he would already find her much nicer; at the second he would wink; at the third he would say. "If you were only willing, Mam'zelle Desiree——" without ever finishing his sentence; at the fourth he would try to hold her back by her skirt in order to kiss her; and when he went as high as ten it was Father Auban who brought him the remaining drinks.

The old innkeeper, who knew all the tricks of the trade, made Desiree walk about between the tables in order to increase the consumption of drinks; and Desiree, who was a worthy daughter of Father Auban, flitted around among the benches and joked with them, her lips smiling and her eyes sparkling.

Patin got so well accustomed to Desiree's face that he thought of it even while at sea, when throwing out his nets, in storms or in calms, on moonlit or dark evenings. He thought of her while holding the tiller in the stern of his boat, while his four companions were slumbering with their heads on their arms. He always saw her, smiling, pouring out the yellow brandy with a peculiar shoulder movement and then exclaiming as she turned away: "There, now; are you satisfied?"

He saw her so much in his mind's eye that he was overcome by an irresistible desire to marry her, and, not being able to hold out any longer, he asked for her hand.

He was rich, owned his own vessel, his nets and a little house at the foot of the hill on the Retenue, whereas Father Auban had nothing. The marriage was therefore eagerly agreed upon and the wedding took place as soon as possible, as both parties were desirous for the affair to be concluded as early as convenient.

Three days after the wedding Patin could no longer understand how he had ever imagined Desiree to be different from other women. What a fool he had been to encumber himself with a penniless creature, who had undoubtedly inveigled him with some drug which she had put in his brandy!

He would curse all day lung, break his pipe with his teeth and maul his crew. After he had sworn by every known term at everything that came his way he would rid himself of his remaining anger on the fish and lobsters, which he pulled from the nets and threw into the baskets amid oaths and foul language. When he returned home he would find his wife, Father Auban's daughter, within reach of his mouth and hand, and it was not long before he treated her like the lowest creature in the world. As she listened calmly, accustomed to paternal violence, he grew exasperated at her quiet, and one evening he beat her. Then life at his home became unbearable.

For ten years the principal topic of conversation on the Retenue was about the beatings that Patin gave his wife and his manner of cursing at her for the least thing. He could, indeed, curse with a richness of vocabulary in a roundness of tone unequalled by any other man in Fecamp. As soon as his ship was sighted at the entrance of the harbor, returning from the fishing expedition, every one awaited the first volley he would hurl from the bridge as soon as he perceived his wife's white cap.

Standing at the stern he would steer, his eye fixed on the bows and on the sail, and, notwithstanding the difficulty of the narrow passage and the height of the turbulent waves, he would search among the watching women and try to recognize his wife, Father Auban's daughter, the wretch!

Then, as soon as he saw her, notwithstanding the noise of the wind and waves, he would let loose upon her with such power and volubility that every one would laugh, although they pitied her greatly. When he arrived at the dock he would relieve his mind, while unloading the fish, in such an expressive manner that he attracted around him all the loafers of the neighborhood. The words left his mouth sometimes like shots from a cannon, short and terrible, sometimes like peals of thunder, which roll and rumble for five minutes, such a hurricane of oaths that he seemed to have in his lungs one of the storms of the Eternal Father.

When he left his ship and found himself face to face with her, surrounded by all the gossips of the neighborhood, he would bring up a new cargo of insults and bring her back to their dwelling, she in front, he behind, she weeping, he yelling at her.

At last, when alone with her behind closed doors, he would thrash her on the slightest pretext. The least thing was sufficient to make him raise his hand, and when he had once begun he did not stop, but he would throw into her face the true motive for his anger. At each blow he would roar: "There, you beggar! There, you wretch! There, you pauper! What a bright thing I did when I rinsed my mouth with your rascal of a father's apology for brandy."

The poor woman lived in continual fear, in a ceaseless trembling of body and soul, in everlasting expectation of outrageous thrashings.

This lasted ten years. She was so timorous that she would grow pale whenever she spoke to any one, and she thought of nothing but the blows with which she was threatened; and she became thinner, more yellow and drier than a smoked fish.

II

One night, when her husband was at sea, she was suddenly awakened by the wild roaring of the wind!

She sat up in her bed, trembling, but, as she hear nothing more, she lay down again; almost immediately there was a roar in the chimney which shook the entire house; it seemed to cross the heavens like a pack of furious animals snorting and roaring.

Then she arose and rushed to the harbor. Other women were arriving from all sides, carrying lanterns. The men also were gathering, and all were watching the foaming crests of the breaking wave.

The storm lasted fifteen hours. Eleven sailors never returned; Patin was among them.

In the neighborhood of Dieppe the wreck of his bark, the Jeune-Amelie, was found. The bodies of his sailors were found near Saint-Valery, but his body was never recovered. As his vessel seemed to have been cut in two, his wife expected and feared his return for a long time, for if there had been a collision he alone might have been picked up and carried afar off.

Little by little she grew accustomed to the thought that she was rid of him, although she would start every time that a neighbor, a beggar or a peddler would enter suddenly.

One afternoon, about four years after the disappearance of her husband, while she was walking along the Rue aux Juifs, she stopped before the house of an old sea captain who had recently died and whose furniture was for sale. Just at that moment a parrot was at auction. He had green feathers and a blue head and was watching everybody with a displeased look. "Three francs!" cried the auctioneer. "A bird that can talk like a lawyer, three francs!"

A friend of the Patin woman nudged her and said:

"You ought to buy that, you who are rich. It would be good company for you. That bird is worth more than thirty francs. Anyhow, you can always sell it for twenty or twenty-five!"

Patin's widow added fifty centimes, and the bird was given her in a little cage, which she carried away. She took it home, and, as she was opening the wire door in order to give it something to drink, he bit her finger and drew blood.

"Oh, how naughty he is!" she said.

Nevertheless she gave it some hemp-seed and corn and watched it pruning its feathers as it glanced warily at its new home and its new mistress. On the following morning, just as day was breaking, the Patin woman distinctly heard a loud, deep, roaring voice calling: "Are you going to get up, carrion?"

Her fear was so great that she hid her head under the sheets, for when Patin was with her as soon as he would open his eyes he would shout those well-known words into her ears.

Trembling, rolled into a ball, her back prepared for the thrashing which she already expected, her face buried in the pillows, she murmured: "Good Lord! he is here! Good Lord! he is here! Good Lord! he has come back!"

Minutes passed; no noise disturbed the quiet room. Then, trembling, she stuck her head out of the bed, sure that he was there, watching, ready to beat her. Except for a ray of sun shining through the window, she saw nothing, and she said to her self: "He must be hidden."

She waited a long time and then, gaining courage, she said to herself: "I must have dreamed it, seeing there is nobody here."

A little reassured, she closed her eyes, when from quite near a furious voice, the thunderous voice of the drowned man, could be heard crying: "Say! when in the name of all that's holy are you going to get up, you b——?"

She jumped out of bed, moved by obedience, by the passive obedience of a woman accustomed to blows and who still remembers and always will remember that voice! She said: "Here I am, Patin; what do you want?"

Put Patin did not answer. Then, at a complete loss, she looked around her, then in the chimney and under the bed and finally sank into a chair, wild with anxiety, convinced that Patin's soul alone was there, near her, and that he had returned in order to torture her.

Suddenly she remembered the loft, in order to reach which one had to take a ladder. Surely he must have hidden there in order to surprise her. He must have been held by savages on some distant shore, unable to escape until now, and he had returned, worse that ever. There was no doubting the quality of that voice. She raised her head and asked: "Are you up there, Patin?"

Patin did not answer. Then, with a terrible fear which made her heart tremble, she climbed the ladder, opened the skylight, looked, saw nothing, entered, looked about and found nothing. Sitting on some straw, she began to cry, but while she was weeping, overcome by a poignant and supernatural terror, she heard Patin talking in the room below.

He seemed less angry and he was saying: "Nasty weather! Fierce wind! Nasty weather! I haven't eaten, damn it!"

She cried through the ceiling: "Here I am, Patin; I am getting your meal ready. Don't get angry."

She ran down again. There was no one in the room. She felt herself growing weak, as if death were touching her, and she tried to run and get help from the neighbors, when a voice near her cried out: "I haven't had my breakfast, by G—!"

And the parrot in his cage watched her with his round, knowing, wicked eye. She, too, looked at him wildly, murmuring: "Ah! so it's you!"

He shook his head and continued: "Just you wait! I'll teach you how to loaf."

What happened within her? She felt, she understood that it was he, the dead man, who had come back, who had disguised himself in the feathers of this bird in order to continue to torment her; that he would curse, as formerly, all day long, and bite her, and swear at her, in order to attract the neighbors and make them laugh. Then she rushed for the cage and seized the bird, which scratched and tore her flesh with its claws and beak. But she held it with all her strength between her hands. She threw it on the ground and rolled over it with the frenzy of one possessed. She crushed it and finally made of it nothing but a little green, flabby lump which no longer moved or spoke. Then she wrapped it in a cloth, as in a shroud, and she went out in her nightgown, barefoot; she crossed the dock, against which the choppy waves of the sea were beating, and she shook the cloth and let drop this little, dead thing, which looked like so much grass. Then she returned, threw herself on her knees before the empty cage, and, overcome by what she had done, kneeled and prayed for forgiveness, as if she had committed some heinous crime.

THE PIECE OF STRING

It was market-day, and from all the country round Goderville the peasants and their wives were coming toward the town. The men walked slowly, throwing the whole body forward at every step of their long, crooked legs. They were deformed from pushing the plough which makes the left-shoulder higher, and bends their figures side-ways; from reaping the grain, when they have to spread their legs so as to keep on their feet. Their starched blue blouses, glossy as though varnished, ornamented at collar and cuffs with a little embroidered design and blown out around their bony bodies, looked very much like balloons about to soar, whence issued two arms and two feet.

Some of these fellows dragged a cow or a calf at the end of a rope. And just behind the animal followed their wives beating it over the back with a leaf-covered branch to hasten its pace, and carrying large baskets out of which protruded the heads of chickens or ducks. These women walked more quickly and energetically than the men, with their erect, dried-up figures, adorned with scanty little shawls pinned over their flat bosoms, and their heads wrapped round with a white cloth, enclosing the hair and surmounted by a cap.

Now a char-a-banc passed by, jogging along behind a nag and shaking up strangely the two men on the seat, and the woman at the bottom of the cart who held fast to its sides to lessen the hard jolting.

In the market-place at Goderville was a great crowd, a mingled multitude of men and beasts. The horns of cattle, the high, long-napped hats of wealthy peasants, the head-dresses of the women came to the surface of that sea. And the sharp, shrill, barking voices made a continuous, wild din, while above it occasionally rose a huge burst of laughter from the sturdy lungs of a merry peasant or a prolonged bellow from a cow tied fast to the wall of a house.

It all smelled of the stable, of milk, of hay and of perspiration, giving off that half-human, half-animal odor which is peculiar to country folks.

Maitre Hauchecorne, of Breaute, had just arrived at Goderville and was making his way toward the square when he perceived on the ground a little piece of string. Maitre Hauchecorne, economical as are all true Normans, reflected that everything was worth picking up which could be of any use, and he stooped down, but painfully, because he suffered from rheumatism. He took the bit of thin string from the ground and was carefully preparing to roll it up when he saw Maitre Malandain, the harness maker, on his doorstep staring at him. They had once had a quarrel about a halter, and they had borne each other malice ever since. Maitre Hauchecorne was overcome with a sort of shame at being seen by his enemy picking up a bit of string in the road. He quickly hid it beneath his blouse and then slipped it into his breeches, pocket, then pretended to be still looking for something on the ground which he did not discover and finally went off toward the market-place, his head bent forward and his body almost doubled in two by rheumatic pains.

He was at once lost in the crowd, which kept moving about slowly and noisily as it chaffered and bargained. The peasants examined the cows, went off, came back, always in doubt for fear of being cheated, never quite daring to decide, looking the seller square in the eye in the effort to discover the tricks of the man and the defect in the beast.

The women, having placed their great baskets at their feet, had taken out the poultry, which lay upon the ground, their legs tied together, with terrified eyes and scarlet combs.

They listened to propositions, maintaining their prices in a decided manner with an impassive face or perhaps deciding to accept the smaller price offered, suddenly calling out to the customer who was starting to go away:

"All right, I'll let you have them, Mait' Anthime."

Then, little by little, the square became empty, and when the Angelus struck midday those who lived at a distance poured into the inns.

At Jourdain's the great room was filled with eaters, just as the vast court was filled with vehicles of every sort—wagons, gigs, chars-a-bancs, tilburies, innumerable vehicles which have no name, yellow with mud, misshapen, pieced together, raising their shafts to heaven like two arms, or it may be with their nose on the ground and their rear in the air.

Just opposite to where the diners were at table the huge fireplace, with its bright flame, gave out a burning heat on the backs of those who sat at the right. Three spits were turning, loaded with chickens, with pigeons and with joints of mutton, and a delectable odor of roast meat and of gravy flowing over crisp brown skin arose from the hearth, kindled merriment, caused mouths to water.

All the aristocracy of the plough were eating there at Mait' Jourdain's, the innkeeper's, a dealer in horses also and a sharp fellow who had made a great deal of money in his day.

The dishes were passed round, were emptied, as were the jugs of yellow cider. Every one told of his affairs, of his purchases and his sales. They exchanged news about the crops. The weather was good for greens, but too wet for grain.

Suddenly the drum began to beat in the courtyard before the house. Every one, except some of the most indifferent, was on their feet at once and ran to the door, to the windows, their mouths full and napkins in their hand.

When the public crier had finished his tattoo he called forth in a jerky voice, pausing in the wrong places:

"Be it known to the inhabitants of Goderville and in general to all persons present at the market that there has been lost this morning on the Beuzeville road, between nine and ten o'clock, a black leather pocketbook containing five hundred francs and business papers. You are requested to return it to the mayor's office at once or to Maitre Fortune Houlbreque, of Manneville. There will be twenty francs reward."

Then the man went away. They heard once more at a distance the dull beating of the drum and the faint voice of the crier. Then they all began to talk of this incident, reckoning up the chances which Maitre Houlbreque had of finding or of not finding his pocketbook again.

The meal went on. They were finishing their coffee when the corporal of gendarmes appeared on the threshold.

He asked:

"Is Maitre Hauchecorne, of Breaute, here?"

Maitre Hauchecorne, seated at the other end of the table answered:

"Here I am, here I am."

And he followed the corporal.

The mayor was waiting for him, seated in an armchair. He was the notary of the place, a tall, grave man of pompous speech.

"Maitre Hauchecorne," said he, "this morning on the Beuzeville road, you were seen to pick up the pocketbook lost by Maitre Houlbreque, of Manneville."

The countryman looked at the mayor in amazement frightened already at this suspicion which rested on him, he knew not why.

"I—I picked up that pocketbook?"

"Yes, YOU."

"I swear I don't even know anything about it."

"You were seen."

"I was seen—I? Who saw me?"

"M. Malandain, the harness-maker."

Then the old man remembered, understood, and, reddening with anger, said:

"Ah! he saw me, did he, the rascal? He saw me picking up this string here, M'sieu le Maire."

And fumbling at the bottom of his pocket, he pulled out of it the little end of string.

But the mayor incredulously shook his head:

"You will not make me believe, Maitre Hauchecorne, that M. Malandain, who is a man whose word can be relied on, has mistaken this string for a pocketbook."

The peasant, furious, raised his hand and spat on the ground beside him as if to attest his good faith, repeating:

"For all that, it is God's truth, M'sieu le Maire. There! On my soul's salvation, I repeat it."

The mayor continued:

"After you picked up the object in question, you even looked about for some time in the mud to see if a piece of money had not dropped out of it."

The good man was choking with indignation and fear.

"How can they tell—how can they tell such lies as that to slander an honest man! How can they?"

His protestations were in vain; he was not believed.

He was confronted with M. Malandain, who repeated and sustained his testimony. They railed at one another for an hour. At his own request Maitre Hauchecorne was searched. Nothing was found on him.

At last the mayor, much perplexed, sent him away, warning him that he would inform the public prosecutor and ask for orders.

The news had spread. When he left the mayor's office the old man was surrounded, interrogated with a curiosity which was serious or mocking, as the case might be, but into which no indignation entered. And he began to tell the story of the string. They did not believe him. They laughed.

He passed on, buttonholed by every one, himself buttonholing his acquaintances, beginning over and over again his tale and his protestations, showing his pockets turned inside out to prove that he had nothing in them.

They said to him:

"You old rogue!"

He grew more and more angry, feverish, in despair at not being believed, and kept on telling his story.

The night came. It was time to go home. He left with three of his neighbors, to whom he pointed out the place where he had picked up the string, and all the way he talked of his adventure.

That evening he made the round of the village of Breaute for the purpose of telling every one. He met only unbelievers.

He brooded over it all night long.

The next day, about one in the afternoon, Marius Paumelle, a farm hand of Maitre Breton, the market gardener at Ymauville, returned the pocketbook and its contents to Maitre Holbreque, of Manneville.

This man said, indeed, that he had found it on the road, but not knowing how to read, he had carried it home and given it to his master.

The news spread to the environs. Maitre Hauchecorne was informed. He started off at once and began to relate his story with the denoument. He was triumphant.

"What grieved me," said he, "was not the thing itself, do you understand, but it was being accused of lying. Nothing does you so much harm as being in disgrace for lying."

All day he talked of his adventure. He told it on the roads to the people who passed, at the cabaret to the people who drank and next Sunday when they came out of church. He even stopped strangers to tell them about it. He was easy now, and yet something worried him without his knowing exactly what it was. People had a joking manner while they listened. They did not seem convinced. He seemed to feel their remarks behind his back.

On Tuesday of the following week he went to market at Goderville, prompted solely by the need of telling his story.

Malandain, standing on his doorstep, began to laugh as he saw him pass. Why?

He accosted a farmer of Criquetot, who did not let him finish, and giving him a punch in the pit of the stomach cried in his face: "Oh, you great rogue!" Then he turned his heel upon him.

Maitre Hauchecorne remained speechless and grew more and more uneasy. Why had they called him "great rogue"?

When seated at table in Jourdain's tavern he began again to explain the whole affair.

A horse dealer of Montivilliers shouted at him:

"Get out, get out, you old scamp! I know all about your old string."

Hauchecorne stammered:

"But since they found it again, the pocketbook!"

But the other continued:

"Hold your tongue, daddy; there's one who finds it and there's another who returns it. And no one the wiser."

The farmer was speechless. He understood at last. They accused him of having had the pocketbook brought back by an accomplice, by a confederate.

He tried to protest. The whole table began to laugh.

He could not finish his dinner, and went away amid a chorus of jeers.

He went home indignant, choking with rage, with confusion, the more cast down since with his Norman craftiness he was, perhaps, capable of having done what they accused him of and even of boasting of it as a good trick. He was dimly conscious that it was impossible to prove his innocence, his craftiness being so well known. He felt himself struck to the heart by the injustice of the suspicion.

He began anew to tell his tale, lengthening his recital every day, each day adding new proofs, more energetic declarations and more sacred oaths, which he thought of, which he prepared in his hours of solitude, for his mind was entirely occupied with the story of the string. The more he denied it, the more artful his arguments, the less he was believed.

"Those are liars proofs," they said behind his back.

He felt this. It preyed upon him and he exhausted himself in useless efforts.

He was visibly wasting away.

Jokers would make him tell the story of "the piece of string" to amuse them, just as you make a soldier who has been on a campaign tell his story of the battle. His mind kept growing weaker and about the end of December he took to his bed.

He passed away early in January, and, in the ravings of death agony, he protested his innocence, repeating:

"A little bit of string—a little bit of string. See, here it is, M'sieu le Maire."

He could not finish his dinner, and went away amid their jeering jests.

VOLUME IX

TOINE

He was known for thirty miles round was father Toine—fat Toine, Toine-my-extra, Antoine Macheble, nicknamed Burnt-Brandy—the innkeeper of Tournevent.

It was he who had made famous this hamlet buried in a niche in the valley that led down to the sea, a poor little peasants' hamlet consisting of ten Norman cottages surrounded by ditches and trees.

The houses were hidden behind a curve which had given the place the name of Tournevent. It seemed to have sought shelter in this ravine overgrown with grass and rushes, from the keen, salt sea wind—the ocean wind that devours and burns like fire, that drys up and withers like the sharpest frost of winter, just as birds seek shelter in the furrows of the fields in time of storm.

But the whole hamlet seemed to be the property of Antoine Macheble, nicknamed Burnt-Brandy, who was called also Toine, or Toine-My-Extra-Special, the latter in consequence of a phrase current in his mouth:

"My Extra-Special is the best in France:"

His "Extra-Special" was, of course, his cognac.

For the last twenty years he had served the whole countryside with his Extra-Special and his "Burnt-Brandy," for whenever he was asked: "What shall I drink, Toine?" he invariably answered: "A burnt-brandy, my son-in-law; that warms the inside and clears the head—there's nothing better for your body."

He called everyone his son-in-law, though he had no daughter, either married or to be married.

Well known indeed was Toine Burnt-Brandy, the stoutest man in all Normandy. His little house seemed ridiculously small, far too small and too low to hold him; and when people saw him standing at his door, as he did all day long, they asked one another how he could possibly get through the door. But he went in whenever a customer appeared, for it was only right that Toine should be invited to take his thimbleful of whatever was drunk in his wine shop.

His inn bore the sign: "The Friends' Meeting-Place"—and old Toine was, indeed, the friend of all. His customers came from Fecamp and Montvilliers, just for the fun of seeing him and hearing him talk; for fat Toine would have made a tombstone laugh. He had a way of chaffing people without offending them, or of winking to express what he didn't say, of slapping his thighs when he was merry in such a way as to make you hold your sides, laughing. And then, merely to see him drink was a curiosity. He drank everything that was offered him, his roguish eyes twinkling, both with the enjoyment of drinking and at the thought of the money he was taking in. His was a double pleasure: first, that of drinking; and second, that of piling up the cash.

You should have heard him quarrelling with his wife! It was worth paying for to see them together. They had wrangled all the thirty years they had been married; but Toine was good-humored, while his better-half grew angry. She was a tall peasant woman, who walked with long steps like a stork, and had a head resembling that of an angry screech-owl. She spent her time rearing chickens in a little poultry-yard behind the inn, and she was noted for her success in fattening them for the table.

Whenever the gentry of Fecamp gave a dinner they always had at least one of Madame Toine's chickens to be in the fashion.

But she was born ill-tempered, and she went through life in a mood of perpetual discontent. Annoyed at everyone, she seemed to be particularly annoyed at her husband. She disliked his gaiety, his reputation, his rude health, his embonpoint. She treated him as a good-for-nothing creature because he earned his money without working, and as a glutton because he ate and drank as much as ten ordinary men; and not a day went by without her declaring spitefully:

"You'd be better in the stye along with the pigs! You're so fat it makes me sick to look at you!"

And she would shout in his face:

"Wait! Wait a bit! We'll see! You'll burst one of these fine days like a sack of corn-you old bloat, you!"

Toine would laugh heartily, patting his corpulent person, and replying:

"Well, well, old hen, why don't you fatten up your chickens like that? just try!"

And, rolling his sleeves back from his enormous arm, he said:

"That would make a fine wing now, wouldn't it?"

And the customers, doubled up with laughter, would thump the table with their fists and stamp their feet on the floor.

The old woman, mad with rage, would repeat:

"Wait a bit! Wait a bit! You'll see what'll happen. He'll burst like a sack of grain!"

And off she would go, amid the jeers and laughter of the drinkers.

Toine was, in fact, an astonishing sight, he was so fat, so heavy, so red. He was one of those enormous beings with whom Death seems to be amusing himself—playing perfidious tricks and pranks, investing with an irresistibly comic air his slow work of destruction. Instead of manifesting his approach, as with others, in white hairs, in emaciation, in wrinkles, in the gradual collapse which makes the onlookers say: "Gad! how he has changed!" he took a malicious pleasure in fattening Toine, in making him monstrous and absurd, in tingeing his face with a deep crimson, in giving him the appearance of superhuman health, and the changes he inflicts on all were in the case of Toine laughable, comic, amusing, instead of being painful and distressing to witness.

"Wait a bit! Wait a bit!" said his wife. "You'll see."

At last Toine had an apoplectic fit, and was paralyzed in consequence. The giant was put to bed in the little room behind the partition of the drinking-room that he might hear what was said and talk to his friends, for his head was quite clear although his enormous body was helplessly inert. It was hoped at first that his immense legs would regain some degree of power; but this hope soon disappeared, and Toine spent his days and nights in the bed, which was only made up once a week, with the help of four neighbors who lifted the innkeeper, each holding a limb, while his mattress was turned.

He kept his spirits, nevertheless; but his gaiety was of a different kind—more timid, more humble; and he lived in a constant, childlike fear of his wife, who grumbled from morning till night:

"Look at him there—the great glutton! the good-for-nothing creature, the old boozer! Serve him right, serve him right!"

He no longer answered her. He contented himself with winking behind the old woman's back, and turning over on his other side—the only movement of which he was now capable. He called this exercise a "tack to the north" or a "tack to the south."

His great distraction nowadays was to listen to the conversations in the bar, and to shout through the wall when he recognized a friend's voice:

"Hallo, my son-in-law! Is that you, Celestin?"

And Celestin Maloisel answered:

"Yes, it's me, Toine. Are you getting about again yet, old fellow?"

"Not exactly getting about," answered Toine. "But I haven't grown thin; my carcass is still good."

Soon he got into the way of asking his intimates into his room to keep him company, although it grieved him to see that they had to drink without him. It pained him to the quick that his customers should be drinking without him.

"That's what hurts worst of all," he would say: "that I cannot drink my Extra-Special any more. I can put up with everything else, but going without drink is the very deuce."

Then his wife's screech-owl face would appear at the window, and she would break in with the words:

"Look at him! Look at him now, the good-for-nothing wretch! I've got to feed him and wash him just as if he were a pig!"

And when the old woman had gone, a cock with red feathers would sometimes fly up to the window sill and looking into the room with his round inquisitive eye, would begin to crow loudly. Occasionally, too, a few hens would flutter as far as the foot of the bed, seeking crumbs on the floor. Toine's friends soon deserted the drinking room to come and chat every afternoon beside the invalid's bed. Helpless though he was, the jovial Toine still provided them with amusement. He would have made the devil himself laugh.

Three men were regular in their attendance at the bedside: Celestin Maloisel, a tall, thin fellow, somewhat gnarled, like the trunk of an apple-tree; Prosper Horslaville, a withered little man with a ferret nose, cunning as a fox; and Cesaire Paumelle, who never spoke, but who enjoyed Toine's society all the same.

They brought a plank from the yard, propped it upon the edge of the bed, and played dominoes from two till six.

But Toine's wife soon became insufferable. She could not endure that her fat, lazy husband should amuse himself at games while lying in his bed; and whenever she caught him beginning a game she pounced furiously on the dominoes, overturned the plank, and carried all away into the bar, declaring that it was quite enough to have to feed that fat, lazy pig without seeing him amusing himself, as if to annoy poor people who had to work hard all day long.

Celestin Maloisel and Cesaire Paumelle bent their heads to the storm, but Prosper Horslaville egged on the old woman, and was only amused at her wrath.

One day, when she was more angry than usual, he said:

"Do you know what I'd do if I were you?"

She fixed her owl's eyes on him, and waited for his next words.

Prosper went on:

"Your man is as hot as an oven, and he never leaves his bed—well, I'd make him hatch some eggs."

She was struck dumb at the suggestion, thinking that Prosper could not possibly be in earnest. But he continued:

"I'd put five under one arm, and five under the other, the same day that I set a hen. They'd all come out at the same time; then I'd take your husband's chickens to the hen to bring up with her own. You'd rear a fine lot that way."

"Could it be done?" asked the astonished old woman.

"Could it be done?" echoed the man. "Why not? Since eggs can be hatched in a warm box why shouldn't they be hatched in a warm bed?"

She was struck by this reasoning, and went away soothed and reflective.

A week later she entered Toine's room with her apron full of eggs, and said:

"I've just put the yellow hen on ten eggs. Here are ten for you; try not to break them."

"What do you want?" asked the amazed Toine.

"I want you to hatch them, you lazy creature!" she answered.

He laughed at first; then, finding she was serious, he got angry, and refused absolutely to have the eggs put under his great arms, that the warmth of his body might hatch them.

But the old woman declared wrathfully:

"You'll get no dinner as long as you won't have them. You'll see what'll happen."

Tome was uneasy, but answered nothing.

When twelve o'clock struck, he called out:

"Hullo, mother, is the soup ready?"

"There's no soup for you, lazy-bones," cried the old woman from her kitchen.

He thought she must be joking, and waited a while. Then he begged, implored, swore, "tacked to the north" and "tacked to the south," and beat on the wall with his fists, but had to consent at last to five eggs being placed against his left side; after which he had his soup.

When his friends arrived that afternoon they thought he must be ill, he seemed so constrained and queer.

They started the daily game of dominoes. But Tome appeared to take no pleasure in it, and reached forth his hand very slowly, and with great precaution.

"What's wrong with your arm?" asked Horslaville.

"I have a sort of stiffness in the shoulder," answered Toine.

Suddenly they heard people come into the inn. The players were silent.

It was the mayor with the deputy. They ordered two glasses of Extra-Special, and began to discuss local affairs. As they were talking in somewhat low tones Toine wanted to put his ear to the wall, and, forgetting all about his eggs, he made a sudden "tack to the north," which had the effect of plunging him into the midst of an omelette.

At the loud oath he swore his wife came hurrying into the room, and, guessing what had happened, stripped the bedclothes from him with lightning rapidity. She stood at first without moving or uttering a syllable, speechless with indignation at sight of the yellow poultice sticking to her husband's side.

Then, trembling with fury, she threw herself on the paralytic, showering on him blows such as those with which she cleaned her linen on the seashore. Tome's three friends were choking with laughter, coughing, spluttering and shouting, and the fat innkeeper himself warded his wife's attacks with all the prudence of which he was capable, that he might not also break the five eggs at his other side.

Tome was conquered. He had to hatch eggs, he had to give up his games of dominoes and renounce movement of any sort, for the old woman angrily deprived him of food whenever he broke an egg.

He lay on his back, with eyes fixed on the ceiling, motionless, his arms raised like wings, warming against his body the rudimentary chickens enclosed in their white shells.

He spoke now only in hushed tones; as if he feared a noise as much as motion, and he took a feverish interest in the yellow hen who was accomplishing in the poultry-yard the same task as he.

"Has the yellow hen eaten her food all right?" he would ask his wife.

And the old woman went from her fowls to her husband and from her husband to her fowls, devoured by anxiety as to the welfare of the little chickens who were maturing in the bed and in the nest.

The country people who knew the story came, agog with curiosity, to ask news of Toine. They entered his room on tiptoe, as one enters a sick-chamber, and asked:

"Well! how goes it?"

"All right," said Toine; "only it keeps me fearfully hot."

One morning his wife entered in a state of great excitement, and declared:

"The yellow hen has seven chickens! Three of the eggs were addled."

Toine's heart beat painfully. How many would he have?

"Will it soon be over?" he asked, with the anguish of a woman who is about to become a mother.

"It's to be hoped so!" answered the old woman crossly, haunted by fear of failure.

They waited. Friends of Toine who had got wind that his time was drawing near arrived, and filled the little room.

Nothing else was talked about in the neighboring cottages. Inquirers asked one another for news as they stood at their doors.

About three o'clock Toine fell asleep. He slumbered half his time nowadays. He was suddenly awakened by an unaccustomed tickling under his right arm. He put his left hand on the spot, and seized a little creature covered with yellow down, which fluttered in his hand.

His emotion was so great that he cried out, and let go his hold of the chicken, which ran over his chest. The bar was full of people at the time. The customers rushed to Toine's room, and made a circle round him as they would round a travelling showman; while Madame Toine picked up the chicken, which had taken refuge under her husband's beard.

No one spoke, so great was the tension. It was a warm April day. Outside the window the yellow hen could be heard calling to her newly-fledged brood.

Toine, who was perspiring with emotion and anxiety, murmured:

"I have another now—under the left arm."

His' wife plunged her great bony hand into the bed, and pulled out a second chicken with all the care of a midwife.

The neighbors wanted to see it. It was passed from one to another, and examined as if it were a phenomenon.

For twenty minutes no more hatched out, then four emerged at the same moment from their shells.

There was a great commotion among the lookers-on. And Toine smiled with satisfaction, beginning to take pride in this unusual sort of paternity. There were not many like him! Truly, he was a remarkable specimen of humanity!

"That makes six!" he declared. "Great heavens, what a christening we'll have!"

And a loud laugh rose from all present. Newcomers filled the bar. They asked one another:

"How many are there?"

"Six."

Toine's wife took this new family to the hen, who clucked loudly, bristled her feathers, and spread her wings wide to shelter her growing brood of little ones.

"There's one more!" cried Toine.

He was mistaken. There were three! It was an unalloyed triumph! The last chicken broke through its shell at seven o'clock in the evening. All the eggs were good! And Toine, beside himself with joy, his brood hatched out, exultant, kissed the tiny creature on the back, almost suffocating it. He wanted to keep it in his bed until morning, moved by a mother's tenderness toward the tiny being which he had brought to life, but the old woman carried it away like the others, turning a deaf ear to her husband's entreaties.

The delighted spectators went off to spread the news of the event, and Horslaville, who was the last to go, asked:

"You'll invite me when the first is cooked, won't you, Toine?"

At this idea a smile overspread the fat man's face, and he answered:

"Certainly I'll invite you, my son-in-law."

MADAME HUSSON'S "ROSIER"

We had just left Gisors, where I was awakened to hearing the name of the town called out by the guards, and I was dozing off again when a terrific shock threw me forward on top of a large lady who sat opposite me.

One of the wheels of the engine had broken, and the engine itself lay across the track. The tender and the baggage car were also derailed, and lay beside this mutilated engine, which rattled, groaned, hissed, puffed, sputtered, and resembled those horses that fall in the street with their flanks heaving, their breast palpitating, their nostrils steaming and their whole body trembling, but incapable of the slightest effort to rise and start off again.

There were no dead or wounded; only a few with bruises, for the train was not going at full speed. And we looked with sorrow at the great crippled iron creature that could not draw us along any more, and that blocked the track, perhaps for some time, for no doubt they would have to send to Paris for a special train to come to our aid.

It was then ten o'clock in the morning, and I at once decided to go back to Gisors for breakfast.

As I was walking along I said to myself:

"Gisors, Gisors—why, I know someone there!

"Who is it? Gisors? Let me see, I have a friend in this town." A name suddenly came to my mind, "Albert Marambot." He was an old school friend whom I had not seen for at least twelve years, and who was practicing medicine in Gisors. He had often written, inviting me to come and see him, and I had always promised to do so, without keeping my word. But at last I would take advantage of this opportunity.

I asked the first passer-by:

"Do you know where Dr. Marambot lives?"

He replied, without hesitation, and with the drawling accent of the Normans:

"Rue Dauphine."

I presently saw, on the door of the house he pointed out, a large brass plate on which was engraved the name of my old chum. I rang the bell, but the servant, a yellow-haired girl who moved slowly, said with a Stupid air:

"He isn't here, he isn't here."

I heard a sound of forks and of glasses and I cried:

"Hallo, Marambot!"

A door opened and a large man, with whiskers and a cross look on his face, appeared, carrying a dinner napkin in his hand.

I certainly should not have recognized him. One would have said he was forty-five at least, and, in a second, all the provincial life which makes one grow heavy, dull and old came before me. In a single flash of thought, quicker than the act of extending my hand to him, I could see his life, his manner of existence, his line of thought and his theories of things in general. I guessed at the prolonged meals that had rounded out his stomach, his after-dinner naps from the torpor of a slow indigestion aided by cognac, and his vague glances cast on the patient while he thought of the chicken that was roasting before the fire. His conversations about cooking, about cider, brandy and wine, the way of preparing certain dishes and of blending certain sauces were revealed to me at sight of his puffy red cheeks, his heavy lips and his lustreless eyes.

"You do not recognize me. I am Raoul Aubertin," I said.

He opened his arms and gave me such a hug that I thought he would choke me.

"You have not breakfasted, have you?"

"No."

"How fortunate! I was just sitting down to table and I have an excellent trout."

Five minutes later I was sitting opposite him at breakfast. I said:

"Are you a bachelor?"

"Yes, indeed."

"And do you like it here?"

"Time does not hang heavy; I am busy. I have patients and friends. I eat well, have good health, enjoy laughing and shooting. I get along."

"Is not life very monotonous in this little town?"

"No, my dear boy, not when one knows how to fill in the time. A little town, in fact, is like a large one. The incidents and amusements are less varied, but one makes more of them; one has fewer acquaintances, but one meets them more frequently. When you know all the windows in a street, each one of them interests you and puzzles you more than a whole street in Paris.

"A little town is very amusing, you know, very amusing, very amusing. Why, take Gisors. I know it at the tips of my fingers, from its beginning up to the present time. You have no idea what queer history it has."

"Do you belong to Gisors?"

"I? No. I come from Gournay, its neighbor and rival. Gournay is to Gisors what Lucullus was to Cicero. Here, everything is for glory; they say 'the proud people of Gisors.' At Gournay, everything is for the stomach; they say 'the chewers of Gournay.' Gisors despises Gournay, but Gournay laughs at Gisors. It is a very comical country, this."

I perceived that I was eating something very delicious, hard-boiled eggs wrapped in a covering of meat jelly flavored with herbs and put on ice for a few moments. I said as I smacked my lips to compliment Marambot:

"That is good."

He smiled.

"Two things are necessary, good jelly, which is hard to get, and good eggs. Oh, how rare good eggs are, with the yolks slightly reddish, and with a good flavor! I have two poultry yards, one for eggs and the other for chickens. I feed my laying hens in a special manner. I have my own ideas on the subject. In an egg, as in the meat of a chicken, in beef, or in mutton, in milk, in everything, one perceives, and ought to taste, the juice, the quintessence of all the food on which the animal has fed. How much better food we could have if more attention were paid to this!"

I laughed as I said:

"You are a gourmand?"

"Parbleu. It is only imbeciles who are not. One is a gourmand as one is an artist, as one is learned, as one is a poet. The sense of taste, my friend, is very delicate, capable of perfection, and quite as worthy of respect as the eye and the ear. A person who lacks this sense is deprived of an exquisite faculty, the faculty of discerning the quality of food, just as one may lack the faculty of discerning the beauties of a book or of a work of art; it means to be deprived of an essential organ, of something that belongs to higher humanity; it means to belong to one of those innumerable classes of the infirm, the unfortunate, and the fools of which our race is composed; it means to have the mouth of an animal, in a word, just like the mind of an animal. A man who cannot distinguish one kind of lobster from another; a herring—that admirable fish that has all the flavors, all the odors of the sea—from a mackerel or a whiting; and a Cresane from a Duchess pear, may be compared to a man who should mistake Balzac for Eugene Sue; a symphony of Beethoven for a military march composed by the bandmaster of a regiment; and the Apollo Belvidere for the statue of General de Blaumont.

"Who is General de Blaumont?"

"Oh, that's true, you do not know. It is easy to tell that you do not belong to Gisors. I told you just now, my dear boy, that they called the inhabitants of this town 'the proud people of Gisors,' and never was an epithet better deserved. But let us finish breakfast first, and then I will tell you about our town and take you to see it."

He stopped talking every now and then while he slowly drank a glass of wine which he gazed at affectionately as he replaced the glass on the table.

It was amusing to see him, with a napkin tied around his neck, his cheeks flushed, his eyes eager, and his whiskers spreading round his mouth as it kept working.

He made me eat until I was almost choking. Then, as I was about to return to the railway station, he seized me by the arm and took me through the streets. The town, of a pretty, provincial type, commanded by its citadel, the most curious monument of military architecture of the seventh century to be found in France, overlooks, in its turn, a long, green valley, where the large Norman cows graze and ruminate in the pastures.

The doctor quoted:

"'Gisors, a town of 4,000 inhabitants in the department of Eure, mentioned in Caesar's Commentaries: Caesaris ostium, then Caesartium, Caesortium, Gisortium, Gisors.' I shall not take you to visit the old Roman encampment, the remains of which are still in existence."

I laughed and replied:

"My dear friend, it seems to me that you are affected with a special malady that, as a doctor, you ought to study; it is called the spirit of provincialism."

He stopped abruptly.

"The spirit of provincialism, my friend, is nothing but natural patriotism," he said. "I love my house, my town and my province because I discover in them the customs of my own village; but if I love my country, if I become angry when a neighbor sets foot in it, it is because I feel that my home is in danger, because the frontier that I do not know is the high road to my province. For instance, I am a Norman, a true Norman; well, in spite of my hatred of the German and my desire for revenge, I do not detest them, I do not hate them by instinct as I hate the English, the real, hereditary natural enemy of the Normans; for the English traversed this soil inhabited by my ancestors, plundered and ravaged it twenty times, and my aversion to this perfidious people was transmitted to me at birth by my father. See, here is the statue of the general."

"What general?"

"General Blaumont! We had to have a statue. We are not 'the proud people of Gisors' for nothing! So we discovered General de Blaumont. Look in this bookseller's window."

He drew me towards the bookstore, where about fifteen red, yellow and blue volumes attracted the eye. As I read the titles, I began to laugh idiotically. They read:

Gisors, its origin, its future, by M. X… ., member of several learned societies; History of Gisors, by the Abbe A…; Gisors from the time of Caesar to the present day, by M. B… ., Landowner; Gisors and its environs, by Doctor C. D… .; The Glories of Gisors, by a Discoverer.

"My friend," resumed Marambot, "not a year, not a single year, you understand, passes without a fresh history of Gisors being published here; we now have twenty-three."

"And the glories of Gisors?" I asked.

"Oh, I will not mention them all, only the principal ones. We had first General de Blaumont, then Baron Davillier, the celebrated ceramist who explored Spain and the Balearic Isles, and brought to the notice of collectors the wonderful Hispano-Arabic china. In literature we have a very clever journalist, now dead, Charles Brainne, and among those who are living, the very eminent editor of the Nouvelliste de Rouen, Charles Lapierre ... and many others, many others."

We were traversing along street with a gentle incline, with a June sun beating down on it and driving the residents into their houses.

Suddenly there appeared at the farther end of the street a drunken man who was staggering along, with his head forward his arms and legs limp. He would walk forward rapidly three, six, or ten steps and then stop. When these energetic movements landed him in the middle of the road he stopped short and swayed on his feet, hesitating between falling and a fresh start. Then he would dart off in any direction, sometimes falling against the wall of a house, against which he seemed to be fastened, as though he were trying to get in through the wall. Then he would suddenly turn round and look ahead of him, his mouth open and his eyes blinking in the sunlight, and getting away from the wall by a movement of the hips, he started off once more.

A little yellow dog, a half-starved cur, followed him, barking; stopping when he stopped, and starting off when he started.

"Hallo," said Marambot, "there is Madame Husson's 'Rosier'.

"Madame Husson's 'Rosier'," I exclaimed in astonishment. "What do you mean?"

The doctor began to laugh.

"Oh, that is what we call drunkards round here. The name comes from an old story which has now become a legend, although it is true in all respects."

"Is it an amusing story?"

"Very amusing."

"Well, then, tell it to me."

"I will."

There lived formerly in this town a very upright old lady who was a great guardian of morals and was called Mme. Husson. You know, I am telling you the real names and not imaginary ones.

Mme. Husson took a special interest in good works, in helping the poor and encouraging the deserving. She was a little woman with a quick walk and wore a black wig. She was ceremonious, polite, on very good terms with the Almighty in the person of Abby Malon, and had a profound horror, an inborn horror of vice, and, in particular, of the vice the Church calls lasciviousness. Any irregularity before marriage made her furious, exasperated her till she was beside herself.

Now, this was the period when they presented a prize as a reward of virtue to any girl in the environs of Paris who was found to be chaste. She was called a Rosiere, and Mme. Husson got the idea that she would institute a similar ceremony at Gisors. She spoke about it to Abbe Malon, who at once made out a list of candidates.

However, Mme. Husson had a servant, an old woman called Francoise, as upright as her mistress. As soon as the priest had left, madame called the servant and said:

"Here, Francoise, here are the girls whose names M. le cure has submitted to me for the prize of virtue; try and find out what reputation they bear in the district."

And Francoise set out. She collected all the scandal, all the stories, all the tattle, all the suspicions. That she might omit nothing, she wrote it all down together with her memoranda in her housekeeping book, and handed it each morning to Mme. Husson, who, after adjusting her spectacles on her thin nose, read as follows:

Bread...........................four sous

Milk............................two sous

Butter ....eight sous

Malvina Levesque got into trouble last year with Mathurin Poilu.

Leg of mutton...................twenty-five sous

Salt............................one sou

Rosalie Vatinel was seen in the Riboudet woods with Cesaire Pienoir, by

Mme. Onesime, the ironer, on July the 20th about dusk.

Radishes........................one sou

Vinegar..........................two sous

Oxalic acid......................two sous

Josephine Durdent, who is not believed to have committed a fault, although she corresponds with young Oportun, who is in service in Rouen, and who sent her a present of a cap by diligence.

Not one came out unscathed in this rigorous inquisition. Francoise inquired of everyone, neighbors, drapers, the principal, the teaching sisters at school, and gathered the slightest details.

As there is not a girl in the world about whom gossips have not found something to say, there was not found in all the countryside one young girl whose name was free from some scandal.

But Mme. Husson desired that the "Rosiere" of Gisors, like Caesar's wife, should be above suspicion, and she was horrified, saddened and in despair at the record in her servant's housekeeping account-book.

They then extended their circle of inquiries to the neighboring villages; but with no satisfaction.

They consulted the mayor. His candidates failed. Those of Dr. Barbesol were equally unlucky, in spite of the exactness of his scientific vouchers.

But one morning Francoise, on returning from one of her expeditions, said to her mistress:

"You see, madame, that if you wish to give a prize to anyone, there is only Isidore in all the country round."

Mme. Husson remained thoughtful. She knew him well, this Isidore, the son of Virginie the greengrocer. His proverbial virtue had been the delight of Gisors for several years, and served as an entertaining theme of conversation in the town, and of amusement to the young girls who loved to tease him. He was past twenty-one, was tall, awkward, slow and timid; helped his mother in the business, and spent his days picking over fruit and vegetables, seated on a chair outside the door.

He had an abnormal dread of a petticoat and cast down his eyes whenever a female customer looked at him smilingly, and this well-known timidity made him the butt of all the wags in the country.

Bold words, coarse expressions, indecent allusions, brought the color to his cheeks so quickly that Dr. Barbesol had nicknamed him "the thermometer of modesty." Was he as innocent as he looked? ill-natured people asked themselves. Was it the mere presentiment of unknown and shameful mysteries or else indignation at the relations ordained as the concomitant of love that so strongly affected the son of Virginie the greengrocer? The urchins of the neighborhood as they ran past the shop would fling disgusting remarks at him just to see him cast down his eyes. The girls amused themselves by walking up and down before him, cracking jokes that made him go into the store. The boldest among them teased him to his face just to have a laugh, to amuse themselves, made appointments with him and proposed all sorts of things.

So Madame Husson had become thoughtful.

Certainly, Isidore was an exceptional case of notorious, unassailable virtue. No one, among the most sceptical, most incredulous, would have been able, would have dared, to suspect Isidore of the slightest infraction of any law of morality. He had never been seen in a cafe, never been seen at night on the street. He went to bed at eight o'clock and rose at four. He was a perfection, a pearl.

But Mme. Husson still hesitated. The idea of substituting a boy for a girl, a "rosier" for a "rosiere," troubled her, worried her a little, and she resolved to consult Abbe Malon.

The abbe responded:

"What do you desire to reward, madame? It is virtue, is it not, and nothing but virtue? What does it matter to you, therefore, if it is masculine or feminine? Virtue is eternal; it has neither sex nor country; it is 'Virtue.'"

Thus encouraged, Mme. Husson went to see the mayor.

He approved heartily.

"We will have a fine ceremony," he said. "And another year if we can find a girl as worthy as Isidore we will give the reward to her. It will even be a good example that we shall set to Nanterre. Let us not be exclusive; let us welcome all merit."

Isidore, who had been told about this, blushed deeply and seemed happy.

The ceremony was fixed for the 15th of August, the festival of the Virgin Mary and of the Emperor Napoleon. The municipality had decided to make an imposing ceremony and had built the platform on the couronneaux, a delightful extension of the ramparts of the old citadel where I will take you presently.

With the natural revulsion of public feeling, the virtue of Isidore, ridiculed hitherto, had suddenly become respected and envied, as it would bring him in five hundred francs besides a savings bank book, a mountain of consideration, and glory enough and to spare. The girls now regretted their frivolity, their ridicule, their bold manners; and Isidore, although still modest and timid, had now a little contented air that bespoke his internal satisfaction.

The evening before the 15th of August the entire Rue Dauphine was decorated with flags. Oh, I forgot to tell you why this street had been called Rue Dauphine.

It seems that the wife or mother of the dauphin, I do not remember which one, while visiting Gisors had been feted so much by the authorities that during a triumphal procession through the town she stopped before one of the houses in this street, halting the procession, and exclaimed:

"Oh, the pretty house! How I should like to go through it! To whom does it belong?"

They told her the name of the owner, who was sent for and brought, proud and embarrassed, before the princess. She alighted from her carriage, went into the house, wishing to go over it from top to bottom, and even shut herself in one of the rooms alone for a few seconds.

When she came out, the people, flattered at this honor paid to a citizen of Gisors, shouted "Long live the dauphine!" But a rhymester wrote some words to a refrain, and the street retained the title of her royal highness, for

"The princess, in a hurry,
Without bell, priest, or beadle,
But with some water only,
Had baptized it."

But to come back to Isidore.

They had scattered flowers all along the road as they do for processions at the Fete-Dieu, and the National Guard was present, acting on the orders of their chief, Commandant Desbarres, an old soldier of the Grand Army, who pointed with pride to the beard of a Cossack cut with a single sword stroke from the chin of its owner by the commandant during the retreat in Russia, and which hung beside the frame containing the cross of the Legion of Honor presented to him by the emperor himself.

The regiment that he commanded was, besides, a picked regiment celebrated all through the province, and the company of grenadiers of Gisors was called on to attend all important ceremonies for a distance of fifteen to twenty leagues. The story goes that Louis Philippe, while reviewing the militia of Eure, stopped in astonishment before the company from Gisors, exclaiming:

"Oh, who are those splendid grenadiers?"

"The grenadiers of Gisors," replied the general.

"I might have known it," murmured the king.

So Commandant Desbarres came at the head of his men, preceded by the band, to get Isidore in his mother's store.

After a little air had been played by the band beneath the windows, the "Rosier" himself appeared—on the threshold. He was dressed in white duck from head to foot and wore a straw hat with a little bunch of orange blossoms as a cockade.

The question of his clothes had bothered Mme. Husson a good deal, and she hesitated some time between the black coat of those who make their first communion and an entire white suit. But Francoise, her counsellor, induced her to decide on the white suit, pointing out that the Rosier would look like a swan.

Behind him came his guardian, his godmother, Mme. Husson, in triumph. She took his arm to go out of the store, and the mayor placed himself on the other side of the Rosier. The drums beat. Commandant Desbarres gave the order "Present arms!" The procession resumed its march towards the church amid an immense crowd of people who has gathered from the neighboring districts.

After a short mass and an affecting discourse by Abbe Malon, they continued on their way to the couronneaux, where the banquet was served in a tent.

Before taking their seats at table, the mayor gave an address. This is it, word for word. I learned it by heart:

"Young man, a woman of means, beloved by the poor and respected by the rich, Mme. Husson, whom the whole country is thanking here, through me, had the idea, the happy and benevolent idea, of founding in this town a prize for virtue, which should serve as a valuable encouragement to the inhabitants of this beautiful country.

"You, young man, are the first to be rewarded in this dynasty of goodness and chastity. Your name will remain at the head of this list of the most deserving, and your life, understand me, your whole life, must correspond to this happy commencement. To-day, in presence of this noble woman, of these soldier-citizens who have taken up their arms in your honor, in presence of this populace, affected, assembled to applaud you, or, rather, to applaud virtue, in your person, you make a solemn contract with the town, with all of us, to continue until your death the excellent example of your youth.

"Do not forget, young man, that you are the first seed cast into this field of hope; give us the fruits that we expect of you."

The mayor advanced three steps, opened his arms and pressed Isidore to his heart.

The "Rosier" was sobbing without knowing why, from a confused emotion, from pride and a vague and happy feeling of tenderness.

Then the mayor placed in one hand a silk purse in which gold tingled—five hundred francs in gold!—and in his other hand a savings bank book. And he said in a solemn tone:

"Homage, glory and riches to virtue."

Commandant Desbarres shouted "Bravo!" the grenadiers vociferated, and the crowd applauded.

Mme. Husson wiped her eyes, in her turn. Then they all sat down at the table where the banquet was served.

The repast was magnificent and seemed interminable. One course followed another; yellow cider and red wine in fraternal contact blended in the stomach of the guests. The rattle of plates, the sound of voices, and of music softly played, made an incessant deep hum, and was dispersed abroad in the clear sky where the swallows were flying. Mme. Husson occasionally readjusted her black wig, which would slip over on one side, and chatted with Abbe Malon. The mayor, who was excited, talked politics with Commandant Desbarres, and Isidore ate, drank, as if he had never eaten or drunk before. He helped himself repeatedly to all the dishes, becoming aware for the first time of the pleasure of having one's belly full of good things which tickle the palate in the first place. He had let out a reef in his belt and, without speaking, and although he was a little uneasy at a wine stain on his white waistcoat, he ceased eating in order to take up his glass and hold it to his mouth as long as possible, to enjoy the taste slowly.

It was time for the toasts. They were many and loudly applauded. Evening was approaching and they had been at the table since noon. Fine, milky vapors were already floating in the air in the valley, the light night-robe of streams and meadows; the sun neared the horizon; the cows were lowing in the distance amid the mists of the pasture. The feast was over. They returned to Gisors. The procession, now disbanded, walked in detachments. Mme. Husson had taken Isidore's arm and was giving him a quantity of urgent, excellent advice.

They stopped at the door of the fruit store, and the "Rosier" was left at his mother's house. She had not come home yet. Having been invited by her family to celebrate her son's triumph, she had taken luncheon with her sister after having followed the procession as far as the banqueting tent.

So Isidore remained alone in the store, which was growing dark. He sat down on a chair, excited by the wine and by pride, and looked about him. Carrots, cabbages, and onions gave out their strong odor of vegetables in the closed room, that coarse smell of the garden blended with the sweet, penetrating odor of strawberries and the delicate, slight, evanescent fragrance of a basket of peaches.

The "Rosier" took one of these and ate it, although he was as full as an egg. Then, all at once, wild with joy, he began to dance about the store, and something rattled in his waistcoat.

He was surprised, and put his hand in his pocket and brought out the purse containing the five hundred francs, which he had forgotten in his agitation. Five hundred francs! What a fortune! He poured the gold pieces out on the counter and spread them out with his big hand with a slow, caressing touch so as to see them all at the same time. There were twenty-five, twenty-five round gold pieces, all gold! They glistened on the wood in the dim light and he counted them over and over, one by one. Then he put them back in the purse, which he replaced in his pocket.

Who will ever know or who can tell what a terrible conflict took place in the soul of the "Rosier" between good and evil, the tumultuous attack of Satan, his artifices, the temptations which he offered to this timid virgin heart? What suggestions, what imaginations, what desires were not invented by the evil one to excite and destroy this chosen one? He seized his hat, Mme. Husson's saint, his hat, which still bore the little bunch of orange blossoms, and going out through the alley at the back of the house, he disappeared in the darkness.

Virginie, the fruiterer, on learning that her son had returned, went home at once, and found the house empty. She waited, without thinking anything about it at first; but at the end of a quarter of an hour she made inquiries. The neighbors had seen Isidore come home and had not seen him go out again. They began to look for him, but could not find him. His mother, in alarm, went to the mayor. The mayor knew nothing, except that he had left him at the door of his home. Mme. Husson had just retired when they informed her that her protege had disappeared. She immediately put on her wig, dressed herself and went to Virginie's house. Virginie, whose plebeian soul was readily moved, was weeping copiously amid her cabbages, carrots and onions.

They feared some accident had befallen him. What could it be? Commandant Desbarres notified the police, who made a circuit of the town, and on the high road to Pontoise they found the little bunch of orange blossoms. It was placed on a table around which the authorities were deliberating. The "Rosier" must have been the victim of some stratagem, some trick, some jealousy; but in what way? What means had been employed to kidnap this innocent creature, and with what object?

Weary of looking for him without any result, Virginie, alone, remained watching and weeping.

The following evening, when the coach passed by on its return from Paris, Gisors learned with astonishment that its "Rosier" had stopped the vehicle at a distance of about two hundred metres from the town, had climbed up on it and paid his fare, handing over a gold piece and receiving the change, and that he had quietly alighted in the centre of the great city.

There was great excitement all through the countryside. Letters passed between the mayor and the chief of police in Paris, but brought no result.

The days followed one another, a week passed.

Now, one morning, Dr. Barbesol, who had gone out early, perceived, sitting on a doorstep, a man dressed in a grimy linen suit, who was sleeping with his head leaning against the wall. He approached him and recognized Isidore. He tried to rouse him, but did not succeed in doing so. The ex-"Rosier" was in that profound, invincible sleep that is alarming, and the doctor, in surprise, went to seek assistance to help him in carrying the young man to Boncheval's drugstore. When they lifted him up they found an empty bottle under him, and when the doctor sniffed at it, he declared that it had contained brandy. That gave a suggestion as to what treatment he would require. They succeeded in rousing him.

Isidore was drunk, drunk and degraded by a week of guzzling, drunk and so disgusting that a ragman would not have touched him. His beautiful white duck suit was a gray rag, greasy, muddy, torn, and destroyed, and he smelt of the gutter and of vice.

He was washed, sermonized, shut up, and did not leave the house for four days. He seemed ashamed and repentant. They could not find on him either his purse, containing the five hundred francs, or the bankbook, or even his silver watch, a sacred heirloom left by his father, the fruiterer.

On the fifth day he ventured into the Rue Dauphine, Curious glances followed him and he walked along with a furtive expression in his eyes and his head bent down. As he got outside the town towards the valley they lost sight of him; but two hours later he returned laughing and rolling against the walls. He was drunk, absolutely drunk.

Nothing could cure him.

Driven from home by his mother, he became a wagon driver, and drove the charcoal wagons for the Pougrisel firm, which is still in existence.

His reputation as a drunkard became so well known and spread so far that even at Evreux they talked of Mme. Husson's "Rosier," and the sots of the countryside have been given that nickname.

A good deed is never lost.

Dr. Marambot rubbed his hands as he finished his story. I asked:

"Did you know the 'Rosier'?"

"Yes. I had the honor of closing his eyes."

"What did he die of?"

"An attack of delirium tremens, of course."

We had arrived at the old citadel, a pile of ruined walls dominated by the enormous tower of St. Thomas of Canterbury and the one called the Prisoner's Tower.

Marambot told me the story of this prisoner, who, with the aid of a nail, covered the walls of his dungeon with sculptures, tracing the reflections of the sun as it glanced through the narrow slit of a loophole.

I also learned that Clothaire II had given the patrimony of Gisors to his cousin, Saint Romain, bishop of Rouen; that Gisors ceased to be the capital of the whole of Vexin after the treaty of Saint-Clair-sur-Epte; that the town is the chief strategic centre of all that portion of France, and that in consequence of this advantage she was taken and retaken over and over again. At the command of William the Red, the eminent engineer, Robert de Bellesme, constructed there a powerful fortress that was attacked later by Louis le Gros, then by the Norman barons, was defended by Robert de Candos, was finally ceded to Louis le Gros by Geoffry Plantagenet, was retaken by the English in consequence of the treachery of the Knights-Templars, was contested by Philippe-Augustus and Richard the Lionhearted, was set on fire by Edward III of England, who could not take the castle, was again taken by the English in 1419, restored later to Charles VIII by Richard de Marbury, was taken by the Duke of Calabria occupied by the League, inhabited by Henry IV, etc., etc.

And Marambot, eager and almost eloquent, continued:

"What beggars, those English! And what sots, my boy; they are all 'Rosiers,' those hypocrites!"

Then, after a silence, stretching out his arm towards the tiny river that glistened in the meadows, he said.

"Did you know that Henry Monnier was one of the most untiring fishermen on the banks of the Epte?"

"No, I did not know it."

"And Bouffe, my boy, Bouffe was a painter on glass."

"You are joking!"

"No, indeed. How is it you do not know these things?"

THE ADOPTED SON

The two cottages stood beside each other at the foot of a hill near a little seashore resort. The two peasants labored hard on the unproductive soil to rear their little ones, and each family had four.

Before the adjoining doors a whole troop of urchins played and tumbled about from morning till night. The two eldest were six years old, and the youngest were about fifteen months; the marriages, and afterward the births, having taken place nearly simultaneously in both families.

The two mothers could hardly distinguish their own offspring among the lot, and as for the fathers, they were altogether at sea. The eight names danced in their heads; they were always getting them mixed up; and when they wished to call one child, the men often called three names before getting the right one.

The first of the two cottages, as you came up from the bathing beach, Rolleport, was occupied by the Tuvaches, who had three girls and one boy; the other house sheltered the Vallins, who had one girl and three boys.

They all subsisted frugally on soup, potatoes and fresh air. At seven o'clock in the morning, then at noon, then at six o'clock in the evening, the housewives got their broods together to give them their food, as the gooseherds collect their charges. The children were seated, according to age, before the wooden table, varnished by fifty years of use; the mouths of the youngest hardly reaching the level of the table. Before them was placed a bowl filled with bread, soaked in the water in which the potatoes had been boiled, half a cabbage and three onions; and the whole line ate until their hunger was appeased. The mother herself fed the smallest.

A small pot roast on Sunday was a feast for all; and the father on this day sat longer over the meal, repeating: "I wish we could have this every day."

One afternoon, in the month of August, a phaeton stopped suddenly in front of the cottages, and a young woman, who was driving the horses, said to the gentleman sitting at her side:

"Oh, look at all those children, Henri! How pretty they are, tumbling about in the dust, like that!"

The man did not answer, accustomed to these outbursts of admiration, which were a pain and almost a reproach to him. The young woman continued:

"I must hug them! Oh, how I should like to have one of them—that one there—the little tiny one!"

Springing down from the carriage, she ran toward the children, took one of the two youngest—a Tuvache child—and lifting it up in her arms, she kissed him passionately on his dirty cheeks, on his tousled hair daubed with earth, and on his little hands, with which he fought vigorously, to get away from the caresses which displeased him.

Then she got into the carriage again, and drove off at a lively trot. But she returned the following week, and seating herself on the ground, took the youngster in her arms, stuffed him with cakes; gave candies to all the others, and played with them like a young girl, while the husband waited patiently in the carriage.

She returned again; made the acquaintance of the parents, and reappeared every day with her pockets full of dainties and pennies.

Her name was Madame Henri d'Hubieres.

One morning, on arriving, her husband alighted with her, and without stopping to talk to the children, who now knew her well, she entered the farmer's cottage.

They were busy chopping wood for the fire. They rose to their feet in surprise, brought forward chairs, and waited expectantly.

Then the woman, in a broken, trembling voice, began:

"My good people, I have come to see you, because I should like—I should like to take—your little boy with me—"

The country people, too bewildered to think, did not answer.

She recovered her breath, and continued: "We are alone, my husband and I. We would keep it. Are you willing?"

The peasant woman began to understand. She asked:

"You want to take Charlot from us? Oh, no, indeed!"

Then M. d'Hubieres intervened:

"My wife has not made her meaning clear. We wish to adopt him, but he will come back to see you. If he turns out well, as there is every reason to expect, he will be our heir. If we, perchance, should have children, he will share equally with them; but if he should not reward our care, we should give him, when he comes of age, a sum of twenty thousand francs, which shall be deposited immediately in his name, with a lawyer. As we have thought also of you, we should pay you, until your death, a pension of one hundred francs a month. Do you understand me?"

The woman had arisen, furious.

"You want me to sell you Charlot? Oh, no, that's not the sort of thing to ask of a mother! Oh, no! That would be an abomination!"

The man, grave and deliberate, said nothing; but approved of what his wife said by a continued nodding of his head.

Madame d'Hubieres, in dismay, began to weep; turning to her husband, with a voice full of tears, the voice of a child used to having all its wishes gratified, she stammered:

"They will not do it, Henri, they will not do it."

Then he made a last attempt: "But, my friends, think of the child's future, of his happiness, of—"

The peasant woman, however, exasperated, cut him short:

"It's all considered! It's all understood! Get out of here, and don't let me see you again—the idea of wanting to take away a child like that!"

Madame d'Hubieres remembered that there were two children, quite little, and she asked, through her tears, with the tenacity of a wilful and spoiled woman:

"But is the other little one not yours?"

Father Tuvache answered: "No, it is our neighbors'. You can go to them if you wish." And he went back into his house, whence resounded the indignant voice of his wife.

The Vallins were at table, slowly eating slices of bread which they parsimoniously spread with a little rancid butter on a plate between the two.

M. d'Hubieres recommenced his proposals, but with more insinuations, more oratorical precautions, more shrewdness.

The two country people shook their heads, in sign of refusal, but when they learned that they were to have a hundred francs a month, they considered the matter, consulting one another by glances, much disturbed. They kept silent for a long time, tortured, hesitating. At last the woman asked: "What do you say to it, man?" In a weighty tone he said: "I say that it's not to be despised."

Madame d'Hubieres, trembling with anguish, spoke of the future of their child, of his happiness, and of the money which he could give them later.

The peasant asked: "This pension of twelve hundred francs, will it be promised before a lawyer?"

M. d'Hubieres responded: "Why, certainly, beginning with to-morrow."

The woman, who was thinking it over, continued:

"A hundred francs a month is not enough to pay for depriving us of the child. That child would be working in a few years; we must have a hundred and twenty francs."

Tapping her foot with impatience, Madame d'Hubieres granted it at once, and, as she wished to carry off the child with her, she gave a hundred francs extra, as a present, while her husband drew up a paper. And the young woman, radiant, carried off the howling brat, as one carries away a wished-for knick-knack from a shop.

The Tuvaches, from their door, watched her departure, silent, serious, perhaps regretting their refusal.

Nothing more was heard of little Jean Vallin. The parents went to the lawyer every month to collect their hundred and twenty francs. They had quarrelled with their neighbors, because Mother Tuvache grossly insulted them, continually, repeating from door to door that one must be unnatural to sell one's child; that it was horrible, disgusting, bribery. Sometimes she would take her Charlot in her arms, ostentatiously exclaiming, as if he understood:

"I didn't sell you, I didn't! I didn't sell you, my little one! I'm not rich, but I don't sell my children!"

The Vallins lived comfortably, thanks to the pension. That was the cause of the unappeasable fury of the Tuvaches, who had remained miserably poor. Their eldest went away to serve his time in the army; Charlot alone remained to labor with his old father, to support the mother and two younger sisters.

He had reached twenty-one years when, one morning, a brilliant carriage stopped before the two cottages. A young gentleman, with a gold watch-chain, got out, giving his hand to an aged, white-haired lady. The old lady said to him: "It is there, my child, at the second house." And he entered the house of the Vallins as though at home.

The old mother was washing her aprons; the infirm father slumbered at the chimney-corner. Both raised their heads, and the young man said:

"Good-morning, papa; good-morning, mamma!"

They both stood up, frightened! In a flutter, the peasant woman dropped her soap into the water, and stammered:

"Is it you, my child? Is it you, my child?"

He took her in his arms and hugged her, repeating: "Good-morning, mamma," while the old man, all a-tremble, said, in his calm tone which he never lost: "Here you are, back again, Jean," as if he had just seen him a month ago.

When they had got to know one another again, the parents wished to take their boy out in the neighborhood, and show him. They took him to the mayor, to the deputy, to the cure, and to the schoolmaster.

Charlot, standing on the threshold of his cottage, watched him pass. In the evening, at supper, he said to the old people: "You must have been stupid to let the Vallins' boy be taken."

The mother answered, obstinately: "I wouldn't sell my child."

The father remained silent. The son continued:

"It is unfortunate to be sacrificed like that."

Then Father Tuvache, in an angry tone, said:

"Are you going to reproach us for having kept you?" And the young man said, brutally:

"Yes, I reproach you for having been such fools. Parents like you make the misfortune of their children. You deserve that I should leave you." The old woman wept over her plate. She moaned, as she swallowed the spoonfuls of soup, half of which she spilled: "One may kill one's self to bring up children!"

Then the boy said, roughly: "I'd rather not have been born than be what I am. When I saw the other, my heart stood still. I said to myself: 'See what I should have been now!'" He got up: "See here, I feel that I would do better not to stay here, because I would throw it up to you from morning till night, and I would make your life miserable. I'll never forgive you for that!"

The two old people were silent, downcast, in tears.

He continued: "No, the thought of that would be too much. I'd rather look for a living somewhere else."

He opened the door. A sound of voices came in at the door. The Vallins were celebrating the return of their child.

COWARD

In society he was called "Handsome Signoles." His name was Vicomte Gontran-Joseph de Signoles.

An orphan, and possessed of an ample fortune, he cut quite a dash, as it is called. He had an attractive appearance and manner, could talk well, had a certain inborn elegance, an air of pride and nobility, a good mustache, and a tender eye, that always finds favor with women.

He was in great request at receptions, waltzed to perfection, and was regarded by his own sex with that smiling hostility accorded to the popular society man. He had been suspected of more than one love affair, calculated to enhance the reputation of a bachelor. He lived a happy, peaceful life—a life of physical and mental well-being. He had won considerable fame as a swordsman, and still more as a marksman.

"When the time comes for me to fight a duel," he said, "I shall choose pistols. With such a weapon I am sure to kill my man."

One evening, having accompanied two women friends of his with their husbands to the theatre, he invited them to take some ice cream at Tortoni's after the performance. They had been seated a few minutes in the restaurant when Signoles noticed that a man was staring persistently at one of the ladies. She seemed annoyed, and lowered her eyes. At last she said to her husband:

"There's a man over there looking at me. I don't know him; do you?"

The husband, who had noticed nothing, glanced across at the offender, and said:

"No; not in the least."

His wife continued, half smiling, half angry:

"It's very tiresome! He quite spoils my ice cream."

The husband shrugged his shoulders.

"Nonsense! Don't take any notice of him. If we were to bother our heads about all the ill-mannered people we should have no time for anything else."

But the vicomte abruptly left his seat. He could not allow this insolent fellow to spoil an ice for a guest of his. It was for him to take cognizance of the offence, since it was through him that his friends had come to the restaurant. He went across to the man and said:

"Sir, you are staring at those ladies in a manner I cannot permit. I must ask you to desist from your rudeness."

The other replied:

"Let me alone, will you!"

"Take care, sir," said the vicomte between his teeth, "or you will force me to extreme measures."

The man replied with a single word—a foul word, which could be heard from one end of the restaurant to the other, and which startled every one there. All those whose backs were toward the two disputants turned round; all the others raised their heads; three waiters spun round on their heels like tops; the two lady cashiers jumped, as if shot, then turned their bodies simultaneously, like two automata worked by the same spring.

There was dead silence. Then suddenly a sharp, crisp sound. The vicomte had slapped his adversary's face. Every one rose to interfere. Cards were exchanged.

When the vicomte reached home he walked rapidly up and down his room for some minutes. He was in a state of too great agitation to think connectedly. One idea alone possessed him: a duel. But this idea aroused in him as yet no emotion of any kind. He had done what he was bound to do; he had proved himself to be what he ought to be. He would be talked about, approved, congratulated. He repeated aloud, speaking as one does when under the stress of great mental disturbance:

"What a brute of a man!" Then he sat down, and began to reflect. He would have to find seconds as soon as morning came. Whom should he choose? He bethought himself of the most influential and best-known men of his acquaintance. His choice fell at last on the Marquis de la Tour-Noire and Colonel Bourdin-a nobleman and a soldier. That would be just the thing. Their names would carry weight in the newspapers. He was thirsty, and drank three glasses of water, one after another; then he walked up and down again. If he showed himself brave, determined, prepared to face a duel in deadly earnest, his adversary would probably draw back and proffer excuses. He picked up the card he had taken from his pocket and thrown on a table. He read it again, as he had already read it, first at a glance in the restaurant, and afterward on the way home in the light of each gas lamp: "Georges Lamil, 51 Rue Moncey." That was all.

He examined closely this collection of letters, which seemed to him mysterious, fraught with many meanings. Georges Lamil! Who was the man? What was his profession? Why had he stared so at the woman? Was it not monstrous that a stranger, an unknown, should thus all at once upset one's whole life, simply because it had pleased him to stare rudely at a woman? And the vicomte once more repeated aloud:

"What a brute!"

Then he stood motionless, thinking, his eyes still fixed on the card. Anger rose in his heart against this scrap of paper—a resentful anger, mingled with a strange sense of uneasiness. It was a stupid business altogether! He took up a penknife which lay open within reach, and deliberately stuck it into the middle of the printed name, as if he were stabbing some one.

So he would have to fight! Should he choose swords or pistols?—for he considered himself as the insulted party. With the sword he would risk less, but with the pistol there was some chance of his adversary backing out. A duel with swords is rarely fatal, since mutual prudence prevents the combatants from fighting close enough to each other for a point to enter very deep. With pistols he would seriously risk his life; but, on the other hand, he might come out of the affair with flying colors, and without a duel, after all.

"I must be firm," he said. "The fellow will be afraid."

The sound of his own voice startled him, and he looked nervously round the room. He felt unstrung. He drank another glass of water, and then began undressing, preparatory to going to bed.

As soon as he was in bed he blew out the light and shut his eyes.

"I have all day to-morrow," he reflected, "for setting my affairs in order. I must sleep now, in order to be calm when the time comes."

He was very warm in bed, but he could not succeed in losing consciousness. He tossed and turned, remained for five minutes lying on his back, then changed to his left side, then rolled over to his right. He was thirsty again, and rose to drink. Then a qualm seized him:

"Can it be possible that I am afraid?"

Why did his heart beat so uncontrollably at every well-known sound in his room? When the clock was about to strike, the prefatory grating of its spring made him start, and for several seconds he panted for breath, so unnerved was he.

He began to reason with himself on the possibility of such a thing: "Could I by any chance be afraid?"

No, indeed; he could not be afraid, since he was resolved to proceed to the last extremity, since he was irrevocably determined to fight without flinching. And yet he was so perturbed in mind and body that he asked himself:

"Is it possible to be afraid in spite of one's self?"

And this doubt, this fearful question, took possession of him. If an irresistible power, stronger than his own will, were to quell his courage, what would happen? He would certainly go to the place appointed; his will would force him that far. But supposing, when there, he were to tremble or faint? And he thought of his social standing, his reputation, his name.

And he suddenly determined to get up and look at himself in the glass. He lighted his candle. When he saw his face reflected in the mirror he scarcely recognized it. He seemed to see before him a man whom he did not know. His eyes looked disproportionately large, and he was very pale.

He remained standing before the mirror. He put out his tongue, as if to examine the state of his health, and all at once the thought flashed into his mind:

"At this time the day after to-morrow I may be dead."

And his heart throbbed painfully.

"At this time the day after to-morrow I may be dead. This person in front of me, this 'I' whom I see in the glass, will perhaps be no more. What! Here I am, I look at myself, I feel myself to be alive—and yet in twenty-four hours I may be lying on that bed, with closed eyes, dead, cold, inanimate."

He turned round, and could see himself distinctly lying on his back on the couch he had just quitted. He had the hollow face and the limp hands of death.

Then he became afraid of his bed, and to avoid seeing it went to his smoking-room. He mechanically took a cigar, lighted it, and began walking back and forth. He was cold; he took a step toward the bell, to wake his valet, but stopped with hand raised toward the bell rope.

"He would see that I am afraid!"

And, instead of ringing, he made a fire himself. His hands quivered nervously as they touched various objects. His head grew dizzy, his thoughts confused, disjointed, painful; a numbness seized his spirit, as if he had been drinking.

And all the time he kept on saying:

"What shall I do? What will become of me?"

His whole body trembled spasmodically; he rose, and, going to the window, drew back the curtains.

The day—a summer day-was breaking. The pink sky cast a glow on the city, its roofs, and its walls. A flush of light enveloped the awakened world, like a caress from the rising sun, and the glimmer of dawn kindled new hope in the breast of the vicomte. What a fool he was to let himself succumb to fear before anything was decided—before his seconds had interviewed those of Georges Lamil, before he even knew whether he would have to fight or not!

He bathed, dressed, and left the house with a firm step.

He repeated as he went:

"I must be firm—very firm. I must show that I am not afraid."

His seconds, the marquis and the colonel, placed themselves at his disposal, and, having shaken him warmly by the hand, began to discuss details.

"You want a serious duel?" asked the colonel.

"Yes—quite serious," replied the vicomte.

"You insist on pistols?" put in the marquis.

"Yes."

"Do you leave all the other arrangements in our hands?"

With a dry, jerky voice the vicomte answered:

"Twenty paces—at a given signal—the arm to be raised, not lowered—shots to be exchanged until one or other is seriously wounded."

"Excellent conditions," declared the colonel in a satisfied tone. "You are a good shot; all the chances are in your favor."

And they parted. The vicomte returned home to wait for them. His agitation, only temporarily allayed, now increased momentarily. He felt, in arms, legs and chest, a sort of trembling—a continuous vibration; he could not stay still, either sitting or standing. His mouth was parched, and he made every now and then a clicking movement of the tongue, as if to detach it from his palate.

He attempted, to take luncheon, but could not eat. Then it occurred to him to seek courage in drink, and he sent for a decanter of rum, of which he swallowed, one after another, six small glasses.

A burning warmth, followed by a deadening of the mental faculties, ensued. He said to himself:

"I know how to manage. Now it will be all right!"

But at the end of an hour he had emptied the decanter, and his agitation was worse than ever. A mad longing possessed him to throw himself on the ground, to bite, to scream. Night fell.

A ring at the bell so unnerved him that he had not the strength to rise to receive his seconds.

He dared not even to speak to them, wish them good-day, utter a single word, lest his changed voice should betray him.

"All is arranged as you wished," said the colonel. "Your adversary claimed at first the privilege of the offended part; but he yielded almost at once, and accepted your conditions. His seconds are two military men."

"Thank you," said the vicomte.

The marquis added:

"Please excuse us if we do not stay now, for we have a good deal to see to yet. We shall want a reliable doctor, since the duel is not to end until a serious wound has been inflicted; and you know that bullets are not to be trifled with. We must select a spot near some house to which the wounded party can be carried if necessary. In fact, the arrangements will take us another two or three hours at least."

The vicomte articulated for the second time:

"Thank you."

"You're all right?" asked the colonel. "Quite calm?"

"Perfectly calm, thank you."

The two men withdrew.

When he was once more alone he felt as though he should go mad. His servant having lighted the lamps, he sat down at his table to write some letters. When he had traced at the top of a sheet of paper the words: "This is my last will and testament," he started from his seat, feeling himself incapable of connected thought, of decision in regard to anything.

So he was going to fight! He could no longer avoid it. What, then, possessed him? He wished to fight, he was fully determined to fight, and yet, in spite of all his mental effort, in spite of the exertion of all his will power, he felt that he could not even preserve the strength necessary to carry him through the ordeal. He tried to conjure up a picture of the duel, his own attitude, and that of his enemy.

Every now and then his teeth chattered audibly. He thought he would read, and took down Chateauvillard's Rules of Dueling. Then he said:

"Is the other man practiced in the use of the pistol? Is he well known? How can I find out?"

He remembered Baron de Vaux's book on marksmen, and searched it from end to end. Georges Lamil was not mentioned. And yet, if he were not an adept, would he have accepted without demur such a dangerous weapon and such deadly conditions?

He opened a case of Gastinne Renettes which stood on a small table, and took from it a pistol. Next he stood in the correct attitude for firing, and raised his arm. But he was trembling from head to foot, and the weapon shook in his grasp.

Then he said to himself:

"It is impossible. I cannot fight like this."

He looked at the little black, death-spitting hole at the end of the pistol; he thought of dishonor, of the whispers at the clubs, the smiles in his friends' drawing-rooms, the contempt of women, the veiled sneers of the newspapers, the insults that would be hurled at him by cowards.

He still looked at the weapon, and raising the hammer, saw the glitter of the priming below it. The pistol had been left loaded by some chance, some oversight. And the discovery rejoiced him, he knew not why.

If he did not maintain, in presence of his opponent, the steadfast bearing which was so necessary to his honor, he would be ruined forever. He would be branded, stigmatized as a coward, hounded out of society! And he felt, he knew, that he could not maintain that calm, unmoved demeanor. And yet he was brave, since the thought that followed was not even rounded to a finish in his mind; but, opening his mouth wide, he suddenly plunged the barrel of the pistol as far back as his throat, and pressed the trigger.

When the valet, alarmed at the report, rushed into the room he found his master lying dead upon his back. A spurt of blood had splashed the white paper on the table, and had made a great crimson stain beneath the words:

"This is my last will and testament."

OLD MONGILET

In the office old Mongilet was considered a type. He was a good old employee, who had never been outside Paris but once in his life.

It was the end of July, and each of us, every Sunday, went to roll in the grass, or soak in the water in the country near by. Asnieres, Argenteuil, Chatou, Borgival, Maisons, Poissy, had their habitues and their ardent admirers. We argued about the merits and advantages of all these places, celebrated and delightful to all Parsian employees.

Daddy Mongilet declared:

"You are like a lot of sheep! It must be pretty, this country you talk of!"

"Well, how about you, Mongilet? Don't you ever go on an excursion?"

"Yes, indeed. I go in an omnibus. When I have had a good luncheon, without any hurry, at the wine shop down there, I look up my route with a plan of Paris, and the time table of the lines and connections. And then I climb up on the box, open my umbrella and off we go. Oh, I see lots of things, more than you, I bet! I change my surroundings. It is as though I were taking a journey across the world, the people are so different in one street and another. I know my Paris better than anyone. And then, there is nothing more amusing than the entresols. You would not believe what one sees in there at a glance. One guesses at domestic scenes simply at sight of the face of a man who is roaring; one is amused on passing by a barber's shop, to see the barber leave his customer whose face is covered with lather to look out in the street. One exchanges heartfelt glances with the milliners just for fun, as one has no time to alight. Ah, how many things one sees!

"It is the drama, the real, the true, the drama of nature, seen as the horses trot by. Heavens! I would not give my excursions in the omnibus for all your stupid excursions in the woods."

"Come and try it, Mongilet, come to the country once just to see."

"I was there once," he replied, "twenty years ago, and you will never catch me there again."

"Tell us about it, Mongilet."

"If you wish to hear it. This is how it was:

"You knew Boivin, the old editorial clerk, whom we called Boileau?"

"Yes, perfectly."

"He was my office chum. The rascal had a house at Colombes and always invited me to spend Sunday with him. He would say:

"'Come along, Maculotte [he called me Maculotte for fun]. You will see what a nice excursion we will take.'

"I let myself be entrapped like an animal, and set out, one morning by the 8 o'clock train. I arrived at a kind of town, a country town where there is nothing to see, and I at length found my way to an old wooden door with an iron bell, at the end of an alley between two walls.

"I rang, and waited a long time, and at last the door was opened. What was it that opened it? I could not tell at the first glance. A woman or an ape? The creature was old, ugly, covered with old clothes that looked dirty and wicked. It had chicken's feathers in its hair and looked as though it would devour me.

"'What do you want?' she said.

"'Mr. Boivin.'

"'What do you want of him, of Mr. Boivin?'

"I felt ill at ease on being questioned by this fury. I stammered: 'Why-he expects me.'

"'Ah, it is you who have come to luncheon?'

"'Yes,' I stammered, trembling.

"Then, turning toward the house, she cried in an angry tone:

"'Boivin, here is your man!'

"It was my friend's wife. Little Boivin appeared immediately on the threshold of a sort of barrack of plaster covered with zinc, that looked like a foot stove. He wore white duck trousers covered with stains and a dirty Panama hat.

"After shaking my hands warmly, he took me into what he called his garden. It was at the end of another alleyway enclosed by high walls and was a little square the size of a pocket handkerchief, surrounded by houses that were so high that the sun, could reach it only two or three hours in the day. Pansies, pinks, wallflowers and a few rose bushes were languishing in this well without air, and hot as an oven from the refraction of heat from the roofs.

"'I have no trees,' said Boivin, 'but the neighbors' walls take their place. I have as much shade as in a wood.'

"Then he took hold of a button of my coat and said in a low tone:

"'You can do me a service. You saw the wife. She is not agreeable, eh? To-day, as I had invited you, she gave me clean clothes; but if I spot them all is lost. I counted on you to water my plants.'

"I agreed. I took off my coat, rolled up my sleeves, and began to work the handle of a kind of pump that wheezed, puffed and rattled like a consumptive as it emitted a thread of water like a Wallace drinking fountain. It took me ten minutes to water it and I was in a bath of perspiration. Boivin directed me:

"'Here—this plant—a little more; enough—now this one.'

"The watering pot leaked and my feet got more water than the flowers. The bottoms of my trousers were soaking and covered with mud. And twenty times running I kept it up, soaking my feet afresh each time, and perspiring anew as I worked the handle of the pump. And when I was tired out and wanted to stop, Boivin, in a tone of entreaty, said as he put his hand on my arm:

"Just one more watering pot full—just one, and that will be all.'

"To thank me he gave me a rose, a big rose, but hardly had it touched my button-hole than it fell to pieces, leaving only a hard little green knot as a decoration. I was surprised, but said nothing.

"Mme. Boivin's voice was heard in the distance:

"'Are you ever coming? When you know that luncheon is ready!'

"We went toward the foot stove. If the garden was in the shade, the house, on the other hand, was in the blazing sun, and the sweating room in the Turkish bath is not as hot as was my friend's dining room.

"Three plates at the side of which were some half-washed forks, were placed on a table of yellow wood in the middle of which stood an earthenware dish containing boiled beef and potatoes. We began to eat.

"A large water bottle full of water lightly colored with wine attracted my attention. Boivin, embarrassed, said to his wife:

"'See here, my dear, just on a special occasion, are you not going to give us some plain wine?'

"She looked at him furiously.

"'So that you may both get tipsy, is that it, and stay here gabbing all day? A fig for your special occasion!'

"He said no more. After the stew she brought in another dish of potatoes cooked with bacon. When this dish was finished, still in silence, she announced:

"'That is all! Now get out!'

"Boivin looked at her in astonishment.

"'But the pigeon—the pigeon you plucked this morning?'

"She put her hands on her hips:

"'Perhaps you have not had enough? Because you bring people here is no reason why we should devour all that there is in the house. What is there for me to eat this evening?'

"We rose. Solvin whispered

"'Wait for me a second, and we will skip.'

"He went into the kitchen where his wife had gone, and I overheard him say:

"'Give me twenty sous, my dear.'

"'What do you want with twenty sons?'

"'Why, one does not know what may happen. It is always better to have some money.'

"She yelled so that I should hear:

"'No, I will not give it to you! As the man has had luncheon here, the least he can do is to pay your expenses for the day.'

"Boivin came back to fetch me. As I wished to be polite I bowed to the mistress of the house, stammering:

"'Madame—many thanks—kind welcome.'

"'That's all right,' she replied. 'But do not bring him back drunk, for you will have to answer to me, you know!'

"We set out. We had to cross a perfectly bare plain under the burning sun. I attempted to gather a flower along the road and gave a cry of pain. It had hurt my hand frightfully. They call these plants nettles. And, everywhere, there was a smell of manure, enough to turn your stomach.

"Boivin said, 'Have a little patience and we will reach the river bank.'

"We reached the river. Here there was an odor of mud and dirty water, and the sun blazed down on the water so that it burned my eyes. I begged Boivin to go under cover somewhere. He took me into a kind of shanty filled with men, a river boatmen's tavern.

"He said:

"'This does not look very grand, but it is very comfortable.'

"I was hungry. I ordered an omelet. But to and behold, at the second glass of wine, that beggar, Boivin, lost his head, and I understand why his wife gave him water diluted.

"He got up, declaimed, wanted to show his strength, interfered in a quarrel between two drunken men who were fighting, and, but for the landlord, who came to the rescue, we should both have been killed.

"I dragged him away, holding him up until we reached the first bush where I deposited him. I lay down beside him and, it seems, I fell asleep. We must certainly have slept a long time, for it was dark when I awoke. Boivin was snoring at my side. I shook him; he rose but he was still drunk, though a little less so.

"We set out through the darkness across the plain. Boivin said he knew the way. He made me turn to the left, then to the right, then to the left. We could see neither sky nor earth, and found ourselves lost in the midst of a kind of forest of wooden stakes, that came as high as our noses. It was a vineyard and these were the supports. There was not a single light on the horizon. We wandered about in this vineyard for about an hour or two, hesitating, reaching out our arms without finding any limit, for we kept retracing our steps.

"At length Boivin fell against a stake that tore his cheek and he remained in a sitting posture on the ground, uttering with all his might long and resounding hallos, while I screamed 'Help! Help!' as loud as I could, lighting candle-matches to show the way to our rescuers, and also to keep up my courage.

"At last a belated peasant heard us and put us on our right road. I took Boivin to his home, but as I was leaving him on the threshold of his garden, the door opened suddenly and his wife appeared, a candle in her hand. She frightened me horribly.

"As soon as she saw her husband, whom she must have been waiting for since dark, she screamed, as she darted toward me:

"'Ah, scoundrel, I knew you would bring him back drunk!'

"My, how I made my escape, running all the way to the station, and as I thought the fury was pursuing me I shut myself in an inner room as the train was not due for half an hour.

"That is why I never married, and why I never go out of Paris."

MOONLIGHT

Madame Julie Roubere was expecting her elder sister, Madame Henriette Letore, who had just returned from a trip to Switzerland.

The Letore household had left nearly five weeks before. Madame Henriette had allowed her husband to return alone to their estate in Calvados, where some business required his attention, and had come to spend a few days in Paris with her sister. Night came on. In the quiet parlor Madame Roubere was reading in the twilight in an absent-minded way, raising her, eyes whenever she heard a sound.

At last, she heard a ring at the door, and her sister appeared, wrapped in a travelling cloak. And without any formal greeting, they clasped each other in an affectionate embrace, only desisting for a moment to give each other another hug. Then they talked about their health, about their respective families, and a thousand other things, gossiping, jerking out hurried, broken sentences as they followed each other about, while Madame Henriette was removing her hat and veil.

It was now quite dark. Madame Roubere rang for a lamp, and as soon as it was brought in, she scanned her sister's face, and was on the point of embracing her once more. But she held back, scared and astonished at the other's appearance.

On her temples Madame Letore had two large locks of white hair. All the rest of her hair was of a glossy, raven-black hue; but there alone, at each side of her head, ran, as it were, two silvery streams which were immediately lost in the black mass surrounding them. She was, nevertheless, only twenty-four years old, and this change had come on suddenly since her departure for Switzerland.

Without moving, Madame Roubere gazed at her in amazement, tears rising to her eyes, as she thought that some mysterious and terrible calamity must have befallen her sister. She asked:

"What is the matter with you, Henriette?"

Smiling with a sad face, the smile of one who is heartsick, the other replied:

"Why, nothing, I assure you. Were you noticing my white hair?"

But Madame Roubere impetuously seized her by the shoulders, and with a searching glance at her, repeated:

"What is the matter with you? Tell me what is the matter with you. And if you tell me a falsehood, I'll soon find it out."

They remained face to face, and Madame Henriette, who looked as if she were about to faint, had two pearly tears in the corners of her drooping eyes.

Her sister continued:

"What has happened to you? What is the matter with you? Answer me!"

Then, in a subdued voice, the other murmured:

"I have—I have a lover."

And, hiding her forehead on the shoulder of her younger sister, she sobbed.

Then, when she had grown a little calmer, when the heaving of her breast had subsided, she commenced to unbosom herself, as if to cast forth this secret from herself, to empty this sorrow of hers into a sympathetic heart.

Thereupon, holding each other's hands tightly clasped, the two women went over to a sofa in a dark corner of the room, into which they sank, and the younger sister, passing her arm over the elder one's neck, and drawing her close to her heart, listened.

"Oh! I know that there was no excuse for me; I do not understand myself, and since that day I feel as if I were mad. Be careful, my child, about yourself—be careful! If you only knew how weak we are, how quickly we yield, and fall. It takes so little, so little, so little, a moment of tenderness, one of those sudden fits of melancholy which come over you, one of those longings to open your arms, to love, to cherish something, which we all have at certain moments.

"You know my husband, and you know how fond I am of him; but he is mature and sensible, and cannot even comprehend the tender vibrations of a woman's heart. He is always the same, always good, always smiling, always kind, always perfect. Oh! how I sometimes have wished that he would clasp me roughly in his arms, that he would embrace me with those slow, sweet kisses which make two beings intermingle, which are like mute confidences! How I have wished that he were foolish, even weak, so that he should have need of me, of my caresses, of my tears!

"This all seems very silly; but we women are made like that. How can we help it?

"And yet the thought of deceiving him never entered my mind. Now it has happened, without love, without reason, without anything, simply because the moon shone one night on the Lake of Lucerne.

"During the month when we were travelling together, my husband, with his calm indifference, paralyzed my enthusiasm, extinguished my poetic ardor. When we were descending the mountain paths at sunrise, when as the four horses galloped along with the diligence, we saw, in the transparent morning haze, valleys, woods, streams, and villages, I clasped my hands with delight, and said to him: 'How beautiful it is, dear! Give me a kiss! Kiss me now!' He only answered, with a smile of chilling kindliness: 'There is no reason why we should kiss each other because you like the landscape.'

"And his words froze me to the heart. It seems to me that when people love each other, they ought to feel more moved by love than ever, in the presence of beautiful scenes.

"In fact, I was brimming over with poetry which he kept me from expressing. I was almost like a boiler filled with steam and hermetically sealed.

"One evening (we had for four days been staying in a hotel at Fluelen) Robert, having one of his sick headaches, went to bed immediately after dinner, and I went to take a walk all alone along the edge of the lake.

"It was a night such as one reads of in fairy tales. The full moon showed itself in the middle of the sky; the tall mountains, with their snowy crests, seemed to wear silver crowns; the waters of the lake glittered with tiny shining ripples. The air was mild, with that kind of penetrating warmth which enervates us till we are ready to faint, to be deeply affected without any apparent cause. But how sensitive, how vibrating the heart is at such moments! how quickly it beats, and how intense is its emotion!

"I sat down on the grass, and gazed at that vast, melancholy, and fascinating lake, and a strange feeling arose in me; I was seized with an insatiable need of love, a revolt against the gloomy dullness of my life. What! would it never be my fate to wander, arm in arm, with a man I loved, along a moon-kissed bank like this? Was I never to feel on my lips those kisses so deep, delicious, and intoxicating which lovers exchange on nights that seem to have been made by God for tenderness? Was I never to know ardent, feverish love in the moonlit shadows of a summer's night?

"And I burst out weeping like a crazy woman. I heard something stirring behind me. A man stood there, gazing at me. When I turned my head round, he recognized me, and, advancing, said:

"'You are weeping, madame?'

"It was a young barrister who was travelling with his mother, and whom we had often met. His eyes had frequently followed me.

"I was so confused that I did not know what answer to give or what to think of the situation. I told him I felt ill.

"He walked on by my side in a natural and respectful manner, and began talking to me about what we had seen during our trip. All that I had felt he translated into words; everything that made me thrill he understood perfectly, better than I did myself. And all of a sudden he repeated some verses of Alfred de Musset. I felt myself choking, seized with indescribable emotion. It seemed to me that the mountains themselves, the lake, the moonlight, were singing to me about things ineffably sweet.

"And it happened, I don't know how, I don't know why, in a sort of hallucination.

"As for him, I did not see him again till the morning of his departure.

"He gave me his card!"

And, sinking into her sister's arms, Madame Letore broke into groans—almost into shrieks.

Then, Madame Roubere, with a self-contained and serious air, said very gently:

"You see, sister, very often it is not a man that we love, but love itself. And your real lover that night was the moonlight."

THE FIRST SNOWFALL

The long promenade of La Croisette winds in a curve along the edge of the blue water. Yonder, to the right, Esterel juts out into the sea in the distance, obstructing the view and shutting out the horizon with its pretty southern outline of pointed summits, numerous and fantastic.

To the left, the isles of Sainte Marguerite and Saint Honorat, almost level with the water, display their surface, covered with pine trees.

And all along the great gulf, all along the tall mountains that encircle Cannes, the white villa residences seem to be sleeping in the sunlight. You can see them from a distance, the white houses, scattered from the top to the bottom of the mountains, dotting the dark greenery with specks like snow.

Those near the water have gates opening on the wide promenade which is washed by the quiet waves. The air is soft and balmy. It is one of those warm winter days when there is scarcely a breath of cool air. Above the walls of the gardens may be seen orange trees and lemon trees full of golden fruit. Ladies are walking slowly across the sand of the avenue, followed by children rolling hoops, or chatting with gentlemen.

A young woman has just passed out through the door of her coquettish little house facing La Croisette. She stops for a moment to gaze at the promenaders, smiles, and with an exhausted air makes her way toward an empty bench facing the sea. Fatigued after having gone twenty paces, she sits down out of breath. Her pale face seems that of a dead woman. She coughs, and raises to her lips her transparent fingers as if to stop those paroxysms that exhaust her.

She gazes at the sky full of sunshine and swallows, at the zigzag summits of the Esterel over yonder, and at the sea, the blue, calm, beautiful sea, close beside her.

She smiles again, and murmurs:

"Oh! how happy I am!"

She knows, however, that she is going to die, that she will never see the springtime, that in a year, along the same promenade, these same people who pass before her now will come again to breathe the warm air of this charming spot, with their children a little bigger, with their hearts all filled with hopes, with tenderness, with happiness, while at the bottom of an oak coffin, the poor flesh which is still left to her to-day will have decomposed, leaving only her bones lying in the silk robe which she has selected for a shroud.

She will be no more. Everything in life will go on as before for others. For her, life will be over, over forever. She will be no more. She smiles, and inhales as well as she can, with her diseased lungs, the perfumed air of the gardens.

And she sinks into a reverie.

She recalls the past. She had been married, four years ago, to a Norman gentleman. He was a strong young man, bearded, healthy-looking, with wide shoulders, narrow mind, and joyous disposition.

They had been united through financial motives which she knew nothing about. She would willingly have said No. She said Yes, with a movement of the head, in order not to thwart her father and mother. She was a Parisian, gay, and full of the joy of living.

Her husband brought her home to his Norman chateau. It was a huge stone building surrounded by tall trees of great age. A high clump of pine trees shut out the view in front. On the right, an opening in the trees presented a view of the plain, which stretched out in an unbroken level as far as the distant, farmsteads. A cross-road passed before the gate and led to the high road three kilometres away.

Oh! she recalls everything, her arrival, her first day in her new abode, and her isolated life afterward.

When she stepped out of the carriage, she glanced at the old building, and laughingly exclaimed:

"It does not look cheerful!"

Her husband began to laugh in his turn, and replied:

"Pooh! we get used to it! You'll see. I never feel bored in it, for my part."

That day they passed their time in embracing each other, and she did not find it too long. This lasted fully a month. The days passed one after the other in insignificant yet absorbing occupations. She learned the value and the importance of the little things of life. She knew that people can interest themselves in the price of eggs, which cost a few centimes more or less according to the seasons.

It was summer. She went to the fields to see the men harvesting. The brightness of the sunshine found an echo in her heart.

The autumn came. Her husband went out shooting. He started in the morning with his two dogs Medor and Mirza. She remained alone, without grieving, moreover, at Henry's absence. She was very fond of him, but she did not miss him. When he returned home, her affection was especially bestowed on the dogs. She took care of them every evening with a mother's tenderness, caressed them incessantly, gave them a thousand charming little names which she had no idea of applying to her husband.

He invariably told her all about his sport. He described the places where he found partridges, expressed his astonishment at not having caught any hares in Joseph Ledentu's clever, or else appeared indignant at the conduct of M. Lechapelier, of Havre, who always went along the edge of his property to shoot the game that he, Henry de Parville, had started.

She replied: "Yes, indeed! it is not right," thinking of something else all the while.

The winter came, the Norman winter, cold and rainy. The endless floods of rain came down on the slates of the great gabled roof, rising like a knife blade toward the sky. The roads seemed like rivers of mud, the country a plain of mud, and no sound could be heard save that of water falling; no movement could be seen save the whirling flight of crows that settled down like a cloud on a field and then hurried off again.

About four o'clock, the army of dark, flying creatures came and perched in the tall beeches at the left of the chateau, emitting deafening cries. During nearly an hour, they flew from tree top to tree top, seemed to be fighting, croaked, and made a black disturbance in the gray branches. She gazed at them each evening with a weight at her heart, so deeply was she impressed by the lugubrious melancholy of the darkness falling on the deserted country.

Then she rang for the lamp, and drew near the fire. She burned heaps of wood without succeeding in warming the spacious apartments reeking with humidity. She was cold all day long, everywhere, in the drawing-room, at meals, in her own apartment. It seemed to her she was cold to the marrow of her bones. Her husband only came in to dinner; he was always out shooting, or else he was superintending sowing the seed, tilling the soil, and all the work of the country.

He would come back jovial, and covered with mud, rubbing his hands as he exclaimed:

"What wretched weather!"

Or else:

"A fire looks comfortable!"

Or sometimes:

"Well, how are you to-day? Are you in good spirits?"

He was happy, in good health, without desires, thinking of nothing save this simple, healthy, and quiet life.

About December, when the snow had come, she suffered so much from the icy-cold air of the chateau which seemed to have become chilled in passing through the centuries just as human beings become chilled with years, that she asked her husband one evening:

"Look here, Henry! You ought to have a furnace put into the house; it would dry the walls. I assure you that I cannot keep warm from morning till night."

At first he was stunned at this extravagant idea of introducing a furnace into his manor-house. It would have seemed more natural to him to have his dogs fed out of silver dishes. He gave a tremendous laugh from the bottom of his chest as he exclaimed:

"A furnace here! A furnace here! Ha! ha! ha! what a good joke!"

She persisted:

"I assure you, dear, I feel frozen; you don't feel it because you are always moving about; but all the same, I feel frozen."

He replied, still laughing:

"Pooh! you'll get used to it, and besides it is excellent for the health. You will only be all the better for it. We are not Parisians, damn it! to live in hot-houses. And, besides, the spring is quite near."

About the beginning of January, a great misfortune befell her. Her father and mother died in a carriage accident. She came to Paris for the funeral. And her sorrow took entire possession of her mind for about six months.

The mildness of the beautiful summer days finally roused her, and she lived along in a state of sad languor until autumn.

When the cold weather returned, she was brought face to face, for the first time, with the gloomy future. What was she to do? Nothing. What was going to happen to her henceforth? Nothing. What expectation, what hope, could revive her heart? None. A doctor who was consulted declared that she would never have children.

Sharper, more penetrating still than the year before, the cold made her suffer continually.

She stretched out her shivering hands to the big flames. The glaring fire burned her face; but icy whiffs seemed to glide down her back and to penetrate between her skin and her underclothing. And she shivered from head to foot. Innumerable draughts of air appeared to have taken up their abode in the apartment, living, crafty currents of air as cruel as enemies. She encountered them at every moment; they blew on her incessantly their perfidious and frozen hatred, now on her face, now on her hands, and now on her back.

Once more she spoke of a furnace; but her husband listened to her request as if she were asking for the moon. The introduction of such an apparatus at Parville appeared to him as impossible as the discovery of the Philosopher's Stone.

Having been at Rouen on business one day, he brought back to his wife a dainty foot warmer made of copper, which he laughingly called a "portable furnace"; and he considered that this would prevent her henceforth from ever being cold.

Toward the end of December she understood that she could not always live like this, and she said timidly one evening at dinner:

"Listen, dear! Are we not going to spend a week or two in Paris before spring:"

He was stupefied.

"In Paris? In Paris? But what are we to do there? Ah! no by Jove! We are better off here. What odd ideas come into your head sometimes."

She faltered:

"It might distract us a little."

He did not understand.

"What is it you want to distract you? Theatres, evening parties, dinners in town? You knew, however, when you came here, that you ought not to expect any distractions of this kind!"

She saw a reproach in these words, and in the tone in which they were uttered. She relapsed into silence. She was timid and gentle, without resisting power and without strength of will.

In January the cold weather returned with violence. Then the snow covered the earth.

One evening, as she watched the great black cloud of crows dispersing among the trees, she began to weep, in spite of herself.

Her husband came in. He asked in great surprise:

"What is the matter with you?"

He was happy, quite happy, never having dreamed of another life or other pleasures. He had been born and had grown up in this melancholy district. He felt contented in his own house, at ease in body and mind.

He did not understand that one might desire incidents, have a longing for changing pleasures; he did not understand that it does not seem natural to certain beings to remain in the same place during the four seasons; he seemed not to know that spring, summer, autumn, and winter have, for multitudes of persons, fresh amusements in new places.

She could say nothing in reply, and she quickly dried her eyes. At last she murmured in a despairing tone:

"I am—I—I am a little sad—I am a little bored."

But she was terrified at having even said so much, and added very quickly:

"And, besides—I am—I am a little cold."

This last plea made him angry.

"Ah! yes, still your idea of the furnace. But look here, deuce take it! you have not had one cold since you came here."

Night came on. She went up to her room, for she had insisted on having a separate apartment. She went to bed. Even in bed she felt cold. She thought:

"It will be always like this, always, until I die."

And she thought of her husband. How could he have said:

"You—have not had one cold since you came here"?

She would have to be ill, to cough before he could understand what she suffered!

And she was filled with indignation, the angry indignation of a weak, timid being.

She must cough. Then, perhaps, he would take pity on her. Well, she would cough; he should hear her coughing; the doctor should be called in; he should see, her husband, he should see.

She got out of bed, her legs and her feet bare, and a childish idea made her smile:

"I want a furnace, and I must have it. I shall cough so much that he'll have to put one in the house."

And she sat down in a chair in her nightdress. She waited an hour, two hours. She shivered, but she did not catch cold. Then she resolved on a bold expedient.

She noiselessly left her room, descended the stairs, and opened the gate into the garden.

The earth, covered with snows seemed dead. She abruptly thrust forward her bare foot, and plunged it into the icy, fleecy snow. A sensation of cold, painful as a wound, mounted to her heart. However, she stretched out the other leg, and began to descend the steps slowly.

Then she advanced through the grass saying to herself:

"I'll go as far as the pine trees."

She walked with quick steps, out of breath, gasping every time she plunged her foot into the snow.

She touched the first pine tree with her hand, as if to assure herself that she had carried out her plan to the end; then she went back into the house. She thought two or three times that she was going to fall, so numbed and weak did she feel. Before going in, however, she sat down in that icy fleece, and even took up several handfuls to rub on her chest.

Then she went in and got into bed. It seemed to her at the end of an hour that she had a swarm of ants in her throat, and that other ants were running all over her limbs. She slept, however.

Next day she was coughing and could not get up.

She had inflammation of the lungs. She became delirious, and in her delirium she asked for a furnace. The doctor insisted on having one put in. Henry yielded, but with visible annoyance.

She was incurable. Her lungs were seriously affected, and those about her feared for her life.

"If she remains here, she will not last until the winter," said the doctor.

She was sent south. She came to Cannes, made the acquaintance of the sun, loved the sea, and breathed the perfume of orange blossoms.

Then, in the spring, she returned north.

But she now lived with the fear of being cured, with the fear of the long winters of Normandy; and as soon as she was better she opened her window by night and recalled the sweet shores of the Mediterranean.

And now she is going to die. She knows it and she is happy.

She unfolds a newspaper which she has not already opened, and reads this heading:

"The first snow in Paris."

She shivers and then smiles. She looks across at the Esterel, which is becoming rosy in the rays of the setting sun. She looks at the vast blue sky, so blue, so very blue, and the vast blue sea, so very blue also, and she rises from her seat.

And then she returned to the house with slow steps, only stopping to cough, for she had remained out too long and she was cold, a little cold.

She finds a letter from her husband. She opens it, still smiling, and she reads:

"MY DEAR LOVE: I hope you are well, and that you do not regret too much our beautiful country. For some days last we have had a good frost, which presages snow. For my part, I adore this weather, and you may believe that I do not light your damned furnace."

She ceases reading, quite happy at the thought that she had her furnace put in. Her right hand, which holds the letter, falls slowly on her lap, while she raises her left hand to her mouth, as if to calm the obstinate cough which is racking her chest.

SUNDAYS OF A BOURGEOIS

Preparations for the Excursion

M. Patissot, born in Paris, after having failed in his examinations at the College Henri IV., like many others, had entered the government service through the influence of one of his aunts, who kept a tobacco store where the head of one of the departments bought his provisions.

He advanced very slowly, and would, perhaps, have died a fourth-class clerk without the aid of a kindly Providence, which sometimes watches over our destiny. He is today fifty-two years old, and it is only at this age that he is beginning to explore, as a tourist, all that part of France which lies between the fortifications and the provinces.

The story of his advance might be useful to many employees, just as the tale of his excursions may be of value to many Parisians who will take them as a model for their own outings, and will thus, through his example, avoid certain mishaps which occurred to him.

In 1854 he only enjoyed a salary of 1,800 francs. Through a peculiar trait of his character he was unpopular with all his superiors, who let him languish in the eternal and hopeless expectation of the clerk's ideal, an increase of salary. Nevertheless he worked; but he did not know how to make himself appreciated. He had too much self-respect, he claimed. His self-respect consisted in never bowing to his superiors in a low and servile manner, as did, according to him, certain of his colleagues, whom he would not mention. He added that his frankness embarrassed many people, for, like all the rest, he protested against injustice and the favoritism shown to persons entirely foreign to the bureaucracy. But his indignant voice never passed beyond the little cage where he worked.

First as a government clerk, then as a Frenchman and finally as a man who believed in order he would adhere to whatever government was established, having an unbounded reverence for authority, except for that of his chiefs.

Each time that he got the chance he would place himself where he could see the emperor pass, in order to have the honor of taking his hat off to him; and he would go away puffed up with pride at having bowed to the head of the state.

From his habit of observing the sovereign he did as many others do; he imitated the way he trimmed his beard or arranged his hair, the cut of his clothes, his walk, his mannerisms. Indeed, how many men in each country seemed to be the living images of the head of the government! Perhaps he vaguely resembled Napoleon III., but his hair was black; therefore he dyed it, and then the likeness was complete; and when he met another gentleman in the street also imitating the imperial countenance he was jealous and looked at him disdainfully. This need of imitation soon became his hobby, and, having heard an usher at the Tuilleries imitate the voice of the emperor, he also acquired the same intonations and studied slowness.

He thus became so much like his model that they might easily have been mistaken for each other, and certain high dignitaries were heard to remark that they found it unseemly and even vulgar; the matter was mentioned to the prime minister, who ordered that the employee should appear before him. But at the sight of him he began to laugh and repeated two or three times: "That's funny, really funny!" This was repeated, and the following day Patissot's immediate superior recommended that his subordinate receive an increase of salary of three hundred francs. He received it immediately.

From that time on his promotions came regularly, thanks to his ape-like faculty of imitation. The presentiment that some high honor might come to him some day caused his chiefs to speak to him with deference.

When the Republic was proclaimed it was a disaster for him. He felt lost, done for, and, losing his head, he stopped dyeing his hair, shaved his face clean and had his hair cut short, thus acquiring a paternal and benevolent expression which could not compromise him in any way.

Then his chiefs took revenge for the long time during which he had imposed upon them, and, having all turned Republican through an instinct of self preservation, they cut down his salary and delayed his promotion. He, too, changed his opinions. But the Republic not being a palpable and living person whom one can resemble, and the presidents succeeding each other with rapidity, he found himself plunged in the greatest embarrassment, in terrible distress, and, after an unsuccessful imitation of his last ideal, M. Thiers, he felt a check put on all his attempts at imitation. He needed a new manifestation of his personality. He searched for a long time; then, one morning, he arrived at the office wearing a new hat which had on the side a small red, white and blue rosette. His colleagues were astounded; they laughed all that day, the next day, all the week, all the month. But the seriousness of his demeanor at last disconcerted them, and once more his superiors became anxious. What mystery could be hidden under this sign? Was it a simple manifestation of patriotism, or an affirmation of his allegiance to the Republic, or perhaps the badge of some powerful association? But to wear it so persistently he must surely have some powerful and hidden protection. It would be well to be on one's guard, especially as he received all pleasantries with unruffled calmness. After that he was treated with respect, and his sham courage saved him; he was appointed head clerk on the first of January, 1880. His whole life had been spent indoors. He hated noise and bustle, and because of this love of rest and quiet he had remained a bachelor. He spent his Sundays reading tales of adventure and ruling guide lines which he afterward offered to his colleagues. In his whole existence he had only taken three vacations of a week each, when he was changing his quarters. But sometimes, on a holiday, he would leave by an excursion train for Dieppe or Havre in order to elevate his mind by the inspiring sight of the sea.

He was full of that common sense which borders on stupidity. For a long time he had been living quietly, with economy, temperate through prudence, chaste by temperament, when suddenly he was assailed by a terrible apprehension. One evening in the street he suddenly felt an attack of dizziness which made him fear a stroke of apoplexy. He hastened to a physician and for five francs obtained the following prescription:

M. X-, fifty-five years old, bachelor, clerk. Full-blooded, danger of apoplexy. Cold-water applications, moderate nourishment, plenty of exercise. MONTELLIER, M.D.

Patissot was greatly distressed, and for a whole month, in his office, he kept a wet towel wrapped around his head like a turban while the water continually dripped on his work, which he would have to do over again. Every once in a while he would read the prescription over, probably in the hope of finding some hidden meaning, of penetrating into the secret thought of the physician, and also of discovering some forms of exercise which, might perhaps make him immune from apoplexy.

Then he consulted his friends, showing them the fateful paper. One advised boxing. He immediately hunted up an instructor, and, on the first day, he received a punch in the nose which immediately took away all his ambition in this direction. Single-stick made him gasp for breath, and he grew so stiff from fencing that for two days and two nights he could not get sleep. Then a bright idea struck him. It was to walk, every Sunday, to some suburb of Paris and even to certain places in the capital which he did not know.

For a whole week his mind was occupied with thoughts of the equipment which you need for these excursions; and on Sunday, the 30th of May, he began his preparations. After reading all the extraordinary advertisements which poor, blind and halt beggars distribute on the street corners, he began to visit the stores with the intention of looking about him only and of buying later on. First of all, he visited a so-called American shoe store, where heavy travelling shoes were shown him. The clerk brought out a kind of ironclad contrivance, studded with spikes like a harrow, which he claimed to be made from Rocky Mountain bison skin. He was so carried away with them that he would willingly have bought two pair, but one was sufficient. He carried them away under his arm, which soon became numb from the weight. He next invested in a pair of corduroy trousers, such as carpenters wear, and a pair of oiled canvas leggings. Then he needed a knapsack for his provisions, a telescope so as to recognize villages perched on the slope of distant hills, and finally, a government survey map to enable him to find his way about without asking the peasants toiling in the fields. Lastly, in order more comfortably to stand the heat, he decided to purchase a light alpaca jacket offered by the famous firm of Raminau, according to their advertisement, for the modest sum of six francs and fifty centimes. He went to this store and was welcomed by a distinguished-looking young man with a marvellous head of hair, nails as pink as those of a lady and a pleasant smile. He showed him the garment. It did not correspond with the glowing style of the advertisement. Then Patissot hesitatingly asked, "Well, monsieur, will it wear well?" The young man turned his eyes away in well-feigned embarrassment, like an honest man who does not wish to deceive a customer, and, lowering his eyes, he said in a hesitating manner: "Dear me, monsieur, you understand that for six francs fifty we cannot turn out an article like this for instance." And he showed him a much finer jacket than the first one. Patissot examined it and asked the price. "Twelve francs fifty." It was very tempting, but before deciding, he once more questioned the big young man, who was observing him attentively. "And—is that good? Do you guarantee it?" "Oh! certainly, monsieur, it is quite good! But, of course, you must not get it wet! Yes, it's really quite good, but you understand that there are goods and goods. It's excellent for the price. Twelve francs fifty, just think. Why, that's nothing at all. Naturally a twenty-five-franc coat is much better. For twenty-five francs you get a superior quality, as strong as linen, and which wears even better. If it gets wet a little ironing will fix it right up. The color never fades, and it does not turn red in the sunlight. It is the warmest and lightest material out." He unfolded his wares, holding them up, shaking them, crumpling and stretching them in order to show the excellent quality of the cloth. He talked on convincingly, dispelling all hesitation by words and gesture. Patissot was convinced; he bought the coat. The pleasant salesman, still talking, tied up the bundle and continued praising the value of the purchase. When it was paid for he was suddenly silent. He bowed with a superior air, and, holding the door open, he watched his customer disappear, both arms filled with bundles and vainly trying to reach his hat to bow.

M. Patissot returned home and carefully studied the map. He wished to try on his shoes, which were more like skates than shoes, owing to the spikes. He slipped and fell, promising himself to be more careful in the future. Then he spread out all his purchases on a chair and looked at them for a long time. He went to sleep with this thought: "Isn't it strange that I didn't think before of taking an excursion to the country?"

During the whole week Patissot worked without ambition. He was dreaming of the outing which he had planned for the following Sunday, and he was seized by a sudden longing for the country, a desire of growing tender over nature, this thirst for rustic scenes which overwhelms the Parisians in spring time.

Only one person gave him any attention; it was a silent old copying clerk named Boivin, nicknamed Boileau. He himself lived in the country and had a little garden which he cultivated carefully; his needs were small, and he was perfectly happy, so they said. Patissot was now able to understand his tastes and the similarity of their ideals made them immediately fast friends. Old man Boivin said to him:

"Do I like fishing, monsieur? Why, it's the delight of my life!"

Then Patissot questioned him with deep interest. Boivin named all the fish who frolicked under this dirty water—and Patissot thought he could see them. Boivin told about the different hooks, baits, spots and times suitable for each kind. And Patissot felt himself more like a fisherman than Boivin himself. They decided that the following Sunday they would meet for the opening of the season for the edification of Patissot, who was delighted to have found such an experienced instructor.

FISHING EXCURSION

The day before the one when he was, for the first time in his life, to throw a hook into a river, Monsieur Patissot bought, for eighty centimes, "How to Become a Perfect Fisherman." In this work he learned many useful things, but he was especially impressed by the style, and he retained the following passage:

"In a word, if you wish, without books, without rules, to fish successfully, to the left or to the right, up or down stream, in the masterly manner that halts at no difficulty, then fish before, during and after a storm, when the clouds break and the sky is streaked with lightning, when the earth shakes with the grumbling thunder; it is then that, either through hunger or terror, all the fish forget their habits in a turbulent flight.

"In this confusion follow or neglect all favorable signs, and just go on fishing; you will march to victory!"

In order to catch fish of all sizes, he bought three well-perfected poles, made to be used as a cane in the city, which, on the river, could be transformed into a fishing rod by a simple jerk. He bought some number fifteen hooks for gudgeon, number twelve for bream, and with his number seven he expected to fill his basket with carp. He bought no earth worms because he was sure of finding them everywhere; but he laid in a provision of sand worms. He had a jar full of them, and in the evening he watched them with interest. The hideous creatures swarmed in their bath of bran as they do in putrid meat. Patissot wished to practice baiting his hook. He took up one with disgust, but he had hardly placed the curved steel point against it when it split open. Twenty times he repeated this without success, and he might have continued all night had he not feared to exhaust his supply of vermin.

He left by the first train. The station was full of people equipped with fishing lines. Some, like Patissot's, looked like simple bamboo canes; others, in one piece, pointed their slender ends to the skies. They looked like a forest of slender sticks, which mingled and clashed like swords or swayed like masts over an ocean of broad-brimmed straw hats.

When the train started fishing rods could be seen sticking out of all the windows and doors, giving to the train the appearance of a huge, bristly caterpillar winding through the fields.

Everybody got off at Courbevoie and rushed for the stage for Bezons. A crowd of fishermen crowded on top of the coach, holding their rods in their hands, giving the vehicle the appearance of a porcupine.

All along the road men were travelling in the same direction as though on a pilgrimage to an unknown Jerusalem. They were carrying those long, slender sticks resembling those carried by the faithful returning from Palestine. A tin box on a strap was fastened to their backs. They were in a hurry.

At Bezons the river appeared. People were lined along bath banks, men in frock coats, others in duck suits, others in blouses, women, children and even young girls of marriageable age; all were fishing.

Patissot started for the dam where his friend Boivin was waiting for him. The latter greeted him rather coolly. He had just made the acquaintance of a big, fat man of about fifty, who seemed very strong and whose skin was tanned. All three hired a big boat and lay off almost under the fall of the dam, where the fish are most plentiful.

Boivin was immediately ready. He baited his line and threw it out, and then sat motionless, watching the little float with extraordinary concentration. From time to time he would jerk his line out of the water and cast it farther out. The fat gentleman threw out his well-baited hooks, put his line down beside him, filled his pipe, lit it, crossed his arms, and, without another glance at the cork, he watched the water flow by. Patissot once more began trying to stick sand worms on his hooks. After about five minutes of this occupation he called to Boivin; "Monsieur Boivin, would you be so kind as to help me put these creatures on my hook? Try as I will, I can't seem to succeed." Boivin raised his head: "Please don't disturb me, Monsieur Patissot; we are not here for pleasure!" However, he baited the line, which Patissot then threw out, carefully imitating all the motions of his friend.

The boat was tossing wildly, shaken by the waves, and spun round like a top by the current, although anchored at both ends. Patissot, absorbed in the sport, felt a vague kind of uneasiness; he was uncomfortably heavy and somewhat dizzy.

They caught nothing. Little Boivin, very nervous, was gesticulating and shaking his head in despair. Patissot was as sad as though some disaster had overtaken him. The fat gentleman alone, still motionless, was quietly smoking without paying any attention to his line. At last Patissot, disgusted, turned toward him and said in a mournful voice:

"They are not biting, are they?"

He quietly replied:

"Of course not!"

Patissot surprised, looked at him.

"Do you ever catch many?"

"Never!"

"What! Never?"

The fat man, still smoking like a factory chimney, let out the following words, which completely upset his neighbor:

"It would bother me a lot if they did bite. I don't come here to fish; I come because I'm very comfortable here; I get shaken up as though I were at sea. If I take a line along, it's only to do as others do."

Monsieur Patissot, on the other hand, did not feel at all well. His discomfort, at first vague, kept increasing, and finally took on a definite form. He felt, indeed, as though he were being tossed by the sea, and he was suffering from seasickness. After the first attack had calmed down, he proposed leaving, but Boivin grew so furious that they almost came to blows. The fat man, moved by pity, rowed the boat back, and, as soon as Patissot had recovered from his seasickness, they bethought themselves of luncheon.

Two restaurants presented themselves. One of them, very small, looked like a beer garden, and was patronized by the poorer fishermen. The other one, which bore the imposing name of "Linden Cottage," looked like a middle-class residence and was frequented by the aristocracy of the rod. The two owners, born enemies, watched each other with hatred across a large field, which separated them, and where the white house of the dam keeper and of the inspector of the life-saving department stood out against the green grass. Moreover, these two officials disagreed, one of them upholding the beer garden and the other one defending the Elms, and the internal feuds which arose in these three houses reproduced the whole history of mankind.

Boivin, who knew the beer garden, wished to go there, exclaiming: "The food is very good, and it isn't expensive; you'll see. Anyhow, Monsieur Patissot, you needn't expect to get me tipsy the way you did last Sunday. My wife was furious, you know; and she has sworn never to forgive you!"

The fat gentleman declared that he would only eat at the Elms, because it was an excellent place and the cooking was as good as in the best restaurants in Paris.

"Do as you wish," declared Boivin; "I am going where I am accustomed to go." He left. Patissot, displeased at his friend's actions, followed the fat gentleman.

They ate together, exchanged ideas, discussed opinions and found that they were made for each other.

After the meal everyone started to fish again, but the two new friends left together. Following along the banks, they stopped near the railroad bridge and, still talking, they threw their lines in the water. The fish still refused to bite, but Patissot was now making the best of it.

A family was approaching. The father, whose whiskers stamped him as a judge, was holding an extraordinarily long rod; three boys of different sizes were carrying poles of different lengths, according to age; and the mother, who was very stout, gracefully manoeuvred a charming rod with a ribbon tied to the handle. The father bowed and asked:

"Is this spot good, gentlemen?" Patissot was going to speak, when his friend answered: "Fine!" The whole family smiled and settled down beside the fishermen. The Patissot was seized with a wild desire to catch a fish, just one, any kind, any size, in order to win the consideration of these people; so he began to handle his rod as he had seen Boivin do in the morning. He would let the cork follow the current to the end of the line, jerk the hooks out of the water, make them describe a large circle in the air and throw them out again a little higher up. He had even, as he thought, caught the knack of doing this movement gracefully. He had just jerked his line out rapidly when he felt it caught in something behind him. He tugged, and a scream burst from behind him. He perceived, caught on one of his hooks, and describing in the air a curve like a meteor, a magnificent hat which he placed right in the middle of the river.

He turned around, bewildered, dropping his pole, which followed the hat down the stream, while the fat gentleman, his new friend, lay on his back and roared with laughter. The lady, hatless and astounded, choked with anger; her husband was outraged and demanded the price of the hat, and Patissot paid about three times its value.

Then the family departed in a very dignified manner.

Patissot took another rod, and, until nightfall, he gave baths to sand worms. His neighbor was sleeping peacefully on the grass. Toward seven in the evening he awoke.

"Let's go away from here!" he said.

Then Patissot withdrew his line, gave a cry and sat down hard from astonishment. At the end of the string was a tiny little fish. When they looked at him more closely they found that he had been hooked through the stomach; the hook had caught him as it was being drawn out of the water.

Patissot was filled with a boundless, triumphant joy; he wished to have the fish fried for himself alone.

During the dinner the friends grew still more intimate. He learned that the fat gentleman lived at Argenteuil and had been sailing boats for thirty years without losing interest in the sport. He accepted to take luncheon with him the following Sunday and to take a sail in his friend's clipper, Plongeon. He became so interested in the conversation that he forgot all about his catch. He did not remember it until after the coffee, and he demanded that it be brought him. It was alone in the middle of a platter, and looked like a yellow, twisted match, But he ate it with pride and relish, and at night, on the omnibus, he told his neighbors that he had caught fourteen pounds of fish during the day.

TWO CELEBRITIES

Monsieur Patissot had promised his friend, the boating man, that he would spend the following Sunday with him. An unforeseen occurrence changed his plan. One evening, on the boulevard, he met one of his cousins whom he saw but very seldom. He was a pleasant journalist, well received in all classes of society, who offered to show Patissot many interesting things.

"What are you going to do next Sunday?"

"I'm going boating at Argenteuil."

"Come on! Boating is an awful bore; there is no variety to it. Listen —I'll take you along with me. I'll introduce you to two celebrities. We will visit the homes of two artists."

"But I have been ordered to go to the country!"

"That's just where we'll go. On the way we'll call on Meissonier, at his place in Poissy; then we'll walk over to Medan, where Zola lives. I have been commissioned to obtain his next novel for our newspaper."

Patissot, wild with joy, accepted the invitation. He even bought a new frock coat, as his own was too much worn to make a good appearance. He was terribly afraid of saying something foolish either to the artist or to the man of letters, as do people who speak of an art which they have never professed.

He mentioned his fears to his cousin, who laughed and answered: "Pshaw! Just pay them compliments, nothing but compliments, always compliments; in that way, if you say anything foolish it will be overlooked. Do you know Meissonier's paintings?"

"I should say I do."

"Have you read the Rougon-Macquart series?"

"From first to last."

"That's enough. Mention a painting from time to time, speak of a novel here and there and add:

"'Superb! Extraordinary! Delightful technique! Wonderfully powerful!' In that way you can always get along. I know that those two are very blase about everything, but admiration always pleases an artist."

Sunday morning they left for Poissy.

Just a few steps from the station, at the end of the church square, they found Meissonier's property. After passing through a low door, painted red, which led into a beautiful alley of vines, the journalist stopped and, turning toward his companion, asked: "What is your idea of Meissonier?"

Patissot hesitated. At last he decided: "A little man, well groomed, clean shaven, a soldierly appearance." The other smiled: "All right, come along." A quaint building in the form of a chalet appeared to the left; and to the right side, almost opposite, was the main house. It was a strange-looking building, where there was a mixture of everything, a mingling of Gothic fortress, manor, villa, hut, residence, cathedral, mosque, pyramid, a, weird combination of Eastern and Western architecture. The style was complicated enough to set a classical architect crazy, and yet there was something whimsical and pretty about it. It had been invented and built under the direction of the artist.

They went in; a collection of trunks encumbered a little parlor. A little man appeared, dressed in a jumper. The striking thing about him was his beard. He bowed to the journalist, and said: "My dear sir, I hope that you will excuse me; I only returned yesterday, and everything is all upset here. Please be seated." The other refused, excusing himself: "My dear master, I only dropped in to pay my respects while passing by." Patissot, very much embarrassed, was bowing at every word of his friend's, as though moving automatically, and he murmured, stammering: "What a su—su—superb property!" The artist, flattered, smiled, and suggested visiting it.

He led them first to a little pavilion of feudal aspect, where his former studio was. Then they crossed a parlor, a dining-room, a vestibule full of beautiful works of art, of beautiful Beauvais, Gobelin and Flanders tapestries. But the strange external luxury of ornamentation became, inside, a revel of immense stairways. A magnificent grand stairway, a secret stairway in one tower, a servants' stairway in another, stairways everywhere! Patissot, by chance, opened a door and stepped back astonished. It was a veritable temple, this place of which respectable people only mention the name in English, an original and charming sanctuary in exquisite taste, fitted up like a pagoda, and the decoration of which must certainly have caused a great effort.

They next visited the park, which was complex, varied, with winding paths and full of old trees. But the journalist insisted on leaving; and, with many thanks, he took leave of the master: As they left they met a gardener; Patissot asked him: "Has Monsieur Meissonier owned this place for a long time?" The man answered: "Oh, monsieur! that needs explaining. I guess he bought the grounds in 1846. But, as for the house! he has already torn down and rebuilt that five or six times. It must have cost him at least two millions!" As Patissot left he was seized with an immense respect for this man, not on account of his success, glory or talent, but for putting so much money into a whim, because the bourgeois deprive themselves of all pleasure in order to hoard money.

After crossing Poissy, they struck out on foot along the road to Medan. The road first followed the Seine, which is dotted with charming islands at this place. Then they went up a hill and crossed the pretty village of Villaines, went down a little; and finally reached the neighborhood inhabited by the author of the Rougon-Macquart series.

A pretty old church with two towers appeared on the left. They walked along a short distance, and a passing farmer directed them to the writer's dwelling.

Before entering, they examined the house. A large building, square and new, very high, seemed, as in the fable of the mountain and the mouse, to have given birth to a tiny little white house, which nestled near it. This little house was the original dwelling, and had been built by the former owner. The tower had been erected by Zola.

They rang the bell. An enormous dog, a cross between a Saint Bernard and a Newfoundland, began to howl so terribly that Patissot felt a vague desire to retrace his steps. But a servant ran forward, calmed "Bertrand," opened the door, and took the journalist's card in order to carry it to his master.

"I hope that he will receive us!" murmured Patissot. "It would be too bad if we had come all this distance not to see him."

His companion smiled and answered: "Never fear, I have a plan for getting in."

But the servant, who had returned, simply asked them to follow him.

They entered the new building, and Patissot, who was quite enthusiastic, was panting as he climbed a stairway of ancient style which led to the second story.

At the same time he was trying to picture to himself this man whose glorious name echoes at present in all corners of the earth, amid the exasperated hatred of some, the real or feigned indignation of society, the envious scorn of several of his colleagues, the respect of a mass of readers, and the frenzied admiration of a great number. He expected to see a kind of bearded giant, of awe-inspiring aspect, with a thundering voice and an appearance little prepossessing at first.

The door opened on a room of uncommonly large dimensions, broad and high, lighted by an enormous window looking out over the valley. Old tapestries covered the walls; on the left, a monumental fireplace, flanked by two stone men, could have burned a century-old oak in one day. An immense table littered with books, papers and magazines stood in the middle of this apartment so vast and grand that it first engrossed the eye, and the attention was only afterward drawn to the man, stretched out when they entered on an Oriental divan where twenty persons could have slept. He took a few steps toward them, bowed, motioned to two seats, and turned back to his divan, where he sat with one leg drawn under him. A book lay open beside him, and in his right hand he held an ivory paper-cutter, the end of which he observed from time to time with one eye, closing the other with the persistency of a near-sighted person.

While the journalist explained the purpose of the visit, and the writer listened to him without yet answering, at times staring at him fixedly, Patissot, more and more embarrassed, was observing this celebrity.

Hardly forty, he was of medium height, fairly stout, and with a good-natured look. His head (very similar to those found in many Italian paintings of the sixteenth century), without being beautiful in the plastic sense of the word, gave an impression of great strength of character, power and intelligence. Short hair stood up straight on the high, well-developed forehead. A straight nose stopped short, as if cut off suddenly above the upper lip which was covered with a black mustache; over the whole chin was a closely-cropped beard. The dark, often ironical look was piercing, one felt that behind it there was a mind always actively at work observing people, interpreting words, analyzing gestures, uncovering the heart. This strong, round head was appropriate to his name, quick and short, with the bounding resonance of the two vowels.

When the journalist had fully explained his proposition, the writer answered him that he did not wish to make any definite arrangement, that he would, however, think the matter over, that his plans were not yet sufficiently defined. Then he stopped. It was a dismissal, and the two men, a little confused, arose. A desire seized Patissot; he wished this well-known person to say something to him, anything, some word which he could repeat to his colleagues; and, growing bold, he stammered: "Oh, monsieur! If you knew how I appreciate your works!" The other bowed, but answered nothing. Patissot became very bold and continued: "It is a great honor for me to speak to you to-day." The writer once more bowed, but with a stiff and impatient look. Patissot noticed it, and, completely losing his head, he added as he retreated: "What a su—su—superb property!"

Then, in the heart of the man of letters, the landowner awoke, and, smiling, he opened the window to show them the immense stretch of view. An endless horizon broadened out on all sides, giving a view of Triel, Pisse-Fontaine, Chanteloup, all the heights of Hautrie, and the Seine as far as the eye could see. The two visitors, delighted, congratulated him, and the house was opened to them. They saw everything, down to the dainty kitchen, whose walls and even ceilings were covered with porcelain tiles ornamented with blue designs, which excited the wonder of the farmers.

"How did you happen to buy this place?" asked the journalist.

The novelist explained that, while looking for a cottage to hire for the summer, he had found the little house, which was for sale for several thousand francs, a song, almost nothing. He immediately bought it.

"But everything that you have added must have cost you a good deal!"

The writer smiled, and answered: "Yes, quite a little."

The two men left. The journalist, taking Patissot by the arm, was philosophizing in a low voice:

"Every general has his Waterloo," he said; "every Balzac has his Jardies, and every artist living in the country feels like a landed proprietor."

They took the train at the station of Villaines, and, on the way home, Patissot loudly mentioned the names of the famous painter and of the great novelist as though they were his friends. He even allowed people to think that he had taken luncheon with one and dinner with the other.

BEFORE THE CELEBRATION

The celebration is approaching and preliminary quivers are already running through the streets, just as the ripples disturb the water preparatory to a storm. The shops, draped with flags, display a variety of gay-colored bunting materials, and the dry-goods people deceive one about the three colors as grocers do about the weight of candles. Little by little, hearts warm up to the matter; people speak about it in the street after dinner; ideas are exchanged:

"What a celebration it will be, my friend; what a celebration!"

"Have you heard the news? All the rulers are coming incognito, as bourgeois, in order to see it."

"I hear that the Emperor of Russia has arrived; he expects to go about everywhere with the Prince of Wales."

"It certainly will be a fine celebration!"

It is going to a celebration; what Monsieur Patissot, Parisian bourgeois, calls a celebration; one of these nameless tumults which, for fifteen hours, roll from one end of the city to the other, every ugly specimen togged out in its finest, a mob of perspiring bodies, where side by side are tossed about the stout gossip bedecked in red, white and blue ribbons, grown fat behind her counter and panting from lack of breath, the rickety clerk with his wife and brat in tow, the laborer carrying his youngster astride his neck, the bewildered provincial with his foolish, dazed expression, the groom, barely shaved and still spreading the perfume of the stable. And the foreigners dressed like monkeys, English women like giraffes, the water-carrier, cleaned up for the occasion, and the innumerable phalanx of little bourgeois, inoffensive little people, amused at everything. All this crowding and pressing, the sweat and dust, and the turmoil, all these eddies of human flesh, trampling of corns beneath the feet of your neighbors, this city all topsy-turvy, these vile odors, these frantic efforts toward nothing, the breath of millions of people, all redolent of garlic, give to Monsieur Patissot all the joy which it is possible for his heart to hold.

After reading the proclamation of the mayor on the walls of his district he had made his preparations.

This bit of prose said:

I wish to call your attention particularly to the part of individuals in this celebration. Decorate your homes, illuminate your windows. Get together, open up a subscription in order to give to your houses and to your street a more brilliant and more artistic appearance than the neighboring houses and streets.

Then Monsieur Patissot tried to imagine how he could give to his home an artistic appearance.

One serious obstacle stood in the way. His only window looked out on a courtyard, a narrow, dark shaft, where only the rats could have seen his three Japanese lanterns.

He needed a public opening. He found it. On the first floor of his house lived a rich man, a nobleman and a royalist, whose coachman, also a reactionary, occupied a garret-room on the sixth floor, facing the street. Monsieur Patissot supposed that by paying (every conscience can be bought) he could obtain the use of the room for the day. He proposed five francs to this citizen of the whip for the use of his room from noon till midnight. The offer was immediately accepted.

Then he began to busy himself with the decorations. Three flags, four lanterns, was that enough to give to this box an artistic appearance—to express all the noble feelings of his soul? No; assuredly not! But, notwithstanding diligent search and nightly meditation, Monsieur Patissot could think of nothing else. He consulted his neighbors, who were surprised at the question; he questioned his colleagues—every one had bought lanterns and flags, some adding, for the occasion, red, white and blue bunting.

Then he began to rack his brains for some original idea. He frequented the cafes, questioning the patrons; they lacked imagination. Then one morning he went out on top of an omnibus. A respectable-looking gentleman was smoking a cigar beside him, a little farther away a laborer was smoking his pipe upside down, near the driver two rough fellows were joking, and clerks of every description were going to business for three cents.

Before the stores stacks of flags were resplendent under the rising sun. Patissot turned to his neighbor.

"It is going to be a fine celebration," he said. The gentleman looked at him sideways and answered in a haughty manner:

"That makes no difference to me!"

"You are not going to take part in it?" asked the surprised clerk. The other shook his head disdainfully and declared:

"They make me tired with their celebrations! Whose celebration is it? The government's? I do not recognize this government, monsieur!"

But Patissot, as government employee, took on his superior manner, and answered in a stern voice:

"Monsieur, the Republic is the government."

His neighbor was not in the least disturbed, and, pushing his hands down in his pockets, he exclaimed:

"Well, and what then? It makes no difference to me. Whether it's for the Republic or something else, I don't care! What I want, monsieur, is to know my government. I saw Charles X. and adhered to him, monsieur; I saw Louis-Philippe and adhered to him, monsieur; I saw Napoleon and adhered to him; but I have never seen the Republic."

Patissot, still serious, answered:

"The Republic, monsieur, is represented by its president!"

The other grumbled:

"Well, them, show him to me!"

Patissot shrugged his shoulders.

"Every one can see him; he's not shut up in a closet!"

Suddenly the fat man grew angry.

"Excuse me, monsieur, he cannot be seen. I have personally tried more than a hundred times, monsieur. I have posted myself near the Elysee; he did not come out. A passer-by informed me that he was playing billiards in the cafe opposite; I went to the cafe opposite; he was not there. I had been promised that he would go to Melun for the convention; I went to Melun, I did not see him. At last I became weary. I did not even see Monsieur Gambetta, and I do not know a single deputy."

He was, growing excited:

"A government, monsieur, is made to be seen; that's what it's there for, and for nothing else. One must be able to know that on such and such a day at such an hour the government will pass through such and such a street. Then one goes there and is satisfied."

Patissot, now calm, was enjoying his arguments.

"It is true," he said, "that it is agreeable to know the people by whom one is governed."

The gentleman continued more gently:

"Do you know how I would manage the celebration? Well, monsieur, I would have a procession of gilded cars, like the chariots used at the crowning of kings; in them I would parade all the members of the government, from the president to the deputies, throughout Paris all day long. In that manner, at least, every one would know by sight the personnel of the state."

But one of the toughs near the coachman turned around, exclaiming:

"And the fatted ox, where would you put him?"

A laugh ran round the two benches. Patissot understood the objection, and murmured:

"It might not perhaps be very dignified."

The gentleman thought the matter over and admitted it.

"Then," he said, "I would place them in view some place, so that every one could see them without going out of his way; on the Triumphal Arch at the Place de l'Etoile, for instance; and I would have the whole population pass before them. That would be very imposing."

Once more the tough turned round and said:

"You'd have to take telescopes to see their faces."

The gentleman did not answer; he continued:

"It's just like the presentation of the flags! There ought to be some pretext, a mimic war ought to be organized, and the banners would be awarded to the troops as a reward. I had an idea about which I wrote to the minister; but he has not deigned to answer me. As the taking of the Bastille has been chosen for the date of the national celebration, a reproduction of this event might be made; there would be a pasteboard Bastille, fixed up by a scene-painter and concealing within its walls the whole Column of July. Then, monsieur, the troop would attack. That would be a magnificent spectacle as well as a lesson, to see the army itself overthrow the ramparts of tyranny. Then this Bastille would be set fire to and from the midst of the flames would appear the Column with the genius of Liberty, symbol of a new order and of the freedom of the people."

This time every one was listening to him and finding his idea excellent. An old gentleman exclaimed:

"That is a great idea, monsieur, which does you honor. It is to be regretted that the government did not adopt it."

A young man declared that actors ought to recite the "Iambes" of Barbier through the streets in order to teach the people art and liberty simultaneously.

These propositions excited general enthusiasm. Each one wished to have his word; all were wrought up. From a passing hand-organ a few strains of the Marseillaise were heard; the laborer started the song, and everybody joined in, roaring the chorus. The exalted nature of the song and its wild rhythm fired the driver, who lashed his horses to a gallop. Monsieur Patissot was bawling at the top of his lungs, and the passengers inside, frightened, were wondering what hurricane had struck them.

At last they stopped, and Monsieur Patissot, judging his neighbor to be a man of initiative, consulted him about the preparations which he expected to make:

"Lanterns and flags are all right,'" said Patissot; "but I prefer something better."

The other thought for a long time, but found nothing. Then, in despair, the clerk bought three flags and four lanterns.

AN EXPERIMENT IN LOVE

Many poets think that nature is incomplete without women, and hence, doubtless, come all the flowery comparisons which, in their songs, make our natural companion in turn a rose, a violet, a tulip, or something of that order. The need of tenderness which seizes us at dusk, when the evening mist begins to roll in from the hills, and when all the perfumes of the earth intoxicate us, is but imperfectly satisfied by lyric invocations. Monsieur Patissot, like all others, was seized with a wild desire for tenderness, for sweet kisses exchanged along a path where sunshine steals in at times, for the pressure of a pair of small hands, for a supple waist bending under his embrace.

He began to look at love as an unbounded pleasure, and, in his hours of reverie, he thanked the Great Unknown for having put so much charm into the caresses of human beings. But he needed a companion, and he did not know where to find one. On the advice of a friend, he went to the Folies-Bergere. There he saw a complete assortment. He was greatly perplexed to choose between them, for the desires of his heart were chiefly composed of poetic impulses, and poetry did not seem to be the strong point of these young ladies with penciled eyebrows who smiled at him in such a disturbing manner, showing the enamel of their false teeth. At last his choice fell on a young beginner who seemed poor and timid and whose sad look seemed to announce a nature easily influenced by poetry.

He made an appointment with her for the following day at nine o'clock at the Saint-Lazare station. She did not come, but she was kind enough to send a friend in her stead.

She was a tall, red-haired girl, patriotically dressed in three colors, and covered by an immense tunnel hat, of which her head occupied the centre. Monsieur Patissot, a little disappointed, nevertheless accepted this substitute. They left for Maisons-Laffite, where regattas and a grand Venetian festival had been announced.

As soon as they were in the car, which was already occupied by two gentlemen who wore the red ribbon and three ladies who must at least have been duchesses, they were so dignified, the big red-haired girl, who answered the name of Octavie, announced to Patissot, in a screeching voice, that she was a fine girl fond of a good time and loving the country because there she could pick flowers and eat fried fish. She laughed with a shrillness which almost shattered the windows, familiarly calling her companion "My big darling."

Shame overwhelmed Patissot, who as a government employee, had to observe a certain amount of decorum. But Octavie stopped talking, glancing at her neighbors, seized with the overpowering desire which haunts all women of a certain class to make the acquaintance of respectable women. After about five minutes she thought she had found an opening, and, drawing from her pocket a Gil-Blas, she politely offered it to one of the amazed ladies, who declined, shaking her head. Then the big, red-haired girl began saying things with a double meaning, speaking of women who are stuck up without being any better than the others; sometimes she would let out a vulgar word which acted like a bomb exploding amid the icy dignity of the passengers.

At last they arrived. Patissot immediately wished to gain the shady nooks of the park, hoping that the melancholy of the forest would quiet the ruffled temper of his companion. But an entirely different effect resulted. As soon as she was amid the leaves and grass she began to sing at the top of her lungs snatches from operas which had stuck in her frivolous mind, warbling and trilling, passing from "Robert le Diable" to the "Muette," lingering especially on a sentimental love-song, whose last verses she sang in a voice as piercing as a gimlet.

Then suddenly she grew hungry. Patissot, who was still awaiting the hoped-for tenderness, tried in vain to retain her. Then she grew angry, exclaiming:

"I am not here for a dull time, am I?"

He had to take her to the Petit-Havre restaurant, which was near the place where the regatta was to be held.

She ordered an endless luncheon, a succession of dishes substantial enough to feed a regiment. Then, unable to wait, she called for relishes. A box of sardines was brought; she started in on it as though she intended to swallow the box itself. But when she had eaten two or three of the little oily fish she declared that she was no longer hungry and that she wished to see the preparations for the race.

Patissot, in despair and in his turn seized with hunger, absolutely refused to move. She started off alone, promising to return in time for the dessert. He began to eat in lonely silence, not knowing how to lead this rebellious nature to the realization of his dreams.

As she did not return he set out in search of her. She had found some friends, a troop of boatmen, in scanty garb, sunburned to the tips of their ears, and gesticulating, who were loudly arranging the details of the race in front of the house of Fourmaise, the builder.

Two respectable-looking gentlemen, probably the judges, were listening attentively. As soon as she saw Patissot, Octavie, who was leaning on the tanned arm of a strapping fellow who probably had more muscle than brains, whispered a few words in his ears. He answered:

"That's an agreement."

She returned to the clerk full of joy, her eyes sparkling, almost caressing.

"Let's go for a row," said she.

Pleased to see her so charming, he gave in to this new whim and procured a boat. But she obstinately refused to go to the races, notwithstanding Patissot's wishes.

"I had rather be alone with you, darling."

His heart thrilled. At last!

He took off his coat and began to row madly.

An old dilapidated mill, whose worm-eaten wheels hung over the water, stood with its two arches across a little arm of the river. Slowly they passed beneath it, and, when they were on the other side, they noticed before them a delightful little stretch of river, shaded by great trees which formed an arch over their heads. The little stream flowed along, winding first to the right and then to the left, continually revealing new scenes, broad fields on one side and on the other side a hill covered with cottages. They passed before a bathing establishment almost entirely hidden by the foliage, a charming country spot where gentlemen in clean gloves and beribboned ladies displayed all the ridiculous awkwardness of elegant people in the country. She cried joyously:

"Later on we will take a dip there."

Farther on, in a kind of bay, she wished to stop, coaxing:

"Come here, honey, right close to me."

She put her arm around his neck and, leaning her head on his shoulder, she murmured:

"How nice it is! How delightful it is on the water!"

Patissot was reveling in happiness. He was thinking of those foolish boatmen who, without ever feeling the penetrating charm of the river banks and the delicate grace of the reeds, row along out of breath, perspiring and tired out, from the tavern where they take luncheon to the tavern where they take dinner.

He was so comfortable that he fell asleep. When he awoke, he was alone. He called, but no one answered. Anxious, he climbed up on the side of the river, fearing that some accident might have happened.

Then, in the distance, coming in his direction, he saw a long, slender gig which four oarsmen as black as negroes were driving through the water like an arrow. It came nearer, skimming over the water; a woman was holding the tiller. Heavens! It looked—it was she! In order to regulate the rhythm of the stroke, she was singing in her shrill voice a boating song, which she interrupted for a minute as she got in front of Patissot. Then, throwing him a kiss, she cried:

"You big goose!"

A DINNER AND SOME OPINIONS

On the occasion of the national celebration Monsieur Antoine Perdrix, chief of Monsieur Patissot's department, was made a knight of the Legion of Honor. He had been in service for thirty years under preceding governments, and for ten years under the present one. His employees, although grumbling a little at being thus rewarded in the person of their chief, thought it wise, nevertheless, to offer him a cross studded with paste diamonds. The new knight, in turn, not wishing to be outdone, invited them all to dinner for the following Sunday, at his place at Asnieres.

The house, decorated with Moorish ornaments, looked like a cafe concert, but its location gave it value, as the railroad cut through the whole garden, passing within a hundred and fifty feet of the porch. On the regulation plot of grass stood a basin of Roman cement, containing goldfish and a stream of water the size of that which comes from a syringe, which occasionally made microscopic rainbows at which the guests marvelled.

The feeding of this irrigator was the constant preoccupation of Monsieur Perdrix, who would sometimes get up at five o'clock in the morning in order to fill the tank. Then, in his shirt sleeves, his big stomach almost bursting from his trousers, he would pump wildly, so that on returning from the office he could have the satisfaction of letting the fountain play and of imagining that it was cooling off the garden.

On the night of the official dinner all the guests, one after the other, went into ecstasies over the surroundings, and each time they heard a train in the distance, Monsieur Perdrix would announce to them its destination: Saint-Germain, Le Havre, Cherbourg, or Dieppe, and they would playfully wave to the passengers leaning from the windows.

The whole office force was there. First came Monsieur Capitaine, the assistant chief; Monsieur Patissot, chief clerk; then Messieurs de Sombreterre and Vallin, elegant young employees who only came to the office when they had to; lastly Monsieur Rade, known throughout the ministry for the absurd doctrines which he upheld, and the copying clerk, Monsieur Boivin.

Monsieur Rade passed for a character. Some called him a dreamer or an idealist, others a revolutionary; every one agreed that he was very clumsy. Old, thin and small, with bright eyes and long, white hair, he had all his life professed a profound contempt for administrative work. A book rummager and a great reader, with a nature continually in revolt against everything, a seeker of truth and a despiser of popular prejudices, he had a clear and paradoxical manner of expressing his opinions which closed the mouths of self-satisfied fools and of those that were discontented without knowing why. People said: "That old fool of a Rade," or else: "That harebrained Rade"; and the slowness, of his promotion seemed to indicate the reason, according to commonplace minds. His freedom of speech often made—his colleagues tremble; they asked themselves with terror how he had been able to keep his place as long as he had. As soon as they had seated themselves, Monsieur Perdrix thanked his "collaborators" in a neat little speech, promising them his protection, the more valuable as his power grew, and he ended with a stirring peroration in which he thanked and glorified a government so liberal and just that it knows how to seek out the worthy from among the humble.

Monsieur Capitaine, the assistant chief, answered in the name of the office, congratulated, greeted, exalted, sang the praises of all; frantic applause greeted these two bits of eloquence. After that they settled down seriously to the business of eating.

Everything went well up to the dessert; lack of conversation went unnoticed. But after the coffee a discussion arose, and Monsieur Rade let himself loose and soon began to overstep the bounds of discretion.

They naturally discussed love, and a breath of chivalry intoxicated this room full of bureaucrats; they praised and exalted the superior beauty of woman, the delicacy of her soul, her aptitude for exquisite things, the correctness of her judgment, and the refinement of her sentiments. Monsieur Rade began to protest, energetically refusing to credit the so-called "fair" sex with all the qualities they ascribed to it; then, amidst the general indignation, he quoted some authors:

"Schopenhauer, gentlemen, Schopenhauer, the great philosopher, revered by all Germany, says: 'Man's intelligence must have been terribly deadened by love in order to call this sex with the small waist, narrow shoulders, large hips and crooked legs, the fair sex. All its beauty lies in the instinct of love. Instead of calling it the fair, it would have been better to call it the unaesthetic sex. Women have neither the appreciation nor the knowledge of music, any more than they have of poetry or of the plastic arts; with them it is merely an apelike imitation, pure pretence, affectation cultivated from their desire to please.'"

"The man who said that is an idiot," exclaimed Monsieur de Sombreterre.

Monsieur Rade smilingly continued:

"And how about Rousseau, gentlemen? Here is his opinion: 'Women, as a rule, love no art, are skilled in none, and have no talent.'"

Monsieur de Sombreterre disdainfully shrugged his shoulders: "Then Rousseau is as much of a fool as the other, that's all."

Monsieur Rade, still smiling, went on:

"And this is what Lord Byron said, who, nevertheless, loved women: 'They should be well fed and well dressed, but not allowed to mingle with society. They should also be taught religion, but they should ignore poetry and politics, only being allowed to read religious works or cook-books.'"

Monsieur Rade continued:

"You see, gentlemen, all of them study painting and music. But not a single one of them has ever painted a remarkable picture or composed a great opera! Why, gentlemen? Because they are the 'sexes sequior', the secondary sex in every sense of the word, made to be kept apart, in the background."

Monsieur Patissot was growing angry, and exclaimed:

"And how about Madame Sand, monsieur?"

"She is the one exception, monsieur, the one exception. I will quote to you another passage from another great philosopher, this one an Englishman, Herbert Spencer. Here is what he says: 'Each sex is capable, under the influence of abnormal stimulation, of manifesting faculties ordinarily reserved for the other one. Thus, for instance, in extreme cases a special excitement may cause the breasts of men to give milk; children deprived of their mothers have often thus been saved in time of famine. Nevertheless, we do not place this faculty of giving milk among the male attributes. It is the same with female intelligence, which, in certain cases, will give superior products, but which is not to be considered in an estimate of the feminine nature as a social factor.'"

All Monsieur Patissot's chivalric instincts were wounded and he declared:

"You are not a Frenchman, monsieur. French gallantry is a form of patriotism."

Monsieur Rade retorted:

"I have very little patriotism, monsieur, as little as I can get along with."

A coolness settled over the company, but he continued quietly:

"Do you admit with me that war is a barbarous thing; that this custom of killing off people constitutes a condition of savagery; that it is odious, when life is the only real good, to see governments, whose duty is to protect the lives of their subjects, persistently looking for means of destruction? Am I not right? Well, if war is a terrible thing, what about patriotism, which is the idea at the base of it? When a murderer kills he has a fixed idea; it is to steal. When a good man sticks his bayonet through another good man, father of a family, or, perhaps, a great artist, what idea is he following out?"

Everybody was shocked.

"When one has such thoughts, one should not express them in public."

M. Patissot continued:

"There are, however, monsieur, principles which all good people recognize."

M. Rade asked: "Which ones?"

Then very solemnly, M. Patissot pronounced: "Morality, monsieur."

M. Rade was beaming; he exclaimed:

"Just let me give you one example, gentlemen, one little example. What is your opinion of the gentlemen with the silk caps who thrive along the boulevard's on the delightful traffic which you know, and who make a living out of it?"

A look of disgust ran round the table:

"Well, gentlemen! only a century ago, when an elegant gentleman, very ticklish about his honor, had for—friend—a beautiful and rich lady, it was considered perfectly proper to live at her expense and even to squander her whole fortune. This game was considered delightful. This only goes to show that the principles of morality are by no means settled—and that—"

M. Perdrix, visibly embarrassed, stopped him:

"M. Rade, you are sapping the very foundations of society. One must always have principles. Thus, in politics, here is M. de Sombreterre, who is a Legitimist; M. Vallin, an Orleanist; M. Patissot and myself, Republicans; we all have very different principles, and yet we agree very well because we have them."

But M. Rade exclaimed:

"I also have principles, gentlemen, very distinct ones."

M. Patissot raised his head and coldly asked:

"It would please me greatly to know them, monsieur."

M. Rade did not need to be coaxed.

"Here they are, monsieur:

"First principle—Government by one person is a monstrosity.

"Second principle—Restricted suffrage is an injustice.

"Third principle—Universal suffrage is idiotic.

"To deliver up millions of men, superior minds, scientists, even geniuses, to the caprice and will of a being who, in an instant of gaiety, madness, intoxication or love, would not hesitate to sacrifice everything for his exalted fancy, would spend the wealth of the country amassed by others with difficulty, would have thousands of men slaughtered on the battle-fields, all this appears to me—a simple logician—a monstrous aberration.

"But, admitting that a country must govern itself, to exclude, on some always debatable pretext, a part of the citizens from the administration of affairs is such an injustice that it seems to me unworthy of a further discussion.

"There remains universal suffrage. I suppose that you will agree with me that geniuses are a rarity. Let us be liberal and say that there are at present five in France. Now, let us add, perhaps, two hundred men with a decided talent, one thousand others possessing various talents, and ten thousand superior intellects. This is a staff of eleven thousand two hundred and five minds. After that you have the army of mediocrities followed by the multitude of fools. As the mediocrities and the fools always form the immense majority, it is impossible for them to elect an intelligent government.

"In order to be fair I admit that logically universal suffrage seems to me the only admissible principle, but it is impracticable. Here are the reasons why:

"To make all the living forces of the country cooperate in the government, to represent all the interests, to take into account all the rights, is an ideal dream, but hardly practicable, because the only force which can be measured is that very one which should be neglected, the stupid strength of numbers, According to your method, unintelligent numbers equal genius, knowledge, learning, wealth and industry. When you are able to give to a member of the Institute ten thousand votes to a ragman's one, one hundred votes for a great land-owner as against his farmer's ten, then you will have approached an equilibrium of forces and obtained a national representation which will really represent the strength of the nation. But I challenge you to do it.

"Here are my conclusions:

"Formerly, when a man was a failure at every other profession he turned photographer; now he has himself elected a deputy. A government thus composed will always be sadly lacking, incapable of evil as well as of good. On the other hand, a despot, if he be stupid, can do a lot of harm, and, if he be intelligent (a thing which is very scarce), he may do good.

"I cannot decide between these two forms of government; I declare myself to be an anarchist, that is to say, a partisan of that power which is the most unassuming, the least felt, the most liberal, in the broadest sense of the word, and revolutionary at the same time; by that I mean the everlasting enemy of this same power, which can in no way be anything but defective. That's all!"

Cries of indignation rose about the table, and all, whether Legitimist, Orleanist or Republican through force of circumstances, grew red with anger. M. Patissot especially was choking with rage, and, turning toward M. Rade, he cried:

"Then, monsieur, you believe in nothing?"

The other answered quietly:

"You're absolutely correct, monsieur."

The anger felt by all the guests prevented M. Rade from continuing, and M. Perdrix, as chief, closed the discussion.

"Enough, gentlemen! We each have our opinion, and we have no intention of changing it."

All agreed with the wise words. But M. Rade, never satisfied, wished to have the last word.

"I have, however, one moral," said he. "It is simple and always applicable. One sentence embraces the whole thought; here it is: 'Never do unto another that which you would not have him do unto you.' I defy you to pick any flaw in it, while I will undertake to demolish your most sacred principles with three arguments."

This time there was no answer. But as they were going home at night, by couples, each one was saying to his companion: "Really, M. Rade goes much too far. His mind must surely be unbalanced. He ought to be appointed assistant chief at the Charenton Asylum."

A RECOLLECTION

How many recollections of youth come to me in the soft sunlight of early spring! It was an age when all was pleasant, cheerful, charming, intoxicating. How exquisite are the remembrances of those old springtimes!

Do you recall, old friends and brothers, those happy years when life was nothing but a triumph and an occasion for mirth? Do you recall the days of wanderings around Paris, our jolly poverty, our walks in the fresh, green woods, our drinks in the wine-shops on the banks of the Seine and our commonplace and delightful little flirtations?

I will tell you about one of these. It was twelve years ago and already appears to me so old, so old that it seems now as if it belonged to the other end of life, before middle age, this dreadful middle age from which I suddenly perceived the end of the journey.

I was then twenty-five. I had just come to Paris. I was in a government office, and Sundays were to me like unusual festivals, full of exuberant happiness, although nothing remarkable occurred.

Now it is Sunday every day, but I regret the time when I had only one Sunday in the week. How enjoyable it was! I had six francs to spend!

On this particular morning I awoke with that sense of freedom that all clerks know so well—the sense of emancipation, of rest, of quiet and of independence.

I opened my window. The weather was charming. A blue sky full of sunlight and swallows spread above the town.

I dressed quickly and set out, intending to spend the day in the woods breathing the air of the green trees, for I am originally a rustic, having been brought up amid the grass and the trees.

Paris was astir and happy in the warmth and the light. The front of the houses was bathed in sunlight, the janitress' canaries were singing in their cages and there was an air of gaiety in the streets, in the faces of the inhabitants, lighting them up with a smile as if all beings and all things experienced a secret satisfaction at the rising of the brilliant sun.

I walked towards the Seine to take the Swallow, which would land me at Saint-Cloud.

How I loved waiting for the boat on the wharf:

It seemed to me that I was about to set out for the ends of the world, for new and wonderful lands. I saw the boat approaching yonder, yonder under the second bridge, looking quite small with its plume of smoke, then growing larger and ever larger, as it drew near, until it looked to me like a mail steamer.

It came up to the wharf and I went on board. People were there already in their Sunday clothes, startling toilettes, gaudy ribbons and bright scarlet designs. I took up a position in the bows, standing up and looking at the quays, the trees, the houses and the bridges disappearing behind us. And suddenly I perceived the great viaduct of Point du Jour which blocked the river. It was the end of Paris, the beginning of the country, and behind the double row of arches the Seine, suddenly spreading out as though it had regained space and liberty, became all at once the peaceful river which flows through the plains, alongside the wooded hills, amid the meadows, along the edge of the forests.

After passing between two islands the Swallow went round a curved verdant slope dotted with white houses. A voice called out: "Bas Meudon" and a little further on, "Sevres," and still further, "Saint-Cloud."

I went on shore and walked hurriedly through the little town to the road leading to the wood.

I had brought with me a map of the environs of Paris, so that I might not lose my way amid the paths which cross in every direction these little forests where Parisians take their outings.

As soon as I was unperceived I began to study my guide, which seemed to be perfectly clear. I was to turn to the right, then to the left, then again to the left and I should reach Versailles by evening in time for dinner.

I walked slowly beneath the young leaves, drinking in the air, fragrant with the odor of young buds and sap. I sauntered along, forgetful of musty papers, of the offices, of my chief, my colleagues, my documents, and thinking of the good things that were sure to come to me, of all the veiled unknown contained in the future. A thousand recollections of childhood came over me, awakened by these country odors, and I walked along, permeated with the fragrant, living enchantment, the emotional enchantment of the woods warmed by the sun of June.

At times I sat down to look at all sorts of little flowers growing on a bank, with the names of which I was familiar. I recognized them all just as if they were the ones I had seen long ago in the country. They were yellow, red, violet, delicate, dainty, perched on long stems or close to the ground. Insects of all colors and shapes, short, long, of peculiar form, frightful, and microscopic monsters, climbed quietly up the stalks of grass which bent beneath their weight.

Then I went to sleep for some hours in a hollow and started off again, refreshed by my doze.

In front of me lay an enchanting pathway and through its somewhat scanty foliage the sun poured down drops of light on the marguerites which grew there. It stretched out interminably, quiet and deserted, save for an occasional big wasp, who would stop buzzing now and then to sip from a flower, and then continue his way.

All at once I perceived at the end of the path two persons, a man and a woman, coming towards me. Annoyed at being disturbed in my quiet walk, I was about to dive into the thicket, when I thought I heard someone calling me. The woman was, in fact, shaking her parasol, and the man, in his shirt sleeves, his coat over one arm, was waving the other as a signal of distress.

I went towards them. They were walking hurriedly, their faces very red, she with short, quick steps and he with long strides. They both looked annoyed and fatigued.

The woman asked:

"Can you tell me, monsieur, where we are? My fool of a husband made us lose our way, although he pretended he knew the country perfectly."

I replied confidently:

"Madame, you are going towards Saint-Cloud and turning your back on Versailles."

With a look of annoyed pity for her husband, she exclaimed:

"What, we are turning our back on Versailles? Why, that is just where we want to dine!"

"I am going there also, madame."

"Mon Dieu, mon Dieu, mon Dieu!" she repeated, shrugging her shoulders, and in that tone of sovereign contempt assumed by women to express their exasperation.

She was quite young, pretty, a brunette with a slight shadow on her upper lip.

As for him, he was perspiring and wiping his forehead. It was assuredly a little Parisian bourgeois couple. The man seemed cast down, exhausted and distressed.

"But, my dear friend, it was you—" he murmured.

She did not allow him to finish his sentence.

"It was I! Ah, it is my fault now! Was it I who wanted to go out without getting any information, pretending that I knew how to find my way? Was it I who wanted to take the road to the right on top of the hill, insisting that I recognized the road? Was it I who undertook to take charge of Cachou—"

She had not finished speaking when her husband, as if he had suddenly gone crazy, gave a piercing scream, a long, wild cry that could not be described in any language, but which sounded like 'tuituit'.

The young woman did not appear to be surprised or moved and resumed:

"No, really, some people are so stupid and they pretend they know everything. Was it I who took the train to Dieppe last year instead of the train to Havre—tell me, was it I? Was it I who bet that M. Letourneur lived in Rue des Martyres? Was it I who would not believe that Celeste was a thief?"

She went on, furious, with a surprising flow of language, accumulating the most varied, the most unexpected and the most overwhelming accusations drawn from the intimate relations of their daily life, reproaching her husband for all his actions, all his ideas, all his habits, all his enterprises, all his efforts, for his life from the time of their marriage up to the present time.

He strove to check her, to calm her and stammered:

"But, my dear, it is useless—before monsieur. We are making ourselves ridiculous. This does not interest monsieur."

And he cast mournful glances into the thicket as though he sought to sound its peaceful and mysterious depths, in order to flee thither, to escape and hide from all eyes, and from time to time he uttered a fresh scream, a prolonged and shrill "tuituit." I took this to be a nervous affection.

The young woman, suddenly turning towards me: and changing her tone with singular rapidity, said:

"If monsieur will kindly allow us, we will accompany him on the road, so as not to lose our way again, and be obliged, possibly, to sleep in the wood."

I bowed. She took my arm and began to talk about a thousand things —about herself, her life, her family, her business. They were glovers in the Rue Saint-Lazare.

Her husband walked beside her, casting wild glances into the thick wood and screaming "tuituit" every few moments.

At last I inquired:

"Why do you scream like that?"

"I have lost my poor dog," he replied in a tone of discouragement and despair.

"How is that—you have lost your dog?"

"Yes. He was just a year old. He had never been outside the shop. I wanted to take him to have a run in the woods. He had never seen the grass nor the leaves and he was almost wild. He began to run about and bark and he disappeared in the wood. I must also add that he was greatly afraid of the train. That may have driven him mad. I kept on calling him, but he has not come back. He will die of hunger in there."

Without turning towards her husband, the young woman said:

"If you had left his chain on, it would not have happened. When people are as stupid as you are they do not keep a dog."

"But, my dear, it was you—" he murmured timidly.

She stopped short, and looking into his eyes as if she were going to tear them out, she began again to cast in his face innumerable reproaches.

It was growing dark. The cloud of vapor that covers the country at dusk was slowly rising and there was a poetry in the air, induced by the peculiar and enchanting freshness of the atmosphere that one feels in the woods at nightfall.

Suddenly the young man stopped, and feeling his body feverishly, exclaimed:

"Oh, I think that I—"

She looked at him.

"Well, what?"

"I did not notice that I had my coat on my arm."

"Well—?"

"I have lost my pocketbook—my money was in it."

She shook with anger and choked with indignation.

"That was all that was lacking. How stupid you are! how stupid you are! Is it possible that I could have married such an idiot! Well, go and look for it, and see that you find it. I am going on to Versailles with monsieur. I do not want to sleep in the wood."

"Yes, my dear," he replied gently. "Where shall I find you?"

A restaurant had been recommended to me. I gave him the address.

He turned back and, stooping down as he searched the ground with anxious eyes, he moved away, screaming "tuituit" every few moments.

We could see him for some time until the growing darkness concealed all but his outline, but we heard his mournful "tuituit," shriller and shriller as the night grew darker.

As for me, I stepped along quickly and happily in the soft twilight, with this little unknown woman leaning on my arm. I tried to say pretty things to her, but could think of nothing. I remained silent, disturbed, enchanted.

Our path was suddenly crossed by a high road. To the right I perceived a town lying in a valley.

What was this place? A man was passing. I asked him. He replied:

"Bougival."

I was dumfounded.

"What, Bougival? Are you sure?"

"Parbleu, I belong there!"

The little woman burst into an idiotic laugh.

I proposed that we should take a carriage and drive to Versailles. She replied:

"No, indeed. This is very funny and I am very hungry. I am really quite calm. My husband will find his way all right. It is a treat to me to be rid of him for a few hours."

We went into a restaurant beside the water and I ventured to ask for a private compartment. We had some supper. She sang, drank champagne, committed all sorts of follies.

That was my first serious flirtation.

OUR LETTERS

Eight hours of railway travel induce sleep for some persons and insomnia for others; with me, any journey prevents my sleeping on the following night.

At about five o'clock I arrived at the estate of Abelle, which belongs to my friends, the Murets d'Artus, to spend three weeks there. It is a pretty house, built by one of their grandfathers in the style of the latter half of the last century. Therefore it has that intimate character of dwellings that have always been inhabited, furnished and enlivened by the same people. Nothing changes; nothing alters the soul of the dwelling, from which the furniture has never been taken out, the tapestries never unnailed, thus becoming worn out, faded, discolored, on the same walls. None of the old furniture leaves the place; only from time to time it is moved a little to make room for a new piece, which enters there like a new-born infant in the midst of brothers and sisters.

The house is on a hill in the center of a park which slopes down to the river, where there is a little stone bridge. Beyond the water the fields stretch out in the distance, and here one can see the cows wandering around, pasturing on the moist grass; their eyes seem full of the dew, mist and freshness of the pasture. I love this dwelling, just as one loves a thing which one ardently desires to possess. I return here every autumn with infinite delight; I leave with regret.

After I had dined with this friendly family, by whom I was received like a relative, I asked my friend, Paul Muret: "Which room did you give me this year?"

"Aunt Rose's room."

An hour later, followed by her three children, two little girls and a boy, Madame Muret d'Artus installed me in Aunt Rose's room, where I had not yet slept.

When I was alone I examined the walls, the furniture, the general aspect of the room, in order to attune my mind to it. I knew it but little, as I had entered it only once or twice, and I looked indifferently at a pastel portrait of Aunt Rose, who gave her name to the room.

This old Aunt Rose, with her curls, looking at me from behind the glass, made very little impression on my mind. She looked to me like a woman of former days, with principles and precepts as strong on the maxims of morality as on cooking recipes, one of these old aunts who are the bugbear of gaiety and the stern and wrinkled angel of provincial families.

I never had heard her spoken of; I knew nothing of her life or of her death. Did she belong to this century or to the preceding one? Had she left this earth after a calm or a stormy existence? Had she given up to heaven the pure soul of an old maid, the calm soul of a spouse, the tender one of a mother, or one moved by love? What difference did it make? The name alone, "Aunt Rose," seemed ridiculous, common, ugly.

I picked up a candle and looked at her severe face, hanging far up in an old gilt frame. Then, as I found it insignificant, disagreeable, even unsympathetic, I began to examine the furniture. It dated from the period of Louis XVI, the Revolution and the Directorate. Not a chair, not a curtain had entered this room since then, and it gave out the subtle odor of memories, which is the combined odor of wood, cloth, chairs, hangings, peculiar to places wherein have lived hearts that have loved and suffered.

I retired but did not sleep. After I had tossed about for an hour or two, I decided to get up and write some letters.

I opened a little mahogany desk with brass trimmings, which was placed between the two windows, in hope of finding some ink and paper; but all I found was a quill-pen, very much worn, and chewed at the end. I was about to close this piece of furniture, when a shining spot attracted my attention it looked like the yellow head of a nail. I scratched it with my finger, and it seemed to move. I seized it between two finger-nails, and pulled as hard as I could.

It came toward me gently. It was a long gold pin which had been slipped into a hole in the wood and remained hidden there.

Why? I immediately thought that it must have served to work some spring which hid a secret, and I looked. It took a long time. After about two hours of investigation, I discovered another hole opposite the first one, but at the bottom of a groove. Into this I stuck my pin: a little shelf sprang toward my face, and I saw two packages of yellow letters, tied with a blue ribbon.

I read them. Here are two of them:

So you wish me to return to you your letters, my dearest friend. Here they are, but it pains me to obey. Of what are you afraid? That I might lose them? But they are under lock and key. Do you fear that they might be stolen? I guard against that, for they are my dearest treasure.

Yes, it pains me deeply. I wondered whether, perhaps you might not be feeling some regret! Not regret at having loved me, for I know that you still do, but the regret of having expressed on white paper this living love in hours when your heart did not confide in me, but in the pen that you held in your hand. When we love, we have need of confession, need of talking or writing, and we either talk or write. Words fly away, those sweet words made of music, air and tenderness, warm and light, which escape as soon as they are uttered, which remain in the memory alone, but which one can neither see, touch nor kiss, as one can with the words written by your hand.

Your letters? Yes, I am returning them to you! But with what sorrow!

Undoubtedly, you must have had an after thought of delicate shame at expressions that are ineffaceable. In your sensitive and timid soul you must have regretted having written to a man that you loved him. You remembered sentences that called up recollections, and you said to yourself: "I will make ashes of those words."

Be satisfied, be calm. Here are your letters. I love you.

MY FRIEND:

No, you have not understood me, you have not guessed. I do not regret, and I never shall, that I told you of my affection.

I will always write to you, but you must return my letters to me as soon as you have read them.

I shall shock you, my friend, when I tell you the reason for this demand. It is not poetic, as you imagined, but practical. I am afraid, not of you, but of some mischance. I am guilty. I do not wish my fault to affect others than myself.

Understand me well. You and I may both die. You might fall off your horse, since you ride every day; you might die from a sudden attack, from a duel, from heart disease, from a carriage accident, in a thousand ways. For, if there is only one death, there are more ways of its reaching us than there are days or us to live.

Then your sisters, your brother, or your sister-in-law might find my letters! Do you think that they love me? I doubt it. And then, even if they adored me, is it possible for two women and one man to know a secret—such a secret!—and not to tell of it?

I seem to be saying very disagreeable things, speaking first of your death, and then suspecting the discreetness of your relatives.

But don't all of us die sooner or later? And it is almost certain that one of us will precede the other under the ground. We must therefore foresee all dangers, even that one.

As for me, I will keep your letters beside mine, in the secret of my little desk. I will show them to you there, sleeping side by side in their silken hiding place, full of our love, like lovers in a tomb.

You will say to me: "But if you should die first, my dear, your husband will find these letters."

Oh! I fear nothing. First of all, he does not know the secret of my desk, and then he will not look for it. And even if he finds it after my death, I fear nothing.

Did you ever stop to think of all the love letters that have been found after death? I have been thinking of this for a long time, and that is the reason I decided to ask you for my letters.

Think that never, do you understand, never, does a woman burn, tear or destroy the letters in which it is told her that she is loved. That is our whole life, our whole hope, expectation and dream. These little papers which bear our name in caressing terms are relics which we adore; they are chapels in which we are the saints. Our love letters are our titles to beauty, grace, seduction, the intimate vanity of our womanhood; they are the treasures of our heart. No, a woman does not destroy these secret and delicious archives of her life.

But, like everybody else, we die, and then—then these letters are found! Who finds them? The husband. Then what does he do? Nothing. He burns them.

Oh, I have thought a great deal about that! Just think that every day women are dying who have been loved; every day the traces and proofs of their fault fall into the hands of their husbands, and that there is never a scandal, never a duel.

Think, my dear, of what a man's heart is. He avenges himself on a living woman; he fights with the man who has dishonored her, kills him while she lives, because, well, why? I do not know exactly why. But, if, after her death, he finds similar proofs, he burns them and no one is the wiser, and he continues to shake hands with the friend of the dead woman, and feels quite at ease that these letters should not have fallen into strange hands, and that they are destroyed.

Oh, how many men I know among my friends who must have burned such proofs, and who pretend to know nothing, and yet who would have fought madly had they found them when she was still alive! But she is dead. Honor has changed. The tomb is the boundary of conjugal sinning.

Therefore, I can safely keep our letters, which, in your hands, would be a menace to both of us. Do you dare to say that I am not right?

I love you and kiss you.

I raised my eyes to the portrait of Aunt Rose, and as I looked at her severe, wrinkled face, I thought of all those women's souls which we do not know, and which we suppose to be so different from what they really are, whose inborn and ingenuous craftiness we never can penetrate, their quiet duplicity; and a verse of De Vigny returned to my memory:

"Always this comrade whose heart is uncertain."

THE LOVE OF LONG AGO

The old-fashioned chateau was built on a wooded knoll in the midst of tall trees with dark-green foliage; the park extended to a great distance, in one direction to the edge of the forest, in another to the distant country. A few yards from the front of the house was a huge stone basin with marble ladies taking a bath; other, basins were seen at intervals down to the foot of the slope, and a stream of water fell in cascades from one basin to another.

From the manor house, which preserved the grace of a superannuated coquette, down to the grottos incrusted with shell-work, where slumbered the loves of a bygone age, everything in this antique demesne had retained the physiognomy of former days. Everything seemed to speak still of ancient customs, of the manners of long ago, of former gallantries, and of the elegant trivialities so dear to our grandmothers.

In a parlor in the style of Louis XV, whose walls were covered with shepherds paying court to shepherdesses, beautiful ladies in hoop-skirts, and gallant gentlemen in wigs, a very old woman, who seemed dead as soon as she ceased to move, was almost lying down in a large easy-chair, at each side of which hung a thin, mummy-like hand.

Her dim eyes were gazing dreamily toward the distant horizon as if they sought to follow through the park the visions of her youth. Through the open window every now and then came a breath of air laden with the odor of grass and the perfume of flowers. It made her white locks flutter around her wrinkled forehead and old memories float through her brain.

Beside her, on a tapestried stool, a young girl, with long fair hair hanging in braids down her back, was embroidering an altar-cloth. There was a pensive expression in her eyes, and it was easy to see that she was dreaming, while her agile fingers flew over her work.

But the old lady turned round her head, and said:

"Berthe, read me something out of the newspapers, that I may still know sometimes what is going on in the world."

The young girl took up a newspaper, and cast a rapid glance over it.

"There is a great deal about politics, grandmamma; shall I pass that over?"

"Yes, yes, darling. Are there no love stories? Is gallantry, then, dead in France, that they no longer talk about abductions or adventures as they did formerly?"

The girl made a long search through the columns of the newspaper.

"Here is one," she said. "It is entitled 'A Love Drama!'"

The old woman smiled through her wrinkles. "Read that for me," she said.

And Berthe commenced. It was a case of vitriol throwing. A wife, in order to avenge herself on her husband's mistress, had burned her face and eyes. She had left the Court of Assizes acquitted, declared to be innocent, amid the applause of the crowd.

The grandmother moved about excitedly in her chair, and exclaimed:

"This is horrible—why, it is perfectly horrible!

"See whether you can find anything else to read to me, darling."

Berthe again made a search; and farther down among the reports of criminal cases, she read:

"'Gloomy Drama. A shop girl, no longer young, allowed herself to be led astray by a young man. Then, to avenge herself on her lover, whose heart proved fickle, she shot him with a revolver. The unhappy man is maimed for life. The jury, all men of moral character, condoning the illicit love of the murderess, honorably acquitted her.'"

This time the old grandmother appeared quite shocked, and, in a trembling voice, she said:

"Why, you people are mad nowadays. You are mad! The good God has given you love, the only enchantment in life. Man has added to this gallantry the only distraction of our dull hours, and here you are mixing up with it vitriol and revolvers, as if one were to put mud into a flagon of Spanish wine."

Berthe did not seem to understand her grandmother's indignation.

"But, grandmamma, this woman avenged herself. Remember she was married, and her husband deceived her."

The grandmother gave a start.

"What ideas have they been filling your head with, you young girls of today?"

Berthe replied:

"But marriage is sacred, grandmamma."

The grandmother's heart, which had its birth in the great age of gallantry, gave a sudden leap.

"It is love that is sacred," she said. "Listen, child, to an old woman who has seen three generations, and who has had a long, long experience of men and women. Marriage and love have nothing in common. We marry to found a family, and we form families in order to constitute society. Society cannot dispense with marriage. If society is a chain, each family is a link in that chain. In order to weld those links, we always seek metals of the same order. When we marry, we must bring together suitable conditions; we must combine fortunes, unite similar races and aim at the common interest, which is riches and children. We marry only once my child, because the world requires us to do so, but we may love twenty times in one lifetime because nature has made us like this. Marriage, you see, is law, and love is an instinct which impels us, sometimes along a straight, and sometimes along a devious path. The world has made laws to combat our instincts—it was necessary to make them; but our instincts are always stronger, and we ought not to resist them too much, because they come from God; while the laws only come from men. If we did not perfume life with love, as much love as possible, darling, as we put sugar into drugs for children, nobody would care to take it just as it is."

Berthe opened her eyes wide in astonishment. She murmured:

"Oh! grandmamma, we can only love once."

The grandmother raised her trembling hands toward Heaven, as if again to invoke the defunct god of gallantries. She exclaimed indignantly:

"You have become a race of serfs, a race of common people. Since the Revolution, it is impossible any longer to recognize society. You have attached big words to every action, and wearisome duties to every corner of existence; you believe in equality and eternal passion. People have written poetry telling you that people have died of love. In my time poetry was written to teach men to love every woman. And we! when we liked a gentleman, my child, we sent him a page. And when a fresh caprice came into our hearts, we were not slow in getting rid of the last Lover—unless we kept both of them."

The old woman smiled a keen smile, and a gleam of roguery twinkled in her gray eye, the intellectual, skeptical roguery of those people who did not believe that they were made of the same clay as the rest, and who lived as masters for whom common beliefs were not intended.

The young girl, turning very pale, faltered out:

"So, then, women have no honor?"

The grandmother ceased to smile. If she had kept in her soul some of Voltaire's irony, she had also a little of Jean Jacques's glowing philosophy: "No honor! because we loved, and dared to say so, and even boasted of it? But, my child, if one of us, among the greatest ladies in France, had lived without a lover, she would have had the entire court laughing at her. Those who wished to live differently had only to enter a convent. And you imagine, perhaps, that your husbands will love but you alone, all their lives. As if, indeed, this could be the case. I tell you that marriage is a thing necessary in order that society should exist, but it is not in the nature of our race, do you understand? There is only one good thing in life, and that is love. And how you misunderstand it! how you spoil it! You treat it as something solemn like a sacrament, or something to be bought, like a dress."

The young girl caught the old woman's trembling hands in her own.

"Hold your tongue, I beg of you, grandmamma!"

And, on her knees, with tears in her eyes, she prayed to Heaven to bestow on her a great passion, one sole, eternal passion in accordance with the dream of modern poets, while the grandmother, kissing her on the forehead, quite imbued still with that charming, healthy reason with which gallant philosophers tinctured the thought of the eighteenth century, murmured:

"Take care, my poor darling! If you believe in such folly as that, you will be very unhappy."

FRIEND JOSEPH

They had been great friends all winter in Paris. As is always the case, they had lost sight of each other after leaving school, and had met again when they were old and gray-haired. One of them had married, but the other had remained in single blessedness.

M. de Meroul lived for six months in Paris and for six months in his little chateau at Tourbeville. Having married the daughter of a neighboring squire, he had lived a good and peaceful life in the indolence of a man who has nothing to do. Of a calm and quiet disposition, and not over-intelligent he used to spend his time quietly regretting the past, grieving over the customs and institutions of the day and continually repeating to his wife, who would lift her eyes, and sometimes her hands, to heaven, as a sign of energetic assent: "Good gracious! What a government!"

Madame de Meroul resembled her husband intellectually as though she had been his sister. She knew, by tradition, that one should above all respect the Pope and the King!

And she loved and respected them from the bottom of her heart, without knowing them, with a poetic fervor, with an hereditary devotion, with the tenderness of a wellborn woman. She was good to, the marrow of her bones. She had had no children, and never ceased mourning the fact.

On meeting his old friend, Joseph Mouradour, at a ball, M. de Meroul was filled with a deep and simple joy, for in their youth they had been intimate friends.

After the first exclamations of surprise at the changes which time had wrought in their bodies and countenances, they told each other about their lives since they had last met.

Joseph Mouradour, who was from the south of France, had become a government official. His manner was frank; he spoke rapidly and without restraint, giving his opinions without any tact. He was a Republican, one of those good fellows who do not believe in standing on ceremony, and who exercise an almost brutal freedom of speech.

He came to his friend's house and was immediately liked for his easy cordiality, in spite of his radical ideas. Madame de Meroul would exclaim:

"What a shame! Such a charming man!"

Monsieur de Meroul would say to his friend in a serious and confidential tone of voice; "You have no idea the harm that you are doing your country." He loved him all the same, for nothing is stronger than the ties of childhood taken up again at a riper age. Joseph Mouradour bantered the wife and the husband, calling them "my amiable snails," and sometimes he would solemnly declaim against people who were behind the times, against old prejudices and traditions.

When he was once started on his democratic eloquence, the couple, somewhat ill at ease, would keep silent from politeness and good-breeding; then the husband would try to turn the conversation into some other channel in order to avoid a clash. Joseph Mouradour was only seen in the intimacy of the family.

Summer came. The Merouls had no greater pleasure than to receive their friends at their country home at Tourbeville. It was a good, healthy pleasure, the enjoyments of good people and of country proprietors. They would meet their friends at the neighboring railroad station and would bring them back in their carriage, always on the lookout for compliments on the country, on its natural features, on the condition of the roads, on the cleanliness of the farm-houses, on the size of the cattle grazing in the fields, on everything within sight.

They would call attention to the remarkable speed with which their horse trotted, surprising for an animal that did heavy work part of the year behind a plow; and they would anxiously await the opinion of the newcomer on their family domain, sensitive to the least word, and thankful for the slightest good intention.

Joseph Mouradour was invited, and he accepted the invitation.

Husband and wife had come to the train, delighted to welcome him to their home. As soon as he saw them, Joseph Mouradour jumped from the train with a briskness which increased their satisfaction. He shook their hands, congratulated them, overwhelmed them with compliments.

All the way home he was charming, remarking on the height of the trees, the goodness of the crops and the speed of the horse.

When he stepped on the porch of the house, Monsieur de Meroul said, with a certain friendly solemnity:

"Consider yourself at home now."

Joseph Mouradour answered:

"Thanks, my friend; I expected as much. Anyhow, I never stand on ceremony with my friends. That's how I understand hospitality."

Then he went upstairs to dress as a farmer, he said, and he came back all togged out in blue linen, with a little straw hat and yellow shoes, a regular Parisian dressed for an outing. He also seemed to become more vulgar, more jovial, more familiar; having put on with his country clothes a free and easy manner which he judged suitable to the surroundings. His new manners shocked Monsieur and Madame de Meroul a little, for they always remained serious and dignified, even in the country, as though compelled by the two letters preceding their name to keep up a certain formality even in the closest intimacy.

After lunch they all went out to visit the farms, and the Parisian astounded the respectful peasants by his tone of comradeship.

In the evening the priest came to dinner, an old, fat priest, accustomed to dining there on Sundays, but who had been especially invited this day in honor of the new guest.

Joseph, on seeing him, made a wry face. Then he observed him with surprise, as though he were a creature of some peculiar race, which he had never been able to observe at close quarters. During the meal he told some rather free stories, allowable in the intimacy of the family, but which seemed to the Merouls a little out of place in the presence of a minister of the Church.

He did not say, "Monsieur l'abbe," but simply, "Monsieur." He embarrassed the priest greatly by philosophical discussions about diverse superstitions current all over the world. He said: "Your God, monsieur, is of those who should be respected, but also one of those who should be discussed. Mine is called Reason; he has always been the enemy of yours."

The Merouls, distressed, tried to turn the trend of the conversation. The priest left very early.

Then the husband said, very quietly:

"Perhaps you went a little bit too far with the priest."

But Joseph immediately exclaimed:

"Well, that's pretty good! As if I would be on my guard with a shaveling! And say, do me the pleasure of not imposing him on me any more at meals. You can both make use of him as much as you wish, but don't serve him up to your friends, hang it!"

"But, my friends, think of his holy—"

Joseph Mouradour interrupted him:

"Yes, I know; they have to be treated like 'rosieres.' But let them respect my convictions, and I will respect theirs!"

That was all for that day.

As soon as Madame de Meroul entered the parlor, the next morning, she noticed in the middle of the table three newspapers which made her start the Voltaire, the Republique-Francaise and the Justice. Immediately Joseph Mouradour, still in blue, appeared on the threshold, attentively reading the Intransigeant. He cried:

"There's a great article in this by Rochefort. That fellow is a wonder!"

He read it aloud, emphasizing the parts which especially pleased him, so carried away by enthusiasm that he did not notice his friend's entrance. Monsieur de Meroul was holding in his hand the Gaulois for himself, the Clarion for his wife.

The fiery prose of the master writer who overthrew the empire, spouted with violence, sung in the southern accent, rang throughout the peaceful parsons seemed to spatter the walls and century-old furniture with a hail of bold, ironical and destructive words.

The man and the woman, one standing, the other sitting, were listening with astonishment, so shocked that they could not move.

In a burst of eloquence Mouradour finished the last paragraph, then exclaimed triumphantly:

"Well! that's pretty strong!"

Then, suddenly, he noticed the two sheets which his friend was carrying, and he, in turn, stood speechless from surprise. Quickly walking toward him he demanded angrily:

"What are you doing with those papers?"

Monsieur de Meroul answered hesitatingly:

"Why—those—those are my papers!"

"Your papers! What are you doing—making fun of me? You will do me the pleasure of reading mine; they will limber up your ideas, and as for yours—there! that's what I do with them."

And before his astonished host could stop him, he had seized the two newspapers and thrown them out of the window. Then he solemnly handed the Justice to Madame de Meroul, the Voltaire to her husband, while he sank down into an arm-chair to finish reading the Intransigeant.

The couple, through delicacy, made a pretense of reading a little, they then handed him back the Republican sheets, which they handled gingerly, as though they might be poisoned.

He laughed and declared:

"One week of this regime and I will have you converted to my ideas."

In truth, at the end of a week he ruled the house. He had closed the door against the priest, whom Madame de Meroul had to visit secretly; he had forbidden the Gaulois and the Clarion to be brought into the house, so that a servant had to go mysteriously to the post-office to get them, and as soon as he entered they would be hidden under sofa cushions; he arranged everything to suit himself—always charming, always good-natured, a jovial and all-powerful tyrant.

Other friends were expected, pious and conservative friends. The unhappy couple saw the impossibility of having them there then, and, not knowing what to do, one evening they announced to Joseph Mouradour that they would be obliged to absent themselves for a few days, on business, and they begged him to stay on alone. He did not appear disturbed, and answered:

"Very well, I don't mind! I will wait here as long as you wish. I have already said that there should be no formality between friends. You are perfectly right-go ahead and attend to your business. It will not offend me in the least; quite the contrary, it will make me feel much more completely one of the family. Go ahead, my friends, I will wait for you!"

Monsieur and Madame de Meroul left the following day.

He is still waiting for them.

THE EFFEMINATES

How often we hear people say, "He is charming, that man, but he is a girl, a regular girl." They are alluding to the effeminates, the bane of our land.

For we are all girl-like men in France—that is, fickle, fanciful, innocently treacherous, without consistency in our convictions or our will, violent and weak as women are.

But the most irritating of girl—men is assuredly the Parisian and the boulevardier, in whom the appearance of intelligence is more marked and who combines in himself all the attractions and all the faults of those charming creatures in an exaggerated degree in virtue of his masculine temperament.

Our Chamber of Deputies is full of girl-men. They form the greater number of the amiable opportunists whom one might call "The Charmers." These are they who control by soft words and deceitful promises, who know how to shake hands in such a manner as to win hearts, how to say "My dear friend" in a certain tactful way to people he knows the least, to change his mind without suspecting it, to be carried away by each new idea, to be sincere in their weathercock convictions, to let themselves be deceived as they deceive others, to forget the next morning what he affirmed the day before.

The newspapers are full of these effeminate men. That is probably where one finds the most, but it is also where they are most needed. The Journal des Debats and the Gazette de France are exceptions.

Assuredly, every good journalist must be somewhat effeminate—that is, at the command of the public, supple in following unconsciously the shades of public opinion, wavering and varying, sceptical and credulous, wicked and devout, a braggart and a true man, enthusiastic and ironical, and always convinced while believing in nothing.

Foreigners, our anti-types, as Mme. Abel called them, the stubborn English and the heavy Germans, regard us with a certain amazement mingled with contempt, and will continue to so regard us till the end of time. They consider us frivolous. It is not that, it is that we are girls. And that is why people love us in spite of our faults, why they come back to us despite the evil spoken of us; these are lovers' quarrels! The effeminate man, as one meets him in this world, is so charming that he captivates you after five minutes' chat. His smile seems made for you; one cannot believe that his voice does not assume specially tender intonations on their account. When he leaves you it seems as if one had known him for twenty years. One is quite ready to lend him money if he asks for it. He has enchanted you, like a woman.

If he commits any breach of manners towards you, you cannot bear any malice, he is so pleasant when you next meet him. If he asks your pardon you long to ask pardon of him. Does he tell lies? You cannot believe it. Does he put you off indefinitely with promises that he does not keep? One lays as much store by his promises as though he had moved heaven and earth to render them a service.

When he admires anything he goes into such raptures that he convinces you. He once adored Victor Hugo, whom he now treats as a back number. He would have fought for Zola, whom he has abandoned for Barbey and d'Aurevilly. And when he admires, he permits no limitation, he would slap your face for a word. But when he becomes scornful, his contempt is unbounded and allows of no protest.

In fact, he understands nothing.

Listen to two girls talking.

"Then you are angry with Julia?" "I slapped her face." "What had she done?" "She told Pauline that I had no money thirteen months out of twelve, and Pauline told Gontran—you understand." "You were living together in the Rue Clanzel?" "We lived together four years in the Rue Breda; we quarrelled about a pair of stockings that she said I had worn —it wasn't true—silk stockings that she had bought at Mother Martin's. Then I gave her a pounding and she left me at once. I met her six months ago and she asked me to come and live with her, as she has rented a flat that is twice too large."

One goes on one's way and hears no more. But on the following Sunday as one is on the way to Saint Germain two young women get into the same railway carriage. One recognizes one of them at once; it is Julia's enemy. The other is Julia!

And there are endearments, caresses, plans. "Say, Julia—listen, Julia," etc.

The girl-man has his friendships of this kind. For three months he cannot bear to leave his old Jack, his dear Jack. There is no one but Jack in the world. He is the only one who has any intelligence, any sense, any talent. He alone amounts to anything in Paris. One meets them everywhere together, they dine together, walk about in company, and every evening walk home with each other back and forth without being able to part with one another.

Three months later, if Jack is mentioned:

"There is a drinker, a sorry fellow, a scoundrel for you. I know him well, you may be sure. And he is not even honest, and ill bred," etc., etc.

Three months later, and they are living together.

But one morning one hears that they have fought a duel, then embraced each other, amid tears, on the duelling ground.

Just now they are the dearest friends in the world, furious with each other half the year, abusing and loving each other by turns, squeezing each other's hands till they almost crush the bones, and ready to run each other through the body for a misunderstanding.

For the relations of these effeminate men are uncertain. Their temper is by fits and starts, their delight unexpected, their affection turn-about-face, their enthusiasm subject to eclipse. One day they love you, the next day they will hardly look at you, for they have in fact a girl's nature, a girl's charm, a girl's temperament, and all their sentiments are like the affections of girls.

They treat their friends as women treat their pet dogs.

It is the dear little Toutou whom they hug, feed with sugar, allow to sleep on the pillow, but whom they would be just as likely to throw out of a window in a moment of impatience, whom they turn round like a sling, holding it by the tail, squeeze in their arms till they almost strangle it, and plunge, without any reason, in a pail of cold water.

Then, what a strange thing it is when one of these beings falls in love with a real girl! He beats her, she scratches him, they execrate each other, cannot bear the sight of each other and yet cannot part, linked together by no one knows what mysterious psychic bonds. She deceives him, he knows it, sobs and forgives her. He despises and adores her without seeing that she would be justified in despising him. They are both atrociously unhappy and yet cannot separate. They cast invectives, reproaches and abominable accusations at each other from morning till night, and when they have reached the climax and are vibrating with rage and hatred, they fall into each other's arms and kiss each other ardently.

The girl-man is brave and a coward at the same time. He has, more than another, the exalted sentiment of honor, but is lacking in the sense of simple honesty, and, circumstances favoring him, would defalcate and commit infamies which do not trouble his conscience, for he obeys without questioning the oscillations of his ideas, which are always impulsive.

To him it seems permissible and almost right to cheat a haberdasher. He considers it honorable not to pay his debts, unless they are gambling debts—that is, somewhat shady. He dupes people whenever the laws of society admit of his doing so. When he is short of money he borrows in all ways, not always being scrupulous as to tricking the lenders, but he would, with sincere indignation, run his sword through anyone who should suspect him of only lacking in politeness.

OLD AMABLE

PART I

The humid gray sky seemed to weigh down on the vast brown plain. The odor of autumn, the sad odor of bare, moist lands, of fallen leaves, of dead grass made the stagnant evening air more thick and heavy. The peasants were still at work, scattered through the fields, waiting for the stroke of the Angelus to call them back to the farmhouses, whose thatched roofs were visible here and there through the branches of the leafless trees which protected the apple-gardens against the wind.

At the side of the road, on a heap of clothes, a very small boy seated with his legs apart was playing with a potato, which he now and then let fall on his dress, whilst five women were bending down planting slips of colza in the adjoining plain. With a slow, continuous movement, all along the mounds of earth which the plough had just turned up, they drove in sharp wooden stakes and in the hole thus formed placed the plant, already a little withered, which sank on one side; then they patted down the earth and went on with their work.

A man who was passing, with a whip in his hand, and wearing wooden shoes, stopped near the child, took it up and kissed it. Then one of the women rose up and came across to him. She was a big, red haired girl, with large hips, waist and shoulders, a tall Norman woman, with yellow hair in which there was a blood-red tint.

She said in a resolute voice:

"Why, here you are, Cesaire—well?"

The man, a thin young fellow with a melancholy air, murmured:

"Well, nothing at all—always the same thing."

"He won't have it?"

"He won't have it."

"What are you going to do?"

"What do you say I ought to do?"

"Go see the cure."

"I will."

"Go at once!"

"I will."

And they stared at each other. He held the child in his arms all the time. He kissed it once more and then put it down again on the woman's clothes.

In the distance, between two farm-houses, could be seen a plough drawn by a horse and driven by a man. They moved on very gently, the horse, the plough and the laborer, in the dim evening twilight.

The woman went on:

"What did your father say?"

"He said he would not have it."

"Why wouldn't he have it?"

The young man pointed toward the child whom he had just put back on the ground, then with a glance he drew her attention to the man drawing the plough yonder there.

And he said emphatically:

"Because 'tis his—this child of yours."

The girl shrugged her shoulders and in an angry tone said:

"Faith, every one knows it well—that it is Victor's. And what about it after all? I made a slip. Am I the only woman that did? My mother also made a slip before me, and then yours did the same before she married your dad! Who is it that hasn't made a slip in the country? I made a slip with Victor because he took advantage of me while I was asleep in the barn, it's true, and afterward it happened between us when I wasn't asleep. I certainly would have married him if he weren't a servant man. Am I a worse woman for that?"

The man said simply:

"As for me, I like you just as you are, with or without the child. It's only my father that opposes me. All the same, I'll see about settling the business."

She answered:

"Go to the cure at once."

"I'm going to him."

And he set forth with his heavy peasant's tread, while the girl, with her hands on her hips, turned round to plant her colza.

In fact, the man who thus went off, Cesaire Houlbreque, the son of deaf old Amable Houlbreque, wanted to marry, in spite of his father, Celeste Levesque, who had a child by Victor Lecoq, a mere laborer on her parents' farm, who had been turned out of doors for this act.

The hierarchy of caste, however, does not exist in the country, and if the laborer is thrifty, he becomes, by taking a farm in his turn, the equal of his former master.

So Cesaire Houlbieque went off, his whip under his arm, brooding over his own thoughts and lifting up one after the other his heavy wooden shoes daubed with clay. Certainly he desired to marry Celeste Levesque. He wanted her with her child because she was the wife he wanted. He could not say why, but he knew it, he was sure of it. He had only to look at her to be convinced of it, to feel quite queer, quite stirred up, simply stupid with happiness. He even found a pleasure in kissing the little boy, Victor's little boy, because he belonged to her.

And he gazed, without hate, at the distant outline of the man who was driving his plough along the horizon.

But old Amable did not want this marriage. He opposed it with the obstinacy of a deaf man, with a violent obstinacy.

Cesaire in vain shouted in his ear, in that ear which still heard a few sounds:

"I'll take good care of you, daddy. I tell you she's a good girl and strong, too, and also thrifty."

The old man repeated:

"As long as I live I won't see her your wife."

And nothing could get the better of him, nothing could make him waver. One hope only was left to Cesaire. Old Amable was afraid of the cure through the apprehension of death which he felt drawing nigh; he had not much fear of God, nor of the Devil, nor of Hell, nor of Purgatory, of which he had no conception, but he dreaded the priest, who represented to him burial, as one might fear the doctors through horror of diseases. For the last tight days Celeste, who knew this weakness of the old man, had been urging Cesaire to go and find the cure, but Cesaire always hesitated, because he had not much liking for the black robe, which represented to him hands always stretched out for collections or for blessed bread.

However, he had made up his mind, and he proceeded toward the presbytery, thinking in what manner he would speak about his case.

The Abbe Raffin, a lively little priest, thin and never shaved, was awaiting his dinner-hour while warming his feet at his kitchen fire.

As soon as he saw the peasant entering he asked, merely turning his head:

"Well, Cesaire, what do you want?"

"I'd like to have a talk with you, M. le Cure."

The man remained standing, intimidated, holding his cap in one hand and his whip in the other.

"Well, talk."

Cesaire looked at the housekeeper, an old woman who dragged her feet while putting on the cover for her master's dinner at the corner of the table in front of the window.

He stammered:

"'Tis—'tis a sort of confession."

Thereupon the Abbe Raffin carefully surveyed his peasant. He saw his confused countenance, his air of constraint, his wandering eyes, and he gave orders to the housekeeper in these words:

"Marie, go away for five minutes to your room, while I talk to Cesaire."

The servant cast on the man an angry glance and went away grumbling.

The clergyman went on:

"Come, now, tell your story."

The young fellow still hesitated, looked down at his wooden shoes, moved about his cap, then, all of a sudden, he made up his mind:

"Here it is: I want to marry Celeste Levesque."

"Well, my boy, what's there to prevent you?"

"The father won't have it."

"Your father?"

"Yes, my father."

"What does your father say?"

"He says she has a child."

"She's not the first to whom that happened, since our Mother Eve."

"A child by Victor Lecoq, Anthime Loisel's servant man."

"Ha! ha! So he won't have it?"

"He won't have it."

"What! not at all?"

"No, no more than an ass that won't budge an inch, saving your presence."

"What do you say to him yourself in order to make him decide?"

"I say to him that she's a good girl, and strong, too, and thrifty also."

"And this does not make him agree to it. So you want me to speak to him?"

"Exactly. You speak to him."

"And what am I to tell your father?"

"Why, what you tell people in your sermons to make them give you sous."

In the peasant's mind every effort of religion consisted in loosening the purse strings, in emptying the pockets of men in order to fill the heavenly coffer. It was a kind of huge commercial establishment, of which the cures were the clerks; sly, crafty clerks, sharp as any one must be who does business for the good God at the expense of the country people.

He knew full well that the priests rendered services, great services to the poorest, to the sick and dying, that they assisted, consoled, counselled, sustained, but all this by means of money, in exchange for white pieces, for beautiful glittering coins, with which they paid for sacraments and masses, advice and protection, pardon of sins and indulgences, purgatory and paradise according to the yearly income and the generosity of the sinner.

The Abbe Raffin, who knew his man and who never lost his temper, burst out laughing.

"Well, yes, I'll tell your father my little story; but you, my lad, you'll come to church."

Houlbreque extended his hand in order to give a solemn assurance:

"On the word of a poor man, if you do this for me, I promise that I will."

"Come, that's all right. When do you wish me to go and find your father?"

"Why, the sooner the better-to-night, if you can."

"In half an hour, then, after supper."

"In half an hour."

"That's understood. So long, my lad."

"Good-by till we meet again, Monsieur le Cure; many thanks."

"Not at all, my lad."

And Cesaire Houlbreque returned home, his heart relieved of a great weight.

He held on lease a little farm, quite small, for they were not rich, his father and he. Alone with a female servant, a little girl of fifteen, who made the soup, looked after the fowls, milked the cows and churned the butter, they lived frugally, though Cesaire was a good cultivator. But they did not possess either sufficient lands or sufficient cattle to earn more than the indispensable.

The old man no longer worked. Sad, like all deaf people, crippled with pains, bent double, twisted, he went through the fields leaning on his stick, watching the animals and the men with a hard, distrustful eye. Sometimes he sat down on the side of the road and remained there without moving for hours, vaguely pondering over the things that had engrossed his whole life, the price of eggs, and corn, the sun and the rain which spoil the crops or make them grow. And, worn out with rheumatism, his old limbs still drank in the humidity of the soul, as they had drunk in for the past sixty years, the moisture of the walls of his low house thatched with damp straw.

He came back at the close of the day, took his place at the end of the table in the kitchen and when the earthen bowl containing the soup had been placed before him he placed round it his crooked fingers, which seemed to have kept the round form of the bowl and, winter and summer, he warmed his hands, before commencing to eat, so as to lose nothing, not even a particle of the heat that came from the fire, which costs a great deal, neither one drop of soup into which fat and salt have to be put, nor one morsel of bread, which comes from the wheat.

Then he climbed up a ladder into a loft, where he had his straw-bed, while his son slept below stairs at the end of a kind of niche near the chimneypiece and the servant shut herself up in a kind of cellar, a black hole which was formerly used to store the potatoes.

Cesaire and his father scarcely ever talked to each other. From time to time only, when there was a question of selling a crop or buying a calf, the young man would ask his father's advice, and, making a speaking-trumpet of his two hands, he would bawl out his views into his ear, and old Amable either approved of them or opposed them in a slow, hollow voice that came from the depths of his stomach.

So one evening Cesaire, approaching him as if about to discuss the purchase of a horse or a heifer, communicated to him at the top of his voice his intention to marry Celeste Levesque.

Then the father got angry. Why? On the score of morality? No, certainly. The virtue of a girl is of slight importance in the country. But his avarice, his deep, fierce instinct for saving, revolted at the idea that his son should bring up a child which he had not begotten himself. He had thought suddenly, in one second, of the soup the little fellow would swallow before becoming useful on the farm. He had calculated all the pounds of bread, all the pints of cider that this brat would consume up to his fourteenth year, and a mad anger broke loose from him against Cesaire, who had not bestowed a thought on all this.

He replied in an unusually strong voice:

"Have you lost your senses?"

Thereupon Cesaire began to enumerate his reasons, to speak about Celeste's good qualities, to prove that she would be worth a thousand times what the child would cost. But the old man doubted these advantages, while he could have no doubts as to the child's existence; and he replied with emphatic repetition, without giving any further explanation:

"I will not have it! I will not have it! As long as I live, this won't be done!" And at this point they had remained for the last three months without one or the other giving in, resuming at least once a week the same discussion, with the same arguments, the same words, the same gestures and the same fruitlessness.

It was then that Celeste had advised Cesaire to go and ask for the cure's assistance.

On arriving home the peasant found his father already seated at table, for he came late through his visit to the presbytery.

They dined in silence, face to face, ate a little bread and butter after the soup and drank a glass of cider. Then they remained motionless in their chairs, with scarcely a glimmer of light, the little servant girl having carried off the candle in order to wash the spoons, wipe the glasses and cut the crusts of bread to be ready for next morning's breakfast.

There was a knock, at the door, which was immediately opened, and the priest appeared. The old man raised toward him an anxious eye full of suspicion, and, foreseeing danger, he was getting ready to climb up his ladder when the Abbe Raffin laid his hand on his shoulder and shouted close to his temple:

"I want to have a talk with you, Father Amable."

Cesaire had disappeared, taking advantage of the door being open. He did not want to listen, for he was afraid and did not want his hopes to crumble slowly with each obstinate refusal of his father. He preferred to learn the truth at once, good or bad, later on; and he went out into the night. It was a moonless, starless night, one of those misty nights when the air seems thick with humidity. A vague odor of apples floated through the farmyard, for it was the season when the earliest applies were gathered, the "early ripe," as they are called in the cider country. As Cesaire passed along by the cattlesheds the warm smell of living beasts asleep on manure was exhaled through the narrow windows, and he heard the stamping of the horses, who were standing at the end of the stable, and the sound of their jaws tearing and munching the hay on the racks.

He went straight ahead, thinking about Celeste. In this simple nature, whose ideas were scarcely more than images generated directly by objects, thoughts of love only formulated themselves by calling up before the mind the picture of a big red-haired girl standing in a hollow road and laughing, with her hands on her hips.

It was thus he saw her on the day when he first took a fancy for her. He had, however, known her from infancy, but never had he been so struck by her as on that morning. They had stopped to talk for a few minutes and then he went away, and as he walked along he kept repeating:

"Faith, she's a fine girl, all the same. 'Tis a pity she made a slip with Victor."

Till evening he kept thinking of her and also on the following morning.

When he saw her again he felt something tickling the end of his throat, as if a cock's feather had been driven through his mouth into his chest, and since then, every time he found himself near her, he was astonished at this nervous tickling which always commenced again.

In three months he made up his mind to marry her, so much did she please him. He could not have said whence came this power over him, but he explained it in these words:

"I am possessed by her," as if the desire for this girl within him were as dominating as one of the powers of hell. He scarcely bothered himself about her transgression. It was a pity, but, after all, it did her no harm, and he bore no grudge against Victor Lecoq.

But if the cure should not succeed, what was he to do? He did not dare to think of it, the anxiety was such a torture to him.

He reached the presbytery and seated himself near the little gateway to wait for the priest's return.

He was there perhaps half an hour when he heard steps on the road, and although the night was very dark, he presently distinguished the still darker shadow of the cassock.

He rose up, his legs giving way under him, not even venturing to speak, not daring to ask a question.

The clergyman perceived him and said gaily:

"Well, my lad, it's all right."

Cesaire stammered:

"All right, 'tisn't possible."

"Yes, my lad, but not without trouble. What an old ass your father is!"

The peasant repeated:

"'Tisn't possible!"

"Why, yes. Come and look me up to-morrow at midday in order to settle about the publication of the banns."

The young man seized the cure's hand. He pressed it, shook it, bruised it as he stammered:

"True-true-true, Monsieur le Cure, on the word of an honest man, you'll see me to-morrow-at your sermon."

PART II

The wedding took place in the middle of December. It was simple, the bridal pair not being rich. Cesaire, attired in new clothes, was ready since eight o'clock in the morning to go and fetch his betrothed and bring her to the mayor's office, but it was too early. He seated himself before the kitchen table and waited for the members of the family and the friends who were to accompany him.

For the last eight days it had been snowing, and the brown earth, the earth already fertilized by the autumn sowing, had become a dead white, sleeping under a great sheet of ice.

It was cold in the thatched houses adorned with white caps, and the round apples in the trees of the enclosures seemed to be flowering, covered with white as they had been in the pleasant month of their blossoming.

This day the big clouds to the north, the big great snow clouds, had disappeared and the blue sky showed itself above the white earth on which the rising sun cast silvery reflections.

Cesaire looked straight before him through the window, thinking of nothing, quite happy.

The door opened, two women entered, peasant women in their Sunday clothes, the aunt and the cousin of the bridegroom; then three men, his cousins; then a woman who was a neighbor. They sat down on chairs and remained, motionless and silent, the women on one side of the kitchen, the men on the other, suddenly seized with timidity, with that embarrassed sadness which takes possession of people assembled for a ceremony. One of the cousins soon asked:

"Is it not the hour?"

Cesaire replied:

"I am much afraid it is."

"Come on! Let us start," said another.

Those rose up. Then Cesaire, whom a feeling of uneasiness had taken possession of, climbed up the ladder of the loft to see whether his father was ready. The old man, always as a rule an early riser, had not yet made his appearance. His son found him on his bed of straw, wrapped up in his blanket, with his eyes open and a malicious gleam in them.

He bawled into his ear: "Come, daddy, get up. It's time for the wedding."

The deaf man murmured-in a doleful tone:

"I can't get up. I have a sort of chill over me that freezes my back. I can't stir."

The young man, dumbfounded, stared at him, guessing that this was a dodge.

"Come, daddy; you must make an effort."

"I can't do it."

"Look here! I'll help you."

And he stooped toward the old man, pulled off his blanket, caught him by the arm and lifted him up. But old Amable began to whine, "Ooh! ooh! ooh! What suffering! Ooh! I can't. My back is stiffened up. The cold wind must have rushed in through this cursed roof."

"Well, you'll get no dinner, as I'm having a spread at Polyte's inn. This will teach you what comes of acting mulishly."

And he hurried down the ladder and started out, accompanied by his relatives and guests.

The men had turned up the bottoms of their trousers so as not to get them wet in the snow. The women held up their petticoats and showed their lean ankles with gray woollen stockings and their bony shanks resembling broomsticks. And they all moved forward with a swinging gait, one behind the other, without uttering a word, moving cautiously, for fear of losing the road which was-hidden beneath the flat, uniform, uninterrupted stretch of snow.

As they approached the farmhouses they saw one or two persons waiting to join them, and the procession went on without stopping and wound its way forward, following the invisible outlines of the road, so that it resembled a living chaplet of black beads undulating through the white countryside.

In front of the bride's door a large group was stamping up and down the open space awaiting the bridegroom. When he appeared they gave him a loud greeting, and presently Celeste came forth from her room, clad in a blue dress, her shoulders covered with a small red shawl and her head adorned with orange flowers.

But every one asked Cesaire:

"Where's your father?"

He replied with embarrassment:

"He couldn't move on account of the pains."

And the farmers tossed their heads with a sly, incredulous air.

They directed their steps toward the mayor's office. Behind the pair about to be wedded a peasant woman carried Victor's child, as if it were going to be baptized; and the peasants, in pairs now, with arms linked, walked through the snow with the movements of a sloop at sea.

After having been united by the mayor in the little municipal house the pair were made one by the cure, in his turn, in the modest house of God. He blessed their union by promising them fruitfulness, then he preached to them on the matrimonial virtues, the simple and healthful virtues of the country, work, concord and fidelity, while the child, who was cold, began to fret behind the bride.

As soon as the couple reappeared on the threshold of the church shots were discharged from the ditch of the cemetery. Only the barrels of the guns could be seen whence came forth rapid jets of smoke; then a head could be seen gazing at the procession. It was Victor Lecoq celebrating the marriage of his old sweetheart, wishing her happiness and sending her his good wishes with explosions of powder. He had employed some friends of his, five or six laboring men, for these salvos of musketry. It was considered a nice attention.

The repast was given in Polyte Cacheprune's inn. Twenty covers were laid in the great hall where people dined on market days, and the big leg of mutton turning before the spit, the fowls browned under their own gravy, the chitterlings sputtering over the bright, clear fire filled the house with a thick odor of live coal sprinkled with fat—the powerful, heavy odor of rustic fare.

They sat down to table at midday and the soup was poured at once into the plates. All faces had already brightened up; mouths opened to utter loud jokes and eyes were laughing with knowing winks. They were going to amuse themselves and no mistake.

The door opened, and old Amable appeared. He seemed in a bad humor and his face wore a scowl as he dragged himself forward on his sticks, whining at every step to indicate his suffering. As soon as they saw him they stopped talking, but suddenly his neighbor, Daddy Malivoire, a big joker, who knew all the little tricks and ways of people, began to yell, just as Cesaire used to do, by making a speaking-trumpet of his hands.

"Hallo, my cute old boy, you have a good nose on you to be able to smell Polyte's cookery from your own house!"

A roar of laughter burst forth from the throats of those present. Malivoire, excited by his success, went on:

"There's nothing for the rheumatics like a chitterling poultice! It keeps your belly warm, along with a glass of three-six!"

The men uttered shouts, banged the table with their fists, laughed, bending on one side and raising up their bodies again as if they were working a pump. The women clucked like hens, while the servants wriggled, standing against the walls. Old Amable was the only one that did not laugh, and, without making any reply, waited till they made room for him.

They found a place for him in the middle of the table, facing his daughter-in-law, and, as soon as he was seated, he began to eat. It was his son who was paying, after all; it was right he should take his share. With each ladleful of soup that went into his stomach, with each mouthful of bread or meat crushed between his gums, with each glass of cider or wine that flowed through his gullet he thought he was regaining something of his own property, getting back a little of his money which all those gluttons were devouring, saving in fact a portion of his own means. And he ate in silence with the obstinacy of a miser who hides his coppers, with the same gloomy persistence with which he formerly performed his daily labors.

But all of a sudden he noticed at the end of the table Celeste's child on a woman's lap, and his eye remained fixed on the little boy. He went on eating, with his glance riveted on the youngster, into whose mouth the woman who minded him every now and then put a little morsel which he nibbled at. And the old man suffered more from the few mouthfuls sucked by this little chap than from all that the others swallowed.

The meal lasted till evening. Then every one went back home.

Cesaire raised up old Amable.

"Come, daddy, we must go home," said he.

And he put the old man's two sticks in his hands.

Celeste took her child in her arms, and they went on slowly through the pale night whitened by the snow. The deaf old man, three-fourths tipsy, and even more malicious under the influence of drink, refused to go forward. Several times he even sat down with the object of making his daughter-in-law catch cold, and he kept whining, without uttering a word, giving vent to a sort of continuous groaning as if he were in pain.

When they reached home he at once climbed up to his loft, while Cesaire made a bed for the child near the deep niche where he was going to lie down with his wife. But as the newly wedded pair could not sleep immediately, they heard the old man for a long time moving about on his bed of straw, and he even talked aloud several times, whether it was that he was dreaming or that he let his thoughts escape through his mouth, in spite of himself, not being able to keep them back, under the obsession of a fixed idea.

When he came down his ladder next morning he saw his daughter-in-law looking after the housekeeping.

She cried out to him:

"Come, daddy, hurry on! Here's some good soup."

And she placed at the end of the table the round black earthen bowl filled with steaming liquid. He sat down without giving any answer, seized the hot bowl, warmed his hands with it in his customary fashion, and, as it was very cold, even pressed it against his breast to try to make a little of the living heat of the boiling liquid enter into him, into his old body stiffened by so many winters.

Then he took his sticks and went out into the fields, covered with ice, till it was time for dinner, for he had seen Celeste's youngster still asleep in a big soap-box.

He did not take his place in the household. He lived in the thatched house, as in bygone days, but he seemed not to belong to it any longer, to be no longer interested in anything, to look upon those people, his son, the wife and the child as strangers whom he did not know, to whom he never spoke.

The winter glided by. It was long and severe.

Then the early spring made the seeds sprout forth again, and the peasants once more, like laborious ants, passed their days in the fields, toiling from morning till night, under the wind and under the rain, along the furrows of brown earth which brought forth the bread of men.

The year promised well for the newly married pair. The crops grew thick and strong. There were no late frosts, and the apples bursting into bloom scattered on the grass their rosy white snow which promised a hail of fruit for the autumn.

Cesaire toiled hard, rose early and left off work late, in order to save the expense of a hired man.

His wife said to him sometimes:

"You'll make yourself ill in the long run."

He replied:

"Certainly not. I'm a good judge."

Nevertheless one evening he came home so fatigued that he had to get to bed without supper. He rose up next morning at the usual hour, but he could not eat, in spite of his fast on the previous night, and he had to come back to the house in the middle of the afternoon in order to go to bed again. In the course of the night he began to cough; he turned round on his straw couch, feverish, with his forehead burning, his tongue dry and his throat parched by a burning thirst.

However, at daybreak he went toward his grounds, but next morning the doctor had to be sent for and pronounced him very ill with inflammation of the lungs.

And he no longer left the dark recess in which he slept. He could be heard coughing, gasping and tossing about in this hole. In order to see him, to give his medicine and to apply cupping-glasses they had to-bring a candle to the entrance. Then one could see his narrow head with his long matted beard underneath a thick lacework of spiders' webs, which hung and floated when stirred by the air. And the hands of the sick man seemed dead under the dingy sheets.

Celeste watched him with restless activity, made him take physic, applied blisters to him, went back and forth in the house, while old Amable remained at the edge of his loft, watching at a distance the gloomy cavern where his son lay dying. He did not come near him, through hatred of the wife, sulking like an ill-tempered dog.

Six more days passed, then one morning, as Celeste, who now slept on the ground on two loose bundles of straw, was going to see whether her man was better, she no longer heard his rapid breathing from the interior of his recess. Terror stricken, she asked:

"Well Cesaire, what sort of a night had you?"

He did not answer. She put out her hand to touch him, and the flesh on his face felt cold as ice. She uttered a great cry, the long cry of a woman overpowered with fright. He was dead.

At this cry the deaf old man appeared at the top of his ladder, and when he saw Celeste rushing to call for help, he quickly descended, placed his hand on his son's face, and suddenly realizing what had happened, went to shut the door from the inside, to prevent the wife from re-entering and resuming possession of the dwelling, since his son was no longer living.

Then he sat down on a chair by the dead man's side.

Some of the neighbors arrived, called out and knocked. He did not hear them. One of them broke the glass of the window and jumped into the room. Others followed. The door was opened again and Celeste reappeared, all in tears, with swollen face and bloodshot eyes. Then old Amable, vanquished, without uttering a word, climbed back to his loft.

The funeral took place next morning. Then, after the ceremony, the father-in-law and the daughter-in-law found themselves alone in the farmhouse with the child.

It was the usual dinner hour. She lighted the fire, made some soup and placed the plates on the table, while the old man sat on the chair waiting without appearing to look at her. When the meal was ready she bawled in his ear—

"Come, daddy, you must eat." He rose up, took his seat at the end of the table, emptied his soup bowl, masticated his bread and butter, drank his two glasses of cider and then took himself off.

It was one of those warm days, one of those enjoyable days when life ferments, pulsates, blooms all over the surface of the soil.

Old Amable pursued a little path across the fields. He looked at the young wheat and the young oats, thinking that his son was now under the earth, his poor boy! He walked along wearily, dragging his legs after him in a limping fashion. And, as he was all alone in the plain, all alone under the blue sky, in the midst of the growing crops, all alone with the larks which he saw hovering above his head, without hearing their light song, he began to weep as he proceeded on his way.

Then he sat down beside a pond and remained there till evening, gazing at the little birds that came there to drink. Then, as the night was falling, he returned to the house, supped without saying a word and climbed up to his loft. And his life went on as in the past. Nothing was changed, except that his son Cesaire slept in the cemetery.

What could he, an old man, do? He could work no longer; he was now good for nothing except to swallow the soup prepared by his daughter-in-law. And he ate it in silence, morning and evening, watching with an eye of rage the little boy also taking soup, right opposite him, at the other side of the table. Then he would go out, prowl about the fields after the fashion of a vagabond, hiding behind the barns where he would sleep for an hour or two as if he were afraid of being seen and then come back at the approach of night.

But Celeste's mind began to be occupied by graver anxieties. The farm needed a man to look after it and cultivate it. Somebody should be there always to go through the fields, not a mere hired laborer, but a regular farmer, a master who understood the business and would take an interest in the farm. A lone woman could not manage the farming, watch the price of corn and direct the sale and purchase of cattle. Then ideas came into her head, simple practical ideas, which she had turned over in her head at night. She could not marry again before the end of the year, and it was necessary at once to take care of pressing interests, immediate interests.

Only one man could help her out of her difficulties, Victor Lecoq, the father of her child. He was strong and understood farming; with a little money in his pocket he would make an excellent cultivator. She was aware of his skill, having known him while he was working on her parents' farm.

So one morning, seeing him passing along the road with a cart of manure, she went out to meet him. When he perceived her, he drew up his horses and she said to him as if she had met him the night before:

"Good-morrow, Victor—are you quite well, the same as ever?"

He replied:

"I'm quite well, the same as ever—and how are you?"

"Oh, I'd be all right, only that I'm alone in the house, which bothers me on account of the farm."

Then they remained chatting for a long time, leaning against the wheel of the heavy cart. The man every now and then lifted up his cap to scratch his forehead and began thinking, while she, with flushed cheeks, went on talking warmly, told him about her views, her plans; her projects for the future. At last he said in a low tone:

"Yes, it can be done."

She opened her hand like a countryman clinching a bargain and asked:

"Is it agreed?"

He pressed her outstretched hand.

"'Tis agreed."

"It's settled, then, for next Sunday?"

"It's settled for next Sunday"

"Well, good-morning, Victor."

"Good-morning, Madame Houlbreque."

PART III

This particular Sunday was the day of the village festival, the annual festival in honor of the patron saint, which in Normandy is called the assembly.

For the last eight days quaint-looking vehicles in which live the families of strolling fair exhibitors, lottery managers, keepers of shooting galleries and other forms of amusement or exhibitors of curiosities whom the peasants call "wonder-makers" could be seen coming along the roads drawn slowly by gray or sorrel horses.

The dirty wagons with their floating curtains, accompanied by a melancholy-looking dog, who trotted, with his head down, between the wheels, drew up one after the other on the green in front of the town hall. Then a tent was erected in front of each ambulant abode, and inside this tent could be seen, through the holes in the canvas, glittering things which excited the envy or the curiosity of the village youngsters.

As soon as the morning of the fete arrived all the booths were opened, displaying their splendors of glass or porcelain, and the peasants on their way to mass looked with genuine satisfaction at these modest shops which they saw again, nevertheless, each succeeding year.

Early in the afternoon there was a crowd on the green. From every neighboring village the farmers arrived, shaken along with their wives and children in the two-wheeled open chars-a-bancs, which rattled along, swaying like cradles. They unharnessed at their friends' houses and the farmyards were filled with strange-looking traps, gray, high, lean, crooked, like long-clawed creatures from the depths of the sea. And each family, with the youngsters in front and the grown-up ones behind, came to the assembly with tranquil steps, smiling countenances and open hands, big hands, red and bony, accustomed to work and apparently tired of their temporary rest.

A clown was blowing a trumpet. The barrel-organ accompanying the carrousel sent through the air its shrill jerky notes. The lottery-wheel made a whirring sound like that of cloth tearing, and every moment the crack of the rifle could be heard. And the slow-moving throng passed on quietly in front of the booths resembling paste in a fluid condition, with the motions of a flock of sheep and the awkwardness of heavy animals who had escaped by chance.

The girls, holding one another's arms in groups of six or eight, were singing; the youths followed them, making jokes, with their caps over their ears and their blouses stiffened with starch, swollen out like blue balloons.

The whole countryside was there—masters, laboring men and women servants.

Old Amable himself, wearing his old-fashioned green frock coat, had wished to see the assembly, for he never failed to attend on such an occasion.

He looked at the lotteries, stopped in front of the shooting galleries to criticize the shots and interested himself specially in a very simple game which consisted in throwing a big wooden ball into the open mouth of a mannikin carved and painted on a board.

Suddenly he felt a tap on his shoulder. It was Daddy Malivoire, who exclaimed:

"Ha, daddy! Come and have a glass of brandy."

And they sat down at the table of an open-air restaurant.

They drank one glass of brandy, then two, then three, and old Amable once more began wandering through the assembly. His thoughts became slightly confused, he smiled without knowing why, he smiled in front of the lotteries, in front of the wooden horses and especially in front of the killing game. He remained there a long time, filled with delight, when he saw a holiday-maker knocking down the gendarme or the cure, two authorities whom he instinctively distrusted. Then he went back to the inn and drank a glass of cider to cool himself. It was late, night came on. A neighbor came to warn him:

"You'll get back home late for the stew, daddy."

Then he set out on his way to the farmhouse. A soft shadow, the warm shadow of a spring night, was slowly descending on the earth.

When he reached the front door he thought he saw through the window which was lighted up two persons in the house. He stopped, much surprised, then he went in, and he saw Victor Lecoq seated at the table, with a plate filled with potatoes before him, taking his supper in the very same place where his son had sat.

And he turned round suddenly as if he wanted to go away. The night was very dark now. Celeste started up and shouted at him:

"Come quick, daddy! Here's some good stew to finish off the assembly with."

He complied through inertia and sat down, watching in turn the man, the woman and the child. Then he began to eat quietly as on ordinary days.

Victor Lecoq seemed quite at home, talked from time to time to Celeste, took up the child in his lap and kissed him. And Celeste again served him with food, poured out drink for him and appeared happy while speaking to him. Old Amable's eyes followed them attentively, though he could not hear what they were saying.

When he had finished supper (and he had scarcely eaten anything, there was such a weight at his heart) he rose up, and instead of ascending to his loft as he did every night he opened the gate of the yard and went out into the open air.

When he had gone, Celeste, a little uneasy, asked:

"What is he going to do?"

Victor replied in an indifferent tone:

"Don't bother yourself. He'll come back when he's tired."

Then she saw after the house, washed the plates and wiped the table, while the man quietly took off his clothes. Then he slipped into the dark and hollow bed in which she had slept with Cesaire.

The yard gate opened and old Amable again appeared. As soon as he entered the house he looked round on every side with the air of an old dog on the scent. He was in search of Victor Lecoq. As he did not see him, he took the candle off the table and approached the dark niche in which his son had died. In the interior of it he perceived the man lying under the bed clothes and already asleep. Then the deaf man noiselessly turned round, put back the candle and went out into the yard.

Celeste had finished her work. She put her son into his bed, arranged everything and waited for her father-in-law's return before lying down herself.

She remained sitting on a chair, without moving her hands and with her eyes fixed on vacancy.

As he did not come back, she murmured in a tone of impatience and annoyance:

"This good-for-nothing old man will make us burn four sous' worth of candles."

Victor answered from under the bed clothes:

"It's over an hour since he went out. We ought to see whether he fell asleep on the bench outside the door."

"I'll go and see," she said.

She rose up, took the light and went out, shading the light with her hand in order to see through the darkness.

She saw nothing in front of the door, nothing on the bench, nothing on the dung heap, where the old man used sometimes to sit in hot weather.

But, just as she was on the point of going in again, she chanced to raise her eyes toward the big apple tree, which sheltered the entrance to the farmyard, and suddenly she saw two feet—two feet at the height of her face belonging to a man who was hanging.

She uttered terrible cries:

"Victor! Victor! Victor!"

He ran out in his shirt. She could not utter another word, and turning aside her head so as not to see, she pointed toward the tree with her outstretched arm.

Not understanding what she meant, he took the candle in order to find out, and in the midst of the foliage lit up from below he saw old Amable hanging high up with a stable-halter round his neck.

A ladder was leaning against the trunk of the apple tree.

Victor ran to fetch a bill-hook, climbed up the tree and cut the halter. But the old man was already cold and his tongue protruded horribly with a frightful grimace.

VOLUME X

THE CHRISTENING

"Well doctor, a little brandy?"

"With pleasure."

The old ship's surgeon, holding out his glass, watched it as it slowly filled with the golden liquid. Then, holding it in front of his eyes, he let the light from the lamp stream through it, smelled it, tasted a few drops and smacked his lips with relish. Then he said:

"Ah! the charming poison! Or rather the seductive murderer, the delightful destroyer of peoples!

"You people do not know it the way I do. You may have read that admirable book entitled L'Assommoir, but you have not, as I have, seen alcohol exterminate a whole tribe of savages, a little kingdom of negroes—alcohol calmly unloaded by the barrel by red-bearded English seamen.

"Right near here, in a little village in Brittany near Pont-l'Abbe, I once witnessed a strange and terrible tragedy caused by alcohol. I was spending my vacation in a little country house left me by my father. You know this flat coast where the wind whistles day and night, where one sees, standing or prone, these giant rocks which in the olden times were regarded as guardians, and which still retain something majestic and imposing about them. I always expect to see them come to life and start to walk across the country with the slow and ponderous tread of giants, or to unfold enormous granite wings and fly toward the paradise of the Druids.

"Everywhere is the sea, always ready on the slightest provocation to rise in its anger and shake its foamy mane at those bold enough to brave its wrath.

"And the men who travel on this terrible sea, which, with one motion of its green back, can overturn and swallow up their frail barks—they go out in the little boats, day and night, hardy, weary and drunk. They are often drunk. They have a saying which says: 'When the bottle is full you see the reef, but when it is empty you see it no more.'

"Go into one of their huts; you will never find the father there. If you ask the woman what has become of her husband, she will stretch her arms out over the dark ocean which rumbles and roars along the coast. He remained, there one night, when he had had too much to drink; so did her oldest son. She has four more big, strong, fair-haired boys. Soon it will be their time.

"As I said, I was living in a little house near Pont-l'Abbe. I was there alone with my servant, an old sailor, and with a native family which took care of the grounds in my absence. It consisted of three persons, two sisters and a man, who had married one of them, and who attended to the garden.

"A short time before Christmas my gardener's wife presented him with a boy. The husband asked me to stand as god-father. I could hardly deny the request, and so he borrowed ten francs from me for the cost of the christening, as he said.

"The second day of January was chosen as the date of the ceremony. For a week the earth had been covered by an enormous white carpet of snow, which made this flat, low country seem vast and limitless. The ocean appeared to be black in contrast with this white plain; one could see it rolling, raging and tossing its waves as though wishing to annihilate its pale neighbor, which appeared to be dead, it was so calm, quiet and cold.

"At nine o'clock the father, Kerandec, came to my door with his sister-in-law, the big Kermagan, and the nurse, who carried the infant wrapped up in a blanket. We started for the church. The weather was so cold that it seemed to dry up the skin and crack it open. I was thinking of the poor little creature who was being carried on ahead of us, and I said to myself that this Breton race must surely be of iron, if their children were able, as soon as they were born, to stand such an outing.

"We came to the church, but the door was closed; the priest was late.

"Then the nurse sat down on one of the steps and began to undress the child. At first I thought there must have been some slight accident, but I saw that they were leaving the poor little fellow naked completely naked, in the icy air. Furious at such imprudence, I protested:

"'Why, you are crazy! You will kill the child!'

"The woman answered quietly: 'Oh, no, sir; he must wait naked before the Lord.'

"The father and the aunt looked on undisturbed. It was the custom. If it were not adhered to misfortune was sure to attend the little one.

"I scolded, threatened and pleaded. I used force to try to cover the frail creature. All was in vain. The nurse ran away from me through the snow, and the body of the little one turned purple. I was about to leave these brutes when I saw the priest coming across the country, followed. by the sexton and a young boy. I ran towards him and gave vent to my indignation. He showed no surprise nor did he quicken his pace in the least. He answered:

"'What can you expect, sir? It's the custom. They all do it, and it's of no use trying to stop them.'

"'But at least hurry up!' I cried.

"He answered: 'But I can't go any faster.'

"He entered the vestry, while we remained outside on the church steps. I was suffering. But what about the poor little creature who was howling from the effects of the biting cold.

"At last the door opened. He went into the church. But the poor child had to remain naked throughout the ceremony. It was interminable. The priest stammered over the Latin words and mispronounced them horribly. He walked slowly and with a ponderous tread. His white surplice chilled my heart. It seemed as though, in the name of a pitiless and barbarous god, he had wrapped himself in another kind of snow in order to torture this little piece of humanity that suffered so from the cold.

"Finally the christening was finished according to the rites and I saw the nurse once more take the frozen, moaning child and wrap it up in the blanket.

"The priest said to me: 'Do you wish to sign the register?'

"Turning to my gardener, I said: 'Hurry up and get home quickly so that you can warm that child.' I gave him some advice so as to ward off, if not too late, a bad attack of pneumonia. He promised to follow my instructions and left with his sister-in-law and the nurse. I followed the priest into the vestry, and when I had signed he demanded five francs for expenses.

"As I had already given the father ten francs, I refused to pay twice. The priest threatened to destroy the paper and to annul the ceremony. I, in turn, threatened him with the district attorney. The dispute was long, and I finally paid five francs.

"As soon as I reached home I went down to Kerandec's to find out whether everything was all right. Neither father, nor sister-in-law, nor nurse had yet returned. The mother, who had remained alone, was in bed, shivering with cold and starving, for she had had nothing to eat since the day before.

"'Where the deuce can they have gone?' I asked. She answered without surprise or anger, 'They're going to drink something to celebrate: It was the custom. Then I thought, of my ten francs which were to pay the church and would doubtless pay for the alcohol.

"I sent some broth to the mother and ordered a good fire to be built in the room. I was uneasy and furious and promised myself to drive out these brutes, wondering with terror what was going to happen to the poor infant.

"It was already six, and they had not yet returned. I told my servant to wait for them and I went to bed. I soon fell asleep and slept like a top. At daybreak I was awakened by my servant, who was bringing me my hot water.

"As soon as my eyes were open I asked: 'How about Kerandec?'

"The man hesitated and then stammered: 'Oh! he came back, all right, after midnight, and so drunk that he couldn't walk, and so were Kermagan and the nurse. I guess they must have slept in a ditch, for the little one died and they never even noticed it.'

"I jumped up out of bed, crying:

"'What! The child is dead?'

"'Yes, sir. They brought it back to Mother Kerandec. When she saw it she began to cry, and now they are making her drink to console her.'

"'What's that? They are making her drink!'

"'Yes, sir. I only found it out this morning. As Kerandec had no more brandy or money, he took some wood alcohol, which monsieur gave him for the lamp, and all four of them are now drinking that. The mother is feeling pretty sick now.'

"I had hastily put on some clothes, and seizing a stick, with the intention of applying it to the backs of these human beasts, I hastened towards the gardener's house.

"The mother was raving drunk beside the blue body of her dead baby. Kerandec, the nurse, and the Kermagan woman were snoring on the floor. I had to take care of the mother, who died towards noon."

The old doctor was silent. He took up the brandy-bottle and poured out another glass. He held it up to the lamp, and the light streaming through it imparted to the liquid the amber color of molten topaz. With one gulp he swallowed the treacherous drink.

THE FARMER'S WIFE

Said the Baron Rene du Treilles to me:

"Will you come and open the hunting season with me at my farm at Marinville? I shall be delighted if you will, my dear boy. In the first place, I am all alone. It is rather a difficult ground to get at, and the place I live in is so primitive that I can invite only my most intimate friends."

I accepted his invitation, and on Saturday we set off on the train going to Normandy. We alighted at a station called Almivare, and Baron Rene, pointing to a carryall drawn by a timid horse and driven by a big countryman with white hair, said:

"Here is our equipage, my dear boy."

The driver extended his hand to his landlord, and the baron pressed it warmly, asking:

"Well, Maitre Lebrument, how are you?"

"Always the same, M'sieu le Baron."

We jumped into this swinging hencoop perched on two enormous wheels, and the young horse, after a violent swerve, started into a gallop, pitching us into the air like balls. Every fall backward on the wooden bench gave me the most dreadful pain.

The peasant kept repeating in his calm, monotonous voice:

"There, there! All right all right, Moutard, all right!"

But Moutard scarcely heard, and kept capering along like a goat.

Our two dogs behind us, in the empty part of the hencoop, were standing up and sniffing the air of the plains, where they scented game.

The baron gazed with a sad eye into the distance at the vast Norman landscape, undulating and melancholy, like an immense English park, where the farmyards, surrounded by two or four rows of trees and full of dwarfed apple trees which hid the houses, gave a vista as far as the eye could see of forest trees, copses and shrubbery such as landscape gardeners look for in laying out the boundaries of princely estates.

And Rene du Treilles suddenly exclaimed:

"I love this soil; I have my very roots in it."

He was a pure Norman, tall and strong, with a slight paunch, and of the old race of adventurers who went to found kingdoms on the shores of every ocean. He was about fifty years of age, ten years less perhaps than the farmer who was driving us.

The latter was a lean peasant, all skin and bone, one of those men who live a hundred years.

After two hours' travelling over stony roads, across that green and monotonous plain, the vehicle entered one of those orchard farmyards and drew up before in old structure falling into decay, where an old maid-servant stood waiting beside a young fellow, who took charge of the horse.

We entered the farmhouse. The smoky kitchen was high and spacious. The copper utensils and the crockery shone in the reflection of the hearth. A cat lay asleep on a chair, a dog under the table. One perceived an odor of milk, apples, smoke, that indescribable smell peculiar to old farmhouses; the odor of the earth, of the walls, of furniture, the odor of spilled stale soup, of former wash-days and of former inhabitants, the smell of animals and of human beings combined, of things and of persons, the odor of time, and of things that have passed away.

I went out to have a look at the farmyard. It was very large, full of apple trees, dwarfed and crooked, and laden with fruit which fell on the grass around them. In this farmyard the Norman smell of apples was as strong as that of the bloom of orange trees on the shores of the south of France.

Four rows of beeches surrounded this inclosure. They were so tall that they seemed to touch the clouds at this hour of nightfall, and their summits, through which the night winds passed, swayed and sang a mournful, interminable song.

I reentered the house.

The baron was warming his feet at the fire, and was listening to the farmer's talk about country matters. He talked about marriages, births and deaths, then about the fall in the price of grain and the latest news about cattle. The "Veularde" (as he called a cow that had been bought at the fair of Veules) had calved in the middle of June. The cider had not been first-class last year. Apricots were almost disappearing from the country.

Then we had dinner. It was a good rustic meal, simple and abundant, long and tranquil. And while we were dining I noticed the special kind of friendly familiarity which had struck me from the start between the baron and the peasant.

Outside, the beeches continued sighing in the night wind, and our two dogs, shut up in a shed, were whining and howling in an uncanny fashion. The fire was dying out in the big fireplace. The maid-servant had gone to bed. Maitre Lebrument said in his turn:

"If you don't mind, M'sieu le Baron, I'm going to bed. I am not used to staying up late."

The baron extended his hand toward him and said: "Go, my friend," in so cordial a tone that I said, as soon as the man had disappeared:

"He is devoted to you, this farmer?"

"Better than that, my dear fellow! It is a drama, an old drama, simple and very sad, that attaches him to me. Here is the story:

"You know that my father was colonel in a cavalry regiment. His orderly was this young fellow, now an old man, the son of a farmer. When my father retired from the army he took this former soldier, then about forty; as his servant. I was at that time about thirty. We were living in our old chateau of Valrenne, near Caudebec-en-Caux.

"At this period my mother's chambermaid was one of the prettiest girls you could see, fair-haired, slender and sprightly in manner, a genuine soubrette of the old type that no longer exists. To-day these creatures spring up into hussies before their time. Paris, with the aid of the railways, attracts them, calls them, takes hold of them, as soon as they are budding into womanhood, these little sluts who in old times remained simple maid-servants. Every man passing by, as recruiting sergeants did formerly, looking for recruits, with conscripts, entices and ruins them —these foolish lassies—and we have now only the scum of the female sex for servant maids, all that is dull, nasty, common and ill-formed, too ugly, even for gallantry.

"Well, this girl was charming, and I often gave her a kiss in dark corners; nothing more, I swear to you! She was virtuous, besides; and I had some respect for my mother's house, which is more than can be said of the blackguards of the present day.

"Now, it happened that my man-servant, the ex-soldier, the old farmer you have just seen, fell madly in love with this girl, perfectly daft. The first thing we noticed was that he forgot everything, he paid no attention to anything.

"My father said incessantly:

"'See here, Jean, what's the matter with you? Are you ill?'

"He replied:

"'No, no, M'sieu le Baron. There's nothing the matter with me.'

"He grew thin; he broke glasses and let plates fall when waiting on the table. We thought he must have been attacked by some nervous affection, and sent for the doctor, who thought he could detect symptoms of spinal disease. Then my father, full of anxiety about his faithful man-servant, decided to place him in a private hospital. When the poor fellow heard of my father's intentions he made a clean breast of it.

"'M'sieu le Baron'

"'Well, my boy?'

"'You see, the thing I want is not physic.'

"'Ha! what is it, then?'

"'It's marriage!'

"My father turned round and stared at him in astonishment.

"'What's that you say, eh?'

"'It's marriage."

"'Marriage! So, then, you jackass, you're to love.'

"'That's how it is, M'sieu le Baron.'

"And my father began to laugh so immoderately that my mother called out through the wall of the next room:

"'What in the world is the matter with you, Gontran?'

"He replied:

"'Come here, Catherine.'

"And when she came in he told her, with tears in his eyes from sheer laughter, that his idiot of a servant-man was lovesick.

"But my mother, instead of laughing, was deeply affected.

"'Who is it that you have fallen in love with, my poor fellow?' she asked.

"He answered without hesitation:

"'With Louise, Madame le Baronne.'

"My mother said with the utmost gravity: 'We must try to arrange this matter the best way we can.'

"So Louise was sent for and questioned by my mother; and she said in reply that she knew all about Jean's liking for her, that in fact Jean had spoken to her about it several times, but that she did not want him. She refused to say why.

"And two months elapsed during which my father and mother never ceased to urge this girl to marry Jean. As she declared she was not in love with any other man, she could not give any serious reason for her refusal. My father at last overcame her resistance by means of a big present of money, and started the pair of them on a farm—this very farm. I did not see them for three years, and then I learned that Louise had died of consumption. But my father and mother died, too, in their turn, and it was two years more before I found myself face to face with Jean.

"At last one autumn day about the end of October the idea came into my head to go hunting on this part of my estate, which my father had told me was full of game.

"So one evening, one wet evening, I arrived at this house. I was shocked to find my father's old servant with perfectly white hair, though he was not more than forty-five or forty-six years of age. I made him dine with me, at the very table where we are now sitting. It was raining hard. We could hear the rain battering at the roof, the walls, and the windows, flowing in a perfect deluge into the farmyard; and my dog was howling in the shed where the other dogs are howling to-night.

"All of a sudden, when the servant-maid had gone to bed, the man said in a timid voice:

"'M'sieu le Baron.'

"'What is it, my dear Jean?'

"'I have something to tell you.'

"'Tell it, my dear Jean.'

"'You remember Louise, my wife.'

"'Certainly, I remember her.'

"'Well, she left me a message for you.'

"'What was it?'

"'A—a—well, it was what you might call a confession.'

"'Ha—and what was it about?'

"'It was—it was—I'd rather, all the same, tell you nothing about it—but I must—I must. Well, it's this—it wasn't consumption she died of at all. It was grief—well, that's the long and short of it. As soon as she came to live here after we were married, she grew thin; she changed so that you wouldn't know her, M'sieu le Baron. She was just as I was before I married her, but it was just the opposite, just the opposite.

"'I sent for the doctor. He said it was her liver that was affected—he said it was what he called a "hepatic" complaint—I don't know these big words, M'sieu le Baron. Then I bought medicine for her, heaps on heaps of bottles that cost about three hundred francs. But she'd take none of them; she wouldn't have them; she said: "It's no use, my poor Jean; it wouldn't do me any good." I saw well that she had some hidden trouble; and then I found her one time crying, and I didn't know what to do, no, I didn't know what to do. I bought her caps, and dresses, and hair oil, and earrings. Nothing did her any good. And I saw that she was going to die. And so one night at the end of November, one snowy night, after she had been in bed the whole day, she told me to send for the cure. So I went for him. As soon as he came—'

"'Jean,' she said, 'I am going to make a confession to you. I owe it to you, Jean. I have never been false to you, never! never, before or after you married me. M'sieu le Cure is there, and can tell you so; he knows my soul. Well, listen, Jean. If I am dying, it is because I was not able to console myself for leaving the chateau, because I was too fond of the young Baron Monsieur Rene, too fond of him, mind you, Jean, there was no harm in it! This is the thing that's killing me. When I could see him no more I felt that I should die. If I could only have seen him, I might have lived, only seen him, nothing more. I wish you'd tell him some day, by and by, when I am no longer here. You will tell him, swear you, will, Jean—swear it—in the presence of M'sieu le Cure! It will console me to know that he will know it one day, that this was the cause of my death! Swear it!'

"'Well, I gave her my promise, M'sieu le Baron, and on the faith of an honest man I have kept my word.'

"And then he ceased speaking, his eyes filling with tears.

"Good God! my dear boy, you can't form any idea of the emotion that filled me when I heard this poor devil, whose wife I had killed without suspecting it, telling me this story on that wet night in this very kitchen.

"I exclaimed: 'Ah! my poor Jean! my poor Jean!'

"He murmured: 'Well, that's all, M'sieu le Baron. I could not help it, one way or the other—and now it's all over!'

"I caught his hand across the table, and I began to weep.

"He asked, 'Will you come and see her grave?' I nodded assent, for I couldn't speak. He rose, lighted a lantern, and we walked through the blinding rain by the light of the lantern.

"He opened a gate, and I saw some crosses of black wood.

"Suddenly he stopped before a marble slab and said: 'There it is,' and he flashed the lantern close to it so that I could read the inscription:

"'TO LOUISE HORTENSE MARINET,

"'Wife of Jean-Francois Lebrument, Farmer,

"'SHE WAS A FAITHFUL WIFE. GOD REST HER SOUL.'

"We fell on our knees in the damp grass, he and I, with the lantern between us, and I saw the rain beating on the white marble slab. And I thought of the heart of her sleeping there in her grave. Ah! poor heart! poor heart! Since then I come here every year. And I don't know why, but I feel as if I were guilty of some crime in the presence of this man who always looks as if he forgave me."

THE DEVIL

The peasant and the doctor stood on opposite sides of the bed, beside the old, dying woman. She was calm and resigned and her mind quite clear as she looked at them and listened to their conversation. She was going to die, and she did not rebel at it, for her time was come, as she was ninety-two.

The July sun streamed in at the window and the open door and cast its hot flames on the uneven brown clay floor, which had been stamped down by four generations of clodhoppers. The smell of the fields came in also, driven by the sharp wind and parched by the noontide heat. The grass-hoppers chirped themselves hoarse, and filled the country with their shrill noise, which was like that of the wooden toys which are sold to children at fair time.

The doctor raised his voice and said: "Honore, you cannot leave your mother in this state; she may die at any moment." And the peasant, in great distress, replied: "But I must get in my wheat, for it has been lying on the ground a long time, and the weather is just right for it; what do you say about it, mother?" And the dying old woman, still tormented by her Norman avariciousness, replied yes with her eyes and her forehead, and thus urged her son to get in his wheat, and to leave her to die alone.

But the doctor got angry, and, stamping his foot, he said: "You are no better than a brute, do you hear, and I will not allow you to do it, do you understand? And if you must get in your wheat today, go and fetch Rapet's wife and make her look after your mother; I will have it, do you understand me? And if you do not obey me, I will let you die like a dog, when you are ill in your turn; do you hear?"

The peasant, a tall, thin fellow with slow movements, who was tormented by indecision, by his fear of the doctor and his fierce love of saving, hesitated, calculated, and stammered out: "How much does La Rapet charge for attending sick people?" "How should I know?" the doctor cried. "That depends upon how long she is needed. Settle it with her, by Heaven! But I want her to be here within an hour, do you hear?"

So the man decided. "I will go for her," he replied; "don't get angry, doctor." And the latter left, calling out as he went: "Be careful, be very careful, you know, for I do not joke when I am angry!" As soon as they were alone the peasant turned to his mother and said in a resigned voice: "I will go and fetch La Rapet, as the man will have it. Don't worry till I get back."

And he went out in his turn.

La Rapet, old was an old washerwoman, watched the dead and the dying of the neighborhood, and then, as soon as she had sewn her customers into that linen cloth from which they would emerge no more, she went and took up her iron to smooth out the linen of the living. Wrinkled like a last year's apple, spiteful, envious, avaricious with a phenomenal avarice, bent double, as if she had been broken in half across the loins by the constant motion of passing the iron over the linen, one might have said that she had a kind of abnormal and cynical love of a death struggle. She never spoke of anything but of the people she had seen die, of the various kinds of deaths at which she had been present, and she related with the greatest minuteness details which were always similar, just as a sportsman recounts his luck.

When Honore Bontemps entered her cottage, he found her preparing the starch for the collars of the women villagers, and he said: "Good-evening; I hope you are pretty well, Mother Rapet?"

She turned her head round to look at him, and said: "As usual, as usual, and you?" "Oh! as for me, I am as well as I could wish, but my mother is not well." "Your mother?" "Yes, my mother!" "What is the matter with her?" "She is going to turn up her toes, that's what's the matter with her!"

The old woman took her hands out of the water and asked with sudden sympathy: "Is she as bad as all that?" "The doctor says she will not last till morning." "Then she certainly is very bad!" Honore hesitated, for he wanted to make a few preparatory remarks before coming to his proposition; but as he could hit upon nothing, he made up his mind suddenly.

"How much will you ask to stay with her till the end? You know that I am not rich, and I can not even afford to keep a servant girl. It is just that which has brought my poor mother to this state—too much worry and fatigue! She did the work of ten, in spite of her ninety-two years. You don't find any made of that stuff nowadays!"

La Rapet answered gravely: "There are two prices: Forty sous by day and three francs by night for the rich, and twenty sous by day and forty by night for the others. You shall pay me the twenty and forty." But the, peasant reflected, for he knew his mother well. He knew how tenacious of life, how vigorous and unyielding she was, and she might last another week, in spite of the doctor's opinion; and so he said resolutely: "No, I would rather you would fix a price for the whole time until the end. I will take my chance, one way or the other. The doctor says she will die very soon. If that happens, so much the better for you, and so much the worse for her, but if she holds out till to-morrow or longer, so much the better for her and so much the worse for you!"

The nurse looked at the man in astonishment, for she had never treated a death as a speculation, and she hesitated, tempted by the idea of the possible gain, but she suspected that he wanted to play her a trick. "I can say nothing until I have seen your mother," she replied.

"Then come with me and see her."

She washed her hands, and went with him immediately.

They did not speak on the road; she walked with short, hasty steps, while he strode on with his long legs, as if he were crossing a brook at every step.

The cows lying down in the fields, overcome by the heat, raised their heads heavily and lowed feebly at the two passers-by, as if to ask them for some green grass.

When they got near the house, Honore Bontemps murmured: "Suppose it is all over?" And his unconscious wish that it might be so showed itself in the sound of his voice.

But the old woman was not dead. She was lying on her back, on her wretched bed, her hands covered with a purple cotton counterpane, horribly thin, knotty hands, like the claws of strange animals, like crabs, half closed by rheumatism, fatigue and the work of nearly a century which she had accomplished.

La Rapet went up to the bed and looked at the dying woman, felt her pulse, tapped her on the chest, listened to her breathing, and asked her questions, so as to hear her speak; and then, having looked at her for some time, she went out of the room, followed by Honore. Her decided opinion was that the old woman would not last till night. He asked: "Well?" And the sick-nurse replied: "Well, she may last two days, perhaps three. You will have to give me six francs, everything included."

"Six francs! six francs!" he shouted. "Are you out of your mind? I tell you she cannot last more than five or six hours!" And they disputed angrily for some time, but as the nurse said she must go home, as the time was going by, and as his wheat would not come to the farmyard of its own accord, he finally agreed to her terms.

"Very well, then, that is settled; six francs, including everything, until the corpse is taken out."

And he went away, with long strides, to his wheat which was lying on the ground under the hot sun which ripens the grain, while the sick-nurse went in again to the house.

She had brought some work with her, for she worked without ceasing by the side of the dead and dying, sometimes for herself, sometimes for the family which employed her as seamstress and paid her rather more in that capacity. Suddenly, she asked: "Have you received the last sacraments, Mother Bontemps?"

The old peasant woman shook her head, and La Rapet, who was very devout, got up quickly:

"Good heavens, is it possible? I will go and fetch the cure"; and she rushed off to the parsonage so quickly that the urchins in the street thought some accident had happened, when they saw her running.

The priest came immediately in his surplice, preceded by a choir boy who rang a bell to announce the passage of the Host through the parched and quiet country. Some men who were working at a distance took off their large hats and remained motionless until the white vestment had disappeared behind some farm buildings; the women who were making up the sheaves stood up to make the sign of the cross; the frightened black hens ran away along the ditch until they reached a well-known hole, through which they suddenly disappeared, while a foal which was tied in a meadow took fright at the sight of the surplice and began to gallop round and round, kicking cut every now and then. The acolyte, in his red cassock, walked quickly, and the priest, with his head inclined toward one shoulder and his square biretta on his head, followed him, muttering some prayers; while last of all came La Rapet, bent almost double as if she wished to prostrate herself, as she walked with folded hands as they do in church.

Honore saw them pass in the distance, and he asked: "Where is our priest going?" His man, who was more intelligent, replied: "He is taking the sacrament to your mother, of course!"

The peasant was not surprised, and said: "That may be," and went on with his work.

Mother Bontemps confessed, received absolution and communion, and the priest took his departure, leaving the two women alone in the suffocating room, while La Rapet began to look at the dying woman, and to ask herself whether it could last much longer.

The day was on the wane, and gusts of cooler air began to blow, causing a view of Epinal, which was fastened to the wall by two pins, to flap up and down; the scanty window curtains, which had formerly been white, but were now yellow and covered with fly-specks, looked as if they were going to fly off, as if they were struggling to get away, like the old woman's soul.

Lying motionless, with her eyes open, she seemed to await with indifference that death which was so near and which yet delayed its coming. Her short breathing whistled in her constricted throat. It would stop altogether soon, and there would be one woman less in the world; no one would regret her.

At nightfall Honore returned, and when he went up to the bed and saw that his mother was still alive, he asked: "How is she?" just as he had done formerly when she had been ailing, and then he sent La Rapet away, saying to her: "To-morrow morning at five o'clock, without fail." And she replied: "To-morrow, at five o'clock."

She came at daybreak, and found Honore eating his soup, which he had made himself before going to work, and the sick-nurse asked him: "Well, is your mother dead?" "She is rather better, on the contrary," he replied, with a sly look out of the corner of his eyes. And he went out.

La Rapet, seized with anxiety, went up to the dying woman, who remained in the same state, lethargic and impassive, with her eyes open and her hands clutching the counterpane. The nurse perceived that this might go on thus for two days, four days, eight days, and her avaricious mind was seized with fear, while she was furious at the sly fellow who had tricked her, and at the woman who would not die.

Nevertheless, she began to work, and waited, looking intently at the wrinkled face of Mother Bontemps. When Honore returned to breakfast he seemed quite satisfied and even in a bantering humor. He was decidedly getting in his wheat under very favorable circumstances.

La Rapet was becoming exasperated; every minute now seemed to her so much time and money stolen from her. She felt a mad inclination to take this old woman, this, headstrong old fool, this obstinate old wretch, and to stop that short, rapid breath, which was robbing her of her time and money, by squeezing her throat a little. But then she reflected on the danger of doing so, and other thoughts came into her head; so she went up to the bed and said: "Have you ever seen the Devil?" Mother Bontemps murmured: "No."

Then the sick-nurse began to talk and to tell her tales which were likely to terrify the weak mind of the dying woman. Some minutes before one dies the Devil appears, she said, to all who are in the death throes. He has a broom in his hand, a saucepan on his head, and he utters loud cries. When anybody sees him, all is over, and that person has only a few moments longer to live. She then enumerated all those to whom the Devil had appeared that year: Josephine Loisel, Eulalie Ratier, Sophie Padaknau, Seraphine Grospied.

Mother Bontemps, who had at last become disturbed in mind, moved about, wrung her hands, and tried to turn her head to look toward the end of the room. Suddenly La Rapet disappeared at the foot of the bed. She took a sheet out of the cupboard and wrapped herself up in it; she put the iron saucepan on her head, so that its three short bent feet rose up like horns, and she took a broom in her right hand and a tin pail in her left, which she threw up suddenly, so that it might fall to the ground noisily.

When it came down, it certainly made a terrible noise. Then, climbing upon a chair, the nurse lifted up the curtain which hung at the bottom of the bed, and showed herself, gesticulating and uttering shrill cries into the iron saucepan which covered her face, while she menaced the old peasant woman, who was nearly dead, with her broom.

Terrified, with an insane expression on her face, the dying woman made a superhuman effort to get up and escape; she even got her shoulders and chest out of bed; then she fell back with a deep sigh. All was over, and La Rapet calmly put everything back into its place; the broom into the corner by the cupboard the sheet inside it, the saucepan on the hearth, the pail on the floor, and the chair against the wall. Then, with professional movements, she closed the dead woman's large eyes, put a plate on the bed and poured some holy water into it, placing in it the twig of boxwood that had been nailed to the chest of drawers, and kneeling down, she fervently repeated the prayers for the dead, which she knew by heart, as a matter of business.

And when Honore returned in the evening he found her praying, and he calculated immediately that she had made twenty sows out of him, for she had only spent three days and one night there, which made five francs altogether, instead of the six which he owed her.

THE SNIPE

Old Baron des Ravots had for forty years been the champion sportsman of his province. But a stroke of paralysis had kept him in his chair for the last five or six years. He could now only shoot pigeons from the window of his drawing-room or from the top of his high doorsteps.

He spent his time in reading.

He was a good-natured business man, who had much of the literary spirit of a former century. He worshipped anecdotes, those little risque anecdotes, and also true stories of events that happened in his neighborhood. As soon as a friend came to see him he asked:

"Well, anything new?"

And he knew how to worm out information like an examining lawyer.

On sunny days he had his large reclining chair, similar to a bed, wheeled to the hall door. A man servant behind him held his guns, loaded them and handed them to his master. Another valet, hidden in the bushes, let fly a pigeon from time to time at irregular intervals, so that the baron should be unprepared and be always on the watch.

And from morning till night he fired at the birds, much annoyed if he were taken by surprise and laughing till he cried when the animal fell straight to the earth or, turned over in some comical and unexpected manner. He would turn to the man who was loading the gun and say, almost choking with laughter:

"Did that get him, Joseph? Did you see how he fell?" Joseph invariably replied:

"Oh, monsieur le baron never misses them."

In autumn, when the shooting season opened, he invited his friends as he had done formerly, and loved to hear them firing in the distance. He counted the shots and was pleased when they followed each other rapidly. And in the evening he made each guest give a faithful account of his day. They remained three hours at table telling about their sport.

They were strange and improbable adventures in which the romancing spirit of the sportsmen delighted. Some of them were memorable stories and were repeated regularly. The story of a rabbit that little Vicomte de Bourril had missed in his vestibule convulsed them with laughter each year anew. Every five minutes a fresh speaker would say:

"I heard 'birr! birr!' and a magnificent covey rose at ten paces from me. I aimed. Pif! paf! and I saw a shower, a veritable shower of birds. There were seven of them!"

And they all went into raptures, amazed, but reciprocally credulous.

But there was an old custom in the house called "The Story of the Snipe."

Whenever this queen of birds was in season the same ceremony took place at each dinner. As they worshipped this incomparable bird, each guest ate one every evening, but the heads were all left in the dish.

Then the baron, acting the part of a bishop, had a plate brought to him containing a little fat, and he carefully anointed the precious heads, holding them by the tip of their slender, needle-like beak. A lighted candle was placed beside him and everyone was silent in an anxiety of expectation.

Then he took one of the heads thus prepared, stuck a pin through it and stuck the pin on a cork, keeping the whole contrivance steady by means of little crossed sticks, and carefully placed this object on the neck of a bottle in the manner of a tourniquet.

All the guests counted simultaneously in a loud tone—

"One-two-three."

And the baron with a fillip of the finger made this toy whirl round.

The guest to whom the long beak pointed when the head stopped became the possessor of all the heads, a feast fit for a king, which made his neighbors look askance.

He took them one by one and toasted them over the candle. The grease sputtered, the roasting flesh smoked and the lucky winner ate the head, holding it by the beak and uttering exclamations of enjoyment.

And at each head the diners, raising their glasses, drank to his health.

When he had finished the last head he was obliged, at the baron's orders, to tell an anecdote to compensate the disappointed ones.

Here are some of the stories.

THE WILL

I knew that tall young fellow, Rene de Bourneval. He was an agreeable man, though rather melancholy and seemed prejudiced against everything, was very skeptical, and he could with a word tear down social hypocrisy. He would often say:

"There are no honorable men, or, at least, they are only relatively so when compared with those lower than themselves."

He had two brothers, whom he never saw, the Messieurs de Courcils. I always supposed they were by another father, on account of the difference in the name. I had frequently heard that the family had a strange history, but did not know the details. As I took a great liking to Rene we soon became intimate friends, and one evening, when I had been dining with him alone, I asked him, by chance: "Are you a son of the first or second marriage?" He grew rather pale, and then flushed, and did not speak for a few moments; he was visibly embarrassed. Then he smiled in the melancholy, gentle manner, which was peculiar to him, and said:

"My dear friend, if it will not weary you, I can give you some very strange particulars about my life. I know that you are a sensible man, so I do not fear that our friendship will suffer by my revelations; and should it suffer, I should not care about having you for my friend any longer.

"My mother, Madame de Courcils, was a poor little, timid woman, whom her husband had married for the sake of her fortune, and her whole life was one of martyrdom. Of a loving, timid, sensitive disposition, she was constantly being ill-treated by the man who ought to have been my father, one of those boors called country gentlemen. A month after their marriage he was living a licentious life and carrying on liaisons with the wives and daughters of his tenants. This did not prevent him from having three children by his wife, that is, if you count me in. My mother said nothing, and lived in that noisy house like a little mouse. Set aside, unnoticed, nervous, she looked at people with her bright, uneasy, restless eyes, the eyes of some terrified creature which can never shake off its fear. And yet she was pretty, very pretty and fair, a pale blonde, as if her hair had lost its color through her constant fear.

"Among the friends of Monsieur de Courcils who constantly came to her chateau, there was an ex-cavalry officer, a widower, a man who was feared, who was at the same time tender and violent, capable of the most determined resolves, Monsieur de Bourneval, whose name I bear. He was a tall, thin man, with a heavy black mustache. I am very like him. He was a man who had read a great deal, and his ideas were not like those of most of his class. His great-grandmother had been a friend of J. J. Rousseau's, and one might have said that he had inherited something of this ancestral connection. He knew the Contrat Social, and the Nouvelle Heloise by heart, and all those philosophical books which prepared in advance the overthrow of our old usages, prejudices, superannuated laws and imbecile morality.

"It seems that he loved my mother, and she loved him, but their liaison was carried on so secretly that no one guessed at its existence. The poor, neglected, unhappy woman must have clung to him in despair, and in her intimacy with him must have imbibed all his ways of thinking, theories of free thought, audacious ideas of independent love; but being so timid she never ventured to speak out, and it was all driven back, condensed, shut up in her heart.

"My two brothers were very hard towards her, like their father, and never gave her a caress, and, accustomed to seeing her count for nothing in the house, they treated her rather like a servant. I was the only one of her sons who really loved her and whom she loved.

"When she died I was seventeen, and I must add, in order that you may understand what follows, that a lawsuit between my father and mother had been decided in my mother's favor, giving her the bulk of the property, and, thanks to the tricks of the law, and the intelligent devotion of a lawyer to her interests, the right to make her will in favor of whom she pleased.

"We were told that there was a will at the lawyer's office and were invited to be present at the reading of it. I can remember it, as if it were yesterday. It was an imposing scene, dramatic, burlesque and surprising, occasioned by the posthumous revolt of that dead woman, by the cry for liberty, by the demands of that martyred one who had been crushed by our oppression during her lifetime and who, from her closed tomb, uttered a despairing appeal for independence.

"The man who believed he was my father, a stout, ruddy-faced man, who looked like a butcher, and my brothers, two great fellows of twenty and twenty-two, were waiting quietly in their chairs. Monsieur de Bourneval, who had been invited to be present, came in and stood behind me. He was very pale and bit his mustache, which was turning gray. No doubt he was prepared for what was going to happen. The lawyer double-locked the door and began to read the will, after having opened, in our presence, the envelope, sealed with red wax, of the contents of which he was ignorant."

My friend stopped talking abruptly, and rising, took from his writing-table an old paper, unfolded it, kissed it and then continued: "This is the will of my beloved mother:

"'I, the undersigned, Anne Catherine-Genevieve-Mathilde de Croixluce, the legitimate wife of Leopold-Joseph Gontran de Councils sound in body and mind, here express my last wishes.

"I first of all ask God, and then my dear son Rene to pardon me for the act I am about to commit. I believe that my child's heart is great enough to understand me, and to forgive me. I have suffered my whole life long. I was married out of calculation, then despised, misunderstood, oppressed and constantly deceived by my husband.

"'I forgive him, but I owe him nothing.

"'My elder sons never loved me, never petted me, scarcely treated me as a mother, but during my whole life I did my duty towards them, and I owe them nothing more after my death. The ties of blood cannot exist without daily and constant affection. An ungrateful son is less than a stranger; he is a culprit, for he has no right to be indifferent towards his mother.

"'I have always trembled before men, before their unjust laws, their inhuman customs, their shameful prejudices. Before God, I have no longer any fear. Dead, I fling aside disgraceful hypocrisy; I dare to speak my thoughts, and to avow and to sign the secret of my heart.

"'I therefore leave that part of my fortune of which the law allows me to dispose, in trust to my dear lover, Pierre-Germer-Simon de Bourneval, to revert afterwards to our dear son Rene.

"'(This bequest is specified more precisely in a deed drawn up by a notary.)

"'And I declare before the Supreme Judge who hears me, that I should have cursed heaven and my own existence, if I had not found the deep, devoted, tender, unshaken affection of my lover; if I had not felt in his arms that the Creator made His creatures to love, sustain and console each other, and to weep together in the hours of sadness.

"'Monsieur de Courcils is the father of my two eldest sons; Rene, alone, owes his life to Monsieur de Bourneval. I pray the Master of men and of their destinies, to place father and son above social prejudices, to make them love each other until they die, and to love me also in my coffin.

"'These are my last thoughts, and my last wish.

"'MATHILDE DE CROIXLUCE.'"

"Monsieur de Courcils had risen and he cried:

"'It is the will of a madwoman.'

"Then Monsieur de Bourneval stepped forward and said in a loud, penetrating voice: 'I, Simon de Bourneval, solemnly declare that this writing contains nothing but the strict truth, and I am ready to prove it by letters which I possess.'

"On hearing that, Monsieur de Courcils went up to him, and I thought that they were going to attack each other. There they stood, both of them tall, one stout and the other thin, both trembling. My mother's husband stammered out: 'You are a worthless wretch!' And the other replied in a loud, dry voice: 'We will meet elsewhere, monsieur. I should have already slapped your ugly face and challenged you long since if I had not, before everything else, thought of the peace of mind during her lifetime of that poor woman whom you caused to suffer so greatly.'

"Then, turning to me, he said: 'You are my son; will you come with me? I have no right to take you away, but I shall assume it, if you are willing to come with me: I shook his hand without replying, and we went out together. I was certainly three parts mad.

"Two days later Monsieur de Bourneval killed Monsieur de Courcils in a duel. My brothers, to avoid a terrible scandal, held their tongues. I offered them and they accepted half the fortune which my mother had left me. I took my real father's name, renouncing that which the law gave me, but which was not really mine. Monsieur de Bourneval died three years later and I am still inconsolable."

He rose from his chair, walked up and down the room, and, standing in front of me, said:

"Well, I say that my mother's will was one of the most beautiful, the most loyal, as well as one of the grandest acts that a woman could perform. Do you not think so?"

I held out both hands to him, saying:

"I most certainly do, my friend."

WALTER SCHNAFFS' ADVENTURE

Ever since he entered France with the invading army Walter Schnaffs had considered himself the most unfortunate of men. He was large, had difficulty in walking, was short of breath and suffered frightfully with his feet, which were very flat and very fat. But he was a peaceful, benevolent man, not warlike or sanguinary, the father of four children whom he adored, and married to a little blonde whose little tendernesses, attentions and kisses he recalled with despair every evening. He liked to rise late and retire early, to eat good things in a leisurely manner and to drink beer in the saloon. He reflected, besides, that all that is sweet in existence vanishes with life, and he maintained in his heart a fearful hatred, instinctive as well as logical, for cannon, rifles, revolvers and swords, but especially for bayonets, feeling that he was unable to dodge this dangerous weapon rapidly enough to protect his big paunch.

And when night fell and he lay on the ground, wrapped in his cape beside his comrades who were snoring, he thought long and deeply about those he had left behind and of the dangers in his path. "If he were killed what would become of the little ones? Who would provide for them and bring them up?" Just at present they were not rich, although he had borrowed when he left so as to leave them some money. And Walter Schnaffs wept when he thought of all this.

At the beginning of a battle his legs became so weak that he would have fallen if he had not reflected that the entire army would pass over his body. The whistling of the bullets gave him gooseflesh.

For months he had lived thus in terror and anguish.

His company was marching on Normandy, and one day he was sent to reconnoitre with a small detachment, simply to explore a portion of the territory and to return at once. All seemed quiet in the country; nothing indicated an armed resistance.

But as the Prussians were quietly descending into a little valley traversed by deep ravines a sharp fusillade made them halt suddenly, killing twenty of their men, and a company of sharpshooters, suddenly emerging from a little wood as large as your hand, darted forward with bayonets at the end of their rifles.

Walter Schnaffs remained motionless at first, so surprised and bewildered that he did not even think of making his escape. Then he was seized with a wild desire to run away, but he remembered at once that he ran like a tortoise compared with those thin Frenchmen, who came bounding along like a lot of goats. Perceiving a large ditch full of brushwood covered with dead leaves about six paces in front of him, he sprang into it with both feet together, without stopping to think of its depth, just as one jumps from a bridge into the river.

He fell like an arrow through a thick layer of vines and thorny brambles that tore his face and hands and landed heavily in a sitting posture on a bed of stones. Raising his eyes, he saw the sky through the hole he had made in falling through. This aperture might betray him, and he crawled along carefully on hands and knees at the bottom of this ditch beneath the covering of interlacing branches, going as fast as he could and getting away from the scene of the skirmish. Presently he stopped and sat down, crouched like a hare amid the tall dry grass.

He heard firing and cries and groans going on for some time. Then the noise of fighting grew fainter and ceased. All was quiet and silent.

Suddenly something stirred, beside him. He was frightfully startled. It was a little bird which had perched on a branch and was moving the dead leaves. For almost an hour Walter Schnaffs' heart beat loud and rapidly.

Night fell, filling the ravine with its shadows. The soldier began to think. What was he to do? What was to become of him? Should he rejoin the army? But how? By what road? And he began over again the horrible life of anguish, of terror, of fatigue and suffering that he had led since the commencement of the war. No! He no longer had the courage! He would not have the energy necessary to endure long marches and to face the dangers to which one was exposed at every moment.

But what should he do? He could not stay in this ravine in concealment until the end of hostilities. No, indeed! If it were not for having to eat, this prospect would not have daunted him greatly. But he had to eat, to eat every day.

And here he was, alone, armed and in uniform, on the enemy's territory, far from those who would protect him. A shiver ran over him.

All at once he thought: "If I were only a prisoner!" And his heart quivered with a longing, an intense desire to be taken prisoner by the French. A prisoner, he would be saved, fed, housed, sheltered from bullets and swords, without any apprehension whatever, in a good, well-kept prison. A prisoner! What a dream:

His resolution was formed at once.

"I will constitute myself a prisoner."

He rose, determined to put this plan into execution without a moment's delay. But he stood motionless, suddenly a prey to disturbing reflections and fresh terrors.

Where would he make himself a prisoner and how? In What direction? And frightful pictures, pictures of death came into his mind.

He would run terrible danger in venturing alone through the country with his pointed helmet.

Supposing he should meet some peasants. These peasants seeing a Prussian who had lost his way, an unprotected Prussian, would kill him as if he were a stray dog! They would murder him with their forks, their picks, their scythes and their shovels. They would make a stew of him, a pie, with the frenzy of exasperated, conquered enemies.

If he should meet the sharpshooters! These sharpshooters, madmen without law or discipline, would shoot him just for amusement to pass an hour; it would make them laugh to see his head. And he fancied he was already leaning against a wall in-front of four rifles whose little black apertures seemed to be gazing at him.

Supposing he should meet the French army itself. The vanguard would take him for a scout, for some bold and sly trooper who had set off alone to reconnoitre, and they would fire at him. And he could already hear, in imagination, the irregular shots of soldiers lying in the brush, while he himself, standing in the middle of the field, was sinking to the earth, riddled like a sieve with bullets which he felt piercing his flesh.

He sat down again in despair. His situation seemed hopeless.

It was quite a dark, black and silent night. He no longer budged, trembling at all the slight and unfamiliar sounds that occur at night. The sound of a rabbit crouching at the edge of his burrow almost made him run. The cry of an owl caused him positive anguish, giving him a nervous shock that pained like a wound. He opened his big eyes as wide as possible to try and see through the darkness, and he imagined every moment that he heard someone walking close beside him.

After interminable hours in which he suffered the tortures of the damned, he noticed through his leafy cover that the sky was becoming bright. He at once felt an intense relief. His limbs stretched out, suddenly relaxed, his heart quieted down, his eyes closed; he fell asleep.

When he awoke the sun appeared to be almost at the meridian. It must be noon. No sound disturbed the gloomy silence. Walter Schnaffs noticed that he was exceedingly hungry.

He yawned, his mouth watering at the thought of sausage, the good sausage the soldiers have, and he felt a gnawing at his stomach.

He rose from the ground, walked a few steps, found that his legs were weak and sat down to reflect. For two or three hours he again considered the pros and cons, changing his mind every moment, baffled, unhappy, torn by the most conflicting motives.

Finally he had an idea that seemed logical and practical. It was to watch for a villager passing by alone, unarmed and with no dangerous tools of his trade, and to run to him and give himself up, making him understand that he was surrendering.

He took off his helmet, the point of which might betray him, and put his head out of his hiding place with the utmost caution.

No solitary pedestrian could be perceived on the horizon. Yonder, to the right, smoke rose from the chimney of a little village, smoke from kitchen fires! And yonder, to the left, he saw at the end of an avenue of trees a large turreted chateau. He waited till evening, suffering frightfully from hunger, seeing nothing but flights of crows, hearing nothing but the silent expostulation of his empty stomach.

And darkness once more fell on him.

He stretched himself out in his retreat and slept a feverish sleep, haunted by nightmares, the sleep of a starving man.

Dawn again broke above his head and he began to make his observations. But the landscape was deserted as on the previous day, and a new fear came into Walter Schnaffs' mind—the fear of death by hunger! He pictured himself lying at full length on his back at the bottom of his hiding place, with his two eyes closed, and animals, little creatures of all kinds, approached and began to feed on his dead body, attacking it all over at once, gliding beneath his clothing to bite his cold flesh, and a big crow pecked out his eyes with its sharp beak.

He almost became crazy, thinking he was going to faint and would not be able to walk. And he was just preparing to rush off to the village, determined to dare anything, to brave everything, when he perceived three peasants walking to the fields with their forks across their shoulders, and he dived back into his hiding place.

But as soon as it grew dark he slowly emerged from the ditch and started off, stooping and fearful, with beating heart, towards the distant chateau, preferring to go there rather than to the village, which seemed to him as formidable as a den of tigers.

The lower windows were brilliantly lighted. One of them was open and from it escaped a strong odor of roast meat, an odor which suddenly penetrated to the olfactories and to the stomach of Walter Schnaffs, tickling his nerves, making him breathe quickly, attracting him irresistibly and inspiring his heart with the boldness of desperation.

And abruptly, without reflection, he placed himself, helmet on head, in front of the window.

Eight servants were at dinner around a large table. But suddenly one of the maids sat there, her mouth agape, her eyes fixed and letting fall her glass. They all followed the direction of her gaze.

They saw the enemy!

Good God! The Prussians were attacking the chateau!

There was a shriek, only one shriek made up of eight shrieks uttered in eight different keys, a terrific screaming of terror, then a tumultuous rising from their seats, a jostling, a scrimmage and a wild rush to the door at the farther end. Chairs fell over, the men knocked the women down and walked over them. In two seconds the room was empty, deserted, and the table, covered with eatables, stood in front of Walter Schnaffs, lost in amazement and still standing at the window.

After some moments of hesitation he climbed in at the window and approached the table. His fierce hunger caused him to tremble as if he were in a fever, but fear still held him back, numbed him. He listened. The entire house seemed to shudder. Doors closed, quick steps ran along the floor above. The uneasy Prussian listened eagerly to these confused sounds. Then he heard dull sounds, as though bodies were falling to the ground at the foot of the walls, human beings jumping from the first floor.

Then all motion, all disturbance ceased, and the great chateau became as silent as the grave.

Walter Schnaffs sat down before a clean plate and began to eat. He took great mouthfuls, as if he feared he might be interrupted before he had swallowed enough. He shovelled the food into his mouth, open like a trap, with both hands, and chunks of food went into his stomach, swelling out his throat as it passed down. Now and then he stopped, almost ready to burst like a stopped-up pipe. Then he would take the cider jug and wash down his esophagus as one washes out a clogged rain pipe.

He emptied all the plates, all the dishes and all the bottles. Then, intoxicated with drink and food, besotted, red in the face, shaken by hiccoughs, his mind clouded and his speech thick, he unbuttoned his uniform in order to breathe or he could not have taken a step. His eyes closed, his mind became torpid; he leaned his heavy forehead on his folded arms on the table and gradually lost all consciousness of things and events.

The last quarter of the moon above the trees in the park shed a faint light on the landscape. It was the chill hour that precedes the dawn.

Numerous silent shadows glided among the trees and occasionally a blade of steel gleamed in the shadow as a ray of moonlight struck it.

The quiet chateau stood there in dark outline. Only two windows were still lighted up on the ground floor.

Suddenly a voice thundered:

"Forward! nom d'un nom! To the breach, my lads!"

And in an instant the doors, shutters and window panes fell in beneath a wave of men who rushed in, breaking, destroying everything, and took the house by storm. In a moment fifty soldiers, armed to the teeth, bounded into the kitchen, where Walter Schnaffs was peacefully sleeping, and placing to his breast fifty loaded rifles, they overturned him, rolled him on the floor, seized him and tied his head and feet together.

He gasped in amazement, too besotted to understand, perplexed, bruised and wild with fear.

Suddenly a big soldier, covered with gold lace, put his foot on his stomach, shouting:

"You are my prisoner. Surrender!"

The Prussian heard only the one word "prisoner" and he sighed, "Ya, ya, ya."

He was raised from the floor, tied in a chair and examined with lively curiosity by his victors, who were blowing like whales. Several of them sat down, done up with excitement and fatigue.

He smiled, actually smiled, secure now that he was at last a prisoner.

Another officer came into the room and said:

"Colonel, the enemy has escaped; several seem to have been wounded. We are in possession."

The big officer, who was wiping his forehead, exclaimed: "Victory!"

And he wrote in a little business memorandum book which he took from his pocket:

"After a desperate encounter the Prussians were obliged to beat a retreat, carrying with them their dead and wounded, the number of whom is estimated at fifty men. Several were taken prisoners."

The young officer inquired:

"What steps shall I take, colonel?"

"We will retire in good order," replied the colonel, "to avoid having to return and make another attack with artillery and a larger force of men."

And he gave the command to set out.

The column drew up in line in the darkness beneath the walls of the chateau and filed out, a guard of six soldiers with revolvers in their hands surrounding Walter Schnaffs, who was firmly bound.

Scouts were sent ahead to reconnoitre. They advanced cautiously, halting from time to time.

At daybreak they arrived at the district of La Roche-Oysel, whose national guard had accomplished this feat of arms.

The uneasy and excited inhabitants were expecting them. When they saw the prisoner's helmet tremendous shouts arose. The women raised their arms in wonder, the old people wept. An old grandfather threw his crutch at the Prussian and struck the nose of one of their own defenders.

The colonel roared:

"See that the prisoner is secure!"

At length they reached the town hall. The prison was opened and Walter Schnaffs, freed from his bonds, cast into it. Two hundred armed men mounted guard outside the building.

Then, in spite of the indigestion that had been troubling him for some time, the Prussian, wild with joy, began to dance about, to dance frantically, throwing out his arms and legs and uttering wild shouts until he fell down exhausted beside the wall.

He was a prisoner-saved!

That was how the Chateau de Charnpignet was taken from the enemy after only six hours of occupation.

Colonel Ratier, a cloth merchant, who had led the assault at the head of a body of the national guard of La Roche-Oysel, was decorated with an order.

AT SEA

The following paragraphs recently appeared in the papers:

"Boulogne-Sur-Mer, January 22.—Our correspondent writes:

"A fearful accident has thrown our sea-faring population, which has suffered so much in the last two years, into the greatest consternation. The fishing smack commanded by Captain Javel, on entering the harbor was wrecked on the rocks of the harbor breakwater.

"In spite of the efforts of the life boat and the shooting of life lines from the shore four sailors and the cabin boy were lost.

"The rough weather continues. Fresh disasters are anticipated."

Who is this Captain Javel? Is he the brother of the one-armed man?

If the poor man tossed about in the waves and dead, perhaps, beneath his wrecked boat, is the one I am thinking of, he took part, just eighteen years ago, in another tragedy, terrible and simple as are all these fearful tragedies of the sea.

Javel, senior, was then master of a trawling smack.

The trawling smack is the ideal fishing boat. So solidly built that it fears no weather, with a round bottom, tossed about unceasingly on the waves like a cork, always on top, always thrashed by the harsh salt winds of the English Channel, it ploughs the sea unweariedly with bellying sail, dragging along at its side a huge trawling net, which scours the depths of the ocean, and detaches and gathers in all the animals asleep in the rocks, the flat fish glued to the sand, the heavy crabs with their curved claws, and the lobsters with their pointed mustaches.

When the breeze is fresh and the sea choppy, the boat starts in to trawl. The net is fastened all along a big log of wood clamped with iron and is let down by two ropes on pulleys at either end of the boat. And the boat, driven by the wind and the tide, draws along this apparatus which ransacks and plunders the depths of the sea.

Javel had on board his younger brother, four sailors and a cabin boy. He had set sail from Boulogne on a beautiful day to go trawling.

But presently a wind sprang up, and a hurricane obliged the smack to run to shore. She gained the English coast, but the high sea broke against the rocks and dashed on the beach, making it impossible to go into port, filling all the harbor entrances with foam and noise and danger.

The smack started off again, riding on the waves, tossed, shaken, dripping, buffeted by masses of water, but game in spite of everything; accustomed to this boisterous weather, which sometimes kept it roving between the two neighboring countries without its being able to make port in either.

At length the hurricane calmed down just as they were in the open, and although the sea was still high the captain gave orders to cast the net.

So it was lifted overboard, and two men in the bows and two in the stern began to unwind the ropes that held it. It suddenly touched bottom, but a big wave made the boat heel, and Javel, junior, who was in the bows directing the lowering of the net, staggered, and his arm was caught in the rope which the shock had slipped from the pulley for an instant. He made a desperate effort to raise the rope with the other hand, but the net was down and the taut rope did not give.

The man cried out in agony. They all ran to his aid. His brother left the rudder. They all seized the rope, trying to free the arm it was bruising. But in vain. "We must cut it," said a sailor, and he took from his pocket a big knife, which, with two strokes, could save young Javel's arm.

But if the rope were cut the trawling net would be lost, and this net was worth money, a great deal of money, fifteen hundred francs. And it belonged to Javel, senior, who was tenacious of his property.

"No, do not cut, wait, I will luff," he cried, in great distress. And he ran to the helm and turned the rudder. But the boat scarcely obeyed it, being impeded by the net which kept it from going forward, and prevented also by the force of the tide and the wind.

Javel, junior, had sunk on his knees, his teeth clenched, his eyes haggard. He did not utter a word. His brother came back to him, in dread of the sailor's knife.

"Wait, wait," he said. "We will let down the anchor."

They cast anchor, and then began to turn the capstan to loosen the moorings of the net. They loosened them at length and disengaged the imprisoned arm, in its bloody woolen sleeve.

Young Javel seemed like an idiot. They took off his jersey and saw a horrible sight, a mass of flesh from which the blood spurted as if from a pump. Then the young man looked at his arm and murmured: "Foutu" (done for).

Then, as the blood was making a pool on the deck of the boat, one of the sailors cried: "He will bleed to death, we must bind the vein."

So they took a cord, a thick, brown, tarry cord, and twisting it around the arm above the wound, tightened it with all their might. The blood ceased to spurt by slow degrees, and, presently, stopped altogether.

Young Javel rose, his arm hanging at his side. He took hold of it with the other hand, raised it, turned it over, shook it. It was all mashed, the bones broken, the muscles alone holding it together. He looked at it sadly, reflectively. Then he sat down on a folded sail and his comrades advised him to keep wetting the arm constantly to prevent it from mortifying.

They placed a pail of water beside him, and every few minutes he dipped a glass into it and bathed the frightful wound, letting the clear water trickle on to it.

"You would be better in the cabin," said his brother. He went down, but came up again in an hour, not caring to be alone. And, besides, he preferred the fresh air. He sat down again on his sail and began to bathe his arm.

They made a good haul. The broad fish with their white bellies lay beside him, quivering in the throes of death; he looked at them as he continued to bathe his crushed flesh.

As they were about to return to Boulogne the wind sprang up anew, and the little boat resumed its mad course, bounding and tumbling about, shaking up the poor wounded man.

Night came on. The sea ran high until dawn. As the sun rose the English coast was again visible, but, as the weather had abated a little, they turned back towards the French coast, tacking as they went.

Towards evening Javel, junior, called his comrades and showed them some black spots, all the horrible tokens of mortification in the portion of the arm below the broken bones.

The sailors examined it, giving their opinion.

"That might be the 'Black,'" thought one.

"He should put salt water on it," said another.

They brought some salt water and poured it on the wound. The injured man became livid, ground his teeth and writhed a little, but did not exclaim.

Then, as soon as the smarting had abated, he said to his brother:

"Give me your knife."

The brother handed it to him.

"Hold my arm up, quite straight, and pull it."

They did as he asked them.

Then he began to cut off his arm. He cut gently, carefully, severing all the tendons with this blade that was sharp as a razor. And, presently, there was only a stump left. He gave a deep sigh and said:

"It had to be done. It was done for."

He seemed relieved and breathed loud. He then began again to pour water on the stump of arm that remained.

The sea was still rough and they could not make the shore.

When the day broke, Javel, junior, took the severed portion of his arm and examined it for a long time. Gangrene had set in. His comrades also examined it and handed it from one to the other, feeling it, turning it over, and sniffing at it.

"You must throw that into the sea at once," said his brother.

But Javel, junior, got angry.

"Oh, no! Oh, no! I don't want to. It belongs to me, does it not, as it is my arm?"

And he took and placed it between his feet.

"It will putrefy, just the same," said the older brother. Then an idea came to the injured man. In order to preserve the fish when the boat was long at sea, they packed it in salt, in barrels. He asked:

"Why can I not put it in pickle?"

"Why, that's a fact," exclaimed the others.

Then they emptied one of the barrels, which was full from the haul of the last few days; and right at the bottom of the barrel they laid the detached arm. They covered it with salt, and then put back the fish one by one.

One of the sailors said by way of joke:

"I hope we do not sell it at auction."

And everyone laughed, except the two Javels.

The wind was still boisterous. They tacked within sight of Boulogne until the following morning at ten o'clock. Young Javel continued to bathe his wound. From time to time he rose and walked from one end to the other of the boat.

His brother, who was at the tiller, followed him with glances, and shook his head.

At last they ran into harbor.

The doctor examined the wound and pronounced it to be in good condition. He dressed it properly and ordered the patient to rest. But Javel would not go to bed until he got back his severed arm, and he returned at once to the dock to look for the barrel which he had marked with a cross.

It was emptied before him and he seized the arm, which was well preserved in the pickle, had shrunk and was freshened. He wrapped it up in a towel he had brought for the purpose and took it home.

His wife and children looked for a long time at this fragment of their father, feeling the fingers, and removing the grains of salt that were under the nails. Then they sent for a carpenter to make a little coffin.

The next day the entire crew of the trawling smack followed the funeral of the detached arm. The two brothers, side by side, led the procession; the parish beadle carried the corpse under his arm.

Javel, junior, gave up the sea. He obtained a small position on the dock, and when he subsequently talked about his accident, he would say confidentially to his auditors:

"If my brother had been willing to cut away the net, I should still have my arm, that is sure. But he was thinking only of his property."

MINUET

Great misfortunes do not affect me very much, said John Bridelle, an old bachelor who passed for a sceptic. I have seen war at quite close quarters; I walked across corpses without any feeling of pity. The great brutal facts of nature, or of humanity, may call forth cries of horror or indignation, but do not cause us that tightening of the heart, that shudder that goes down your spine at sight of certain little heartrending episodes.

The greatest sorrow that anyone can experience is certainly the loss of a child, to a mother; and the loss of his mother, to a man. It is intense, terrible, it rends your heart and upsets your mind; but one is healed of these shocks, just as large bleeding wounds become healed. Certain meetings, certain things half perceived, or surmised, certain secret sorrows, certain tricks of fate which awake in us a whole world of painful thoughts, which suddenly unclose to us the mysterious door of moral suffering, complicated, incurable; all the deeper because they appear benign, all the more bitter because they are intangible, all the more tenacious because they appear almost factitious, leave in our souls a sort of trail of sadness, a taste of bitterness, a feeling of disenchantment, from which it takes a long time to free ourselves.

I have always present to my mind two or three things that others would surely not have noticed, but which penetrated my being like fine, sharp incurable stings.

You might not perhaps understand the emotion that I retained from these hasty impressions. I will tell you one of them. She was very old, but as lively as a young girl. It may be that my imagination alone is responsible for my emotion.

I am fifty. I was young then and studying law. I was rather sad, somewhat of a dreamer, full of a pessimistic philosophy and did not care much for noisy cafes, boisterous companions, or stupid girls. I rose early and one of my chief enjoyments was to walk alone about eight o'clock in the morning in the nursery garden of the Luxembourg.

You people never knew that nursery garden. It was like a forgotten garden of the last century, as pretty as the gentle smile of an old lady. Thick hedges divided the narrow regular paths,—peaceful paths between two walls of carefully trimmed foliage. The gardener's great shears were pruning unceasingly these leafy partitions, and here and there one came across beds of flowers, lines of little trees looking like schoolboys out for a walk, companies of magnificent rose bushes, or regiments of fruit trees.

An entire corner of this charming spot was in habited by bees. Their straw hives skillfully arranged at distances on boards had their entrances—as large as the opening of a thimble—turned towards the sun, and all along the paths one encountered these humming and gilded flies, the true masters of this peaceful spot, the real promenaders of these quiet paths.

I came there almost every morning. I sat down on a bench and read. Sometimes I let my book fall on my knees, to dream, to listen to the life of Paris around me, and to enjoy the infinite repose of these old-fashioned hedges.

But I soon perceived that I was not the only one to frequent this spot as soon as the gates were opened, and I occasionally met face to face, at a turn in the path, a strange little old man.

He wore shoes with silver buckles, knee-breeches, a snuff-colored frock coat, a lace jabot, and an outlandish gray hat with wide brim and long-haired surface that might have come out of the ark.

He was thin, very thin, angular, grimacing and smiling. His bright eyes were restless beneath his eyelids which blinked continuously. He always carried in his hand a superb cane with a gold knob, which must have been for him some glorious souvenir.

This good man astonished me at first, then caused me the intensest interest. I watched him through the leafy walls, I followed him at a distance, stopping at a turn in the hedge so as not to be seen.

And one morning when he thought he was quite alone, he began to make the most remarkable motions. First he would give some little springs, then make a bow; then, with his slim legs, he would give a lively spring in the air, clapping his feet as he did so, and then turn round cleverly, skipping and frisking about in a comical manner, smiling as if he had an audience, twisting his poor little puppet-like body, bowing pathetic and ridiculous little greetings into the empty air. He was dancing.

I stood petrified with amazement, asking myself which of us was crazy, he or I.

He stopped suddenly, advanced as actors do on the stage, then bowed and retreated with gracious smiles, and kissing his hand as actors do, his trembling hand, to the two rows of trimmed bushes.

Then he continued his walk with a solemn demeanor.

After that I never lost sight of him, and each morning he began anew his outlandish exercises.

I was wildly anxious to speak to him. I decided to risk it, and one day, after greeting him, I said:

"It is a beautiful day, monsieur."

He bowed.

"Yes, sir, the weather is just as it used to be."

A week later we were friends and I knew his history. He had been a dancing master at the opera, in the time of Louis XV. His beautiful cane was a present from the Comte de Clermont. And when we spoke about dancing he never stopping talking.

One day he said to me:

"I married La Castris, monsieur. I will introduce you to her if you wish it, but she does not get here till later. This garden, you see, is our delight and our life. It is all that remains of former days. It seems as though we could not exist if we did not have it. It is old and distingue, is it not? I seem to breathe an air here that has not changed since I was young. My wife and I pass all our afternoons here, but I come in the morning because I get up early."

As soon as I had finished luncheon I returned to the Luxembourg, and presently perceived my friend offering his arm ceremoniously to a very old little lady dressed in black, to whom he introduced me. It was La Castris, the great dancer, beloved by princes, beloved by the king, beloved by all that century of gallantry that seems to have left behind it in the world an atmosphere of love.

We sat down on a bench. It was the month of May. An odor of flowers floated in the neat paths; a hot sun glided its rays between the branches and covered us with patches of light. The black dress of La Castris seemed to be saturated with sunlight.

The garden was empty. We heard the rattling of vehicles in the distance.

"Tell me," I said to the old dancer, "what was the minuet?"

He gave a start.

"The minuet, monsieur, is the queen of dances, and the dance of queens, do you understand? Since there is no longer any royalty, there is no longer any minuet."

And he began in a pompous manner a long dithyrambic eulogy which I could not understand. I wanted to have the steps, the movements, the positions, explained to me. He became confused, was amazed at his inability to make me understand, became nervous and worried.

Then suddenly, turning to his old companion who had remained silent and serious, he said:

"Elise, would you like—say—would you like, it would be very nice of you, would you like to show this gentleman what it was?"

She turned eyes uneasily in all directions, then rose without saying a word and took her position opposite him.

Then I witnessed an unheard-of thing.

They advanced and retreated with childlike grimaces, smiling, swinging each other, bowing, skipping about like two automaton dolls moved by some old mechanical contrivance, somewhat damaged, but made by a clever workman according to the fashion of his time.

And I looked at them, my heart filled with extraordinary emotions, my soul touched with an indescribable melancholy. I seemed to see before me a pathetic and comical apparition, the out-of-date ghost of a former century.

They suddenly stopped. They had finished all the figures of the dance. For some seconds they stood opposite each other, smiling in an astonishing manner. Then they fell on each other's necks sobbing.

I left for the provinces three days later. I never saw them again. When I returned to Paris, two years later, the nursery had been destroyed. What became of them, deprived of the dear garden of former days, with its mazes, its odor of the past, and the graceful windings of its hedges?

Are they dead? Are they wandering among modern streets like hopeless exiles? Are they dancing—grotesque spectres—a fantastic minuet in the moonlight, amid the cypresses of a cemetery, along the pathways bordered by graves?

Their memory haunts me, obsesses me, torments me, remains with me like a wound. Why? I do not know.

No doubt you think that very absurd?

THE SON

The two old friends were walking in the garden in bloom, where spring was bringing everything to life.

One was a senator, the other a member of the French Academy, both serious men, full of very logical but solemn arguments, men of note and reputation.

They talked first of politics, exchanging opinions; not on ideas, but on men, personalities in this regard taking the predominance over ability. Then they recalled some memories. Then they walked along in silence, enervated by the warmth of the air.

A large bed of wallflowers breathed out a delicate sweetness. A mass of flowers of all species and color flung their fragrance to the breeze, while a cytisus covered with yellow clusters scattered its fine pollen abroad, a golden cloud, with an odor of honey that bore its balmy seed across space, similar to the sachet-powders of perfumers.

The senator stopped, breathed in the cloud of floating pollen, looked at the fertile shrub, yellow as the sun, whose seed was floating in the air, and said:

"When one considers that these imperceptible fragrant atoms will create existences at a hundred leagues from here, will send a thrill through the fibres and sap of female trees and produce beings with roots, growing from a germ, just as we do, mortal like ourselves, and who will be replaced by other beings of the same order, like ourselves again!"

And, standing in front of the brilliant cytisus, whose live pollen was shaken off by each breath of air, the senator added:

"Ah, old fellow, if you had to keep count of all your children you would be mightily embarrassed. Here is one who generates freely, and then lets them go without a pang and troubles himself no more about them."

"We do the same, my friend," said the academician.

"Yes, I do not deny it; we let them go sometimes," resumed the senator, "but we are aware that we do, and that constitutes our superiority."

"No, that is not what I mean," said the other, shaking his head. "You see, my friend, that there is scarcely a man who has not some children that he does not know, children—'father unknown'—whom he has generated almost unconsciously, just as this tree reproduces.

"If we had to keep account of our amours, we should be just as embarrassed as this cytisus which you apostrophized would be in counting up his descendants, should we not?

"From eighteen to forty years, in fact, counting in every chance cursory acquaintanceship, we may well say that we have been intimate with two or three hundred women.

"Well, then, my friend, among this number can you be sure that you have not had children by at least one of them, and that you have not in the streets, or in the bagnio, some blackguard of a son who steals from and murders decent people, i.e., ourselves; or else a daughter in some disreputable place, or, if she has the good fortune to be deserted by her mother, as cook in some family?

"Consider, also, that almost all those whom we call 'prostitutes' have one or two children of whose paternal parentage they are ignorant, generated by chance at the price of ten or twenty francs. In every business there is profit and loss. These wildings constitute the 'loss' in their profession. Who generated them? You—I—we all did, the men called 'gentlemen'! They are the consequences of our jovial little dinners, of our gay evenings, of those hours when our comfortable physical being impels us to chance liaisons.

"Thieves, marauders, all these wretches, in fact, are our children. And that is better for us than if we were their children, for those scoundrels generate also!

"I have in my mind a very horrible story that I will relate to you. It has caused me incessant remorse, and, further than that, a continual doubt, a disquieting uncertainty, that, at times, torments me frightfully.

"When I was twenty-five I undertook a walking tour through Brittany with one of my friends, now a member of the cabinet.

"After walking steadily for fifteen or twenty days and visiting the Cotes-du-Nord and part of Finistere we reached Douarnenez. From there we went without halting to the wild promontory of Raz by the bay of Les Trepaases, and passed the night in a village whose name ends in 'of.' The next morning a strange lassitude kept my friend in bed; I say bed from habit, for our couch consisted simply of two bundles of straw.

"It would never do to be ill in this place. So I made him get up, and we reached Andierne about four or five o'clock in the evening.

"The following day he felt a little better, and we set out again. But on the road he was seized with intolerable pain, and we could scarcely get as far as Pont Labbe.

"Here, at least, there was an inn. My friend went to bed, and the doctor, who had been sent for from Quimper, announced that he had a high fever, without being able to determine its nature.

"Do you know Pont Labbe? No? Well, then, it is the most Breton of all this Breton Brittany, which extends from the promontory of Raz to the Morbihan, of this land which contains the essence of the Breton manners, legends and customs. Even to-day this corner of the country has scarcely changed. I say 'even to-day,' for I now go there every year, alas!

"An old chateau laves the walls of its towers in a great melancholy pond, melancholy and frequented by flights of wild birds. It has an outlet in a river on which boats can navigate as far as the town. In the narrow streets with their old-time houses the men wear big hats, embroidered waistcoats and four coats, one on top of the other; the inside one, as large as your hand, barely covering the shoulder-blades, and the outside one coming to just above the seat of the trousers.

"The girls, tall, handsome and fresh have their bosoms crushed in a cloth bodice which makes an armor, compresses them, not allowing one even to guess at their robust and tortured neck. They also wear a strange headdress. On their temples two bands embroidered in colors frame their face, inclosing the hair, which falls in a shower at the back of their heads, and is then turned up and gathered on top of the head under a singular cap, often woven with gold or silver thread.

"The servant at our inn was eighteen at most, with very blue eyes, a pale blue with two tiny black pupils, short teeth close together, which she showed continually when she laughed, and which seemed strong enough to grind granite.

"She did not know a word of French, speaking only Breton, as did most of her companions.

"As my friend did not improve much, and although he had no definite malady, the doctor forbade him to continue his journey yet, ordering complete rest. I spent my days with him, and the little maid would come in incessantly, bringing either my dinner or some herb tea.

"I teased her a little, which seemed to amuse her, but we did not chat, of course, as we could not understand each other.

"But one night, after I had stayed quite late with my friend and was going back to my room, I passed the girl, who was going to her room. It was just opposite my open door, and, without reflection, and more for fun than anything else, I abruptly seized her round the waist, and before she recovered from her astonishment I had thrown her down and locked her in my room. She looked at me, amazed, excited, terrified, not daring to cry out for fear of a scandal and of being probably driven out, first by her employers and then, perhaps, by her father.

"I did it as a joke at first. She defended herself bravely, and at the first chance she ran to the door, drew back the bolt and fled.

"I scarcely saw her for several days. She would not let me come near her. But when my friend was cured and we were to get out on our travels again I saw her coming into my room about midnight the night before our departure, just after I had retired.

"She threw herself into my arms and embraced me passionately, giving me all the assurances of tenderness and despair that a woman can give when she does not know a word of our language.

"A week later I had forgotten this adventure, so common and frequent when one is travelling, the inn servants being generally destined to amuse travellers in this way.

"I was thirty before I thought of it again, or returned to Pont Labbe.

"But in 1876 I revisited it by chance during a trip into Brittany, which I made in order to look up some data for a book and to become permeated with the atmosphere of the different places.

"Nothing seemed changed. The chateau still laved its gray wall in the pond outside the little town; the inn was the same, though it had been repaired, renovated and looked more modern. As I entered it I was received by two young Breton girls of eighteen, fresh and pretty, bound up in their tight cloth bodices, with their silver caps and wide embroidered bands on their ears.

"It was about six o'clock in the evening. I sat down to dinner, and as the host was assiduous in waiting on me himself, fate, no doubt, impelled me to say:

"'Did you know the former proprietors of this house? I spent about ten days here thirty years ago. I am talking old times.'

"'Those were my parents, monsieur,' he replied.

"Then I told him why we had stayed over at that time, how my comrade had been delayed by illness. He did not let me finish.

"'Oh, I recollect perfectly. I was about fifteen or sixteen. You slept in the room at the end and your friend in the one I have taken for myself, overlooking the street.'

"It was only then that the recollection of the little maid came vividly to my mind. I asked: 'Do you remember a pretty little servant who was then in your father's employ, and who had, if my memory does not deceive me, pretty eyes and fresh-looking teeth?'

"'Yes, monsieur; she died in childbirth some time after.'

"And, pointing to the courtyard where a thin, lame man was stirring up the manure, he added:

"'That is her son.'

"I began to laugh:

"'He is not handsome and does not look much like his mother. No doubt he looks like his father.'

"'That is very possible,' replied the innkeeper; 'but we never knew whose child it was. She died without telling any one, and no one here knew of her having a beau. Every one was hugely astonished when they heard she was enceinte, and no one would believe it.'

"A sort of unpleasant chill came over me, one of those painful surface wounds that affect us like the shadow of an impending sorrow. And I looked at the man in the yard. He had just drawn water for the horses and was carrying two buckets, limping as he walked, with a painful effort of his shorter leg. His clothes were ragged, he was hideously dirty, with long yellow hair, so tangled that it looked like strands of rope falling down at either side of his face.

"'He is not worth much,' continued the innkeeper; 'we have kept him for charity's sake. Perhaps he would have turned out better if he had been brought up like other folks. But what could one do, monsieur? No father, no mother, no money! My parents took pity on him, but he was not their child, you understand.'

"I said nothing.

"I slept in my old room, and all night long I thought of this frightful stableman, saying to myself: 'Supposing it is my own son? Could I have caused that girl's death and procreated this being? It was quite possible!'

"I resolved to speak to this man and to find out the exact date of his birth. A variation of two months would set my doubts at rest.

"I sent for him the next day. But he could not speak French. He looked as if he could not understand anything, being absolutely ignorant of his age, which I had inquired of him through one of the maids. He stood before me like an idiot, twirling his hat in 'his knotted, disgusting hands, laughing stupidly, with something of his mother's laugh in the corners of his mouth and of his eyes.

"The landlord, appearing on the scene, went to look for the birth certificate of this wretched being. He was born eight months and twenty-six days after my stay at Pont Labbe, for I recollect perfectly that we reached Lorient on the fifteenth of August. The certificate contained this description: 'Father unknown.' The mother called herself Jeanne Kerradec.

"Then my heart began to beat rapidly. I could not utter a word, for I felt as if I were choking. I looked at this animal whose long yellow hair reminded me of a straw heap, and the beggar, embarrassed by my gaze, stopped laughing, turned his head aside, and wanted to get away.

"All day long I wandered beside the little river, giving way to painful reflections. But what was the use of reflection? I could be sure of nothing. For hours and hours I weighed all the pros and cons in favor of or against the probability of my being the father, growing nervous over inexplicable suppositions, only to return incessantly to the same horrible uncertainty, then to the still more atrocious conviction that this man was my son.

"I could eat no dinner, and went to my room.

"I lay awake for a long time, and when I finally fell asleep I was haunted by horrible visions. I saw this laborer laughing in my face and calling me 'papa.' Then he changed into a dog and bit the calves of my legs, and no matter how fast I ran he still followed me, and instead of barking, talked and reviled me. Then he appeared before my colleagues at the Academy, who had assembled to decide whether I was really his father; and one of them cried out: 'There can be no doubt about it! See how he resembles him.' And, indeed, I could see that this monster looked like me. And I awoke with this idea fixed in my mind and with an insane desire to see the man again and assure myself whether or not we had similar features.

"I joined him as he was going to mass (it was Sunday) and I gave him five francs as I gazed at him anxiously. He began to laugh in an idiotic manner, took the money, and then, embarrassed afresh at my gaze, he ran off, after stammering an almost inarticulate word that, no doubt, meant 'thank you.'

"My day passed in the same distress of mind as on the previous night. I sent for the landlord, and, with the greatest caution, skill and tact, I told him that I was interested in this poor creature, so abandoned by every one and deprived of everything, and I wished to do something for him.

"But the man replied: 'Oh, do not think of it, monsieur; he is of no account; you will only cause yourself annoyance. I employ him to clean out the stable, and that is all he can do. I give him his board and let him sleep with the horses. He needs nothing more. If you have an old pair of trousers, you might give them to him, but they will be in rags in a week.'

"I did not insist, intending to think it over.

"The poor wretch came home that evening frightfully drunk, came near setting fire to the house, killed a horse by hitting it with a pickaxe, and ended up by lying down to sleep in the mud in the midst of the pouring rain, thanks to my donation.

"They begged me next day not to give him any more money. Brandy drove him crazy, and as soon as he had two sous in his pocket he would spend it in drink. The landlord added: 'Giving him money is like trying to kill him.' The man had never, never in his life had more than a few centimes, thrown to him by travellers, and he knew of no destination for this metal but the wine shop.

"I spent several hours in my room with an open book before me which I pretended to read, but in reality looking at this animal, my son! my son! trying to discover if he looked anything like me. After careful scrutiny I seemed to recognize a similarity in the lines of the forehead and the root of the nose, and I was soon convinced that there was a resemblance, concealed by the difference in garb and the man's hideous head of hair.

"I could not stay here any longer without arousing suspicion, and I went away, my heart crushed, leaving with the innkeeper some money to soften the existence of his servant.

"For six years now I have lived with this idea in my mind, this horrible uncertainty, this abominable suspicion. And each year an irresistible force takes me back to Pont Labbe. Every year I condemn myself to the torture of seeing this animal raking the manure, imagining that he resembles me, and endeavoring, always vainly, to render him some assistance. And each year I return more uncertain, more tormented, more worried.

"I tried to have him taught, but he is a hopeless idiot. I tried to make his life less hard. He is an irreclaimable drunkard, and spends in drink all the money one gives him, and knows enough to sell his new clothes in order to get brandy.

"'I tried to awaken his master's sympathy, so that he should look after him, offering to pay him for doing so. The innkeeper, finally surprised, said, very wisely: 'All that you do for him, monsieur, will only help to destroy him. He must be kept like a prisoner. As soon as he has any spare time, or any comfort, he becomes wicked. If you wish to do good, there is no lack of abandoned children, but select one who will appreciate your attention.'

"What could I say?

"If I allowed the slightest suspicion of the doubts that tortured me to escape, this idiot would assuredly become cunning, in order to blackmail me, to compromise me and ruin me. He would call out 'papa,' as in my dream.

"And I said to myself that I had killed the mother and lost this atrophied creature, this larva of the stable, born and raised amid the manure, this man who, if brought up like others, would have been like others.

"And you cannot imagine what a strange, embarrassed and intolerable feeling comes over me when he stands before me and I reflect that he came from myself, that he belongs to me through the intimate bond that links father and son, that, thanks to the terrible law of heredity, he is my own self in a thousand ways, in his blood and his flesh, and that he has even the same germs of disease, the same leaven of emotions.

"I have an incessant restless, distressing longing to see him, and the sight of him causes me intense suffering, as I look down from my window and watch him for hours removing and carting the horse manure, saying to myself: 'That is my son.'

"And I sometimes feel an irresistible longing to embrace him. I have never even touched his dirty hand."

The academician was silent. His companion, a tactful man, murmured: "Yes, indeed, we ought to take a closer interest in children who have no father."

A gust of wind passing through the tree shook its yellow clusters, enveloping in a fragrant and delicate mist the two old men, who inhaled in the fragrance with deep breaths.

The senator added: "It is good to be twenty-five and even to have children like that."

THAT PIG OF A MORIN

"Here, my friend," I said to Labarbe, "you have just repeated those five words, that pig of a Morin. Why on earth do I never hear Morin's name mentioned without his being called a pig?"

Labarbe, who is a deputy, looked at me with his owl-like eyes and said: "Do you mean to say that you do not know Morin's story and you come from La Rochelle?" I was obliged to declare that I did not know Morin's story, so Labarbe rubbed his hands and began his recital.

"You knew Morin, did you not, and you remember his large linen-draper's shop on the Quai de la Rochelle?"

"Yes, perfectly."

"Well, then. You must know that in 1862 or '63 Morin went to spend a fortnight in Paris for pleasure; or for his pleasures, but under the pretext of renewing his stock, and you also know what a fortnight in Paris means to a country shopkeeper; it fires his blood. The theatre every evening, women's dresses rustling up against you and continual excitement; one goes almost mad with it. One sees nothing but dancers in tights, actresses in very low dresses, round legs, fat shoulders, all nearly within reach of one's hands, without daring, or being able, to touch them, and one scarcely tastes food. When one leaves the city one's heart is still all in a flutter and one's mind still exhilarated by a sort of longing for kisses which tickles one's lips.

"Morin was in that condition when he took his ticket for La Rochelle by the eight-forty night express. As he was walking up and down the waiting-room at the station he stopped suddenly in front of a young lady who was kissing an old one. She had her veil up, and Morin murmured with delight: 'By Jove what a pretty woman!'

"When she had said 'good-by' to the old lady she went into the waiting-room, and Morin followed her; then she went on the platform and Morin still followed her; then she got into an empty carriage, and he again followed her. There were very few travellers on the express. The engine whistled and the train started. They were alone. Morin devoured her with his eyes. She appeared to be about nineteen or twenty and was fair, tall, with a bold look. She wrapped a railway rug round her and stretched herself on the seat to sleep.

"Morin asked himself: 'I wonder who she is?' And a thousand conjectures, a thousand projects went through his head. He said to himself: 'So many adventures are told as happening on railway journeys that this may be one that is going to present itself to me. Who knows? A piece of good luck like that happens very suddenly, and perhaps I need only be a little venturesome. Was it not Danton who said: "Audacity, more audacity and always audacity"? If it was not Danton it was Mirabeau, but that does not matter. But then I have no audacity, and that is the difficulty. Oh! If one only knew, if one could only read people's minds! I will bet that every day one passes by magnificent opportunities without knowing it, though a gesture would be enough to let me know her mind.'

"Then he imagined to himself combinations which conducted him to triumph. He pictured some chivalrous deed or merely some slight service which he rendered her, a lively, gallant conversation which ended in a declaration.

"But he could find no opening, had no pretext, and he waited for some fortunate circumstance, with his heart beating and his mind topsy-turvy. The night passed and the pretty girl still slept, while Morin was meditating his own fall. The day broke and soon the first ray of sunlight appeared in the sky, a long, clear ray which shone on the face of the sleeping girl and woke her. She sat up, looked at the country, then at Morin and smiled. She smiled like a happy woman, with an engaging and bright look, and Morin trembled. Certainly that smile was intended for him; it was discreet invitation, the signal which he was waiting for. That smile meant to say: 'How stupid, what a ninny, what a dolt, what a donkey you are, to have sat there on your seat like a post all night!

"'Just look at me, am I not charming? And you have sat like that for the whole night, when you have been alone with a pretty woman, you great simpleton!'

"She was still smiling as she looked at him; she even began to laugh; and he lost his head trying to find something suitable to say, no matter what. But he could think of nothing, nothing, and then, seized with a coward's courage, he said to himself:

"'So much the worse, I will risk everything,' and suddenly, without the slightest warning, he went toward her, his arms extended, his lips protruding, and, seizing her in his arms, he kissed her.

"She sprang up immediately with a bound, crying out: 'Help! help!' and screaming with terror; and then she opened the carriage door and waved her arm out, mad with terror and trying to jump out, while Morin, who was almost distracted and feeling sure that she would throw herself out, held her by the skirt and stammered: 'Oh, madame! oh, madame!'

"The train slackened speed and then stopped. Two guards rushed up at the young woman's frantic signals. She threw herself into their arms, stammering: 'That man wanted—wanted—to—to—' And then she fainted.

"They were at Mauze station, and the gendarme on duty arrested Morin. When the victim of his indiscreet admiration had regained her consciousness, she made her charge against him, and the police drew it up. The poor linen draper did not reach home till night, with a prosecution hanging over him for an outrage to morals in a public place." II

"At that time I was editor of the Fanal des Charentes, and I used to meet Morin every day at the Cafe du Commerce, and the day after his adventure. he came to see me, as he did not know what to do. I did not hide my opinion from him, but said to him: 'You are no better than a pig. No decent man behaves like that.'

"He cried. His wife had given him a beating, and he foresaw his trade ruined, his name dragged through the mire and dishonored, his friends scandalized and taking no notice of him. In the end he excited my pity, and I sent for my colleague, Rivet, a jocular but very sensible little man, to give us his advice.

"He advised me to see the public prosecutor, who was a friend of mine, and so I sent Morin home and went to call on the magistrate. He told me that the woman who had been insulted was a young lady, Mademoiselle Henriette Bonnel, who had just received her certificate as governess in Paris and spent her holidays with her uncle and aunt, who were very respectable tradespeople in Mauze. What made Morin's case all the more serious was that the uncle had lodged a complaint, but the public official had consented to let the matter drop if this complaint were withdrawn, so we must try and get him to do this.

"I went back to Morin's and found him in bed, ill with excitement and distress. His wife, a tall raw-boned woman with a beard, was abusing him continually, and she showed me into the room, shouting at me: 'So you have come to see that pig of a Morin. Well, there he is, the darling!' And she planted herself in front of the bed, with her hands on her hips. I told him how matters stood, and he begged me to go and see the girl's uncle and aunt. It was a delicate mission, but I undertook it, and the poor devil never ceased repeating: 'I assure you I did not even kiss her; no, not even that. I will take my oath to it!'

"I replied: 'It is all the same; you are nothing but a pig.' And I took a thousand francs which he gave me to employ as I thought best, but as I did not care to venture to her uncle's house alone, I begged Rivet to go with me, which he agreed to do on condition that we went immediately, for he had some urgent business at La Rochelle that afternoon. So two hours later we rang at the door of a pretty country house. An attractive girl came and opened the door to us assuredly the young lady in question, and I said to Rivet in a low voice: 'Confound it! I begin to understand Morin!'

"The uncle, Monsieur Tonnelet, subscribed to the Fanal, and was a fervent political coreligionist of ours. He received us with open arms and congratulated us and wished us joy; he was delighted at having the two editors in his house, and Rivet whispered to me: 'I think we shall be able to arrange the matter of that pig of a Morin for him.'

"The niece had left the room and I introduced the delicate subject. I waved the spectre of scandal before his eyes; I accentuated the inevitable depreciation which the young lady would suffer if such an affair became known, for nobody would believe in a simple kiss, and the good man seemed undecided, but he could not make up his mind about anything without his wife, who would not be in until late that evening. But suddenly he uttered an exclamation of triumph: 'Look here, I have an excellent idea; I will keep you here to dine and sleep, and when my wife comes home I hope we shall be able to arrange matters:

"Rivet resisted at first, but the wish to extricate that pig of a Morin decided him, and we accepted the invitation, and the uncle got up radiant, called his niece and proposed that we should take a stroll in his grounds, saying: 'We will leave serious matters until the morning.' Rivet and he began to talk politics, while I soon found myself lagging a little behind with 'the girl who was really charming—charming—and with the greatest precaution I began to speak to her about her adventure and try to make her my ally. She did not, however, appear the least confused, and listened to me like a person who was enjoying the whole thing very much.

"I said to her: 'Just think, mademoiselle, how unpleasant it will be for you. You will have to appear in court, to encounter malicious looks, to speak before everybody and to recount that unfortunate occurrence in the railway carriage in public. Do you not think, between ourselves, that it would have been much better for you to have put that dirty scoundrel back in his place without calling for assistance, and merely to change your carriage?' She began to laugh and replied: 'What you say is quite true, but what could I do? I was frightened, and when one is frightened one does not stop to reason with one's self. As soon as I realized the situation I was very sorry, that I had called out, but then it was too late. You must also remember that the idiot threw himself upon me like a madman, without saying a word and looking like a lunatic. I did not even know what he wanted of me.'

"She looked me full in the face without being nervous or intimidated and I said to myself: 'She is a queer sort of girl, that: I can quite see how that pig Morin came to make a mistake,' and I went on jokingly: 'Come, mademoiselle, confess that he was excusable, for, after all, a man cannot find himself opposite such a pretty girl as you are without feeling a natural desire to kiss her.'

"She laughed more than ever and showed her teeth and said: 'Between the desire and the act, monsieur, there is room for respect.' It was an odd expression to use, although it was not very clear, and I asked abruptly: 'Well, now, suppose I were to kiss you, what would you do?' She stopped to look at me from head to foot and then said calmly: 'Oh, you? That is quite another matter.'

"I knew perfectly well, by Jove, that it was not the same thing at all, as everybody in the neighborhood called me 'Handsome Labarbe'—I was thirty years old in those days—but I asked her: 'And why, pray?' She shrugged her shoulders and replied: 'Well! because you are not so stupid as he is.' And then she added, looking at me slyly: 'Nor so ugly, either: And before she could make a movement to avoid me I had implanted a hearty kiss on her cheek. She sprang aside, but it was too late, and then she said: 'Well, you are not very bashful, either! But don't do that sort of thing again.'

"I put on a humble look and said in a low voice: 'Oh, mademoiselle! as for me, if I long for one thing more than another it is to be summoned before a magistrate for the same reason as Morin.'

"'Why?' she asked. And, looking steadily at her, I replied: 'Because you are one of the most beautiful creatures living; because it would be an honor and a glory for me to have wished to offer you violence, and because people would have said, after seeing you: "Well, Labarbe has richly deserved what he has got, but he is a lucky fellow, all the same."'

"She began to laugh heartily again and said: 'How funny you are!' And she had not finished the word 'funny' before I had her in my arms and was kissing her ardently wherever I could find a place, on her forehead, on her eyes, on her lips occasionally, on her cheeks, all over her head, some part of which she was obliged to leave exposed, in spite of herself, to defend the others; but at last she managed to release herself, blushing and angry. 'You are very unmannerly, monsieur,' she said, 'and I am sorry I listened to you.'

"I took her hand in some confusion and stammered out: 'I beg your pardon. I beg your pardon, mademoiselle. I have offended you; I have acted like a brute! Do not be angry with me for what I have done. If you knew—' I vainly sought for some excuse, and in a few moments she said: 'There is nothing for me to know, monsieur.' But I had found something to say, and I cried: 'Mademoiselle, I love you!'

"She was really surprised and raised her eyes to look at me, and I went on: 'Yes, mademoiselle, and pray listen to me. I do not know

Morin, and I do not care anything about him. It does not matter to me the least if he is committed for trial and locked up meanwhile. I saw you here last year, and I was so taken with you that the thought of you has never left me since, and it does not matter to me whether you believe me or not. I thought you adorable, and the remembrance of you took such a hold on me that I longed to see you again, and so I made use of that fool Morin as a pretext, and here I am. Circumstances have made me exceed the due limits of respect, and I can only beg you to pardon me.'

"She looked at me to see if I was in earnest and was ready to smile again. Then she murmured: 'You humbug!' But I raised my hand and said in a sincere voice (and I really believe that I was sincere): 'I swear to you that I am speaking the truth,' and she replied quite simply: 'Don't talk nonsense!'

"We were alone, quite alone, as Rivet and her uncle had disappeared down a sidewalk, and I made her a real declaration of love, while I squeezed and kissed her hands, and she listened to it as to something new and agreeable, without exactly knowing how much of it she was to believe, while in the end I felt agitated, and at last really myself believed what I said. I was pale, anxious and trembling, and I gently put my arm round her waist and spoke to her softly, whispering into the little curls over her ears. She seemed in a trance, so absorbed in thought was she.

"Then her hand touched mine, and she pressed it, and I gently squeezed her waist with a trembling, and gradually firmer, grasp. She did not move now, and I touched her cheek with my lips, and suddenly without seeking them my lips met hers. It was a long, long kiss, and it would have lasted longer still if I had not heard a hm! hm! just behind me, at which she made her escape through the bushes, and turning round I saw Rivet coming toward me, and, standing in the middle of the path, he said without even smiling: 'So that is the way you settle the affair of that pig of a Morin.' And I replied conceitedly: 'One does what one can, my dear fellow. But what about the uncle? How have you got on with him? I will answer for the niece.' 'I have not been so fortunate with him,' he replied.

"Whereupon I took his arm and we went indoors." III

"Dinner made me lose my head altogether. I sat beside her, and my hand continually met hers under the tablecloth, my foot touched hers and our glances met.

"After dinner we took a walk by moonlight, and I whispered all the tender things I could think of to her. I held her close to me, kissed her every moment, while her uncle and Rivet were arguing as they walked in front of us. They went in, and soon a messenger brought a telegram from her aunt, saying that she would not return until the next morning at seven o'clock by the first train.

"'Very well, Henriette,' her uncle said, 'go and show the gentlemen their rooms.' She showed Rivet his first, and he whispered to me: 'There was no danger of her taking us into yours first.' Then she took me to my room, and as soon as she was alone with me I took her in my arms again and tried to arouse her emotion, but when she saw the danger she escaped out of the room, and I retired very much put out and excited and feeling rather foolish, for I knew that I should not sleep much, and I was wondering how I could have committed such a mistake, when there was a gentle knock at my door, and on my asking who was there a low voice replied: 'I'

"I dressed myself quickly and opened the door, and she came in. 'I forgot to ask you what you take in the morning,' she said; 'chocolate, tea or coffee?' I put my arms round her impetuously and said, devouring her with kisses: 'I will take—I will take—'

"But she freed herself from my arms, blew out my candle and disappeared and left me alone in the dark, furious, trying to find some matches, and not able to do so. At last I got some and I went into the passage, feeling half mad, with my candlestick in my hand.

"What was I about to do? I did not stop to reason, I only wanted to find her, and I would. I went a few steps without reflecting, but then I suddenly thought: 'Suppose I should walk into the uncle's room what should I say?' And I stood still, with my head a void and my heart beating. But in a few moments I thought of an answer: 'Of course, I shall say that I was looking for Rivet's room to speak to him about an important matter,' and I began to inspect all the doors, trying to find hers, and at last I took hold of a handle at a venture, turned it and went in. There was Henriette, sitting on her bed and looking at me in tears. So I gently turned the key, and going up to her on tiptoe I said: 'I forgot to ask you for something to read, mademoiselle.'

"I was stealthily returning to my room when a rough hand seized me and a voice—it was Rivet's—whispered in my ear: 'So you have not yet quite settled that affair of Morin's?'

"At seven o'clock the next morning Henriette herself brought me a cup of chocolate. I never have drunk anything like it, soft, velvety, perfumed, delicious. I could hardly take away my lips from the cup, and she had hardly left the room when Rivet came in. He seemed nervous and irritable, like a man who had not slept, and he said to me crossly:

"'If you go on like this you will end by spoiling the affair of that pig of a Morin!'

"At eight o'clock the aunt arrived. Our discussion was very short, for they withdrew their complaint, and I left five hundred francs for the poor of the town. They wanted to keep us for the day, and they arranged an excursion to go and see some ruins. Henriette made signs to me to stay, behind her parents' back, and I accepted, but Rivet was determined to go, and though I took him aside and begged and prayed him to do this for me, he appeared quite exasperated and kept saying to me: 'I have had enough of that pig of a Morin's affair, do you hear?'

"Of course I was obliged to leave also, and it was one of the hardest moments of my life. I could have gone on arranging that business as long as I lived, and when we were in the railway carriage, after shaking hands with her in silence, I said to Rivet: 'You are a mere brute!' And he replied: 'My dear fellow, you were beginning to annoy me confoundedly.'

"On getting to the Fanal office, I saw a crowd waiting for us, and as soon as they saw us they all exclaimed: 'Well, have you settled the affair of that pig of a Morin?' All La Rochelle was excited about it, and Rivet, who had got over his ill-humor on the journey, had great difficulty in keeping himself from laughing as he said: 'Yes, we have managed it, thanks to Labarbe: And we went to Morin's.

"He was sitting in an easy-chair with mustard plasters on his legs and cold bandages on his head, nearly dead with misery. He was coughing with the short cough of a dying man, without any one knowing how he had caught it, and his wife looked at him like a tigress ready to eat him, and as soon as he saw us he trembled so violently as to make his hands and knees shake, so I said to him immediately: 'It is all settled, you dirty scamp, but don't do such a thing again.'

"He got up, choking, took my hands and kissed them as if they had belonged to a prince, cried, nearly fainted, embraced Rivet and even kissed Madame Morin, who gave him such a push as to send him staggering back into his chair; but he never got over the blow; his mind had been too much upset. In all the country round, moreover, he was called nothing but 'that pig of a Morin,' and that epithet went through him like a sword-thrust every time he heard it. When a street boy called after him 'Pig!' he turned his head instinctively. His friends also overwhelmed him with horrible jokes and used to ask him, whenever they were eating ham, 'Is it a bit of yourself?' He died two years later.

"As for myself, when I was a candidate for the Chamber of Deputies in 1875, I called on the new notary at Fousserre, Monsieur Belloncle, to solicit his vote, and a tall, handsome and evidently wealthy lady received me. 'You do not know me again?' she said. And I stammered out: 'Why—no—madame.' 'Henriette Bonnel.' 'Ah!' And I felt myself turning pale, while she seemed perfectly at her ease and looked at me with a smile.

"As soon as she had left me alone with her husband he took both my hands, and, squeezing them as if he meant to crush them, he said: 'I have been intending to go and see you for a long time, my dear sir, for my wife has very often talked to me about you. I know—yes, I know under what painful circumstances you made her acquaintance, and I know also how perfectly you behaved, how full of delicacy, tact and devotion you showed yourself in the affair—' He hesitated and then said in a lower tone, as if he had been saying something low and coarse, 'in the affair of that pig of a Morin.'"

SAINT ANTHONY

They called him Saint Anthony, because his name was Anthony, and also, perhaps, because he was a good fellow, jovial, a lover of practical jokes, a tremendous eater and a heavy drinker and a gay fellow, although he was sixty years old.

He was a big peasant of the district of Caux, with a red face, large chest and stomach, and perched on two legs that seemed too slight for the bulk of his body.

He was a widower and lived alone with his two men servants and a maid on his farm, which he conducted with shrewd economy. He was careful of his own interests, understood business and the raising of cattle, and farming. His two sons and his three daughters, who had married well, were living in the neighborhood and came to dine with their father once a month. His vigor of body was famous in all the countryside. "He is as strong as Saint Anthony," had become a kind of proverb.

At the time of the Prussian invasion Saint Anthony, at the wine shop, promised to eat an army, for he was a braggart, like a true Norman, a bit of a coward and a blusterer. He banged his fist on the wooden table, making the cups and the brandy glasses dance, and cried with the assumed wrath of a good fellow, with a flushed face and a sly look in his eye: "I shall have to eat some of them, nom de Dieu!" He reckoned that the Prussians would not come as far as Tanneville, but when he heard they were at Rautot he never went out of the house, and constantly watched the road from the little window of his kitchen, expecting at any moment to see the bayonets go by.

One morning as he was eating his luncheon with the servants the door opened and the mayor of the commune, Maitre Chicot, appeared, followed by a soldier wearing a black copper-pointed helmet. Saint Anthony bounded to his feet and his servants all looked at him, expecting to see him slash the Prussian. But he merely shook hands with the mayor, who said:

"Here is one for you, Saint Anthony. They came last night. Don't do anything foolish, above all things, for they talked of shooting and burning everything if there is the slightest unpleasantness, I have given you warning. Give him something to eat; he looks like a good fellow. Good-day. I am going to call on the rest. There are enough for all." And he went out.

Father Anthony, who had turned pale, looked at the Prussian. He was a big, young fellow with plump, white skin, blue eyes, fair hair, unshaven to his cheek bones, who looked stupid, timid and good. The shrewd Norman read him at once, and, reassured, he made him a sign to sit down. Then he said: "Will you take some soup?"

The stranger did not understand. Anthony then became bolder, and pushing a plateful of soup right under his nose, he said: "Here, swallow that, big pig!"

The soldier answered "Ya," and began to eat greedily, while the farmer, triumphant, feeling he had regained his reputation, winked his eye at the servants, who were making strange grimaces, what with their terror and their desire to laugh.

When the Prussian had devoured his soup, Saint Anthony gave him another plateful, which disappeared in like manner; but he flinched at the third which the farmer tried to insist on his eating, saying: "Come, put that into your stomach; 'twill fatten you or it is your own fault, eh, pig!"

The soldier, understanding only that they wanted to make him eat all his soup, laughed in a contented manner, making a sign to show that he could not hold any more.

Then Saint Anthony, become quite familiar, tapped him on the stomach, saying: "My, there is plenty in my pig's belly!" But suddenly he began to writhe with laughter, unable to speak. An idea had struck him which made him choke with mirth. "That's it, that's it, Saint Anthony and his pig. There's my pig!" And the three servants burst out laughing in their turn.

The old fellow was so pleased that he had the brandy brought in, good stuff, 'fil en dix', and treated every one. They clinked glasses with the Prussian, who clacked his tongue by way of flattery to show that he enjoyed it. And Saint Anthony exclaimed in his face: "Eh, is not that superfine? You don't get anything like that in your home, pig!"

From that time Father Anthony never went out without his Prussian. He had got what he wanted. This was his vengeance, the vengeance of an old rogue. And the whole countryside, which was in terror, laughed to split its sides at Saint Anthony's joke. Truly, there was no one like him when it came to humor. No one but he would have thought of a thing like that. He was a born joker!

He went to see his neighbors every day, arm in arm with his German, whom he introduced in a jovial manner, tapping him on the shoulder: "See, here is my pig; look and see if he is not growing fat, the animal!"

And the peasants would beam with smiles. "He is so comical, that reckless fellow, Antoine!"

"I will sell him to you, Cesaire, for three pistoles" (thirty francs).

"I will take him, Antoine, and I invite you to eat some black pudding."

"What I want is his feet."

"Feel his belly; you will see that it is all fat."

And they all winked at each other, but dared not laugh too loud, for fear the Prussian might finally suspect they were laughing at him. Anthony, alone growing bolder every day, pinched his thighs, exclaiming, "Nothing but fat"; tapped him on the back, shouting, "That is all bacon"; lifted him up in his arms as an old Colossus that could have lifted an anvil, declaring, "He weighs six hundred and no waste."

He had got into the habit of making people offer his "pig" something to eat wherever they went together. This was the chief pleasure, the great diversion every day. "Give him whatever you please, he will swallow everything." And they offered the man bread and butter, potatoes, cold meat, chitterlings, which caused the remark, "Some of your own, and choice ones."

The soldier, stupid and gentle, ate from politeness, charmed at these attentions, making himself ill rather than refuse, and he was actually growing fat and his uniform becoming tight for him. This delighted Saint Anthony, who said: "You know, my pig, that we shall have to have another cage made for you."

They had, however, become the best friends in the world, and when the old fellow went to attend to his business in the neighborhood the Prussian accompanied him for the simple pleasure of being with him.

The weather was severe; it was freezing hard. The terrible winter of 1870 seemed to bring all the scourges on France at one time.

Father Antoine, who made provision beforehand, and took advantage of every opportunity, foreseeing that manure would be scarce for the spring farming, bought from a neighbor who happened to be in need of money all that he had, and it was agreed that he should go every evening with his cart to get a load.

So every day at twilight he set out for the farm of Haules, half a league distant, always accompanied by his "pig." And each time it was a festival, feeding the animal. All the neighbors ran over there as they would go to high mass on Sunday.

But the soldier began to suspect something, be mistrustful, and when they laughed too loud he would roll his eyes uneasily, and sometimes they lighted up with anger.

One evening when he had eaten his fill he refused to swallow another morsel, and attempted to rise to leave the table. But Saint Anthony stopped him by a turn of the wrist and, placing his two powerful hands on his shoulders, he sat him down again so roughly that the chair smashed under him.

A wild burst of laughter broke forth, and Anthony, beaming, picked up his pig, acted as though he were dressing his wounds, and exclaimed: "Since you will not eat, you shall drink, nom de Dieu!" And they went to the wine shop to get some brandy.

The soldier rolled his eyes, which had a wicked expression, but he drank, nevertheless; he drank as long as they wanted him, and Saint Anthony held his head to the great delight of his companions.

The Norman, red as a tomato, his eyes ablaze, filled up the glasses and clinked, saying: "Here's to you!". And the Prussian, without speaking a word, poured down one after another glassfuls of cognac.

It was a contest, a battle, a revenge! Who would drink the most, nom d'un nom! They could neither of them stand any more when the liter was emptied. But neither was conquered. They were tied, that was all. They would have to begin again the next day.

They went out staggering and started for home, walking beside the dung cart which was drawn along slowly by two horses.

Snow began to fall and the moonless night was sadly lighted by this dead whiteness on the plain. The men began to feel the cold, and this aggravated their intoxication. Saint Anthony, annoyed at not being the victor, amused himself by shoving his companion so as to make him fall over into the ditch. The other would dodge backwards, and each time he did he uttered some German expression in an angry tone, which made the peasant roar with laughter. Finally the Prussian lost his temper, and just as Anthony was rolling towards him he responded with such a terrific blow with his fist that the Colossus staggered.

Then, excited by the brandy, the old man seized the pugilist round the waist, shook him for a few moments as he would have done with a little child, and pitched him at random to the other side of the road. Then, satisfied with this piece of work, he crossed his arms and began to laugh afresh.

But the soldier picked himself up in a hurry, his head bare, his helmet having rolled off, and drawing his sword he rushed over to Father Anthony.

When he saw him coming the peasant seized his whip by the top of the handle, his big holly wood whip, straight, strong and supple as the sinew of an ox.

The Prussian approached, his head down, making a lunge with his sword, sure of killing his adversary. But the old fellow, squarely hitting the blade, the point of which would have pierced his stomach, turned it aside, and with the butt end of the whip struck the soldier a sharp blow on the temple and he fell to the ground.

Then he, gazed aghast, stupefied with amazement, at the body, twitching convulsively at first and then lying prone and motionless. He bent over it, turned it on its back, and gazed at it for some time. The man's eyes were closed, and blood trickled from a wound at the side of his forehead. Although it was dark, Father Anthony could distinguish the bloodstain on the white snow.

He remained there, at his wit's end, while his cart continued slowly on its way.

What was he to do? He would be shot! They would burn his farm, ruin his district! What should he do? What should he do? How could he hide the body, conceal the fact of his death, deceive the Prussians? He heard voices in the distance, amid the utter stillness of the snow. All at once he roused himself, and picking up the helmet he placed it on his victim's head. Then, seizing him round the body, he lifted him up in his arms, and thus running with him, he overtook his team, and threw the body on top of the manure. Once in his own house he would think up some plan.

He walked slowly, racking his brain, but without result. He saw, he felt, that he was lost. He entered his courtyard. A light was shining in one of the attic windows; his maid was not asleep. He hastily backed his wagon to the edge of the manure hollow. He thought that by overturning the manure the body lying on top of it would fall into the ditch and be buried beneath it, and he dumped the cart.

As he had foreseen, the man was buried beneath the manure. Anthony evened it down with his fork, which he stuck in the ground beside it. He called his stableman, told him to put up the horses, and went to his room.

He went to bed, still thinking of what he had best do, but no ideas came to him. His apprehension increased in the quiet of his room. They would shoot him! He was bathed in perspiration from fear, his teeth chattered, he rose shivering, not being able to stay in bed.

He went downstairs to the kitchen, took the bottle of brandy from the sideboard and carried it upstairs. He drank two large glasses, one after another, adding a fresh intoxication to the late one, without quieting his mental anguish. He had done a pretty stroke of work, nom de Dieu, idiot!

He paced up and down, trying to think of some stratagem, some explanations, some cunning trick, and from time to time he rinsed his mouth with a swallow of "fil en dix" to give him courage.

But no ideas came to him, not one.

Towards midnight his watch dog, a kind of cross wolf called "Devorant," began to howl frantically. Father Anthony shuddered to the marrow of his bones, and each time the beast began his long and lugubrious wail the old man's skin turned to goose flesh.

He had sunk into a chair, his legs weak, stupefied, done up, waiting anxiously for "Devorant" to set up another howl, and starting convulsively from nervousness caused by terror.

The clock downstairs struck five. The dog was still howling. The peasant was almost insane. He rose to go and let the dog loose, so that he should not hear him. He went downstairs, opened the hall door, and stepped out into the darkness. The snow was still falling. The earth was all white, the farm buildings standing out like black patches. He approached the kennel. The dog was dragging at his chain. He unfastened it. "Devorant" gave a bound, then stopped short, his hair bristling, his legs rigid, his muzzle in the air, his nose pointed towards the manure heap.

Saint Anthony, trembling from head to foot, faltered:

"What's the matter with you, you dirty hound?" and he walked a few steps forward, gazing at the indistinct outlines, the sombre shadow of the courtyard.

Then he saw a form, the form of a man sitting on the manure heap!

He gazed at it, paralyzed by fear, and breathing hard. But all at once he saw, close by, the handle of the manure fork which was sticking in the ground. He snatched it up and in one of those transports of fear that will make the greatest coward brave he rushed forward to see what it was.

It was he, his Prussian, come to life, covered with filth from his bed of manure which had kept him warm. He had sat down mechanically, and remained there in the snow which sprinkled down, all covered with dirt and blood as he was, and still stupid from drinking, dazed by the blow and exhausted from his wound.

He perceived Anthony, and too sodden to understand anything, he made an attempt to rise. But the moment the old man recognized him, he foamed with rage like a wild animal.

"Ah, pig! pig!" he sputtered. "You are not dead! You are going to denounce me now—wait—wait!"

And rushing on the German with all the strength of leis arms he flung the raised fork like a lance and buried the four prongs full length in his breast.

The soldier fell over on his back, uttering a long death moan, while the old peasant, drawing the fork out of his breast, plunged it over and over again into his abdomen, his stomach, his throat, like a madman, piercing the body from head to foot, as it still quivered, and the blood gushed out in streams.

Finally he stopped, exhausted by his arduous work, swallowing great mouthfuls of air, calmed down at the completion of the murder.

As the cocks were beginning to crow in the poultry yard and it was near daybreak, he set to work to bury the man.

He dug a hole in the manure till he reached the earth, dug down further, working wildly, in a frenzy of strength with frantic motions of his arms and body.

When the pit was deep enough he rolled the corpse into it with the fork, covered it with earth, which he stamped down for some time, and then put back the manure, and he smiled as he saw the thick snow finishing his work and covering up its traces with a white sheet.

He then stuck the fork in the manure and went into the house. His bottle, still half full of brandy stood on the table. He emptied it at a draught, threw himself on his bed and slept heavily.

He woke up sober, his mind calm and clear, capable of judgment and thought.

At the end of an hour he was going about the country making inquiries everywhere for his soldier. He went to see the Prussian officer to find out why they had taken away his man.

As everyone knew what good friends they were, no one suspected him. He even directed the research, declaring that the Prussian went to see the girls every evening.

An old retired gendarme who had an inn in the next village, and a pretty daughter, was arrested and shot.

LASTING LOVE

It was the end of the dinner that opened the shooting season. The Marquis de Bertrans with his guests sat around a brightly lighted table, covered with fruit and flowers. The conversation drifted to love. Immediately there arose an animated discussion, the same eternal discussion as to whether it were possible to love more than once. Examples were given of persons who had loved once; these were offset by those who had loved violently many times. The men agreed that passion, like sickness, may attack the same person several times, unless it strikes to kill. This conclusion seemed quite incontestable. The women, however, who based their opinion on poetry rather than on practical observation, maintained that love, the great passion, may come only once to mortals. It resembles lightning, they said, this love. A heart once touched by it becomes forever such a waste, so ruined, so consumed, that no other strong sentiment can take root there, not even a dream. The marquis, who had indulged in many love affairs, disputed this belief.

"I tell you it is possible to love several times with all one's heart and soul. You quote examples of persons who have killed themselves for love, to prove the impossibility of a second passion. I wager that if they had not foolishly committed suicide, and so destroyed the possibility of a second experience, they would have found a new love, and still another, and so on till death. It is with love as with drink. He who has once indulged is forever a slave. It is a thing of temperament."

They chose the old doctor as umpire. He thought it was as the marquis had said, a thing of temperament.

"As for me," he said, "I once knew of a love which lasted fifty-five years without one day's respite, and which ended only with death." The wife of the marquis clasped her hands.

"That is beautiful! Ah, what a dream to be loved in such a way! What bliss to live for fifty-five years enveloped in an intense, unwavering affection! How this happy being must have blessed his life to be so adored!"

The doctor smiled.

"You are not mistaken, madame, on this point the loved one was a man. You even know him; it is Monsieur Chouquet, the chemist. As to the woman, you also know her, the old chair-mender, who came every year to the chateau." The enthusiasm of the women fell. Some expressed their contempt with "Pouah!" for the loves of common people did not interest them. The doctor continued: "Three months ago I was called to the deathbed of the old chair-mender. The priest had preceded me. She wished to make us the executors of her will. In order that we might understand her conduct, she told us the story of her life. It is most singular and touching: Her father and mother were both chair-menders. She had never lived in a house. As a little child she wandered about with them, dirty, unkempt, hungry. They visited many towns, leaving their horse, wagon and dog just outside the limits, where the child played in the grass alone until her parents had repaired all the broken chairs in the place. They seldom spoke, except to cry, 'Chairs! Chairs! Chair-mender!'

"When the little one strayed too far away, she would be called back by the harsh, angry voice of her father. She never heard a word of affection. When she grew older, she fetched and carried the broken chairs. Then it was she made friends with the children in the street, but their parents always called them away and scolded them for speaking to the barefooted child. Often the boys threw stones at her. Once a kind woman gave her a few pennies. She saved them most carefully.

"One day—she was then eleven years old—as she was walking through a country town she met, behind the cemetery, little Chouquet, weeping bitterly, because one of his playmates had stolen two precious liards (mills). The tears of the small bourgeois, one of those much-envied mortals, who, she imagined, never knew trouble, completely upset her. She approached him and, as soon as she learned the cause of his grief, she put into his hands all her savings. He took them without hesitation and dried his eyes. Wild with joy, she kissed him. He was busy counting his money, and did not object. Seeing that she was not repulsed, she threw her arms round him and gave him a hug—then she ran away.

"What was going on in her poor little head? Was it because she had sacrificed all her fortune that she became madly fond of this youngster, or was it because she had given him the first tender kiss? The mystery is alike for children and for those of riper years. For months she dreamed of that corner near the cemetery and of the little chap. She stole a sou here and, there from her parents on the chair money or groceries she was sent to buy. When she returned to the spot near the cemetery she had two francs in her pocket, but he was not there. Passing his father's drug store, she caught sight of him behind the counter. He was sitting between a large red globe and a blue one. She only loved him the more, quite carried away at the sight of the brilliant-colored globes. She cherished the recollection of it forever in her heart. The following year she met him near the school playing marbles. She rushed up to him, threw her arms round him, and kissed him so passionately that he screamed, in fear. To quiet him, she gave him all her money. Three francs and twenty centimes! A real gold mine, at which he gazed with staring eyes.

"After this he allowed her to kiss him as much as she wished. During the next four years she put into his hands all her savings, which he pocketed conscientiously in exchange for kisses. At one time it was thirty sous, at another two francs. Again, she only had twelve sous. She wept with grief and shame, explaining brokenly that it had been a poor year. The next time she brought five francs, in one whole piece, which made her laugh with joy. She no longer thought of any one but the boy, and he watched for her with impatience; sometimes he would run to meet her. This made her heart thump with joy. Suddenly he disappeared. He had gone to boarding school. She found this out by careful investigation. Then she used great diplomacy to persuade her parents to change their route and pass by this way again during vacation. After a year of scheming she succeeded. She had not seen him for two years, and scarcely recognized him, he was so changed, had grown taller, better looking and was imposing in his uniform, with its brass buttons. He pretended not to see her, and passed by without a glance. She wept for two days and from that time loved and suffered unceasingly.

"Every year he came home and she passed him, not daring to lift her eyes. He never condescended to turn his head toward her. She loved him madly, hopelessly. She said to me:

"'He is the only man whom I have ever seen. I don't even know if another exists.' Her parents died. She continued their work.

"One day, on entering the village, where her heart always remained, she saw Chouquet coming out of his pharmacy with a young lady leaning on his arm. She was his wife. That night the chair-mender threw herself into the river. A drunkard passing the spot pulled her out and took her to the drug store. Young Chouquet came down in his dressing gown to revive her. Without seeming to know who she was he undressed her and rubbed her; then he said to her, in a harsh voice:

"'You are mad! People must not do stupid things like that.' His voice brought her to life again. He had spoken to her! She was happy for a long time. He refused remuneration for his trouble, although she insisted.

"All her life passed in this way. She worked, thinking always of him. She began to buy medicines at his pharmacy; this gave her a chance to talk to him and to see him closely. In this way, she was still able to give him money.

"As I said before, she died this spring. When she had closed her pathetic story she entreated me to take her earnings to the man she loved. She had worked only that she might leave him something to remind him of her after her death. I gave the priest fifty francs for her funeral expenses. The next morning I went to see the Chouquets. They were finishing breakfast, sitting opposite each other, fat and red, important and self-satisfied. They welcomed me and offered me some coffee, which I accepted. Then I began my story in a trembling voice, sure that they would be softened, even to tears. As soon as Chouquet understood that he had been loved by 'that vagabond! that chair-mender! that wanderer!' he swore with indignation as though his reputation had been sullied, the respect of decent people lost, his personal honor, something precious and dearer to him than life, gone. His exasperated wife kept repeating: 'That beggar! That beggar!'

"Seeming unable to find words suitable to the enormity, he stood up and began striding about. He muttered: 'Can you understand anything so horrible, doctor? Oh, if I had only known it while she was alive, I should have had her thrown into prison. I promise you she would not have escaped.'

"I was dumfounded; I hardly knew what to think or say, but I had to finish my mission. 'She commissioned me,' I said, 'to give you her savings, which amount to three thousand five hundred francs. As what I have just told you seems to be very disagreeable, perhaps you would prefer to give this money to the poor.'

"They looked at me, that man and woman,' speechless with amazement. I took the few thousand francs from out of my pocket. Wretched-looking money from every country. Pennies and gold pieces all mixed together. Then I asked:

"'What is your decision?'

"Madame Chouquet spoke first. 'Well, since it is the dying woman's wish, it seems to me impossible to refuse it.'

"Her husband said, in a shamefaced manner: 'We could buy something for our children with it.'

"I answered dryly: 'As you wish.'

"He replied: 'Well, give it to us anyhow, since she commissioned you to do so; we will find a way to put it to some good purpose.'

"I gave them the money, bowed and left.

"The next day Chouquet came to me and said brusquely:

"'That woman left her wagon here—what have you done with it?'

"'Nothing; take it if you wish.'

"'It's just what I wanted,' he added, and walked off. I called him back and said:

"'She also left her old horse and two dogs. Don't you need them?'

"He stared at me surprised: 'Well, no! Really, what would I do with them?'

"'Dispose of them as you like.'

"He laughed and held out his hand to me. I shook it. What could I do? The doctor and the druggist in a country village must not be at enmity. I have kept the dogs. The priest took the old horse. The wagon is useful to Chouquet, and with the money he has bought railroad stock. That is the only deep, sincere love that I have ever known in all my life."

The doctor looked up. The marquise, whose eyes were full of tears, sighed and said:

"There is no denying the fact, only women know how to love."

PIERROT

Mme. Lefevre was a country dame, a widow, one of these half peasants, with ribbons and bonnets with trimming on them, one of those persons who clipped her words and put on great airs in public, concealing the soul of a pretentious animal beneath a comical and bedizened exterior, just as the country-folks hide their coarse red hands in ecru silk gloves.

She had a servant, a good simple peasant, called Rose.

The two women lived in a little house with green shutters by the side of the high road in Normandy, in the centre of the country of Caux. As they had a narrow strip of garden in front of the house, they grew some vegetables.

One night someone stole twelve onions. As soon as Rose became aware of the theft, she ran to tell madame, who came downstairs in her woolen petticoat. It was a shame and a disgrace! They had robbed her, Mme. Lefevre! As there were thieves in the country, they might come back.

And the two frightened women examined the foot tracks, talking, and supposing all sorts of things.

"See, they went that way! They stepped on the wall, they jumped into the garden!"

And they became apprehensive for the future. How could they sleep in peace now!

The news of the theft spread. The neighbors came, making examinations and discussing the matter in their turn, while the two women explained to each newcomer what they had observed and their opinion.

A farmer who lived near said to them:

"You ought to have a dog."

That is true, they ought to have a dog, if it were only to give the alarm. Not a big dog. Heavens! what would they do with a big dog? He would eat their heads off. But a little dog (in Normandy they say "quin"), a little puppy who would bark.

As soon as everyone had left, Mme. Lefevre discussed this idea of a dog for some time. On reflection she made a thousand objections, terrified at the idea of a bowl full of soup, for she belonged to that race of parsimonious country women who always carry centimes in their pocket to give alms in public to beggars on the road and to put in the Sunday collection plate.

Rose, who loved animals, gave her opinion and defended it shrewdly. So it was decided that they should have a dog, a very small dog.

They began to look for one, but could find nothing but big dogs, who would devour enough soup to make one shudder. The grocer of Rolleville had one, a tiny one, but he demanded two francs to cover the cost of sending it. Mme. Lefevre declared that she would feed a "quin," but would not buy one.

The baker, who knew all that occurred, brought in his wagon one morning a strange little yellow animal, almost without paws, with the body of a crocodile, the head of a fox, and a curly tail—a true cockade, as big as all the rest of him. Mme. Lefevre thought this common cur that cost nothing was very handsome. Rose hugged it and asked what its name was.

"Pierrot," replied the baker.

The dog was installed in an old soap box and they gave it some water which it drank. They then offered it a piece of bread. He ate it. Mme. Lefevre, uneasy, had an idea.

"When he is thoroughly accustomed to the house we can let him run. He can find something to eat, roaming about the country."

They let him run, in fact, which did not prevent him from being famished. Also he never barked except to beg for food, and then he barked furiously.

Anyone might come into the garden, and Pierrot would run up and fawn on each one in turn and not utter a bark.

Mme. Lefevre, however, had become accustomed to the animal. She even went so far as to like it and to give it from time to time pieces of bread soaked in the gravy on her plate.

But she had not once thought of the dog tax, and when they came to collect eight francs—eight francs, madame—for this puppy who never even barked, she almost fainted from the shock.

It was immediately decided that they must get rid of Pierrot. No one wanted him. Every one declined to take him for ten leagues around. Then they resolved, not knowing what else to do, to make him "piquer du mas."

"Piquer du mas" means to eat chalk. When one wants to get rid of a dog they make him "Piquer du mas."

In the midst of an immense plain one sees a kind of hut, or rather a very small roof standing above the ground. This is the entrance to the clay pit. A big perpendicular hole is sunk for twenty metres underground and ends in a series of long subterranean tunnels.

Once a year they go down into the quarry at the time they fertilize the ground. The rest of the year it serves as a cemetery for condemned dogs, and as one passed by this hole plaintive howls, furious or despairing barks and lamentable appeals reach one's ear.

Sportsmen's dogs and sheep dogs flee in terror from this mournful place, and when one leans over it one perceives a disgusting odor of putrefaction.

Frightful dramas are enacted in the darkness.

When an animal has suffered down there for ten or twelve days, nourished on the foul remains of his predecessors, another animal, larger and more vigorous, is thrown into the hole. There they are, alone, starving, with glittering eyes. They watch each other, follow each other, hesitate in doubt. But hunger impels them; they attack each other, fight desperately for some time, and the stronger eats the weaker, devours him alive.

When it was decided to make Pierrot "piquer du mas" they looked round for an executioner. The laborer who mended the road demanded six sous to take the dog there. That seemed wildly exorbitant to Mme. Lefevre. The neighbor's hired boy wanted five sous; that was still too much. So Rose having observed that they had better carry it there themselves, as in that way it would not be brutally treated on the way and made to suspect its fate, they resolved to go together at twilight.

They offered the dog that evening a good dish of soup with a piece of butter in it. He swallowed every morsel of it, and as he wagged his tail with delight Rose put him in her apron.

They walked quickly, like thieves, across the plain. They soon perceived the chalk pit and walked up to it. Mme. Lefevre leaned over to hear if any animal was moaning. No, there were none there; Pierrot would be alone. Then Rose, who was crying, kissed the dog and threw him into the chalk pit, and they both leaned over, listening.

First they heard a dull sound, then the sharp, bitter, distracting cry of an animal in pain, then a succession of little mournful cries, then despairing appeals, the cries of a dog who is entreating, his head raised toward the opening of the pit.

He yelped, oh, how he yelped!

They were filled with remorse, with terror, with a wild inexplicable fear, and ran away from the spot. As Rose went faster Mme. Lefevre cried: "Wait for me, Rose, wait for me!"

At night they were haunted by frightful nightmares.

Mme. Lefevre dreamed she was sitting down at table to eat her soup, but when she uncovered the tureen Pierrot was in it. He jumped out and bit her nose.

She awoke and thought she heard him yelping still. She listened, but she was mistaken.

She fell asleep again and found herself on a high road, an endless road, which she followed. Suddenly in the middle of the road she perceived a basket, a large farmer's basket, lying there, and this basket frightened her.

She ended by opening it, and Pierrot, concealed in it, seized her hand and would not let go. She ran away in terror with the dog hanging to the end of her arm, which he held between his teeth.

At daybreak she arose, almost beside herself, and ran to the chalk pit.

He was yelping, yelping still; he had yelped all night. She began to sob and called him by all sorts of endearing names. He answered her with all the tender inflections of his dog's voice.

Then she wanted to see him again, promising herself that she would give him a good home till he died.

She ran to the chalk digger, whose business it was to excavate for chalk, and told him the situation. The man listened, but said nothing. When she had finished he said:

"You want your dog? That will cost four francs." She gave a jump. All her grief was at an end at once.

"Four francs!" she said. "You would die of it! Four francs!"

"Do you suppose I am going to bring my ropes, my windlass, and set it up, and go down there with my boy and let myself be bitten, perhaps, by your cursed dog for the pleasure of giving it back to you? You should not have thrown it down there."

She walked away, indignant. Four francs!

As soon as she entered the house she called Rose and told her of the quarryman's charges. Rose, always resigned, repeated:

"Four francs! That is a good deal of money, madame." Then she added: "If we could throw him something to eat, the poor dog, so he will not die of hunger."

Mme. Lefevre approved of this and was quite delighted. So they set out again with a big piece of bread and butter.

They cut it in mouthfuls, which they threw down one after the other, speaking by turns to Pierrot. As soon as the dog finished one piece he yelped for the next.

They returned that evening and the next day and every day. But they made only one trip.

One morning as they were just letting fall the first mouthful they suddenly heard a tremendous barking in the pit. There were two dogs there. Another had been thrown in, a large dog.

"Pierrot!" cried Rose. And Pierrot yelped and yelped. Then they began to throw down some food. But each time they noticed distinctly a terrible struggle going on, then plaintive cries from Pierrot, who had been bitten by his companion, who ate up everything as he was the stronger.

It was in vain that they specified, saying:

"That is for you, Pierrot." Pierrot evidently got nothing.

The two women, dumfounded, looked at each other and Mme. Lefevre said in a sour tone:

"I could not feed all the dogs they throw in there! We must give it up."

And, suffocating at the thought of all the dogs living at her expense, she went away, even carrying back what remained of the bread, which she ate as she walked along.

Rose followed her, wiping her eyes on the corner of her blue apron.

A NORMANDY JOKE

It was a wedding procession that was coming along the road between the tall trees that bounded the farms and cast their shadow on the road. At the head were the bride and groom, then the family, then the invited guests, and last of all the poor of the neighborhood. The village urchins who hovered about the narrow road like flies ran in and out of the ranks or climbed up the trees to see it better.

The bridegroom was a good-looking young fellow, Jean Patu, the richest farmer in the neighborhood, but he was above all things, an ardent sportsman who seemed to take leave of his senses in order to satisfy that passion, and who spent large sums on his dogs, his keepers, his ferrets and his guns. The bride, Rosalie Roussel, had been courted by all the likely young fellows in the district, for they all thought her handsome and they knew that she would have a good dowry. But she had chosen Patu; partly, perhaps, because she liked him better than she did the others, but still more, like a careful Normandy girl, because he had more crown pieces.

As they entered the white gateway of the husband's farm, forty shots resounded without their seeing those who fired, as they were hidden in the ditches. The noise seemed to please the men, who were slouching along heavily in their best clothes, and Patu left his wife, and running up to a farm servant whom he perceived behind a tree, took his gun and fired a shot himself, as frisky as a young colt. Then they went on, beneath the apple trees which were heavy with fruit, through the high grass and through the midst of the calves, who looked at them with their great eyes, got up slowly and remained standing, with their muzzles turned toward the wedding party.

The men became serious when they came within measurable distance of the wedding dinner. Some of them, the rich ones, had on tall, shining silk hats, which seemed altogether out of place there; others had old head-coverings with a long nap, which might have been taken for moleskin, while the humblest among them wore caps. All the women had on shawls, which they wore loosely on their back, holding the tips ceremoniously under their arms. They were red, parti-colored, flaming shawls, and their brightness seemed to astonish the black fowls on the dung-heap, the ducks on the side of the pond and the pigeons on the thatched roofs.

The extensive farm buildings seemed to be waiting there at the end of that archway of apple trees, and a sort of vapor came out of open door and windows and an almost overpowering odor of eatables was exhaled from the vast building, from all its openings and from its very walls. The string of guests extended through the yard; but when the foremost of them reached the house, they broke the chain and dispersed, while those behind were still coming in at the open gate. The ditches were now lined with urchins and curious poor people, and the firing did not cease, but came from every side at once, and a cloud of smoke, and that odor which has the same intoxicating effect as absinthe, blended with the atmosphere. The women were shaking their dresses outside the door, to get rid of the dust, were undoing their cap-strings and pulling their shawls over their arms, and then they went into the house to lay them aside altogether for the time. The table was laid in the great kitchen that would hold a hundred persons; they sat down to dinner at two o'clock; and at eight o'clock they were still eating, and the men, in their shirt-sleeves, with their waistcoats unbuttoned and with red faces, were swallowing down the food and drink as if they had been whirlpools. The cider sparkled merrily, clear and golden in the large glasses, by the side of the dark, blood-colored wine, and between every dish they made a "hole," the Normandy hole, with a glass of brandy which inflamed the body and put foolish notions into the head. Low jokes were exchanged across the table until the whole arsenal of peasant wit was exhausted. For the last hundred years the same broad stories had served for similar occasions, and, although every one knew them, they still hit the mark and made both rows of guests roar with laughter.

At one end of the table four young fellows, who were neighbors, were preparing some practical jokes for the newly married couple, and they seemed to have got hold of a good one by the way they whispered and laughed, and suddenly one of them, profiting by a moment of silence, exclaimed: "The poachers will have a good time to-night, with this moon! I say, Jean, you will not be looking at the moon, will you?" The bridegroom turned to him quickly and replied: "Only let them come, that's all!" But the other young fellow began to laugh, and said: "I do not think you will pay much attention to them!"

The whole table was convulsed with laughter, so that the glasses shook, but the bridegroom became furious at the thought that anybody would profit by his wedding to come and poach on his land, and repeated: "I only say-just let them come!"

Then there was a flood of talk with a double meaning which made the bride blush somewhat, although she was trembling with expectation; and when they had emptied the kegs of brandy they all went to bed. The young couple went into their own room, which was on the ground floor, as most rooms in farmhouses are. As it was very warm, they opened the window and closed the shutters. A small lamp in bad taste, a present from the bride's father, was burning on the chest of drawers, and the bed stood ready to receive the young people.

The young woman had already taken off her wreath and her dress, and she was in her petticoat, unlacing her boots, while Jean was finishing his cigar and looking at her out of the corners of his eyes. Suddenly, with a brusque movement, like a man who is about to set to work, he took off his coat. She had already taken off her boots, and was now pulling off her stockings, and then she said to him: "Go and hide yourself behind the curtains while I get into bed."

He seemed as if he were about to refuse; but at last he did as she asked him, and in a moment she unfastened her petticoat, which slipped down, fell at her feet and lay on the ground. She left it there, stepped over it in her loose chemise and slipped into the bed, whose springs creaked beneath her weight. He immediately went up to the bed, and, stooping over his wife, he sought her lips, which she hid beneath the pillow, when a shot was heard in the distance, in the direction of the forest of Rapees, as he thought.

He raised himself anxiously, with his heart beating, and running to the window, he opened the shutters. The full moon flooded the yard with yellow light, and the reflection of the apple trees made black shadows at their feet, while in the distance the fields gleamed, covered with the ripe corn. But as he was leaning out, listening to every sound in the still night, two bare arms were put round his neck, and his wife whispered, trying to pull him back: "Do leave them alone; it has nothing to do with you. Come to bed."

He turned round, put his arms round her, and drew her toward him, but just as he was laying her on the bed, which yielded beneath her weight, they heard another report, considerably nearer this time, and Jean, giving way to his tumultuous rage, swore aloud: "Damn it! They will think I do not go out and see what it is because of you! Wait, wait a few minutes!" He put on his shoes again, took down his gun, which was always hanging within reach against the wall, and, as his wife threw herself on her knees in her terror, imploring him not to go, he hastily freed himself, ran to the window and jumped into the yard.

She waited one hour, two hours, until daybreak, but her husband did not return. Then she lost her head, aroused the house, related how angry Jean was, and said that he had gone after the poachers, and immediately all the male farm-servants, even the boys, went in search of their master. They found him two leagues from the farm, tied hand and foot, half dead with rage, his gun broken, his trousers turned inside out, and with three dead hares hanging round his neck, and a placard on his chest with these words: "Who goes on the chase loses his place."

In later years, when he used to tell this story of his wedding night, he usually added: "Ah! as far as a joke went it was a good joke. They caught me in a snare, as if I had been a rabbit, the dirty brutes, and they shoved my head into a bag. But if I can only catch them some day they had better look out for themselves!"

That is how they amuse themselves in Normandy on a wedding day.

FATHER MATTHEW

We had just left Rouen and were galloping along the road to Jumieges. The light carriage flew along across the level country. Presently the horse slackened his pace to walk up the hill of Cantelen.

One sees there one of the most magnificent views in the world. Behind us lay Rouen, the city of churches, with its Gothic belfries, sculptured like ivory trinkets; before us Saint Sever, the manufacturing suburb, whose thousands of smoking chimneys rise amid the expanse of sky, opposite the thousand sacred steeples of the old city.

On the one hand the spire of the cathedral, the highest of human monuments, on the other the engine of the power-house, its rival, and almost as high, and a metre higher than the tallest pyramid in Egypt.

Before us wound the Seine, with its scattered islands and bordered by white banks, covered with a forest on the right and on the left immense meadows, bounded by another forest yonder in the distance.

Here and there large ships lay at anchor along the banks of the wide river. Three enormous steam boats were starting out, one behind the other, for Havre, and a chain of boats, a bark, two schooners and a brig, were going upstream to Rouen, drawn by a little tug that emitted a cloud of black smoke.

My companion, a native of the country, did not glance at this wonderful landscape, but he smiled continually; he seemed to be amused at his thoughts. Suddenly he cried:

"Ah, you will soon see something comical—Father Matthew's chapel. That is a sweet morsel, my boy."

I looked at him in surprise. He continued:

"I will give you a whiff of Normandy that will stay by you. Father Matthew is the handsomest Norman in the province and his chapel is one of the wonders of the world, nothing more nor less. But I will first give you a few words of explanation.

"Father Matthew, who is also called Father 'La Boisson,' is an old sergeant-major who has come back to his native land. He combines in admirable proportions, making a perfect whole, the humbug of the old soldier and the sly roguery of the Norman. On his return to Normandy, thanks to influence and incredible cleverness, he was made doorkeeper of a votive chapel, a chapel dedicated to the Virgin and frequented chiefly by young women who have gone astray … . He composed and had painted a special prayer to his 'Good Virgin.' This prayer is a masterpiece of unintentional irony, of Norman wit, in which jest is blended with fear of the saint and with the superstitious fear of the secret influence of something. He has not much faith in his protectress, but he believes in her a little through prudence, and he is considerate of her through policy.

"This is how this wonderful prayer begins:

"'Our good Madame Virgin Mary, natural protectress of girl mothers in this land and all over the world, protect your servant who erred in a moment of forgetfulness …'

"It ends thus:

"'Do not forget me, especially when you are with your holy spouse, and intercede with God the Father that he may grant me a good husband, like your own.'

"This prayer, which was suppressed by the clergy of the district, is sold by him privately, and is said to be very efficacious for those who recite it with unction.

"In fact he talks of the good Virgin as the valet de chambre of a redoubted prince might talk of his master who confided in him all his little private secrets. He knows a number of amusing anecdotes at his expense which he tells confidentially among friends as they sit over their glasses.

"But you will see for yourself.

"As the fees coming from the Virgin did not appear sufficient to him, he added to the main figure a little business in saints. He has them all, or nearly all. There was not room enough in the chapel, so he stored them in the wood-shed and brings them forth as soon as the faithful ask for them. He carved these little wooden statues himself—they are comical in the extreme—and painted them all bright green one year when they were painting his house. You know that saints cure diseases, but each saint has his specialty, and you must not confound them or make any blunders. They are as jealous of each other as mountebanks.

"In order that they may make no mistake, the old women come and consult Matthew.

"'For diseases of the ear which saint is the best?'

"'Why, Saint Osyme is good and Saint Pamphilius is not bad.' But that is not all.

"As Matthew has some time to spare, he drinks; but he drinks like a professional, with conviction, so much so that he is intoxicated regularly every evening. He is drunk, but he is aware of it. He is so well aware of it that he notices each day his exact degree of intoxication. That is his chief occupation; the chapel is a secondary matter.

"And he has invented—listen and catch on—he has invented the 'Saoulometre.'

"There is no such instrument, but Matthew's observations are as precise as those of a mathematician. You may hear him repeating incessantly: 'Since Monday I have had more than forty-five,' or else 'I was between fifty-two and fifty-eight,' or else 'I had at least sixty-six to seventy,' or 'Hullo, cheat, I thought I was in the fifties and here I find I had had seventy-five!'

"He never makes a mistake.

"He declares that he never reached his limit, but as he acknowledges that his observations cease to be exact when he has passed ninety, one cannot depend absolutely on the truth of that statement.

"When Matthew acknowledges that he has passed ninety, you may rest assured that he is blind drunk.

"On these occasions his wife, Melie, another marvel, flies into a fury. She waits for him at the door of the house, and as he enters she roars at him:

"'So there you are, slut, hog, giggling sot!'

"Then Matthew, who is not laughing any longer, plants himself opposite her and says in a severe tone:

"'Be still, Melie; this is no time to talk; wait till to-morrow.'

"If she keeps on shouting at him, he goes up to her and says in a shaky voice:

"'Don't bawl any more. I have had about ninety; I am not counting any more. Look out, I am going to hit you!'

"Then Melie beats a retreat.

"If, on the following day, she reverts to the subject, he laughs in her face and says:

"'Come, come! We have said enough. It is past. As long as I have not reached my limit there is no harm done. But if I go past that, I will allow you to correct me, my word on it!'"

We had reached the top of the hill. The road entered the delightful forest of Roumare.

Autumn, marvellous autumn, blended its gold and purple with the remaining traces of verdure. We passed through Duclair. Then, instead of going on to Jumieges, my friend turned to the left and, taking a crosscut, drove in among the trees.

And presently from the top of a high hill we saw again the magnificent valley of the Seine and the winding river beneath us.

At our right a very small slate-covered building, with a bell tower as large as a sunshade, adjoined a pretty house with green Venetian blinds, and all covered with honeysuckle and roses.

"Here are some friends!" cried a big voice, and Matthew appeared on the threshold. He was a man about sixty, thin and with a goatee and long, white mustache.

My friend shook him by the hand and introduced me, and Matthew took us into a clean kitchen, which served also as a dining-room. He said:

"I have no elegant apartment, monsieur. I do not like to get too far away from the food. The saucepans, you see, keep me company." Then, turning to my friend:

"Why did you come on Thursday? You know quite well that this is the day I consult my Guardian Saint. I cannot go out this afternoon."

And running to the door, he uttered a terrific roar: "Melie!" which must have startled the sailors in the ships along the stream in the valley below.

Melie did not reply.

Then Matthew winked his eye knowingly.

"She is not pleased with me, you see, because yesterday I was in the nineties."

My friend began to laugh. "In the nineties, Matthew! How did you manage it?"

"I will tell you," said Matthew. "Last year I found only twenty rasieres (an old dry measure) of apricots. There are no more, but those are the only things to make cider of. So I made some, and yesterday I tapped the barrel. Talk of nectar! That was nectar. You shall tell me what you think of it. Polyte was here, and we sat down and drank a glass and another without being satisfied (one could go on drinking it until to-morrow), and at last, with glass after glass, I felt a chill at my stomach. I said to Polyte: 'Supposing we drink a glass of cognac to warm ourselves?' He agreed. But this cognac, it sets you on fire, so that we had to go back to the cider. But by going from chills to heat and heat to chills, I saw that I was in the nineties. Polyte was not far from his limit."

The door opened and Melie appeared. At once, before bidding us good-day, she cried:

"Great hog, you have both of you reached your limit!"

"Don't say that, Melie; don't say that," said Matthew, getting angry. "I have never reached my limit."

They gave us a delicious luncheon outside beneath two lime trees, beside the little chapel and overlooking the vast landscape. And Matthew told us, with a mixture of humor and unexpected credulity, incredible stories of miracles.

We had drunk a good deal of delicious cider, sparkling and sweet, fresh and intoxicating, which he preferred to all other drinks, and were smoking our pipes astride our chairs when two women appeared.

They were old, dried up and bent. After greeting us they asked for Saint Blanc. Matthew winked at us as he replied:

"I will get him for you." And he disappeared in his wood shed. He remained there fully five minutes. Then he came back with an expression of consternation. He raised his hands.

"I don't know where he is. I cannot find him. I am quite sure that I had him." Then making a speaking trumpet of his hands, he roared once more:

"Meli-e-a!"

"What's the matter?" replied his wife from the end of the garden.

"Where's Saint Blanc? I cannot find him in the wood shed."

Then Melie explained it this way:

"Was not that the one you took last week to stop up a hole in the rabbit hutch?"

Matthew gave a start.

"By thunder, that may be!" Then turning to the women, he said: "Follow me."

They followed him. We did the same, almost choking with suppressed laughter.

Saint Blanc was indeed stuck into the earth like an ordinary stake, covered with mud and dirt, and forming a corner for the rabbit hutch.

As soon as they perceived him, the two women fell on their knees, crossed themselves and began to murmur an "Oremus." But Matthew darted toward them.

"Wait," he said, "you are in the mud; I will get you a bundle of straw."

He went to fetch the straw and made them a priedieu. Then, looking at his muddy saint and doubtless afraid of bringing discredit on his business, he added:

"I will clean him off a little for you."

He took a pail of water and a brush and began to scrub the wooden image vigorously, while the two old women kept on praying.

When he had finished he said:

"Now he is all right." And he took us back to the house to drink another glass.

As he was carrying the glass to his lips he stopped and said in a rather confused manner:

"All the same, when I put Saint Blanc out with the rabbits I thought he would not make any more money. For two years no one had asked for him. But the saints, you see, they are never out of date."

VOLUME XI

THE UMBRELLA

Mme. Oreille was a very economical woman; she knew the value of a centime, and possessed a whole storehouse of strict principles with regard to the multiplication of money, so that her cook found the greatest difficulty in making what the servants call their market-penny, and her husband was hardly allowed any pocket money at all. They were, however, very comfortably off, and had no children; but it really pained Mme. Oreille to see any money spent; it was like tearing at her heartstrings when she had to take any of those nice crown-pieces out of her pocket; and whenever she had to spend anything, no matter how necessary it might be, she slept badly the next night.

Oreille was continually saying to his wife:

"You really might be more liberal, as we have no children, and never spend our income."

"You don't know what may happen," she used to reply. "It is better to have too much than too little."

She was a little woman of about forty, very active, rather hasty, wrinkled, very neat and tidy, and with a very short temper.

Her husband frequently complained of all the privations she made him endure; some of them were particularly painful to him, as they touched his vanity.

He was one of the head clerks in the War Office, and only stayed on there in obedience to his wife's wish, to increase their income which they did not nearly spend.

For two years he had always come to the office with the same old patched umbrella, to the great amusement of his fellow clerks. At last he got tired of their jokes, and insisted upon his wife buying him a new one. She bought one for eight francs and a half, one of those cheap articles which large houses sell as an advertisement. When the men in the office saw the article, which was being sold in Paris by the thousand, they began their jokes again, and Oreille had a dreadful time of it. They even made a song about it, which he heard from morning till night all over the immense building.

Oreille was very angry, and peremptorily told his wife to get him a new one, a good silk one, for twenty francs, and to bring him the bill, so that he might see that it was all right.

She bought him one for eighteen francs, and said, getting red with anger as she gave it to her husband:

"This will last you for five years at least."

Oreille felt quite triumphant, and received a small ovation at the office with his new acquisition.

When he went home in the evening his wife said to him, looking at the umbrella uneasily:

"You should not leave it fastened up with the elastic; it will very likely cut the silk. You must take care of it, for I shall not buy you a new one in a hurry."

She took it, unfastened it, and remained dumfounded with astonishment and rage; in the middle of the silk there was a hole as big as a six-penny-piece; it had been made with the end of a cigar.

"What is that?" she screamed.

Her husband replied quietly, without looking at it:

"What is it? What do you mean?"

She was choking with rage, and could hardly get out a word.

"You—you—have—burned—your umbrella! Why—you must be—mad! Do you wish to ruin us outright?"

He turned round, and felt that he was growing pale.

"What are you talking about?"

"I say that you have burned your umbrella. Just look here."

And rushing at him, as if she were going to beat him, she violently thrust the little circular burned hole under his nose.

He was so utterly struck dumb at the sight of it that he could only stammer out:

"What-what is it? How should I know? I have done nothing, I will swear. I don't know what is the matter with the umbrella."

"You have been playing tricks with it at the office; you have been playing the fool and opening it, to show it off!" she screamed.

"I only opened it once, to let them see what a nice one it was, that is all, I swear."

But she shook with rage, and got up one of those conjugal scenes which make a peaceable man dread the domestic hearth more than a battlefield where bullets are raining.

She mended it with a piece of silk cut out of the old umbrella, which was of a different color, and the next day Oreille went off very humbly with the mended article in his hand. He put it into a cupboard, and thought no more of it than of some unpleasant recollection.

But he had scarcely got home that evening when his wife took the umbrella from him, opened it, and nearly had a fit when she saw what had befallen it, for the disaster was irreparable. It was covered with small holes, which evidently proceeded from burns, just as if some one had emptied the ashes from a lighted pipe on to it. It was done for utterly, irreparably.

She looked at it without a word, in too great a passion to be able to say anything. He, also, when he saw the damage, remained almost dumfounded, in a state of frightened consternation.

They looked at each other, then he looked at the floor; and the next moment she threw the useless article at his head, screaming out in a transport of the most violent rage, for she had recovered her voice by that time:

"Oh! you brute! you brute! You did it on purpose, but I will pay you out for it. You shall not have another."

And then the scene began again, and after the storm had raged for an hour, he at last was able to explain himself. He declared that he could not understand it at all, and that it could only proceed from malice or from vengeance.

A ring at the bell saved him; it was a friend whom they were expecting to dinner.

Mme. Oreille submitted the case to him. As for buying a new umbrella, that was out of the question; her husband should not have another. The friend very sensibly said that in that case his clothes would be spoiled, and they were certainly worth more than the umbrella. But the little woman, who was still in a rage, replied:

"Very well, then, when it rains he may have the kitchen umbrella, for I will not give him a new silk one."

Oreille utterly rebelled at such an idea.

"All right," he said; "then I shall resign my post. I am not going to the office with the kitchen umbrella."

The friend interposed.

"Have this one re-covered; it will not cost much."

But Mme. Oreille, being in the temper that she was, said:

"It will cost at least eight francs to re-cover it. Eight and eighteen are twenty-six. Just fancy, twenty-six francs for an umbrella! It is utter madness!"

The friend, who was only a poor man of the middle classes, had an inspiration:

"Make your fire assurance pay for it. The companies pay for all articles that are burned, as long as the damage has been done in your own house."

On hearing this advice the little woman calmed down immediately, and then, after a moment's reflection, she said to her husband:

"To-morrow, before going to your office, you will go to the Maternelle Assurance Company, show them the state your umbrella is in, and make them pay for the damage."

M. Oreille fairly jumped, he was so startled at the proposal.

"I would not do it for my life! It is eighteen francs lost, that is all. It will not ruin us."

The next morning he took a walking-stick when he went out, and, luckily, it was a fine day.

Left at home alone, Mme. Oreille could not get over the loss of her eighteen francs by any means. She had put the umbrella on the dining-room table, and she looked at it without being able to come to any determination.

Every moment she thought of the assurance company, but she did not dare to encounter the quizzical looks of the gentlemen who might receive her, for she was very timid before people, and blushed at a mere nothing, and was embarrassed when she had to speak to strangers.

But the regret at the loss of the eighteen francs pained her as if she had been wounded. She tried not to think of it any more, and yet every moment the recollection of the loss struck her painfully. What was she to do, however? Time went on, and she could not decide; but suddenly, like all cowards, on making a resolve, she became determined.

"I will go, and we will see what will happen."

But first of all she was obliged to prepare the umbrella so that the disaster might be complete, and the reason of it quite evident. She took a match from the mantelpiece, and between the ribs she burned a hole as big as the palm of her hand; then she delicately rolled it up, fastened it with the elastic band, put on her bonnet and shawl, and went quickly toward the Rue de Rivoli, where the assurance office was.

But the nearer she got, the slower she walked. What was she going to say, and what reply would she get?

She looked at the numbers of the houses; there were still twenty-eight. That was all right, so she had time to consider, and she walked slower and slower. Suddenly she saw a door on which was a large brass plate with "La Maternelle Fire Assurance Office" engraved on it. Already! She waited a moment, for she felt nervous and almost ashamed; then she walked past, came back, walked past again, and came back again.

At last she said to herself:

"I must go in, however, so I may as well do it sooner as later."

She could not help noticing, however, how her heart beat as she entered. She went into an enormous room with grated doors all round it, and above them little openings at which a man's head appeared, and as a gentleman carrying a number of papers passed her, she stopped him and said timidly: "I beg your pardon, monsieur, but can you tell me where I must apply for payment for anything that has been accidentally burned?"

He replied in a sonorous voice:

"The first door on the left; that is the department you want."

This frightened her still more, and she felt inclined to run away, to put in no claim, to sacrifice her eighteen francs. But the idea of that sum revived her courage, and she went upstairs, out of breath, stopping at almost every other step.

She knocked at a door which she saw on the first landing, and a clear voice said, in answer:

"Come in!"

She obeyed mechanically, and found herself in a large room where three solemn gentlemen, all with a decoration in their buttonholes, were standing talking.

One of them asked her: "What do you want, madame?"

She could hardly get out her words, but stammered: "I have come—I have come on account of an accident, something—".

He very politely pointed out a seat to her,

"If you will kindly sit down I will attend to you in a moment."

And, returning to the other two, he went on with the conversation.

"The company, gentlemen, does not consider that it is under any obligation to you for more than four hundred thousand francs, and we can pay no attention to your claim to the further sum of a hundred thousand, which you wish to make us pay. Besides that, the surveyor's valuation—"

One of the others interrupted him:

"That is quite enough, monsieur; the law courts will decide between us, and we have nothing further to do than to take our leave." And they went out after mutual ceremonious bows.

Oh! if she could only have gone away with them, how gladly she would have done it; she would have run away and given up everything. But it was too late, for the gentleman came back, and said, bowing:

"What can I do for you, madame?"

She could scarcely speak, but at last she managed to say:

"I have come-for this."

The manager looked at the object which she held out to him in mute astonishment.

With trembling fingers she tried to undo the elastic, and succeeding, after several attempts, she hastily opened the damaged remains of the umbrella.

"It looks to me to be in a very bad state of health," he said compassionately.

"It cost me twenty francs," she said, with some hesitation.

He seemed astonished. "Really! As much as that?"

"Yes, it was a capital article, and I wanted you to see the condition it is in."

"Yes, yes, I see; very well. But I really do not understand what it can have to do with me."

She began to feel uncomfortable; perhaps this company did not pay for such small articles, and she said:

"But—it is burned."

He could not deny it.

"I see that very well," he replied.

She remained open-mouthed, not knowing what to say next; then, suddenly recollecting that she had left out the main thing, she said hastily:

"I am Mme. Oreille; we are assured in La Maternelle, and I have come to claim the value of this damage."

"I only want you to have it re-covered," she added quickly, fearing a positive refusal.

The manager was rather embarrassed, and said: "But, really, madame, we do not sell umbrellas; we cannot undertake such kinds of repairs."

The little woman felt her courage reviving; she was not going to give up without a struggle; she was not even afraid any more, and said:

"I only want you to pay me the cost of repairing it; I can quite well get it done myself."

The gentleman seemed rather confused.

"Really, madame, it is such a very small matter! We are never asked to give compensation for such trivial losses. You must allow that we cannot make good pocket-handkerchiefs, gloves, brooms, slippers, all the small articles which are every day exposed to the chances of being burned."

She got red in the face, and felt inclined to fly into a rage.

"But, monsieur, last December one of our chimneys caught fire, and caused at least five hundred francs' damage; M. Oreille made no claim on the company, and so it is only just that it should pay for my umbrella now."

The manager, guessing that she was telling a lie, said, with a smile:

"You must acknowledge, madame, that it is very surprising that M. Oreille should have asked no compensation for damages amounting to five hundred francs, and should now claim five or six francs for mending an umbrella."

She was not the least put out, and replied:

"I beg your pardon, monsieur, the five hundred francs affected M. Oreille's pocket, whereas this damage, amounting to eighteen francs, concerns Mme. Oreille's pocket only, which is a totally different matter."

As he saw that he had no chance of getting rid of her, and that he would only be wasting his time, he said resignedly:

"Will you kindly tell me how the damage was done?"

She felt that she had won the victory, and said:

"This is how it happened, monsieur: In our hall there is a bronze stick and umbrella stand, and the other day, when I came in, I put my umbrella into it. I must tell you that just above there is a shelf for the candlesticks and matches. I put out my hand, took three or four matches, and struck one, but it missed fire, so I struck another, which ignited, but went out immediately, and a third did the same."

The manager interrupted her to make a joke.

"I suppose they were government matches, then?"

She did not understand him, and went on:

"Very likely. At any rate, the fourth caught fire, and I lit my candle, and went into my room to go to bed; but in a quarter of an hour I fancied that I smelt something burning, and I have always been terribly afraid of fire. If ever we have an accident it will not be my fault, I assure you. I am terribly nervous since our chimney was on fire, as I told you; so I got up, and hunted about everywhere, sniffing like a dog after game, and at last I noticed that my umbrella was burning. Most likely a match had fallen between the folds and burned it. You can see how it has damaged it."

The manager had taken his cue, and asked her: "What do you estimate the damage at?"

She did not know what to say, as she was not certain what value to put on it, but at last she replied:

"Perhaps you had better get it done yourself. I will leave it to you."

He, however, naturally refused.

"No, madame, I cannot do that. Tell me the amount of your claim, that is all I want to know."

"Well, I think that—Look here, monsieur, I do not want to make any money out of you, so I will tell you what we will do. I will take my umbrella to the maker, who will re-cover it in good, durable silk, and I will bring the bill to you. Will that suit you, monsieur?"

"Perfectly, madame; we will settle it so. Here is a note for the cashier, who will repay you whatever it costs you."

He gave Mme. Oreille a slip of paper, who took it, got up and went out, thanking him, for she was in a hurry to escape lest he should change his mind.

She went briskly through the streets, looking out for a really good umbrella maker, and when she found a shop which appeared to be a first-class one, she went in, and said, confidently:

"I want this umbrella re-covered in silk, good silk. Use the very best and strongest you have; I don't mind what it costs."

BELHOMME'S BEAST

The coach for Havre was ready to leave Criquetot, and all the passengers were waiting for their names to be called out, in the courtyard of the Commercial Hotel kept by Monsieur Malandain, Jr.

It was a yellow wagon, mounted on wheels which had once been yellow, but were now almost gray through the accumulation of mud. The front wheels were very small, the back ones, high and fragile, carried the large body of the vehicle, which was swollen like the belly of an animal. Three white horses, with enormous heads and great round knees, were the first things one noticed. They were harnessed ready to draw this coach, which had something of the appearance of a monster in its massive structure. The horses seemed already asleep in front of the strange vehicle.

The driver, Cesaire Horlaville, a little man with a big paunch, supple nevertheless, through his constant habit of climbing over the wheels to the top of the wagon, his face all aglow from exposure to the brisk air of the plains, to rain and storms, and also from the use of brandy, his eyes twitching from the effect of constant contact with wind and hail, appeared in the doorway of the hotel, wiping his mouth on the back of his hand. Large round baskets, full of frightened poultry, were standing in front of the peasant women. Cesaire Horlaville took them one after the other and packed them on the top of his coach; then more gently, he loaded on those containing eggs; finally he tossed up from below several little bags of grain, small packages wrapped in handkerchiefs, pieces of cloth, or paper. Then he opened the back door, and drawing a list from his pocket he called:

"Monsieur le cure de Gorgeville."

The priest advanced. He was a large, powerful, robust man with a red face and a genial expression. He hitched up his cassock to lift his foot, just as the women hold up their skirts, and climbed into the coach.

"The schoolmaster of Rollebose-les-Grinets."

The man hastened forward, tall, timid, wearing a long frock coat which fell to his knees, and he in turn disappeared through the open door.

"Maitre Poiret, two seats."

Poiret approached, a tall, round-shouldered man, bent by the plow, emaciated through abstinence, bony, with a skin dried by a sparing use of water. His wife followed him, small and thin, like a tired animal, carrying a large green umbrella in her hands.

"Maitre Rabot, two seats."

Rabot hesitated, being of an undecided nature. He asked:

"You mean me?"

The driver was going to answer with a jest, when Rabot dived head first towards the door, pushed forward by a vigorous shove from his wife, a tall, square woman with a large, round stomach like a barrel, and hands as large as hams.

Rabot slipped into the wagon like a rat entering a hole.

"Maitre Caniveau."

A large peasant, heavier than an ox, made the springs bend, and was in turn engulfed in the interior of the yellow chest.

"Maitre Belhomme."

Belhomme, tall and thin, came forward, his neck bent, his head hanging, a handkerchief held to his ear as if he were suffering from a terrible toothache.

All these people wore the blue blouse over quaint and antique coats of a black or greenish cloth, Sunday clothes which they would only uncover in the streets of Havre. Their heads were covered by silk caps at high as towers, the emblem of supreme elegance in the small villages of Normandy.

Cesaire Horlaville closed the door, climbed up on his box and snapped his whip.

The three horses awoke and, tossing their heads, shook their bells.

The driver then yelling "Get up!" as loud as he could, whipped up his horses. They shook themselves, and, with an effort, started off at a slow, halting gait. And behind them came the coach, rattling its shaky windows and iron springs, making a terrible clatter of hardware and glass, while the passengers were tossed hither and thither like so many rubber balls.

At first all kept silent out of respect for the priest, that they might not shock him. Being of a loquacious and genial disposition, he started the conversation.

"Well, Maitre Caniveau," said he, "how are you getting along?"

The enormous farmer who, on account of his size, girth and stomach, felt a bond of sympathy for the representative of the Church, answered with a smile:

"Pretty well, Monsieur le cure, pretty well. And how are you?"

"Oh! I'm always well and healthy."

"And you, Maitre Poiret?" asked the abbe.

"Oh! I'd be all right only the colzas ain't a-goin' to give much this year, and times are so hard that they are the only things worth while raisin'."

"Well, what can you expect? Times are hard."

"Hub! I should say they were hard," sounded the rather virile voice of Rabot's big consort.

As she was from a neighboring village, the priest only knew her by name.

"Is that you, Blondel?" he said.

"Yes, I'm the one that married Rabot."

Rabot, slender, timid, and self-satisfied, bowed smilingly, bending his head forward as though to say: "Yes, I'm the Rabot whom Blondel married."

Suddenly Maitre Belhomme, still holding his handkerchief to his ear, began groaning in a pitiful fashion. He was going "Oh-oh-oh!" and stamping his foot in order to show his terrible suffering.

"You must have an awful toothache," said the priest.

The peasant stopped moaning for a minute and answered:

"No, Monsieur le cure, it is not the teeth. It's my ear-away down at the bottom of my ear."

"Well, what have you got in your ear? A lump of wax?"

"I don't know whether it's wax; but I know that it is a bug, a big bug, that crawled in while I was asleep in the haystack."

"A bug! Are you sure?"

"Am I sure? As sure as I am of heaven, Monsieur le cure! I can feel it gnawing at the bottom of my ear! It's eating my head for sure! It's eating my head! Oh-oh-oh!" And he began to stamp his foot again.

Great interest had been aroused among the spectators. Each one gave his bit of advice. Poiret claimed that it was a spider, the teacher, thought it might be a caterpillar. He had already seen such a thing once, at Campemuret, in Orne, where he had been for six years. In this case the caterpillar had gone through the head and out at the nose. But the man remained deaf in that ear ever after, the drum having been pierced.

"It's more likely to be a worm," said the priest.

Maitre Belhomme, his head resting against the door, for he had been the last one to enter, was still moaning.

"Oh—oh—oh! I think it must be an ant, a big ant—there it is biting again. Oh, Monsieur le cure, how it hurts! how it hurts!"

"Have you seen the doctor?" asked Caniveau.

"I should say not!"

"Why?"

The fear of the doctor seemed to cure Belhomme. He straightened up without, however, dropping his handkerchief.

"What! You have money for them, for those loafers? He would have come once, twice, three times, four times, five times! That means two five-franc pieces, two five-franc pieces, for sure. And what would he have done, the loafer, tell me, what would he have done? Can you tell me?"

Caniveau was laughing.

"No, I don't know. Where are you going?"

"I am going to Havre, to see Chambrelan."

"Who is Chambrelan?"

"The healer, of course."

"What healer?"

"The healer who cured my father."

"Your father?"

"Yes, the healer who cured my father years ago."

"What was the matter with your father?"

"A draught caught him in the back, so that he couldn't move hand or foot."

"Well, what did your friend Chambrelan do to him?"

"He kneaded his back with both hands as though he were making bread! And he was all right in a couple of hours!"

Belhomme thought that Chambrelan must also have used some charm, but he did not dare say so before the priest. Caniveau replied, laughing:

"Are you sure it isn't a rabbit that you have in your ear? He might have taken that hole for his home. Wait, I'll make him run away."

Whereupon Caniveau, making a megaphone of his hands, began to mimic the barking of hounds. He snapped, howled, growled, barked. And everybody in the carriage began to roar, even the schoolmaster, who, as a rule, never ever smiled.

However, as Belhomme seemed angry at their making fun of him, the priest changed the conversation and turning to Rabot's big wife, said:

"You have a large family, haven't you?"

"Oh, yes, Monsieur le cure—and it's a pretty hard matter to bring them up!"

Rabot agreed, nodding his head as though to say: "Oh, yes, it's a hard thing to bring up!"

"How many children?"

She replied authoritatively in a strong, clear voice:

"Sixteen children, Monsieur le cure, fifteen of them by my husband!"

And Rabot smiled broadly, nodding his head. He was responsible for fifteen, he alone, Rabot! His wife said so! Therefore there could be no doubt about it. And he was proud!

And whose was the sixteenth? She didn't tell. It was doubtless the first. Perhaps everybody knew, for no one was surprised. Even Caniveau kept mum.

But Belhomme began to moan again:

"Oh-oh-oh! It's scratching about in the bottom of my ear! Oh, dear, oh, dear!"

The coach just then stopped at the Cafe Polyto. The priest said:

"If someone were to pour a little water into your ear, it might perhaps drive it out. Do you want to try?"

"Sure! I am willing."

And everybody got out in order to witness the operation. The priest asked for a bowl, a napkin and a glass of water, then he told the teacher to hold the patient's head over on one side, and, as soon as the liquid should have entered the ear, to turn his head over suddenly on the other side.

But Caniveau, who was already peering into Belhomme's ear to see if he couldn't discover the beast, shouted:

"Gosh! What a mess! You'll have to clear that out, old man. Your rabbit could never get through that; his feet would stick."

The priest in turn examined the passage and saw that it was too narrow and too congested for him to attempt to expel the animal. It was the teacher who cleared out this passage by means of a match and a bit of cloth. Then, in the midst of the general excitement, the priest poured into the passage half a glass of water, which trickled over the face through the hair and down the neck of the patient. Then the schoolmaster quickly twisted the head round over the bowl, as though he were trying to unscrew it. A couple of drops dripped into the white bowl. All the passengers rushed forward. No insect had come out.

However, Belhomme exclaimed: "I don't feel anything any more." The priest triumphantly exclaimed: "Certainly it has been drowned." Everybody was happy and got back into the coach.

But hardly had they started when Belhomme began to cry out again. The bug had aroused itself and had become furious. He even declared that it had now entered his head and was eating his brain. He was howling with such contortions that Poiret's wife, thinking him possessed by the devil, began to cry and to cross herself. Then, the pain abating a little, the sick man began to tell how it was running round in his ear. With his finger he imitated the movements of the body, seeming to see it, to follow it with his eyes: "There it goes up again! Oh—oh—oh—what torture!"

Caniveau was getting impatient. "It's the water that is making the bug angry. It is probably more accustomed to wine."

Everybody laughed, and he continued: "When we get to the Cafe Bourbeux, give it some brandy, and it won't bother you any more, I wager."

But Belhomme could contain himself no longer; he began howling as though his soul were being torn from his body. The priest was obliged to hold his head for him. They asked Cesaire Horlaville to stop at the nearest house. It was a farmhouse at the side of the road. Belhomme was carried into it and laid on the kitchen table in order to repeat the operation. Caniveau advised mixing brandy and water in order to benumb and perhaps kill the insect. But the priest preferred vinegar.

They poured the liquid in drop by drop this time, that it might penetrate down to the bottom, and they left it several minutes in the organ that the beast had chosen for its home.

A bowl had once more been brought; Belhomme was turned over bodily by the priest and Caniveau, while the schoolmaster was tapping on the healthy ear in order to empty the other.

Cesaire Horlaville himself, whip in hand, had come in to observe the proceedings.

Suddenly, at the bottom of the bowl appeared a little brown spot, no bigger than a tiny seed. However, it was moving. It was a flea! First there were cries of astonishment and then shouts of laughter. A flea! Well, that was a good joke, a mighty good one! Caniveau was slapping his thigh, Cesaire Horlaville snapped his whip, the priest laughed like a braying donkey, the teacher cackled as though he were sneezing, and the two women were giving little screams of joy, like the clucking of hens.

Belhomme had seated himself on the table and had taken the bowl between his knees; he was observing, with serious attention and a vengeful anger in his eye, the conquered insect which was twisting round in the water. He grunted, "You rotten little beast!" and he spat on it.

The driver, wild with joy, kept repeating: "A flea, a flea, ah! there you are, damned little flea, damned little flea, damned little flea!" Then having calmed down a little, he cried: "Well, back to the coach! We've lost enough time."

DISCOVERY

The steamer was crowded with people and the crossing promised to be good. I was going from Havre to Trouville.

The ropes were thrown off, the whistle blew for the last time, the whole boat started to tremble, and the great wheels began to revolve, slowly at first, and then with ever-increasing rapidity.

We were gliding along the pier, black with people. Those on board were waving their handkerchiefs, as though they were leaving for America, and their friends on shore were answering in the same manner.

The big July sun was shining down on the red parasols, the light dresses, the joyous faces and on the ocean, barely stirred by a ripple. When we were out of the harbor, the little vessel swung round the big curve and pointed her nose toward the distant shore which was barely visible through the early morning mist. On our left was the broad estuary of the Seine, her muddy water, which never mingles with that of the ocean, making large yellow streaks clearly outlined against the immense sheet of the pure green sea.

As soon as I am on a boat I feel the need of walking to and fro, like a sailor on watch. Why? I do not know. Therefore I began to thread my way along the deck through the crowd of travellers. Suddenly I heard my name called. I turned around. I beheld one of my old friends, Henri Sidoine, whom I had not seen for ten years.

We shook hands and continued our walk together, talking of one thing or another. Suddenly Sidoine, who had been observing the crowd of passengers, cried out angrily:

"It's disgusting, the boat is full of English people!"

It was indeed full of them. The men were standing about, looking over the ocean with an all-important air, as though to say: "We are the English, the lords of the sea! Here we are!"

The young girls, formless, with shoes which reminded one of the naval constructions of their fatherland, wrapped in multicolored shawls, were smiling vacantly at the magnificent scenery. Their small heads, planted at the top of their long bodies, wore English hats of the strangest build.

And the old maids, thinner yet, opening their characteristic jaws to the wind, seemed to threaten one with their long, yellow teeth. On passing them, one could notice the smell of rubber and of tooth wash.

Sidoine repeated, with growing anger:

"Disgusting! Can we never stop their coming to France?"

I asked, smiling:

"What have you got against them? As far as I am concerned, they don't worry me."

He snapped out:

"Of course they don't worry you! But I married one of them."

I stopped and laughed at him.

"Go ahead and tell me about it. Does she make you very unhappy?"

He shrugged his shoulders.

"No, not exactly."

"Then she—is not true to you?"

"Unfortunately, she is. That would be cause for a divorce, and I could get rid of her."

"Then I'm afraid I don't understand!"

"You don't understand? I'm not surprised. Well, she simply learned how to speak French—that's all! Listen.

"I didn't have the least desire of getting married when I went to spend the summer at Etretat two years ago. There is nothing more dangerous than watering-places. You have no idea how it suits young girls. Paris is the place for women and the country for young girls.

"Donkey rides, surf-bathing, breakfast on the grass, all these things are traps set for the marriageable man. And, really, there is nothing prettier than a child about eighteen, running through a field or picking flowers along the road.

"I made the acquaintance of an English family who were stopping at the same hotel where I was. The father looked like those men you see over there, and the mother was like all other Englishwomen.

"They had two sons, the kind of boys who play rough games with balls, bats or rackets from morning till night; then came two daughters, the elder a dry, shrivelled-up Englishwoman, the younger a dream of beauty, a heavenly blonde. When those chits make up their minds to be pretty, they are divine. This one had blue eyes, the kind of blue which seems to contain all the poetry, all the dreams, all the hopes and happiness of the world!

"What an infinity of dreams is caused by two such eyes! How well they answer the dim, eternal question of our heart!

"It must not be forgotten either that we Frenchmen adore foreign women. As soon as we meet a Russian, an Italian, a Swede, a Spaniard, or an Englishwoman with a pretty face, we immediately fall in love with her. We enthuse over everything which comes from outside—clothes, hats, gloves, guns and—women. But what a blunder!

"I believe that that which pleases us in foreign women is their accent. As soon as a woman speaks our language badly we think she is charming, if she uses the wrong word she is exquisite and if she jabbers in an entirely unintelligible jargon, she becomes irresistible.

"My little English girl, Kate, spoke a language to be marvelled at. At the beginning I could understand nothing, she invented so many new words; then I fell absolutely in love with this queer, amusing dialect. All maimed, strange, ridiculous terms became delightful in her mouth. Every evening, on the terrace of the Casino, we had long conversations which resembled spoken enigmas.

"I married her! I loved her wildly, as one can only love in a dream. For true lovers only love a dream which has taken the form of a woman.

"Well, my dear fellow, the most foolish thing I ever did was to give my wife a French teacher. As long as she slaughtered the dictionary and tortured the grammar I adored her. Our conversations were simple. They revealed to me her surprising gracefulness and matchless elegance; they showed her to me as a wonderful speaking jewel, a living doll made to be kissed, knowing, after a fashion, how to express what she loved. She reminded me of the pretty little toys which say 'papa' and 'mamma' when you pull a string.

"Now she talks—badly—very badly. She makes as many mistakes as ever—but I can understand her.

"I have opened my doll to look inside—and I have seen. And now I have to talk to her!

"Ah! you don't know, as I do, the opinions, the ideas, the theories of a well-educated young English girl, whom I can blame in nothing, and who repeats to me from morning till night sentences from a French reader prepared in England for the use of young ladies' schools.

"You have seen those cotillon favors, those pretty gilt papers, which enclose candies with an abominable taste. I have one of them. I tore it open. I wished to eat what was inside and it disgusted me so that I feel nauseated at seeing her compatriots.

"I have married a parrot to whom some old English governess might have taught French. Do you understand?"

The harbor of Trouville was now showing its wooden piers covered with people.

I said:

"Where is your wife?"

He answered:

"I took her back to Etretat."

"And you, where are you going?"

"I? Oh, I am going to rest up here at Trouville."

Then, after a pause, he added:

"You have no idea what a fool a woman can be at times!"

THE ACCURSED BREAD

Daddy Taille had three daughters: Anna, the eldest, who was scarcely ever mentioned in the family; Rose, the second girl, who was eighteen, and Clara, the youngest, who was a girl of fifteen.

Old Taille was a widower and a foreman in M. Lebrument's button manufactory. He was a very upright man, very well thought of, abstemious; in fact, a sort of model workman. He lived at Havre, in the Rue d'Angouleme.

When Anna ran away from home the old man flew into a fearful rage. He threatened to kill the head clerk in a large draper's establishment in that town, whom he suspected. After a time, when he was told by various people that she was very steady and investing money in government securities, that she was no gadabout, but was a great friend of Monsieur Dubois, who was a judge of the Tribunal of Commerce, the father was appeased.

He even showed some anxiety as to how she was getting on, and asked some of her old friends who had been to see her, and when told that she had her own furniture, and that her mantelpiece was covered with vases and the walls with pictures, that there were clocks and carpets everywhere, he gave a broad contented smile. He had been working for thirty years to get together a wretched five or six thousand francs. This girl was evidently no fool.

One fine morning the son of Touchard, the cooper, at the other end of the street, came and asked him for the hand of Rose, the second girl. The old man's heart began to beat, for the Touchards were rich and in a good position. He was decidedly lucky with his girls.

The marriage was agreed upon, and it was settled that it should be a grand affair, and the wedding dinner was to be held at Sainte-Adresse, at Mother Jusa's restaurant. It would cost a lot certainly, but never mind, it did not matter just for once in a way.

But one morning, just as the old man was going home to luncheon with his two daughters, the door opened suddenly, and Anna appeared. She was well dressed and looked undeniably pretty and nice. She threw her arms round her father's neck before he could say a word, then fell into her sisters' arms with many tears and then asked for a plate, so that she might share the family soup. Taille was moved to tears in his turn and said several times:

"That is right, dear, that is right."

Then she told them about herself. She did not wish Rose's wedding to take place at Sainte-Adresse—certainly not. It should take place at her house and would cost her father nothing. She had settled everything and arranged everything, so it was "no good to say any more about it—there!"

"Very well, my dear! very well!" the old man said; "we will leave it so." But then he felt some doubt. Would the Touchards consent? But Rose, the bride-elect, was surprised and asked: "Why should they object, I should like to know? Just leave that to me; I will talk to Philip about it."

She mentioned it to her lover the very same day, and he declared it would suit him exactly. Father and Mother Touchard were naturally delighted at the idea of a good dinner which would cost them nothing and said:

"You may be quite sure that everything will be in first-rate style."

They asked to be allowed to bring a friend, Madame Florence, the cook on the first floor, and Anna agreed to everything.

The wedding was fixed for the last Tuesday of the month.

After the civil formalities and the religious ceremony the wedding party went to Anna's house. Among those whom the Tailles had brought was a cousin of a certain age, a Monsieur Sauvetanin, a man given to philosophical reflections, serious, and always very self-possessed, and Madame Lamondois, an old aunt.

Monsieur Sautevanin had been told off to give Anna his arm, as they were looked upon as the two most important persons in the company.

As soon as they had arrived at the door of Anna's house she let go her companion's arm, and ran on ahead, saying: "I will show you the way," and ran upstairs while the invited guests followed more slowly; and, when they got upstairs, she stood on one side to let them pass, and they rolled their eyes and turned their heads in all directions to admire this mysterious and luxurious dwelling.

The table was laid in the drawing-room, as the dining-room had been thought too small. Extra knives, forks and spoons had been hired from a neighboring restaurant, and decanters stood full of wine under the rays of the sun which shone in through the window.

The ladies went into the bedroom to take off their shawls and bonnets, and Father Touchard, who was standing at the door, made funny and suggestive signs to the men, with many a wink and nod. Daddy Taille, who thought a great deal of himself, looked with fatherly pride at his child's well-furnished rooms and went from one to the other, holding his hat in his hand, making a mental inventory of everything, and walking like a verger in a church.

Anna went backward and forward, ran about giving orders and hurrying on the wedding feast. Soon she appeared at the door of the dining-room and cried: "Come here, all of you, for a moment," and as the twelve guests entered the room they saw twelve glasses of Madeira on a small table.

Rose and her husband had their arms round each other's waists and were kissing each other in every corner. Monsieur Sauvetanin never took his eyes off Anna.

They sat down, and the wedding breakfast began, the relations sitting at one end of the table and the young people at the other. Madame Touchard, the mother, presided on the right and the bride on the left. Anna looked after everybody, saw that the glasses were kept filled and the plates well supplied. The guests evidently felt a certain respectful embarrassment at the sight of all the sumptuousness of the rooms and at the lavish manner in which they were treated. They all ate heartily of the good things provided, but there were no jokes such as are prevalent at weddings of that sort; it was all too grand, and it made them feel uncomfortable. Old

Madame Touchard, who was fond of a bit of fun, tried to enliven matters a little, and at the beginning of the dessert she exclaimed: "I say, Philip, do sing us something." The neighbors in their street considered that he had the finest voice in all Havre.

The bridegroom got up, smiled, and, turning to his sister-in-law, from politeness and gallantry, tried to think of something suitable for the occasion, something serious and correct, to harmonize with the seriousness of the repast.

Anna had a satisfied look on her face, and leaned back in her chair to listen, and all assumed looks of attention, though prepared to smile should smiles be called for.

The singer announced "The Accursed Bread," and, extending his right arm, which made his coat ruck up into his neck, he began.

It was decidedly long, three verses of eight lines each, with the last line and the last but one repeated twice.

All went well for the first two verses; they were the usual commonplaces about bread gained by honest labor and by dishonesty. The aunt and the bride wept outright. The cook, who was present, at the end of the first verse looked at a roll which she held in her hand, with streaming eyes, as if it applied to her, while all applauded vigorously. At the end of the second verse the two servants, who were standing with their backs to the wall, joined loudly in the chorus, and the aunt and the bride wept outright.

Daddy Taille blew his nose with the noise of a trombone, and old Touchard brandished a whole loaf half over the table, and the cook shed silent tears on the crust which she was still holding.

Amid the general emotion Monsieur Sauvetanin said:

"That is the right sort of song; very different from the nasty, risky things one generally hears at weddings."

Anna, who was visibly affected, kissed her hand to her sister and pointed to her husband with an affectionate nod, as if to congratulate her.

Intoxicated by his success, the young man continued, and unfortunately the last verse contained words about the "bread of dishonor" gained by young girls who had been led astray. No one took up the refrain about this bread, supposed to be eaten with tears, except old Touchard and the two servants. Anna had grown deadly pale and cast down her eyes, while the bridegroom looked from one to the other without understanding the reason for this sudden coldness, and the cook hastily dropped the crust as if it were poisoned.

Monsieur Sauvetanin said solemnly, in order to save the situation: "That last couplet is not at all necessary"; and Daddy Taille, who had got red up to his ears, looked round the table fiercely.

Then Anna, her eyes swimming in tears, told the servants in the faltering voice of a woman trying to stifle her sobs, to bring the champagne.

All the guests were suddenly seized with exuberant joy, and all their faces became radiant again. And when old Touchard, who had seen, felt and understood nothing of what was going on, and pointing to the guests so as to emphasize his words, sang the last words of the refrain:

"Children, I warn you all to eat not of that bread," the whole company, when they saw the champagne bottles, with their necks covered with gold foil, appear, burst out singing, as if electrified by the sight:

"Children, I warn you all to eat not of that bread."

THE DOWRY

The marriage of Maitre Simon Lebrument with Mademoiselle Jeanne Cordier was a surprise to no one. Maitre Lebrument had bought out the practice of Maitre Papillon; naturally, he had to have money to pay for it; and Mademoiselle Jeanne Cordier had three hundred thousand francs clear in currency, and in bonds payable to bearer.

Maitre Lebrument was a handsome man. He was stylish, although in a provincial way; but, nevertheless, he was stylish—a rare thing at Boutigny-le-Rebours.

Mademoiselle Cordier was graceful and fresh-looking, although a trifle awkward; nevertheless, she was a handsome girl, and one to be desired.

The marriage ceremony turned all Boutigny topsy-turvy. Everybody admired the young couple, who quickly returned home to domestic felicity, having decided simply to take a short trip to Paris, after a few days of retirement.

This tete-a-tete was delightful, Maitre Lebrument having shown just the proper amount of delicacy. He had taken as his motto: "Everything comes to him who waits." He knew how to be at the same time patient and energetic. His success was rapid and complete.

After four days, Madame Lebrument adored her husband. She could not get along without him. She would sit on his knees, and taking him by the ears she would say: "Open your mouth and shut your eyes." He would open his mouth wide and partly close his eyes, and he would try to nip her fingers as she slipped some dainty between his teeth. Then she would give him a kiss, sweet and long, which would make chills run up and down his spine. And then, in his turn, he would not have enough caresses to please his wife from morning to night and from night to morning.

When the first week was over, he said to his young companion:

"If you wish, we will leave for Paris next Tuesday. We will be like two lovers, we will go to the restaurants, the theatres, the concert halls, everywhere, everywhere!"

She was ready to dance for joy.

"Oh! yes, yes. Let us go as soon as possible."

He continued:

"And then, as we must forget nothing, ask your father to have your dowry ready; I shall pay Maitre Papillon on this trip."

She answered:

"All right: I will tell him to-morrow morning."

And he took her in his arms once more, to renew those sweet games of love which she had so enjoyed for the past week.

The following Tuesday, father-in-law and mother-in-law went to the station with their daughter and their son-in-law who were leaving for the capital.

The father-in-law said:

"I tell you it is very imprudent to carry so much money about in a pocketbook." And the young lawyer smiled.

"Don't worry; I am accustomed to such things. You understand that, in my profession, I sometimes have as much as a million about me. In this manner, at least we avoid a great amount of red tape and delay. You needn't worry."

The conductor was crying:

"All aboard for Paris!"

They scrambled into a car, where two old ladies were already seated.

Lebrument whispered into his wife's ear:

"What a bother! I won't be able to smoke."

She answered in a low voice

"It annoys me too, but not an account of your cigar."

The whistle blew and the train started. The trip lasted about an hour, during which time they did not say very much to each other, as the two old ladies did not go to sleep.

As soon as they were in front of the Saint-Lazare Station, Maitre Lebrument said to his wife:

"Dearie, let us first go over to the Boulevard and get something to eat; then we can quietly return and get our trunk and bring it to the hotel."

She immediately assented.

"Oh! yes. Let's eat at the restaurant. Is it far?"

He answered:

"Yes, it's quite a distance, but we will take the omnibus."

She was surprised:

"Why don't we take a cab?"

He began to scold her smilingly:

"Is that the way you save money? A cab for a five minutes' ride at six cents a minute! You would deprive yourself of nothing."

"That's so," she said, a little embarrassed.

A big omnibus was passing by, drawn by three big horses, which were trotting along. Lebrument called out:

"Conductor! Conductor!"

The heavy carriage stopped. And the young lawyer, pushing his wife, said to her quickly:

"Go inside; I'm going up on top, so that I may smoke at least one cigarette before lunch."

She had no time to answer. The conductor, who had seized her by the arm to help her up the step, pushed her inside, and she fell into a seat, bewildered, looking through the back window at the feet of her husband as he climbed up to the top of the vehicle.

And she sat there motionless, between a fat man who smelled of cheap tobacco and an old woman who smelled of garlic.

All the other passengers were lined up in silence—a grocer's boy, a young girl, a soldier, a gentleman with gold-rimmed spectacles and a big silk hat, two ladies with a self-satisfied and crabbed look, which seemed to say: "We are riding in this thing, but we don't have to," two sisters of charity and an undertaker. They looked like a collection of caricatures.

The jolting of the wagon made them wag their heads and the shaking of the wheels seemed to stupefy them—they all looked as though they were asleep.

The young woman remained motionless.

"Why didn't he come inside with me?" she was saying to herself. An unaccountable sadness seemed to be hanging over her. He really need not have acted so.

The sisters motioned to the conductor to stop, and they got off one after the other, leaving in their wake the pungent smell of camphor. The bus started tip and soon stopped again. And in got a cook, red-faced and out of breath. She sat down and placed her basket of provisions on her knees. A strong odor of dish-water filled the vehicle.

"It's further than I imagined," thought Jeanne.

The undertaker went out, and was replaced by a coachman who seemed to bring the atmosphere of the stable with him. The young girl had as a successor a messenger, the odor of whose feet showed that he was continually walking.

The lawyer's wife began to feel ill at ease, nauseated, ready to cry without knowing why.

Other persons left and others entered. The stage went on through interminable streets, stopping at stations and starting again.

"How far it is!" thought Jeanne. "I hope he hasn't gone to sleep! He has been so tired the last few days."

Little by little all the passengers left. She was left alone, all alone. The conductor cried:

"Vaugirard!"

Seeing that she did not move, he repeated:

"Vaugirard!"

She looked at him, understanding that he was speaking to her, as there was no one else there. For the third time the man said:

"Vaugirard!"

Then she asked:

"Where are we?"

He answered gruffly:

"We're at Vaugirard, of course! I have been yelling it for the last half hour!"

"Is it far from the Boulevard?" she said.

"Which boulevard?"

"The Boulevard des Italiens."

"We passed that a long time ago!"

"Would you mind telling my husband?"

"Your husband! Where is he?"

"On the top of the bus."

"On the top! There hasn't been anybody there for a long time."

She started, terrified.

"What? That's impossible! He got on with me. Look well! He must be there."

The conductor was becoming uncivil:

"Come on, little one, you've talked enough! You can find ten men for every one that you lose. Now run along. You'll find another one somewhere."

Tears were coming to her eyes. She insisted:

"But, monsieur, you are mistaken; I assure you that you must be mistaken. He had a big portfolio under his arm."

The man began to laugh:

"A big portfolio! Oh, yes! He got off at the Madeleine. He got rid of you, all right! Ha! ha! ha!"

The stage had stopped. She got out and, in spite of herself, she looked up instinctively to the roof of the bus. It was absolutely deserted.

Then she began to cry, and, without thinking that anybody was listening or watching her, she said out loud:

"What is going to become of me?"

An inspector approached:

"What's the matter?"

The conductor answered, in a bantering tone of voice:

"It's a lady who got left by her husband during the trip."

The other continued:

"Oh! that's nothing. You go about your business."

Then he turned on his heels and walked away.

She began to walk straight ahead, too bewildered, too crazed even to understand what had happened to her. Where was she to go? What could she do? What could have happened to him? How could he have made such a mistake? How could he have been so forgetful?

She had two francs in her pocket. To whom could she go? Suddenly she remembered her cousin Barral, one of the assistants in the offices of the Ministry of the Navy.

She had just enough to pay for a cab. She drove to his house. He met her just as he was leaving for his office. He was carrying a large portfolio under his arm, just like Lebrument.

She jumped out of the carriage.

"Henry!" she cried.

He stopped, astonished:

"Jeanne! Here—all alone! What are you doing? Where have you come from?"

Her eyes full of tears, she stammered:

"My husband has just got lost!"

"Lost! Where?"

"On an omnibus."

"On an omnibus?"

Weeping, she told him her whole adventure.

He listened, thought, and then asked:

"Was his mind clear this morning?"

"Yes."

"Good. Did he have much money with him?"

"Yes, he was carrying my dowry."

"Your dowry! The whole of it?"

"The whole of it—in order to pay for the practice which he bought."

"Well, my dear cousin, by this time your husband must be well on his way to Belgium."

She could not understand. She kept repeating:

"My husband—you say—"

"I say that he has disappeared with your—your capital—that's all!"

She stood there, a prey to conflicting emotions, sobbing.

"Then he is—he is—he is a villain!"

And, faint from excitement, she leaned her head on her cousin's shoulder and wept.

As people were stopping to look at them, he pushed her gently into the vestibule of his house, and, supporting her with his arm around her waist, he led her up the stairs, and as his astonished servant opened the door, he ordered:

"Sophie, run to the restaurant and get a luncheon for two. I am not going to the office to-day."

THE DIARY OF A MADMAN

He was dead—the head of a high tribunal, the upright magistrate whose irreproachable life was a proverb in all the courts of France. Advocates, young counsellors, judges had greeted him at sight of his large, thin, pale face lighted up by two sparkling deep-set eyes, bowing low in token of respect.

He had passed his life in pursuing crime and in protecting the weak. Swindlers and murderers had no more redoubtable enemy, for he seemed to read the most secret thoughts of their minds.

He was dead, now, at the age of eighty-two, honored by the homage and followed by the regrets of a whole people. Soldiers in red trousers had escorted him to the tomb and men in white cravats had spoken words and shed tears that seemed to be sincere beside his grave.

But here is the strange paper found by the dismayed notary in the desk where he had kept the records of great criminals! It was entitled: WHY?

20th June, 1851. I have just left court. I have condemned Blondel to death! Now, why did this man kill his five children? Frequently one meets with people to whom the destruction of life is a pleasure. Yes, yes, it should be a pleasure, the greatest of all, perhaps, for is not killing the next thing to creating? To make and to destroy! These two words contain the history of the universe, all the history of worlds, all that is, all! Why is it not intoxicating to kill?

25th June. To think that a being is there who lives, who walks, who runs. A being? What is a being? That animated thing, that bears in it the principle of motion and a will ruling that motion. It is attached to nothing, this thing. Its feet do not belong to the ground. It is a grain of life that moves on the earth, and this grain of life, coming I know not whence, one can destroy at one's will. Then nothing—nothing more. It perishes, it is finished.

26th June. Why then is it a crime to kill? Yes, why? On the contrary, it is the law of nature. The mission of every being is to kill; he kills to live, and he kills to kill. The beast kills without ceasing, all day, every instant of his existence. Man kills without ceasing, to nourish himself; but since he needs, besides, to kill for pleasure, he has invented hunting! The child kills the insects he finds, the little birds, all the little animals that come in his way. But this does not suffice for the irresistible need to massacre that is in us. It is not enough to kill beasts; we must kill man too. Long ago this need was satisfied by human sacrifices. Now the requirements of social life have made murder a crime. We condemn and punish the assassin! But as we cannot live without yielding to this natural and imperious instinct of death, we relieve ourselves, from time to time, by wars. Then a whole nation slaughters another nation. It is a feast of blood, a feast that maddens armies and that intoxicates civilians, women and children, who read, by lamplight at night, the feverish story of massacre.

One might suppose that those destined to accomplish these butcheries of men would be despised! No, they are loaded with honors. They are clad in gold and in resplendent garments; they wear plumes on their heads and ornaments on their breasts, and they are given crosses, rewards, titles of every kind. They are proud, respected, loved by women, cheered by the crowd, solely because their mission is to shed human blood; They drag through the streets their instruments of death, that the passer-by, clad in black, looks on with envy. For to kill is the great law set by nature in the heart of existence! There is nothing more beautiful and honorable than killing!

30th June. To kill is the law, because nature loves eternal youth. She seems to cry in all her unconscious acts: "Quick! quick! quick!" The more she destroys, the more she renews herself.

2d July. A human being—what is a human being? Through thought it is a reflection of all that is; through memory and science it is an abridged edition of the universe whose history it represents, a mirror of things and of nations, each human being becomes a microcosm in the macrocosm.

3d July. It must be a pleasure, unique and full of zest, to kill; to have there before one the living, thinking being; to make therein a little hole, nothing but a little hole, to see that red thing flow which is the blood, which makes life; and to have before one only a heap of limp flesh, cold, inert, void of thought!

5th August. I, who have passed my life in judging, condemning, killing by the spoken word, killing by the guillotine those who had killed by the knife, I, I, if I should do as all the assassins have done whom I have smitten, I—I—who would know it?

10th August. Who would ever know? Who would ever suspect me, me, me, especially if I should choose a being I had no interest in doing away with?

15th August. The temptation has come to me. It pervades my whole being; my hands tremble with the desire to kill.

22d August. I could resist no longer. I killed a little creature as an experiment, for a beginning. Jean, my servant, had a goldfinch in a cage hung in the office window. I sent him on an errand, and I took the little bird in my hand, in my hand where I felt its heart beat. It was warm. I went up to my room. From time to time I squeezed it tighter; its heart beat faster; this was atrocious and delicious. I was near choking it. But I could not see the blood.

Then I took scissors, short-nail scissors, and I cut its throat with three slits, quite gently. It opened its bill, it struggled to escape me, but I held it, oh! I held it—I could have held a mad dog—and I saw the blood trickle.

And then I did as assassins do—real ones. I washed the scissors, I washed my hands. I sprinkled water and took the body, the corpse, to the garden to hide it. I buried it under a strawberry-plant. It will never be found. Every day I shall eat a strawberry from that plant. How one can enjoy life when one knows how!

My servant cried; he thought his bird flown. How could he suspect me? Ah! ah!

25th August. I must kill a man! I must—

30th August. It is done. But what a little thing! I had gone for a walk in the forest of Vernes. I was thinking of nothing, literally nothing. A child was in the road, a little child eating a slice of bread and butter.

He stops to see me pass and says, "Good-day, Mr. President."

And the thought enters my head, "Shall I kill him?"

I answer: "You are alone, my boy?"

"Yes, sir."

"All alone in the wood?"

"Yes, sir."

The wish to kill him intoxicated me like wine. I approached him quite softly, persuaded that he was going to run away. And, suddenly, I seized him by the throat. He looked at me with terror in his eyes—such eyes! He held my wrists in his little hands and his body writhed like a feather over the fire. Then he moved no more. I threw the body in the ditch, and some weeds on top of it. I returned home, and dined well. What a little thing it was! In the evening I was very gay, light, rejuvenated; I passed the evening at the Prefect's. They found me witty. But I have not seen blood! I am tranquil.

31st August. The body has been discovered. They are hunting for the assassin. Ah! ah!

1st September. Two tramps have been arrested. Proofs are lacking.

2d September. The parents have been to see me. They wept! Ah! ah!

6th October. Nothing has been discovered. Some strolling vagabond must have done the deed. Ah! ah! If I had seen the blood flow, it seems to me I should be tranquil now! The desire to kill is in my blood; it is like the passion of youth at twenty.

20th October. Yet another. I was walking by the river, after breakfast. And I saw, under a willow, a fisherman asleep. It was noon. A spade was standing in a potato-field near by, as if expressly, for me.

I took it. I returned; I raised it like a club, and with one blow of the edge I cleft the fisherman's head. Oh! he bled, this one! Rose-colored blood. It flowed into the water, quite gently. And I went away with a grave step. If I had been seen! Ah! ah! I should have made an excellent assassin.

25th October. The affair of the fisherman makes a great stir. His nephew, who fished with him, is charged with the murder.

26th October. The examining magistrate affirms that the nephew is guilty. Everybody in town believes it. Ah! ah!

27th October. The nephew makes a very poor witness. He had gone to the village to buy bread and cheese, he declared. He swore that his uncle had been killed in his absence! Who would believe him?

28th October. The nephew has all but confessed, they have badgered him so. Ah! ah! justice!

15th November. There are overwhelming proofs against the nephew, who was his uncle's heir. I shall preside at the sessions.

25th January. To death! to death! to death! I have had him condemned to death! Ah! ah! The advocate-general spoke like an angel! Ah! ah! Yet another! I shall go to see him executed!

10th March. It is done. They guillotined him this morning. He died very well! very well! That gave me pleasure! How fine it is to see a man's head cut off!

Now, I shall wait, I can wait. It would take such a little thing to let myself be caught.

The manuscript contained yet other pages, but without relating any new crime.

Alienist physicians to whom the awful story has been submitted declare that there are in the world many undiscovered madmen as adroit and as much to be feared as this monstrous lunatic.

THE MASK

There was a masquerade ball at the Elysee-Montmartre that evening. It was the 'Mi-Careme', and the crowds were pouring into the brightly lighted passage which leads to the dance ball, like water flowing through the open lock of a canal. The loud call of the orchestra, bursting like a storm of sound, shook the rafters, swelled through the whole neighborhood and awoke, in the streets and in the depths of the houses, an irresistible desire to jump, to get warm, to have fun, which slumbers within each human animal.

The patrons came from every quarter of Paris; there were people of all classes who love noisy pleasures, a little low and tinged with debauch. There were clerks and girls—girls of every description, some wearing common cotton, some the finest batiste; rich girls, old and covered with diamonds, and poor girls of sixteen, full of the desire to revel, to belong to men, to spend money. Elegant black evening suits, in search of fresh or faded but appetizing novelty, wandering through the excited crowds, looking, searching, while the masqueraders seemed moved above all by the desire for amusement. Already the far-famed quadrilles had attracted around them a curious crowd. The moving hedge which encircled the four dancers swayed in and out like a snake, sometimes nearer and sometimes farther away, according to the motions of the performers. The two women, whose lower limbs seemed to be attached to their bodies by rubber springs, were making wonderful and surprising motions with their legs. Their partners hopped and skipped about, waving their arms about. One could imagine their panting breath beneath their masks.

One of them, who had taken his place in the most famous quadrille, as substitute for an absent celebrity, the handsome "Songe-au-Gosse," was trying to keep up with the tireless "Arete-de-Veau" and was making strange fancy steps which aroused the joy and sarcasm of the audience.

He was thin, dressed like a dandy, with a pretty varnished mask on his face. It had a curly blond mustache and a wavy wig. He looked like a wax figure from the Musee Grevin, like a strange and fantastic caricature of the charming young man of fashion plates, and he danced with visible effort, clumsily, with a comical impetuosity. He appeared rusty beside the others when he tried to imitate their gambols: he seemed overcome by rheumatism, as heavy as a great Dane playing with greyhounds. Mocking bravos encouraged him. And he, carried away with enthusiasm, jigged about with such frenzy that suddenly, carried away by a wild spurt, he pitched head foremost into the living wall formed by the audience, which opened up before him to allow him to pass, then closed around the inanimate body of the dancer, stretched out on his face.

Some men picked him up and carried him away, calling for a doctor. A gentleman stepped forward, young and elegant, in well-fitting evening clothes, with large pearl studs. "I am a professor of the Faculty of Medicine," he said in a modest voice. He was allowed to pass, and he entered a small room full of little cardboard boxes, where the still lifeless dancer had been stretched out on some chairs. The doctor at first wished to take off the mask, and he noticed that it was attached in a complicated manner, with a perfect network of small metal wires which cleverly bound it to his wig and covered the whole head. Even the neck was imprisoned in a false skin which continued the chin and was painted the color of flesh, being attached to the collar of the shirt.

All this had to be cut with strong scissors. When the physician had slit open this surprising arrangement, from the shoulder to the temple, he opened this armor and found the face of an old man, worn out, thin and wrinkled. The surprise among those who had brought in this seemingly young dancer was so great that no one laughed, no one said a word.

All were watching this sad face as he lay on the straw chairs, his eyes closed, his face covered with white hair, some long, falling from the forehead over the face, others short, growing around the face and the chin, and beside this poor head, that pretty little, neat varnished, smiling mask.

The man regained consciousness after being inanimate for a long time, but he still seemed to be so weak and sick that the physician feared some dangerous complication. He asked: "Where do you live?"

The old dancer seemed to be making an effort to remember, and then he mentioned the name of the street, which no one knew. He was asked for more definite information about the neighborhood. He answered with a great slowness, indecision and difficulty, which revealed his upset state of mind. The physician continued:

"I will take you home myself."

Curiosity had overcome him to find out who this strange dancer, this phenomenal jumper might be. Soon the two rolled away in a cab to the other side of Montmartre.

They stopped before a high building of poor appearance. They went up a winding staircase. The doctor held to the banister, which was so grimy that the hand stuck to it, and he supported the dizzy old man, whose forces were beginning to return. They stopped at the fourth floor.

The door at which they had knocked was opened by an old woman, neat looking, with a white nightcap enclosing a thin face with sharp features, one of those good, rough faces of a hard-working and faithful woman. She cried out:

"For goodness sake! What's the matter?"

He told her the whole affair in a few words. She became reassured and even calmed the physician himself by telling him that the same thing had happened many times. She said: "He must be put to bed, monsieur, that is all. Let him sleep and tomorrow he will be all right."

The doctor continued: "But he can hardly speak."

"Oh! that's just a little drink, nothing more; he has eaten no dinner, in order to be nimble, and then he took a few absinthes in order to work himself up to the proper pitch. You see, drink gives strength to his legs, but it stops his thoughts and words. He is too old to dance as he does. Really, his lack of common sense is enough to drive one mad!"

The doctor, surprised, insisted:

"But why does he dance like that at his age?"

She shrugged her shoulders and turned red from the anger which was slowly rising within her and she cried out:

"Ah! yes, why? So that the people will think him young under his mask; so that the women will still take him for a young dandy and whisper nasty things into his ears; so that he can rub up against all their dirty skins, with their perfumes and powders and cosmetics. Ah! it's a fine business! What a life I have had for the last forty years! But we must first get him to bed, so that he may have no ill effects. Would you mind helping me? When he is like that I can't do anything with him alone."

The old man was sitting on his bed, with a tipsy look, his long white hair falling over his face. His companion looked at him with tender yet indignant eyes. She continued:

"Just see the fine head he has for his age, and yet he has to go and disguise himself in order to make people think that he is young. It's a perfect shame! Really, he has a fine head, monsieur! Wait, I'll show it to you before putting him to bed."

She went to a table on which stood the washbasin a pitcher of water, soap and a comb and brush. She took the brush, returned to the bed and pushed back the drunkard's tangled hair. In a few seconds she made him look like a model fit for a great painter, with his long white locks flowing on his neck. Then she stepped back in order to observe him, saying: "There! Isn't he fine for his age?"

"Very," agreed the doctor, who was beginning to be highly amused.

She added: "And if you had known him when he was twenty-five! But we must get him to bed, otherwise the drink will make him sick. Do you mind drawing off that sleeve? Higher-like that-that's right. Now the trousers. Wait, I will take his shoes off—that's right. Now, hold him upright while I open the bed. There—let us put him in. If you think that he is going to disturb himself when it is time for me to get in you are mistaken. I have to find a little corner any place I can. That doesn't bother him! Bah! You old pleasure seeker!"

As soon as he felt himself stretched out in his sheets the old man closed his eyes, opened them closed them again, and over his whole face appeared an energetic resolve to sleep. The doctor examined him with an ever-increasing interest and asked: "Does he go to all the fancy balls and try to be a young man?" "To all of them, monsieur, and he comes back to me in the morning in a deplorable condition. You see, it's regret that leads him on and that makes him put a pasteboard face over his own. Yes, the regret of no longer being what he was and of no longer making any conquests!"

He was sleeping now and beginning to snore. She looked at him with a pitying expression and continued: "Oh! how many conquests that man has made! More than one could believe, monsieur, more than the finest gentlemen of the world, than all the tenors and all the generals."

"Really? What did he do?"

"Oh! it will surprise you at first, as you did not know him in his palmy days. When I met him it was also at a ball, for he has always frequented them. As soon as I saw him I was caught—caught like a fish on a hook. Ah! how pretty he was, monsieur, with his curly raven locks and black eyes as large as saucers! Indeed, he was good looking! He took me away that evening and I never have left him since, never, not even for a day, no matter what he did to me! Oh! he has often made it hard for me!"

The doctor asked: "Are you married?"

She answered simply: "Yes, monsieur, otherwise he would have dropped me as he did the others. I have been his wife and his servant, everything, everything that he wished. How he has made me cry—tears which I did not show him; for he would tell all his adventures to me—to me, monsieur—without understanding how it hurt me to listen."

"But what was his business?"

"That's so. I forgot to tell you. He was the foreman at Martel's—a foreman such as they never had had—an artist who averaged ten francs an hour."

"Martel?—who is Martel?"

"The hairdresser, monsieur, the great hairdresser of the Opera, who had all the actresses for customers. Yes, sir, all the smartest actresses had their hair dressed by Ambrose and they would give him tips that made a fortune for him. Ah! monsieur, all the women are alike, yes, all of them. When a man pleases their fancy they offer themselves to him. It is so easy—and it hurt me so to hear about it. For he would tell me everything—he simply could not hold his tongue—it was impossible. Those things please the men so much! They seem to get even more enjoyment out of telling than doing.

"When I would see him coming in the evening, a little pale, with a pleased look and a bright eye, would say to myself: 'One more. I am sure that he has caught one more.' Then I felt a wild desire to question him and then, again, not to know, to stop his talking if he should begin. And we would look at each other.

"I knew that he would not keep still, that he would come to the point. I could feel that from his manner, which seemed to laugh and say: 'I had a fine adventure to-day, Madeleine.' I would pretend to notice nothing, to guess nothing; I would set the table, bring on the soup and sit down opposite him.

"At those times, monsieur, it was as if my friendship for him had been crushed in my body as with a stone. It hurt. But he did not understand; he did not know; he felt a need to tell all those things to some one, to boast, to show how much he was loved, and I was the only one he had to whom he could talk-the only one. And I would have to listen and drink it in, like poison.

"He would begin to take his soup and then he would say: 'One more, Madeleine.'

"And I would think: 'Here it comes! Goodness! what a man! Why did I ever meet him?'

"Then he would begin: 'One more! And a beauty, too.' And it would be some little one from the Vaudeville or else from the Varietes, and some of the big ones, too, some of the most famous. He would tell me their names, how their apartments were furnished, everything, everything, monsieur. Heartbreaking details. And he would go over them and tell his story over again from beginning to end, so pleased with himself that I would pretend to laugh so that he would not get angry with me.

"Everything may not have been true! He liked to glorify himself and was quite capable of inventing such things! They may perhaps also have been true! On those evenings he would pretend to be tired and wish to go to bed after supper. We would take supper at eleven, monsieur, for he could never get back from work earlier.

"When he had finished telling about his adventure he would walk round the room and smoke cigarettes, and he was so handsome, with his mustache and curly hair, that I would think: 'It's true, just the same, what he is telling. Since I myself am crazy about that man, why should not others be the same?' Then I would feel like crying, shrieking, running away and jumping out of the window while I was clearing the table and he was smoking. He would yawn in order to show how tired he was, and he would say two or three times before going to bed: 'Ah! how well I shall sleep this evening!'

"I bear him no ill will, because he did not know how he was hurting me. No, he could not know! He loved to boast about the women just as a peacock loves to show his feathers. He got to the point where he thought that all of them looked at him and desired him.

"It was hard when he grew old. Oh, monsieur, when I saw his first white hair I felt a terrible shock and then a great joy—a wicked joy—but so great, so great! I said to myself: 'It's the end-it's the end.' It seemed as if I were about to be released from prison. At last I could have him to myself, all to myself, when the others would no longer want him.

"It was one morning in bed. He was still sleeping and I leaned over him to wake him up with a kiss, when I noticed in his curls, over his temple, a little thread which shone like silver. What a surprise! I should not have thought it possible! At first I thought of tearing it out so that he would not see it, but as I looked carefully I noticed another farther up. White hair! He was going to have white hair! My heart began to thump and perspiration stood out all over me, but away down at the bottom I was happy.

"It was mean to feel thus, but I did my housework with a light heart that morning, without waking him up, and, as soon as he opened his eyes of his own accord, I said to him: 'Do you know what I discovered while you were asleep?'

"'No.'

"'I found white hairs.'

"He started up as if I had tickled him and said angrily: 'It's not true!'

"'Yes, it is. There are four of them over your left temple.'

"He jumped out of bed and ran over to the mirror. He could not find them. Then I showed him the first one, the lowest, the little curly one, and I said: 'It's no wonder, after the life that you have been leading. In two years all will be over for you.'

"Well, monsieur, I had spoken true; two years later one could not recognize him. How quickly a man changes! He was still handsome, but he had lost his freshness, and the women no longer ran after him. Ah! what a life I led at that time! How he treated me! Nothing suited him. He left his trade to go into the hat business, in which he ate up all his money. Then he unsuccessfully tried to be an actor, and finally he began to frequent public balls. Fortunately, he had had common sense enough to save a little something on which we now live. It is sufficient, but it is not enormous. And to think that at one time he had almost a fortune.

"Now you see what he does. This habit holds him like a frenzy. He has to be young; he has to dance with women who smell of perfume and cosmetics. You poor old darling!"

She was looking at her old snoring husband fondly, ready to cry. Then, gently tiptoeing up to him, she kissed his hair. The physician had risen and was getting ready to leave, finding nothing to say to this strange couple. Just as he was leaving she asked:

"Would you mind giving me your address? If he should grow worse, I could go and get you."

THE PENGUINS' ROCK

This is the season for penguins.

From April to the end of May, before the Parisian visitors arrive, one sees, all at once, on the little beach at Etretat several old gentlemen, booted and belted in shooting costume. They spend four or five days at the Hotel Hauville, disappear, and return again three weeks later. Then, after a fresh sojourn, they go away altogether.

One sees them again the following spring.

These are the last penguin hunters, what remain of the old set. There were about twenty enthusiasts thirty or forty years ago; now there are only a few of the enthusiastic sportsmen.

The penguin is a very rare bird of passage, with peculiar habits. It lives the greater part of the year in the latitude of Newfoundland and the islands of St. Pierre and Miquelon. But in the breeding season a flight of emigrants crosses the ocean and comes every year to the same spot to lay their eggs, to the Penguins' Rock near Etretat. They are found nowhere else, only there. They have always come there, have always been chased away, but return again, and will always return. As soon as the young birds are grown they all fly away, and disappear for a year.

Why do they not go elsewhere? Why not choose some other spot on the long white, unending cliff that extends from the Pas-de-Calais to Havre? What force, what invincible instinct, what custom of centuries impels these birds to come back to this place?

What first migration, what tempest, possibly, once cast their ancestors on this rock? And why do the children, the grandchildren, all the descendants of the first parents always return here?

There are not many of them, a hundred at most, as if one single family, maintaining the tradition, made this annual pilgrimage.

And each spring, as soon as the little wandering tribe has taken up its abode an the rock, the same sportsmen also reappear in the village. One knew them formerly when they were young; now they are old, but constant to the regular appointment which they have kept for thirty or forty years. They would not miss it for anything in the world.

It was an April evening in one of the later years. Three of the old sportsmen had arrived; one was missing—M. d'Arnelles.

He had written to no one, given no account of himself. But he was not dead, like so many of the rest; they would have heard of it. At length, tired of waiting for him, the other three sat down to table. Dinner was almost over when a carriage drove into the yard of the hotel, and the late comer presently entered the dining room.

He sat down, in a good humor, rubbing his hands, and ate with zest. When one of his comrades remarked with surprise at his being in a frock-coat, he replied quietly:

"Yes, I had no time to change my clothes."

They retired on leaving the table, for they had to set out before daybreak in order to take the birds unawares.

There is nothing so pretty as this sport, this early morning expedition.

At three o'clock in the morning the sailors awoke the sportsmen by throwing sand against the windows. They were ready in a few minutes and went down to the beach. Although it was still dark, the stars had paled a little. The sea ground the shingle on the beach. There was such a fresh breeze that it made one shiver slightly in spite of one's heavy clothing.

Presently two boats were pushed down the beach, by the sailors, with a sound as of tearing cloth, and were floated on the nearest waves. The brown sail was hoisted, swelled a little, fluttered, hesitated and swelling out again as round as a paunch, carried the boats towards the large arched entrance that could be faintly distinguished in the darkness.

The sky became clearer, the shadows seemed to melt away. The coast still seemed veiled, the great white coast, perpendicular as a wall.

They passed through the Manne-Porte, an enormous arch beneath which a ship could sail; they doubled the promontory of La Courtine, passed the little valley of Antifer and the cape of the same name; and suddenly caught sight of a beach on which some hundreds of seagulls were perched.

That was the Penguins' Rock. It was just a little protuberance of the cliff, and on the narrow ledges of rock the birds' heads might be seen watching the boats.

They remained there, motionless, not venturing to fly off as yet. Some of them perched on the edges, seated upright, looked almost like bottles, for their little legs are so short that when they walk they glide along as if they were on rollers. When they start to fly they cannot make a spring and let themselves fall like stones almost down to the very men who are watching them.

They know their limitation and the danger to which it subjects them, and cannot make up their minds to fly away.

But the boatmen begin to shout, beating the sides of the boat with the wooden boat pins, and the birds, in affright, fly one by one into space until they reach the level of the waves. Then, moving their wings rapidly, they scud, scud along until they reach the open sea; if a shower of lead does not knock them into the water.

For an hour the firing is kept up, obliging them to give up, one after another. Sometimes the mother birds will not leave their nests, and are riddled with shot, causing drops of blood to spurt out on the white cliff, and the animal dies without having deserted her eggs.

The first day M. d'Arnelles fired at the birds with his habitual zeal; but when the party returned toward ten o'clock, beneath a brilliant sun, which cast great triangles of light on the white cliffs along the coast he appeared a little worried, and absentminded, contrary to his accustomed manner.

As soon as they got on shore a kind of servant dressed in black came up to him and said something in a low tone. He seemed to reflect, hesitate, and then replied:

"No, to-morrow."

The following day they set out again. This time M, d'Arnelles frequently missed his aim, although the birds were close by. His friends teased him, asked him if he were in love, if some secret sorrow was troubling his mind and heart. At length he confessed.

"Yes, indeed, I have to leave soon, and that annoys me."

"What, you must leave? And why?"

"Oh, I have some business that calls me back. I cannot stay any longer."

They then talked of other matters.

As soon as breakfast was over the valet in black appeared. M. d'Arnelles ordered his carriage, and the man was leaving the room when the three sportsmen interfered, insisting, begging, and praying their friend to stay. One of them at last said:

"Come now, this cannot be a matter of such importance, for you have already waited two days."

M. d'Arnelles, altogether perplexed, began to think, evidently baffled, divided between pleasure and duty, unhappy and disturbed.

After reflecting for some time he stammered:

"The fact is—the fact is—I am not alone here. I have my son-in-law."

There were exclamations and shouts of "Your son-in-law! Where is he?"

He suddenly appeared confused and his face grew red.

"What! do you not know? Why—why—he is in the coach house. He is dead."

They were all silent in amazement.

M. d'Arnelles continued, more and more disturbed:

"I had the misfortune to lose him; and as I was taking the body to my house, in Briseville, I came round this way so as not to miss our appointment. But you can see that I cannot wait any longer."

Then one of the sportsmen, bolder than the rest said:

"Well, but—since he is dead—it seems to me that he can wait a day longer."

The others chimed in:

"That cannot be denied."

M. d'Arnelles appeared to be relieved of a great weight, but a little uneasy, nevertheless, he asked:

"But, frankly—do you think—"

The three others, as one man, replied:

"Parbleu! my dear boy, two days more or less can make no difference in his present condition."

And, perfectly calmly, the father-in-law turned to the undertaker's assistant, and said:

"Well, then, my friend, it will be the day after tomorrow."

A FAMILY

I was to see my old friend, Simon Radevin, of whom I had lost sight for fifteen years. At one time he was my most intimate friend, the friend who knows one's thoughts, with whom one passes long, quiet, happy evenings, to whom one tells one's secret love affairs, and who seems to draw out those rare, ingenious, delicate thoughts born of that sympathy that gives a sense of repose.

For years we had scarcely been separated; we had lived, travelled, thought and dreamed together; had liked the same things, had admired the same books, understood the same authors, trembled with the same sensations, and very often laughed at the same individuals, whom we understood completely by merely exchanging a glance.

Then he married. He married, quite suddenly, a little girl from the provinces, who had come to Paris in search of a husband. How in the world could that little thin, insipidly fair girl, with her weak hands, her light, vacant eyes, and her clear, silly voice, who was exactly like a hundred thousand marriageable dolls, have picked up that intelligent, clever young fellow? Can any one understand these things? No doubt he had hoped for happiness, simple, quiet and long-enduring happiness, in the arms of a good, tender and faithful woman; he had seen all that in the transparent looks of that schoolgirl with light hair.

He had not dreamed of the fact that an active, living and vibrating man grows weary of everything as soon as he understands the stupid reality, unless, indeed, he becomes so brutalized that he understands nothing whatever.

What would he be like when I met him again? Still lively, witty, light-hearted and enthusiastic, or in a state of mental torpor induced by provincial life? A man may change greatly in the course of fifteen years!

The train stopped at a small station, and as I got out of the carriage, a stout, a very stout man with red cheeks and a big stomach rushed up to me with open arms, exclaiming: "George!" I embraced him, but I had not recognized him, and then I said, in astonishment: "By Jove! You have not grown thin!" And he replied with a laugh:

"What did you expect? Good living, a good table and good nights! Eating and sleeping, that is my existence!"

I looked at him closely, trying to discover in that broad face the features I held so dear. His eyes alone had not changed, but I no longer saw the same expression in them, and I said to myself: "If the expression be the reflection of the mind, the thoughts in that head are not what they used to be formerly; those thoughts which I knew so well."

Yet his eyes were bright, full of happiness and friendship, but they had not that clear, intelligent expression which shows as much as words the brightness of the intellect. Suddenly he said:

"Here are my two eldest children." A girl of fourteen, who was almost a woman, and a boy of thirteen, in the dress of a boy from a Lycee, came forward in a hesitating and awkward manner, and I said in a low voice: "Are they yours?" "Of course they are," he replied, laughing. "How many have you?" "Five! There are three more at home."

He said this in a proud, self-satisfied, almost triumphant manner, and I felt profound pity, mingled with a feeling of vague contempt, for this vainglorious and simple reproducer of his species.

I got into a carriage which he drove himself, and we set off through the town, a dull, sleepy, gloomy town where nothing was moving in the streets except a few dogs and two or three maidservants. Here and there a shopkeeper, standing at his door, took off his hat, and Simon returned his salute and told me the man's name; no doubt to show me that he knew all the inhabitants personally, and the thought struck me that he was thinking of becoming a candidate for the Chamber of Deputies, that dream of all those who bury themselves in the provinces.

We were soon out of the town, and the carriage turned into a garden that was an imitation of a park, and stopped in front of a turreted house, which tried to look like a chateau.

"That is my den," said Simon, so that I might compliment him on it. "It is charming," I replied.

A lady appeared on the steps, dressed for company, and with company phrases all ready prepared. She was no longer the light-haired, insipid girl I had seen in church fifteen years previously, but a stout lady in curls and flounces, one of those ladies of uncertain age, without intellect, without any of those things that go to make a woman. In short, she was a mother, a stout, commonplace mother, a human breeding machine which procreates without any other preoccupation but her children and her cook-book.

She welcomed me, and I went into the hall, where three children, ranged according to their height, seemed set out for review, like firemen before a mayor, and I said: "Ah! ah! so there are the others?" Simon, radiant with pleasure, introduced them: "Jean, Sophie and Gontran."

The door of the drawing-room was open. I went in, and in the depths of an easy-chair, I saw something trembling, a man, an old, paralyzed man. Madame Radevin came forward and said: "This is my grandfather, monsieur; he is eighty-seven." And then she shouted into the shaking old man's ears: "This is a friend of Simon's, papa." The old gentleman tried to say "good-day" to me, and he muttered: "Oua, oua, oua," and waved his hand, and I took a seat saying: "You are very kind, monsieur."

Simon had just come in, and he said with a laugh: "So! You have made grandpapa's acquaintance. He is a treasure, that old man; he is the delight of the children. But he is so greedy that he almost kills himself at every meal; you have no idea what he would eat if he were allowed to do as he pleased. But you will see, you will see. He looks at all the sweets as if they were so many girls. You never saw anything so funny; you will see presently."

I was then shown to my room, to change my dress for dinner, and hearing a great clatter behind me on the stairs, I turned round and saw that all the children were following me behind their father; to do me honor, no doubt.

My windows looked out across a dreary, interminable plain, an ocean of grass, of wheat and of oats, without a clump of trees or any rising ground, a striking and melancholy picture of the life which they must be leading in that house.

A bell rang; it was for dinner, and I went downstairs. Madame Radevin took my arm in a ceremonious manner, and we passed into the dining-room. A footman wheeled in the old man in his armchair. He gave a greedy and curious look at the dessert, as he turned his shaking head with difficulty from one dish to the other.

Simon rubbed his hands: "You will be amused," he said; and all the children understanding that I was going to be indulged with the sight of their greedy grandfather, began to laugh, while their mother merely smiled and shrugged her shoulders, and Simon, making a speaking trumpet of his hands, shouted at the old man: "This evening there is sweet creamed rice!" The wrinkled face of the grandfather brightened, and he trembled more violently, from head to foot, showing that he had understood and was very pleased. The dinner began.

"Just look!" Simon whispered. The old man did not like the soup, and refused to eat it; but he was obliged to do it for the good of his health, and the footman forced the spoon into his mouth, while the old man blew so energetically, so as not to swallow the soup, that it was scattered like a spray all over the table and over his neighbors. The children writhed with laughter at the spectacle, while their father, who was also amused, said: "Is not the old man comical?"

During the whole meal they were taken up solely with him. He devoured the dishes on the table with his eyes, and tried to seize them and pull them over to him with his trembling hands. They put them almost within his reach, to see his useless efforts, his trembling clutches at them, the piteous appeal of his whole nature, of his eyes, of his mouth and of his nose as he smelt them, and he slobbered on his table napkin with eagerness, while uttering inarticulate grunts. And the whole family was highly amused at this horrible and grotesque scene.

Then they put a tiny morsel on his plate, and he ate with feverish gluttony, in order to get something more as soon as possible, and when the sweetened rice was brought in, he nearly had a fit, and groaned with greediness, and Gontran called out to him:

"You have eaten too much already; you can have no more." And they pretended not to give him any. Then he began to cry; he cried and trembled more violently than ever, while all the children laughed. At last, however, they gave him his helping, a very small piece; and as he ate the first mouthful, he made a comical noise in his throat, and a movement with his neck as ducks do when they swallow too large a morsel, and when he had swallowed it, he began to stamp his feet, so as to get more.

I was seized with pity for this saddening and ridiculous Tantalus, and interposed on his behalf:

"Come, give him a little more rice!" But Simon replied: "Oh! no, my dear fellow, if he were to eat too much, it would harm him, at his age."

I held my tongue, and thought over those words. Oh, ethics! Oh, logic! Oh, wisdom! At his age! So they deprived him of his only remaining pleasure out of regard for his health! His health! What would he do with it, inert and trembling wreck that he was? They were taking care of his life, so they said. His life? How many days? Ten, twenty, fifty, or a hundred? Why? For his own sake? Or to preserve for some time longer the spectacle of his impotent greediness in the family.

There was nothing left for him to do in this life, nothing whatever. He had one single wish left, one sole pleasure; why not grant him that last solace until he died?

After we had played cards for a long time, I went up to my room and to bed; I was low-spirited and sad, sad, sad! and I sat at my window. Not a sound could be heard outside but the beautiful warbling of a bird in a tree, somewhere in the distance. No doubt the bird was singing in a low voice during the night, to lull his mate, who was asleep on her eggs. And I thought of my poor friend's five children, and pictured him to myself, snoring by the side of his ugly wife.

SUICIDES

To Georges Legrand.

Hardly a day goes by without our reading a news item like the following in some newspaper:

"On Wednesday night the people living in No. 40 Rue de——, were awakened by two successive shots. The explosions seemed to come from the apartment occupied by M. X——. The door was broken in and the man was found bathed in his blood, still holding in one hand the revolver with which he had taken his life.

"M. X——was fifty-seven years of age, enjoying a comfortable income, and had everything necessary to make him happy. No cause can be found for his action."

What terrible grief, what unknown suffering, hidden despair, secret wounds drive these presumably happy persons to suicide? We search, we imagine tragedies of love, we suspect financial troubles, and, as we never find anything definite, we apply to these deaths the word "mystery."

A letter found on the desk of one of these "suicides without cause," and written during his last night, beside his loaded revolver, has come into our hands. We deem it rather interesting. It reveals none of those great catastrophes which we always expect to find behind these acts of despair; but it shows us the slow succession of the little vexations of life, the disintegration of a lonely existence, whose dreams have disappeared; it gives the reason for these tragic ends, which only nervous and high-strung people can understand.

Here it is:

"It is midnight. When I have finished this letter I shall kill myself. Why? I shall attempt to give the reasons, not for those who may read these lines, but for myself, to kindle my waning courage, to impress upon myself the fatal necessity of this act which can, at best, be only deferred.

"I was brought up by simple-minded parents who were unquestioning believers. And I believed as they did.

"My dream lasted a long time. The last veil has just been torn from my eyes.

"During the last few years a strange change has been taking place within me. All the events of Life, which formerly had to me the glow of a beautiful sunset, are now fading away. The true meaning of things has appeared to me in its brutal reality; and the true reason for love has bred in me disgust even for this poetic sentiment: 'We are the eternal toys of foolish and charming illusions, which are always being renewed.'

"On growing older, I had become partly reconciled to the awful mystery of life, to the uselessness of effort; when the emptiness of everything appeared to me in a new light, this evening, after dinner.

"Formerly, I was happy! Everything pleased me: the passing women, the appearance of the streets, the place where I lived; and I even took an interest in the cut of my clothes. But the repetition of the same sights has had the result of filling my heart with weariness and disgust, just as one would feel were one to go every night to the same theatre.

"For the last thirty years I have been rising at the same hour; and, at the same restaurant, for thirty years, I have been eating at the same hours the same dishes brought me by different waiters.

"I have tried travel. The loneliness which one feels in strange places terrified me. I felt so alone, so small on the earth that I quickly started on my homeward journey.

"But here the unchanging expression of my furniture, which has stood for thirty years in the same place, the smell of my apartments (for, with time, each dwelling takes on a particular odor) each night, these and other things disgust me and make me sick of living thus.

"Everything repeats itself endlessly. The way in which I put my key in the lock, the place where I always find my matches, the first object which meets my eye when I enter the room, make me feel like jumping out of the window and putting an end to those monotonous events from which we can never escape.

"Each day, when I shave, I feel an inordinate desire to cut my throat; and my face, which I see in the little mirror, always the same, with soap on my cheeks, has several times made me weak from sadness.

"Now I even hate to be with people whom I used to meet with pleasure; I know them so well, I can tell just what they are going to say and what I am going to answer. Each brain is like a circus, where the same horse keeps circling around eternally. We must circle round always, around the same ideas, the same joys, the same pleasures, the same habits, the same beliefs, the same sensations of disgust.

"The fog was terrible this evening. It enfolded the boulevard, where the street lights were dimmed and looked like smoking candles. A heavier weight than usual oppressed me. Perhaps my digestion was bad.

"For good digestion is everything in life. It gives the inspiration to the artist, amorous desires to young people, clear ideas to thinkers, the joy of life to everybody, and it also allows one to eat heartily (which is one of the greatest pleasures). A sick stomach induces scepticism unbelief, nightmares and the desire for death. I have often noticed this fact. Perhaps I would not kill myself, if my digestion had been good this evening.

"When I sat down in the arm-chair where I have been sitting every day for thirty years, I glanced around me, and just then I was seized by such a terrible distress that I thought I must go mad.

"I tried to think of what I could do to run away from myself. Every occupation struck me as being worse even than inaction. Then I bethought me of putting my papers in order.

"For a long time I have been thinking of clearing out my drawers; for, for the last thirty years, I have been throwing my letters and bills pell-mell into the same desk, and this confusion has often caused me considerable trouble. But I feel such moral and physical laziness at the sole idea of putting anything in order that I have never had the courage to begin this tedious business.

"I therefore opened my desk, intending to choose among my old papers and destroy the majority of them.

"At first I was bewildered by this array of documents, yellowed by age, then I chose one.

"Oh! if you cherish life, never disturb the burial place of old letters!

"And if, perchance, you should, take the contents by the handful, close your eyes that you may not read a word, so that you may not recognize some forgotten handwriting which may plunge you suddenly into a sea of memories; carry these papers to the fire; and when they are in ashes, crush them to an invisible powder, or otherwise you are lost—just as I have been lost for an hour.

"The first letters which I read did not interest me greatly. They were recent, and came from living men whom I still meet quite often, and whose presence does not move me to any great extent. But all at once one envelope made me start. My name was traced on it in a large, bold handwriting; and suddenly tears came to my eyes. That letter was from my dearest friend, the companion of my youth, the confidant of my hopes; and he appeared before me so clearly, with his pleasant smile and his hand outstretched, that a cold shiver ran down my back. Yes, yes, the dead come back, for I saw him! Our memory is a more perfect world than the universe: it gives back life to those who no longer exist.

"With trembling hand and dimmed eyes I reread everything that he told me, and in my poor sobbing heart I felt a wound so painful that I began to groan as a man whose bones are slowly being crushed.

"Then I travelled over my whole life, just as one travels along a river. I recognized people, so long forgotten that I no longer knew their names. Their faces alone lived in me. In my mother's letters I saw again the old servants, the shape of our house and the little insignificant odds and ends which cling to our minds.

"Yes, I suddenly saw again all my mother's old gowns, the different styles which she adopted and the several ways in which she dressed her hair. She haunted me especially in a silk dress, trimmed with old lace; and I remembered something she said one day when she was wearing this dress. She said: 'Robert, my child, if you do not stand up straight you will be round-shouldered all your life.'

"Then, opening another drawer, I found myself face to face with memories of tender passions: a dancing-pump, a torn handkerchief, even a garter, locks of hair and dried flowers. Then the sweet romances of my life, whose living heroines are now white-haired, plunged me into the deep melancholy of things. Oh, the young brows where blond locks curl, the caress of the hands, the glance which speaks, the hearts which beat, that smile which promises the lips, those lips which promise the embrace! And the first kiss-that endless kiss which makes you close your eyes, which drowns all thought in the immeasurable joy of approaching possession!

"Taking these old pledges of former love in both my hands, I covered them with furious caresses, and in my soul, torn by these memories, I saw them each again at the hour of surrender; and I suffered a torture more cruel than all the tortures invented in all the fables about hell.

"One last letter remained. It was written by me and dictated fifty years ago by my writing teacher. Here it is:

"'MY DEAR LITTLE MAMMA:

"'I am seven years old to-day. It is the age of reason. I take advantage of it to thank you for having brought me into this world.

"'Your little son, who loves you

"'ROBERT.'

"It is all over. I had gone back to the beginning, and suddenly I turned my glance on what remained to me of life. I saw hideous and lonely old age, and approaching infirmities, and everything over and gone. And nobody near me!

"My revolver is here, on the table. I am loading it . . . . Never reread your old letters!"

And that is how many men come to kill themselves; and we search in vain to discover some great sorrow in their lives.

AN ARTIFICE

The old doctor sat by the fireside, talking to his fair patient who was lying on the lounge. There was nothing much the matter with her, except that she had one of those little feminine ailments from which pretty women frequently suffer—slight anaemia, a nervous attack, etc.

"No, doctor," she said; "I shall never be able to understand a woman deceiving her husband. Even allowing that she does not love him, that she pays no heed to her vows and promises, how can she give herself to another man? How can she conceal the intrigue from other people's eyes? How can it be possible to love amid lies and treason?"

The doctor smiled, and replied: "It is perfectly easy, and I can assure you that a woman does not think of all those little subtle details when she has made up her mind to go astray.

"As for dissimulation, all women have plenty of it on hand for such occasions, and the simplest of them are wonderful, and extricate themselves from the greatest dilemmas in a remarkable manner."

The young woman, however, seemed incredulous.

"No, doctor," she said; "one never thinks until after it has happened of what one ought to have done in a critical situation, and women are certainly more liable than men to lose their head on such occasions:"

The doctor raised his hands. "After it has happened, you say! Now I will tell you something that happened to one of my female patients, whom I always considered an immaculate woman.

"It happened in a provincial town, and one night when I was asleep, in that deep first sleep from which it is so difficult to rouse us, it seemed to me, in my dreams, as if the bells in the town were sounding a fire alarm, and I woke up with a start. It was my own bell, which was ringing wildly, and as my footman did not seem to be answering the door, I, in turn, pulled the bell at the head of my bed, and soon I heard a banging, and steps in the silent house, and Jean came into my room, and handed me a letter which said: 'Madame Lelievre begs Dr. Simeon to come to her immediately.'

"I thought for a few moments, and then I said to myself: 'A nervous attack, vapors; nonsense, I am too tired.' And so I replied: 'As Dr. Simeon is not at all well, he must beg Madame Lelievre to be kind enough to call in his colleague, Monsieur Bonnet.' I put the note into an envelope and went to sleep again, but about half an hour later the street bell rang again, and Jean came to me and said: 'There is somebody downstairs; I do not quite know whether it is a man or a woman, as the individual is so wrapped up, but they wish to speak to you immediately. They say it is a matter of life and death for two people.' Whereupon I sat up in bed and told him to show the person in.

"A kind of black phantom appeared and raised her veil as soon as Jean had left the room. It was Madame Berthe Lelievre, quite a young woman, who had been married for three years to a large merchant in the town, who was said to have married the prettiest girl in the neighborhood.

"She was terribly pale, her face was contracted as the faces of insane people are, occasionally, and her hands trembled violently. Twice she tried to speak without being able to utter a sound, but at last she stammered out: 'Come—quick—quick, doctor. Come—my—friend has just died in my bedroom.' She stopped, half suffocated with emotion, and then went on: 'My husband will be coming home from the club very soon.'

"I jumped out of bed without even considering that I was only in my nightshirt, and dressed myself in a few moments, and then I said: 'Did you come a short time ago?' 'No,' she said, standing like a statue petrified with horror. 'It was my servant—she knows.' And then, after a short silence, she went on: 'I was there—by his side.' And she uttered a sort of cry of horror, and after a fit of choking, which made her gasp, she wept violently, and shook with spasmodic sobs for a minute: or two. Then her tears suddenly ceased, as if by an internal fire, and with an air of tragic calmness, she said: 'Let us make haste.'

"I was ready, but exclaimed: 'I quite forgot to order my carriage.' 'I have one,' she said; 'it is his, which was waiting for him!' She wrapped herself up, so as to completely conceal her face, and we started.

"When she was by my side in the carriage she suddenly seized my hand, and crushing it in her delicate fingers, she said, with a shaking voice, that proceeded from a distracted heart: 'Oh! if you only knew, if you only knew what I am suffering! I loved him, I have loved him distractedly, like a madwoman, for the last six months.' 'Is anyone up in your house?' I asked. 'No, nobody except those, who knows everything.'

"We stopped at the door, and evidently everybody was asleep. We went in without making any noise, by means of her latch-key, and walked upstairs on tiptoe. The frightened servant was sitting on the top of the stairs with a lighted candle by her side, as she was afraid to remain with the dead man, and I went into the room, which was in great disorder. Wet towels, with which they had bathed the young man's temples, were lying on the floor, by the side of a washbasin and a glass, while a strong smell of vinegar pervaded the room.

"The dead man's body was lying at full length in the middle of the room, and I went up to it, looked at it, and touched it. I opened the eyes and felt the hands, and then, turning to the two women, who were shaking as if they were freezing, I said to them: 'Help me to lift him on to the bed.' When we had laid him gently on it, I listened to his heart and put a looking-glass to his lips, and then said: 'It is all over.' It was a terrible sight!

"I looked at the man, and said: 'You ought to arrange his hair a little.' The girl went and brought her mistress' comb and brush, but as she was trembling, and pulling out his long, matted hair in doing it, Madame Lelievre took the comb out of her hand, and arranged his hair as if she were caressing him. She parted it, brushed his beard, rolled his mustaches gently round her fingers, then, suddenly, letting go of his hair, she took the dead man's inert head in her hands and looked for a long time in despair at the dead face, which no longer could smile at her, and then, throwing herself on him, she clasped him in her arms and kissed him ardently. Her kisses fell like blows on his closed mouth and eyes, his forehead and temples; and then, putting her lips to his ear, as if he could still hear her, and as if she were about to whisper something to him, she said several times, in a heartrending voice:

"'Good-by, my darling!'

"Just then the clock struck twelve, and I started up. 'Twelve o'clock!' I exclaimed. 'That is the time when the club closes. Come, madame, we have not a moment to lose!' She started up, and I said:

"'We must carry him into the drawing-room.' And when we had done this, I placed him on a sofa, and lit the chandeliers, and just then the front door was opened and shut noisily. 'Rose, bring me the basin and the towels, and make the room look tidy. Make haste, for Heaven's sake! Monsieur Lelievre is coming in.'

"I heard his steps on the stairs, and then his hands feeling along the walls. 'Come here, my dear fellow,' I said; 'we have had an accident.'

"And the astonished husband appeared in the door with a cigar in his mouth, and said: 'What is the matter? What is the meaning of this?' 'My dear friend,' I said, going up to him, 'you find us in great embarrassment. I had remained late, chatting with your wife and our friend, who had brought me in his carriage, when he suddenly fainted, and in spite of all we have done, he has remained unconscious for two hours. I did not like to call in strangers, and if you will now help me downstairs with him, I shall be able to attend to him better at his own house.'

"The husband, who was surprised, but quite unsuspicious, took off his hat, and then he took his rival, who would be quite inoffensive for the future, under the arms. I got between his two legs, as if I had been a horse between the shafts, and we went downstairs, while his wife held a light for us. When we got outside I stood the body up, so as to deceive the coachman, and said: 'Come, my friend; it is nothing; you feel better already I expect. Pluck up your courage, and make an effort. It will soon be over.' But as I felt that he was slipping out of my hands, I gave him a slap on the shoulder, which sent him forward and made him fall into the carriage, and then I got in after him. Monsieur Lelievre, who was rather alarmed, said to me: 'Do you think it is anything serious?' To which I replied: 'No,' with a smile, as I looked at his wife, who had put her arm into that of her husband, and was trying to see into the carriage.

"I shook hands with them and told my coachman to start, and during the whole drive the dead man kept falling against me. When we got to his house I said that he had become unconscious on the way home, and helped to carry him upstairs, where I certified that he was dead, and acted another comedy to his distracted family, and at last I got back to bed, not without swearing at lovers."

The doctor ceased, though he was still smiling, and the young woman, who was in a very nervous state, said: "Why have you told me that terrible story?"

He gave her a gallant bow, and replied:

"So that I may offer you my services if they should be needed."

DREAMS

They had just dined together, five old friends, a writer, a doctor and three rich bachelors without any profession.

They had talked about everything, and a feeling of lassitude came over them, that feeling which precedes and leads to the departure of guests after festive gatherings. One of those present, who had for the last five minutes been gazing silently at the surging boulevard dotted with gas-lamps, with its rattling vehicles, said suddenly:

"When you've nothing to do from morning till night, the days are long."

"And the nights too," assented the guest who sat next to him. "I sleep very little; pleasures fatigue me; conversation is monotonous. Never do I come across a new idea, and I feel, before talking to any one, a violent longing to say nothing and to listen to nothing. I don't know what to do with my evenings."

The third idler remarked:

"I would pay a great deal for anything that would help me to pass just two pleasant hours every day."

The writer, who had just thrown his overcoat across his arm, turned round to them, and said:

"The man who could discover a new vice and introduce it among his fellow creatures, even if it were to shorten their lives, would render a greater service to humanity than the man who found the means of securing to them eternal salvation and eternal youth."

The doctor burst out laughing, and, while he chewed his cigar, he said:

"Yes, but it is not so easy to discover it. Men have however crudely, been seeking for—and working for the object you refer to since the beginning of the world. The men who came first reached perfection at once in this way. We are hardly equal to them."

One of the three idlers murmured:

"What a pity!"

Then, after a minute's pause, he added:

"If we could only sleep, sleep well, without feeling hot or cold, sleep with that perfect unconsciousness we experience on nights when we are thoroughly fatigued, sleep without dreams."

"Why without dreams?" asked the guest sitting next to him.

The other replied:

"Because dreams are not always pleasant; they are always fantastic, improbable, disconnected; and because when we are asleep we cannot have the sort of dreams we like. We ought to dream waking."

"And what's to prevent you?" asked the writer.

The doctor flung away the end of his cigar.

"My dear fellow, in order to dream when you are awake, you need great power and great exercise of will, and when you try to do it, great weariness is the result. Now, real dreaming, that journey of our thoughts through delightful visions, is assuredly the sweetest experience in the world; but it must come naturally, it must not be provoked in a painful, manner, and must be accompanied by absolute bodily comfort. This power of dreaming I can give you, provided you promise that you will not abuse it."

The writer shrugged his shoulders:

"Ah! yes, I know—hasheesh, opium, green tea—artificial paradises. I have read Baudelaire, and I even tasted the famous drug, which made me very sick."

But the doctor, without stirring from his seat, said:

"No; ether, nothing but ether; and I would suggest that you literary men should use it sometimes."

The three rich bachelors drew closer to the doctor.

One of them said:

"Explain to us the effects of it."

And the doctor replied:

"Let us put aside big words, shall we not? I am not talking of medicine or morality; I am talking of pleasure. You give yourselves up every day to excesses which consume your lives. I want to indicate to you a new sensation, possible only to intelligent men—let us say even very intelligent men—dangerous, like everything else that overexcites our organs, but exquisite. I might add that you would require a certain preparation, that is to say, practice, to feel in all their completeness the singular effects of ether.

"They are different from the effects of hasheesh, of opium, or morphia, and they cease as soon as the absorption of the drug is interrupted, while the other generators of day dreams continue their action for hours.

"I am now going to try to analyze these feelings as clearly as possible. But the thing is not easy, so facile, so delicate, so almost imperceptible, are these sensations.

"It was when I was attacked by violent neuralgia that I made use of this remedy, which since then I have, perhaps, slightly abused.

"I had acute pains in my head and neck, and an intolerable heat of the skin, a feverish restlessness. I took up a large bottle of ether, and, lying down, I began to inhale it slowly.

"At the end of some minutes I thought I heard a vague murmur, which ere long became a sort of humming, and it seemed to me that all the interior of my body had become light, light as air, that it was dissolving into vapor.

"Then came a sort of torpor, a sleepy sensation of comfort, in spite of the pains which still continued, but which had ceased to make themselves felt. It was one of those sensations which we are willing to endure and not any of those frightful wrenches against which our tortured body protests.

"Soon the strange and delightful sense of emptiness which I felt in my chest extended to my limbs, which, in their turn, became light, as light as if the flesh and the bones had been melted and the skin only were left, the skin necessary to enable me to realize the sweetness of living, of bathing in this sensation of well-being. Then I perceived that I was no longer suffering. The pain had gone, melted away, evaporated. And I heard voices, four voices, two dialogues, without understanding what was said. At one time there were only indistinct sounds, at another time a word reached my ear. But I recognized that this was only the humming I had heard before, but emphasized. I was not asleep; I was not awake; I comprehended, I felt, I reasoned with the utmost clearness and depth, with extraordinary energy and intellectual pleasure, with a singular intoxication arising from this separation of my mental faculties.

"It was not like the dreams caused by hasheesh or the somewhat sickly visions that come from opium; it was an amazing acuteness of reasoning, a new way of seeing, judging and appreciating the things of life, and with the certainty, the absolute consciousness that this was the true way.

"And the old image of the Scriptures suddenly came back to my mind. It seemed to me that I had tasted of the Tree of Knowledge, that all the mysteries were unveiled, so much did I find myself under the sway of a new, strange and irrefutable logic. And arguments, reasonings, proofs rose up in a heap before my brain only to be immediately displaced by some stronger proof, reasoning, argument. My head had, in fact, become a battleground of ideas. I was a superior being, armed with invincible intelligence, and I experienced a huge delight at the manifestation of my power.

"It lasted a long, long time. I still kept inhaling the ether from my flagon. Suddenly I perceived that it was empty."

The four men exclaimed at the same time:

"Doctor, a prescription at once for a liter of ether!"

But the doctor, putting on his hat, replied:

"As to that, certainly not; go and let some one else poison you!"

And he left them.

Ladies and gentlemen, what is your opinion on the subject?

SIMON'S PAPA

Noon had just struck. The school door opened and the youngsters darted out, jostling each other in their haste to get out quickly. But instead of promptly dispersing and going home to dinner as usual, they stopped a few paces off, broke up into knots, and began whispering.

The fact was that, that morning, Simon, the son of La Blanchotte, had, for the first time, attended school.

They had all of them in their families heard talk of La Blanchotte; and, although in public she was welcome enough, the mothers among themselves treated her with a somewhat disdainful compassion, which the children had imitated without in the least knowing why.

As for Simon himself, they did not know him, for he never went out, and did not run about with them in the streets of the village, or along the banks of the river. And they did not care for him; so it was with a certain delight, mingled with considerable astonishment, that they met and repeated to each other what had been said by a lad of fourteen or fifteen who appeared to know all about it, so sagaciously did he wink. "You know—Simon—well, he has no papa."

Just then La Blanchotte's son appeared in the doorway of the school.

He was seven or eight years old, rather pale, very neat, with a timid and almost awkward manner.

He was starting home to his mother's house when the groups of his schoolmates, whispering and watching him with the mischievous and heartless eyes of children bent upon playing a nasty trick, gradually closed in around him and ended by surrounding him altogether. There he stood in their midst, surprised and embarrassed, not understanding what they were going to do with him. But the lad who had brought the news, puffed up with the success he had met with already, demanded:

"What is your name, you?"

He answered: "Simon."

"Simon what?" retorted the other.

The child, altogether bewildered, repeated: "Simon."

The lad shouted at him: "One is named Simon something—that is not a name—Simon indeed."

The child, on the brink of tears, replied for the third time:

"My name is Simon."

The urchins began to laugh. The triumphant tormentor cried: "You can see plainly that he has no papa."

A deep silence ensued. The children were dumfounded by this extraordinary, impossible, monstrous thing—a boy who had not a papa; they looked upon him as a phenomenon, an unnatural being, and they felt that hitherto inexplicable contempt of their mothers for La Blanchotte growing upon them. As for Simon, he had leaned against a tree to avoid falling, and he remained as if prostrated by an irreparable disaster. He sought to explain, but could think of nothing-to say to refute this horrible charge that he had no papa. At last he shouted at them quite recklessly: "Yes, I have one."

"Where is he?" demanded the boy.

Simon was silent, he did not know. The children roared, tremendously excited; and those country boys, little more than animals, experienced that cruel craving which prompts the fowls of a farmyard to destroy one of their number as soon as it is wounded. Simon suddenly espied a little neighbor, the son of a widow, whom he had seen, as he himself was to be seen, always alone with his mother.

"And no more have you," he said; "no more have you a papa."

"Yes," replied the other, "I have one."

"Where is he?" rejoined Simon.

"He is dead," declared the brat, with superb dignity; "he is in the cemetery, is my papa."

A murmur of approval rose among the little wretches as if this fact of possessing a papa dead in a cemetery had caused their comrade to grow big enough to crush the other one who had no papa at all. And these boys, whose fathers were for the most part bad men, drunkards, thieves, and who beat their wives, jostled each other to press closer and closer, as though they, the legitimate ones, would smother by their pressure one who was illegitimate.

The boy who chanced to be next Simon suddenly put his tongue out at him with a mocking air and shouted at him:

"No papa! No papa!"

Simon seized him by the hair with both hands and set to work to disable his legs with kicks, while he bit his cheek ferociously. A tremendous struggle ensued between the two combatants, and Simon found himself beaten, torn, bruised, rolled on the ground in the midst of the ring of applauding schoolboys. As he arose, mechanically brushing with his hand his little blouse all covered with dust, some one shouted at him:

"Go and tell your papa."

Then he felt a great sinking at his heart. They were stronger than he was, they had beaten him, and he had no answer to give them, for he knew well that it was true that he had no papa. Full of pride, he attempted for some moments to struggle against the tears which were choking him. He had a feeling of suffocation, and then without any sound he commenced to weep, with great shaking sobs. A ferocious joy broke out among his enemies, and, with one accord, just like savages in their fearful festivals, they took each other by the hand and danced round him in a circle, repeating as a refrain:

"No papa! No papa!"

But suddenly Simon ceased sobbing. He became ferocious. There were stones under his feet; he picked them up and with all his strength hurled them at his tormentors. Two or three were struck and rushed off yelling, and so formidable did he appear that the rest became panic-stricken. Cowards, as the mob always is in presence of an exasperated man, they broke up and fled. Left alone, the little fellow without a father set off running toward the fields, for a recollection had been awakened in him which determined his soul to a great resolve. He made up his mind to drown himself in the river.

He remembered, in fact, that eight days before, a poor devil who begged for his livelihood had thrown himself into the water because he had no more money. Simon had been there when they fished him out again; and the wretched man, who usually seemed to him so miserable, and ugly, had then struck him as being so peaceful with his pale cheeks, his long drenched beard, and his open eyes full of calm. The bystanders had said:

"He is dead."

And some one had said:

"He is quite happy now."

And Simon wished to drown himself also, because he had no father, just like the wretched being who had no money.

He reached the water and watched it flowing. Some fish were sporting briskly in the clear stream and occasionally made a little bound and caught the flies flying on the surface. He stopped crying in order to watch them, for their maneuvers interested him greatly. But, at intervals, as in a tempest intervals of calm alternate suddenly with tremendous gusts of wind, which snap off the trees and then lose themselves in the horizon, this thought would return to him with intense pain:

"I am going to drown myself because I have no papa."

It was very warm, fine weather. The pleasant sunshine warmed the grass. The water shone like a mirror. And Simon enjoyed some minutes of happiness, of that languor which follows weeping, and felt inclined to fall asleep there upon the grass in the warm sunshine.

A little green frog leaped from under his feet. He endeavored to catch it. It escaped him. He followed it and lost it three times in succession. At last he caught it by one of its hind legs and began to laugh as he saw the efforts the creature made to escape. It gathered itself up on its hind legs and then with a violent spring suddenly stretched them out as stiff as two bars; while it beat the air with its front legs as though they were hands, its round eyes staring in their circle of yellow. It reminded him of a toy made of straight slips of wood nailed zigzag one on the other; which by a similar movement regulated the movements of the little soldiers fastened thereon. Then he thought of his home, and then of his mother, and, overcome by sorrow, he again began to weep. A shiver passed over him. He knelt down and said his prayers as before going to bed. But he was unable to finish them, for tumultuous, violent sobs shook his whole frame. He no longer thought, he no longer saw anything around him, and was wholly absorbed in crying.

Suddenly a heavy hand was placed upon his shoulder, and a rough voice asked him:

"What is it that causes you so much grief, my little man?"

Simon turned round. A tall workman with a beard and black curly hair was staring at him good-naturedly. He answered with his eyes and throat full of tears:

"They beat me—because—I—I have no—papa—no papa."

"What!" said the man, smiling; "why, everybody has one."

The child answered painfully amid his spasms of grief:

"But I—I—I have none."

Then the workman became serious. He had recognized La Blanchotte's son, and, although himself a new arrival in the neighborhood, he had a vague idea of her history.

"Well," said he, "console yourself, my boy, and come with me home to your mother. They will give you—a papa."

And so they started on the way, the big fellow holding the little fellow by the hand, and the man smiled, for he was not sorry to see this Blanchotte, who was, it was said, one of the prettiest girls of the countryside, and, perhaps, he was saying to himself, at the bottom of his heart, that a lass who had erred might very well err again.

They arrived in front of a very neat little white house.

"There it is," exclaimed the child, and he cried, "Mamma!"

A woman appeared, and the workman instantly left off smiling, for he saw at once that there was no fooling to be done with the tall pale girl who stood austerely at her door as though to defend from one man the threshold of that house where she had already been betrayed by another. Intimidated, his cap in his hand, he stammered out:

"See, madame, I have brought you back your little boy who had lost himself near the river."

But Simon flung his arms about his mother's neck and told her, as he again began to cry:

"No, mamma, I wished to drown myself, because the others had beaten me—had beaten me—because I have no papa."

A burning redness covered the young woman's cheeks; and, hurt to the quick, she embraced her child passionately, while the tears coursed down her face. The man, much moved, stood there, not knowing how to get away.

But Simon suddenly ran to him and said:

"Will you be my papa?"

A deep silence ensued. La Blanchotte, dumb and tortured with shame, leaned herself against the wall, both her hands upon her heart. The child, seeing that no answer was made him, replied:

"If you will not, I shall go back and drown myself."

The workman took the matter as a jest and answered, laughing:

"Why, yes, certainly I will."

"What is your name," went on the child, "so that I may tell the others when they wish to know your name?"

"Philip," answered the man:

Simon was silent a moment so that he might get the name well into his head; then he stretched out his arms, quite consoled, as he said:

"Well, then, Philip, you are my papa."

The workman, lifting him from the ground, kissed him hastily on both cheeks, and then walked away very quickly with great strides. When the child returned to school next day he was received with a spiteful laugh, and at the end of school, when the lads were on the point of recommencing, Simon threw these words at their heads as he would have done a stone: "He is named Philip, my papa."

Yells of delight burst out from all sides.

"Philip who? Philip what? What on earth is Philip? Where did you pick up your Philip?"

Simon answered nothing; and, immovable in his faith, he defied them with his eye, ready to be martyred rather than fly before them. The school master came to his rescue and he returned home to his mother.

During three months, the tall workman, Philip, frequently passed by La Blanchotte's house, and sometimes he made bold to speak to her when he saw her sewing near the window. She answered him civilly, always sedately, never joking with him, nor permitting him to enter her house. Notwithstanding, being, like all men, a bit of a coxcomb, he imagined that she was often rosier than usual when she chatted with him.

But a lost reputation is so difficult to regain and always remains so fragile that, in spite of the shy reserve of La Blanchotte, they already gossiped in the neighborhood.

As for Simon he loved his new papa very much, and walked with him nearly every evening when the day's work was done. He went regularly to school, and mixed with great dignity with his schoolfellows without ever answering them back.

One day, however, the lad who had first attacked him said to him:

"You have lied. You have not a papa named Philip."

"Why do you say that?" demanded Simon, much disturbed.

The youth rubbed his hands. He replied:

"Because if you had one he would be your mamma's husband."

Simon was confused by the truth of this reasoning; nevertheless, he retorted:

"He is my papa, all the same."

"That can very well be," exclaimed the urchin with a sneer, "but that is not being your papa altogether."

La Blanchotte's little one bowed his head and went off dreaming in the direction of the forge belonging to old Loizon, where Philip worked. This forge was as though buried beneath trees. It was very dark there; the red glare of a formidable furnace alone lit up with great flashes five blacksmiths; who hammered upon their anvils with a terrible din. They were standing enveloped in flame, like demons, their eyes fixed on the red-hot iron they were pounding; and their dull ideas rose and fell with their hammers.

Simon entered without being noticed, and went quietly to pluck his friend by the sleeve. The latter turned round. All at once the work came to a standstill, and all the men looked on, very attentive. Then, in the midst of this unaccustomed silence, rose the slender pipe of Simon:

"Say, Philip, the Michaude boy told me just now that you were not altogether my papa."

"Why not?" asked the blacksmith,

The child replied with all innocence:

"Because you are not my mamma's husband."

No one laughed. Philip remained standing, leaning his forehead upon the back of his great hands, which supported the handle of his hammer standing upright upon the anvil. He mused. His four companions watched him, and Simon, a tiny mite among these giants, anxiously waited. Suddenly, one of the smiths, answering to the sentiment of all, said to Philip:

"La Blanchotte is a good, honest girl, and upright and steady in spite of her misfortune, and would make a worthy wife for an honest man."

"That is true," remarked the three others.

The smith continued:

"Is it the girl's fault if she went wrong? She had been promised marriage; and I know more than one who is much respected to-day, and who sinned every bit as much."

"That is true," responded the three men in chorus.

He resumed:

"How hard she has toiled, poor thing, to bring up her child all alone, and how she has wept all these years she has never gone out except to church, God only knows."

"This is also true," said the others.

Then nothing was heard but the bellows which fanned the fire of the furnace. Philip hastily bent himself down to Simon:

"Go and tell your mother that I am coming to speak to her this evening." Then he pushed the child out by the shoulders. He returned to his work, and with a single blow the five hammers again fell upon their anvils. Thus they wrought the iron until nightfall, strong, powerful, happy, like contented hammers. But just as the great bell of a cathedral resounds upon feast days above the jingling of the other bells, so Philip's hammer, sounding above the rest, clanged second after second with a deafening uproar. And he stood amid the flying sparks plying his trade vigorously.

The sky was full of stars as he knocked at La Blanchotte's door. He had on his Sunday blouse, a clean shirt, and his beard was trimmed. The young woman showed herself upon the threshold, and said in a grieved tone:

"It is ill to come thus when night has fallen, Mr. Philip."

He wished to answer, but stammered and stood confused before her.

She resumed:

"You understand, do you not, that it will not do for me to be talked about again."

"What does that matter to me, if you will be my wife!"

No voice replied to him, but he believed that he heard in the shadow of the room the sound of a falling body. He entered quickly; and Simon, who had gone to bed, distinguished the sound of a kiss and some words that his mother murmured softly. Then, all at once, he found himself lifted up by the hands of his friend, who, holding him at the length of his herculean arms, exclaimed:

"You will tell them, your schoolmates, that your papa is Philip Remy, the blacksmith, and that he will pull the ears of all who do you any harm."

On the morrow, when the school was full and lessons were about to begin, little Simon stood up, quite pale with trembling lips:

"My papa," said he in a clear voice, "is Philip Remy, the blacksmith, and he has promised to pull the ears of all who does me any harm."

This time no one laughed, for he was very well known, was Philip Remy, the blacksmith, and was a papa of whom any one in the world would have been proud.

VOLUME XII

THE CHILD

Lemonnier had remained a widower with one child. He had loved his wife devotedly, with a tender and exalted love, without a slip, during their entire married life. He was a good, honest man, perfectly simple, sincere, without suspicion or malice.

He fell in love with a poor neighbor, proposed and was accepted. He was making a very comfortable living out of the wholesale cloth business, and he did not for a minute suspect that the young girl might have accepted him for anything else but himself.

She made him happy. She was everything to him; he only thought of her, looked at her continually, with worshiping eyes. During meals he would make any number of blunders, in order not to have to take his eyes from the beloved face; he would pour the wine in his plate and the water in the salt-cellar, then he would laugh like a child, repeating:

"You see, I love you too much; that makes me crazy."

She would smile with a calm and resigned look; then she would look away, as though embarrassed by the adoration of her husband, and try to make him talk about something else; but he would take her hand under the table and he would hold it in his, whispering:

"My little Jeanne, my darling little Jeanne!"

She sometimes lost patience and said:

"Come, come, be reasonable; eat and let me eat."

He would sigh and break off a mouthful of bread, which he would then chew slowly.

For five years they had no children. Then suddenly she announced to him that this state of affairs would soon cease. He was wild with joy. He no longer left her for a minute, until his old nurse, who had brought him up and who often ruled the house, would push him out and close the door behind him, in order to compel him to go out in the fresh air.

He had grown very intimate with a young man who had known his wife since childhood, and who was one of the prefect's secretaries. M. Duretour would dine three times a week with the Lemonniers, bringing flowers to madame, and sometimes a box at the theater; and often, at the end of the dinner, Lemonnier, growing tender, turning towards his wife, would explain: "With a companion like you and a friend like him, a man is completely happy on earth."

She died in childbirth. The shock almost killed him. But the sight of the child, a poor, moaning little creature, gave him courage.

He loved it with a passionate and sorrowful love, with a morbid love in which stuck the memory of death, but in which lived something of his worship for the dead mother. It was the flesh of his wife, her being continued, a sort of quintessence of herself. This child was her very life transferred to another body; she had disappeared that it might exist, and the father would smother it in with kisses. But also, this child had killed her; he had stolen this beloved creature, his life was at the cost of hers. And M. Lemonnier would place his son in the cradle and would sit down and watch him. He would sit this way by the hour, looking at him, dreaming of thousands of things, sweet or sad. Then, when the little one was asleep, he would bend over him and sob.

The child grew. The father could no longer spend an hour away from him; he would stay near him, take him out for walks, and himself dress him, wash him, make him eat. His friend, M. Duretour, also seemed to love the boy; he would kiss him wildly, in those frenzies of tenderness which are characteristic of parents. He would toss him in his arms, he would trot him on his knees, by the hour, and M. Lemonnier, delighted, would mutter:

"Isn't he a darling? Isn't he a darling?"

And M. Duretour would hug the child in his arms and tickle his neck with his mustache.

Celeste, the old nurse, alone, seemed to have no tenderness for the little one. She would grow angry at his pranks, and seemed impatient at the caresses of the two men. She would exclaim:

"How can you expect to bring a child up like that? You'll make a perfect monkey out of him."

Years went by, and Jean was nine years old. He hardly knew how to read; he had been so spoiled, and only did as he saw fit. He was willful, stubborn and quick-tempered. The father always gave in to him and let him have his own way. M. Duretour would always buy him all the toys he wished, and he fed him on cake and candies. Then Celeste would grow angry and exclaim:

"It's a shame, monsieur, a shame. You are spoiling this child. But it will have to stop; yes, sir, I tell you it will have to stop, and before long, too."

M. Lemonnier would answer, smiling:

"What can you expect? I love him too much, I can't resist him; you must get used to it."

Jean was delicate, rather. The doctor said that he was anaemic, prescribed iron, rare meat and broth.

But the little fellow loved only cake and refused all other nourishment; and the father, in despair, stuffed him with cream-puffs and chocolate eclairs.

One evening, as they were sitting down to supper, Celeste brought on the soup with an air of authority and an assurance which she did not usually have. She took off the cover and, dipping the ladle into the dish, she declared:

"Here is some broth such as I have never made; the young one will have to take some this time."

M. Lemonnier, frightened, bent his head. He saw a storm brewing.

Celeste took his plate, filled it herself and placed it in front of him.

He tasted the soup and said:

"It is, indeed, excellent."

The servant took the boy's plate and poured a spoonful of soup in it. Then she retreated a few steps and waited.

Jean smelled the food and pushed his plate away with an expression of disgust. Celeste, suddenly pale, quickly stepped forward and forcibly poured a spoonful down the child's open mouth.

He choked, coughed, sneezed, spat; howling, he seized his glass and threw it at his nurse. She received it full in the stomach. Then, exasperated, she took the young shaver's head under her arm and began pouring spoonful after spoonful of soup down his throat. He grew as red as a beet, and he would cough it up, stamping, twisting, choking, beating the air with his hands.

At first the father was so surprised that he could not move. Then, suddenly, he rushed forward, wild with rage, seized the servant by the throat and threw her up against the wall stammering:

"Out! Out! Out! you brute!"

But she shook him off, and, her hair streaming down her back, her eyes snapping, she cried out:

"What's gettin' hold of you? You're trying to thrash me because I am making this child eat soup when you are filling him with sweet stuff!"

He kept repeating, trembling from head to foot:

"Out! Get out-get out, you brute!"

Then, wild, she turned to him and, pushing her face up against his, her voice trembling:

"Ah!—you think-you think that you can treat me like that? Oh! no. And for whom?—for that brat who is not even yours. No, not yours! No, not yours—not yours! Everybody knows it, except yourself! Ask the grocer, the butcher, the baker, all of them, any one of them!"

She was growling and mumbling, choked with passion; then she stopped and looked at him.

He was motionless livid, his arms hanging by his sides. After a short pause, he murmured in a faint, shaky voice, instinct with deep feeling:

"You say? you say? What do you say?"

She remained silent, frightened by his appearance. Once more he stepped forward, repeating:

"You say—what do you say?"

Then in a calm voice, she answered:

"I say what I know, what everybody knows."

He seized her and, with the fury of a beast, he tried to throw her down. But, although old, she was strong and nimble. She slipped under his arm, and running around the table once more furious, she screamed:

"Look at him, just look at him, fool that you are! Isn't he the living image of M. Durefour? just look at his nose and his eyes! Are yours like that? And his hair! Is it like his mother's? I tell you that everyone knows it, everyone except yourself! It's the joke of the town! Look at him!"

She went to the door, opened it, and disappeared.

Jean, frightened, sat motionless before his plate of soup.

At the end of an hour, she returned gently, to see how matters stood. The child, after doing away with all the cakes and a pitcher full of cream and one of syrup, was now emptying the jam-pot with his soup-spoon.

The father had gone out.

Celeste took the child, kissed him, and gently carried him to his room and put him to bed. She came back to the dining-room, cleared the table, put everything in place, feeling very uneasy all the time.

Not a single sound could be heard throughout the house. She put her ear against her master's door. He seemed to be perfectly still. She put her eye to the keyhole. He was writing, and seemed very calm.

Then she returned to the kitchen and sat down, ready for any emergency. She slept on a chair and awoke at daylight.

She did the rooms as she had been accustomed to every morning; she swept and dusted, and, towards eight o'clock, prepared M. Lemonnier's breakfast.

But she did not dare bring it to her master, knowing too well how she would be received; she waited for him to ring. But he did not ring. Nine o'clock, then ten o'clock went by.

Celeste, not knowing what to think, prepared her tray and started up with it, her heart beating fast.

She stopped before the door and listened. Everything was still. She knocked; no answer. Then, gathering up all her courage, she opened the door and entered. With a wild shriek, she dropped the breakfast tray which she had been holding in her hand.

In the middle of the room, M. Lemonnier was hanging by a rope from a ring in the ceiling. His tongue was sticking out horribly. His right slipper was lying on the ground, his left one still on his foot. An upturned chair had rolled over to the bed.

Celeste, dazed, ran away shrieking. All the neighbors crowded together. The physician declared that he had died at about midnight.

A letter addressed to M. Duretdur was found on the table of the suicide. It contained these words:

"I leave and entrust the child to you!"

A COUNTRY EXCURSION

For five months they had been talking of going to take luncheon in one of the country suburbs of Paris on Madame Dufour's birthday, and as they were looking forward very impatiently to the outing, they rose very early that morning. Monsieur Dufour had borrowed the milkman's wagon and drove himself. It was a very tidy, two-wheeled conveyance, with a cover supported by four iron rods, with curtains that had been drawn up, except the one at the back, which floated out like a sail. Madame Dufour, resplendent in a wonderful, cherry colored silk dress, sat by the side of her husband.

The old grandmother and a girl sat behind them on two chairs, and a boy with yellow hair was lying at the bottom of the wagon, with nothing to be seen of him except his head.

When they reached the bridge of Neuilly, Monsieur Dufour said: "Here we are in the country at last!" and at that signal his wife grew sentimental about the beauties of nature. When they got to the crossroads at Courbevoie they were seized with admiration for the distant landscape. On the right was Argenteuil with its bell tower, and above it rose the hills of Sannois and the mill of Orgemont, while on the left the aqueduct of Marly stood out against the clear morning sky, and in the distance they could see the terrace of Saint-Germain; and opposite them, at the end of a low chain of hills, the new fort of Cormeilles. Quite in the distance; a very long way off, beyond the plains and village, one could see the sombre green of the forests.

The sun was beginning to burn their faces, the dust got into their eyes, and on either side of the road there stretched an interminable tract of bare, ugly country with an unpleasant odor. One might have thought that it had been ravaged by a pestilence, which had even attacked the buildings, for skeletons of dilapidated and deserted houses, or small cottages, which were left in an unfinished state, because the contractors had not been paid, reared their four roofless walls on each side.

Here and there tall factory chimneys rose up from the barren soil. The only vegetation on that putrid land, where the spring breezes wafted an odor of petroleum and slate, blended with another odor that was even less agreeable. At last, however, they crossed the Seine a second time, and the bridge was a delight. The river sparkled in the sun, and they had a feeling of quiet enjoyment, felt refreshed as they drank in the purer air that was not impregnated by the black smoke of factories nor by the miasma from the deposits of night soil. A man whom they met told them that the name of the place was Bezons. Monsieur Dufour pulled up and read the attractive announcement outside an eating house: Restaurant Poulin, matelottes and fried fish, private rooms, arbors, and swings.

"Well, Madame Dufour, will this suit you? Will you make up your mind at last?"

She read the announcement in her turn and then looked at the house for some time.

It was a white country inn, built by the roadside, and through the open door she could see the bright zinc of the counter, at which sat two workmen in their Sunday clothes. At last she made up her mind and said:

"Yes, this will do; and, besides, there is a view."

They drove into a large field behind the inn, separated from the river by the towing path, and dismounted. The husband sprang out first and then held out his arms for his wife, and as the step was very high Madame Dufour, in order to reach him, had to show the lower part of her limbs, whose former slenderness had disappeared in fat, and Monsieur Dufour, who was already getting excited by the country air, pinched her calf, and then, taking her in his arms, he set her on the ground, as if she had been some enormous bundle.

She shook the dust out of the silk dress and then looked round to see in what sort of a place she was.

She was a stout woman, of about thirty-six, full-blown, and delightful to look at. She could hardly breathe, as her corsets were laced too tightly, and their pressure forced her superabundant bosom up to her double chin. Next the girl placed her hand on her father's shoulder and jumped down lightly. The boy with the yellow hair had got down by stepping on the wheel, and he helped Monsieur Dufour to lift his grandmother out. Then they unharnessed the horse, which they had tied to a tree, and the carriage fell back, with both shafts in the air. The men took off their coats and washed their hands in a pail of water and then went and joined the ladies, who had already taken possession of the swings.

Mademoiselle Dufour was trying to swing herself standing up, but she could not succeed in getting a start. She was a pretty girl of about eighteen, one of those women who suddenly excite your desire when you meet them in the street and who leave you with a vague feeling of uneasiness and of excited senses. She was tall, had a small waist and large hips, with a dark skin, very large eyes and very black hair. Her dress clearly marked the outlines of her firm, full figure, which was accentuated by the motion of her hips as she tried to swing herself higher. Her arms were stretched upward to hold the rope, so that her bosom rose at every movement she made. Her hat, which a gust of wind had blown off, was hanging behind her, and as the swing gradually rose higher and higher, she showed her delicate limbs up to the knees each time, and the breeze from her flying skirts, which was more heady than the fumes of wine, blew into the faces of the two men, who were looking at her and smiling.

Sitting in the other swing, Madame Dufour kept saying in a monotonous voice:

"Cyprian, come and swing me; do come and swing me, Cyprian!"

At last he went, and turning up his shirt sleeves, as if undertaking a hard piece of work, with much difficulty he set his wife in motion. She clutched the two ropes and held her legs out straight, so as not to touch the ground. She enjoyed feeling dizzy at the motion of the swing, and her whole figure shook like a jelly on a dish, but as she went higher and higher; she became too giddy and was frightened.

Each time the swing came down she uttered a piercing scream, which made all the little urchins in the neighborhood come round, and down below, beneath the garden hedge, she vaguely saw a row of mischievous heads making various grimaces as they laughed.

When a servant girl came out they ordered luncheon.

"Some fried fish, a rabbit saute, salad and dessert," Madame Dufour said, with an important air.

"Bring two quarts of beer and a bottle of claret," her husband said.

"We will have lunch on the grass," the girl added.

The grandmother, who had an affection for cats, had been running after one that belonged to the house, trying to coax it to come to her for the last ten minutes. The animal, who was no doubt secretly flattered by her attentions, kept close to the good woman, but just out of reach of her hand, and quietly walked round the trees, against which she rubbed herself, with her tail up, purring with pleasure.

"Hello!" suddenly exclaimed the young man with the yellow hair, who was wandering about. "Here are two swell boats!" They all went to look at them and saw two beautiful canoes in a wooden shed; they were as beautifully finished as if they had been ornamental furniture. They hung side by side, like two tall, slender girls, in their narrow shining length, and made one wish to float in them on warm summer mornings and evenings along the flower-covered banks of the river, where the trees dip their branches into the water, where the rushes are continually rustling in the breeze and where the swift kingfishers dart about like flashes of blue lightning.

The whole family looked at them with great respect.

"Oh, they are indeed swell boats!" Monsieur Dufour repeated gravely, as he examined them like a connoiseur. He had been in the habit of rowing in his younger days, he said, and when he had spat in his hands—and he went through the action of pulling the oars—he did not care a fig for anybody. He had beaten more than one Englishman formerly at the Joinville regattas. He grew quite excited at last and offered to make a bet that in a boat like that he could row six leagues an hour without exerting himself.

"Luncheon is ready," the waitress said, appearing at the entrance to the boathouse, and they all hurried off. But two young men had taken the very seats that Madame Dufour had selected and were eating their luncheon. No doubt they were the owners of the sculls, for they were in boating costume. They were stretched out, almost lying on the chairs; they were sun-browned and their thin cotton jerseys, with short sleeves, showed their bare arms, which were as strong as a blacksmith's. They were two strong, athletic fellows, who showed in all their movements that elasticity and grace of limb which can only be acquired by exercise and which is so different to the deformity with which monotonous heavy work stamps the mechanic.

They exchanged a rapid smile when they saw the mother and then a glance on seeing the daughter.

"Let us give up our place," one of them said; "it will make us acquainted with them."

The other got up immediately, and holding his black and red boating cap in his hand, he politely offered the ladies the only shady place in the garden. With many excuses they accepted, and that it might be more rural, they sat on the grass, without either tables or chairs.

The two young men took their plates, knives, forks, etc., to a table a little way off and began to eat again, and their bare arms, which they showed continually, rather embarrassed the girl. She even pretended to turn her head aside and not to see them, while Madame Dufour, who was rather bolder, tempted by feminine curiosity, looked at them every moment, and, no doubt, compared them with the secret unsightliness of her husband. She had squatted herself on ground, with her legs tucked under her, after the manner of tailors, and she kept moving about restlessly, saying that ants were crawling about her somewhere. Monsieur Dufour, annoyed at the presence of the polite strangers, was trying to find a comfortable position which he did not, however, succeed in doing, and the young man with the yellow hair was eating as silently as an ogre.

"It is lovely weather, monsieur," the stout lady said to one of the boating men. She wished to be friendly because they had given up their place.

"It is, indeed, madame," he replied. "Do you often go into the country?"

"Oh, only once or twice a year to get a little fresh air. And you, monsieur?"

"I come and sleep here every night."

"Oh, that must be very nice!"

"Certainly it is, madame." And he gave them such a practical account of his daily life that it awakened afresh in the hearts of these shopkeepers who were deprived of the meadows and who longed for country walks, to that foolish love of nature which they all feel so strongly the whole year round behind the counter in their shop.

The girl raised her eyes and looked at the oarsman with emotion and Monsieur Dufour spoke for the first time.

"It is indeed a happy life," he said. And then he added: "A little more rabbit, my dear?"

"No, thank you," she replied, and turning to the young men again, and pointing to their arms, asked: "Do you never feel cold like that?"

They both began to laugh, and they astonished the family with an account of the enormous fatigue they could endure, of their bathing while in a state of tremendous perspiration, of their rowing in the fog at night; and they struck their chests violently to show how hollow they sounded.

"Ah! You look very strong," said the husband, who did not talk any more of the time when he used to beat the English. The girl was looking at them sideways now, and the young fellow with the yellow hair, who had swallowed some wine the wrong way, was coughing violently and bespattering Madame Dufour's cherry-colored silk dress. She got angry and sent for some water to wash the spots.

Meanwhile it had grown unbearably hot, the sparkling river looked like a blaze of fire and the fumes of the wine were getting into their heads. Monsieur Dufour, who had a violent hiccough, had unbuttoned his waistcoat and the top button of his trousers, while his wife, who felt choking, was gradually unfastening her dress. The apprentice was shaking his yellow wig in a happy frame of mind, and kept helping himself to wine, and the old grandmother, feeling the effects of the wine, was very stiff and dignified. As for the girl, one noticed only a peculiar brightness in her eyes, while the brown cheeks became more rosy.

The coffee finished, they suggested singing, and each of them sang or repeated a couplet, which the others applauded frantically. Then they got up with some difficulty, and while the two women, who were rather dizzy, were trying to get a breath of air, the two men, who were altogether drunk, were attempting gymnastics. Heavy, limp and with scarlet faces they hung or, awkwardly to the iron rings, without being able to raise themselves.

Meanwhile the two boating men had got their boats into the water, and they came back and politely asked the ladies whether they would like a row.

"Would you like one, Monsieur Dufour?" his wife exclaimed. "Please come!"

He merely gave her a drunken nod, without understanding what she said. Then one of the rowers came up with two fishing rods in his hands, and the hope of catching a gudgeon, that great vision of the Parisian shopkeeper, made Dufour's dull eyes gleam, and he politely allowed them to do whatever they liked, while he sat in the shade under the bridge, with his feet dangling over the river, by the side of the young man with the yellow hair, who was sleeping soundly.

One of the boating men made a martyr of himself and took the mother.

"Let us go to the little wood on the Ile aux Anglais!" he called out as he rowed off. The other boat went more slowly, for the rower was looking at his companion so intently that he thought of nothing else, and his emotion seemed to paralyze his strength, while the girl, who was sitting in the bow, gave herself up to the enjoyment of being on the water. She felt a disinclination to think, a lassitude in her limbs and a total enervation, as if she were intoxicated, and her face was flushed and her breathing quickened. The effects of the wine, which were increased by the extreme heat, made all the trees on the bank seem to bow as she passed. A vague wish for enjoyment and a fermentation of her blood seemed to pervade her whole body, which was excited by the heat of the day, and she was also disturbed at this tete-a-tete on the water, in a place which seemed depopulated by the heat, with this young man who thought her pretty, whose ardent looks seemed to caress her skin and were as penetrating and pervading as the sun's rays.

Their inability to speak increased their emotion, and they looked about them. At last, however, he made an effort and asked her name.

"Henriette," she said.

"Why, my name is Henri," he replied. The sound of their voices had calmed them, and they looked at the banks. The other boat had passed them and seemed to be waiting for them, and the rower called out:

"We will meet you in the wood; we are going as far as Robinson's, because Madame Dufour is thirsty." Then he bent over his oars again and rowed off so quickly that he was soon out of sight.

Meanwhile a continual roar, which they had heard for some time, came nearer, and the river itself seemed to shiver, as if the dull noise were rising from its depths.

"What is that noise?" she asked. It was the noise of the weir which cut the river in two at the island, and he was explaining it to her, when, above the noise of the waterfall, they heard the song of a bird, which seemed a long way off.

"Listen!" he said; "the nightingales are singing during the day, so the female birds must be sitting."

A nightingale! She had never heard one before, and the idea of listening to one roused visions of poetic tenderness in her heart. A nightingale! That is to say, the invisible witness of her love trysts which Juliet invoked on her balcony; that celestial music which it attuned to human kisses, that eternal inspirer of all those languorous romances which open an ideal sky to all the poor little tender hearts of sensitive girls!

She was going to hear a nightingale.

"We must not make a noise," her companion said, "and then we can go into the wood, and sit down close beside it."

The boat seemed to glide. They saw the trees on the island, the banks of which were so low that they could look into the depths of the thickets. They stopped, he made the boat fast, Henriette took hold of Henri's arm, and they went beneath the trees.

"Stoop," he said, so she stooped down, and they went into an inextricable thicket of creepers, leaves and reed grass, which formed an undiscoverable retreat, and which the young man laughingly called "his private room."

Just above their heads, perched in one of the trees which hid them, the bird was still singing. He uttered trills and roulades, and then loud, vibrating notes that filled the air and seemed to lose themselves on the horizon, across the level country, through that burning silence which weighed upon the whole landscape. They did not speak for fear of frightening it away. They were sitting close together, and, slowly, Henri's arm stole round the girl's waist and squeezed it gently. She took that daring hand without any anger, and kept removing it whenever he put it round her; without, however, feeling at all embarrassed by this caress, just as if it had been something quite natural, which she was resisting just as naturally.

She was listening to the bird in ecstasy. She felt an infinite longing for happiness, for some sudden demonstration of tenderness, for the revelation of superhuman poetry, and she felt such a softening at her heart, and relaxation of her nerves, that she began to cry, without knowing why. The young man was now straining her close to him, yet she did not remove his arm; she did not think of it. Suddenly the nightingale stopped, and a voice called out in the distance:

"Henriette!"

"Do not reply," he said in a low voice; "you will drive the bird away."

But she had no idea of doing so, and they remained in the same position for some time. Madame Dufour had sat down somewhere or other, for from time to time they heard the stout lady break out into little bursts of laughter.

The girl was still crying; she was filled with strange sensations. Henri's head was on her shoulder, and suddenly he kissed her on the lips. She was surprised and angry, and, to avoid him, she stood up.

They were both very pale when they left their grassy retreat. The blue sky appeared to them clouded and the ardent sun darkened; and they felt the solitude and the silence. They walked rapidly, side by side, without speaking or touching each other, for they seemed to have become irreconcilable enemies, as if disgust and hatred had arisen between them, and from time to time Henriette called out: "Mamma!"

By and by they heard a noise behind a bush, and the stout lady appeared, looking rather confused, and her companion's face was wrinkled with smiles which he could not check.

Madame Dufour took his arm, and they returned to the boats, and Henri, who was ahead, walked in silence beside the young girl.

At last they got back to Bezons. Monsieur Dufour, who was now sober, was waiting for them very impatiently, while the young man with the yellow hair was having a mouthful of something to eat before leaving the inn. The carriage was waiting in the yard, and the grandmother, who had already got in, was very frightened at the thought of being overtaken by night before they reached Paris, as the outskirts were not safe.

They all shook bands, and the Dufour family drove off.

"Good-by, until we meet again!" the oarsmen cried, and the answer they got was a sigh and a tear.

Two months later, as Henri was going along the Rue des Martyrs, he saw Dufour, Ironmonger, over a door, and so he went in, and saw the stout lady sitting at the counter. They recognized each other immediately, and after an interchange of polite greetings, he asked after them all.

"And how is Mademoiselle Henriette?" he inquired specially.

"Very well, thank you; she is married."

"Ah!" He felt a certain emotion, but said: "Whom did she marry?"

"That young man who accompanied us, you know; he has joined us in business."

"I remember him perfectly."

He was going out, feeling very unhappy, though scarcely knowing why, when madame called him back.

"And how is your friend?" she asked rather shyly.

"He is very well, thank you."

"Please give him our compliments, and beg him to come and call, when he is in the neighborhood."

She then added: "Tell him it will give me great pleasure."

"I will be sure to do so. Adieu!"

"Do not say that; come again very soon."

The next year, one very hot Sunday, all the details of that adventure, which Henri had never forgotten, suddenly came back to him so clearly that he returned alone to their room in the wood, and was overwhelmed with astonishment when he went in. She was sitting on the grass, looking very sad, while by her side, still in his shirt sleeves, the young man with the yellow hair was sleeping soundly, like some animal.

She grew so pale when she saw Henri that at first he thought she was going to faint; then, however, they began to talk quite naturally. But when he told her that he was very fond of that spot, and went there frequently on Sundays to indulge in memories, she looked into his eyes for a long time.

"I too, think of it," she replied.

"Come, my dear," her husband said, with a yawn. "I think it is time for us to be going."

ROSE

The two young women appear to be buried under a blanket of flowers. They are alone in the immense landau, which is filled with flowers like a giant basket. On the front seat are two small hampers of white satin filled with violets, and on the bearskin by which their knees are covered there is a mass of roses, mimosas, pinks, daisies, tuberoses and orange blossoms, interwoven with silk ribbons; the two frail bodies seem buried under this beautiful perfumed bed, which hides everything but the shoulders and arms and a little of the dainty waists.

The coachman's whip is wound with a garland of anemones, the horses' traces are dotted with carnations, the spokes of the wheels are clothed in mignonette, and where the lanterns ought to be are two enormous round bouquets which look as though they were the eyes of this strange, rolling, flower-bedecked creature.

The landau drives rapidly along the road, through the Rue d'Antibes, preceded, followed, accompanied, by a crowd of other carriages covered with flowers, full of women almost hidden by a sea of violets. It is the flower carnival at Cannes.

The carriage reaches the Boulevard de la Fonciere, where the battle is waged. All along the immense avenue a double row of flower-bedecked vehicles are going and coming like an endless ribbon. Flowers are thrown from one to the other. They pass through the air like balls, striking fresh faces, bouncing and falling into the dust, where an army of youngsters pick them up.

A thick crowd is standing on the sidewalks looking on and held in check by the mounted police, who pass brutally along pushing back the curious pedestrians as though to prevent the common people from mingling with the rich.

In the carriages, people call to each other, recognize each other and bombard each other with roses. A chariot full of pretty women, dressed in red, like devils, attracts the eyes of all. A gentleman, who looks like the portraits of Henry IV., is throwing an immense bouquet which is held back by an elastic. Fearing the shock, the women hide their eyes and the men lower their heads, but the graceful, rapid and obedient missile describes a curve and returns to its master, who immediately throws it at some new face.

The two young women begin to throw their stock of flowers by handfuls, and receive a perfect hail of bouquets; then, after an hour of warfare, a little tired, they tell the coachman to drive along the road which follows the seashore.

The sun disappears behind Esterel, outlining the dark, rugged mountain against the sunset sky. The clear blue sea, as calm as a mill-pond, stretches out as far as the horizon, where it blends with the sky; and the fleet, anchored in the middle of the bay, looks like a herd of enormous beasts, motionless on the water, apocalyptic animals, armored and hump-backed, their frail masts looking like feathers, and with eyes which light up when evening approaches.

The two young women, leaning back under the heavy robes, look out lazily over the blue expanse of water. At last one of them says:

"How delightful the evenings are! How good everything seems! Don't you think so, Margot?"

"Yes, it is good. But there is always something lacking."

"What is lacking? I feel perfectly happy. I don't need anything else."

"Yes, you do. You are not thinking of it. No matter how contented we may be, physically, we always long for something more—for the heart."

The other asked with a smile:

"A little love?"

"Yes."

They stopped talking, their eyes fastened on the distant horizon, then the one called Marguerite murmured: "Life without that seems to me unbearable. I need to be loved, if only by a dog. But we are all alike, no matter what you may say, Simone."

"Not at all, my dear. I had rather not be loved at all than to be loved by the first comer. Do you think, for instance, that it would be pleasant to be loved by—by—"

She was thinking by whom she might possibly be loved, glancing across the wide landscape. Her eyes, after traveling around the horizon, fell on the two bright buttons which were shining on the back of the coachman's livery, and she continued, laughing: "by my coachman?"

Madame Margot barely smiled, and said in a low tone of voice:

"I assure you that it is very amusing to be loved by a servant. It has happened to me two or three times. They roll their eyes in such a funny manner—it's enough to make you die laughing! Naturally, the more in love they are, the more severe one must be with them, and then, some day, for some reason, you dismiss them, because, if anyone should notice it, you would appear so ridiculous."

Madame Simone was listening, staring straight ahead of her, then she remarked:

"No, I'm afraid that my footman's heart would not satisfy me. Tell me how you noticed that they loved you."

"I noticed it the same way that I do with other men—when they get stupid."

"The others don't seem stupid to me, when they love me."

"They are idiots, my dear, unable to talk, to answer, to understand anything."

"But how did you feel when you were loved by a servant? Were you—moved—flattered?"

"Moved? no, flattered—yes a little. One is always flattered to be loved by a man, no matter who he may be."

"Oh, Margot!"

"Yes, indeed, my dear! For instance, I will tell you of a peculiar incident which happened to me. You will see how curious and complex our emotions are, in such cases.

"About four years ago I happened to be without a maid. I had tried five or six, one right after the other, and I was about ready to give up in despair, when I saw an advertisement in a newspaper of a young girl knowing how to cook, embroider, dress hair, who was looking for a position and who could furnish the best of references. Besides all these accomplishments, she could speak English.

"I wrote to the given address, and the next day the person in question presented herself. She was tall, slender, pale, shy-looking. She had beautiful black eyes and a charming complexion; she pleased me immediately. I asked for her certificates; she gave me one in English, for she came, as she said, from Lady Rymwell's, where she had been for ten years.

"The certificate showed that the young girl had left of her own free will, in order to return to France, and the only thing which they had had to find fault in her during her long period of service was a little French coquettishness.

"This prudish English phrase even made me smile, and I immediately engaged this maid.

"She came to me the same day. Her name was Rose.

"At the end of a month I would have been helpless without her. She was a treasure, a pearl, a phenomenon.

"She could dress my hair with infinite taste; she could trim a hat better than most milliners, and she could even make my dresses.

"I was astonished at her accomplishments. I had never before been waited on in such a manner.

"She dressed me rapidly and with a surprisingly light touch. I never felt her fingers on my skin, and nothing is so disagreeable to me as contact with a servant's hand. I soon became excessively lazy; it was so pleasant to be dressed from head to foot, and from lingerie to gloves, by this tall, timid girl, always blushing a little, and never saying a word. After my bath she would rub and massage me while I dozed a little on my couch; I almost considered her more of a friend than a servant.

"One morning the janitor asked, mysteriously, to speak to me. I was surprised, and told him to come in. He was a good, faithful man, an old soldier, one of my husband's former orderlies.

"He seemed to be embarrassed by what he had to say to me. At last he managed to mumble:

"'Madame, the superintendent of police is downstairs.'

"I asked quickly:

"'What does he wish?'

"'He wishes to search the house.'

"Of course the police are useful, but I hate them. I do not think that it is a noble profession. I answered, angered and hurt:

"'Why this search? For what reason? He shall not come in.'

"The janitor continued:

"'He says that there is a criminal hidden in the house.'

"This time I was frightened and I told him to bring the inspector to me, so that I might get some explanation. He was a man with good manners and decorated with the Legion of Honor. He begged my pardon for disturbing me, and then informed me that I had, among my domestics, a convict.

"I was shocked; and I answered that I could guarantee every servant in the house, and I began to enumerate them.

"'The janitor, Pierre Courtin, an old soldier.'

"'It's not he.'

"'A stable-boy, son of farmers whom I know, and a groom whom you have just seen.'

"'It's not he.'

"'Then, monsieur, you see that you must be mistaken.'

"'Excuse me, madame, but I am positive that I am not making a mistake.

"As the conviction of a notable criminal is at stake, would you be so kind as to send for all your servants?"

"At first I refused, but I finally gave in, and sent downstairs for everybody, men and women.

"The inspector glanced at them and then declared:

"'This isn't all.'

"'Excuse me, monsieur, there is no one left but my maid, a young girl whom you could not possibly mistake for a convict.'

"He asked:

"'May I also see her?'

"'Certainly.'

"I rang for Rose, who immediately appeared. She had hardly entered the room, when the inspector made a motion, and two men whom I had not seen, hidden behind the door, sprang forward, seized her and tied her hands behind her back.

"I cried out in anger and tried to rush forward to defend her. The inspector stopped me:

"'This girl, madame, is a man whose name is Jean Nicolas Lecapet, condemned to death in 1879 for assaulting a woman and injuring her so that death resulted. His sentence was commuted to imprisonment for life. He escaped four months ago. We have been looking for him ever since.'

"I was terrified, bewildered. I did not believe him. The commissioner continued, laughing:

"'I can prove it to you. His right arm is tattooed.'

"'The sleeve was rolled up. It was true. The inspector added, with bad taste:

"'You can trust us for the other proofs.'

"And they led my maid away!

"Well, would you believe me, the thing that moved me most was not anger at having thus been played upon, deceived and made ridiculous, it was not the shame of having thus been dressed and undressed, handled and touched by this man—but a deep humiliation—a woman's humiliation. Do you understand?"

"I am afraid I don't."

"Just think—this man had been condemned for—for assaulting a woman. Well! I thought of the one whom he had assaulted—and—and I felt humiliated—There! Do you understand now?"

Madame Margot did not answer. She was looking straight ahead, her eyes fastened on the two shining buttons of the livery, with that sphinx-like smile which women sometimes have.

ROSALIE PRUDENT

There was a real mystery in this affair which neither the jury, nor the president, nor the public prosecutor himself could understand.

The girl Prudent (Rosalie), servant at the Varambots', of Nantes, having become enceinte without the knowledge of her masters, had, during the night, killed and buried her child in the garden.

It was the usual story of the infanticides committed by servant girls. But there was one inexplicable circumstance about this one. When the police searched the girl Prudent's room they discovered a complete infant's outfit, made by Rosalie herself, who had spent her nights for the last three months in cutting and sewing it. The grocer from whom she had bought her candles, out of her own wages, for this long piece of work had come to testify. It came out, moreover, that the sage-femme of the district, informed by Rosalie of her condition, had given her all necessary instructions and counsel in case the event should happen at a time when it might not be possible to get help. She had also procured a place at Poissy for the girl Prudent, who foresaw that her present employers would discharge her, for the Varambot couple did not trifle with morality.

There were present at the trial both the man and the woman, a middle-class pair from the provinces, living on their income. They were so exasperated against this girl, who had sullied their house, that they would have liked to see her guillotined on the spot without a trial. The spiteful depositions they made against her became accusations in their mouths.

The defendant, a large, handsome girl of Lower Normandy, well educated for her station in life, wept continuously and would not answer to anything.

The court and the spectators were forced to the opinion that she had committed this barbarous act in a moment of despair and madness, since there was every indication that she had expected to keep and bring up her child.

The president tried for the last time to make her speak, to get some confession, and, having urged her with much gentleness, he finally made her understand that all these men gathered here to pass judgment upon her were not anxious for her death and might even have pity on her.

Then she made up her mind to speak.

"Come, now, tell us, first, who is the father of this child?" he asked.

Until then she had obstinately refused to give his name.

But she replied suddenly, looking at her masters who had so cruelly calumniated her:

"It is Monsieur Joseph, Monsieur Varambot's nephew."

The couple started in their seats and cried with one voice—"That's not true! She lies! This is infamous!"

The president had them silenced and continued, "Go on, please, and tell us how it all happened."

Then she suddenly began to talk freely, relieving her pent-up heart, that poor, solitary, crushed heart—laying bare her sorrow, her whole sorrow, before those severe men whom she had until now taken for enemies and inflexible judges.

"Yes, it was Monsieur Joseph Varambot, when he came on leave last year."

"What does Mr. Joseph Varambot do?"

"He is a non-commissioned officer in the artillery, monsieur. Well, he stayed two months at the house, two months of the summer. I thought nothing about it when he began to look at me, and then flatter me, and make love to me all day long. And I let myself be taken in, monsieur. He kept saying to me that I was a handsome girl, that I was good company, that I just suited him—and I, I liked him well enough. What could I do? One listens to these things when one is alone—all alone—as I was. I am alone in the world, monsieur. I have no one to talk to—no one to tell my troubles to. I have no father, no mother, no brother, no sister, nobody. And when he began to talk to me it was as if I had a brother who had come back. And then he asked me to go with him to the river one evening, so that we might talk without disturbing any one. I went—I don't know—I don't know how it happened. He had his arm around me. Really I didn't want to—no—no—I could not—I felt like crying, the air was so soft —the moon was shining. No, I swear to you—I could not—he did what he wanted. That went on three weeks, as long as he stayed. I could have followed him to the ends of the world. He went away. I did not know that I was enceinte. I did not know it until the month after—"

She began to cry so bitterly that they had to give her time to collect herself.

Then the president resumed with the tone of a priest at the confessional: "Come, now, go on."

She began to talk again: "When I realized my condition I went to see Madame Boudin, who is there to tell you, and I asked her how it would be, in case it should come if she were not there. Then I made the outfit, sewing night after night, every evening until one o'clock in the morning; and then I looked for another place, for I knew very well that I should be sent away, but I wanted to stay in the house until the very last, so as to save my pennies, for I have not got very much and I should need my money for the little one."

"Then you did not intend to kill him?"

"Oh, certainly not, monsieur!"

"Why did you kill him, then?"

"It happened this way. It came sooner than I expected. It came upon me in the kitchen, while I was doing the dishes. Monsieur and Madame Varambot were already asleep, so I went up, not without difficulty, dragging myself up by the banister, and I lay down on the bare floor. It lasted perhaps one hour, or two, or three; I don't know, I had such pain; and then I pushed him out with all my strength. I felt that he came out and I picked him up.

"Ah! but I was glad, I assure you! I did all that Madame Boudin told me to do. And then I laid him on my bed. And then such a pain griped me again that I thought I should die. If you knew what it meant, you there, you would not do so much of this. I fell on my knees, and then toppled over backward on the floor; and it griped me again, perhaps one hour, perhaps two. I lay there all alone—

and then another one comes—another little one—two, yes, two, like this. I took him up as I did the first one, and then I put him on the bed, the two side by side. Is it possible, tell me, two children, and I who get only twenty francs a month? Say, is it possible? One, yes, that can be managed by going without things, but not two. That turned my head. What do I know about it? Had I any choice, tell me?

"What could I do? I felt as if my last hour had come. I put the pillow over them, without knowing why. I could not keep them both; and then I threw myself down, and I lay there, rolling over and over and crying until I saw the daylight come into the window. Both of them were quite dead under the pillow. Then I took them under my arms and went down the stairs out in the vegetable garden. I took the gardener's spade and I buried them under the earth, digging as deep a hole as I could, one here and the other one there, not together, so that they might not talk of their mother if these little dead bodies can talk. What do I know about it?

"And then, back in my bed, I felt so sick that I could not get up. They sent for the doctor and he understood it all. I'm telling you the truth, Your Honor. Do what you like with me; I'm ready."

Half of the jury were blowing their noses violently to keep from crying. The women in the courtroom were sobbing.

The president asked her:

"Where did you bury the other one?"

"The one that you have?" she asked.

"Why, this one—this one was in the artichokes."

"Oh, then the other one is among the strawberries, by the well."

And she began to sob so piteously that no one could hear her unmoved.

The girl Rosalie Prudent was acquitted.

REGRET

Monsieur Saval, who was called in Mantes "Father Saval," had just risen from bed. He was weeping. It was a dull autumn day; the leaves were falling. They fell slowly in the rain, like a heavier and slower rain. M. Saval was not in good spirits. He walked from the fireplace to the window, and from the window to the fireplace. Life has its sombre days. It would no longer have any but sombre days for him, for he had reached the age of sixty-two. He is alone, an old bachelor, with nobody about him. How sad it is to die alone, all alone, without any one who is devoted to you!

He pondered over his life, so barren, so empty. He recalled former days, the days of his childhood, the home, the house of his parents; his college days, his follies; the time he studied law in Paris, his father's illness, his death. He then returned to live with his mother. They lived together very quietly, and desired nothing more. At last the mother died. How sad life is! He lived alone since then, and now, in his turn, he, too, will soon be dead. He will disappear, and that will be the end. There will be no more of Paul Saval upon the earth. What a frightful thing! Other people will love, will laugh. Yes, people will go on amusing themselves, and he will no longer exist! Is it not strange that people can laugh, amuse themselves, be joyful under that eternal certainty of death? If this death were only probable, one could then have hope; but no, it is inevitable, as inevitable as that night follows the day.

If, however, his life had been full! If he had done something; if he had had adventures, great pleasures, success, satisfaction of some kind or another. But no, nothing. He had done nothing, nothing but rise from bed, eat, at the same hours, and go to bed again. And he had gone on like that to the age of sixty-two years. He had not even taken unto himself a wife, as other men do. Why? Yes, why was it that he had not married? He might have done so, for he possessed considerable means. Had he lacked an opportunity? Perhaps! But one can create opportunities. He was indifferent; that was all. Indifference had been his greatest drawback, his defect, his vice. How many men wreck their lives through indifference! It is so difficult for some natures to get out of bed, to move about, to take long walks, to speak, to study any question.

He had not even been loved. No woman had reposed on his bosom, in a complete abandon of love. He knew nothing of the delicious anguish of expectation, the divine vibration of a hand in yours, of the ecstasy of triumphant passion.

What superhuman happiness must overflow your heart, when lips encounter lips for the first time, when the grasp of four arms makes one being of you, a being unutterably happy, two beings infatuated with one another.

M. Saval was sitting before the fire, his feet on the fender, in his dressing gown. Assuredly his life had been spoiled, completely spoiled. He had, however, loved. He had loved secretly, sadly, and indifferently, in a manner characteristic of him in everything. Yes, he had loved his old friend, Madame Sandres, the wife of his old companion, Sandres. Ah! if he had known her as a young girl! But he had met her too late; she was already married. Unquestionably, he would have asked her hand! How he had loved her, nevertheless, without respite, since the first day he set eyes on her!

He recalled his emotion every time he saw her, his grief on leaving her, the many nights that he could not sleep, because he was thinking of her.

On rising in the morning he was somewhat more rational than on the previous evening.

Why?

How pretty she was formerly, so dainty, with fair curly hair, and always laughing. Sandres was not the man she should have chosen. She was now fifty-two years of age. She seemed happy. Ah! if she had only loved him in days gone by; yes, if she had only loved him!

And why should she not have loved him, he, Saval, seeing that he loved her so much, yes, she, Madame Sandres!

If only she could have guessed. Had she not guessed anything, seen anything, comprehended anything? What would she have thought? If he had spoken, what would she have answered?

And Saval asked himself a thousand other things. He reviewed his whole life, seeking to recall a multitude of details.

He recalled all the long evenings spent at the house of Sandres, when the latter's wife was young, and so charming.

He recalled many things that she had said to him, the intonations of her voice, the little significant smiles that meant so much.

He recalled their walks, the three of them together, along the banks of the Seine, their luncheon on the grass on Sundays, for Sandres was employed at the sub-prefecture. And all at once the distinct recollection came to him of an afternoon spent with her in a little wood on the banks of the river.

They had set out in the morning, carrying their provisions in baskets. It was a bright spring morning, one of those days which intoxicate one. Everything smells fresh, everything seems happy. The voices of the birds sound more joyous, and they fly more swiftly. They had luncheon on the grass, under the willow trees, quite close to the water, which glittered in the sun's rays. The air was balmy, charged with the odors of fresh vegetation; they drank it in with delight. How pleasant everything was on that day!

After lunch, Sandres went to sleep on the broad of his back. "The best nap he had in his life," said he, when he woke up.

Madame Sandres had taken the arm of Saval, and they started to walk along the river bank.

She leaned tenderly on his arm. She laughed and said to him: "I am intoxicated, my friend, I am quite intoxicated." He looked at her, his heart going pit-a-pat. He felt himself grow pale, fearful that he might have looked too boldly at her, and that the trembling of his hand had revealed his passion.

She had made a wreath of wild flowers and water-lilies, and she asked him: "Do I look pretty like that?"

As he did not answer—for he could find nothing to say, he would have liked to go down on his knees—she burst out laughing, a sort of annoyed, displeased laugh, as she said: "Great goose, what ails you? You might at least say something."

He felt like crying, but could not even yet find a word to say.

All these things came back to him now, as vividly as on the day when they took place. Why had she said this to him, "Great goose, what ails you? You might at least say something!"

And he recalled how tenderly she had leaned on his arm. And in passing under a shady tree he had felt her ear brushing his cheek, and he had moved his head abruptly, lest she should suppose he was too familiar.

When he had said to her: "Is it not time to return?" she darted a singular look at him. "Certainly," she said, "certainly," regarding him at the same time in a curious manner. He had not thought of it at the time, but now the whole thing appeared to him quite plain.

"Just as you like, my friend. If you are tired let us go back."

And he had answered: "I am not fatigued; but Sandres may be awake now."

And she had said: "If you are afraid of my husband's being awake, that is another thing. Let us return."

On their way back she remained silent, and leaned no longer on his arm. Why?

At that time it had never occurred to him, to ask himself "why." Now he seemed to apprehend something that he had not then understood.

Could it?

M. Saval felt himself blush, and he got up at a bound, as if he were thirty years younger and had heard Madame Sandres say, "I love you."

Was it possible? That idea which had just entered his mind tortured him. Was it possible that he had not seen, had not guessed?

Oh! if that were true, if he had let this opportunity of happiness pass without taking advantage of it!

He said to himself: "I must know. I cannot remain in this state of doubt. I must know!" He thought: "I am sixty-two years of age, she is fifty-eight; I may ask her that now without giving offense."

He started out.

The Sandres' house was situated on the other side of the street, almost directly opposite his own. He went across and knocked at the door, and a little servant opened it.

"You here at this hour, Saval! Has some accident happened to you?"

"No, my girl," he replied; "but go and tell your mistress that I want to speak to her at once."

"The fact is madame is preserving pears for the winter, and she is in the preserving room. She is not dressed, you understand."

"Yes, but go and tell her that I wish to see her on a very important matter."

The little servant went away, and Saval began to walk, with long, nervous strides, up and down the drawing-room. He did not feel in the least embarrassed, however. Oh! he was merely going to ask her something, as he would have asked her about some cooking recipe. He was sixty-two years of age!

The door opened and madame appeared. She was now a large woman, fat and round, with full cheeks and a sonorous laugh. She walked with her arms away from her sides and her sleeves tucked up, her bare arms all covered with fruit juice. She asked anxiously: "What is the matter with you, my friend? You are not ill, are you?"

"No, my dear friend; but I wish to ask you one thing, which to me is of the first importance, something which is torturing my heart, and I want you to promise that you will answer me frankly."

She laughed, "I am always frank. Say on."

"Well, then. I have loved you from the first day I ever saw you. Can you have any doubt of this?"

She responded, laughing, with something of her former tone of voice.

"Great goose! what ails you? I knew it from the very first day!"

Saval began to tremble. He stammered out: "You knew it? Then ..."

He stopped.

She asked:

"Then?"

He answered:

"Then—what did you think? What—what—what would you have answered?"

She broke into a peal of laughter. Some of the juice ran off the tips of her fingers on to the carpet.

"What?"

"I? Why, you did not ask me anything. It was not for me to declare myself!"

He then advanced a step toward her.

"Tell me—tell me … . You remember the day when Sandres went to sleep on the grass after lunch … when we had walked together as far as the bend of the river, below …"

He waited, expectantly. She had ceased to laugh, and looked at him, straight in the eyes.

"Yes, certainly, I remember it."

He answered, trembling all over:

"Well—that day—if I had been—if I had been—venturesome—what would you have done?"

She began to laugh as only a happy woman can laugh, who has nothing to regret, and responded frankly, in a clear voice tinged with irony:

"I would have yielded, my friend."

She then turned on her heels and went back to her jam-making.

Saval rushed into the street, cast down, as though he had met with some disaster. He walked with giant strides through the rain, straight on, until he reached the river bank, without thinking where he was going. He then turned to the right and followed the river. He walked a long time, as if urged on by some instinct. His clothes were running with water, his hat was out of shape, as soft as a rag, and dripping like a roof. He walked on, straight in front of him. At last, he came to the place where they had lunched on that day so long ago, the recollection of which tortured his heart. He sat down under the leafless trees, and wept.

A SISTER'S CONFESSION

Marguerite de Therelles was dying. Although she was only fifty-six years old she looked at least seventy-five. She gasped for breath, her face whiter than the sheets, and had spasms of violent shivering, with her face convulsed and her eyes haggard as though she saw a frightful vision.

Her elder sister, Suzanne, six years older than herself, was sobbing on her knees beside the bed. A small table close to the dying woman's couch bore, on a white cloth, two lighted candles, for the priest was expected at any moment to administer extreme unction and the last communion.

The apartment wore that melancholy aspect common to death chambers; a look of despairing farewell. Medicine bottles littered the furniture; linen lay in the corners into which it had been kicked or swept. The very chairs looked, in their disarray, as if they were terrified and had run in all directions. Death—terrible Death—was in the room, hidden, awaiting his prey.

This history of the two sisters was an affecting one. It was spoken of far and wide; it had drawn tears from many eyes.

Suzanne, the elder, had once been passionately loved by a young man, whose affection she returned. They were engaged to be married, and the wedding day was at hand, when Henry de Sampierre suddenly died.

The young girl's despair was terrible, and she took an oath never to marry. She faithfully kept her vow and adopted widow's weeds for the remainder of her life.

But one morning her sister, her little sister Marguerite, then only twelve years old, threw herself into Suzanne's arms, sobbing: "Sister, I don't want you to be unhappy. I don't want you to mourn all your life. I'll never leave you—never, never, never! I shall never marry, either. I'll stay with you always—always!"

Suzanne kissed her, touched by the child's devotion, though not putting any faith in her promise.

But the little one kept her word, and, despite her parents' remonstrances, despite her elder sister's prayers, never married. She was remarkably pretty and refused many offers. She never left her sister.

They spent their whole life together, without a single day's separation. They went everywhere together and were inseparable. But Marguerite was pensive, melancholy, sadder than her sister, as if her sublime sacrifice had undermined her spirits. She grew older more quickly; her hair was white at thirty; and she was often ill, apparently stricken with some unknown, wasting malady.

And now she would be the first to die.

She had not spoken for twenty-four hours, except to whisper at daybreak:

"Send at once for the priest."

And she had since remained lying on her back, convulsed with agony, her lips moving as if unable to utter the dreadful words that rose in her heart, her face expressive of a terror distressing to witness.

Suzanne, distracted with grief, her brow pressed against the bed, wept bitterly, repeating over and over again the words:

"Margot, my poor Margot, my little one!"

She had always called her "my little one," while Marguerite's name for the elder was invariably "sister."

A footstep sounded on the stairs. The door opened. An acolyte appeared, followed by the aged priest in his surplice. As soon as she saw him the dying woman sat up suddenly in bed, opened her lips, stammered a few words and began to scratch the bed-clothes, as if she would have made hole in them.

Father Simon approached, took her hand, kissed her on the forehead and said in a gentle voice:

"May God pardon your sins, my daughter. Be of good courage. Now is the moment to confess them—speak!"

Then Marguerite, shuddering from head to foot, so that the very bed shook with her nervous movements, gasped:

"Sit down, sister, and listen."

The priest stooped toward the prostrate Suzanne, raised her to her feet, placed her in a chair, and, taking a hand of each of the sisters, pronounced:

"Lord God! Send them strength! Shed Thy mercy upon them."

And Marguerite began to speak. The words issued from her lips one by one—hoarse, jerky, tremulous.

"Pardon, pardon, sister! pardon me! Oh, if only you knew how I have dreaded this moment all my life!"

Suzanne faltered through her tears:

"But what have I to pardon, little one? You have given me everything, sacrificed all to me. You are an angel."

But Marguerite interrupted her:

"Be silent, be silent! Let me speak! Don't stop me! It is terrible. Let me tell all, to the very end, without interruption. Listen. You remember—you remember—Henry—"

Suzanne trembled and looked at her sister. The younger one went on:

"In order to understand you must hear everything. I was twelve years old—only twelve—you remember, don't you? And I was spoilt; I did just as I pleased. You remember how everybody spoilt me? Listen. The first time he came he had on his riding boots; he dismounted, saying that he had a message for father. You remember, don't you? Don't speak. Listen. When I saw him I was struck with admiration. I thought him so handsome, and I stayed in a corner of the drawing-room all the time he was talking. Children are strange—and terrible. Yes, indeed, I dreamt of him.

"He came again—many times. I looked at him with all my eyes, all my heart. I was large for my age and much more precocious than—any one suspected. He came often. I thought only of him. I often whispered to myself:

"'Henry-Henry de Sampierre!'

"Then I was told that he was going to marry you. That was a blow! Oh, sister, a terrible blow—terrible! I wept all through three sleepless nights.

"He came every afternoon after lunch. You remember, don't you? Don't answer. Listen. You used to make cakes that he was very fond of—with flour, butter and milk. Oh, I know how to make them. I could make them still, if necessary. He would swallow them at one mouthful and wash them down with a glass of wine, saying: 'Delicious!' Do you remember the way he said it?

"I was jealous—jealous! Your wedding day was drawing near. It was only a fortnight distant. I was distracted. I said to myself: 'He shall not marry Suzanne—no, he shall not! He shall marry me when I am old enough! I shall never love any one half so much.' But one evening, ten days before the wedding, you went for a stroll with him in the moonlight before the house—and yonder—under the pine tree, the big pine tree—he kissed you—kissed you—and held you in his arms so long—so long! You remember, don't you? It was probably the first time. You were so pale when you came back to the drawing-room!

"I saw you. I was there in the shrubbery. I was mad with rage! I would have killed you both if I could!

"I said to myself: 'He shall never marry Suzanne—never! He shall marry no one! I could not bear it.' And all at once I began to hate him intensely.

"Then do you know what I did? Listen. I had seen the gardener prepare pellets for killing stray dogs. He would crush a bottle into small pieces with a stone and put the ground glass into a ball of meat.

"I stole a small medicine bottle from mother's room. I ground it fine with a hammer and hid the glass in my pocket. It was a glistening powder. The next day, when you had made your little cakes; I opened them with a knife and inserted the glass. He ate three. I ate one myself. I threw the six others into the pond. The two swans died three days later. You remember? Oh, don't speak! Listen, listen. I, I alone did not die. But I have always been ill. Listen—he died—you know—listen—that was not the worst. It was afterward, later—always—the most terrible—listen.

"My life, all my life—such torture! I said to myself: 'I will never leave my sister. And on my deathbed I will tell her all.' And now I have told. And I have always thought of this moment—the moment when all would be told. Now it has come. It is terrible—oh!—sister—

"I have always thought, morning and evening, day and night: 'I shall have to tell her some day!' I waited. The horror of it! It is done. Say nothing. Now I am afraid—I am afraid! Oh! Supposing I should see him again, by and by, when I am dead! See him again! Only to think of it! I dare not—yet I must. I am going to die. I want you to forgive me. I insist on it. I cannot meet him without your forgiveness. Oh, tell her to forgive me, Father! Tell her. I implore you! I cannot die without it."

She was silent and lay back, gasping for breath, still plucking at the sheets with her fingers.

Suzanne had hidden her face in her hands and did not move. She was thinking of him whom she had loved so long. What a life of happiness they might have had together! She saw him again in the dim and distant past-that past forever lost. Beloved dead! how the thought of them rends the heart! Oh! that kiss, his only kiss! She had retained the memory of it in her soul. And, after that, nothing, nothing more throughout her whole existence!

The priest rose suddenly and in a firm, compelling voice said:

"Mademoiselle Suzanne, your sister is dying!"

Then Suzanne, raising her tear-stained face, put her arms round her sister, and kissing her fervently, exclaimed:

"I forgive you, I forgive you, little one!"

COCO

Throughout the whole countryside the Lucas farn, was known as "the Manor." No one knew why. The peasants doubtless attached to this word, "Manor," a meaning of wealth and of splendor, for this farm was undoubtedly the largest, richest and the best managed in the whole neighborhood.

The immense court, surrounded by five rows of magnificent trees, which sheltered the delicate apple trees from the harsh wind of the plain, inclosed in its confines long brick buildings used for storing fodder and grain, beautiful stables built of hard stone and made to accommodate thirty horses, and a red brick residence which looked like a little chateau.

Thanks for the good care taken, the manure heaps were as little offensive as such things can be; the watch-dogs lived in kennels, and countless poultry paraded through the tall grass.

Every day, at noon, fifteen persons, masters, farmhands and the women folks, seated themselves around the long kitchen table where the soup was brought in steaming in a large, blue-flowered bowl.

The beasts-horses, cows, pigs and sheep-were fat, well fed and clean. Maitre Lucas, a tall man who was getting stout, would go round three times a day, overseeing everything and thinking of everything.

A very old white horse, which the mistress wished to keep until its natural death, because she had brought it up and had always used it, and also because it recalled many happy memories, was housed, through sheer kindness of heart, at the end of the stable.

A young scamp about fifteen years old, Isidore Duval by name, and called, for convenience, Zidore, took care of this pensioner, gave him his measure of oats and fodder in winter, and in summer was supposed to change his pasturing place four times a day, so that he might have plenty of fresh grass.

The animal, almost crippled, lifted with difficulty his legs, large at the knees and swollen above the hoofs. His coat, which was no longer curried, looked like white hair, and his long eyelashes gave to his eyes a sad expression.

When Zidore took the animal to pasture, he had to pull on the rope with all his might, because it walked so slowly; and the youth, bent over and out of breath, would swear at it, exasperated at having to care for this old nag.

The farmhands, noticing the young rascal's anger against Coco, were amused and would continually talk of the horse to Zidore, in order to exasperate him. His comrades would make sport with him. In the village he was called Coco-Zidore.

The boy would fume, feeling an unholy desire to revenge himself on the horse. He was a thin, long-legged, dirty child, with thick, coarse, bristly red hair. He seemed only half-witted, and stuttered as though ideas were unable to form in his thick, brute-like mind.

For a long time he had been unable to understand why Coco should be kept, indignant at seeing things wasted on this useless beast. Since the horse could no longer work, it seemed to him unjust that he should be fed; he revolted at the idea of wasting oats, oats which were so expensive, on this paralyzed old plug. And often, in spite of the orders of Maitre Lucas, he would economize on the nag's food, only giving him half measure. Hatred grew in his confused, childlike mind, the hatred of a stingy, mean, fierce, brutal and cowardly peasant.

When summer came he had to move the animal about in the pasture. It was some distance away. The rascal, angrier every morning, would start, with his dragging step, across the wheat fields. The men working in the fields would shout to him, jokingly: "Hey, Zidore, remember me to Coco."

He would not answer; but on the way he would break off a switch, and, as soon as he had moved the old horse, he would let it begin grazing; then, treacherously sneaking up behind it, he would slash its legs. The animal would try to escape, to kick, to get away from the blows, and run around in a circle about its rope, as though it had been inclosed in a circus ring. And the boy would slash away furiously, running along behind, his teeth clenched in anger.

Then he would go away slowly, without turning round, while the horse watched him disappear, his ribs sticking out, panting as a result of his unusual exertions. Not until the blue blouse of the young peasant was out of sight would he lower his thin white head to the grass.

As the nights were now warm, Coco was allowed to sleep out of doors, in the field behind the little wood. Zidore alone went to see him. The boy threw stones at him to amuse himself. He would sit down on an embankment about ten feet away and would stay there about half an hour, from time to time throwing a sharp stone at the old horse, which remained standing tied before his enemy, watching him continually and not daring to eat before he was gone.

This one thought persisted in the mind of the young scamp: "Why feed this horse, which is no longer good for anything?" It seemed to him that this old nag was stealing the food of the others, the goods of man and God, that he was even robbing him, Zidore, who was working.

Then, little by little, each day, the boy began to shorten the length of rope which allowed the horse to graze.

The hungry animal was growing thinner, and starving. Too feeble to break his bonds, he would stretch his head out toward the tall, green, tempting grass, so near that he could smell, and yet so far that he could not touch it.

But one morning Zidore had an idea: it was, not to move Coco any more. He was tired of walking so far for that old skeleton. He came, however, in order to enjoy his vengeance. The beast watched him anxiously. He did not beat him that day. He walked around him with his hands in his pockets. He even pretended to change his place, but he sank the stake in exactly the same hole, and went away overjoyed with his invention.

The horse, seeing him leave, neighed to call him back; but the rascal began to run, leaving him alone, entirely alone in his field, well tied down and without a blade of grass within reach.

Starving, he tried to reach the grass which he could touch with the end of his nose. He got on his knees, stretching out his neck and his long, drooling lips. All in vain. The old animal spent the whole day in useless, terrible efforts. The sight of all that green food, which stretched out on all sides of him, served to increase the gnawing pangs of hunger.

The scamp did not return that day. He wandered through the woods in search of nests.

The next day he appeared upon the scene again. Coco, exhausted, had lain down. When he saw the boy, he got up, expecting at last to have his place changed.

But the little peasant did not even touch the mallet, which was lying on the ground. He came nearer, looked at the animal, threw at his head a clump of earth which flattened out against the white hair, and he started off again, whistling.

The horse remained standing as long as he could see him; then, knowing that his attempts to reach the near-by grass would be hopeless, he once more lay down on his side and closed his eyes.

The following day Zidore did not come.

When he did come at last, he found Coco still stretched out; he saw that he was dead.

Then he remained standing, looking at him, pleased with what he had done, surprised that it should already be all over. He touched him with his foot, lifted one of his legs and then let it drop, sat on him and remained there, his eyes fixed on the grass, thinking of nothing. He returned to the farm, but did not mention the accident, because he wished to wander about at the hours when he used to change the horse's pasture. He went to see him the next day. At his approach some crows flew away. Countless flies were walking over the body and were buzzing around it. When he returned home, he announced the event. The animal was so old that nobody was surprised. The master said to two of the men:

"Take your shovels and dig a hole right where he is."

The men buried the horse at the place where he had died of hunger. And the grass grew thick, green and vigorous, fed by the poor body.

DEAD WOMAN'S SECRET

The woman had died without pain, quietly, as a woman should whose life had been blameless. Now she was resting in her bed, lying on her back, her eyes closed, her features calm, her long white hair carefully arranged as though she had done it up ten minutes before dying. The whole pale countenance of the dead woman was so collected, so calm, so resigned that one could feel what a sweet soul had lived in that body, what a quiet existence this old soul had led, how easy and pure the death of this parent had been.

Kneeling beside the bed, her son, a magistrate with inflexible principles, and her daughter, Marguerite, known as Sister Eulalie, were weeping as though their hearts would break. She had, from childhood up, armed them with a strict moral code, teaching them religion, without weakness, and duty, without compromise. He, the man, had become a judge and handled the law as a weapon with which he smote the weak ones without pity. She, the girl, influenced by the virtue which had bathed her in this austere family, had become the bride of the Church through her loathing for man.

They had hardly known their father, knowing only that he had made their mother most unhappy, without being told any other details.

The nun was wildly-kissing the dead woman's hand, an ivory hand as white as the large crucifix lying across the bed. On the other side of the long body the other hand seemed still to be holding the sheet in the death grasp; and the sheet had preserved the little creases as a memory of those last movements which precede eternal immobility.

A few light taps on the door caused the two sobbing heads to look up, and the priest, who had just come from dinner, returned. He was red and out of breath from his interrupted digestion, for he had made himself a strong mixture of coffee and brandy in order to combat the fatigue of the last few nights and of the wake which was beginning.

He looked sad, with that assumed sadness of the priest for whom death is a bread winner. He crossed himself and approaching with his professional gesture: "Well, my poor children! I have come to help you pass these last sad hours." But Sister Eulalie suddenly arose. "Thank you, father, but my brother and I prefer to remain alone with her. This is our last chance to see her, and we wish to be together, all three of us, as we—we—used to be when we were small and our poor mo—mother——"

Grief and tears stopped her; she could not continue.

Once more serene, the priest bowed, thinking of his bed. "As you wish, my children." He kneeled, crossed himself, prayed, arose and went out quietly, murmuring: "She was a saint!"

They remained alone, the dead woman and her children. The ticking of the clock, hidden in the shadow, could be heard distinctly, and through the open window drifted in the sweet smell of hay and of woods, together with the soft moonlight. No other noise could be heard over the land except the occasional croaking of the frog or the chirping of some belated insect. An infinite peace, a divine melancholy, a silent serenity surrounded this dead woman, seemed to be breathed out from her and to appease nature itself.

Then the judge, still kneeling, his head buried in the bed clothes, cried in a voice altered by grief and deadened by the sheets and blankets: "Mamma, mamma, mamma!" And his sister, frantically striking her forehead against the woodwork, convulsed, twitching and trembling as in an epileptic fit, moaned: "Jesus, Jesus, mamma, Jesus!" And both of them, shaken by a storm of grief, gasped and choked.

The crisis slowly calmed down and they began to weep quietly, just as on the sea when a calm follows a squall.

A rather long time passed and they arose and looked at their dead. And the memories, those distant memories, yesterday so dear, to-day so torturing, came to their minds with all the little forgotten details, those little intimate familiar details which bring back to life the one who has left. They recalled to each other circumstances, words, smiles, intonations of the mother who was no longer to speak to them. They saw her again happy and calm. They remembered things which she had said, and a little motion of the hand, like beating time, which she often used when emphasizing something important.

And they loved her as they never had loved her before. They measured the depth of their grief, and thus they discovered how lonely they would find themselves.

It was their prop, their guide, their whole youth, all the best part of their lives which was disappearing. It was their bond with life, their mother, their mamma, the connecting link with their forefathers which they would thenceforth miss. They now became solitary, lonely beings; they could no longer look back.

The nun said to her brother: "You remember how mamma used always to read her old letters; they are all there in that drawer. Let us, in turn, read them; let us live her whole life through tonight beside her! It would be like a road to the cross, like making the acquaintance of her mother, of our grandparents, whom we never knew, but whose letters are there and of whom she so often spoke, do you remember?"

Out of the drawer they took about ten little packages of yellow paper, tied with care and arranged one beside the other. They threw these relics on the bed and chose one of them on which the word "Father" was written. They opened and read it.

It was one of those old-fashioned letters which one finds in old family desk drawers, those epistles which smell of another century. The first one started: "My dear," another one: "My beautiful little girl," others: "My dear child," or: "My dear (laughter)." And suddenly the nun began to read aloud, to read over to the dead woman her whole history, all her tender memories. The judge, resting his elbow on the bed, was listening with his eyes fastened on his mother. The motionless body seemed happy.

Sister Eulalie, interrupting herself, said suddenly:

"These ought to be put in the grave with her; they ought to be used as a shroud and she ought to be buried in it." She took another package, on which no name was written. She began to read in a firm voice: "My adored one, I love you wildly. Since yesterday I have been suffering the tortures of the damned, haunted by our memory. I feel your lips against mine, your eyes in mine, your breast against mine. I love you, I love you! You have driven me mad. My arms open, I gasp, moved by a wild desire to hold you again. My whole soul and body cries out for you, wants you. I have kept in my mouth the taste of your kisses—"

The judge had straightened himself up. The nun stopped reading. He snatched the letter from her and looked for the signature. There was none, but only under the words, "The man who adores you," the name "Henry." Their father's name was Rene. Therefore this was not from him. The son then quickly rummaged through the package of letters, took one out and read: "I can no longer live without your caresses." Standing erect, severe as when sitting on the bench, he looked unmoved at the dead woman. The nun, straight as a statue, tears trembling in the corners of her eyes, was watching her brother, waiting. Then he crossed the room slowly, went to the window and stood there, gazing out into the dark night.

When he turned around again Sister Eulalie, her eyes dry now, was still standing near the bed, her head bent down.

He stepped forward, quickly picked up the letters and threw them pell-mell back into the drawer. Then he closed the curtains of the bed.

When daylight made the candles on the table turn pale the son slowly left his armchair, and without looking again at the mother upon whom he had passed sentence, severing the tie that united her to son and daughter, he said slowly: "Let us now retire, sister."

A HUMBLE DRAMA

Meetings that are unexpected constitute the charm of traveling. Who has not experienced the joy of suddenly coming across a Parisian, a college friend, or a neighbor, five hundred miles from home? Who has not passed a night awake in one of those small, rattling country stage-coaches, in regions where steam is still a thing unknown, beside a strange young woman, of whom one has caught only a glimpse in the dim light of the lantern, as she entered the carriage in front of a white house in some small country town?

And the next morning, when one's head and ears feel numb with the continuous tinkling of the bells and the loud rattling of the windows, what a charming sensation it is to see your pretty neighbor open her eyes, startled, glance around her, arrange her rebellious hair with her slender fingers, adjust her hat, feel with sure hand whether her corset is still in place, her waist straight, and her skirt not too wrinkled.

She glances at you coldly and curiously. Then she leans back and no longer seems interested in anything but the country.

In spite of yourself, you watch her; and in spite of yourself you keep on thinking of her. Who is she? Whence does she come? Where is she going? In spite of yourself you spin a little romance around her. She is pretty; she seems charming! Happy he who … Life might be delightful with her. Who knows? She is perhaps the woman of our dreams, the one suited to our disposition, the one for whom our heart calls.

And how delicious even the disappointment at seeing her get out at the gate of a country house! A man stands there, who is awaiting her, with two children and two maids. He takes her in his arms and kisses as he lifts her out. Then she stoops over the little ones, who hold up their hands to her; she kisses them tenderly; and then they all go away together, down a path, while the maids catch the packages which the driver throws down to them from the coach.

Adieu! It is all over. You never will see her again! Adieu to the young woman who has passed the night by your side. You know her no more, you have not spoken to her; all the same, you feel a little sad to see her go. Adieu!

I have had many of these souvenirs of travel, some joyous and some sad.

Once I was in Auvergne, tramping through those delightful French mountains, that are not too high, not too steep, but friendly and familiar. I had climbed the Sancy, and entered a little inn, near a pilgrim's chapel called Notre-Dame de Vassiviere, when I saw a queer, ridiculous-looking old woman breakfasting alone at the end table.

She was at least seventy years old, tall, skinny, and angular, and her white hair was puffed around her temples in the old-fashioned style. She was dressed like a traveling Englishwoman, in awkward, queer clothing, like a person who is indifferent to dress. She was eating an omelet and drinking water.

Her face was peculiar, with restless eyes and the expression of one with whom fate has dealt unkindly. I watched her, in spite of myself, thinking: "Who is she? What is the life of this woman? Why is she wandering alone through these mountains?"

She paid and rose to leave, drawing up over her shoulders an astonishing little shawl, the two ends of which hung over her arms. From a corner of the room she took an alpenstock, which was covered with names traced with a hot iron; then she went out, straight, erect, with the long steps of a letter-carrier who is setting out on his route.

A guide was waiting for her at the door, and both went away. I watched them go down the valley, along the road marked by a line of high wooden crosses. She was taller than her companion, and seemed to walk faster than he.

Two hours later I was climbing the edge of the deep funnel that incloses Lake Pavin in a marvelous and enormous basin of verdure, full of trees, bushes, rocks, and flowers. This lake is so round that it seems as if the outline had been drawn with a pair of compasses, so clear and blue that one might deem it a flood of azure come down from the sky, so charming that one would like to live in a hut on the wooded slope which dominates this crater, where the cold, still water is sleeping. The Englishwoman was standing there like a statue, gazing upon the transparent sheet down in the dead volcano. She was straining her eyes to penetrate below the surface down to the unknown depths, where monstrous trout which have devoured all the other fish are said to live. As I was passing close by her, it seemed to me that two big tears were brimming her eyes. But she departed at a great pace, to rejoin her guide, who had stayed behind in an inn at the foot of the path leading to the lake.

I did not see her again that day.

The next day, at nightfall, I came to the chateau of Murol. The old fortress, an enormous tower standing on a peak in the midst of a large valley, where three valleys intersect, rears its brown, uneven, cracked surface into the sky; it is round, from its large circular base to the crumbling turrets on its pinnacles.

It astonishes the eye more than any other ruin by its simple mass, its majesty, its grave and imposing air of antiquity. It stands there, alone, high as a mountain, a dead queen, but still the queen of the valleys stretched out beneath it. You go up by a slope planted with firs, then you enter a narrow gate, and stop at the foot of the walls, in the first inclosure, in full view of the entire country.

Inside there are ruined halls, crumbling stairways, unknown cavities, dungeons, walls cut through in the middle, vaulted roofs held up one knows not how, and a mass of stones and crevices, overgrown with grass, where animals glide in and out.

I was exploring this ruin alone.

Suddenly I perceived behind a bit of wall a being, a kind of phantom, like the spirit of this ancient and crumbling habitation.

I was taken aback with surprise, almost with fear, when I recognized the old lady whom I had seen twice.

She was weeping, with big tears in her eyes, and held her handkerchief in her hand.

I turned around to go away, when she spoke to me, apparently ashamed to have been surprised in her grief.

"Yes, monsieur, I am crying. That does not happen often to me."

"Pardon me, madame, for having disturbed you," I stammered, confused, not knowing what to say. "Some misfortune has doubtless come to you."

"Yes. No—I am like a lost dog," she murmured, and began to sob, with her handkerchief over her eyes.

Moved by these contagious tears, I took her hand, trying to calm her. Then brusquely she told me her history, as if no longer ably to bear her grief alone.

"Oh! Oh! Monsieur—if you knew—the sorrow in which I live—in what sorrow.

"Once I was happy. I have a house down there—a home. I cannot go back to it any more; I shall never go back to it again, it is too hard to bear.

"I have a son. It is he! it is he! Children don't know. Oh, one has such a short time to live! If I should see him now I should perhaps not recognize him. How I loved him? How I loved him! Even before he was born, when I felt him move. And after that! How I have kissed and caressed and cherished him! If you knew how many nights I have passed in watching him sleep, and how many in thinking of him. I was crazy about him. When he was eight years old his father sent him to boarding-school. That was the end. He no longer belonged to me. Oh, heavens! He came to see me every Sunday. That was all!

"He went to college in Paris. Then he came only four times a year, and every time I was astonished to see how he had changed, to find him taller without having seen him grow. They stole his childhood from me, his confidence, and his love which otherwise would not have gone away from me; they stole my joy in seeing him grow, in seeing him become a little man.

"I saw him four times a year. Think of it! And at every one of his visits his body, his eye, his movements, his voice his laugh, were no longer the same, were no longer mine. All these things change so quickly in a child; and it is so sad if one is not there to see them change; one no longer recognizes him.

"One year he came with down on his cheek! He! my son! I was dumfounded —would you believe it? I hardly dared to kiss him. Was it really he, my little, little curly head of old, my dear; dear child, whom I had held in his diapers or my knee, and who had nursed at my breast with his little greedy lips—was it he, this tall, brown boy, who no longer knew how to kiss me, who seemed to love me as a matter of duty, who called me 'mother' for the sake of politeness, and who kissed me on the forehead, when I felt like crushing him in my arms?

"My husband died. Then my parents, and then my two sisters. When Death enters a house it seems as if he were hurrying to do his utmost, so as not to have to return for a long time after that. He spares only one or two to mourn the others.

"I remained alone. My tall son was then studying law. I was hoping to live and die near him, and I went to him so that we could live together. But he had fallen into the ways of young men, and he gave me to understand that I was in his way. So I left. I was wrong in doing so, but I suffered too much in feeling myself in his way, I, his mother! And I came back home.

"I hardly ever saw him again.

"He married. What a joy! At last we should be together for good. I should have grandchildren. His wife was an Englishwoman, who took a dislike to me. Why? Perhaps she thought that I loved him too much.

"Again I was obliged to go away. And I was alone. Yes, monsieur.

"'Then he went to England, to live with them, with his wife's parents. Do you understand? They have him—they have my son for themselves. They have stolen him from me. He writes to me once a month. At first he came to see me. But now he no longer comes.

"It is now four years since I saw him last. His face then was wrinkled and his hair white. Was that possible? This man, my son, almost an old man? My little rosy child of old? No doubt I shall never see him again.

"And so I travel about all the year. I go east and west, as you see, with no companion.

"I am like a lost dog. Adieu, monsieur! don't stay here with me for it hurts me to have told you all this."

I went down the hill, and on turning round to glance back, I saw the old woman standing on a broken wall, looking out upon the mountains, the long valley and Lake Chambon in the distance.

And her skirt and the queer little shawl which she wore around her thin shoulders were fluttering tike a flag in the wind.

MADEMOISELLE COCOTTE

We were just leaving the asylum when I saw a tall, thin man in a corner of the court who kept on calling an imaginary dog. He was crying in a soft, tender voice: "Cocotte! Come here, Cocotte, my beauty!" and slapping his thigh as one does when calling an animal. I asked the physician, "Who is that man?" He answered: "Oh! he is not at all interesting. He is a coachman named Francois, who became insane after drowning his dog."

I insisted: "Tell me his story. The most simple and humble things are sometimes those which touch our hearts most deeply."

Here is this man's adventure, which was obtained from a friend of his, a groom:

There was a family of rich bourgeois who lived in a suburb of Paris. They had a villa in the middle of a park, at the edge of the Seine. Their coachman was this Francois, a country fellow, somewhat dull, kind-hearted, simple and easy to deceive.

One evening, as he was returning home, a dog began to follow him. At first he paid no attention to it, but the creature's obstinacy at last made him turn round. He looked to see if he knew this dog. No, he had never seen it. It was a female dog and frightfully thin. She was trotting behind him with a mournful and famished look, her tail between her legs, her ears flattened against her head and stopping and starting whenever he did.

He tried to chase this skeleton away and cried:

"Run along! Get out! Kss! kss!" She retreated a few steps, then sat down and waited. And when the coachman started to walk again she followed along behind him.

He pretended to pick up some stones. The animal ran a little farther away, but came back again as soon as the man's back was turned.

Then the coachman Francois took pity on the beast and called her. The dog approached timidly. The man patted her protruding ribs, moved by the beast's misery, and he cried: "Come! come here!" Immediately she began to wag her tail, and, feeling herself taken in, adopted, she began to run along ahead of her new master.

He made her a bed on the straw in the stable, then he ran to the kitchen for some bread. When she had eaten all she could she curled up and went to sleep.

When his employers heard of this the next day they allowed the coachman to keep the animal. It was a good beast, caressing and faithful, intelligent and gentle.

Nevertheless Francois adored Cocotte, and he kept repeating: "That beast is human. She only lacks speech."

He had a magnificent red leather collar made for her which bore these words engraved on a copper plate: "Mademoiselle Cocotte, belonging to the coachman Francois."

She was remarkably prolific and four times a year would give birth to a batch of little animals belonging to every variety of the canine race. Francois would pick out one which he would leave her and then he would unmercifully throw the others into the river. But soon the cook joined her complaints to those of the gardener. She would find dogs under the stove, in the ice box, in the coal bin, and they would steal everything they came across.

Finally the master, tired of complaints, impatiently ordered Francois to get rid of Cocotte. In despair the man tried to give her away. Nobody wanted her. Then he decided to lose her, and he gave her to a teamster, who was to drop her on the other side of Paris, near Joinville-le-Pont.

Cocotte returned the same day. Some decision had to be taken. Five francs was given to a train conductor to take her to Havre. He was to drop her there.

Three days later she returned to the stable, thin, footsore and tired out.

The master took pity on her and let her stay. But other dogs were attracted as before, and one evening, when a big dinner party was on, a stuffed turkey was carried away by one of them right under the cook's nose, and she did not dare to stop him.

This time the master completely lost his temper and said angrily to Francois: "If you don't throw this beast into the water before—to-morrow morning, I'll put you out, do you hear?"

The man was dumbfounded, and he returned to his room to pack his trunk, preferring to leave the place. Then he bethought himself that he could find no other situation as long as he dragged this animal about with him. He thought of his good position, where he was well paid and well fed, and he decided that a dog was really not worth all that. At last he decided to rid himself of Cocotte at daybreak.

He slept badly. He rose at dawn, and taking a strong rope, went to get the dog. She stood up slowly, shook herself, stretched and came to welcome her master.

Then his courage forsook him, and he began to pet her affectionately, stroking her long ears, kissing her muzzle and calling her tender names.

But a neighboring clock struck six. He could no longer hesitate. He opened the door, calling: "Come!" The beast wagged her tail, understanding that she was to be taken out.

They reached the beach, and he chose a place where the water seemed deep. Then he knotted the rope round the leather collar and tied a heavy stone to the other end. He seized Cocotte in his arms and kissed her madly, as though he were taking leave of some human being. He held her to his breast, rocked her and called her "my dear little Cocotte, my sweet little Cocotte," and she grunted with pleasure.

Ten times he tried to throw her into the water and each time he lost courage.

But suddenly he made up his mind and threw her as far from him as he could. At first she tried to swim, as she did when he gave her a bath, but her head, dragged down by the stone, kept going under, and she looked at her master with wild, human glances as she struggled like a drowning person. Then the front part of her body sank, while her hind legs waved wildly out of the water. Finally those also disappeared.

Then, for five minutes, bubbles rose to the surface as though the river were boiling, and Francois, haggard, his heart beating, thought that he saw Cocotte struggling in the mud, and, with the simplicity of a peasant, he kept saying to himself: "What does the poor beast think of me now?"

He almost lost his mind. He was ill for a month and every night he dreamed of his dog. He could feel her licking his hands and hear her barking. It was necessary to call in a physician. At last he recovered, and toward the 2nd of June his employers took him to their estate at Biesard, near Rouen.

There again he was near the Seine. He began to take baths. Each morning he would go down with the groom and they would swim across the river.

One day, as they were disporting themselves in the water, Francois suddenly cried to his companion: "Look what's coming! I'm going to give you a chop!"

It was an enormous, swollen corpse that was floating down with its feet sticking straight up in the air.

Francois swam up to it, still joking: "Whew! it's not fresh. What a catch, old man! It isn't thin, either!" He kept swimming about at a distance from the animal that was in a state of decomposition. Then, suddenly, he was silent and looked at it: attentively. This time he came near enough to touch, it. He looked fixedly at the collar, then he stretched out his arm, seized the neck, swung the corpse round and drew it up close to him and read on the copper which had turned green and which still stuck to the discolored leather: "Mademoiselle Cocotte, belonging to the coachman Francois."

The dead dog had come more than a hundred miles to find its master.

He let out a frightful shriek and began to swim for the beach with all his might, still howling; and as soon as he touched land he ran away wildly, stark naked, through the country. He was insane!

THE CORSICAN BANDIT

The road ascended gently through the forest of Aitone. The large pines formed a solemn dome above our heads, and that mysterious sound made by the wind in the trees sounded like the notes of an organ.

After walking for three hours, there was a clearing, and then at intervals an enormous pine umbrella, and then we suddenly came to the edge of the forest, some hundred meters below, the pass leading to the wild valley of Niolo.

On the two projecting heights which commanded a view of this pass, some old trees, grotesquely twisted, seemed to have mounted with painful efforts, like scouts sent in advance of the multitude in the rear. When we turned round, we saw the entire forest stretched beneath our feet, like a gigantic basin of verdure, inclosed by bare rocks whose summits seemed to reach the sky.

We resumed our walk, and, ten minutes later, found ourselves in the pass.

Then I beheld a remarkable landscape. Beyond another forest stretched a valley, but a valley such as I had never seen before; a solitude of stone, ten leagues long, hollowed out between two high mountains, without a field or a tree to be seen. This was the Niolo valley, the fatherland of Corsican liberty, the inaccessible citadel, from which the invaders had never been able to drive out the mountaineers.

My companion said to me: “This is where all our bandits have taken refuge?”

Ere long we were at the further end of this gorge, so wild, so inconceivably beautiful.

Not a blade of grass, not a plant-nothing but granite. As far as our eyes could reach, we saw in front of us a desert of glittering stone, heated like an oven by a burning sun, which seemed to hang for that very purpose right above the gorge. When we raised our eyes towards the crests, we stood dazzled and stupefied by what we saw. They looked like a festoon of coral; all the summits are of porphyry; and the sky overhead was violet, purple, tinged with the coloring of these strange mountains. Lower down, the granite was of scintillating gray, and seemed ground to powder beneath our feet. At our right, along a long and irregular course, roared a tumultuous torrent. And we staggered along under this heat, in this light, in this burning, arid, desolate valley cut by this torrent of turbulent water which seemed to be ever hurrying onward, without fertilizing the rocks, lost in this furnace which greedily drank it up without being saturated or refreshed by it.

But, suddenly, there was visible at our right a little wooden cross sunk in a little heap of stones. A man had been killed there; and I said to my companion.

"Tell me about your bandits."

He replied:

"I knew the most celebrated of them, the terrible St. Lucia. I will tell you his history.

"His father was killed in a quarrel by a young man of the district, it is said; and St. Lucia was left alone with his sister. He was a weak, timid youth, small, often ill, without any energy. He did not proclaim vengeance against the assassin of his father. All his relatives came to see him, and implored of him to avenge his death; he remained deaf to their menaces and their supplications.

"Then, following the old Corsican custom, his sister, in her indignation carried away his black clothes, in order that he might not wear mourning for a dead man who had not been avenged. He was insensible to even this affront, and rather than take down from the rack his father's gun, which was still loaded, he shut himself up, not daring to brave the looks of the young men of the district.

"He seemed to have even forgotten the crime, and lived with his sister in the seclusion of their dwelling.

"But, one day, the man who was suspected of having committed the murder, was about to get married. St. Lucia did not appear to be moved by this news, but, out of sheer bravado, doubtless, the bridegroom, on his way to the church, passed before the house of the two orphans.

"The brother and the sister, at their window, were eating frijoles, when the young man saw the bridal procession going by. Suddenly he began to tremble, rose to his feet without uttering a word, made the sign of the cross, took the gun which was hanging over the fireplace, and went out.

"When he spoke of this later on, he said: 'I don't know what was the matter with me; it was like fire in my blood; I felt that I must do it, that, in spite of everything, I could not resist, and I concealed the gun in a cave on the road to Corte.

"An hour later, he came back, with nothing in his hand, and with his habitual air of sad weariness. His sister believed that there was nothing further in his thoughts.

"But when night fell he disappeared.

"His enemy had, the same evening, to repair to Corte on foot, accompanied by his two groomsmen.

"He was walking along, singing as he went, when St. Lucia stood before him, and looking straight in the murderer's face, exclaimed: 'Now is the time!' and shot him point-blank in the chest.

"One of the men fled; the other stared at, the young man, saying:

"'What have you done, St. Lucia?' and he was about to hasten to Corte for help, when St. Lucia said in a stern tone:

"'If you move another step, I'll shoot you in the leg.'

"The other, aware of his timidity hitherto, replied: 'You would not dare to do it!' and was hurrying off when he fell instantaneously, his thigh shattered by a bullet.

"And St. Lucia, coming over to where he lay, said:

"'I am going to look at your wound; if it is not serious, I'll leave you there; if it is mortal I'll finish you off."

"He inspected the wound, considered it mortal, and slowly reloading his gun, told the wounded man to say a prayer, and shot him through the head.

"Next day he was in the mountains.

"And do you know what this St. Lucia did after this?

"All his family were arrested by the gendarmes. His uncle, the cure, who was suspected of having incited him to this deed of vengeance, was himself put in prison, and accused by the dead man's relatives. But he escaped, took a gun in his turn, and went to join his nephew in the brush.

"Next, St. Lucia killed, one after the other, his uncle's accusers, and tore out their eyes to teach the others never to state what they had seen with their eyes.

"He killed all the relatives, all the connections of his enemy's family. He slew during his life fourteen gendarmes, burned down the houses of his adversaries, and was, up to the day of his death, the most terrible of all the bandits whose memory we have preserved."

The sun disappeared behind Monte Cinto and the tall shadow of the granite mountain went to sleep on the granite of the valley. We quickened our pace in order to reach before night the little village of Albertaccio, nothing but a pile of stones welded into the stone flanks of a wild gorge. And I said as I thought of the bandit:

"What a terrible custom your vendetta is!"

My companion answered with an air of resignation:

"What would you have? A man must do his duty!"

THE GRAVE

The seventeenth of July, one thousand eight hundred and eighty-three, at half-past two in the morning, the watchman in the cemetery of Besiers, who lived in a small cottage on the edge of this field of the dead, was awakened by the barking of his dog, which was shut up in the kitchen.

Going down quickly, he saw the animal sniffing at the crack of the door and barking furiously, as if some tramp had been sneaking about the house. The keeper, Vincent, therefore took his gun and went out.

His dog, preceding him, at once ran in the direction of the Avenue General Bonnet, stopping short at the monument of Madame Tomoiseau.

The keeper, advancing cautiously, soon saw a faint light on the side of the Avenue Malenvers, and stealing in among the graves, he came upon a horrible act of profanation.

A man had dug up the coffin of a young woman who had been buried the evening before and was dragging the corpse out of it.

A small dark lantern, standing on a pile of earth, lighted up this hideous scene.

Vincent sprang upon the wretch, threw him to the ground, bound his hands and took him to the police station.

It was a young, wealthy and respected lawyer in town, named Courbataille.

He was brought into court. The public prosecutor opened the case by referring to the monstrous deeds of the Sergeant Bertrand.

A wave of indignation swept over the courtroom. When the magistrate sat down the crowd assembled cried: "Death! death!" With difficulty the presiding judge established silence.

Then he said gravely:

"Defendant, what have you to say in your defense?"

Courbataille, who had refused counsel, rose. He was a handsome fellow, tall, brown, with a frank face, energetic manner and a fearless eye.

Paying no attention to the whistlings in the room, he began to speak in a voice that was low and veiled at first, but that grew more firm as he proceeded.

"Monsieur le President, gentlemen of the jury: I have very little to say. The woman whose grave I violated was my sweetheart. I loved her.

"I loved her, not with a sensual love and not with mere tenderness of heart and soul, but with an absolute, complete love, with an overpowering passion.

"Hear me:

"When I met her for the first time I felt a strange sensation. It was not astonishment nor admiration, nor yet that which is called love at first sight, but a feeling of delicious well-being, as if I had been plunged into a warm bath. Her gestures seduced me, her voice enchanted me, and it was with infinite pleasure that I looked upon her person. It seemed to me as if I had seen her before and as if I had known her a long time. She had within her something of my spirit.

"She seemed to me like an answer to a cry uttered by my soul, to that vague and unceasing cry with which we call upon Hope during our whole life.

"When I knew her a little better, the mere thought of seeing her again filled me with exquisite and profound uneasiness; the touch of her hand in mine was more delightful to me than anything that I had imagined; her smile filled me with a mad joy, with the desire to run, to dance, to fling myself upon the ground.

"So we became lovers.

"Yes, more than that: she was my very life. I looked for nothing further on earth, and had no further desires. I longed for nothing further.

"One evening, when we had gone on a somewhat long walk by the river, we were overtaken by the rain, and she caught cold. It developed into pneumonia the next day, and a week later she was dead.

"During the hours of her suffering astonishment and consternation prevented my understanding and reflecting upon it, but when she was dead I was so overwhelmed by blank despair that I had no thoughts left. I wept.

"During all the horrible details of the interment my keen and wild grief was like a madness, a kind of sensual, physical grief.

"Then when she was gone, when she was under the earth, my mind at once found itself again, and I passed through a series of moral sufferings so terrible that even the love she had vouchsafed to me was dear at that price.

"Then the fixed idea came to me: I shall not see her again.

"When one dwells on this thought for a whole day one feels as if he were going mad. Just think of it! There is a woman whom you adore, a unique woman, for in the whole universe there is not a second one like her. This woman has given herself to you and has created with you the mysterious union that is called Love. Her eye seems to you more vast than space, more charming than the world, that clear eye smiling with her tenderness. This woman loves you. When she speaks to you her voice floods you with joy.

"And suddenly she disappears! Think of it! She disappears, not only for you, but forever. She is dead. Do you understand what that means? Never, never, never, not anywhere will she exist any more. Nevermore will that eye look upon anything again; nevermore will that voice, nor any voice like it, utter a word in the same way as she uttered it.

"Nevermore will a face be born that is like hers. Never, never! The molds of statues are kept; casts are kept by which one can make objects with the same outlines and forms. But that one body and that one face will never more be born again upon the earth. And yet millions and millions of creatures will be born, and more than that, and this one woman will not reappear among all the women of the future. Is it possible? It drives one mad to think of it.

"She lived for twenty years, not more, and she has disappeared forever, forever, forever! She thought, she smiled, she loved me. And now nothing! The flies that die in the autumn are as much as we are in this world. And now nothing! And I thought that her body, her fresh body, so warm, so sweet, so white, so lovely, would rot down there in that box under the earth. And her soul, her thought, her love—where is it?

"Not to see her again! The idea of this decomposing body, that I might yet recognize, haunted me. I wanted to look at it once more.

"I went out with a spade, a lantern and a hammer; I jumped over the cemetery wall and I found the grave, which had not yet been closed entirely; I uncovered the coffin and took up a board. An abominable odor, the stench of putrefaction, greeted my nostrils. Oh, her bed perfumed with orris!

"Yet I opened the coffin, and, holding my lighted lantern down into it I saw her. Her face was blue, swollen, frightful. A black liquid had oozed out of her mouth.

"She! That was she! Horror seized me. But I stretched out my arm to draw this monstrous face toward me. And then I was caught.

"All night I have retained the foul odor of this putrid body, the odor of my well beloved, as one retains the perfume of a woman after a love embrace.

"Do with me what you will."

A strange silence seemed to oppress the room. They seemed to be waiting for something more. The jury retired to deliberate.

When they came back a few minutes later the accused showed no fear and did not even seem to think.

The president announced with the usual formalities that his judges declared him to be not guilty.

He did not move and the room applauded.

The Grave appeared in Gil Blas, July 29, 1883, under the signature of "Maufrigneuse."

VOLUME XIII

OLD JUDAS

This entire stretch of country was amazing; it was characterized by a grandeur that was almost religious, and yet it had an air of sinister desolation.

A great, wild lake, filled with stagnant, black water, in which thousands of reeds were waving to and fro, lay in the midst of a vast circle of naked hills, where nothing grew but broom, or here and there an oak curiously twisted by the wind.

Just one house stood on the banks of that dark lake, a small, low house inhabited by Uncle Joseph, an old boatman, who lived on what he could make by his fishing. Once a week he carried the fish he caught into the surrounding villages, returning with the few provisions that he needed for his sustenance.

I went to see this old hermit, who offered to take me with him to his nets, and I accepted.

His boat was old, worm-eaten and clumsy, and the skinny old man rowed with a gentle and monotonous stroke that was soothing to the soul, already oppressed by the sadness of the land round about.

It seemed to me as if I were transported to olden times, in the midst of that ancient country, in that primitive boat, which was propelled by a man of another age.

He took up his nets and threw the fish into the bottom of the boat, as the fishermen of the Bible might have done. Then he took me down to the end of the lake, where I suddenly perceived a ruin on the other side of the bank a dilapidated hut, with an enormous red cross on the wall that looked as if it might have been traced with blood, as it gleamed in the last rays of the setting sun.

"What is that?" I asked.

"That is where Judas died," the man replied, crossing himself.

I was not surprised, being almost prepared for this strange answer.

Still I asked:

"Judas? What Judas?"

"The Wandering Jew, monsieur," he added.

I asked him to tell me this legend.

But it was better than a legend, being a true story, and quite a recent one, since Uncle Joseph had known the man.

This hut had formerly been occupied by a large woman, a kind of beggar, who lived on public charity.

Uncle Joseph did not remember from whom she had this hut. One evening an old man with a white beard, who seemed to be at least two hundred years old, and who could hardly drag himself along, asked alms of this forlorn woman, as he passed her dwelling.

"Sit down, father," she replied; "everything here belongs to all the world, since it comes from all the world."

He sat down on a stone before the door. He shared the woman's bread, her bed of leaves, and her house.

He did not leave her again, for he had come to the end of his travels.

"It was Our Lady the Virgin who permitted this, monsieur," Joseph added, "it being a woman who had opened her door to a Judas, for this old vagabond was the Wandering Jew. It was not known at first in the country, but the people suspected it very soon, because he was always walking; it had become a sort of second nature to him."

And suspicion had been aroused by still another thing. This woman, who kept that stranger with her, was thought to be a Jewess, for no one had ever seen her at church. For ten miles around no one ever called her anything else but the Jewess.

When the little country children saw her come to beg they cried out: "Mamma, mamma, here is the Jewess!"

The old man and she began to go out together into the neighboring districts, holding out their hands at all the doors, stammering supplications into the ears of all the passers. They could be seen at all hours of the day, on by-paths, in the villages, or again eating bread, sitting in the noon heat under the shadow of some solitary tree. And the country people began to call the beggar Old Judas.

One day he brought home in his sack two little live pigs, which a farmer had given him after he had cured the farmer of some sickness.

Soon he stopped begging, and devoted himself entirely to his pigs. He took them out to feed by the lake, or under isolated oaks, or in the near-by valleys. The woman, however, went about all day begging, but she always came back to him in the evening.

He also did not go to church, and no one ever had seen him cross himself before the wayside crucifixes. All this gave rise to much gossip:

One night his companion was attacked by a fever and began to tremble like a leaf in the wind. He went to the nearest town to get some medicine, and then he shut himself up with her, and was not seen for six days.

The priest, having heard that the "Jewess" was about to die, came to offer the consolation of his religion and administer the last sacrament. Was she a Jewess? He did not know. But in any case, he wished to try to save her soul.

Hardly had he knocked at the door when old Judas appeared on the threshold, breathing hard, his eyes aflame, his long beard agitated, like rippling water, and he hurled blasphemies in an unknown language, extending his skinny arms in order to prevent the priest from entering.

The priest attempted to speak, offered his purse and his aid, but the old man kept on abusing him, making gestures with his hands as if throwing; stones at him.

Then the priest retired, followed by the curses of the beggar.

The companion of old Judas died the following day. He buried her himself, in front of her door. They were people of so little account that no one took any interest in them.

Then they saw the man take his pigs out again to the lake and up the hillsides. And he also began begging again to get food. But the people gave him hardly anything, as there was so much gossip about him. Every one knew, moreover, how he had treated the priest.

Then he disappeared. That was during Holy Week, but no one paid any attention to him.

But on Easter Sunday the boys and girls who had gone walking out to the lake heard a great noise in the hut. The door was locked; but the boys broke it in, and the two pigs ran out, jumping like gnats. No one ever saw them again.

The whole crowd went in; they saw some old rags on the floor, the beggar's hat, some bones, clots of dried blood and bits of flesh in the hollows of the skull.

His pigs had devoured him.

"This happened on Good Friday, monsieur." Joseph concluded his story, "three hours after noon."

"How do you know that?" I asked him.

"There is no doubt about that," he replied.

I did not attempt to make him understand that it could easily happen that the famished animals had eaten their master, after he had died suddenly in his hut.

As for the cross on the wall, it had appeared one morning, and no one knew what hand traced it in that strange color.

Since then no one doubted any longer that the Wandering Jew had died on this spot.

I myself believed it for one hour.

THE LITTLE CASK

He was a tall man of forty or thereabout, this Jules Chicot, the innkeeper of Spreville, with a red face and a round stomach, and said by those who knew him to be a smart business man. He stopped his buggy in front of Mother Magloire's farmhouse, and, hitching the horse to the gatepost, went in at the gate.

Chicot owned some land adjoining that of the old woman, which he had been coveting for a long while, and had tried in vain to buy a score of times, but she had always obstinately refused to part with it.

"I was born here, and here I mean to die," was all she said.

He found her peeling potatoes outside the farmhouse door. She was a woman of about seventy-two, very thin, shriveled and wrinkled, almost dried up in fact and much bent but as active and untiring as a girl. Chicot patted her on the back in a friendly fashion and then sat down by her on a stool.

"Well mother, you are always pretty well and hearty, I am glad to see."

"Nothing to complain of, considering, thank you. And how are you, Monsieur Chicot?"

"Oh, pretty well, thank you, except a few rheumatic pains occasionally; otherwise I have nothing to complain of."

"So much the better."

And she said no more, while Chicot watched her going on with her work. Her crooked, knotted fingers, hard as a lobster's claws, seized the tubers, which were lying in a pail, as if they had been a pair of pincers, and she peeled them rapidly, cutting off long strips of skin with an old knife which she held in the other hand, throwing the potatoes into the water as they were done. Three daring fowls jumped one after the other into her lap, seized a bit of peel and then ran away as fast as their legs would carry them with it in their beak.

Chicot seemed embarrassed, anxious, with something on the tip of his tongue which he could not say. At last he said hurriedly:

"Listen, Mother Magloire—"

"Well, what is it?"

"You are quite sure that you do not want to sell your land?"

"Certainly not; you may make up your mind to that. What I have said I have said, so don't refer to it again."

"Very well; only I think I know of an arrangement that might suit us both very well."

"What is it?"

"Just this. You shall sell it to me and keep it all the same. You don't understand? Very well, then follow me in what I am going to say."

The old woman left off peeling potatoes and looked at the innkeeper attentively from under her heavy eyebrows, and he went on:

"Let me explain myself. Every month I will give you a hundred and fifty francs. You understand me! suppose! Every month I will come and bring you thirty crowns, and it will not make the slightest difference in your life—not the very slightest. You will have your own home just as you have now, need not trouble yourself about me, and will owe me nothing; all you will have to do will be to take my money. Will that arrangement suit you?"

He looked at her good-humoredly, one might almost have said benevolently, and the old woman returned his looks distrustfully, as if she suspected a trap, and said:

"It seems all right as far as I am concerned, but it will not give you the farm."

"Never mind about that," he said; "you may remain here as long as it pleases God Almighty to let you live; it will be your home. Only you will sign a deed before a lawyer making it over to me; after your death. You have no children, only nephews and nieces for whom you don't care a straw. Will that suit you? You will keep everything during your life, and I will give you the thirty crowns a month. It is pure gain as far as you are concerned."

The old woman was surprised, rather uneasy, but, nevertheless, very much tempted to agree, and answered:

"I don't say that I will not agree to it, but I must think about it. Come back in a week, and we will talk it over again, and I will then give you my definite answer."

And Chicot went off as happy as a king who had conquered an empire.

Mother Magloire was thoughtful, and did not sleep at all that night; in fact, for four days she was in a fever of hesitation. She suspected that there was something underneath the offer which was not to her advantage; but then the thought of thirty crowns a month, of all those coins clinking in her apron, falling to her, as it were, from the skies, without her doing anything for it, aroused her covetousness.

She went to the notary and told him about it. He advised her to accept Chicot's offer, but said she ought to ask for an annuity of fifty instead of thirty, as her farm was worth sixty thousand francs at the lowest calculation.

"If you live for fifteen years longer," he said, "even then he will only have paid forty-five thousand francs for it."

The old woman trembled with joy at this prospect of getting fifty crowns a month, but she was still suspicious, fearing some trick, and she remained a long time with the lawyer asking questions without being able to make up her mind to go. At last she gave him instructions to draw up the deed and returned home with her head in a whirl, just as if she had drunk four jugs of new cider.

When Chicot came again to receive her answer she declared, after a lot of persuading, that she could not make up her mind to agree to his proposal, though she was all the time trembling lest he should not consent to give the fifty crowns, but at last, when he grew urgent, she told him what she expected for her farm.

He looked surprised and disappointed and refused.

Then, in order to convince him, she began to talk about the probable duration of her life.

"I am certainly not likely to live more than five or six years longer. I am nearly seventy-three, and far from strong, even considering my age. The other evening I thought I was going to die, and could hardly manage to crawl into bed."

But Chicot was not going to be taken in.

"Come, come, old lady, you are as strong as the church tower, and will live till you are a hundred at least; you will no doubt see me put under ground first."

The whole day was spent in discussing the money, and as the old woman would not give in, the innkeeper consented to give the fifty crowns, and she insisted upon having ten crowns over and above to strike the bargain.

Three years passed and the old dame did not seem to have grown a day older. Chicot was in despair, and it seemed to him as if he had been paying that annuity for fifty years, that he had been taken in, done, ruined. From time to time he went to see the old lady, just as one goes in July to see when the harvest is likely to begin. She always met him with a cunning look, and one might have supposed that she was congratulating herself on the trick she had played him. Seeing how well and hearty she seemed he very soon got into his buggy again, growling to himself:

"Will you never die, you old hag?"

He did not know what to do, and he felt inclined to strangle her when he saw her. He hated her with a ferocious, cunning hatred, the hatred of a peasant who has been robbed, and began to cast about for some means of getting rid of her.

One day he came to see her again, rubbing his hands as he did the first time he proposed the bargain, and, after having chatted for a few minutes, he said:

"Why do you never come and have a bit of dinner at my place when you are in Spreville? The people are talking about it, and saying we are not on friendly terms, and that pains me. You know it will cost you nothing if you come, for I don't look at the price of a dinner. Come whenever you feel inclined; I shall be very glad to see you."

Old Mother Magloire did not need to be asked twice, and the next day but one, as she had to go to the town in any case, it being market day, she let her man drive her to Chicot's place, where the buggy was put in the barn while she went into the house to get her dinner.

The innkeeper was delighted and treated her like a lady, giving her roast fowl, black pudding, leg of mutton and bacon and cabbage. But she ate next to nothing. She had always been a small eater, and had generally lived on a little soup and a crust of bread and butter.

Chicot was disappointed and pressed her to eat more, but she refused, and she would drink little, and declined coffee, so he asked her:

"But surely you will take a little drop of brandy or liqueur?"

"Well, as to that, I don't know that I will refuse." Whereupon he shouted out:

"Rosalie, bring the superfine brandy—the special—you know."

The servant appeared, carrying a long bottle ornamented with a paper vine-leaf, and he filled two liqueur glasses.

"Just try that; you will find it first rate."

The good woman drank it slowly in sips, so as to make the pleasure last all the longer, and when she had finished her glass, she said:

"Yes, that is first rate!"

Almost before she had said it Chicot had poured her out another glassful. She wished to refuse, but it was too late, and she drank it very slowly, as she had done the first, and he asked her to have a third. She objected, but he persisted.

"It is as mild as milk, you know; I can drink ten or a dozen glasses without any ill effects; it goes down like sugar and does not go to the head; one would think that it evaporated on the tongue: It is the most wholesome thing you can drink."

She took it, for she really enjoyed it, but she left half the glass.

Then Chicot, in an excess of generosity, said:

"Look here, as it is so much to your taste, I will give you a small keg of it, just to show that you and I are still excellent friends." So she took one away with her, feeling slightly overcome by the effects of what she had drunk.

The next day the innkeeper drove into her yard and took a little iron-hooped keg out of his gig. He insisted on her tasting the contents, to make sure it was the same delicious article, and, when they had each of them drunk three more glasses, he said as he was going away:

"Well, you know when it is all gone there is more left; don't be modest, for I shall not mind. The sooner it is finished the better pleased I shall be."

Four days later he came again. The old woman was outside her door cutting up the bread for her soup.

He went up to her and put his face close to hers, so that he might smell her breath; and when he smelt the alcohol he felt pleased.

"I suppose you will give me a glass of the Special?" he said. And they had three glasses each.

Soon, however, it began to be whispered abroad that Mother Magloire was in the habit of getting drunk all by herself. She was picked up in her kitchen, then in her yard, then in the roads in the neighborhood, and she was often brought home like a log.

The innkeeper did not go near her any more, and, when people spoke to him about her, he used to say, putting on a distressed look:

"It is a great pity that she should have taken to drink at her age, but when people get old there is no remedy. It will be the death of her in the long run."

And it certainly was the death of her. She died the next winter. About Christmas time she fell down, unconscious, in the snow, and was found dead the next morning.

And when Chicot came in for the farm, he said:

"It was very stupid of her; if she had not taken to drink she would probably have lived ten years longer."

BOITELLE

Father Boitelle (Antoine) made a specialty of undertaking dirty jobs all through the countryside. Whenever there was a ditch or a cesspool to be cleaned out, a dunghill removed, a sewer cleansed, or any dirt hole whatever, he way always employed to do it.

He would come with the instruments of his trade, his sabots covered with dirt, and set to work, complaining incessantly about his occupation. When people asked him then why he did this loathsome work, he would reply resignedly:

"Faith, 'tis for my children, whom I must support. This brings me in more than anything else."

He had, indeed, fourteen children. If any one asked him what had become of them, he would say with an air of indifference:

"There are only eight of them left in the house. One is out at service and five are married."

When the questioner wanted to know whether they were well married, he replied vivaciously:

"I did not oppose them. I opposed them in nothing. They married just as they pleased. We shouldn't go against people's likings, it turns out badly. I am a night scavenger because my parents went against my likings. But for that I would have become a workman like the others."

Here is the way his parents had thwarted him in his likings:

He was at the time a soldier stationed at Havre, not more stupid than another, or sharper either, a rather simple fellow, however. When he was not on duty, his greatest pleasure was to walk along the quay, where the bird dealers congregate. Sometimes alone, sometimes with a soldier from his own part of the country, he would slowly saunter along by cages containing parrots with green backs and yellow heads from the banks of the Amazon, or parrots with gray backs and red heads from Senegal, or enormous macaws, which look like birds reared in hot-houses, with their flower-like feathers, their plumes and their tufts. Parrots of every size, who seem painted with minute care by the miniaturist, God Almighty, and the little birds, all the smaller birds hopped about, yellow, blue and variegated, mingling their cries with the noise of the quay; and adding to the din caused by unloading the vessels, as well as by passengers and vehicles, a violent clamor, loud, shrill and deafening, as if from some distant forest of monsters.

Boitelle would pause, with wondering eyes, wide-open mouth, laughing and enraptured, showing his teeth to the captive cockatoos, who kept nodding their white or yellow topknots toward the glaring red of his breeches and the copper buckle of his belt. When he found a bird that could talk he put questions to it, and if it happened at the time to be disposed to reply and to hold a conversation with him he would carry away enough amusement to last him till evening. He also found heaps of amusement in looking at the monkeys, and could conceive no greater luxury for a rich man than to own these animals as one owns cats and dogs. This kind of taste for the exotic he had in his blood, as people have a taste for the chase, or for medicine, or for the priesthood. He could not help returning to the quay every time the gates of the barracks opened, drawn toward it by an irresistible longing.

On one occasion, having stopped almost in ecstasy before an enormous macaw, which was swelling out its plumes, bending forward and bridling up again as if making the court curtseys of parrot-land, he saw the door of a little cafe adjoining the bird dealer's shop open, and a young negress appeared, wearing on her head a red silk handkerchief. She was sweeping into the street the corks and sand of the establishment.

Boitelle's attention was soon divided between the bird and the woman, and he really could not tell which of these two beings he contemplated with the greater astonishment and delight.

The negress, having swept the rubbish into the street, raised her eyes, and, in her turn, was dazzled by the soldier's uniform.

There she stood facing him with her broom in her hands as if she were bringing him a rifle, while the macaw continued bowing. But at the end of a few seconds the soldier began to feel embarrassed at this attention, and he walked away quietly so as not to look as if he were beating a retreat.

But he came back. Almost every day he passed before the Cafe des Colonies, and often he could distinguish through the window the figure of the little black-skinned maid serving "bocks" or glasses of brandy to the sailors of the port. Frequently, too, she would come out to the door on seeing him; soon, without even having exchanged a word, they smiled at one another like acquaintances; and Boitelle felt his heart touched when he suddenly saw, glittering between the dark lips of the girl, a shining row of white teeth. At length, one day he ventured to enter, and was quite surprised to find that she could speak French like every one else. The bottle of lemonade, of which she was good enough to accept a glassful, remained in the soldier's recollection memorably delicious, and it became a custom with him to come and absorb in this little tavern on the quay all the agreeable drinks which he could afford.

For him it was a treat, a happiness, on which his thoughts dwelt constantly, to watch the black hand of the little maid pouring something into his glass while her teeth laughed more than her eyes. At the end of two months they became fast friends, and Boitelle, after his first astonishment at discovering that this negress had as good principles as honest French girls, that she exhibited a regard for economy, industry, religion and good conduct, loved her more on that account, and was so charmed with her that he wanted to marry her.

He told her his intentions, which made her dance with joy. She had also a little money, left her by a female oyster dealer, who had picked her up when she had been left on the quay at Havre by an American captain. This captain had found her, when she was only about six years old, lying on bales of cotton in the hold of his ship, some hours after his departure from New York. On his arrival in Havre he abandoned to the care of this compassionate oyster dealer the little black creature, who had been hidden on board his vessel, he knew not why or by whom.

The oyster woman having died, the young negress became a servant at the Colonial Tavern.

Antoine Boitelle added: "This will be all right if my parents don't oppose it. I will never go against them, you understand, never! I'm going to say a word or two to them the first time I go back to the country."

On the following week, in fact, having obtained twenty-four hours' leave, he went to see his family, who cultivated a little farm at Tourteville, near Yvetot.

He waited till the meal was finished, the hour when the coffee baptized with brandy makes people more open-hearted, before informing his parents that he had found a girl who satisfied his tastes, all his tastes, so completely that there could not exist any other in all the world so perfectly suited to him.

The old people, on hearing this, immediately assumed a cautious manner and wanted explanations. He had concealed nothing from them except the color of her skin.

She was a servant, without much means, but strong, thrifty, clean, well-conducted and sensible. All these things were better than money would be in the hands of a bad housewife. Moreover, she had a few sous, left her by a woman who had reared her, a good number of sous, almost a little dowry, fifteen hundred francs in the savings bank. The old people, persuaded by his talk, and relying also on their own judgment, were gradually weakening, when he came to the delicate point. Laughing in rather a constrained fashion, he said:

"There's only one thing you may not like. She is not a white slip."

They did not understand, and he had to explain at some length and very cautiously, to avoid shocking them, that she belonged to the dusky race of which they had only seen samples in pictures at Epinal. Then they became restless, perplexed, alarmed, as if he had proposed a union with the devil.

The mother said: "Black? How much of her is black? Is the whole of her?"

He replied: "Certainly. Everywhere, just as you are white everywhere."

The father interposed: "Black? Is it as black as the pot?"

The son answered: "Perhaps a little less than that. She is black, but not disgustingly black. The cure's cassock is black, but it is not uglier than a surplice which is white."

The father said: "Are there more black people besides her in her country?"

And the son, with an air of conviction, exclaimed: "Certainly!"

But the old man shook his head.

"That must be unpleasant."

And the son:

"It isn't more disagreeable than anything else when you get accustomed to it."

The mother asked:

"It doesn't soil the underwear more than other skins, this black skin?"

"Not more than your own, as it is her proper color."

Then, after many other questions, it was agreed that the parents should see this girl before coming; to any decision, and that the young fellow, whose, term of military service would be over in a month, should bring her to the house in order that they might examine her and decide by talking the matter over whether or not she was too dark to enter the Boitelle family.

Antoine accordingly announced that on Sunday, the 22d of May, the day of his discharge, he would start for Tourteville with his sweetheart.

She had put on, for this journey to the house of her lover's parents, her most beautiful and most gaudy clothes, in which yellow, red and blue were the prevailing colors, so that she looked as if she were adorned for a national festival.

At the terminus, as they were leaving Havre, people stared at her, and Boitelle was proud of giving his arm to a person who commanded so much attention. Then, in the third-class carriage, in which she took a seat by his side, she aroused so much astonishment among the country folks that the people in the adjoining compartments stood up on their benches to look at her over the wooden partition which divides the compartments. A child, at sight of her, began to cry with terror, another concealed his face in his mother's apron. Everything went off well, however, up to their arrival at their destination. But when the train slackened its rate of motion as they drew near Yvetot, Antoine felt ill at ease, as he would have done at a review when; he did not know his drill practice. Then, as he; leaned his head out, he recognized in the distance: his father, holding the bridle of the horse harnessed to a carryall, and his mother, who had come forward to the grating, behind which stood those who were expecting friends.

He alighted first, gave his hand to his sweetheart, and holding himself erect, as if he were escorting a general, he went to meet his family.

The mother, on seeing this black lady in variegated costume in her son's company, remained so stupefied that she could not open her mouth; and the father found it hard to hold the horse, which the engine or the negress caused to rear continuously. But Antoine, suddenly filled with unmixed joy at seeing once more the old people, rushed forward with open arms, embraced his mother, embraced his father, in spite of the nag's fright, and then turning toward his companion, at whom the passengers on the platform stopped to stare with amazement, he proceeded to explain:

"Here she is! I told you that, at first sight, she is not attractive; but as soon as you know her, I can assure you there's not a better sort in the whole world. Say good-morning to her so that she may not feel badly."

Thereupon Mere Boitelle, almost frightened out of her wits, made a sort of curtsy, while the father took off his cap, murmuring:

"I wish you good luck!"

Then, without further delay, they climbed into the carryall, the two women at the back, on seats which made them jump up and down as the vehicle went jolting along the road, and the two men in front on the front seat.

Nobody spoke. Antoine, ill at ease, whistled a barrack-room air; his father whipped the nag; and his mother, from where she sat in the corner, kept casting sly glances at the negress, whose forehead and cheekbones shone in the sunlight like well-polished shoes.

Wishing to break the ice, Antoine turned round.

"Well," said he, "we don't seem inclined to talk."

"We must have time," replied the old woman.

He went on:

"Come! Tell us the little story about that hen of yours that laid eight eggs."

It was a funny anecdote of long standing in the family. But, as his mother still remained silent, paralyzed by her emotion, he undertook himself to tell the story, laughing as he did so at the memorable incident. The father, who knew it by heart brightened at the opening words of the narrative; his wife soon followed his example; and the negress herself, when he reached the drollest part of it, suddenly gave vent to a laugh, such a loud, rolling torrent of laughter that the horse, becoming excited, broke into a gallop for a while.

This served to cement their acquaintance. They all bezgan to chat.

They had scarcely reached the house and had all alighted, when Antoine conducted his sweetheart to a room, so that she might take off her dress, to avoid staining it, as she was going to prepare a nice dish, intended to win the old people's affections through their stomachs. He drew his parents outside the house, and, with beating heart, asked:

"Well, what do you say now?"

The father said nothing. The mother, less timid, exclaimed:

"She is too black. No, indeed, this is too much for me. It turns my blood."

"You will get used to it," said Antoine.

"Perhaps so, but not at first."

They went into the house, where the good woman was somewhat affected at the spectacle of the negress engaged in cooking. She at once proceeded to assist her, with petticoats tucked up, active in spite of her age.

The meal was an excellent one, very long, very enjoyable. When they were taking a turn after dinner, Antoine took his father aside.

"Well, dad, what do you say about it?"

The peasant took care never to compromise himself.

"I have no opinion about it. Ask your mother."

So Antoine went back to his mother, and, detaining her behind the rest, said:

"Well, mother, what do you think of her?"

"My poor lad, she is really too black. If she were only a little less black, I would not go against you, but this is too much. One would think it was Satan!"

He did not press her, knowing how obstinate the old woman had always been, but he felt a tempest of disappointment sweeping over his heart. He was turning over in his mind what he ought to do, what plan he could devise, surprised, moreover, that she had not conquered them already as she had captivated himself. And they, all four, walked along through the wheat fields, having gradually relapsed into silence. Whenever they passed a fence they saw a countryman sitting on the stile, and a group of brats climbed up to stare at them, and every one rushed out into the road to see the "black" whore young Boitelle had brought home with him. At a distance they noticed people scampering across the fields just as when the drum beats to draw public attention to some living phenomenon. Pere and Mere Boitelle, alarmed at this curiosity, which was exhibited everywhere through the country at their approach, quickened their pace, walking side by side, and leaving their son far behind. His dark companion asked what his parents thought of her.

He hesitatingly replied that they had not yet made up their minds.

But on the village green people rushed out of all the houses in a flutter of excitement; and, at the sight of the gathering crowd, old Boitelle took to his heels, and regained his abode, while Antoine; swelling with rage, his sweetheart on his arm, advanced majestically under the staring eyes, which opened wide in amazement.

He understood that it was at an end, and there was no hope for him, that he could not marry his negress. She also understood it; and as they drew near the farmhouse they both began to weep. As soon as they had got back to the house, she once more took off her dress to aid the mother in the household duties, and followed her everywhere, to the dairy, to the stable, to the hen house, taking on herself the hardest part of the work, repeating always: "Let me do it, Madame Boitelle," so that, when night came on, the old woman, touched but inexorable, said to her son: "She is a good girl, all the same. It's a pity she is so black; but indeed she is too black. I could not get used to it. She must go back again. She is too, too black!"

And young Boitelle said to his sweetheart:

"She will not consent. She thinks you are too black. You must go back again. I will go with you to the train. No matter—don't fret. I am going to talk to them after you have started."

He then took her to the railway station, still cheering her with hope, and, when he had kissed her, he put her into the train, which he watched as it passed out of sight, his eyes swollen with tears.

In vain did he appeal to the old people. They would never give their consent.

And when he had told this story, which was known all over the country, Antoine Boitelle would always add:

"From that time forward I have had no heart for anything—for anything at all. No trade suited me any longer, and so I became what I am—a night scavenger."

People would say to him:

"Yet you got married."

"Yes, and I can't say that my wife didn't please me, seeing that I have fourteen children; but she is not the other one, oh, no—certainly not! The other one, mark you, my negress, she had only to give me one glance, and I felt as if I were in Heaven."

A WIDOW

This story was told during the hunting season at the Chateau Baneville. The autumn had been rainy and sad. The red leaves, instead of rustling under the feet, were rotting under the heavy downfalls.

The forest was as damp as it could be. From it came an odor of must, of rain, of soaked grass and wet earth; and the sportsmen, their backs hunched under the downpour, mournful dogs, with tails between their legs and hairs sticking to their sides, and the young women, with their clothes drenched, returned every evening, tired in body and in mind.

After dinner, in the large drawing-room, everybody played lotto, without enjoyment, while the wind whistled madly around the house. Then they tried telling stories like those they read in books, but no one was able to invent anything amusing. The hunters told tales of wonderful shots and of the butchery of rabbits; and the women racked their brains for ideas without revealing the imagination of Scheherezade. They were about to give up this diversion when a young woman, who was idly caressing the hand of an old maiden aunt, noticed a little ring made of blond hair, which she had often seen, without paying any attention to it.

She fingered it gently and asked, "Auntie, what is this ring? It looks as if it were made from the hair of a child."

The old lady blushed, grew pale, then answered in a trembling voice: "It is sad, so sad that I never wish to speak of it. All the unhappiness of my life comes from that. I was very young then, and the memory has remained so painful that I weep every time I think of it."

Immediately everybody wished to know the story, but the old lady refused to tell it. Finally, after they had coaxed her for a long time, she yielded. Here is the story:

"You have often heard me speak of the Santeze family, now extinct. I knew the last three male members of this family. They all died in the same manner; this hair belongs to the last one. He was thirteen when he killed himself for me. That seems strange to you, doesn't it?

"Oh! it was a strange family—mad, if you will, but a charming madness, the madness of love. From father to son, all had violent passions which filled their whole being, which impelled them to do wild things, drove them to frantic enthusiasm, even to crime. This was born in them, just as burning devotion is in certain souls. Trappers have not the same nature as minions of the drawing-room. There was a saying: 'As passionate as a Santeze.' This could be noticed by looking at them. They all had wavy hair, falling over their brows, curly beards and large eyes whose glance pierced and moved one, though one could not say why.

"The grandfather of the owner of this hair, of whom it is the last souvenir, after many adventures, duels and elopements, at about sixty-five fell madly in love with his farmer's daughter. I knew them both. She was blond, pale, distinguished-looking, with a slow manner of talking, a quiet voice and a look so gentle that one might have taken her for a Madonna. The old nobleman took her to his home and was soon so captivated with her that he could not live without her for a minute. His daughter and daughter-in-law, who lived in the chateau, found this perfectly natural, love was such a tradition in the family. Nothing in regard to a passion surprised them, and if one spoke before them of parted lovers, even of vengeance after treachery, both said in the same sad tone: 'Oh, how he must have suffered to come to that point!' That was all. They grew sad over tragedies of love, but never indignant, even when they were criminal.

"Now, one day a young man named Monsieur de Gradelle, who had been invited for the shooting, eloped with the young girl.

"Monsieur de Santeze remained calm as if nothing had happened, but one morning he was found hanging in the kennels, among his dogs.

"His son died in the same manner in a hotel in Paris during a journey which he made there in 1841, after being deceived by a singer from the opera.

"He left a twelve-year-old child and a widow, my mother's sister. She came to my father's house with the boy, while we were living at Bertillon. I was then seventeen.

"You have no idea how wonderful and precocious this Santeze child was. One might have thought that all the tenderness and exaltation of the whole race had been stored up in this last one. He was always dreaming and walking about alone in a great alley of elms leading from the chateau to the forest. I watched from my window this sentimental boy, who walked with thoughtful steps, his hands behind his back, his head bent, and at times stopping to raise his eyes as if he could see and understand things that were not comprehensible at his age.

"Often, after dinner on clear evenings, he would say to me: 'Let us go outside and dream, cousin.' And we would go outside together in the park. He would stop quickly before a clearing where the white vapor of the moon lights the woods, and he would press my hand, saying: 'Look! look! but you don't understand me; I feel it. If you understood me, we should be happy. One must love to know! I would laugh and then kiss this child, who loved me madly.

"Often, after dinner, he would sit on my mother's knees. 'Come, auntie,' he would say, 'tell me some love-stories.' And my mother, as a joke, would tell him all the old legends of the family, all the passionate adventures of his forefathers, for thousands of them were current, some true and some false. It was their reputation for love and gallantry which was the ruin of every one of these men; they gloried in it and then thought that they had to live up to the renown of their house.

"The little fellow became exalted by these tender or terrible stories, and at times he would clap his hands, crying: 'I, too, I, too, know how to love, better than all of them!'

"Then, he began to court me in a timid and tender manner, at which every one laughed, it was, so amusing. Every morning I had some flowers picked by him, and every evening before going to his room he would kiss my hand and murmur: 'I love you!'

"I was guilty, very guilty, and I grieved continually about it, and I have been doing penance all my life; I have remained an old maid—or, rather, I have lived as a widowed fiancee, his widow.

"I was amused at this childish tenderness, and I even encouraged him. I was coquettish, as charming as with a man, alternately caressing and severe. I maddened this child. It was a game for me and a joyous diversion for his mother and mine. He was twelve! think of it! Who would have taken this atom's passion seriously? I kissed him as often as he wished; I even wrote him little notes, which were read by our respective mothers; and he answered me by passionate letters, which I have kept. Judging himself as a man, he thought that our loving intimacy was secret. We had forgotten that he was a Santeze.

"This lasted for about a year. One evening in the park he fell at my feet and, as he madly kissed the hem of my dress, he kept repeating: 'I love you! I love you! I love you! If ever you deceive me, if ever you leave me for another, I'll do as my father did.' And he added in a hoarse voice, which gave me a shiver: 'You know what he did!'

"I stood there astonished. He arose, and standing on the tips of his toes in order to reach my ear, for I was taller than he, he pronounced my first name: 'Genevieve!' in such a gentle, sweet, tender tone that I trembled all over. I stammered: 'Let us return! let us return!' He said no more and followed me; but as we were going up the steps of the porch, he stopped me, saying: 'You know, if ever you leave me, I'll kill myself.'

"This time I understood that I had gone too far, and I became quite reserved. One day, as he was reproaching me for this, I answered: 'You are now too old for jesting and too young for serious love. I'll wait.'

"I thought that this would end the matter. In the autumn he was sent to a boarding-school. When he returned the following summer I was engaged to be married. He understood immediately, and for a week he became so pensive that I was quite anxious.

"On the morning of the ninth day I saw a little paper under my door as I got up. I seized it, opened it and read: 'You have deserted me and you know what I said. It is death to which you have condemned me. As I do not wish to be found by another than you, come to the park just where I told you last year that I loved you and look in the air.'

"I thought that I should go mad. I dressed as quickly as I could and ran wildly to the place that he had mentioned. His little cap was on the ground in the mud. It had been raining all night. I raised my eyes and saw something swinging among the leaves, for the wind was blowing a gale.

"I don't know what I did after that. I must have screamed at first, then fainted and fallen, and finally have run to the chateau. The next thing that I remember I was in bed, with my mother sitting beside me.

"I thought that I had dreamed all this in a frightful nightmare. I stammered: 'And what of him, what of him, Gontran?' There was no answer. It was true!

"I did not dare see him again, but I asked for a lock of his blond hair. Here—here it is!"

And the old maid stretched out her trembling hand in a despairing gesture. Then she blew her nose several times, wiped her eyes and continued:

"I broke off my marriage—without saying why. And I—I always have remained the—the widow of this thirteen-year-old boy." Then her head fell on her breast and she wept for a long time.

As the guests were retiring for the night a large man, whose quiet she had disturbed, whispered in his neighbor's ear: "Isn't it unfortunate to, be so sentimental?"

THE ENGLISHMAN OF ETRETAT

A great English poet has just crossed over to France in order to greet Victor Hugo. All the newspapers are full of his name and he is the great topic of conversation in all drawing-rooms. Fifteen years ago I had occasion several times to meet Algernon Charles Swinburne. I will attempt to show him just as I saw him and to give an idea of the strange impression he made on me, which will remain with me throughout time.

I believe it was in 1867 or in 1868 that an unknown young Englishman came to Etretat and bought a little hut hidden under great trees. It was said that he lived there, always alone, in a strange manner; and he aroused the inimical surprise of the natives, for the inhabitants were sullen and foolishly malicious, as they always are in little towns.

They declared that this whimsical Englishman ate nothing but boiled, roasted or stewed monkey; that he would see no one; that he talked to himself hours at a time and many other surprising things that made people think that he was different from other men. They were surprised that he should live alone with a monkey. Had it been a cat or a dog they would have said nothing. But a monkey! Was that not frightful? What savage tastes the man must have!

I knew this young man only from seeing him in the streets. He was short, plump, without being fat, mild-looking, and he wore a little blond mustache, which was almost invisible.

Chance brought us together. This savage had amiable and pleasing manners, but he was one of those strange Englishmen that one meets here and there throughout the world.

Endowed with remarkable intelligence, he seemed to live in a fantastic dream, as Edgar Poe must have lived. He had translated into English a volume of strange Icelandic legends, which I ardently desired to see translated into French. He loved the supernatural, the dismal and grewsome, but he spoke of the most marvellous things with a calmness that was typically English, to which his gentle and quiet voice gave a semblance of reality that was maddening.

Full of a haughty disdain for the world, with its conventions, prejudices and code of morality, he had nailed to his house a name that was boldly impudent. The keeper of a lonely inn who should write on his door: "Travellers murdered here!" could not make a more sinister jest. I never had entered his dwelling, when one day I received an invitation to luncheon, following an accident that had occurred to one of his friends, who had been almost drowned and whom I had attempted to rescue.

Although I was unable to reach the man until he had already been rescued, I received the hearty thanks of the two Englishmen, and the following day I called upon them.

The friend was a man about thirty years old. He bore an enormous head on a child's body—a body without chest or shoulders. An immense forehead, which seemed to have engulfed the rest of the man, expanded like a dome above a thin face which ended in a little pointed beard. Two sharp eyes and a peculiar mouth gave one the impression of the head of a reptile, while the magnificent brow suggested a genius.

A nervous twitching shook this peculiar being, who walked, moved, acted by jerks like a broken spring.

This was Algernon Charles Swinburne, son of an English admiral and grandson, on the maternal side, of the Earl of Ashburnham.

He strange countenance was transfigured when he spoke. I have seldom seen a man more impressive, more eloquent, incisive or charming in conversation. His rapid, clear, piercing and fantastic imagination seemed to creep into his voice and to lend life to his words. His brusque gestures enlivened his speech, which penetrated one like a dagger, and he had bursts of thought, just as lighthouses throw out flashes of fire, great, genial lights that seemed to illuminate a whole world of ideas.

The home of the two friends was pretty and by no means commonplace. Everywhere were paintings, some superb, some strange, representing different conceptions of insanity. Unless I am mistaken, there was a water-color which represented the head of a dead man floating in a rose-colored shell on a boundless ocean, under a moon with a human face.

Here and there I came across bones. I clearly remember a flayed hand on which was hanging some dried skin and black muscles, and on the snow-white bones could be seen the traces of dried blood.

The food was a riddle which I could not solve. Was it good? Was it bad? I could not say. Some roast monkey took away all desire to make a steady diet of this animal, and the great monkey who roamed about among us at large and playfully pushed his head into my glass when I wished to drink cured me of any desire I might have to take one of his brothers as a companion for the rest of my days.

As for the two men, they gave me the impression of two strange, original, remarkable minds, belonging to that peculiar race of talented madmen from among whom have arisen Poe, Hoffmann and many others.

If genius is, as is commonly believed, a sort of aberration of great minds, then Algernon Charles Swinburne is undoubtedly a genius.

Great minds that are healthy are never considered geniuses, while this sublime qualification is lavished on brains that are often inferior but are slightly touched by madness.

At any rate, this poet remains one of the first of his time, through his originality and polished form. He is an exalted lyrical singer who seldom bothers about the good and humble truth, which French poets are now seeking so persistently and patiently. He strives to set down dreams, subtle thoughts, sometimes great, sometimes visibly forced, but sometimes magnificent.

Two years later I found the house closed and its tenants gone. The furniture was being sold. In memory of them I bought the hideous flayed hand. On the grass an enormous square block of granite bore this simple word: "Nip." Above this a hollow stone offered water to the birds. It was the grave of the monkey, who had been hanged by a young, vindictive negro servant. It was said that this violent domestic had been forced to flee at the point of his exasperated master's revolver. After wandering about without home or food for several days, he returned and began to peddle barley-sugar in the streets. He was expelled from the country after he had almost strangled a displeased customer.

The world would be gayer if one could often meet homes like that.

This story appeared in the "Gaulois," November 29, 1882. It was the original sketch for the introductory study of Swinburne, written by Maupassant for the French translation by Gabriel Mourey of "Poems and Ballads."

MAGNETISM

It was a men's dinner party, and they were sitting over their cigars and brandy and discussing magnetism. Donato's tricks and Charcot's experiments. Presently, the sceptical, easy-going men, who cared nothing for religion of any sort, began telling stories of strange occurrences, incredible things which, nevertheless, had really occurred, so they said, falling back into superstitious beliefs, clinging to these last remnants of the marvellous, becoming devotees of this mystery of magnetism, defending it in the name of science. There was only one person who smiled, a vigorous young fellow, a great ladies' man who was so incredulous that he would not even enter upon a discussion of such matters.

He repeated with a sneer:

"Humbug! humbug! humbug! We need not discuss Donato, who is merely a very smart juggler. As for M. Charcot, who is said to be a remarkable man of science, he produces on me the effect of those story-tellers of the school of Edgar Poe, who end by going mad through constantly reflecting on queer cases of insanity. He has authenticated some cases of unexplained and inexplicable nervous phenomena; he makes his way into that unknown region which men are exploring every day, and unable always to understand what he sees, he recalls, perhaps, the ecclesiastical interpretation of these mysteries. I should like to hear what he says himself."

The words of the unbeliever were listened to with a kind of pity, as if he had blasphemed in an assembly of monks.

One of these gentlemen exclaimed:

"And yet miracles were performed in olden times."

"I deny it," replied the other: "Why cannot they be performed now?"

Then, each mentioned some fact, some fantastic presentiment some instance of souls communicating with each other across space, or some case of the secret influence of one being over another. They asserted and maintained that these things had actually occurred, while the sceptic angrily repeated:

"Humbug! humbug! humbug!"

At last he rose, threw away his cigar, and with his hands in his pockets, said: "Well, I also have two stories to tell you, which I will afterwards explain. Here they are:

"In the little village of Etretat, the men, who are all seafaring folk, go every year to Newfoundland to fish for cod. One night the little son of one of these fishermen woke up with a start, crying out that his father was dead. The child was quieted, and again he woke up exclaiming that his father was drowned. A month later the news came that his father had, in fact, been swept off the deck of his smack by a billow. The widow then remembered how her son had woke up and spoken of his father's death. Everyone said it was a miracle, and the affair caused a great sensation. The dates were compared, and it was found that the accident and the dream were almost coincident, whence they concluded that they had happened on the same night and at the same hour. And there is a mystery of magnetism."

The story-teller stopped suddenly.

Thereupon, one of those who had heard him, much affected by the narrative, asked:

"And can you explain this?"

"Perfectly, monsieur. I have discovered the secret. The circumstance surprised me and even perplexed me very much; but you see, I do not believe on principle. Just as others begin by believing, I begin by doubting; and when I cannot understand, I continue to deny that there can be any telepathic communication between souls; certain that my own intelligence will be able to explain it. Well, I kept on inquiring into the matter, and by dint of questioning all the wives of the absent seamen, I was convinced that not a week passed without one of them, or one of their children dreaming and declaring when they woke up that the father was drowned. The horrible and continual fear of this accident makes them always talk about it. Now, if one of these frequent predictions coincides, by a very simple chance, with the death of the person referred to, people at once declare it to be a miracle; for they suddenly lose sight of all the other predictions of misfortune that have remained unfulfilled. I have myself known fifty cases where the persons who made the prediction forgot all about it a week afterwards. But, if, then one happens to die, then the recollection of the thing is immediately revived, and people are ready to believe in the intervention of God, according to some, and magnetism, according to others."

One of the smokers remarked:

"What you say is right enough; but what about your second story?"

"Oh! my second story is a very delicate matter to relate. It happened to myself, and so I don't place any great value on my own view of the matter. An interested party can never give an impartial opinion. However, here it is:

"Among my acquaintances was a young woman on whom I had never bestowed a thought, whom I had never even looked at attentively, never taken any notice of.

"I classed her among the women of no importance, though she was not bad-looking; she appeared, in fact, to possess eyes, a nose, a mouth, some sort of hair—just a colorless type of countenance. She was one of those beings who awaken only a chance, passing thought, but no special interest, no desire.

"Well, one night, as I was writing some letters by my fireside before going to bed, I was conscious, in the midst of that train of sensuous visions that sometimes pass through one's brain in moments of idle reverie, of a kind of slight influence, passing over me, a little flutter of the heart, and immediately, without any cause, without any logical connection of thought, I saw distinctly, as if I were touching her, saw from head to foot, and disrobed, this young woman to whom I had never given more than three seconds' thought at a time. I suddenly discovered in her a number of qualities which I had never before observed, a sweet charm, a languorous fascination; she awakened in me that sort of restless emotion that causes one to pursue a woman. But

I did not think of her long. I went to bed and was soon asleep. And I dreamed.

"You have all had these strange dreams which make you overcome the impossible, which open to you double-locked doors, unexpected joys, tightly folded arms?

"Which of us in these troubled, excising, breathless slumbers, has not held, clasped, embraced with rapture, the woman who occupied his thoughts? And have you ever noticed what superhuman delight these happy dreams give us? Into what mad intoxication they cast you! with what passionate spasms they shake you! and with what infinite, caressing, penetrating tenderness they fill your heart for her whom you hold clasped in your arms in that adorable illusion that is so like reality!

"All this I felt with unforgettable violence. This woman was mine, so much mine that the pleasant warmth of her skin remained in my fingers, the odor of her skin, in my brain, the taste of her kisses, on my lips, the sound of her voice lingered in my ears, the touch of her clasp still clung to me, and the burning charm of her tenderness still gratified my senses long after the delight but disillusion of my awakening.

"And three times that night I had the same dream.

"When the day dawned she haunted me, possessed me, filled my senses to such an extent that I was not one second without thinking of her.

"At last, not knowing what to do, I dressed myself and went to call on her. As I went upstairs to her apartment, I was so overcome by emotion that I trembled, and my heart beat rapidly.

"I entered the apartment. She rose the moment she heard my name mentioned; and suddenly our eyes met in a peculiar fixed gaze.

"I sat down. I stammered out some commonplaces which she seemed not to hear. I did not know what to say or do. Then, abruptly, clasping my arms round her, my dream was realized so suddenly that I began to doubt whether I was really awake. We were friends after this for two years."

"What conclusion do you draw from it?" said a voice.

The story-teller seemed to hesitate.

"The conclusion I draw from it—well, by Jove, the conclusion is that it was just a coincidence! And then—who can tell? Perhaps it was some glance of hers which I had not noticed and which came back that night to me through one of those mysterious and unconscious —recollections that often bring before us things ignored by our own consciousness, unperceived by our minds!"

"Call it whatever you like," said one of his table companions, when the story was finished; "but if you don't believe in magnetism after that, my dear boy, you are an ungrateful fellow!"

A FATHER'S CONFESSION

All Veziers-le-Rethel had followed the funeral procession of M. Badon-Leremince to the grave, and the last words of the funeral oration pronounced by the delegate of the district remained in the minds of all: "He was an honest man, at least!"

An honest man he had been in all the known acts of his life, in his words, in his examples, his attitude, his behavior, his enterprises, in the cut of his beard and the shape of his hats. He never had said a word that did not set an example, never had given an alms without adding a word of advice, never had extended his hand without appearing to bestow a benediction.

He left two children, a boy and a girl. His son was counselor general, and his daughter, having married a lawyer, M. Poirel de la Voulte, moved in the best society of Veziers.

They were inconsolable at the death of their father, for they loved him sincerely.

As soon as the ceremony was over, the son, daughter and son-in-law returned to the house of mourning, and, shutting themselves in the library, they opened the will, the seals of which were to be broken by them alone and only after the coffin had been placed in the ground. This wish was expressed by a notice on the envelope.

M. Poirel de la Voulte tore open the envelope, in his character of a lawyer used to such operations, and having adjusted his spectacles, he read in a monotonous voice, made for reading the details of contracts:

My children, my dear children, I could not sleep the eternal sleep in peace if I did not make to you from the tomb a confession, the confession of a crime, remorse for which has ruined my life. Yes, I committed a crime, a frightful, abominable crime.

I was twenty-six years old, and I had just been called to the bar in Paris, and was living the life off young men from the provinces who are stranded in this town without acquaintances, relatives, or friends.

I took a sweetheart. There are beings who cannot live alone. I was one of those. Solitude fills me with horrible anguish, the solitude of my room beside my fire in the evening. I feel then as if I were alone on earth, alone, but surrounded by vague dangers, unknown and terrible things; and the partition that separates me from my neighbor, my neighbor whom I do not know, keeps me at as great a distance from him as the stars that I see through my window. A sort of fever pervades me, a fever of impatience and of fear, and the silence of the walls terrifies me. The silence of a room where one lives alone is so intense and so melancholy. It is not only a silence of the mind; when a piece of furniture cracks a shudder goes through you for you expect no noise in this melancholy abode.

How many times, nervous and timid from this motionless silence, I have begun to talk, to repeat words without rhyme or reason, only to make some sound. My voice at those times sounds so strange that I am afraid of that, too. Is there anything more dreadful than talking to one's self in an empty house? One's voice sounds like that of another, an unknown voice talking aimlessly, to no one, into the empty air, with no ear to listen to it, for one knows before they escape into the solitude of the room exactly what words will be uttered. And when they resound lugubriously in the silence, they seem no more than an echo, the peculiar echo of words whispered by ones thought.

My sweetheart was a young girl like other young girls who live in Paris on wages that are insufficient to keep them. She was gentle, good, simple. Her parents lived at Poissy. She went to spend several days with them from time to time.

For a year I lived quietly with her, fully decided to leave her when I should find some one whom I liked well enough to marry. I would make a little provision for this one, for it is an understood thing in our social set that a woman's love should be paid for, in money if she is poor, in presents if she is rich.

But one day she told me she was enceinte. I was thunderstruck, and saw in a second that my life would be ruined. I saw the fetter that I should wear until my death, everywhere, in my future family life, in my old age, forever; the fetter of a woman bound to my life through a child; the fetter of the child whom I must bring up, watch over, protect, while keeping myself unknown to him, and keeping him hidden from the world.

I was greatly disturbed at this news, and a confused longing, a criminal desire, surged through my mind; I did not formulate it, but I felt it in my heart, ready to come to the surface, as if some one hidden behind a portiere should await the signal to come out. If some accident might only happen! So many of these little beings die before they are born!

Oh! I did not wish my sweetheart to die! The poor girl, I loved her very much! But I wished, possibly, that the child might die before I saw it.

He was born. I set up housekeeping in my little bachelor apartment, an imitation home, with a horrible child. He looked like all children; I did not care for him. Fathers, you see, do not show affection until later. They have not the instinctive and passionate tenderness of mothers; their affection has to be awakened gradually, their mind must become attached by bonds formed each day between beings that live in each other's society.

A year passed. I now avoided my home, which was too small, where soiled linen, baby-clothes and stockings the size of gloves were lying round, where a thousand articles of all descriptions lay on the furniture, on the arm of an easy-chair, everywhere. I went out chiefly that I might not hear the child cry, for he cried on the slightest pretext, when he was bathed, when he was touched, when he was put to bed, when he was taken up in the morning, incessantly.

I had made a few acquaintances, and I met at a reception the woman who was to be your mother. I fell in love with her and became desirous to marry her. I courted her; I asked her parents' consent to our marriage and it was granted.

I found myself in this dilemma: I must either marry this young girl whom I adored, having a child already, or else tell the truth and renounce her, and happiness, my future, everything; for her parents, who were people of rigid principles, would not give her to me if they knew.

I passed a month of horrible anguish, of mortal torture, a month haunted by a thousand frightful thoughts; and I felt developing in me a hatred toward my son, toward that little morsel of living, screaming flesh, who blocked my path, interrupted my life, condemned me to an existence without hope, without all those vague expectations that make the charm of youth.

But just then my companion's mother became ill, and I was left alone with the child.

It was in December, and the weather was terribly cold. What a night! My companion had just left. I had dined alone in my little dining-room and I went gently into the room where the little one was asleep.

I sat down in an armchair before the fire. The wind was blowing, making the windows rattle, a dry, frosty wind; and I saw trough the window the stars shining with that piercing brightness that they have on frosty nights.

Then the idea that had obsessed me for a month rose again to the surface. As soon as I was quiet it came to me and harassed me. It ate into my mind like a fixed idea, just as cancers must eat into the flesh. It was there, in my head, in my heart, in my whole body, it seemed to me; and it swallowed me up as a wild beast might have. I endeavored to drive it away, to repulse it, to open my mind to other thoughts, as one opens a window to the fresh morning breeze to drive out the vitiated air; but I could not drive it from my brain, not even for a second. I do not know how to express this torture. It gnawed at my soul, and I felt a frightful pain, a real physical and moral pain.

My life was ruined! How could I escape from this situation? How could I draw back, and how could I confess?

And I loved the one who was to become your mother with a mad passion, which this insurmountable obstacle only aggravated.

A terrible rage was taking possession of me, choking me, a rage that verged on madness! Surely I was crazy that evening!

The child was sleeping. I got up and looked at it as it slept. It was he, this abortion, this spawn, this nothing, that condemned me to irremediable unhappiness!

He was asleep, his mouth open, wrapped in his bed-clothes in a crib beside my bed, where I could not sleep.

How did I ever do what I did? How do I know? What force urged me on? What malevolent power took possession of me? Oh! the temptation to crime came to me without any forewarning. All I recall is that my heart beat tumultuously. It beat so hard that I could hear it, as one hears the strokes of a hammer behind a partition. That is all I can recall—the beating of my heart! In my head there was a strange confusion, a tumult, a senseless disorder, a lack of presence of mind. It was one of those hours of bewilderment and hallucination when a man is neither conscious of his actions nor able to guide his will.

I gently raised the coverings from the body of the child; I turned them down to the foot of the crib, and he lay there uncovered and naked.

He did not wake. Then I went toward the window, softly, quite softly, and I opened it.

A breath of icy air glided in like an assassin; it was so cold that I drew aside, and the two candles flickered. I remained standing near the window, not daring to turn round, as if for fear of seeing what was doing on behind me, and feeling the icy air continually across my forehead, my cheeks, my hands, the deadly air which kept streaming in. I stood there a long time.

I was not thinking, I was not reflecting. All at once a little cough caused me to shudder frightfully from head to foot, a shudder that I feel still to the roots of my hair. And with a frantic movement I abruptly closed both sides of the window and, turning round, ran over to the crib.

He was still asleep, his mouth open, quite naked. I touched his legs; they were icy cold and I covered them up.

My heart was suddenly touched, grieved, filled with pity, tenderness, love for this poor innocent being that I had wished to kill. I kissed his fine, soft hair long and tenderly; then I went and sat down before the fire.

I reflected with amazement with horror on what I had done, asking myself whence come those tempests of the soul in which a man loses all perspective of things, all command over himself and acts as in a condition of mad intoxication, not knowing whither he is going—like a vessel in a hurricane.

The child coughed again, and it gave my heart a wrench. Suppose it should die! O God! O God! What would become of me?

I rose from my chair to go and look at him, and with a candle in my hand I leaned over him. Seeing him breathing quietly I felt reassured, when he coughed a third time. It gave me such a shock tat I started backward, just as one does at sight of something horrible, and let my candle fall.

As I stood erect after picking it up, I noticed that my temples were bathed in perspiration, that cold sweat which is the result of anguish of soul. And I remained until daylight bending over my son, becoming calm when he remained quiet for some time, and filled with atrocious pain when a weak cough came from his mouth.

He awoke with his eyes red, his throat choked, and with an air of suffering.

When the woman came in to arrange my room I sent her at once for a doctor. He came at the end of an hour, and said, after examining the child:

"Did he not catch cold?"

I began to tremble like a person with palsy, and I faltered:

"No, I do not think so."

And then I said:

"What is the matter? Is it serious?"

"I do not know yet," he replied. "I will come again this evening."

He came that evening. My son had remained almost all day in a condition of drowsiness, coughing from time to time. During the night inflammation of the lungs set in.

That lasted ten days. I cannot express what I suffered in those interminable hours that divide morning from night, right from morning.

He died.

And since—since that moment, I have not passed one hour, not a single hour, without the frightful burning recollection, a gnawing recollection, a memory that seems to wring my heart, awaking in me like a savage beast imprisoned in the depth of my soul.

Oh! if I could have gone mad!

M. Poirel de la Voulte raised his spectacles with a motion that was peculiar to him whenever he finished reading a contract; and the three heirs of the defunct looked at one another without speaking, pale and motionless.

At the end of a minute the lawyer resumed:

"That must be destroyed."

The other two bent their heads in sign of assent. He lighted a candle, carefully separated the pages containing the damaging confession from those relating to the disposition of money, then he held them over the candle and threw them into the fireplace.

And they watched the white sheets as they burned, till they were presently reduced to little crumbling black heaps. And as some words were still visible in white tracing, the daughter, with little strokes of the toe of her shoe, crushed the burning paper, mixing it with the old ashes in the fireplace.

Then all three stood there watching it for some time, as if they feared that the destroyed secret might escape from the fireplace.

A MOTHER OF MONSTERS

I recalled this horrible story, the events of which occurred long ago, and this horrible woman, the other day at a fashionable seaside resort, where I saw on the beach a well-known young, elegant and charming Parisienne, adored and respected by everyone.

I had been invited by a friend to pay him a visit in a little provincial town. He took me about in all directions to do the honors of the place, showed me noted scenes, chateaux, industries, ruins. He pointed out monuments, churches, old carved doorways, enormous or distorted trees, the oak of St. Andrew, and the yew tree of Roqueboise.

When I had exhausted my admiration and enthusiasm over all the sights, my friend said with a distressed expression on his face, that there was nothing left to look at. I breathed freely. I would now be able to rest under the shade of the trees. But, all at once, he uttered an exclamation:

"Oh, yes! We have the 'Mother of Monsters'; I must take you to see her."

"Who is that, the 'Mother of Monsters'?" I asked.

"She is an abominable woman," he replied, "a regular demon, a being who voluntarily brings into the world deformed, hideous, frightful children, monstrosities, in fact, and then sells them to showmen who exhibit such things.

"These exploiters of freaks come from time to time to find out if she has any fresh monstrosity, and if it meets with their approval they carry it away with them, paying the mother a compensation.

"She has eleven of this description. She is rich.

"You think I am joking, romancing, exaggerating. No, my friend; I am telling you the truth, the exact truth.

"Let us go and see this woman. Then I will tell you her history."

He took me into one of the suburbs. The woman lived in a pretty little house by the side of the road. It was attractive and well kept. The garden was filled with fragrant flowers. One might have supposed it to be the residence of a retired lawyer.

A maid ushered us into a sort of little country parlor, and the wretch appeared. She was about forty. She was a tall, big woman with hard features, but well formed, vigorous and healthy, the true type of a robust peasant woman, half animal, and half woman.

She was aware of her reputation and received everyone with a humility that smacked of hatred.

"What do the gentlemen wish?" she asked.

"They tell me that your last child is just like an ordinary child, that he does not resemble his brothers at all," replied my friend. "I wanted to be sure of that. Is it true?"

She cast on us a malicious and furious look as she said:

"Oh, no, oh, no, my poor sir! He is perhaps even uglier than the rest. I have no luck, no luck!

"They are all like that, it is heartbreaking! How can the good God be so hard on a poor woman who is all alone in the world, how can He?" She spoke hurriedly, her eyes cast down, with a deprecating air as of a wild beast who is afraid. Her harsh voice became soft, and it seemed strange to hear those tearful falsetto tones issuing from that big, bony frame, of unusual strength and with coarse outlines, which seemed fitted for violent action, and made to utter howls like a wolf.

"We should like to see your little one," said my friend.

I fancied she colored up. I may have been deceived. After a few moments of silence, she said in a louder tone:

"What good will that do you?"

"Why do you not wish to show it to us?" replied my friend. "There are many people to whom you will show it; you know whom I mean."

She gave a start, and resuming her natural voice, and giving free play to her anger, she screamed:

"Was that why you came here? To insult me? Because my children are like animals, tell me? You shall not see him, no, no, you shall not see him! Go away, go away! I do not know why you all try to torment me like that."

She walked over toward us, her hands on her hips. At the brutal tone of her voice, a sort of moaning, or rather a mewing, the lamentable cry of an idiot, came from the adjoining room. I shivered to the marrow of my bones. We retreated before her.

"Take care, Devil" (they called her the Devil); said my friend, "take care; some day you will get yourself into trouble through this."

She began to tremble, beside herself with fury, shaking her fist and roaring:

"Be off with you! What will get me into trouble? Be off with you, miscreants!"

She was about to attack us, but we fled, saddened at what we had seen. When we got outside, my friend said:

"Well, you have seen her, what do you think of her?"

"Tell me the story of this brute," I replied.

And this is what he told me as we walked along the white high road, with ripe crops on either side of it which rippled like the sea in the light breeze that passed over them.

"This woman was once a servant on a farm. She was an honest girl, steady and economical. She was never known to have an admirer, and never suspected of any frailty. But she went astray, as so many do.

"She soon found herself in trouble, and was tortured with fear and shame. Wishing to conceal her misfortune, she bound her body tightly with a corset of her own invention, made of boards and cord. The more she developed, the more she bound herself with this instrument of torture, suffering martyrdom, but brave in her sorrow, not allowing anyone to see, or suspect, anything. She maimed the little unborn being, cramping it with that frightful corset, and made a monster of it. Its head was squeezed and elongated to a point, and its large eyes seemed popping out of its head. Its limbs, exaggeratedly long, and twisted like the stalk of a vine, terminated in fingers like the claws of a spider. Its trunk was tiny, and round as a nut.

"The child was born in an open field, and when the weeders saw it, they fled away, screaming, and the report spread that she had given birth to a demon. From that time on, she was called 'the Devil.'

"She was driven from the farm, and lived on charity, under a cloud. She brought up the monster, whom she hated with a savage hatred, and would have strangled, perhaps, if the priest had not threatened her with arrest.

"One day some travelling showmen heard about the frightful creature, and asked to see it, so that if it pleased them they might take it away. They were pleased, and counted out five hundred francs to the mother. At first, she had refused to let them see the little animal, as she was ashamed; but when she discovered it had a money value, and that these people were anxious to get it, she began to haggle with them, raising her price with all a peasant's persistence.

"She made them draw up a paper, in which they promised to pay her four hundred francs a year besides, as though they had taken this deformity into their employ.

"Incited by the greed of gain, she continued to produce these phenomena, so as to have an assured income like a bourgeoise.

"Some of them were long, some short, some like crabs-all bodies-others like lizards. Several died, and she was heartbroken.

"The law tried to interfere, but as they had no proof they let her continue to produce her freaks.

"She has at this moment eleven alive, and they bring in, on an average, counting good and bad years, from five to six thousand francs a year. One, alone, is not placed, the one she was unwilling to show us. But she will not keep it long, for she is known to all the showmen in the world, who come from time to time to see if she has anything new.

"She even gets bids from them when the monster is valuable."

My friend was silent. A profound disgust stirred my heart, and a feeling of rage, of regret, to think that I had not strangled this brute when I had the opportunity.

I had forgotten this story, when I saw on the beach of a fashionable resort the other day, an elegant, charming, dainty woman, surrounded by men who paid her respect as well as admiration.

I was walking along the beach, arm in arm with a friend, the resident physician. Ten minutes later, I saw a nursemaid with three children, who were rolling in the sand. A pair of little crutches lay on the ground, and touched my sympathy. I then noticed that these three children were all deformed, humpbacked, or crooked; and hideous.

"Those are the offspring of that charming woman you saw just now," said the doctor.

I was filled with pity for her, as well as for them, and exclaimed: "Oh, the poor mother! How can she ever laugh!"

"Do not pity her, my friend. Pity the poor children," replied the doctor. "This is the consequence of preserving a slender figure up to the last. These little deformities were made by the corset. She knows very well that she is risking her life at this game. But what does she care, as long as he can be beautiful and have admirers!"

And then I recalled that other woman, the peasant, the "Devil," who sold her children, her monsters.

AN UNCOMFORTABLE BED

One autumn I went to spend the hunting season with some friends in a chateau in Picardy.

My friends were fond of practical jokes. I do not care to know people who are not.

When I arrived, they gave me a princely reception, which at once awakened suspicion in my mind. They fired off rifles, embraced me, made much of me, as if they expected to have great fun at my expense.

I said to myself:

"Look out, old ferret! They have something in store for you."

During the dinner the mirth was excessive, exaggerated, in fact. I thought: "Here are people who have more than their share of amusement, and apparently without reason. They must have planned some good joke. Assuredly I am to be the victim of the joke. Attention!"

During the entire evening every one laughed in an exaggerated fashion. I scented a practical joke in the air, as a dog scents game. But what was it? I was watchful, restless. I did not let a word, or a meaning, or a gesture escape me. Every one seemed to me an object of suspicion, and I even looked distrustfully at the faces of the servants.

The hour struck for retiring; and the whole household came to escort me to my room. Why?

They called to me: "Good-night." I entered the apartment, shut the door, and remained standing, without moving a single step, holding the wax candle in my hand.

I heard laughter and whispering in the corridor. Without doubt they were spying on me. I cast a glance round the walls, the furniture, the ceiling, the hangings, the floor. I saw nothing to justify suspicion. I heard persons moving about outside my door. I had no doubt they were looking through the keyhole.

An idea came into my head: "My candle may suddenly go out and leave me in darkness."

Then I went across to the mantelpiece and lighted all the wax candles that were on it. After that I cast another glance around me without discovering anything. I advanced with short steps, carefully examining the apartment. Nothing. I inspected every article, one after the other. Still nothing. I went over to the window. The shutters, large wooden shutters, were open. I shut them with great care, and then drew the curtains, enormous velvet curtains, and placed a chair in front of them, so as to have nothing to fear from outside.

Then I cautiously sat down. The armchair was solid. I did not venture to get into the bed. However, the night was advancing; and I ended by coming to the conclusion that I was foolish. If they were spying on me, as I supposed, they must, while waiting for the success of the joke they had been preparing for me, have been laughing immoderately at my terror. So I made up my mind to go to bed. But the bed was particularly suspicious-looking. I pulled at the curtains. They seemed to be secure.

All the same, there was danger. I was going perhaps to receive a cold shower both from overhead, or perhaps, the moment I stretched myself out, to find myself sinking to the floor with my mattress. I searched in my memory for all the practical jokes of which I ever had experience. And I did not want to be caught. Ah! certainly not! certainly not! Then I suddenly bethought myself of a precaution which I considered insured safety. I caught hold of the side of the mattress gingerly, and very slowly drew it toward me. It came away, followed by the sheet and the rest of the bedclothes. I dragged all these objects into the very middle of the room, facing the entrance door. I made my bed over again as best I could at some distance from the suspected bedstead and the corner which had filled me with such anxiety. Then I extinguished all the candles, and, groping my way, I slipped under the bed clothes.

For at least another hour I remained awake, starting at the slightest sound. Everything seemed quiet in the chateau. I fell asleep.

I must have been in a deep sleep for a long time, but all of a sudden I was awakened with a start by the fall of a heavy body tumbling right on top of my own, and, at the same time, I received on my face, on my neck, and on my chest a burning liquid which made me utter a howl of pain. And a dreadful noise, as if a sideboard laden with plates and dishes had fallen down, almost deafened me.

I was smothering beneath the weight that was crushing me and preventing me from moving. I stretched out my hand to find out what was the nature of this object. I felt a face, a nose, and whiskers. Then, with all my strength, I launched out a blow at this face. But I immediately received a hail of cuffings which made me jump straight out of the soaked sheets, and rush in my nightshirt into the corridor, the door of which I found open.

Oh, heavens! it was broad daylight. The noise brought my friends hurrying into my apartment, and we found, sprawling over my improvised bed, the dismayed valet, who, while bringing me my morning cup of tea, had tripped over this obstacle in the middle of the floor and fallen on his stomach, spilling my breakfast over my face in spite of himself.

The precautions I had taken in closing the shutters and going to sleep in the middle of the room had only brought about the practical joke I had been trying to avoid.

Oh, how they all laughed that day!

A PORTRAIT

"Hello! there's Milial!" said somebody near me. I looked at the man who had been pointed out as I had been wishing for a long time to meet this Don Juan.

He was no longer young. His gray hair looked a little like those fur bonnets worn by certain Northern peoples, and his long beard, which fell down over his chest, had also somewhat the appearance of fur. He was talking to a lady, leaning toward her, speaking in a low voice and looking at her with an expression full of respect and tenderness.

I knew his life, or at least as much as was known of it. He had loved madly several times, and there had been certain tragedies with which his name had been connected. When I spoke to women who were the loudest in his praise, and asked them whence came this power, they always answered, after thinking for a while: "I don't know—he has a certain charm about him."

He was certainly not handsome. He had none of the elegance that we ascribe to conquerors of feminine hearts. I wondered what might be his hidden charm. Was it mental? I never had heard of a clever saying of his. In his glance? Perhaps. Or in his voice? The voices of some beings have a certain irresistible attraction, almost suggesting the flavor of things good to eat. One is hungry for them, and the sound of their words penetrates us like a dainty morsel. A friend was passing. I asked him: "Do you know Monsieur Milial?"

"Yes."

"Introduce us."

A minute later we were shaking hands and talking in the doorway. What he said was correct, agreeable to hear; it contained no irritable thought. The voice was sweet, soft, caressing, musical; but I had heard others much more attractive, much more moving. One listened to him with pleasure, just as one would look at a pretty little brook. No tension of the mind was necessary in order to follow him, no hidden meaning aroused curiosity, no expectation awoke interest. His conversation was rather restful, but it did not awaken in one either a desire to answer, to contradict or to approve, and it was as easy to answer him as it was to listen to him. The response came to the lips of its own accord, as soon as he had finished talking, and phrases turned toward him as if he had naturally aroused them.

One thought soon struck me. I had known him for a quarter of an hour, and it seemed as if he were already one of my old friends, that I had known all about him for a long time; his face, his gestures, his voice, his ideas. Suddenly, after a few minutes of conversation, he seemed already to be installed in my intimacy. All constraint disappeared between us, and, had he so desired, I might have confided in him as one confides only in old friends.

Certainly there was some mystery about him. Those barriers that are closed between most people and that are lowered with time when sympathy, similar tastes, equal intellectual culture and constant intercourse remove constraint—those barriers seemed not to exist between him and me, and no doubt this was the case between him and all people, both men and women, whom fate threw in his path.

After half an hour we parted, promising to see each other often, and he gave me his address after inviting me to take luncheon with him in two days.

I forgot what hour he had stated, and I arrived too soon; he was not yet home. A correct and silent domestic showed me into a beautiful, quiet, softly lighted parlor. I felt comfortable there, at home. How often I have noticed the influence of apartments on the character and on the mind! There are some which make one feel foolish; in others, on the contrary, one always feels lively. Some make us sad, although well lighted and decorated in light-colored furniture; others cheer us up, although hung with sombre material. Our eye, like our heart, has its likes and dislikes, of which it does not inform us, and which it secretly imposes on our temperament. The harmony of furniture, walls, the style of an ensemble, act immediately on our mental state, just as the air from the woods, the sea or the mountains modifies our physical natures.

I sat down on a cushion-covered divan and felt myself suddenly carried and supported by these little silk bags of feathers, as if the outline of my body had been marked out beforehand on this couch.

Then I looked about. There was nothing striking about the room; every-where were beautiful and modest things, simple and rare furniture, Oriental curtains which did not seem to come from a department store but from the interior of a harem; and exactly opposite me hung the portrait of a woman. It was a portrait of medium size, showing the head and the upper part of the body, and the hands, which were holding a book. She was young, bareheaded; ribbons were woven in her hair; she was smiling sadly. Was it because she was bareheaded, was it merely her natural expression? I never have seen a portrait of a lady which seemed so much in its place as that one in that dwelling. Of all those I knew I have seen nothing like that one. All those that I know are on exhibition, whether the lady be dressed in her gaudiest gown, with an attractive headdress and a look which shows that she is posing first of all before the artist and then before those who will look at her or whether they have taken a comfortable attitude in an ordinary gown. Some are standing majestically in all their beauty, which is not at all natural to them in life. All of them have something, a flower or, a jewel, a crease in the dress or a curve of the lip, which one feels to have been placed there for effect by the artist. Whether they wear a hat or merely their hair one can immediately notice that they are not entirely natural. Why? One cannot say without knowing them, but the effect is there. They seem to be calling somewhere, on people whom they wish to please and to whom they wish to appear at their best advantage; and they have studied their attitudes, sometimes modest, Sometimes haughty.

What could one say about this one? She was at home and alone. Yes, she was alone, for she was smiling as one smiles when thinking in solitude of something sad or sweet, and not as one smiles when one is being watched. She seemed so much alone and so much at home that she made the whole large apartment seem absolutely empty. She alone lived in it, filled it, gave it life. Many people might come in and converse, laugh, even sing; she would still be alone with a solitary smile, and she alone would give it life with her pictured gaze.

That look also was unique. It fell directly on me, fixed and caressing, without seeing me. All portraits know that they are being watched, and they answer with their eyes, which see, think, follow us without leaving us, from the very moment we enter the apartment they inhabit. This one did not see me; it saw nothing, although its look was fixed directly on me. I remembered the surprising verse of Baudelaire:

And your eyes, attractive as those of a portrait.

They did indeed attract me in an irresistible manner; those painted eyes which had lived, or which were perhaps still living, threw over me a strange, powerful spell. Oh, what an infinite and tender charm, like a passing breeze, like a dying sunset of lilac rose and blue, a little sad like the approaching night, which comes behind the sombre frame and out of those impenetrable eyes! Those eyes, created by a few strokes from a brush, hide behind them the mystery of that which seems to be and which does not exist, which can appear in the eyes of a woman, which can make love blossom within us.

The door opened and M. Milial entered. He excused himself for being late. I excused myself for being ahead of time. Then I said: "Might I ask you who is this lady?"

He answered: "That is my mother. She died very young."

Then I understood whence came the inexplicable attraction of this man.

THE DRUNKARD

The north wind was blowing a hurricane, driving through the sky big, black, heavy clouds from which the rain poured down on the earth with terrific violence.

A high sea was raging and dashing its huge, slow, foamy waves along the coast with the rumbling sound of thunder. The waves followed each other close, rolling in as high as mountains, scattering the foam as they broke.

The storm engulfed itself in the little valley of Yport, whistling and moaning, tearing the shingles from the roofs, smashing the shutters, knocking down the chimneys, rushing through the narrow streets in such gusts that one could walk only by holding on to the walls, and children would have been lifted up like leaves and carried over the houses into the fields.

The fishing smacks had been hauled high up on land, because at high tide the sea would sweep the beach. Several sailors, sheltered behind the curved bottoms of their boats, were watching this battle of the sky and the sea.

Then, one by one, they went away, for night was falling on the storm, wrapping in shadows the raging ocean and all the battling elements.

Just two men remained, their hands plunged deep into their pockets, bending their backs beneath the squall, their woolen caps pulled down over their ears; two big Normandy fishermen, bearded, their skin tanned through exposure, with the piercing black eyes of the sailor who looks over the horizon like a bird of prey.

One of them was saying:

"Come on, Jeremie, let's go play dominoes. It's my treat."

The other hesitated a while, tempted on one hand by the game and the thought of brandy, knowing well that, if he went to Paumelle's, he would return home drunk; held back, on the other hand, by the idea of his wife remaining alone in the house.

He asked:

"Any one might think that you had made a bet to get me drunk every night. Say, what good is it doing you, since it's always you that's treating?"

Nevertheless he was smiling at the idea of all this brandy drunk at the expense of another. He was smiling the contented smirk of an avaricious Norman.

Mathurin, his friend, kept pulling him by the sleeve.

"Come on, Jeremie. This isn't the kind of a night to go home without anything to warm you up. What are you afraid of? Isn't your wife going to warm your bed for you?"

Jeremie answered:

"The other night I couldn't find the door—I had to be fished out of the ditch in front of the house!"

He was still laughing at this drunkard's recollection, and he was unconsciously going toward Paumelle's Cafe, where a light was shining in the window; he was going, pulled by Mathurin and pushed by the wind, unable to resist these combined forces.

The low room was full of sailors, smoke and noise. All these men, clad in woolens, their elbows on the tables, were shouting to make themselves heard. The more people came in, the more one had to shout in order to overcome the noise of voices and the rattling of dominoes on the marble tables.

Jeremie and Mathurin sat down in a corner and began a game, and the glasses were emptied in rapid succession into their thirsty throats.

Then they played more games and drank more glasses. Mathurin kept pouring and winking to the saloon keeper, a big, red-faced man, who chuckled as though at the thought of some fine joke; and Jeremie kept absorbing alcohol and wagging his head, giving vent to a roar of laughter and looking at his comrade with a stupid and contented expression.

All the customers were going away. Every time that one of them would open the door to leave a gust of wind would blow into the cafe, making the tobacco smoke swirl around, swinging the lamps at the end of their chains and making their flames flicker, and suddenly one could hear the deep booming of a breaking wave and the moaning of the wind.

Jeremie, his collar unbuttoned, was taking drunkard's poses, one leg outstretched, one arm hanging down and in the other hand holding a domino.

They were alone now with the owner, who had come up to them, interested.

He asked:

"Well, Jeremie, how goes it inside? Feel less thirsty after wetting your throat?"

Jeremie muttered:

"The more I wet it, the drier it gets inside."

The innkeeper cast a sly glance at Mathurin. He said:

"And your brother, Mathurin, where's he now?"

The sailor laughed silently:

"Don't worry; he's warm, all right."

And both of them looked toward Jeremie, who was triumphantly putting down the double six and announcing:

"Game!"

Then the owner declared:

"Well, boys, I'm goin' to bed. I will leave you the lamp and the bottle; there's twenty cents' worth in it. Lock the door when you go, Mathurin, and slip the key under the mat the way you did the other night."

Mathurin answered:

"Don't worry; it'll be all right."

Paumelle shook hands with his two customers and slowly went up the wooden stairs. For several minutes his heavy step echoed through the little house. Then a loud creaking announced that he had got into bed.

The two men continued to play. From time to time a more violent gust of wind would shake the whole house, and the two drinkers would look up, as though some one were about to enter. Then Mathurin would take the bottle and fill Jeremie's glass. But suddenly the clock over the bar struck twelve. Its hoarse clang sounded like the rattling of saucepans. Then Mathurin got up like a sailor whose watch is over.

"Come on, Jeremie, we've got to get out."

The other man rose to his feet with difficulty, got his balance by leaning on the table, reached the door and opened it while his companion was putting out the light.

As soon as they were in the street Mathurin locked the door and then said:

"Well, so long. See you to-morrow night!"

And he disappeared in the darkness.

Jeremie took a few steps, staggered, stretched out his hands, met a wall which supported him and began to stumble along. From time to time a gust of wind would sweep through the street, pushing him forward, making him run for a few steps; then, when the wind would die down, he would stop short, having lost his impetus, and once more he would begin to stagger on his unsteady drunkard's legs.

He went instinctively toward his home, just as birds go to their nests. Finally he recognized his door, and began to feel about for the keyhole and tried to put the key in it. Not finding the hole, he began to swear. Then he began to beat on the door with his fists, calling for his wife to come and help him:

"Melina! Oh, Melina!"

As he leaned against the door for support, it gave way and opened, and Jeremie, losing his prop, fell inside, rolling on his face into the middle of his room, and he felt something heavy pass over him and escape in the night.

He was no longer moving, dazed by fright, bewildered, fearing the devil, ghosts, all the mysterious beings of darkness, and he waited a long time without daring to move. But when he found out that nothing else was moving, a little reason returned to him, the reason of a drunkard.

Gently he sat up. Again he waited a long time, and at last, growing bolder, he called:

"Melina!"

His wife did not answer.

Then, suddenly, a suspicion crossed his darkened mind, an indistinct, vague suspicion. He was not moving; he was sitting there in the dark, trying to gather together his scattered wits, his mind stumbling over incomplete ideas, just as his feet stumbled along.

Once more he asked:

"Who was it, Melina? Tell me who it was. I won't hurt you!"

He waited, no voice was raised in the darkness. He was now reasoning with himself out loud.

"I'm drunk, all right! I'm drunk! And he filled me up, the dog; he did it, to stop my goin' home. I'm drunk!"

And he would continue:

"Tell me who it was, Melina, or somethin'll happen to you."

After having waited again, he went on with the slow and obstinate logic of a drunkard:

"He's been keeping me at that loafer Paumelle's place every night, so as to stop my going home. It's some trick. Oh, you damned carrion!"

Slowly he got on his knees. A blind fury was gaining possession of him, mingling with the fumes of alcohol.

He continued:

"Tell me who it was, Melina, or you'll get a licking—I warn you!"

He was now standing, trembling with a wild fury, as though the alcohol had set his blood on fire. He took a step, knocked against a chair, seized it, went on, reached the bed, ran his hands over it and felt the warm body of his wife.

Then, maddened, he roared:

"So! You were there, you piece of dirt, and you wouldn't answer!"

And, lifting the chair, which he was holding in his strong sailor's grip, he swung it down before him with an exasperated fury. A cry burst from the bed, an agonizing, piercing cry. Then he began to thrash around like a thresher in a barn. And soon nothing more moved. The chair was broken to pieces, but he still held one leg and beat away with it, panting.

At last he stopped to ask:

"Well, are you ready to tell me who it was?"

Melina did not answer.

Then tired out, stupefied from his exertion, he stretched himself out on the ground and slept.

When day came a neighbor, seeing the door open, entered. He saw Jeremie snoring on the floor, amid the broken pieces of a chair, and on the bed a pulp of flesh and blood.

THE WARDROBE

As we sat chatting after dinner, a party of men, the conversation turned on women, for lack of something else.

One of us said:

"Here's a funny thing that happened to me on, that very subject." And he told us the following story:

One evening last winter I suddenly felt overcome by that overpowering sense of misery and languor that takes possession of one from time to time. I was in my own apartment, all alone, and I was convinced that if I gave in to my feelings I should have a terrible attack of melancholia, one of those attacks that lead to suicide when they recur too often.

I put on my overcoat and went out without the slightest idea of what I was going to do. Having gone as far as the boulevards, I began to wander along by the almost empty cafes. It was raining, a fine rain that affects your mind as it does your clothing, not one of those good downpours which come down in torrents, driving breathless passers-by into doorways, but a rain without drops that deposits on your clothing an imperceptible spray and soon covers you with a sort of iced foam that chills you through.

What should I do? I walked in one direction and then came back, looking for some place where I could spend two hours, and discovering for the first time that there is no place of amusement in Paris in the evening. At last I decided to go to the Folies-Bergere, that entertaining resort for gay women.

There were very few people in the main hall. In the long horseshoe curve there were only a few ordinary looking people, whose plebeian origin was apparent in their manners, their clothes, the cut of their hair and beard, their hats, their complexion. It was rarely that one saw from time to time a man whom you suspected of having washed himself thoroughly, and his whole make-up seemed to match. As for the women, they were always the same, those frightful women you all know, ugly, tired looking, drooping, and walking along in their lackadaisical manner, with that air of foolish superciliousness which they assume, I do not know why.

I thought to myself that, in truth, not one of those languid creatures, greasy rather than fat, puffed out here and thin there, with the contour of a monk and the lower extremities of a bow-legged snipe, was worth the louis that they would get with great difficulty after asking five.

But all at once I saw a little creature whom I thought attractive, not in her first youth, but fresh, comical and tantalizing. I stopped her, and stupidly, without thinking, I made an appointment with her for that night. I did not want to go back to my own home alone, all alone; I preferred the company and the caresses of this hussy.

And I followed her. She lived in a great big house in the Rue des Martyrs. The gas was already extinguished on the stairway I ascended the steps slowly, lighting a candle match every few seconds, stubbing my foot against the steps, stumbling and angry as I followed the rustle of the skirt ahead of me.

She stopped on the fourth floor, and having closed the outer door she said:

"Then you will stay till to-morrow?"

"Why, yes. You know that that was the agreement."

"All right, my dear, I just wanted to know. Wait for me here a minute, I will be right back."

And she left me in the darkness. I heard her shutting two doors and then I thought I heard her talking. I was surprised and uneasy. The thought that she had a protector staggered me. But I have good fists and a solid back. "We shall see," I said to myself.

I listened attentively with ear and mind. Some one was stirring about, walking quietly and very carefully. Then another door was opened and I thought I again heard some one talking, but in a very low tone.

She came back carrying a lighted candle.

"You may come in," she said.

She said "thou" in speaking to me, which was an indication of possession. I went in and after passing through a dining room in which it was very evident that no one ever ate, I entered a typical room of all these women, a furnished room with red curtains and a soiled eiderdown bed covering.

"Make yourself at home, 'mon chat'," she said.

I gave a suspicious glance at the room, but there seemed no reason for uneasiness.

As she took off her wraps she began to laugh.

"Well, what ails you? Are you changed into a pillar of salt? Come, hurry up."

I did as she suggested.

Five minutes later I longed to put on my things and get away. But this terrible languor that had overcome me at home took possession of me again, and deprived me of energy enough to move and I stayed in spite of the disgust that I felt for this association. The unusual attractiveness that I supposed I had discovered in this creature over there under the chandeliers of the theater had altogether vanished on closer acquaintance, and she was nothing more to me now than a common woman, like all the others, whose indifferent and complaisant kiss smacked of garlic.

I thought I would say something.

"Have you lived here long?" I asked.

"Over six months on the fifteenth of January."

"Where were you before that?"

"In the Rue Clauzel. But the janitor made me very uncomfortable and I left."

And she began to tell me an interminable story of a janitor who had talked scandal about her.

But, suddenly, I heard something moving quite close to us. First there was a sigh, then a slight, but distinct, sound as if some one had turned round on a chair.

I sat up abruptly and asked.

"What was that noise?"

She answered quietly and confidently:

"Do not be uneasy, my dear boy, it is my neighbor. The partition is so thin that one can hear everything as if it were in the room. These are wretched rooms, just like pasteboard."

I felt so lazy that I paid no further attention to it. We resumed our conversation. Driven by the stupid curiosity that prompts all men to question these creatures about their first experiences, to attempt to lift the veil of their first folly, as though to find in them a trace of pristine innocence, to love them, possibly, in a fleeting memory of their candor and modesty of former days, evoked by a word, I insistently asked her about her earlier lovers.

I knew she was telling me lies. What did it matter? Among all these lies I might, perhaps, discover something sincere and pathetic.

"Come," said I, "tell me who he was."

"He was a boating man, my dear."

"Ah! Tell me about it. Where were you?"

"I was at Argenteuil."

"What were you doing?"

"I was waitress in a restaurant."

"What restaurant?"

"'The Freshwater Sailor.' Do you know it?"

"I should say so, kept by Bonanfan."

"Yes, that's it."

"And how did he make love to you, this boating man?"

"While I was doing his room. He took advantage of me."

But I suddenly recalled the theory of a friend of mine, an observant and philosophical physician whom constant attendance in hospitals has brought into daily contact with girl-mothers and prostitutes, with all the shame and all the misery of women, of those poor women who have become the frightful prey of the wandering male with money in his pocket.

"A woman," he said, "is always debauched by a man of her own class and position. I have volumes of statistics on that subject. We accuse the rich of plucking the flower of innocence among the girls of the people. This is not correct. The rich pay for what they want. They may gather some, but never for the first time."

Then, turning to my companion, I began to laugh.

"You know that I am aware of your history. The boating man was not the first."

"Oh, yes, my dear, I swear it."

"You are lying, my dear."

"Oh, no, I assure you."

"You are lying; come, tell me all."

She seemed to hesitate in astonishment. I continued:

"I am a sorcerer, my dear girl, I am a clairvoyant. If you do not tell me the truth, I will go into a trance sleep and then I can find out."

She was afraid, being as stupid as all her kind. She faltered:

"How did you guess?"

"Come, go on telling me," I said.

"Oh, the first time didn't amount to anything.

"There was a festival in the country. They had sent for a special chef, M. Alexandre. As soon as he came he did just as he pleased in the house. He bossed every one, even the proprietor and his wife, as if he had been a king. He was a big handsome man, who did not seem fitted to stand beside a kitchen range. He was always calling out, 'Come, some butter—some eggs—some Madeira!' And it had to be brought to him at once in a hurry, or he would get cross and say things that would make us blush all over.

"When the day was over he would smoke a pipe outside the door. And as I was passing by him with a pile of plates he said to me, like that: 'Come, girlie, come down to the water with me and show me the country.' I went with him like a fool, and we had hardly got down to the bank of the river when he took advantage of me so suddenly that I did not even know what he was doing. And then he went away on the nine o'clock train. I never saw him again."

"Is that all?" I asked.

She hesitated.

"Oh, I think Florentin belongs to him."

"Who is Florentin?"

"My little boy."

"Oh! Well, then, you made the boating man believe that he was the father, did you not?"

"You bet!"

"Did he have any money, this boating man?"

"Yes, he left me an income of three hundred francs, settled on Florentin."

I was beginning to be amused and resumed:

"All right, my girl, all right. You are all of you less stupid than one would imagine, all the same. And how old is he now, Florentin?"

She replied:

"He is now twelve. He will make his first communion in the spring."

"That is splendid. And since then you have carried on your business conscientiously?"

She sighed in a resigned manner.

"I must do what I can."

But a loud noise just then coming from the room itself made me start up with a bound. It sounded like some one falling and picking themselves up again by feeling along the wall with their hands.

I had seized the candle and was looking about me, terrified and furious. She had risen also and was trying to hold me back to stop me, murmuring:

"That's nothing, my dear, I assure you it's nothing."

But I had discovered what direction the strange noise came from. I walked straight towards a door hidden at the head of the bed and I opened it abruptly and saw before me, trembling, his bright, terrified eyes opened wide at sight of me, a little pale, thin boy seated beside a large wicker chair off which he had fallen.

As soon as he saw me he began to cry. Stretching out his arms to his mother, he cried:

"It was not my fault, mamma, it was not my fault. I was asleep, and I fell off. Do not scold me, it was not my fault."

I turned to the woman and said:

"What does this mean?"

She seemed confused and worried, and said in a broken voice:

"What do you want me to do? I do not earn enough to put him to school! I have to keep him with me, and I cannot afford to pay for another room, by heavens! He sleeps with me when I am alone. If any one comes for one hour or two he can stay in the wardrobe; he keeps quiet, he understands it. But when people stay all night, as you have done, it tires the poor child to sleep on a chair.

"It is not his fault. I should like to see you sleep all night on a chair—you would have something to say."

She was getting angry and excited and was talking loud.

The child was still crying. A poor delicate timid little fellow, a veritable child of the wardrobe, of the cold, dark closet, a child who from time to time was allowed to get a little warmth in the bed if it chanced to be unoccupied.

I also felt inclined to cry.

And I went home to my own bed.

THE MOUNTAIN POOL

Saint Agnes, May 6.
MY DEAR FRIEND:

You asked me to write to you often and to tell you in particular about the things I might see. You also begged me to rummage among my recollections of travels for some of those little anecdotes gathered from a chance peasant, from an innkeeper, from some strange traveling acquaintance, which remain as landmarks in the memory. With a landscape depicted in a few lines, and a little story told in a few sentences you think one can give the true characteristics of a country, make it living, visible, dramatic. I will try to do as you wish. I will, therefore, send you from time to time letters in which I will mention neither you nor myself, but only the landscape and the people who move about in it. And now I will begin.

Spring is a season in which one ought, it seems to me, to drink and eat the landscape. It is the season of chills, just as autumn is the season of reflection. In spring the country rouses the physical senses, in autumn it enters into the soul.

I desired this year to breathe the odor of orange blossoms and I set out for the South of France just at the time that every one else was returning home. I visited Monaco, the shrine of pilgrims, rival of Mecca and Jerusalem, without leaving any gold in any one else's pockets, and I climbed the high mountain beneath a covering of lemon, orange and olive branches.

Have you ever slept, my friend, in a grove of orange trees in flower? The air that one inhales with delight is a quintessence of perfumes. The strong yet sweet odor, delicious as some dainty, seems to blend with our being, to saturate us, to intoxicate us, to enervate us, to plunge us into a sleepy, dreamy torpor. As though it were an opium prepared by the hands of fairies and not by those of druggists.

This is a country of ravines. The surface of the mountains is cleft, hollowed out in all directions, and in these sinuous crevices grow veritable forests of lemon trees. Here and there where the steep gorge is interrupted by a sort of step, a kind of reservoir has been built which holds the water of the rain storms.

They are large holes with slippery walls with nothing for any one to grasp hold of should they fall in.

I was walking slowly in one of these ascending valleys or gorges, glancing through the foliage at the vivid-hued fruit that remained on the branches. The narrow gorge made the heavy odor of the flowers still more penetrating; the air seemed to be dense with it. A feeling of lassitude came over me and I looked for a place to sit down. A few drops of water glistened in the grass. I thought that there was a spring near by and I climbed a little further to look for it. But I only reached the edge of one of these large, deep reservoirs.

I sat down tailor fashion, with my legs crossed under me, and remained there in a reverie before this hole, which looked as if it were filled with ink, so black and stagnant was the liquid it contained. Down yonder, through the branches, I saw, like patches, bits of the Mediterranean gleaming so that they fairly dazzled my eyes. But my glance always returned to the immense somber well that appeared to be inhabited by no aquatic animals, so motionless was its surface. Suddenly a voice made me tremble. An old gentleman who was picking flowers—this country is the richest in Europe for herbalists—asked me:

"Are you a relation of those poor children, monsieur?"

I looked at him in astonishment.

"What children, monsieur?"

He seemed embarrassed and answered with a bow:

"I beg your pardon. On seeing you sitting thus absorbed in front of this reservoir I thought you were recalling the frightful tragedy that occurred here."

Now I wanted to know about it, and I begged him to tell me the story.

It is very dismal and very heart-rending, my dear friend, and very trivial at the same time. It is a simple news item. I do not know whether to attribute my emotion to the dramatic manner in which the story was told to me, to the setting of the mountains, to the contrast between the joy of the sunlight and the flowers and this black, murderous hole, but my heart was wrung, all my nerves unstrung by this tale which, perhaps, may not appear so terribly harrowing to you as you read it in your room without having the scene of the tragedy before your eyes.

It was one spring in recent years. Two little boys frequently came to play on the edge of this cistern while their tutor lay under a tree reading a book. One warm afternoon a piercing cry awoke the tutor who was dozing and the sound of splashing caused by something falling into the water made him jump to his feet abruptly. The younger of the children, eight years of age, was shouting, as he stood beside the reservoir, the surface of which was stirred and eddying at the spot where the older boy had fallen in as he ran along the stone coping.

Distracted, without waiting or stopping to think what was best to do, the tutor jumped into the black water and did not rise again, having struck his head at the bottom of the cistern.

At the same moment the young boy who had risen to the surface was waving his stretched-out arms toward his brother. The little fellow on land lay down full length, while the other tried to swim, to approach the wall, and presently the four little hands clasped each other, tightened in each other's grasp, contracted as though they were fastened together. They both felt the intense joy of an escape from death, a shudder at the danger past.

The older boy tried to climb up to the edge, but could not manage it, as the wall was perpendicular, and his brother, who was too weak, was sliding slowly towards the hole.

Then they remained motionless, filled anew with terror. And they waited.

The little fellow squeezed his brother's hands with all his might and wept from nervousness as he repeated: "I cannot drag you out, I cannot drag you out." And all at once he began to shout, "Help!

Help!" But his light voice scarcely penetrated beyond the dome of foliage above their heads.

They remained thus a long time, hours and hours, facing each other, these two children, with one thought, one anguish of heart and the horrible dread that one of them, exhausted, might let go the hands of the other. And they kept on calling, but all in vain.

At length the older boy, who was shivering with cold, said to the little one: "I cannot hold out any longer. I am going to fall. Good-by, little brother." And the other, gasping, replied: "Not yet, not yet, wait."

Evening came on, the still evening with its stars mirrored in the water. The older lad, his endurance giving out, said: "Let go my hand, I am going to give you my watch." He had received it as a present a few days before, and ever since it had been his chief amusement. He was able to get hold of it, and held it out to the little fellow who was sobbing and who laid it down on the grass beside him.

It was night now. The two unhappy beings, exhausted, had almost loosened their grasp. The elder, at last, feeling that he was lost, murmured once more: "Good-by, little brother, kiss mamma and papa." And his numbed fingers relaxed their hold. He sank and did not rise again .... The little fellow, left alone, began to shout wildly: "Paul! Paul!" But the other did not come to the surface.

Then he darted across the mountain, falling among the stones, overcome by the most frightful anguish that can wring a child's heart, and with a face like death reached the sitting-room, where his parents were waiting. He became bewildered again as he led them to the gloomy reservoir. He could not find his way. At last he reached the spot. "It is there; yes, it is there!"

But the cistern had to be emptied, and the proprietor would not permit it as he needed the water for his lemon trees.

The two bodies were found, however, but not until the next day.

You see, my dear friend, that this is a simple news item. But if you had seen the hole itself your heart would have been wrung, as mine was, at the thought of the agony of that child hanging to his brother's hands, of the long suspense of those little chaps who were accustomed only to laugh and to play, and at the simple incident of the giving of the watch.

I said to myself: "May Fate preserve me from ever receiving a similar relic!" I know of nothing more terrible than such a recollection connected with a familiar object that one cannot dispose of. Only think of it; each time that he handles this sacred watch the survivor will picture once more the horrible scene; the pool, the wall, the still water, and the distracted face of his brother-alive, and yet as lost as though he were already dead. And all through his life, at any moment, the vision will be there, awakened the instant even the tip of his finger touches his watch pocket.

And I was sad until evening. I left the spot and kept on climbing, leaving the region of orange trees for the region of olive trees, and the region of olive trees for the region of pines; then I came to a valley of stones, and finally reached the ruins of an ancient castle, built, they say, in the tenth century by a Saracen chief, a good man, who was baptized a Christian through love for a young girl. Everywhere around me were mountains, and before me the sea, the sea with an almost imperceptible patch on it: Corsica, or, rather, the shadow of Corsica. But on the mountain summits, blood-red in the glow of the sunset, in the boundless sky and on the sea, in all this superb landscape that I had come here to admire I saw only two poor children, one lying prone on the edge of a hole filled with black water, the other submerged to his neck, their hands intertwined, weeping opposite each other, in despair. And it seemed as though I continually heard a weak, exhausted voice saying: "Good-by, little brother, I am going to give you my watch."

This letter may seem rather melancholy, dear friend. I will try to be more cheerful some other day.

A CREMATION

Last Monday an Indian prince died at Etretat, Bapu Sahib Khanderao Ghatay, a relation of His Highness, the Maharajah Gaikwar, prince of Baroda, in the province of Guzerat, Presidency of Bombay.

For about three weeks there had been seen walking in the streets about ten young East Indians, small, lithe, with dark skins, dressed all in gray and wearing on their heads caps such as English grooms wear. They were men of high rank who had come to Europe to study the military institutions of the principal Western nations. The little band consisted of three princes, a nobleman, an interpreter and three servants.

The head of the commission had just died, an old man of forty-two and father-in-law of Sampatro Kashivao Gaikwar, brother of His Highness, the Gaikwar of Baroda.

The son-in-law accompanied his father-in-law.

The other East Indians were called Ganpatrao Shravanrao Gaikwar, cousin of His Highness Khasherao Gadhav; Vasudev Madhav Samarth, interpreter and secretary; the slaves: Ramchandra Bajaji, Ganu bin Pukiram Kokate, Rhambhaji bin Fabji.

On leaving his native land the one who died recently was overcome with terrible grief, and feeling convinced that he would never return he wished to give up the journey, but he had to obey the wishes of his noble relative, the Prince of Baroda, and he set out.

They came to spend the latter part of the summer at Etretat, and people would go out of curiosity every morning to see them taking their bath at the Etablissment des Roches-Blanches.

Five or six days ago Bapu Sahib Khanderao Ghatay was taken with pains in his gums; then the inflammation spread to the throat and became ulceration. Gangrene set in and, on Monday, the doctors told his young friends that their relative was dying. The final struggle was already beginning, and the breath had almost left the unfortunate man's body when his friends seized him, snatched him from his bed and laid him on the stone floor of the room, so that, stretched out on the earth, our mother, he should yield up his soul, according to the command of Brahma.

They then sent to ask the mayor, M. Boissaye, for a permit to burn the body that very day so as to fulfill the prescribed ceremonial of the Hindoo religion. The mayor hesitated, telegraphed to the prefecture to demand instructions, at the same time sending word that a failure to reply would be considered by him tantamount to a consent. As he had received no reply at 9 o'clock that evening, he decided, in view of the infectious character of the disease of which the East Indian had died, that the cremation of the body should take place that very night, beneath the cliff, on the beach, at ebb tide.

The mayor is being criticized now for this decision, though he acted as an intelligent, liberal and determined man, and was upheld and advised by the three physicians who had watched the case and reported the death.

They were dancing at the Casino that evening. It was an early autumn evening, rather chilly. A pretty strong wind was blowing from the ocean, although as yet there was no sea on, and swift, light, ragged clouds were driving across the sky. They came from the edge of the horizon, looking dark against the background of the sky, but as they approached the moon they grew whiter and passed hurriedly across her face, veiling it for a few seconds without completely hiding it.

The tall straight cliffs that inclose the rounded beach of Etretat and terminate in two celebrated arches, called "the Gates," lay in shadow, and made two great black patches in the softly lighted landscape.

It had rained all day.

The Casino orchestra was playing waltzes, polkas and quadrilles. A rumor was presently circulated among the groups of dancers. It was said that an East Indian prince had just died at the Hotel des Bains and that the ministry had been approached for permission to burn the body. No one believed it, or at least no one supposed that such a thing could occur so foreign was the custom as yet to our customs, and as the night was far advanced every one went home.

At midnight, the lamplighter, running from street to street, extinguished, one after another, the yellow jets of flame that lighted up the sleeping houses, the mud and the puddles of water. We waited, watching for the hour when the little town should be quiet and deserted.

Ever since noon a carpenter had been cutting up wood and asking himself with amazement what was going to be done with all these planks sawn up into little bits, and why one should destroy so much good merchandise. This wood was piled up in a cart which went along through side streets as far as the beach, without arousing the suspicion of belated persons who might meet it. It went along on the shingle at the foot of the cliff, and having dumped its contents on the beach the three Indian servants began to build a funeral pile, a little longer than it was wide. They worked alone, for no profane hand must aid in this solemn duty.

It was one o'clock in the morning when the relations of the deceased were informed that they might accomplish their part of the work.

The door of the little house they occupied was open, and we perceived, lying on a stretcher in the small, dimly lighted vestibule the corpse covered with white silk. We could see him plainly as he lay stretched out on his back, his outline clearly defined beneath this white veil.

The East Indians, standing at his feet, remained motionless, while one of them performed the prescribed rites, murmuring unfamiliar words in a low, monotonous tone. He walked round and round the corpse; touching it occasionally, then, taking an urn suspended from three slender chains, he sprinkled it for some time with the sacred water of the Ganges, that East Indians must always carry with them wherever they go.

Then the stretcher was lifted by four of them who started off at a slow march. The moon had gone down, leaving the muddy, deserted streets in darkness, but the body on the stretcher appeared to be luminous, so dazzlingly white was the silk, and it was a weird sight to see, passing along through the night, the semi-luminous form of this corpse, borne by those men, the dusky skin of whose faces and hands could scarcely be distinguished from their clothing in the darkness.

Behind the corpse came three Indians, and then, a full head taller than themselves and wrapped in an ample traveling coat of a soft gray color, appeared the outline of an Englishman, a kind and superior man, a friend of theirs, who was their guide and counselor in their European travels.

Beneath the cold, misty sky of this little northern beach I felt as if I were taking part in a sort of symbolical drama. It seemed to me that they were carrying there, before me, the conquered genius of India, followed, as in a funeral procession, by the victorious genius of England robed in a gray ulster.

On the shingly beach the four bearers halted a few moments to take breath, and then proceeded on their way. They now walked quickly, bending beneath the weight of their burden. At length they reached the funeral pile. It was erected in an indentation, at the very foot of the cliff, which rose above it perpendicularly a hundred meters high, perfectly white but looking gray in the night.

The funeral pile was about three and a half feet high. The corpse was placed on it and then one of the Indians asked to have the pole star pointed out to him. This was done, and the dead Rajah was laid with his feet turned towards his native country. Then twelve bottles of kerosene were poured over him and he was covered completely with thin slabs of pine wood. For almost another hour the relations and servants kept piling up the funeral pyre which looked like one of those piles of wood that carpenters keep in their yards. Then on top of this was poured the contents of twenty bottles of oil, and on top of all they emptied a bag of fine shavings. A few steps further on, a flame was glimmering in a little bronze brazier, which had remained lighted since the arrival of the corpse.

The moment had arrived. The relations went to fetch the fire. As it was barely alight, some oil was poured on it, and suddenly a flame arose lighting up the great wall of rock from summit to base. An Indian who was leaning over the brazier rose upright, his two hands in the air, his elbows bent, and all at once we saw arising, all black on the immense white cliff, a colossal shadow, the shadow of Buddha in his hieratic posture. And the little pointed toque that the man wore on his head even looked like the head-dress of the god.

The effect was so striking and unexpected that I felt my heart beat as though some supernatural apparition had risen up before me.

That was just what it was—the ancient and sacred image, come from the heart of the East to the ends of Europe, and watching over its son whom they were going to cremate there.

It vanished. They brought fire. The shavings on top of the pyre were lighted and then the wood caught fire and a brilliant light illumined the cliff, the shingle and the foam of the waves as they broke on the beach.

It grew brighter from second to second, lighting up on the sea in the distance the dancing crest of the waves.

The breeze from the ocean blew in gusts, increasing the heat of the flame which flattened down, twisted, then shot up again, throwing out millions of sparks. They mounted with wild rapidity along the cliff and were lost in the sky, mingling with the stars, increasing their number. Some sea birds who had awakened uttered their plaintive cry, and, describing long curves, flew, with their white wings extended, through the gleam from the funeral pyre and then disappeared in the night.

Before long the pile of wood was nothing but a mass of flame, not red but yellow, a blinding yellow, a furnace lashed by the wind. And, suddenly, beneath a stronger gust, it tottered, partially crumbling as it leaned towards the sea, and the corpse came to view, full length, blackened on his couch of flame and burning with long blue flames:

The pile of wood having crumbled further on the right the corpse turned over as a man does in bed. They immediately covered him with fresh wood and the fire started up again more furiously than ever.

The East Indians, seated in a semi-circle on the shingle, looked out with sad, serious faces. And the rest of us, as it was very cold, had drawn nearer to the fire until the smoke and sparks came in our faces. There was no odor save that of burning pine and petroleum.

Hours passed; day began to break. Toward five o'clock in the morning nothing remained but a heap of ashes. The relations gathered them up, cast some of them to the winds, some in the sea, and kept some in a brass vase that they had brought from India. They then retired to their home to give utterance to lamentations.

These young princes and their servants, by the employment of the most inadequate appliances succeeded in carrying out the cremation of their relation in the most perfect manner, with singular skill and remarkable dignity. Everything was done according to ritual, according to the rigid ordinances of their religion. Their dead one rests in peace.

The following morning at daybreak there was an indescribable commotion in Etretat. Some insisted that they had burned a man alive, others that they were trying to hide a crime, some that the mayor would be put in jail, others that the Indian prince had succumbed to an attack of cholera.

The men were amazed, the women indignant. A crowd of people spent the day on the site of the funeral pile, looking for fragments of bone in the shingle that was still warm. They found enough bones to reconstruct ten skeletons, for the farmers on shore frequently throw their dead sheep into the sea. The finders carefully placed these various fragments in their pocketbooks. But not one of them possesses a true particle of the Indian prince.

That very night a deputy sent by the government came to hold an inquest. He, however, formed an estimate of this singular case like a man of intelligence and good sense. But what should he say in his report?

The East Indians declared that if they had been prevented in France from cremating their dead they would have taken him to a freer country where they could have carried out their customs.

Thus, I have seen a man cremated on a funeral pile, and it has given me a wish to disappear in the same manner.

In this way everything ends at once. Man expedites the slow work of nature, instead of delaying it by the hideous coffin in which one decomposes for months. The flesh is dead, the spirit has fled. Fire which purifies disperses in a few hours all that was a human being; it casts it to the winds, converting it into air and ashes, and not into ignominious corruption.

This is clean and hygienic. Putrefaction beneath the ground in a closed box where the body becomes like pap, a blackened, stinking pap, has about it something repugnant and disgusting. The sight of the coffin as it descends into this muddy hole wrings one's heart with anguish. But the funeral pyre which flames up beneath the sky has about it something grand, beautiful and solemn.

MISTI

I was very much interested at that time in a droll little woman. She was married, of course, as I have a horror of unmarried flirts. What enjoyment is there in making love to a woman who belongs to nobody and yet belongs to any one? And, besides, morality aside, I do not understand love as a trade. That disgusts me somewhat.

The especial attraction in a married woman to a bachelor is that she gives him a home, a sweet, pleasant home where every one takes care of you and spoils you, from the husband to the servants. One finds everything combined there, love, friendship, even fatherly interest, bed and board, all, in fact, that constitutes the happiness of life, with this incalculable advantage, that one can change one's family from time to time, take up one's abode in all kinds of society in turn: in summer, in the country with the workman who rents you a room in his house; in winter with the townsfolk, or even with the nobility, if one is ambitious.

I have another weakness; it is that I become attached to the husband as well as the wife. I acknowledge even that some husbands, ordinary or coarse as they may be, give me a feeling of disgust for their wives, however charming they may be. But when the husband is intellectual or charming I invariably become very much attached to him. I am careful if I quarrel with the wife not to quarrel with the husband. In this way I have made some of my best friends, and have also proved in many cases the incontestable superiority of the male over the female in the human species. The latter makes all sorts of trouble-scenes, reproaches, etc.; while the former, who has just as good a right to complain, treats you, on the contrary, as though you were the special Providence of his hearth.

Well, my friend was a quaint little woman, a brunette, fanciful, capricious, pious, superstitious, credulous as a monk, but charming. She had a way of kissing one that I never saw in any one else—but that was not the attraction—and such a soft skin! It gave me intense delight merely to hold her hands. And an eye—her glance was like a slow caress, delicious and unending. Sometimes I would lean my head on her knee and we would remain motionless, she leaning over me with that subtle, enigmatic, disturbing smile that women have, while my eyes would be raised to hers, drinking sweetly and deliciously into my heart, like a form of intoxication, the glance of her limpid blue eyes, limpid as though they were full of thoughts of love, and blue as though they were a heaven of delights.

Her husband, inspector of some large public works, was frequently away from home and left us our evenings free. Sometimes I spent them with her lounging on the divan with my forehead on one of her knees; while on the other lay an enormous black cat called "Misti," whom she adored. Our fingers would meet on the cat's back and would intertwine in her soft silky fur. I felt its warm body against my cheek, trembling with its eternal purring, and occasionally a paw would reach out and place on my mouth, or my eyelid, five unsheathed claws which would prick my eyelids, and then be immediately withdrawn.

Sometimes we would go out on what we called our escapades. They were very innocent, however. They consisted in taking supper at some inn in the suburbs, or else, after dining at her house or at mine, in making the round of the cheap cafes, like students out for a lark.

We would go into the common drinking places and take our seats at the end of the smoky den on two rickety chairs, at an old wooden table. A cloud of pungent smoke, with which blended an odor of fried fish from dinner, filled the room. Men in smocks were talking in loud tones as they drank their petits verres, and the astonished waiter placed before us two cherry brandies.

She, trembling, charmingly afraid, would raise her double black veil as far as her nose, and then take up her glass with the enjoyment that one feels at doing something delightfully naughty.

Each cherry she swallowed made her feel as if she had done something wrong, each swallow of the burning liquor had on her the affect of a delicate and forbidden enjoyment.

Then she would say to me in a low tone: "Let us go." And we would leave, she walking quickly with lowered head between the drinkers who watched her going by with a look of displeasure. And as soon as we got into the street she would give a great sigh of relief, as if we had escaped some terrible danger.

Sometimes she would ask me with a shudder:

"Suppose they, should say something rude to me in those places, what would you do?" "Why, I would defend you, parbleu!" I would reply in a resolute manner. And she would squeeze my arm for happiness, perhaps with a vague wish that she might be insulted and protected, that she might see men fight on her account, even those men, with me!

One evening as we sat at a table in a tavern at Montmartre, we saw an old woman in tattered garments come in, holding in her hand a pack of dirty cards. Perceiving a lady, the old woman at once approached us and offered to tell my friend's fortune. Emma, who in her heart believed in everything, was trembling with longing and anxiety, and she made a place beside her for the old woman.

The latter, old, wrinkled, her eyes with red inflamed rings round them, and her mouth without a single tooth in it, began to deal her dirty cards on the table. She dealt them in piles, then gathered them up, and then dealt them out again, murmuring indistinguishable words. Emma, turning pale, listened with bated breath, gasping with anxiety and curiosity.

The fortune-teller broke silence. She predicted vague happenings: happiness and children, a fair young man, a voyage, money, a lawsuit, a dark man, the return of some one, success, a death. The mention of this death attracted the younger woman's attention. "Whose death? When? In what manner?"

The old woman replied: "Oh, as to that, these cards are not certain enough. You must come to my place to-morrow; I will tell you about it with coffee grounds which never make a mistake."

Emma turned anxiously to me:

"Say, let us go there to-morrow. Oh, please say yes. If not, you cannot imagine how worried I shall be."

I began to laugh.

"We will go if you wish it, dearie."

The old woman gave us her address. She lived on the sixth floor, in a wretched house behind the Buttes-Chaumont. We went there the following day.

Her room, an attic containing two chairs and a bed, was filled with strange objects, bunches of herbs hanging from nails, skins of animals, flasks and phials containing liquids of various colors. On the table a stuffed black cat looked out of eyes of glass. He seemed like the demon of this sinister dwelling.

Emma, almost fainting with emotion, sat down on a chair and exclaimed:

"Oh, dear, look at that cat; how like it is to Misti."

And she explained to the old woman that she had a cat "exactly like that, exactly like that!"

The old woman replied gravely:

"If you are in love with a man, you must not keep it."

Emma, suddenly filled with fear, asked:

"Why not?"

The old woman sat down familiarly beside her and took her hand.

"It was the undoing of my life," she said.

My friend wanted to hear about it. She leaned against the old woman, questioned her, begged her to tell. At length the woman agreed to do so.

"I loved that cat," she said, "as one would love a brother. I was young then and all alone, a seamstress. I had only him, Mouton. One of the tenants had given it to me. He was as intelligent as a child, and gentle as well, and he worshiped me, my dear lady, he worshiped me more than one does a fetish. All day long he would sit on my lap purring, and all night long on my pillow; I could feel his heart beating, in fact.

"Well, I happened to make an acquaintance, a fine young man who was working in a white-goods house. That went on for about three months on a footing of mere friendship. But you know one is liable to weaken, it may happen to any one, and, besides, I had really begun to love him. He was so nice, so nice, and so good. He wanted us to live together, for economy's sake. I finally allowed him to come and see me one evening. I had not made up my mind to anything definite; oh, no! But I was pleased at the idea that we should spend an hour together.

"At first he behaved very well, said nice things to me that made my heart go pit-a-pat. And then he kissed me, madame, kissed me as one does when they love. I remained motionless, my eyes closed, in a paroxysm of happiness. But, suddenly, I felt him start violently and he gave a scream, a scream that I shall never forget. I opened my eyes and saw that Mouton had sprung at his face and was tearing the skin with his claws as if it had been a linen rag. And the blood was streaming down like rain, madame.

"I tried to take the cat away, but he held on tight, scratching all the time; and he bit me, he was so crazy. I finally got him and threw him out of the window, which was open, for it was summer.

"When I began to bathe my poor friend's face, I noticed that his eyes were destroyed, both his eyes!

"He had to go to the hospital. He died of grief at the end of a year. I wanted to keep him with me and provide for him, but he would not agree to it. One would have supposed that he hated me after the occurrence.

"As for Mouton, his back was broken by the fall, The janitor picked up his body. I had him stuffed, for in spite of all I was fond of him. If he acted as he did it was because he loved me, was it not?"

The old woman was silent and began to stroke the lifeless animal whose body trembled on its iron framework.

Emma, with sorrowful heart, had forgotten about the predicted death—or, at least, she did not allude to it again, and she left, giving the woman five francs.

As her husband was to return the following day, I did not go to the house for several days. When I did go I was surprised at not seeing Misti. I asked where he was.

She blushed and replied:

"I gave him away. I was uneasy."

I was astonished.

"Uneasy? Uneasy? What about?"

She gave me a long kiss and said in a low tone:

"I was uneasy about your eyes, my dear."

Misti appeared in. Gil Blas of January 22, 1884, over the signature of "MAUFRIGNEUSE."

MADAME HERMET

Crazy people attract me. They live in a mysterious land of weird dreams, in that impenetrable cloud of dementia where all that they have witnessed in their previous life, all they have loved, is reproduced for them in an imaginary existence, outside of all laws that govern the things of this life and control human thought.

For them there is no such thing as the impossible, nothing is improbable; fairyland is a constant quantity and the supernatural quite familiar. The old rampart, logic; the old wall, reason; the old main stay of thought, good sense, break down, fall and crumble before their imagination, set free and escaped into the limitless realm of fancy, and advancing with fabulous bounds, and nothing can check it. For them everything happens, and anything may happen. They make no effort to conquer events, to overcome resistance, to overturn obstacles. By a sudden caprice of their flighty imagination they become princes, emperors, or gods, are possessed of all the wealth of the world, all the delightful things of life, enjoy all pleasures, are always strong, always beautiful, always young, always beloved! They, alone, can be happy in this world; for, as far as they are concerned, reality does not exist. I love to look into their wandering intelligence as one leans over an abyss at the bottom of which seethes a foaming torrent whose source and destination are both unknown.

But it is in vain that we lean over these abysses, for we shall never discover the source nor the destination of this water. After all, it is only water, just like what is flowing in the sunlight, and we shall learn nothing by looking at it.

It is likewise of no use to ponder over the intelligence of crazy people, for their most weird notions are, in fact, only ideas that are already known, which appear strange simply because they are no longer under the restraint of reason. Their whimsical source surprises us because we do not see it bubbling up. Doubtless the dropping of a little stone into the current was sufficient to cause these ebullitions. Nevertheless crazy people attract me and I always return to them, drawn in spite of myself by this trivial mystery of dementia.

One day as I was visiting one of the asylums the physician who was my guide said:

"Come, I will show you an interesting case."

And he opened the door of a cell where a woman of about forty, still handsome, was seated in a large armchair, looking persistently at her face in a little hand mirror.

As soon as she saw us she rose to her feet, ran to the other end of the room, picked up a veil that lay on a chair, wrapped it carefully round her face, then came back, nodding her head in reply to our greeting.

"Well," said the doctor, "how are you this morning?"

She gave a deep sigh.

"Oh, ill, monsieur, very ill. The marks are increasing every day."

He replied in a tone of conviction:

"Oh, no; oh, no; I assure you that you are mistaken."

She drew near to him and murmured:

"No. I am certain of it. I counted ten pittings more this morning, three on the right cheek, four on the left cheek, and three on the forehead. It is frightful, frightful! I shall never dare to let any one see me, not even my son; no, not even him! I am lost, I am disfigured forever."

She fell back in her armchair and began to sob.

The doctor took a chair, sat down beside her, and said soothingly in a gentle tone:

"Come, let me see; I assure you it is nothing. With a slight cauterization I will make it all disappear."

She shook her head in denial, without speaking. He tried to touch her veil, but she seized it with both hands so violently that her fingers went through it.

He continued to reason with her and reassure her.

"Come, you know very well that I remove those horrid pits every time and that there is no trace of them after I have treated them. If you do not let me see them I cannot cure you."

"I do not mind your seeing them," she murmured, "but I do not know that gentleman who is with you."

"He is a doctor also, who can give you better care than I can."

She then allowed her face to be uncovered, but her dread, her emotion, her shame at being seen brought a rosy flush to her face and her neck, down to the collar of her dress. She cast down her eyes, turned her face aside, first to the right; then to the left, to avoid our gaze and stammered out:

"Oh, it is torture to me to let myself be seen like this! It is horrible, is it not? Is it not horrible?"

I looked at her in much surprise, for there was nothing on her face, not a mark, not a spot, not a sign of one, nor a scar.

She turned towards me, her eyes still lowered, and said:

"It was while taking care of my son that I caught this fearful disease, monsieur. I saved him, but I am disfigured. I sacrificed my beauty to him, to my poor child. However, I did my duty, my conscience is at rest. If I suffer it is known only to God."

The doctor had drawn from his coat pocket a fine water-color paint brush.

"Let me attend to it," he said, "I will put it all right."

She held out her right cheek, and he began by touching it lightly with the brush here and there, as though he were putting little points of paint on it. He did the same with the left cheek, then with the chin, and the forehead, and then exclaimed:

"See, there is nothing there now, nothing at all!"

She took up the mirror, gazed at her reflection with profound, eager attention, with a strong mental effort to discover something, then she sighed:

"No. It hardly shows at all. I am infinitely obliged to you."

The doctor had risen. He bowed to her, ushered me out and followed me, and, as soon as he had locked the door, said:

"Here is the history of this unhappy woman."

Her name is Mme. Hermet. She was once very beautiful, a great coquette, very much beloved and very much in-love with life.

She was one of those women who have nothing but their beauty and their love of admiration to sustain, guide or comfort them in this life. The constant anxiety to retain her freshness, the care of her complexion, of her hands, her teeth, of every portion of body that was visible, occupied all her time and all her attention.

She became a widow, with one son. The boy was brought up as are all children of society beauties. She was, however, very fond of him.

He grew up, and she grew older. Whether she saw the fatal crisis approaching, I cannot say. Did she, like so many others, gaze for hours and hours at her skin, once so fine, so transparent and free from blemish, now beginning to shrivel slightly, to be crossed with a thousand little lines, as yet imperceptible, that will grow deeper day by day, month by month? Did she also see slowly, but surely, increasing traces of those long wrinkles on the forehead, those slender serpents that nothing can check? Did she suffer the torture, the abominable torture of the mirror, the little mirror with the silver handle which one cannot make up one's mind to lay down on the table, but then throws down in disgust only to take it up again in order to look more closely, and still more closely at the hateful and insidious approaches of old age? Did she shut herself up ten times, twenty times a day, leaving her friends chatting in the drawing-room, and go up to her room where, under the protection of bolts and bars, she would again contemplate the work of time on her ripe beauty, now beginning to wither, and recognize with despair the gradual progress of the process which no one else had as yet seemed to perceive, but of which she, herself, was well aware. She knows where to seek the most serious, the gravest traces of age. And the mirror, the little round hand-glass in its carved silver frame, tells her horrible things; for it speaks, it seems to laugh, it jeers and tells her all that is going to occur, all the physical discomforts and the atrocious mental anguish she will suffer until the day of her death, which will be the day of her deliverance.

Did she weep, distractedly, on her knees, her forehead to the ground, and pray, pray, pray to Him who thus slays his creatures and gives them youth only that he may render old age more unendurable, and lends them beauty only that he may withdraw it almost immediately? Did she pray to Him, imploring Him to do for her what He has never yet done for any one, to let her retain until her last day her charm, her freshness and her gracefulness? Then, finding that she was imploring in vain an inflexible Unknown who drives on the years, one after another, did she roll on the carpet in her room, knocking her head against the furniture and stifling in her throat shrieks of despair?

Doubtless she suffered these tortures, for this is what occurred:

One day (she was then thirty-five) her son aged fifteen, fell ill.

He took to his bed without any one being able to determine the cause or nature of his illness.

His tutor, a priest, watched beside him and hardly ever left him, while Mme. Hermet came morning and evening to inquire how he was.

She would come into the room in the morning in her night wrapper, smiling, all powdered and perfumed, and would ask as she entered the door:

"Well, George, are you better?"

The big boy, his face red, swollen and showing the ravages of fever, would reply:

"Yes, little mother, a little better."

She would stay in the room a few seconds, look at the bottles of medicine, and purse her lips as if she were saying "phew," and then would suddenly exclaim: "Oh, I forgot something very important," and would run out of the room leaving behind her a fragrance of choice toilet perfumes.

In the evening she would appear in a decollete dress, in a still greater hurry, for she was always late, and she had just time to inquire:

"Well, what does the doctor say?"

The priest would reply:

"He has not yet given an opinion, madame."

But one evening the abbe replied: "Madame, your son has got the small-pox."

She uttered a scream of terror and fled from the room.

When her maid came to her room the following morning she noticed at once a strong odor of burnt sugar, and she found her mistress, with wide-open eyes, her face pale from lack of sleep, and shivering with terror in her bed.

As soon as the shutters were opened Mme. Herrnet asked:

"How is George?"

"Oh, not at all well to-day, madame."

She did not rise until noon, when she ate two eggs with a cup of tea, as if she herself had been ill, and then she went out to a druggist's to inquire about prophylactic measures against the contagion of small-pox.

She did not come home until dinner time, laden with medicine bottles, and shut herself up at once in her room, where she saturated herself with disinfectants.

The priest was waiting for her in the dining-room. As soon as she saw him she exclaimed in a voice full of emotion:

"Well?"

"No improvement. The doctor is very anxious:"

She began to cry and could eat nothing, she was so worried.

The next day, as soon as it was light, she sent to inquire for her son, but there was no improvement and she spent the whole day in her room, where little braziers were giving out pungent odors. Her maid said also that you could hear her sighing all the evening.

She spent a whole week in this manner, only going out for an hour or two during the afternoon to breathe the air.

She now sent to make inquiries every hour, and would sob when the reports were unfavorable.

On the morning of the eleventh day the priest, having been announced, entered her room, his face grave and pale, and said, without taking the chair she offered him:

"Madame, your son is very ill and wishes to see you."

She fell on her knees, exclaiming:

"Oh, my God! Oh, my God! I would never dare! My God! My God! Help me!"

The priest continued:

"The doctor holds out little hope, madame, and George is expecting you!"

And he left the room.

Two hours later as the young lad, feeling himself dying, again asked for his mother, the abbe went to her again and found her still on her knees, still weeping and repeating:

"I will not .... I will not... . I am too much afraid .... I will not... ."

He tried to persuade her, to strengthen her, to lead her. He only succeeded in bringing on an attack of "nerves" that lasted some time and caused her to shriek.

The doctor when he came in the evening was told of this cowardice and declared that he would bring her in himself, of her own volition, or by force. But after trying all manner of argument and just as he seized her round the waist to carry her into her son's room, she caught hold of the door and clung to it so firmly that they could not drag her away. Then when they let go of her she fell at the feet of the doctor, begging his forgiveness and acknowledging that she was a wretched creature. And then she exclaimed: "Oh, he is not going to die; tell me that he is not going to die, I beg of you; tell him that I love him, that I worship him..."

The young lad was dying. Feeling that he had only a few moments more to live, he entreated that his mother be persuaded to come and bid him a last farewell. With that sort of presentiment that the dying sometimes have, he had understood, had guessed all, and he said: "If she is afraid to come into the room, beg her just to come on the balcony as far as my window so that I may see her, at least, so that I may take a farewell look at her, as I cannot kiss her."

The doctor and the abbe, once more, went together to this woman and assured her: "You will run no risk, for there will be a pane of glass between you and him."

She consented, covered up her head, and took with her a bottle of smelling salts. She took three steps on the balcony; then, all at once, hiding her face in her hands, she moaned: "No ... no ... I would never dare to look at him ... never.... I am too much ashamed ... too much afraid .... No ... I cannot."

They endeavored to drag her along, but she held on with both hands to the railings and uttered such plaints that the passers-by in the street raised their heads. And the dying boy waited, his eyes turned towards that window, waited to die until he could see for the last time the sweet, beloved face, the worshiped face of his mother.

He waited long, and night came on. Then he turned over with his face to the wall and was silent.

When day broke he was dead. The day following she was crazy.

THE MAGIC COUCH

The Seine flowed past my house, without a ripple on its surface, and gleaming in the bright morning sunlight. It was a beautiful, broad, indolent silver stream, with crimson lights here and there; and on the opposite side of the river were rows of tall trees that covered all the bank with an immense wall of verdure.

The sensation of life which is renewed each day, of fresh, happy, loving life trembled in the leaves, palpitated in the air, was mirrored in the water.

The postman had just brought my papers, which were handed to me, and I walked slowly to the river bank in order to read them.

In the first paper I opened I noticed this headline, "Statistics of Suicides," and I read that more than 8,500 persons had killed themselves in that year.

In a moment I seemed to see them! I saw this voluntary and hideous massacre of the despairing who were weary of life. I saw men bleeding, their jaws fractured, their skulls cloven, their breasts pierced by a bullet, slowly dying, alone in a little room in a hotel, giving no thought to their wound, but thinking only of their misfortunes.

I saw others seated before a tumbler in which some matches were soaking, or before a little bottle with a red label.

They would look at it fixedly without moving; then they would drink and await the result; then a spasm would convulse their cheeks and draw their lips together; their eyes would grow wild with terror, for they did not know that the end would be preceded by so much suffering.

They rose to their feet, paused, fell over and with their hands pressed to their stomachs they felt their internal organs on fire, their entrails devoured by the fiery liquid, before their minds began to grow dim.

I saw others hanging from a nail in the wall, from the fastening of the window, from a hook in the ceiling, from a beam in the garret, from a branch of a tree amid the evening rain. And I surmised all that had happened before they hung there motionless, their tongues hanging out of their mouths. I imagined the anguish of their heart, their final hesitation, their attempts to fasten the rope, to determine that it was secure, then to pass the noose round their neck and to let themselves fall.

I saw others lying on wretched beds, mothers with their little children, old men dying of hunger, young girls dying for love, all rigid, suffocated, asphyxiated, while in the center of the room the brasier still gave forth the fumes of charcoal.

And I saw others walking at night along the deserted bridges. These were the most sinister. The water flowed under the arches with a low sound. They did not see it … they guessed at it from its cool breath! They longed for it and they feared it. They dared not do it! And yet, they must. A distant clock sounded the hour and, suddenly, in the vast silence of the night, there was heard the splash of a body falling into the river, a scream or two, the sound of hands beating the water, and all was still. Sometimes, even, there was only the sound of the falling body when they had tied their arms down or fastened a stone to their feet. Oh, the poor things, the poor things, the poor things, how I felt their anguish, how I died in their death! I went through all their wretchedness; I endured in one hour all their tortures. I knew all the sorrows that had led them to this, for I know the deceitful infamy of life, and no one has felt it more than I have.

How I understood them, these who weak, harassed by misfortune, having lost those they loved, awakened from the dream of a tardy compensation, from the illusion of another existence where God will finally be just, after having been ferocious, and their minds disabused of the mirages of happiness, have given up the fight and desire to put an end to this ceaseless tragedy, or this shameful comedy.

Suicide! Why, it is the strength of those whose strength is exhausted, the hope of those who no longer believe, the sublime courage of the conquered! Yes, there is at least one door to this life we can always open and pass through to the other side. Nature had an impulse of pity; she did not shut us up in prison. Mercy for the despairing!

As for those who are simply disillusioned, let them march ahead with free soul and quiet heart. They have nothing to fear since they may take their leave; for behind them there is always this door that the gods of our illusions cannot even lock.

I thought of this crowd of suicides: more than eight thousand five hundred in one year. And it seemed to me that they had combined to send to the world a prayer, to utter a cry of appeal, to demand something that should come into effect later when we understood things better. It seemed to me that all these victims, their throats cut, poisoned, hung, asphyxiated, or drowned, all came together, a frightful horde, like citizens to the polls, to say to society: "Grant us, at least, a gentle death! Help us to die, you who will not help us to live! See, we are numerous, we have the right to speak in these days of freedom, of philosophic independence and of popular suffrage. Give to those who renounce life the charity of a death that will not be repugnant nor terrible."

I began to dream, allowing my fancy to roam at will in weird and mysterious fashion on this subject.

I seemed to be all at once in a beautiful city. It was Paris; but at what period? I walked about the streets, looking at the houses, the theaters, the public buildings, and presently found myself in a square where I remarked a large building; very handsome, dainty and attractive. I was surprised on reading on the facade this inscription in letters of gold, "Suicide Bureau."

Oh, the weirdness of waking dreams where the spirit soars into a world of unrealities and possibilities! Nothing astonishes one, nothing shocks one; and the unbridled fancy makes no distinction between the comic and the tragic.

I approached the building where footmen in knee-breeches were seated in the vestibule in front of a cloak-room as they do at the entrance of a club.

I entered out of curiosity. One of the men rose and said:

"What does monsieur wish?"

"I wish to know what building this is."

"Nothing more?"

"Why, no."

"Then would monsieur like me to take him to the Secretary of the Bureau?"

I hesitated, and asked:

"But will not that disturb him?"

"Oh, no, monsieur, he is here to receive those who desire information."

"Well, lead the way."

He took me through corridors where old gentlemen were chatting, and finally led me into a beautiful office, somewhat somber, furnished throughout in black wood. A stout young man with a corporation was writing a letter as he smoked a cigar, the fragrance of which gave evidence of its quality.

He rose. We bowed to each other, and as soon as the footman had retired he asked:

"What can I do for you?"

"Monsieur," I replied, "pardon my curiosity. I had never seen this establishment. The few words inscribed on the facade filled me with astonishment, and I wanted to know what was going on here."

He smiled before replying, then said in a low tone with a complacent air:

"Mon Dieu, monsieur, we put to death in a cleanly and gentle—I do not venture to say agreeable manner those persons who desire to die."

I did not feel very shocked, for it really seemed to me natural and right. What particularly surprised me was that on this planet, with its low, utilitarian, humanitarian ideals, selfish and coercive of all true freedom, any one should venture on a similar enterprise, worthy of an emancipated humanity.

"How did you get the idea?" I asked.

"Monsieur," he replied, "the number of suicides increased so enormously during the five years succeeding the world exposition of 1889 that some measures were urgently needed. People killed themselves in the streets, at fetes, in restaurants, at the theater, in railway carriages, at the receptions held by the President of the Republic, everywhere. It was not only a horrid sight for those who love life, as I do, but also a bad example for children. Hence it became necessary to centralize suicides."

"What caused this suicidal epidemic?"

"I do not know. The fact is, I believe, the world is growing old. People begin to see things clearly and they are getting disgruntled. It is the same to-day with destiny as with the government, we have found out what it is; people find that they are swindled in every direction, and they just get out of it all. When one discovers that Providence lies, cheats, robs, deceives human beings just as a plain Deputy deceives his constituents, one gets angry, and as one cannot nominate a fresh Providence every three months as we do with our privileged representatives, one just gets out of the whole thing, which is decidedly bad."

"Really!"

"Oh, as for me, I am not complaining."

"Will you inform me how you carry on this establishment?"

"With pleasure. You may become a member when you please. It is a club."

"A club!"

"Yes, monsieur, founded by the most eminent men in the country, by men of the highest intellect and brightest intelligence. And," he added, laughing heartily, "I swear to you that every one gets a great deal of enjoyment out of it."

"In this place?"

"Yes, in this place."

"You surprise me."

"Mon Dieu, they enjoy themselves because they have not that fear of death which is the great killjoy in all our earthly pleasures."

"But why should they be members of this club if they do not kill themselves?"

"One may be a member of the club without being obliged for that reason to commit suicide."

"But then?"

"I will explain. In view of the enormous increase in suicides, and of the hideous spectacle they presented, a purely benevolent society was formed for the protection of those in despair, which placed at their disposal the facilities for a peaceful, painless, if not unforeseen death."

"Who can have authorized such an institution?"

"General Boulanger during his brief tenure of power. He could never refuse anything. However, that was the only good thing he did. Hence, a society was formed of clear-sighted, disillusioned skeptics who desired to erect in the heart of Paris a kind of temple dedicated to the contempt for death. This place was formerly a dreaded spot that no one ventured to approach. Then its founders, who met together here, gave a grand inaugural entertainment with Mmes. Sarah Bernhardt, Judic, Theo, Granier, and twenty others, and Mme. de Reske, Coquelin, Mounet-Sully, Paulus, etc., present, followed by concerts, the comedies of Dumas, of Meilhac, Halevy and Sardon. We had only one thing to mar it, one drama by Becque which seemed sad, but which subsequently had a great success at the Comedie-Francaise. In fact all Paris came. The enterprise was launched."

"In the midst of the festivities! What a funereal joke!"

"Not at all. Death need not be sad, it should be a matter of indifference. We made death cheerful, crowned it with flowers, covered it with perfume, made it easy. One learns to aid others through example; one can see that it is nothing."

"I can well understand that they should come to the entertainments; but did they come to ... Death?"

"Not at first; they were afraid."

"And later?"

"They came."

"Many of them?"

"In crowds. We have had more than forty in a day. One finds hardly any more drowned bodies in the Seine."

"Who was the first?"

"A club member."

"As a sacrifice to the cause?"

"I don't think so. A man who was sick of everything, a 'down and out' who had lost heavily at baccarat for three months."

"Indeed?"

"The second was an Englishman, an eccentric. We then advertised in the papers, we gave an account of our methods, we invented some attractive instances. But the great impetus was given by poor people."

"How do you go to work?"

"Would you like to see? I can explain at the same time."

"Yes, indeed."

He took his hat, opened the door, allowed me to precede him, and we entered a card room, where men sat playing as they, play in all gambling places. They were chatting cheerfully, eagerly. I have seldom seen such a jolly, lively, mirthful club.

As I seemed surprised, the secretary said:

"Oh, the establishment has an unheard of prestige. All the smart people all over the world belong to it so as to appear as though they held death in scorn. Then, once they get here, they feel obliged to be cheerful that they may not appear to be afraid. So they joke and laugh and talk flippantly, they are witty and they become so. At present it is certainly the most frequented and the most entertaining place in Paris. The women are even thinking of building an annex for themselves."

"And, in spite of all this, you have many suicides in the house?"

"As I said, about forty or fifty a day. Society people are rare, but poor devils abound. The middle class has also a large contingent.

"And how … do they do?"

"They are asphyxiated … very slowly."

"In what manner?"

"A gas of our own invention. We have the patent. On the other side of the building are the public entrances—three little doors opening on small streets. When a man or a woman present themselves they are interrogated. Then they are offered assistance, aid, protection. If a client accepts, inquiries are made; and sometimes we have saved their lives."

"Where do you get your money?"

"We have a great deal. There are a large number of shareholders. Besides it is fashionable to contribute to the establishment. The names of the donors are published in Figaro. Then the suicide of every rich man costs a thousand francs. And they look as if they were lying in state. It costs the poor nothing."

"How can you tell who is poor?"

"Oh, oh, monsieur, we can guess! And, besides, they must bring a certificate of indigency from the commissary of police of their district. If you knew how distressing it is to see them come in! I visited their part of our building once only, and I will never go again. The place itself is almost as good as this part, almost as luxurious and comfortable; but they themselves ... they themselves!!! If you could see them arriving, the old men in rags coming to die; persons who have been dying of misery for months, picking up their food at the edges of the curbstone like dogs in the street; women in rags, emaciated, sick, paralyzed, incapable of making a living, who say to us after they have told us their story: 'You see that things cannot go on like that, as I cannot work any longer or earn anything.' I saw one woman of eighty-seven who had lost all her children and grandchildren, and who for the last six weeks had been sleeping out of doors. It made me ill to hear of it. Then we have so many different cases, without counting those who say nothing, but simply ask: 'Where is it?' These are admitted at once and it is all over in a minute."

With a pang at my heart I repeated:

"And ... where is it?"

"Here," and he opened a door, adding:

"Go in; this is the part specially reserved for club members, and the one least used. We have so far had only eleven annihilations here."

"Ah! You call that an ... annihilation!"

"Yes, monsieur. Go in."

I hesitated. At length I went in. It was a wide corridor, a sort of greenhouse in which panes of glass of pale blue, tender pink and delicate green gave the poetic charm of landscapes to the inclosing walls. In this pretty salon there were divans, magnificent palms, flowers, especially roses of balmy fragrance, books on the tables, the Revue des Deuxmondes, cigars in government boxes, and, what surprised me, Vichy pastilles in a bonbonniere.

As I expressed my surprise, my guide said:

"Oh, they often come here to chat." He continued: "The public corridors are similar, but more simply furnished."

In reply to a question of mine, he pointed to a couch covered with creamy crepe de Chine with white embroidery, beneath a large shrub of unknown variety at the foot of which was a circular bed of mignonette.

The secretary added in a lower tone:

"We change the flower and the perfume at will, for our gas, which is quite imperceptible, gives death the fragrance of the suicide's favorite flower. It is volatilized with essences. Would you like to inhale it for a second?"

"'No, thank you," I said hastily, "not yet . . . ."

He began to laugh.

"Oh, monsieur, there is no danger. I have tried it myself several times."

I was afraid he would think me a coward, and I said:

"Well, I'll try it."

"Stretch yourself out on the 'endormeuse.'"

A little uneasy I seated myself on the low couch covered with crepe de Chine and stretched myself full length, and was at once bathed in a delicious odor of mignonette. I opened my mouth in order to breathe it in, for my mind had already become stupefied and forgetful of the past and was a prey, in the first stages of asphyxia, to the enchanting intoxication of a destroying and magic opium.

Some one shook me by the arm.

"Oh, oh, monsieur," said the secretary, laughing, "it looks to me as if you were almost caught."

But a voice, a real voice, and no longer a dream voice, greeted me with the peasant intonation:

"Good morning, m'sieu. How goes it?"

My dream was over. I saw the Seine distinctly in the sunlight, and, coming along a path, the garde champetre of the district, who with his right hand touched his kepi braided in silver. I replied:

"Good morning, Marinel. Where are you going?"

"I am going to look at a drowned man whom they fished up near the Morillons. Another who has thrown himself into the soup. He even took off his trousers in order to tie his legs together with them."